Second Son

To Betty
I hope I got the
dialogue right!
Sylvia

Second Son

A MEMOIR

Sylvia Otani

Contents

Chapter 1   The Beginning Revisited, Pre-1900 1
Chapter 2   Growing Up, 1900-1916. 22
Chapter 3   At Sea, 1916-1920. 55
Chapter 4   New York, 1920-1928. 90
Chapter 5   To Seattle, 1928— 125
Chapter 6   Bachelor Days, 1928-1933 .150
Chapter 7   The Valley, 1900-1931 174
Chapter 8   Marriage and Family, 1933-1940 206
Chapter 9   The Hospital, 1940-1942 251
Chapter 10   The War, 1941 283
Chapter 11   Puyallup, 1942. 312
Chapter 12   Minidoka, the First Year, 1942-1943 345
Chapter 13   Minidoka, the Middle Year, 1943-1944 374
Chapter 14   Minidoka, the Third Year, 1944-1945 409
Chapter 15   Spokane Interval, 1945-1947 437
Chapter 16   Back in Seattle, 1947-1949 472
Chapter 17   High School and Beyond, 1949-1957 503
Chapter 18   The Job, 1957-1966 537
Chapter 19   The Profession, 1963-1970 568
Chapter 20   Epilogue. 600

Author's Notes 613
Names 617
Glossary 623

Seinojo, mother Yasue with infant Yoshi and unidentified woman

CHAPTER 1

The Beginning Revisited, Pre-1900

"Mukashi, mukashi…"

"Stop! Tell me the story in English, Daddy. I don't understand Japanese."

"Hummm… Maybe half and half be all right? I am Japanese; Midori, you are Japanese American. If you listen good, you will understand. *Neh.*"

"Mukashi, mukashi…" Thus, he repeated the words foreign to me and began another remembered tale of old Japan.

When I was young, Father entertained me with those fabled stories. A few he related from memory; the others he found in books. First, he read a page or two of Japanese text. The words were alien to me on first reading, so he did a follow-up with a translation in his unique, fractured English. In time, the rhythm of the language and the repetition of words and phrases became familiar, and I could follow the story with fewer interruptions. Now and then, he wandered from the story line and lost his way. He reminisced about his own life events in that faraway land when those times were not yet so long ago. Real life stories were devoid of ethereal spirits disguised as humans and ghosts surreptitiously roaming our environs when not ensconced in their nether world; tales that were doubly tantalizing in a foreign tongue. My father's reminiscences also lacked the gaggle of wily phantom creatures whose mischievous schemes pervade children's fairy tales that were familiar to me. His own true life stories without those other worldly elements lacked make-believe; I paid less attention and insisted he resume reading the written word.

Those musings of his life and times now fall within the realm of long ago. Times and customs are much changed, and what was then real has been transformed and now resides in the sphere of fantasy along with the magic-filled tales I adored. Father's stories were colored with his point of view and, through the years, details of his stories changed in the telling. It is doubtful they were deliberately altered; more likely, remembered events became blurred by the thickening fog in his mind, and they were lost, too, to witnesses of those events who could verify or contradict and correct him. My own youthful impatience and inattention makes me an unreliable chronicler, but before it all fades from human memory forever, those remembered fragments are here collected and set into a mosaic of his life as well as mine.

"*Mukashi, mukashi*. Ohh, *mukashi…*"

"Long, long ago. A very long time ago…in a faraway land in a village by the sea…"

When there were no sounds of motorcars or of airplanes soaring overhead, only rarely did mechanized noises of any sort intrude upon a person's senses. The quiet of midday could be pierced by creaking wheels of a burdened cart pulled along a rutted roadway or a vendor calling out his wares. Random human voices mingled with the sounds of nature, of lapping sea waves in the distance and of rustling leaves blown by the wind. Only the *uguisu* nightingale's songs from the forested hills rang clear and distinct.

In an island nation dotted with small clusters of dwellings set wherever the land proved hospitable to habitation, in an especially isolated coastal village where homes hugged the narrow spit of negotiable land between steep mountain cliffs and the sea, was the inauspicious setting where the boy baby was born. It was a birth with little fanfare. Alas, there was no grand entrance of tumbling down the river in a peach; Momotaro he was not. Nor did he arrive on the back of a giant tortoise, riding in on a galloping wave. Those phantasmal times were eons ago; this was the dawn of a new and modern era.

The birth was heralded only by the infant's own soft whimper.

The quietness broken, activity resumed in the household as word of the baby's safe delivery spread. Odai had stayed close to the kitchen that morning, knowing the distracted help needed reminding to stay focused on their chores and prepare breakfast.

"Make sure you have added two extra portions. The midwife and her assistant will be hungry, too. Otherwise, the two of you will be eating fish bones and the dregs from the soup pot this morning," Odai warned.

I cooked enough rice, and I can thin the soup with extra water, but… "Go get a couple more fish from the bucket," whispered one maid to the other.

Relieved a minor crisis had been averted, Odai leaned on a post and took in a deep breath to clear her mind.

"*Ah…ya…*" She realized she was tardy in starting her own chores. She sped through the empty walkway with uncharacteristic clatter to the adjacent building, which housed the children, the domestic servants, and her charge's private quarters. Stopping short of the closed *shoji*, she quickly knelt, knocked gently on the wooden frame, and called the room's occupant by his name. No sound. Gently sliding the panel partially open, she peered in and noted there was no activity within. Quickly rising to her feet, she entered, hustled across the room, and pushed aside the screens on the far side, exposing the silent quarters to filtered morning light.

"Kajiro *Ojii-chan*, are you still sleeping?" Odai asked loudly. There was a slight stirring on the futon where he lay. "*Ojii-chan*, do wake up," she persisted. "It's time to wake up. If you sleep too long, worms will eat your eyeballs in their sockets."

The old man opened his eyes to a mere squint and tried to focus. He blankly looked at nothing in particular.

"*Nani*? What?" he muttered.

"Ahh, you're finally awake," she said cheerfully, happy she had gained his attention. "While you slept, a boy baby was born. You have a second grandson."

His eyes opened wider; he turned his head and focused his cloudy eyes on her. "A grandson? You said a new grandson?" He silently repeated to himself, "New baby…boy baby…"

"Yes, your tiny new grandson…" Then, lowering her voice in a conspiring whisper to his ear, she said, "…he has a head shaped like the moon, they say."

"*Nani*?"

"A moon-head grandson."

The fog cleared, and the old man was alert with eyes wide. "A new grandson, you say. Hmm…that calls for a toast. *Onei-san*, bring me some *sake*. Big Sister, it's time to celebrate."

"What are you talking about, *Ojii-chan*?" Odai protested. "We have to clean you up. You have to eat food and drink some nourishing miso soup. You're so thin, I could blow you away with a puff."

The old man countered, "You sound like my daughter-in-law lecturing me. Common sense is, you don't drink and eat at the same time. I said bring the *sake*, *Onei-san*, I'll eat later."

Odai was surprised at the old man's vigorous response. He was more lucid than he had been in weeks. But he's forgotten my name. He's so old and forgetful.

ODAI

When Odai first arrived in the far-off village and began working for the family, *Ojii-chan* had taken an immediate liking to her, and they had soon established an easy, friendly relationship not common between patriarch and employee.

"*Dai-suki-na*, Odai-chan…my fa-vo-rite," the old man would intone in a singsong. Then in whispered confidence, he nuzzled her ear, "Odai, when you're older and start bleeding, I'll make you my mistress."

"Grandfather," she whispered back, "I would also need a young lover, someone capable of more than a tickle, *neh*."

"Ho ho, what insolence!" he guffawed. "I think we'll keep you, anyway. You might change your mind. *Daiji* Odai-*chan*... precious Odai."

The teasing was not continual, but it turned raucous after much heated *sake*.

"Odai, why won't you let me ride on your stomach? Hmm?" he pleaded. "I'm a little old and used, but there's still a lot of spirit. Humph...more spirit than those pip-squeak youngsters like my sons."

Occasionally, Yasue stepped in and admonished *Ojii-chan*. "Even you must treat our help with respect and kindness, Father. Remember, they are here to ease our burdens." The fact was: the family's considerate and generous treatment of their employees was common knowledge in the village, and requests were continually made to employ a daughter or son.

"Odai not only assists me in taking good care of you, Father, but she's more a sister to me. You should treat her like a daughter," Yasue scolded.

Daughter-in-law, never you worry," the old man said. "I treat Odai better and with more respect than I would a...a daughter."

Delighted with his own rancorous counter to Yasue, he could not stop chortling to himself.

The old man surely was a devil when he was younger. All those stories about him are probably true and more. But Yasue kept such thoughts to herself; voicing them was disrespectful, and she was bound by duty to be the traditional wife. Always honor your husband's father even more than one's own husband. Yasue's relationship with her even-tempered and sober husband had been harmonious with little rancor, and so it was with her father-in-law except when he was drinking his *sake*. That was when his wild spirits raged. When sober, he was a likable rascal, and Yasue could not have wanted for a better father-in-law, but it was also her responsibility to promote and maintain a harmonious household, which meant reigning in *Ojii-chan* once in a while.

The demands and irreverent banter had become less frequent as the old man became frail and then bedridden. Odai had assumed most of the caregiving since he still managed to be loudly vocal about preferring her company to others. The arrangement suited the family. Yasue was kept busy: as the mistress of the family, she managed the household, worked in the shop counseling and attending to the women customers' yardage needs for their kimonos, provided advice on accessories and adornments, as well as assuming the role of chief goodwill promoter. She also kept producing babies at regular intervals, as did most traditional, dutiful, and fertile wives in that era.

As Odai continued dressing *Ojii-chan*, she was alternately happy and sad. Glad the old man was unusually alert and feisty like his former self that morning, but sad he no longer remembered her name.

"*Onei-san*, where's the *sake*? I need to wet my lips." He loudly smacked his lips and sucked in his imaginary brew, "…it's been…a long time…ah, tickle my throat…warm, good…"

A wisp of a smile deepened the folds of his wizened face. Slowly, only a flutter crossed his lips; he fell silent, closed his eyes, and drifted back into sleep.

"You've fallen asleep again. All your energy is gone, used up," Odai said. "All you do is sleep day and night. Are there enough dreams to fill your endless sleep?"

"Kajiro, wake up. Wake up. The baby is a boy!"

He woke up with a start. "Heh? A baby…a baby boy? A healthy baby boy?"

"Yes, yes."

"I'm the father of a son…" "Yes, a healthy baby son."

"A boy, you say." Then after a long hesitation, "Maybe…perhaps… perhaps the baby should have been a girl?"

And, yes, the problems brought on by the birth of a boy would have been easier to resolve if the baby had been a girl.

"Now it's double trouble and more work to straighten everything out," the matriarch said. "I'll be mindful to hire less attractive female help for this household in the future." That said, she held her tongue and kept further thoughts unspoken. Yes, Hanako was much too attractive, and unforeseen trouble followed her through our threshold.

Patriarch Kihei reminded his wife, "Our son Kajiro is just a high-spirited boy, and Hanako's constant tempt... er, presence around the house, made her a convenient foil. They indulged in a little merrymaking." Her husband's remark and blasé attitude to their dilemma exacerbated the matriarch's ill-humor, but Kihei merrily continued, "You surely have not forgotten, wife of mine, we men in this family are greatly desired by women. A similar fate could have befallen me on a number of occasions, but that was not to be. I was lucky."

His wife's reply was not recorded.

The matriarch's responsibilities had increased twofold with an unwed mother and her newborn child, her grandson, living in her home. A wet nurse was found for the baby, who was then entrusted to her care for the duration. When Hanako completed her convalescence, a new position was found for the baby's mother in a faraway village with her parents' consent. The child remained with the father and his family as tradition dictated, though they had no intention of keeping him. As the firstborn son of Kajiro, the present *chonan*––or eldest/number one son––of patriarch Kihei, technically the newborn child was positioned to follow his father to become heir apparent, and someday become the family patriarch and inheritor of the properties. That was an untenable situation that had to be changed. The family could not subjugate subsequent generations of their family to be blemished descendants of a person born out of wedlock to a woman without proper bloodlines and credentials. A permanent home had to be found for the baby.

The boy was named Sutekichi, the "throwaway child," an arch example of the Japanese fondness for descriptive names. Innocent of the circumstances of his birth and saddled with a less-than-noble name, the throwaway child prospered despite the handicaps. He was engagingly alert, and his bubbly responses soon ingratiated him to all those around him. Sutekichi was precious. No one wanted to send him off to parts unknown; after all, he was the *chonan's* offspring. The solution to their dilemma was in their midst.

Tadao was the family's trusted employee whose dependable steadfast presence in the *mise* provided stewardship of the store's operation whenever the owner became distracted by other ventures. And his devotion to the family was beyond question. So, when childless Tadao and his wife were offered the throwaway child for their adoption, the couple was overjoyed and received the infant without hesitation. Their relationship with the family was further sealed when they gave Tadao the family surname, Nomura. Thus, the child retained his birth surname, and he was placed in convenient proximity to his birth family.

In China, the family surname was fundamental to the clan system, which incorporated filial piety to a common ancestor and loyalty to a vast extended family. Though the Japanese adopted important aspects of Chinese culture in the sixth and seventh centuries, they had retained their own restrictive system of hierarchy and class, where only nobles had surnames. Japanese commoners only began using surnames with the era of the Meiji Restoration in the mid-nineteenth century. Prior to that time, a surname identified the locale where a person lived, such as "large valley," or Ohtani.

The Family

For centuries, small groups of settlers had lived in the tiny hamlets bordering the sea on the Shima peninsula well south of the sacred shrine in Ise Province. Close in distance to the historical capitals when measured as the crow flies, they were far removed from the well-traveled roadways and the spheres of power ruling the country. The mountainous terrain geographically isolated the inhabitants who settled in those lands and protected them from unwanted intrusions to their lives. They lived primarily off the sea's bounty, as there was little arable land on the narrow stretches between mountain and sea.

The inhabitants of one such community all used the surname Nomura, or "field village," from whence Kajiro's father, Kihei, had come. In search of greater opportunities not available to him there, he left his village and traveled west along mountainous trails, ending his journey in Kamisaki, where he settled.

Kihei, having decided the community was large enough to support several merchants, proceeded to set up a competing dry goods store and opened for business. The store did well; he married and started a family. Kajiro was the firstborn son.

A shopkeeper is a tradesman, and in the feudal hierarchy, he held a low social station, well below the farmer and craftsman. Classed below the tradesman were the dregs of society: criminals and their ilk. On the very bottom were the unmentionable *eta's*. In India, there was once a group designated "Untouchables", who were known as the lowest of the low. Here, a group was designated "Unmentionable"; therefore, they did not exist.

The farmer, a commoner with his prestige position next to the samurai, nevertheless toiled from dawn to dark for survival. Other commoners, fishermen among them, braved the seas and nature's whims to earn their livelihoods. A merchant labors less rigorously, but he must also work diligently, and nurture his reputation as honest and trustworthy to succeed and prosper.

Kihei hired help to run the shop in order to maintain a satisfied customer base, and other men were hired to operate Kihei's small side business ventures. He also employed domestics to assist his wife with the upkeep of their extended family, and for their workers he provided each a meal every working day. The intermingling of family and workers, private and business affairs, generated a constant beehive of activity in their home. The expenses of supporting it all consumed most of the profits, but Kihei was comfortable with their hectic lifestyle and satisfied with his lot. If only...

Once established, the shop maintained its share of the villagers' patronage, but the sparse population precluded further expansion. Itching for another venture, Kihei found one to supplement his existing enterprise.

He acquired a boat to carry freight and began purchasing goods in Nagoya to sell in his shop, thus avoiding the uncertainties encountered with merchandise carted by scheduled transport serving the villages on the peninsula.

The wood hulled, single sail, flat bottomed vessel had a low beamed interior compartment to store goods. It was considerably larger than the villagers' fishing boats, but a great deal smaller than the regularly scheduled transport ships that sailed between Osaka and Tokyo. Its size was adequate for the shorter runs they undertook. Conforming to edicts of pre-Meiji era regulations prohibiting private ownership of ocean going vessels, it was not designed or intended to sail the open seas. The boat sailed within sight of land, permitting easy sighting of the coastal villages along the way. Living quarters on board were rough but adequate for the crew.

Chonan Kajiro was given greater responsibilities and put in charge of the craft to keep him busy, and to quell further mischief making. The new duties suited him well, and he relished the variety of challenges he encountered both at sea and in dealing with tradesmen on land. As a transporter, Kajiro and his crew routinely spent several days in Nagoya to purchase and to load merchandise; they then set sail for home. Along the way, they stopped in the small coastal communities to deal with shop owners, selling them goods they had picked up in Nagoya. After a respite spent at home, they again set sail, returning to the villages visited earlier, picking up foodstuff and fresh fish to sell to merchants in the city. Kajiro had a knack for trade and business and did well. He initiated and invested in various other ventures––some were successful, a few were not. To expand his opportunities as a trader, Kajiro had also become a fish broker, and when he saw a market for fish products like *katsuo* and dried *nori*, the family became involved. Growing silkworms, which was popular at the time, was another endeavor the family undertook. Those who dealt with him, found Kajiro trustworthy and fair in their negotiations, and when the business was done, he was good company when they partied.

"Hello, Cousin, you have come a long way to visit us here in Kamisaki. Is there a special occasion for you and your family's visit? Or did a relative die during my absence?"

"You're teasing me, Kajiro-*san*. Of course you know why I'm here."

"Yae-*san*, I truly don't know. Forgive me for not knowing something I'm supposed to know. Now be a good girl, and let me hear the secret."

Tears came in large droplets from her eyes and fell on her lap.

Alarmed at the girl's response, Kajiro called his mother at the top of his voice. "*Oh-ka! Oh-ka!*" The matriarch promptly appeared.

"*Naze sonna koe...* Why do you call in such a voice?" She spied Yae with tears still streaming down her cheeks. "Have you two had an argument already?"

"No, we have not. I was very polite and asked her why she came to visit."

"Oh, is that all?"

"What? Is there a secret about her visit you failed to tell me?"

"Nothing's a secret when something has been known for at least ten years."

The young cousin started sobbing audibly. "*Okaa*, now you made her cry."

"Son, be nice to Yae-*chan*."

"I have been nice to her. Now tell me what everyone else has known for ten years."

"Hmmm... Somehow, we must have forgotten to tell you." A rapid memory search came up with no "sharing conferences" involving her son. It was time to confess.

"Well...ah...hum... We, Sister and I, decided you would marry her daughter Yae. You two have been engaged since well before that miserable affair with that maid Hanako."

"But...but..."

"We'll follow expected formalities: name a *nakodo*, go-between..." "A total sham..." Kajiro interjected.

"Don't be insulting. You're not entitled to an opinion on this." "And… and what about…?"

"It's legal. Her name is Kato, not Nomura." "That's… I was… You conspired…"

"Son, a *chonan* has privileges as well as responsibilities."

"I understand that, Mother. So what does that have to do with…?"

"We felt this was the perfect alignment for our families. And they were willing to overlook your obvious foibles, and as their daughter's mother-in-law, I would protect her rather than be an antagonist."

"Thank you for telling me, Mother." Then, turning to his bride-to-be, he bowed respectfully. "Please excuse me while I retire to my room to digest this information, Yae-*san*. Tomorrow we can listen to our parents' schem-m-m…plans they've brewed up for us."

He left the women and went to his room and called for the maid, "*Onei-san*, bring me *sake*."

The plan hatched by the two mothers a decade or so earlier was carried out without further ado. By most witnesses' accounts, Yae and Kajiro's marriage was successful. She was a dutiful, traditional wife, and Kajiro continued on with his old bachelor ways when on business away from home. At home and anywhere in proximity to its environs, Kajiro was the image of a kind and solicitous husband, wise and a successful businessman. Altogether, seven children were born to the couple, and they all contributed to the noisy hustle and bustle that prevailed in their household. Sutekichi had been adopted out, but he joined in the household fray more often than naught. Yae's first child, born with disabilities, was followed by a daughter and a second son. The fact that Kajiro's fourth offspring be designated *chonan* was duly accepted, and the three generations lived in harmony most of the time. With the passing of the elder matriarch and Kihei, Yae became matriarch, and Kajiro the patriarch of the clan. He was flexible and smart, and their ventures flourished.

When the Tokugawa Shogunate gave way to the Meiji Reformation, massive changes to the status quo were adopted, and modernization became national policy. The changes were substantial and affected all aspects of their lives. The edicts filtered down to faraway villages a bit more slowly, but everyone fell in step. Cultural changes lagged behind, and some customs hardly changed at all. In the shop, customers were properly greeted and goods brought out for their inspection and discussed, perhaps over a cup of tea...

Not all things were subject to change however, and the man's love for *sake* continued unabated. "*Onei-san*, I told you once, maybe twice. For the third time–– bring me my *sake*!"

GRANDFATHER'S PASSING

News of his moon-head grandson had jostled Kajiro's consciousness; he was aware and lively again for one last brief time, soon after, he fell silent and never spoke again. His eyes remained unfocused, and he barely stirred under his futon. His lips no longer parted to take in nourishment, and liquids rolled from his mouth. Air was his only sustenance.

The household carried on in quiet respect anticipating his forthcoming passing. Unaware of the solemnity of such times, it was moon-head grandson's squeals that pierced the hush. Within days of the birth, the one morning Odai stepped into the languid air of *Ojii-chan's* room, and she knew he had died. He had run out of dreams.

The family had planned to consult with Yasue's brother Shoshun regarding the proper protocol required for *Ojii-chan's* funeral before his passing, since the inevitable was not unanticipated, but the family had been distracted by recent events in the household. They also had not vigorously pursued preplanning a funeral, fearing it might tempt the gods into speeding the demise or worse. When the old man died, the family was unprepared, and much commotion ensued. A dispatch was sent immediately to Shoshun, requesting his presence as soon as possible to oversee the funeral rites. In the meantime, *Ojii-chan's* body was repositioned with the head of the corpse to the north; the direction living persons avoid when sleeping to disarm a similar deathly omen.

The shop was closed for the duration. Members of the family dug deep into their wardrobes searching for their mourning garb that had been put into storage after *Obaa-chan* Yae's passing years before. Kakichi, the *chonan*, now patriarch, was required to wear his mourning outfit for thirteen months, Yasue for fifty days, and other family members were to wear theirs for a lesser prescribed length of time.

The local village priest, who had been summoned, arrived almost immediately. Quickly setting up his props, the priest began rituals for the dead. The Buddhist sutras were chanted to contact and soothe the dead man's spirit now roaming the netherworld before his burial. The spectacle of priest with his assistant, both carrying their ceremonial paraphernalia rushing through the street to the house, had been the silent affirmation alerting the villagers that someone had died. The news of *Ojii-chan's* passing was swift.

The family had begun the first of several prescribed services to honor *Ojii-chan's* memory and death. Dressed in his splendid priestly robes in contrast to the group of simply clothed family members, the priest untoned his sutras in breath-long monotone stanzas, punctured with a loud hissing as he took in air with clenched teeth: "Zzzssh." He tapped the metal bell once, twice, or more times: "Ting…ting, ting," providing punctuation and a wake-up for dozers. The next stanza was chanted, breath exhausted: "Zzzssh." Stanza after stanza, the sutra was read: "Ting, ting."

The original Buddhist sutras in Sanskrit had been translated into Chinese when the religion migrated there from India. When it spread to Japan, the Japanese people continued to read the sutras in Chinese rather than translate them into Japanese. Like a Catholic service in Latin, the words were incomprehensible to the layman, but hearing the chants repeated through a lifetime, they now provided a sense of continuum, that brings comfort to the brethren.

The hair of the deceased was shaved off, much like the shorn head of a priest. The body was washed then clothed in a simple white garment and positioned with knees to the chest, the fetal position to ready his body for burial. That evening, the family kept vigil with burning incense and lit candles until morning. Flower bouquets sent by relatives, close friends, and associates arrived at the house and were placed on display near the entry. When Shoshun arrived from his distant village, he quickly changed into his priestly robes and joined the village priest in the chanting that was in progress.

In the morning, the body in its sitting prenatal position, was set into a tub-shaped wooden casket then set on a litter and carried to the cemetery in a procession of priests, family, relatives, and other mourners. The casket with body was buried, and a headstone was positioned to mark its location.

Although cremation was now practiced in the cities and was spreading to rural areas where conserving scarce land was a practical alternative, people in Kamisaki had deferred. Years earlier, several villagers who had vigorously advocated the practice of cremation over interment were coincidentally stricken with personal tragedies; it was considered a bad omen. No one else wanted to invoke a similar streak of bad luck by committing to cremation. The family had Kajiro *Ojii-chan's* body interred.

Shoshun stayed with the family to participate in the first seventh-day services for the dead. The long sutra intonations, tingling of bells, incense fumes mingling and wafting ever upward, were undertaken in hopes of influencing the gods to grant *Ojii-chan* a noble life in his next incarnation. Six additional "seven-day anniversary" services, for a total of seven, were required. After the seventh service, forty-nine days after the death, a respite from funerary services allowed the family to live a normal life until the next important date, the one-year anniversary service. An annual service would be scheduled thereafter. Payments for services were a priest's primary source of income, so it behooved a priest to diligently remind his parishioners of important upcoming death anniversaries. These tasks kept him busy.

When Yasue's brother departed for home after the significant seventh-day memorial service, he was laden with generous gifts for himself and his wife, in addition to the handsome fee he received for services rendered. Visiting his sister was always well worth the journey for Shoshun. Though the actual map distance to his village and temple were relatively close, the path between the two villages was torturous. The mountainous terrain with sudden steep drops to the roaring ocean below made for narrow winding roads carved in the cliffs, or long circuitous paths around mountainous obstacles. The route had no consistency vertically, as it climbed up or dropped down as the terrain dictated. Shoshun was spared the endurance test on his return by boarding the family's trading boat bound for Nagoya. The crew dropped him off at the pier closest to his village. They hired a laborer to tote his packages up the mountain slope to the temple complex where he lived, then the vessel resumed its journey to trade its wares in the city.

It was the right decision, allowing Yasue to marry a merchant, mused Shoshun. There is more prestige being the wife of a physician, and definitely more as a clergyman's wife. Married to a tradesman, she must work in the *mise*. It's not exactly demeaning labor…but it's… The slight sneer of his upturned nostril completed his line of thought. His mind kept racing. No, she could not have endured the rigors as a clergyman's wife. Yasue, my quiet, unassuming younger sister so easily swayed by others, who could also turn obstinate and immovable like a rock, is best suited to be a merchant's wife; it is her niche.

Shoshun returned home to his wife and their austere cottage without sharing his thoughts. Must not forget we're beneficiaries of generous kinfolk.

The somber funereal atmosphere that had prevailed over the household, along with the weight of adhering to the prescribed protocol attendant with the death of the old patriarch had lifted with Shoshun's departure. The shop reopened for business--too soon for the traditionalists, but too impractical to do otherwise. Family members continued to wear their mourning garments as dictated, but soon the hustle and bustle within the household quickened to its usual pitch.

Kakichi felt he had fulfilled his obligation of providing a dignified and proper departure for his parent, and he was ready to carry on as the family patriarch. Actually, he had been given the title several years before, when his father decided to retire and give up a daily work schedule to live life as a country gentleman. Kakichi knew well the old man's skills in business dealings far exceeded his own abilities, as he had continued to seek Kajiro's advice on major decisions; the decisions were now his alone to make.

Naming the Baby

Yasue did not attend the earlier services, though as matriarch of the family, she had participated behind the scenes making arrangements for many of the funeral functions despite her convalescence. At that time, her concerns had also revolved around her newborn son, who was not as robust as Seinojo and Tameko, her two children who survived. The infant was physically frail like the two who had previously died soon after birth, and she feared losing a third baby. She knew her other duties would keep her from devoting her full attention and time to her sickly child to ensure his survival. She needed help.

"Odai-*san*, I have a very great favor to ask of you," Yasue said. She had treated Odai with inordinate courtesy since her arrival. Though she had been hired primarily to tend to *Ojii-chan's* needs and to look after the children, she was so resourceful she was soon assisting Yasue in all aspects of running the household; the mistress depended on her. She was being enlisted for additional assistance.

"What is the favor you ask, Yasue-*san*?" Odai inquired, calling her by her name rather than by her title as she did in public.

"Little Bot-*chan* is so tiny and sickly, not at all strong. I worry he may not survive. I'm overwhelmed with distractions I'm required to tend to, and he needs so much more devoted attention than I can give.

I feel so helpless." Then, almost voicelessly, Yasue whispered, "I may lose him like the others. I don't want this baby to die, too."

Odai sat silently while the answer to her question was obliquely finding its way to the open.

Yasue continued, "He needs so much attention. I'll soon be busy in the *mise* again. You no longer have Kajiro *Ojii-san* demanding your attention and…will you? Will you help me care for little Bot-*chan*?"

"Yasue-*san*, you need not ask. I acknowledge all the children in my charge."

"I may be asking you to be more than a nursemaid." After a pause, she said more slowly, "He is a sweet, lovely baby despite being so frail. Will you assist me so we'll both see him grow up to have a long, happy life? *Tanomi-masu*, I humbly request." Yasue bowed long and deeply.

The bargain was sealed. Odai took the responsibility to heart and became the infant's unofficial second mother.

Odai had come to pick up the baby after Yasue had nursed him. "Yasue-*san*, Bot-*chan* is such a common term for such a special baby; I'd like to call him by his name. What did you name him?"

"Ah-la… We've been so busy with *Ojii-san's* funeral, we haven't given Bot-*chan* a name! And we didn't register his birth!" Yasue exclaimed.

By law, all births must be registered within a week. More than two weeks had elapsed since Bot-*chan's* arrival. The second problem was easily resolved by changing the birth date to comply with the law. Since the day of birth was a made-up day, they selected an auspicious day that would fall between a Buddhist seventh-day memorial date and a Shinto tenth-day memorial day to avoid incurring any bad luck by setting the birth date on an ancestor's memorial day.

Belatedly, Kakichi consulted with the family to select the infant's name. Everyone agreed the name should incorporate Grandfather Kajiro's name in some way since the infant's birth was the subject of the old man's last known utterances. Bot-*chan* was not the first-born son, a *chonan*; therefore, he could not be given the patriarch's name outright. The test was to select a name using the same written kanji character and meaning, but to apply a second pronunciation and adding a different ending syllable or two.

When the Japanese adopted the Chinese written ideographs rather than develop their own unique written language, it occurred well after

Japan's spoken language had evolved. The Chinese character with its established meaning was assigned to the Japanese word with the same or a similar meaning. However, cultural differences, misinterpretations, and other factors added complexities to the imported system, and irregularities became endemic. A written ideograph can be pronounced in more than one way and have more than one meaning to the Japanese. A spoken word can often be written with different ideographs, and it can have multiple meanings. Such inconsistencies and ambiguities in the language promoted word play as a favorite pastime in Japan, a game not limited to scholars.

The family council began Bot-*chan*'s name selection by combing through their reference books for an alternative pronunciation of Grandfather Kajiro's kanji ideograph. They found the kanji was verbalized as "Yoshi" during samurai eras, although the word was and remained commonly identified with a different ideograph. "*Tsugu*," to come after, was added to the first half, and the name Yoshitsugu was registered.

It was such an archaic and uncommon pronunciation for the kanji, it baffled most people upon first encountering the written name—a frustration the child dealt with the rest of his life.

SETTLING BACK INTO DAILY LIFE

His birth dutifully registered and armed with a four-syllable name, Yoshitsugu joined the bustling family life of traders and shopkeepers. Their lives were not as hardscrabble as some folks, or as dependent on the elements of weather or the sea as the fishermen of the village, but the family's livelihood depended on the villagers' fortunes and goodwill. Just as in the days when Kihei and Kajiro were the patriarchs, Kakichi supported an extended family of three generations who still remained at home. Besides his immediate family, dependents included unmarried siblings and on occasions the families of married siblings, a nanny for the children, and at least two girls hired to clean, wash, and cook for the household, plus other temporary or part-time help who came as needed.

Busy during the day with assigned tasks, at the end of the workday, those who worked for the family, including shop clerks and trading boat crewmen upon their return from a voyage, joined the extended household members and sat down together in haphazard clusters for the evening meal. There were free-wheeling discussions of every sort, about events of the day, or the new edicts from the government and its growing prowess spreading its tentacles to the far reaches of the nation, and its effect on their business and their lives. The family had greater access to such news through their trading contacts in Nagoya and remained more current than most people living in such isolated areas as theirs. Much of the talk was less serious with enough gossip to keep the discussions lively and spicy

The new millennium was approaching, and the Western world was preparing for a centennial celebration. The Japanese had adopted the Gregorian calendar a quarter century before; however, they preferred to date their history by their old traditional methods based on an emperor's reign, so their conversion to the new was partial. In their daily lives, the Japanese used the Western calendar, so New Year's Day was celebrated along with the rest of the world.

For the New Year, the house needed to be cleaned from top to bottom, and old tatami mats replaced with new ones. Preparations for the special foods to be served started well in advance. The womenfolk worked to exhaustion to have it ready on the First. The variety and great quantities of celebratory foods so painstakingly prepared, were planned to be eaten through the following three days with minimal additional time at the stove. Visits with family and friends kept the holiday spirit alive for days. Another incentive to party was a tradition that made New Year's Day everyone's birthday; everyone became a year older the first day of each year. Since a Japanese baby is considered to be one year old at birth, on New Year's Day 1900, three months after his birth, baby Yoshi-*yan* was a two-year old.

Yoshi-*yan*, as he came to be called, was a more fitting three syllable moniker that rolled easily off the tongue, than his four-syllable name. Yoshitsugu was reserved for formal occasions, when it was dusted off and displayed. That such an ingeniously constructed name was bestowed on such an inconsequential and sickly child was a pity. The infant was prone to catching any and all germs lurking around the neighborhood, and Odai was kept busy nursing him back to health. When he was not strapped to Odai's back, Yoshi-*yan* was carried on the back of one or another of the maids while they worked. The child, sleeping contentedly, was not a great burden, and the girls vied with each other to watch the child. When healthy, Yoshi-*yan* was a happy and complacent infant whose smiling responses and gurgles captivated the household, especially the females. Father Kakichi had a few reservations that his son should garner so much cooing and pampering, and he was thankful Seinojo was the *chonan* rather than Yoshi-*yan*.

Kakichi, Yoshi's father

CHAPTER 2

Growing Up, 1900–1916

TWO YEARS AFTER YOSHI-*YAN*'S ARRIVAL, sister Umaye was born, but she died within a year. A year later, baby sister Chisato joined the family. There were now four living children after seven births.

Older siblings, Seinojo, ensconced in his privileged position, and Tameko were both healthy and rambunctious children. Yoshi-*yan* continued to be a frail child, and though he was no longer the youngest, the household kept careful watch over him, and the help continued to keep him close by as they tended to their chores. His genial temperament and ingratiating ways still made him a favorite, although he was known to rile with angry outbursts on rare occasions. At such times, they were reminded, "He was born in the year of the wild boar, and when it bares its fangs, we see his wild side." His audience usually stepped aside and watched in awe as he fumed and fussed.

One day, Tameko came home with the measles, having been exposed at school. It was promptly passed on to Yoshi-*yan*. They were both put to bed. Yoshi-*yan*'s fever climbed, and his survival was in doubt once again. Tameko was down only a short time before she considered herself well and chafed at the mandatory bed rest imposed on her. Still riddled with her red pustules, she snuck out of the sickroom and went outdoors to play with her friends. On her return home, she became seriously ill and died. Yoshi-*yan* eventually recovered and survived to live his third or fourth life. There were only three children in the family again.

Another baby girl was born to replace Tameko within a year. For the sake of Yasue's health, a wet nurse was found for baby Kimiko. The woman insisted on caring for the infant in her own home, and Yasue reluctantly agreed to the arrangement. When the child was ready to be weaned, the wet nurse insisted the child would be better served if she stayed with her. Kimiko was not formally adopted by the other family; she was on permanent loan. The arrangement was not a secret, both families and the siblings acknowledged she was a Nomura child; she just lived and grew up in a separate household. When her foster parents died, she finally returned home.

A Meiji edict a quarter century before had established an educational system requiring all children to attend school. Since the village and its surrounds were sufficiently populated to support a school for the primary grades, the village youngsters were able to attend a school within walking distance of their homes. Most children managed to comply with the mandatory eight years of schooling. There were about fifty students in Yoshi-*yan*'s class, too small to be split into two classes but too large for effective teaching. Academically, Yoshi-*yan* was an average student who was often absent from school due to one illness or other. He did well in subjects he enjoyed, especially literature and history, but mathematics was not a favorite. He endured the daily calisthenics all students participated in; the regimen was mandatory. It was promoted as a symbol of their nation's physical and spiritual fitness, and garnered national pride. Yoshi-*yan*'s attempts at other athletic endeavors were meager, and he was best described as woefully lacking a stellar macho image.

His various illnesses contributed to his slow physical growth, putting Yoshi-*yan* among the runts in the classroom; he was skinny, too. A number of factors kept him from being bullied, as small children are often targets for their larger classmates. Family had some clout, and an older sibling was a presence; ultimately Yoshi-*yan*'s engaging disposition disarmed his enemies sufficiently to keep him from becoming their victim. With the bullies kept at bay, he easily made friends with his classmates and other children in the village.

Even during the ages when the two sexes choose to stay segregated in their activities, Yoshi-*yan* could be found surrounded by girls who found him far more companionable than other boys. Always watched over, lovingly tended to, and adored since infancy, Yoshi-*yan* had been nurtured by the females surrounding him, and he forever continued to bask in their attention, always comfortable in their midst.

The school day started on a wrong note, and Yoshi-*yan*'s usual good humor had vanished. He seethed silently through his classes and waited impatiently for school to end. Single-minded in his mission, he rushed home to confront his mother. Once past the entry threshold, he kicked off his footwear, letting it fly hither and yon for someone else to pick up.

"*Okaa-a-a-san*!" Yoshi hollered as he got past the vestibule. "*Okaa-a…*" He spied his mother. "Today, I saw Yosuke wearing my uniform at school. Mother, how did that happen?"

"Your clothes? Are you sure?"

"Yes, I'm sure. He wasn't wearing his usual tatty things. He had on one of my…the one with a tear on the sleeve. I meant to ask Odai to sew it for me."

"Well, yes, you've worn those clothes, Yoshi-*yan*."

"I knew you were responsible. Why do you give away my things?"

"The clothes were not new, and you have many. Yosuke's mother was overjoyed you wanted to share with them. He doesn't have any other school outfits, *nah*."

"Well, yes… He looked a lot spiffier today…in my outfit. *Okaa-san*, if you had only told me before, I wouldn't have been so surprised and upset."

She did not hear him. I wish I had known about the torn sleeve; I could have found something else for the boy, Yasue mumbled to herself.

Yoshi-*yan* was glad he had checked his temper and had not confronted his classmate. They both saved face with their silence; it was a lesson to be learned.

The men and children were gathered around tables set on the tatami as they ate their evening meal of fish, rice, soup and sides, plus a goodly variety of pickled edibles––a menu that rarely varied. What changed from meal to meal was the species of fish selected and the manner in which the fish was prepared: raw, as sashimi, *tataki,* the Asian ceviche, braised, grilled, fried in a pan, or fried in deep oil.

The women, having served the men and children, were joining the diners to begin their meal while the two maids remained busy refilling rice bowls and cups of tea. They would eat last. In this house, they never ran out of food; sometimes they ran short of the main fish entrée, but there was plenty of *tsukemono* to eat with their blend of rice and tea to fill their stomachs.

"Yoshitsugu," his father, Kakichi, called to him one evening.

He knew immediately he was being put on notice. Everyone in the household knew Yoshi-*yan* called by his full four-syllable name meant the topic was serious.

A quick, respectful reply was called for. "*Hai, Otoo-san* Yes, Father," he said as he put down his rice bowl and chopsticks.

"Yoshitsugu, I received a complaint about you today. I'm sure you know what it's about."

How did he find out? The thought crossed through Yoshi-*yan's* mind. "*Otoo-san*, we returned the boat." His father said nothing, so he continued, "My friends and I decided it was a good day to go fishing. We needed a boat. The boat was just sitting there in the water, and the owner was gone. We just borrowed it for a short time." As an afterthought, he added, "It was a very good day for fishing."

"Humm… In that case, where is the fish you caught? Perhaps you owe the boat's owner, Tainaka-*san*, the fish you caught."

"We let Taro take home the fish, *Otoo-san.* He said his family would enjoy some fresh fish for dinner."

It was common knowledge in the village that Taro's father was ill and the family was experiencing hard times. The fish the boys had caught during their clandestine excursion meant the boy's family had food to eat for days. Kakichi realized his son's caper, which started as a lark, had ultimately been a charitable one, but, he was still obliged to lecture his son to satisfy Tainaka-*san's* affront. "You know the rules, son. A fisherman cleans his boat after using it. Next time you borrow someone else's boat, you must clean your mess and leave it in the condition you found it, especially if you borrow the boat without permission."

"Ah, yes. You must clean the boat," Uncle Katsujiro interjected. "Even the fish in the ocean don't like the smell of a dirty boat." Amused by his own wit, he chuckled and nearly choked on the rice in his mouth.

Everyone who heard the exchange agreed the resolution to the boat "theft" had been wisely handled under the circumstances. Taro's family had food to eat, and Tainaka-*san* would have a clean boat when it was borrowed the next time.

Yoshi-*yan* was relieved the inquisition and reprimand were over and the original infraction had not come to light. He had learned early on that he could pilfer a few stray coins from the till without detection, and he put the skill to the test when he needed a sugar fix. Unknown to him, the staff was aware of his thefts, which were infrequent. As long as they remained a trifle, it was considered the boy's perk––his unofficial allowance to buy the sweets and *manju* he loved. Yoshi-*yan* had made a purchase of goodies paid with his latest ill-gotten gains before he and his friends went fishing that day. Out on the waters, away from peering eyes, the shared sweets tasted ever more delicious, and to their surprise, fish began nibbling on their bait. Paradise could not be better than this.

In a small and isolated village, the villagers know everyone's affairs, their schedules and routines, and their personal habits. There were few secrets. Because everyone knew when each fisherman took his boat out to sea during any given season, the adventurous village boys knew when it was an opportune time to borrow a particular boat without repercussions. It was an ongoing game. Only occasionally were the culprits identified and reprimanded.

"Those *kozo's* have taken my boat out again! I'll hang the rascals by their toenails if I ever catch them, I will!" The boat-owning fisherman cursed loud and long, and with that, the incident was forgotten until the next time.

The family still owned the trading vessel from Kajiro's seagoing trading days, though no one in the extended family had the knack for handling the boat like the old patriarch. Now operated entirely by hired help, landlubber Kakichi sailed aboard infrequently. When business required his presence in the city, travel by water on one's own boat was undeniably more convenient. Yasue went on buying trips to purchase yardage goods semiannually, and she went to witness the new fashion trends in vogue to report back to her customers. Duly noting that the women she saw in Nagoya all displayed their natural ivory toned teeth, she too abandoned the centuries-old custom for married women to blacken their teeth. Unfortunately, the plucked eyebrows never grew back.

Yoshi-*yan* had never expressed much interest in his parents' special shopping trips to Nagoya, although the entire household eagerly awaited their return home for the bountiful *omiyage*, gifts that accompanied them back, as much as for their relief knowing the journey had been safe and successful. Before one such trip when he was still a preschooler, the child told his mother she need not bring him a gift from her forthcoming trip. His parents were dumbfounded. How strange? Of course, every kid wants a treat, they thought.

Yasue consulted immediately with Odai. This being a confidential conversation, she leaned in close to her. "Do you think Yoshi-*yan* is normal in the head? He just told us he did not need any *omiyage* from Nagoya."

Odai laughed and assured Yasue, "He is fine. He would be delighted to have a new picture book; even better, he loves sweets."

"He seems normal, but children don't ever refuse…you…understand… His uncle Katsuji…"

"No. Do not think that," Odai said quickly.

"I'm so relieved. I do worry when my children exhibit strange behavior." Yasue sat back and relaxed. "Now what *omiyage* can I bring back for you? 'Nothing' is not a proper answer." They both laughed in kinship.

Some years later, Yoshi-*yan* was invited to accompany his parents and older brother Seinojo to Nagoya to see for himself from where those *omiyage* had come from. It was a rare treat when a child was taken on such trips, and he reacted with enthusiasm, leaving no doubt in Yasue's mind he was a normal kid.

Streets, alleys, and ditches ran in myriad directions with a hodgepodge of wooden buildings, each a unique specimen bordering the roadways. Hordes of people of every description walked alongside conveyances carrying goods or people. General merchandise stores, specialty shops, and eateries were so abundant Yoshi-*yan* soon lost count. The sights, sounds, and even scents were exotic and consuming, and he was completely captivated by the experience; a new world opened for him. He understood the stories he read in books were not all make-believe.

Yoshi-*yan* was taken on several more trips to Nagoya and also a pilgrimage to visit the grounds of the sacred Grand Shinto Shrine in Ise; otherwise, everyday life in the village continued in the same steady, uneventful pace characteristic of rural villages. That is how it appeared. Actually, progress had been infiltrating their routine insidiously with new innovations and new government regulations since the Reformation—changes so obvious in urban areas. Japan was prospering and becoming a political and military force in the International Arena, and a proliferation of newspapers disseminated the larger news events to reach even the most remote areas in a country with a growing literate populace.

The country was in its ascendency; on the other hand, the family's fortunes had taken a downward trajectory, and their finances were far from robust. The cost of keeping and maintaining their trading boat had become untenable; it was an obsolete relic as the use of steamboats became widespread; the sailing ship was sold. Other business ventures lost money, although their small-scale cottage industries, such as their *katsuo*, dried fish, and silkworm production, were correspondingly profitable on a small scale. The present patriarch was not a business scion. Kakichi was a wannabe with a penchant for failed undertakings.

For a youngster still approaching adolescence, Yoshi-*yan* accepted the changes being wrought by modernization taking place in the outside world as intrinsic progress. At home, changes evolved slowly, the personnel came and went, the crowd at evening meals dwindled, new babies arrived periodically filling the voids, and all was well as Yoshi-*yan* viewed the world.

LEAVING HOME FOR THE FIRST TIME

"Yoshitsugu, your mother wishes to speak to you," his father said. "It is important. Please attend to it immediately."

He didn't have to tell me it's important; he called me by my full name, thought Yoshi-*yan*. Why is he sending me to Mother? Father is always the bearer of important announcements and of meting out the discipline.

Curiosity prompted him to seek out his mother posthaste. He found her alone, kneeling in front of her dresser, adjusting her hair.

She was large with child again, and she sat on several cushions to ease the imbalance created by her protruding midsection. Shifting her weight, she and her cushion slid into a turn, and she faced her son.

"Yoshi-*yan*, you've come. I see you forgot to close the shoji. Do that, will you?" she said. "Now come here and sit close to me. I want to talk to you privately."

Secluded in her room together, mother and son sat facing each other. "I don't know how to start. I want very much for you to understand," she began as she studied him intently. Words began to flow. "We worried and tried very hard to keep you alive when you were little; you were sick so frequently. We succeeded, and you've grown and become quite healthy, but I still worry about you."

Her prelude revealed no clue to the important matter for which Yoshi-*yan* was summoned. She was not blurting it out. She was proceeding in the oblique way etiquette dictated, the usual circuitous approach.

Wondering if she was waiting for him to interject his agreement, he spoke, "*Okaa-san*, I'm ever thank…"

"Please don't interrupt me. Just listen," she snapped. Taken aback by her brusqueness, he hung his head and studied the interwoven strands holding together the tatami they sat on.

"Yes, I still worry about you, Yoshi-*yan*. What will you do when you finish school? You are not suited for manual labor. How will you support yourself?" He knew not to interrupt her when she paused. "I know you love to read and expect to go on to high school like Seinojo, but that would mean leaving home and going to live in Ise to attend school."

"*Okaa-san*, that's still a few years away…"

"Please be quiet, and let me finish," she said firmly. Her eyes downcast, she continued, "Our financial circumstances cannot support you going to high school in the future."

Yoshi-*yan* was dumbstruck. He had never paid much attention to the family business. He took for granted their relatively comfortable lifestyle. They were not rich by any means, but they did not endure real hardships either. He had naturally assumed he would follow Seinojo and continue his schooling in Ise City after finishing his eight years of school in the village. He thought he had the luxury of postponing any decisions about his future for many more years.

He had always known he eventually had to strike out on his own since he was only a second son. Seinojo, the number-one son, would inherit the business, the house, and the properties––everything. That was the custom of the land. In addition to inheriting the estate, the oldest son became the patriarch who was responsible for the support and care of the parents and other dependents in their old age. All other sons were expected to leave home and earn their own livelihoods, and start their own clans. Thus, details of the family business had never been shared with Yoshi-*yan*, nor had he taken any but the most cursory interest in money matters. To learn the family's fortunes had eroded so greatly was disturbing.

"We must be prudent about our spending; it's imperative. I'm afraid your younger brothers and sisters will have fewer privileges than you had." That said, the preliminaries were over, and Yasue sighed with relief.

Yoshi-*yan* sat speechless as he tried to assess the thunderbolt that had just shattered his world.

"I've thought and pondered what you could do in the future… something that wasn't exerting physically…something that would allow you to sit and read to your heart's content." She smiled. "Yoshi-*yan*, my brother Shoshun has agreed to take you on as an apprentice. That is what I had to tell you."

Yoshi-*yan* was pummeled by a second thunderbolt. His world had exploded with the first part of "important matter;" this second part was hurling him into the unknown, away from the shelter and security he took for granted.

His mother continued talking in the same vein, "Priests do not engage in physical labor. They may putter around their shrine dusting off a cobweb or two, and they may pick up litter on the grounds, but they do little physical exercise; they contemplate. That is ideal for my Yoshi-*yan*. You would have all the time to read books. Your friendly and agreeable disposition will make you welcome in any congregation."

He stared at the tatami and said nothing.

"Well, say something; now talk." This was not the response she had expected; she had hoped he would welcome the decision. On the surface, steering her physically frail son toward the priesthood was a good decision, but deep in her heart she knew her son's enthusiasms were for the real world, not a spiritual world. She saw his tears streaming down his cheeks, falling on his folded knees. She could not hold back her own tears, and they spilled onto her kimono. Neither said a word, each engrossed in his or her own thoughts.

Entering the priesthood was the least appealing future Yoshi-*yan* could imagine for himself, to live an aesthetic spiritual life required unfaltering faith and devotion, qualities he did not have. His mother had made the decision to apprentice him to her brother out of her love for him and her deep concern for his uncertain future. She could not be blamed. It was his destiny. Nevertheless, his remorse was overwhelming.

Yoshi-*yan* had thought he had a good many years to contemplate and plan for his own future and had never really focused on the task. He had a few vague dreams of seeking whatever opportunities might allow him to venture beyond his village, beyond Nagoya and perhaps Nihon. He had never articulated his yearnings to participate in the far-off secular world of limitless wonders and enticements he had glimpsed while on his trips to the city and had imagined from the books he read. None of those dreams mattered any longer; that possibility had just slipped away.

Yasue knew her son would never confess his deep disappointment to her. He would explain his tears as gratitude, and he would accept the plans made for him without expressing a negative word. She proceeded to explain the details worked out earlier with her brother. "You'll go and live with Shoshun and his wife in two weeks. They have no children, so you'll be their only son. You'll go to school there, and I'm sure you'll make many new friends."

"Yes, Mother."

"Yoshi-*yan*, you'll soon find such joy in your new life with Uncle Shoshun, you'll forget us in Kamisaki." She knew they were empty words, as did her son.

He had time to say his farewells to friends and relatives, and to settle his affairs of whatever magnitude they were at his young age. The one person he felt compelled to talk with before his departure was Odai. Now that he was twelve, she was not the ever-present nurse and caregiver of his earlier years. She had charge of the younger children: Chisato, Noboru, Shiro, and Hiromu, who kept her as busy as the older ones had before them, though that special bond she felt for Yoshi-*yan* was still intact. And she was happy he sought her out for a private farewell.

"Odai-*san*, you know I am leaving to live with Uncle Shoshun." "Oh yes, everyone has heard. The whole village knows you will be training to become a priest one day."

"Odai-*san*, are you going to miss me?"

"You silly boy, of course your second mother will miss you." "Odai-*san*, will I be happy there?"

Sensing her charge had more serious things to say, she put her arms around him and inquired, "Yoshi-*yan*, what is it you want to tell me?"

He buried his face on her chest and mumbled, "I don't really want to become a priest, you know." She was not surprised by the content of his confession; the surprise was that he revealed it to her. He had been stoic in front of his mother, but he could no longer suppress his true feelings, and he released his crushing disappointment. Odai understood his complete sense of defeat. He would have kept it buried if his feelings had not run so deep. She was powerless to change the circumstances, but she had to ease his grief and loss of spirit; otherwise, he would wither into a mere shell of a human being.

"Yoshi-*yan*, this is your karma," she said to him as she stroked his hair. She had not comforted him in this way in years…ever since he had grown up and started acting like his older brother. His hair is still as soft as a baby's, she thought. "When you were little, your karma was that you would grow up to be a big boy. We didn't know that; we thought we would be burying you with Tameko and your other brother and sisters."

"There is a karma, but this is different," he said defiantly.

"How many times have I told you one's destiny is prewritten by the gods? People cannot change it. One learns to accept it." She was repeating an old lesson.

She felt his body heaving again as his tears flowed in torrents. He may be bigger now, but he's still my baby, the one who responded to a gentle word rather than a command, she remembered.

"It's all a matter of how you accept your destiny," she said quietly. "If you're defiant and inflexible, you'll be defeated. You'll lose and be miserable. The secret is to be flexible…like the bamboo, which flexes in a wind. It doesn't break; it survives."

He had heard all this before, but with this telling, it seemed more meaningful. Now calmer and in control, he told her, "Odai-*san*, I try not to get angry about things which I can't control, but sometimes I explode with fury."

"I know, I know."

"Odai, were you ever as unhappy about your karma as I am now?"

She smiled. "Oh, yes, *mukashi*… After my father died, my mother remarried. Her new husband turned out to be a very mean man. He let me finish school so the prospects of a better marriage were enhanced. He arranged a marriage for me with a much older man who had buried several wives already and was known to be as loathsome as my stepfather. I refused to marry the man because I knew my misery would never end if I agreed."

Yoshi-*yan* sat up, wide-eyed, as he heard her story for the first time.

"My stepfather forced my mother to disown me, and he threw me out of the house and told me to make my own way. I thought mine was the blackest destiny ever. We had been relatively prosperous once, and I had never cooked, washed, or cleaned house. I had learned to perform the tea ceremony and other skills useless for employment."

"How did you find us?"

"I wanted to get as far away from my stepfather as possible so I wouldn't be subjected to any future treachery from him. I was naïve and foolhardy. No one wants to hire someone with no experience and no family references. I was desperate, and I did curse my karma," she confessed.

"I was never curious about your life before you came to our village. I somehow believed you were always here with us." Yoshi-*yan* said, regretting his own gross insensitivity.

Odai continued, "I kept to the smaller villages, hoping someone would take me in, but they are more suspicious of strangers, and there are far fewer families who hire domestics. I was told often enough that if I was so destitute, I should make inquires at a pleasure house." She paused to recollect those times.

"I was in another strange village, whose name I knew not. I was ill, and I collapsed on a frequented road. Those villagers who found me were probably afraid they would incur bad luck and burial expenses if I died in their midst, so they took me to a doctor to be treated. He was elderly, and he lived alone, except a servant girl came every day to cook and clean the cozy house. I was given medicines and nourishing foods, and I began my recovery. There was no way I could pay him. When the doctor heard the details of my predicament, he thought he might have a remedy for that problem, too. 'I have a married daughter who needs assistance running her household. If she's sensible, I'm sure she'd be willing to take you in,' he said to me." Then pausing only briefly, she said, "His daughter was your mother." Odai had not told her story for years, and the memories awakened old emotions.

"Grandfather Uchida, I don't know much about him. Was he like Nomura *Ojii-chan?*" Yoshi-*yan* asked.

"Both of your grandfathers were very old, as all grandfathers are; otherwise they were different as can be on the outside, although they were similar again on the inside. Your grandfather Uchida was dignified and respected as a learned man of medicine, and he was very kind," she replied. "He insisted I stay at his home until I was better. When he thought I could make the journey, he wrote a letter to your mother and told me to deliver it personally. I thought if your mother were like her father, I would surely like her and could be happy working for her. I immediately noticed her responsibilities went beyond the immediate family to include all the employees. She truly needed someone to help her. When she got the letter from her father, she thought it was her karma to be rescued when she most needed the assistance. I was very ragged and looked like a garbage picker, but she let me stay without any hesitation."

"I'm glad you came and stayed."

"You see, I had cursed my karma, too, but it turned out to be a wonderful fate. Not only did I leave my stepfather and avoid a bad marriage, I found a family, and have many children. Do I lack for anything?" she asked.

"But Odai-*san*, you don't have your own husband. You can make your own babies and have someone else take care of them," Yoshi-*yan* said. "If you can't find your own husband, you can wait for me to grow up, and you can marry me!"

They both burst out laughing––only temporarily masking their gnawing sadness.

The walk to Uncle Shoshun's village would take most of the day. The distance was not far when measured in a straight line, but travel on the narrow twisting trail tracing the sides of the mountain ranges separating one remote village from the other was far from straight. The walk was torturous and a test of endurance. Yoshi-*yan* was accompanied by a porter, who packed the boy's possessions on his back. The two travelers rested whenever they found a stream to quench their thirst, and they lightened their loads by eating portions of the huge *obentos* that they had been provided with for the journey. *Okaa-san* had included a special treat of *okashi*, which she knew was Yoshi-*yan*'s favorite. Much as he loved his sweets, he had shared the goodies with his companion. Yoshi-*yan* promptly ate his portion with relish, but the porter, unaccustomed to such riches, savored each delectable bite to prolong the pleasure while the boy watched, fascinated by his companion's self-restraint.

Each step of the journey distanced Yoshi-*yan* further from home and the life he had known, and the real prospect of not returning for a very long time added weight to his steps. The pace of their walk slowed. A good part of the day had lapsed when they finally reached the priest's village, only to flounder about, unable to locate the religious structures. Shoshun's temple was up the hillside toward the mountain, they were told. Their journey had not yet ended, and with weary legs, they started another upward climb.

When they finally arrived at their destination, Yoshi-*yan* was so exhausted he promptly fell asleep.

MAKING ADJUSTMENTS

It was barely daybreak when Yoshi-*yan* woke to chanting, broadcasting from one corner of the house and the movement of someone else working in the kitchen in another corner. The house was small and its furnishings austere. There was no clatter of footsteps rushing around, no screens sliding open and closed in unseen sections of the structure, no cacophony of voices, cries, or random noises; the stillness was disquieting. As if life's breath had been sucked away; death must be close, he thought.

The chanting came to an end, and Uncle Shoshun turned his attention toward his nephew. "Finally awake, I see. Then it is time you're told your daily schedule." Without further ado, he began, "Begin day with morning prayer chants. Eat breakfast, and go to school. On return from school, assist Aunt Emi with chores, and complete school assignments. After supper, you will begin your studies learning the *Okyo*. Your scriptures study shall continue until bedtime."

Shoshun took his Z breath, taking in air with clenched teeth, and continued, "Today was your privileged day. From tomorrow, you are expected to put away your bedding and finish your personal hygiene before morning prayers. Never mind that you don't know them yet. My sister, your mother, has certainly been negligent in her duties to instill the Buddha's teachings upon her children. I will remind her in my next letter."

Yoshi-*yan*'s stomach was growling loudly. He had not eaten a thing since his arrival, and his hunger pangs kept increasing. Uncle showed no notice, and his speech continued without a break. "I shall walk down to the village with you this morning to show you your school. Emi Oba-*san*, your aunt, shall tell…"

When's breakfast? I'll faint from hunger soon. Images of food kept racing through Yoshi-*yan*'s head.

"The Lord Buddha in his infinite wisdom said…" Yoshi-*yan* suppressed a yawn and a growling stomach. "…and hereafter, you shall be addressed as either Yoshitsugu or Yoshi for short. Buddha's disciples are not addressed as Yoshi-*yan*. Phewww."

Yoshi had never in his life been restricted to such a strict regimen. Life at home was chaotic, but he considered it normal and was comfortable with it. In Uncle's home, it was the opposite; things were orderly and the rules strict. Everyone living in the house had set duties and responsibilities, and no deviations were allowed. Yoshi understood he had to conform; he was given no other choices.

Slouching was not allowed even after hours of sitting on one's legs on the tatami. Repressing the sensation of pain was one challenge; learning the scriptures was a different challenge. The lesson began with Shoshun reading a passage of the sacred script. Yoshi was then expected to repeat the same passage with the same pronunciations, intonations, and phrasings. No matter how much he concentrated and focused on memorizing a passage as it was read, he failed the task of repeating it without error. After the second try and every failed attempt thereafter, Shoshun rapped Yoshi's head with a stick. The *Okyo* was written and chanted in Chinese. Thus, it was Yoshi's task to learn the form phonically, syllable by syllable. There was little emphasis on what it all meant.

Another problem for Yoshi were the pauses. Long phrases were intoned in one long breath then came a pause to suck in air with clenched teeth before continuing on to the next phrase. He could not produce a proper sucking-in-air sound. Instead of the high-pitched tenor "shzzz," his sounded like a low-pitched baritone "suzz." Shoshun's anguish was almost audible. No one bothered to discover that the difference in pitch was due to Yoshi's under bite.

"*AH-h-h…mi-i-i…da-a-…*" and so the chants continued on and on. The pleasures await…soaking in the *ofuro*…though the bath water be cool…then to sleep without dreams… When? How much longer must I suffer?

Since his nephew's apprenticeship was starting years late, Shoshun had hoped Yoshi would be a quick study. That expectation was dashed. His progress was slow, very slow. The boy persevered, and his compliant attitude and good manners allayed further harsh words or treatment from Uncle. In addition to his own assigned chores in and around the house and temple, Yoshi found ways to assist his aunt with her work. She had no maids to lighten her workload as his mother had, so he took on the more onerous jobs when possible.

In their hillside domain, they were physically removed from the village proper and its daily activities. Their trips to the village were for necessities and when called upon to provide services; visits were rarely for recreation. Since the villagers' pilgrimages to the temple were infrequent, life on the mountainside was an isolated one saturated with religion. Shoshun relished his austere, contemplative life, but it was a lonely one for his wife. She appreciated Yoshi's company, as they chatted and exchanged stories while working together side by side doing the chores. For Yoshi, the afternoons became his favorite time of day. His homesickness eased, and life became tolerable, except the evening scripture lessons, which remained sheer torture.

The standardized school curriculum in force throughout the country ensured identical school courses were taught at both the new school and his school in Kamisaki. It was not the academic studies that concerned him. In fact, his grades improved from lack of distractions. The real challenges entering a new school without friends or acquaintances were the social interactions that Yoshi had dreaded the most. He was the new boy, the stranger in their midst. It takes time and effort to forge new friendships, especially among suspicious peers, and the regimen dictated by his uncle provided no free time after school hours to pursue such bonding; frivolous activities were unknown to Uncle. Also, Yoshi no longer had the resources to bribe anyone with sweets and favors as he could have back home. He had to make adjustments.

Especially galling and hurtful were times when village boys taunted him by pointing and calling him a religious flunky: "*Teru teru bozu. Teru bozu.*" That insult cut to the bone. The words were innocuous in their meaning: "Temple priest/apprentice." It was what was implied that crushed his ego, his self-image. Yoshi could not hide his role of priest apprentice. He was excused from school whenever he needed to assist his uncle at a funeral or memorial service. His life, he felt, revolved around commemorations for the dead. Usually pious congregants conformed to the seven "service every seventh day" rule for the newly deceased. Even the not-so-pious followed custom and held yearly anniversary services for their longer-gone family members, although their dedication to such services eventually lapsed. The number of residents in the village and surrounding lands were sufficient to keep the priest and his apprentice busy conducting services.

At each service, the same scriptures were repeated endlessly again and again. Yoshi forever struggled to intone the chants exactly the same as Uncle Shoshun; he made progress, slow progress. And the untranslated foreign words he intoned so imperfectly still held no lessons, religious or otherwise, and Yoshi went through the rituals on auto-pilot.

The experience was totally depressing. Yoshi tried to remember Odai's words of advice: "Every dark-negative has a counterforce of light-positive; a person has to seek it." That is not exactly what she said, but words to that effect, thought Yoshi, and he decided to give it a try. After each memorial service, custom required the family of the deceased to provide a meal for the attendants. No matter how humble the circumstances, the food that was served was more elaborate than their daily sustenance. For Yoshi, it was party food compared to the austere meals prepared by his aunt. Yes, the services could be endured since the meal served afterward was usually delicious.

The fresh breezes of mountain air, the vigorous long hikes to school––first down the hillside, then the return up the slopes––and living a regimented orderly life with few indulgences contributed to Yoshi's overall good health. He was still shorter than average but free from the constant illnesses of his childhood. He even began showing signs of developing a muscular physique. Infrequently invited to join in their team sports, Yoshi began practicing on the playground exercise bars; chin-ups gradually led to more complicated routines. Mentally, his horizons also expanded. The solitude gave him time for introspection, time to think. Sometimes his mind drifted during the sutra chanting, and he entered a state of quiet and peace within himself, in spite of the bells tingling by his ear.

A year had passed since his arrival, a date neither noted nor celebrated. Keeping to his schedule, Yoshi-*yan* was busily adjusting the kindling and stoking the fire under the *ofuro* to heat the water for the evening bath when Emi Oba-*san* came alongside. Crouching on her knees beside him she whispered, "I think there's a baby growing in my stomach. I'm quite sure, but I haven't mentioned it to your uncle yet. Please don't tell him. I want to be sure. We've wanted a child for such a long time."

She knew her husband wanted an heir, a son to mold to his specifications. That was fine with her, but she truly wanted a daughter to share confidences with and to keep her company. The prospect of having a child was a godsend.

Yoshi took special care making sure Emi did not over exert herself and kept mum about her secret. A few months later at the start of their *Okyo* session, instead of intoning the chant with his usual robot precision, Uncle Shoshun's voice wavered, and he stopped and loudly cleared his throat not once but three times. He paused and fidgeted.

"What's come over you, Uncle? Are you ill?" Yoshi asked.

"I have something to share with you." His voice quivered. "Your aunt is going to have a baby."

"Uncle, this is good news, indeed. I'm very happy for you. We must take good care of Aunt Emi."

"We'll forgo the lesson today, Nephew. Why don't you go and read a book until bedtime?"

The daily routine of the household continued as before, but there were signs the rules were slowly easing. When a healthy baby boy was born, Shoshun was overjoyed. He now had a true heir. But the once-orderly household had become a shambles. The infant's needs took precedence. Without hired help to share the work, Yoshi pitched in and cleaned, washed, and even tried to cook on occasion. He became a babysitter and diaper changer, too.

The schedule was no longer predictable. Uncle Shoshun told Yoshi he needed to talk to him. On this occasion, Emi *Oba-san*, with child securely strapped to her back, sat in on the meeting

"Yoshi, you realize circumstances here have changed since you first arrived. It was a difficult adjustment for us all in the beginning, but in time everything worked out well. We truly appreciated your willingness to help no matter how menial or unrewarding the task. It took a while to become accustomed to your personality because we thought it replaced internal fortitude and self-discipline. We now know you possess both qualities. You just don't wear it on the surface."

That circuitous speech again. What is he leading up to? Yoshi speculated, but he knew better than to interrupt his uncle.

"We realized almost from the start you were not particularly interested in studying Buddhism, or learning the scriptures, or in becoming a priest.

Unfortunately, the first twelve years of your life were without knowledge of the scriptures; you were exposed to an alternate secular world, a very material world. This was not your fault," Shoshun said. "You accepted your karma when your mother and I decided that perhaps you were suited for the priesthood. Children are not asked if they agree with their parents' decisions; you accepted like a dutiful son."

He doesn't know how Odai had to convince me.

"Now that your aunt and I have been blessed with a son to whom I can teach the scriptures and to lead on pathways toward Buddha from an early age before he is corrupted, he can replace you and become my apprentice. Your aunt and I have decided we must do what is right and release you from the agreement. Your karma appears to be not what we thought. This will allow you to pursue that different destiny."

"What destiny, Uncle?"

"I don't know––only the gods know. Whatever is to be shall be. You will be leaving us to go home to your parents."

"But who will help Emi *Oba-san* with the chores?"

"We'll learn to manage," the uncle said with a smile, realizing the concern expressed was sincere.

Emi *Oba-san* now spoke for the first time, "Yoshi, you have been the best nephew one could ask for. You not only lessened my burdens, but your smiles and kind ways will always be remembered. Maybe your karma nudged ours and helped to make our baby possible and helped us to be happy, *Neh*. Thank you."

Whether it was his aunt's words or the realization that his tenure as an apprentice to the priesthood had ended, the tears could not be stopped. Yoshi knew his uncle considered shedding tears a sign of weakness, but he did not care. The tears that flowed were tears of joy. "Yoshi, you must be ready to leave in two days. Two men from the village will be travel-ing toward Kamisaki, and they're willing to have you accompany them. Their destination is only a few villages away from Kamisaki. Once you get there, you will know the way. I'm sure you're old enough to travel the familiar distance on your own," Shoshun said in his usual businesslike manner. "Your departure date was speeded up when we heard about the men's plans. Your mother will certainly be surprised when she sees you since I have not written her yet. But I knew you wouldn't mind leaving so soon. We'll send your clothes and books by messenger later."

Everything was a blur from that time until Yoshi-*yan* was on the road going home. He made his speedy farewells to the classmates he considered his friends, leaving them with a memento or two, and he managed to complete a few unfinished household tasks. His few belongings were packed in a wicker basket for later delivery. A smaller bundle of personal necessities was placed in a knotted scarf, which he planned to carry on his journey. He said his formal farewells to his uncle and aunt and expressed his gratitude for their guidance and care the past two years. The bows were long and low, as dictated for such occasions.

Shoshun deviated from his set routine that morning, promising himself a longer prayer session in the evening, and walked to the village with Yoshi. He introduced his nephew to the two villagers who would be his travel companions. He wished them a good journey, and they departed without further delay. As they lost sight of the main cluster of houses and started climbing into the mountains, the fog in Yoshi's head finally began to clear, only to be replaced with sadness. A tinge of regret to be leaving the quiet mountainside home and the enriching time he had spent there lingered. He knew now that it had not been such a bad karma after all. The hours upon endless hours of reciting the *Okyo* were fast fading into distant memory.

The two men traveling with Yoshi were middle-aged tradesmen making a business trip. They kept up a steady stream of talk throughout the walk and paid little attention to Yoshi except to glance back on occasion to make sure he was still following behind them. He was two years older now and better able to keep up with the older men's gait. They made few rest stops along the way, but the journey home did not feel strenuous or tiring. Listening to the men's chatter, whose subjects ranged from village gossip to philosophy, was absorbing, and the hours passed without notice.

RETURNING HOME

When the men arrived at their destination, they pointed Yoshi toward the trail that would take him to Kamisaki. They warned him not to meander and make straight for home. They waved him off and went their own way. Now that he was on familiar ground, the trail leading home was an easy sail.

It was late afternoon, and the shadows cast by the sun made the village appear eerily foreign. There were no noticeable changes to the roads or houses leading to the *mise*; nevertheless, things somehow looked different. People who passed by him along the way did not recognize him, and that suited him at the moment. No one was present in front of the building when he finally reached home, so he entered as he would have done after a day at school and called out more loudly than normal, "*Tadai-ma!*" the customary announcement made upon returning home, that is not necessarily addressed to anyone in particular, elicited no response from anyone in other parts of the building. They're all busy, he thought. He made himself comfortable and waited for company to arrive.

A young girl wearing an apron came into the room with intentions of merely passing through when she saw Yoshi sprawled on the tatami in the middle of the reception room and grinning at her.

"*Ah iii…* who are you?" she asked. "Who invited you in?"

"And who are you?" he asked in return. "No one invited me in. I belong here."

"*Ah iii…*you leave right now! Or you'll be in big trouble! Go… Go…" she commanded.

When he ignored her, she spun around and left the room in a huff. She ran through the corridors calling for help, warning everyone there was a young vagrant parked in the house.

Seinojo was the first to arrive, broomstick in hand, ready to boot out the intruder. He leaped inside, pouncing on the floor looking fierce, only to find Yoshi seated cross-legged, facing him with a grin on his face. The culprit asked wearily, "Seinojo, what's all the excitement about?"

"Well, if it isn't my younger brother. When did you arrive?" he asked.

Yasue had rushed to the scene to appease her frantic maid.

She stayed behind the shoji and made a quick sideways tilt of her head glancing through the opening to appraise the situation. "*Da-le?* Who is it? You look like Yoshi-*yan*, but it can't be," she said. She was completely baffled.

"*Okaa-san*, don't you recognize your own son?" Seinojo said.

She entered the room for a closer look. "*Honto?* It's really you, Yoshi-*yan*?" she asked, still doubtful. "Then why didn't you tell us you were coming home? And why did you scare Hiroko like that? You rascal boy," she said as she turned to leave. "I have to let everyone know the dangerous intruder was only Yoshi-*yan* teasing the maid."

Seinojo stayed behind to hear why Yoshi had returned so unexpectedly. When his curiosity was satisfied, it was Yoshi's turn to ask questions.

Hiroko was the new maid. No, the business was not prospering. Yes, there is a new baby. "Let me count, besides you, me, and Chisato, there's Noboru, Shiro, Hiromu, and the baby Shitoshi. I'm not counting Kimiko," Seinojo said.

"We're all boys except Chisato. She probably wanted a sister." "The little guys are always underfoot and making noise. I hope they grow up fast. I'm surprised they didn't come rushing in here. They're probably under a pile of futons still scared to come out. Heh, heh."

The clan was gathered to eat dinner at their various tables, and Yoshi explained to the entire gathering the reasons for his return and recounted a few of his experiences while living away from home. This alleviated having to repeat the same story more than once. His father welcomed him home, saying something about the lost child finding his way home, with everyone nodding in agreement.

"Did you come home with the crows?" piped up four-year-old Shiro.

"*Ka ra su to I sho ni...*" Noboru sang out. Little three-year-old Hiromu completed the nursery rhyme,

"*Ka e ri ma shoooo.*"

The three tots were giggling so hard they could not contain themselves. The gang–of–three had struck again.

Yasue told them singing during dinner was improper. When father Kakichi told them to stop their silliness in a stern, scolding voice, the three complied.

Seinojo leaned over to Yoshi, "Now do you understand what I meant about the noise?"

Yes, it's as chaotic as I remembered, thought Yoshi. But this is home.

He gave his mother the letter Shoshun had written to her explaining the reason for terminating Yoshi's apprenticeship and his nephew's early return home. Yasue sat back to read the multi-page message. The flowery first page of his letter is uncharacteristically formal. This second page chiding me for neglecting the children's religious education is a lecture I've heard before. That the third page reads like a treatise about family values and the need for flexibility etc. etc. is a curiosity. Has fatherhood softened him, or has Yoshi-*yan*'s presence contributed in any way? We'll never know, thought Yasue. A final, fourth page revealed the reasons for Yoshi-*yan*'s return.

She told everyone that Shoshun suggested in a postscript, they follow his example, calling Yoshi-*yan* by a more grown-up name: Yoshi. She agreed that was advice they ought to follow. "Luckily, things have turned out for the better; that is what's important."

Since only minor changes had taken place during his absence, Yoshi-*yan*, now called Yoshi, picked up his life where he had left it. Odai was busier than ever with her four male charges, who sometimes sang nursery rhymes at the dinner table. There were no opportunities for Yoshi to sit and chat with her.

A Bit of Advice

"*Moshi moshi*. Anyone home?" asked the visitor in the entry. The screen slid open, and the visitor let himself in. Hiroko arrived in a rush to greet the guest but found him impatiently kicking off his slippers. "What kind of welcome is this? The FIRST *CHONAN* has arrived," he said gruffly as he walked past her. He headed straight to the dining area, where the family was clustered and the remnants of dinner were still being cleared. He sat down at a table uninvited. He said nothing, heaving his chest with each breath to show his annoyance.

"Sutekichi, why didn't you notify us you were coming?" said Kakichi, completely ignoring his guest's rude behavior. "You just came at an inconvenient time. If you had come earlier, you could have joined us for dinner. We haven't served the sweets yet. Make yourself comfortable and have some tea…"

"Forget the tea. You eat the sweets," Sutekichi interrupted. "Tell Hiroko to warm up some *sake* for me." He was, after all, Kajiro *Ojii-chan*'s "throwaway" offspring, and he liked his *sake*. His mother was not Kajiro's wife, Yae, and he had never been subjected to "the treatment."

Early on in their marriage, Yae realized she could not circumvent her husband's love for drinking, and as his drunken binges were distressful to her, she pledged none of her sons would follow their father in such debauchery. When each son was still an infant—there were a total of four sons—she placed the child in an empty *sake taru* for a day. The wooden barrels reeking of *sake* fumes, and the child crying to be removed from his pungent cradle, Yae refused to pick him up until the end of the day. Her "treatment" worked, and none of her sons took to drink.

The others at the table chimed in their greetings, and after a few sips of heated brew, Sutekichi relaxed and warmed to the congenial company he had joined.

Yoshi could not place the face; it was rounder but curiously fitted with a Nomura nose. He kept scanning his memory trying to remember. Feeling the lad's questioning stare, the older man looked toward the boy, thought a moment, and then blurted out, "Aha, you're the derelict apprentice from the temple. When did you escape? Spent a couple years of mumbo jumbo without achieving enlightenment, *nah*. Lucky for you, you retrieved your future."

"Uncle! You're Uncle Sutekichi," Yoshi called out. "I haven't seen you for so many years. When did you come back?"

"Let's just say I'm back," he answered. "I can't remember your name. Your parents keep producing so many babies, I've lost track of the names."

"My name is Yoshitsugu, Uncle, but everyone calls me Yoshi now."

"Ahhh, yes, the sickly one. Well, you look healthy and grown-up now."

Sutekichi visited often, always unannounced. Since his adoptive parents worked in the *mise*, he had spent as much time in this house as his own while growing up. Always treated as part of the family, he found no reason to change that relationship. His frequent visits were also motivated by his half-brother's tub of *sake* that never ran dry. Kajiro's progeny who followed Sutekichi not only lost a love for *sake*, but the old man's vim and vinegar had also been diluted and replaced by a generous, gentler spirit.

The *sake* loosened Sutekichi's tongue, and he entertained his hosts with stories of his adventures, which differed with each telling. His listeners were an appreciative audience and rarely challenged him about the changes. The tales, whether true or embellished, were always worthy entertainment as rendered by their bombastic kin.

"With my brains and good looks, I managed to gain a position as a trusted aide in the town council."

"Why did you leave, Uncle?"

"Well, I backed the wrong candidate. That was the problem. Our candidate lost, and after his opponent took office the newly elected official claimed he found irregularities in the books. He took revenge," explained Sutekichi. "there was no way to counter the accusations. It was karma. I just disappeared for a while."

By now, everyone knew he had "relocated" to Australia for the duration. Leaving his wife to fend for herself, he took his four sons with him to parts unknown. After drifting about for a spell, he eventually landed in Australia with his eldest son, Shoichi. They made their way in a foreign country as best they could. Then, through enterprise, their circumstances improved, and they lived rather comfortably. Shoichi married and started a family. When Sutekichi learned his oppressor had died and the witch hunt was over, he returned home to Mie. His son chose to stay in Australia.

Sutekichi came home to an empty house. His wife had died, and the three younger sons, who had also accompanied him, did not return to the village with their father. The three had found work as merchant seamen soon after leaving home. Son Shozo continued to work aboard ships, but Kajuro and Torao, after a brief stint on the seas, landed halfway around the world in New York City, occupations unknown. Sutekichi, now a wizened old man, decided to remarry and start a second family.

Occasionally Sutekichi asked Yoshi what he planned for his future since abandoning his pursuit for a religious sainthood. "Go see the world, Yoshi. Don't limit yourself. Leave Kamisaki. Go beyond Nagoya. Just as our country is expanding in the world, you should expand your sights, too."

On another occasion he said to him, "Your brother Seinoijo is stuck here. He has no choice because he is the *chonan*; he'll inherit everything, the family responsibilities, too. You're the second son, and you must find a livelihood to support yourself and a family. Later, those silly little brothers of yours will have to do the same. You must start thinking about your options, Nephew. Don't let others decide for you. You know as well as I, that could bring you a lifetime of misery."

Yoshi knew his uncle's advice was sincerely given; he had faced a similar dilemma. He had not qualified for the number-one son position due to the circumstances of his birth. He was sympathetic.

The description of faraway places intrigued Yoshi, and he listened with rapt attention when Sutekichi started his ramblings.

"The Aborigines in Australia are dark, unlike the white people from Europe who settled the country. They definitely don't look like us Japanese. Chinese and Koreans look like us. Even the Ainu's in Hokkaido resemble us more than those dark Aborigines. Nor do they look like the dark-skinned peoples of the Philippines."

"Uncle, were you ever…" Uncle ignored him and continued his ramblings.

"The Ryukyu inhabitants are unlike those in Taiwan, too, but they're both Oriental; they eat rice."

Yoshi finished his last year of school, and he had made no plans for his future. A few of his classmates continued on to further schooling in Ise City. The *chonan* in his midst stayed on and worked with their families. He was joining the majority, who had to find work. Uncle Sutekichi had fostered his interests in traveling the world, which appealed to him––but how to proceed?

"Yoshi, I have a favor to ask you," Seinojo blurted out without formalities. When they were younger, the five-year age difference led them into separate pursuits and peer groups, and their birth order had eliminated any sense of competition between them. Despite wide-ranging personality differences, their relationship was cordial and supportive.

"*Ni-san*, big brother, you look so serious. What's the favor you want?"

Seinojo hemmed and hawed. "I was wondering if you…"

"Oh, you need help attracting a girl. I'm at your service."

"Don't be sarcastic. I don't need help when it comes to females."

"Well, your girlfriends to date have been…shall we say…Ahh rather *bu-sai-ki?*"

"What? My girlfriend is, ugly? I should have let those bullies beat you up in grade school!"

"You're right. They wanted to leave me in a bloody heap. I haven't forgotten you were my savior and bodyguard after that. What is the favor you ask?"

Seinojo, not noted for his flowery prose, finally said what had been on his mind. "Will you stay here at home until I finish my military service? It would put my mind at ease if you were here to look after our parents and everything in general until I return."

"When is the physical scheduled?"

"Well, not until next month, but I'm sure they'll accept me. When I finish and return, you will be free to go and do as you want, I promise," said Seinojo.

"I trust you'd keep any promise."

"It would mean postponing your future plans for a while, any sea voyages…"

"So you know…"

"I wouldn't ask you if the other boys were older. They're just kids yet."

"Hmm…being temporary *chonan* should prove interesting. I might command a little more respect and…"

"Look, Yoshi, you have never been burdened with responsibilities. *Ka-chan* was always worried you were going to be one of her babies she would bury. You got special treatment."

"Seinojo, you didn't have to tell me that. I had every intention of staying here while you're gone whether you asked me or not."

"Why didn't you say so in the beginning instead of distracting me with other inane talk?"

"That's the difference between you and me, Seinojo. I have never considered females to be an inane subject."

"You're probably right about that, but wrong about homely girlfriends, little brother. And thank you."

The pact was made, and as he had predicted, Seinojo was tagged physically fit, and he went off to serve his military service obligation.

Yoshi was temporarily the oldest son and took the responsibility seriously. The work ethic he acquired while studying with Shoshun he now applied to the projects at hand. In addition to the shop, the family was still involved in the fish brokerage market, the production of dried fish and seaweed, and other small-scale businesses. They were still growing silkworms, but too many ventures failed, like the ill-conceived sardine canning factory, which went broke and sunk the family's income with it. They no longer had an advantage, they were without a trading boat, and their competition was gaining. Kajiro *Ojii-chan's* wily business acumen was missing, and their business fortunes continued to go downhill. Yoshi was able to observe this firsthand and understood the predicament his older brother faced.

Life, though, was not all work, and when he could persuade his friends to go fishing, they rowed out of their protected cove into the ocean proper in pursuit of bigger fish, testing themselves against the rough, unrestrained waves. Still free from commitments to marriages, likely with strangers, they also pursued another sport, their time-tested "let's get acquainted" games. At night, when a girl's parents were asleep, the boy sought to lure the girl to sneak out of the house and join him. Some girls needed much less persuasion than others, and some boys were much more successful with their trysts. The adults were not unaware since it was likely they had participated in the sport when they, too, were young. Scoring a win was sought for the rewards, and the same risks inherent in playing the game remained: avoid getting caught, and avoid a pregnancy.

The two-year reprieve allowing him to stay home before setting off on his own gave Yoshi time to formulate his plans. Uncle Sutekichi gave him names of people and places to contact. Other villagers gave him practical advice of what to expect based on their own experiences outside of Kamisaki. He did not share his plans with his parents, though they surmised he was planning to seek his fortunes far from their village.

"When a boy doesn't show up for his physical examination for military service, there are consequences we wish to avoid, Yoshi. There's a multitude of red tape that is endless. The boy's father or his guardian is constantly harassed to get the errant boy home. I'm still involved with Kuniyuki's disappearance. He isn't even related, but he wrote my name as guardian. What a headache," Kakichi said.

"I understand why you're telling me, *Otoo-san*," Yoshi replied. "I promise to be home when my examinations are scheduled."

"You're a good son," his father said with a loving smile, "and you always have been."

Seinojo wrote Yoshi asking if he would mind postponing any plans for several more months while he stayed in Nagoya to tend to some unfinished business before returning home. Yoshi had a good idea what the intended business involved, but he could not deny his older brother, his protector of long standing, a last fret-free fling before settling down in Kamisaki for the rest of his life.

Yoshi had matured, and he now contemplated his life with a new perspective and appreciated his blessings: the extended family, their home and village, and the good life he had known. It was also his good fortune to have grown up with the constant rhythmic sound of ocean waves lapping the shores and breathing the ever-prevailing salt mist. As a child of such environs, the subliminal bonds with the sea would remain throughout his life. His future was calling him, and it was time to respond.

LEAVING HOME AGAIN

Seinojo returned home after his military duty and prolonged vacation in the city and assumed his role as *chonan*. Responsibilities of a number-one son, even a temporary substitute one, were more grueling than grand, and Yoshi returned the title gladly. The household took no heed to the "changing of the guards," and continued to hum, churn, and crackle, in its own chaotic fashion, reassuring Yoshi all was well.

With a few bundled clothes and a lunch in his knapsack, Yoshi jauntily left home, telling all he was visiting a friend in a distant village and not to expect him back for a few days. He carried such a small bundle, no one suspected he was carrying all the money he owned with him, too. He made his way up the treacherous winding trail, which switched back and forth, back and forth, gaining elevation up the mountain slope.

Near the top of the first mountain range, Yoshi rested to view the circular sheltering cove dotted with thrusting outcroppings of ragged rocks. On one side, the mountain thrust vertically out of the sea. In other areas, there were narrow shelves of land providing a transition between land and sea. Clusters of rooftops, crowded on those land shelves, were a discordant display interrupting the natural surroundings. Almost invisible from the viewpoint was the valley green surrounding the meandering rivulet as it made its way from the slopes above. Beaches spotted the farther reaches of land, defining the land from the sea. He sat, committing the scene to memory. It's so beautiful; why am I leaving?

Travel on the trail was torturous, reminding Yoshi of another journey he had taken. He had been miserable about leaving then; his present journey was undertaken with a lighter heart. He met few people on the road. A person or two bringing goods to market in the inland villages used the pathway, but most found an easier road to take. Yoshi had taken this path deliberately to avoid meeting others, especially inquiring villagers. Once he reached the village on the plateau, the path wound through flatter ground, and he made better time to Ise. After an overnight stay, he caught a train to his destination, the port city of Kobe.

CHAPTER 3

At Sea, 1916-1920

THE COUNTRYSIDE SCROLLED PAST YOSHI'S window as if by magic. Distant landmarks moved barely, and the middle ground paraded past leisurely on its *kaiten* conveyor as foreground objects flashed by as blurred streaks and then were gone. On and on the show unfolded with ever*chan*ging scenes. All Yoshi had to do was to sit back and watch. The clicking sounds of metal wheels rolling on metal rails and the rhythmic sideway rocking of the car was hypnotic. This was Yoshi's first ride on a train, and he embraced the experience whole-heartedly. Whatever regrets Yoshi may have had vanished, and he was anxious to get on with the new.

The train stopped, and passengers rushed out, leaving the cab virtually empty. Within minutes, they were scrambling back in with their obento purchases to be eaten en route. Hungry as he was, Yoshi stayed on board and fasted. His money was limited, consisting of his meager savings from his allowance. Leaving in secret meant he received no *o-senbetsu*, the parting gift of cash given to travelers, nor had he asked his parents for a subsidy. He was, after all, on this journey to reduce their burden of supporting him. Concentrating on the scenery would distract him from his hunger pangs, he hoped.

"Young man, you should have purchased the obento like the rest of us. You're missing a rare treat," the matron sitting across the aisle from him said as she began nibbling on her treat.

"Is it so special?"

55

"That train stop is famous; don't forget. You have to be quick since the stop is short and you want to get back on the train before it starts moving again."

"I'll remember next time."

"Where are you from?"

"Mie, by the ocean; south of Ise-*shi*."

"The backwoods. No wonder you don't know about these things."

Had he taken an express instead of the local run, which stopped at every village along the way, their arrival in Osaka would have been quicker, but he was in no particular hurry, and he was enjoying the journey. His was not a reserved seat, so he decided to stay put and watch passengers leave and new ones board. The incoming passengers were in as much a hurry as those leaving. With frowns and furrowed brows, they hurried down the aisle looking for suitable seats, sometimes trying two or three before settling down and clearing the congested aisle for the short ride to the next town. Once the behemoth vehicle overcame its inertia and chugged out of Osaka, Kobe soon appeared on the horizon, and Yoshi prepared to leave the security of his perch and make his way in the strange city.

The platform was crowded, and people were rushing, each person single-mindedly moving toward his or her own destination. They moved quickly, indifferent to others' plights.

"Don't stand there in the middle. Move to the side." "*Gomen-nasai*, excuse me."

"Get out of the way, boy." It was not always articulated; the facial expression was all that was needed.

After getting his bearings, Yoshi started on his way to the boardinghouse, which he had been advised to seek. "They are from our village. You will be safe there," Cousin Shozo had said, although his directions proved to be less than accurate. For someone not familiar with the old waterfront neighborhood, there was no discernible logic to the street layout or to the address system for the buildings within. He walked circles through narrow alley lanes and choked roadways asking likely tradespeople if they recognized the address or knew the people he was seeking. Eventually, someone pointed him in the direction he sought, rescuing him from spending a sleepless night in the streets. Seto, the proprietor of the boarding house, had left their village in Mie years before to work in the city.

The family took in boarders regularly to supplement their income, and fellow villagers were always welcomed warmly. It was their opportunity to catch up on the latest news and gossip circulating in the *mura*, and they also felt assured their customers could be trusted.

"Nomura-*san*, the Kawachi-ya *mise* family, of course. The entire village knows your family. Welcome."

"*Do-mo...*"

"You said you are son number two? I knew Seinojo when he was a toddler..."

The feeling of trust was mutual, and they exchanged stories and information openly. In the morning, Yoshi made his way to the job placement office for men seeking work on merchant ships. No, he did not have any experience, but he came from a seacoast fishing village and was familiar with the ways of the sea. At that time, jobs for seamen aboard ships were plentiful, and job applicants needed fewer credentials. Europe was at war and had lost many of their ships, while Japan, halfway around the world, plied its trade in the Pacific unencumbered. The no-previous-experience entry-level job was apprentice seaman, the lowest position on a ship; the place where Yoshi started. He was assured they would soon find a ship assignment for him, and he needed to keep them informed about his whereabouts at all times so he could be contacted for his assignment immediately.

"Nomura, Nomura Yoshitsugu..." He was paged in a neighborhood theater two weeks later as he was whiling away the afternoon. He reported to the placement office immediately; he was to replace a crewman who had fallen ill and was to be left behind.

Yoshi had to board before the ship's departure. He sailed out of Kobe two days later.

The ship Yoshi boarded was the Koshu Maru, a 28,000-ton class cargo freighter owned by the Osaka Shoshen Kabushiki Kaisha. It freighted goods primarily between Japan and Taiwan.

Since he was an apprentice seaman, everyone onboard the ship was Yoshi's boss — that meant thirty-five men from the captain down to the fourth-class seamen. He was assigned the most menial of jobs: cleaning quarters and latrines, disposing the garbage, anything and everything too lowly for the other seamen to do. He set the mess tables and served the officers their meals in their quarters. The dirtiest job of all was washing the hatch after the pressed coal cargo was delivered and off-loaded to waiting naval ships. When he finished, he was as black as the natives in Fiji, and his whites were a dingy gray no matter how hard he scrubbed them in the wash.

Seaman Koga called out to Yoshi, telling him they had been assigned to painting detail. "You're new and inexperienced, so why don't you paint the mast in the aft, which has a smaller area. And I'll paint the mast on the bow," he offered. Yoshi agreed, thinking that was decent of Koga. After Yoshi started painting, he noticed the cinders from the smoke stack were sticking to the wet, painted surfaces. No matter how fast he painted, he had to repaint the same areas after removing the particles. The job was endless. It was impossible to paint anything in the aft of a speeding ship. Koga finished his section and wandered back.

"Hey, Nomura, what's taking you so long?" he asked. Then he burst out hooting and slapping his knee. On seeing Yoshi's *oni* monster expression, he hollered some more.

Yoshi was fuming mad. "You outsmarted me this time, Koga, but this is the last time I paint the rear of the ship when it's moving!"

His antagonist wasn't mean-spirited, but as a lowly seaman one step above Yoshi, he could not resist taking advantage of the greenhorn. Koga had graduated out of the apprentice job not so long ago himself, and he had a long road ahead to make his promotions in a job he intended to make his career.

"Don't stay angry, kid. That was just part of your initiation," he said.

Though Yoshi was small physically, he was quick and capable, young in age, still fearless of shipboard dangers, and also unafraid of heights. He accomplished his chores diligently and did what he was asked, all the while learning the upper seaman's work in preparation for an eventual promotion; from apprentice seaman to seaman fourth class usually took at least a year, he was told. There was little time for leisure, but when he finished his assignments, he could indulge his passion for reading his books on Japanese history.

"Ehh. Nomura-*kun*, come join us in a game of cards," the others had often said. "If you don't know the game, we'll teach you."

Whenever the seamen were not on duty, eating, or sleeping, they were into a game of cards or gambling. They had invited Yoshi to participate in the beginning, but when they saw him reading a book, they left him to his own interests. When it became too raucous to continue reading, he sat and watched the action, or he roamed the deck to take in the sea air and quiet.

"This apprentice isn't the youngest we've had, but he's the first one who prefers books over our company," went the talk among the card players.

"He's short on the machismo…"

"And he talks sorta dainty…like my sisters."

"What do you say? Think he's *okaaa*…effeminate?" "Hmm, let's say he was overly coddled by his mother or a bunch of women."

"Seems to me females like that type. Hey, play your hand; we don't have all night."

"As I like to say, why complain? He works hard without bellyaching all the time, and he's generally good-natured unless you pull a fast one on him like Koga did."

"He was cursing like any good sailor that time."

"On second thought, this kid's OK. We don't need another one like that lazy lump head before him."

"Wish he played cards, though. I need an easy prey."

"He doesn't make enough money to make it worth your while."

"Nevertheless…"

The ship's officers took notice of Yoshi's work performance, and he was promoted to seaman fourth class with a pay raise; it was two months, five days after he boarded the ship. Two months later, he was promoted to seaman third class.

When Yoshi was off duty and wanted to be out above deck, he began spending time in the quartermaster's roost when Minoura was on duty. He came from a village down the coast from Mie in Wakayama prefecture, making him practically a neighbor. The older man enjoyed the youth's company, which relieved the monotony of being at the helm alone, and, perhaps for his own self-interest, he began teaching Yoshi how to navigate the ship and chart the course - the skills required to be a quartermaster. After he completed his own chores, Yoshi was taught in private how to handle the ship, and he took over the helm for an hour each night.

"If you have these skills, it'll help your chances for promotion," Minoura said. "If one of us quartermasters falls sick, you will be in a position to step into the job since you will be trained."

Another off-duty viewpoint Yoshi found on the ship was the crow's nest high up the mast. He would scamper up the ropes to survey the vast ocean seascape stretching to the horizon, and his mind followed, expanding beyond the limits of what he could see. He found it an exhilarating place to perch.

A storm had been brewing in the area for days before turning into a full-fledged typhoon heading in their direction. The decision to head the ship away from the storm toward open seas came too late. The safest alternative strategy meant waiting out the storm on the lee shore of the island, where mountain ranges would buffer the worst onslaught of winds.

Conditions on deck became dangerous, and the crew was put on full alert. They slept with their clothes on in case of an emergency. The ship sped toward port for safe harbor ahead of the storm's eye, but by the time they arrived, the winds and waves were battering the ship mercilessly as it was tossed from one roller coaster wave to the next. It was imperative they secure the fiercely rocking ship to the pier before it was smashed against it or blown adrift.

The crew gathered on the ship's leeward deck, where they were totally exposed to the soaking downpour and to almighty gales intent on overturning anything in their path. They had to act. The seamen threw their cables down to the dock again and again, but the ropes kept missing their target. Wind gusts blasted their coiled cables, ripping apart the measured loops, transforming the bundle into an undulating tendril. Whipped wayward and deflected from the dock, the ropes dropped into the sea. The situation was critical as the ship heaved on the waves, ramming the battens in ever-louder crashes.

The crew watched, transfixed. The waves cascaded, winds howled in greater fury, and the rains fell in torrential sheets.

"Koga, grip the rope, and leap to the dock! Hurry!" the first officer barked at the seaman fourth class. "Hurry! We have no time to waste!"

Koga was stunned. "That's SUICIDE! I'll be crushed between the pier and the ship! I CAN'T do it! I don't wanna DIE!" he screamed. He collapsed in sobs.

A thunderous crash in addition to loud creaking responses as the ship bashed into the pier again and again. All on board knew they were facing imminent disaster, and they were petrified. When feuding gods unleash legions of screaming Kamikaze winds as angry Poseidon churns the fury of raging seas, mortals caught in the turmoil can expect no miracle intervention from distracted gods. They must fend for themselves.

Seizing the moment, a foolhardy youth not yet fearing mortality, Yoshi took action. He grabbed the rope and tied it around his waist, swung himself over the rail, and leaped into the wind. He floated, supported momentarily by the wind, then bounced and tossed, while pummeling directly onto the wood wharf below. He was not crushed, just flattened; he scrambled to his feet. The crew lined along the rail witnessed the drama with gaping mouths. Seeing him on his feet, the men breathed a collective sigh of relief before a chorus began shouting instructions, telling him how to secure the ship.

When Yoshi was pulled back aboard ship, it was the first officer who approached him. "Good work, seaman," he said and left the rest unsaid. Everyone else on board remained silent but individually seconded the words by giving Yoshi a bow when they next saw him. Koga bowed his head the lowest, and thenceforth if the slightest shadow was cast besmirching Yoshi's character or actions, Koga was the first to defend him.

The Koshu Maru safely rode out the storm while securely tied to the pier. Later, they learned the ship that had preceded them out of port on their previous call, had not been as lucky and had sunk off Korea the day before.

Yoshi was generally treated kindly by the ship's officers even before the incident, and he continued to receive special favors others did not get. The crew generously felt little resentment. They concurred he deserved his promotions based on merit. Two months after reaching seaman third class rank, Yoshi was promoted to seaman second class, and in another two months, he was promoted again and became a seaman first class. The wonderment was the speed of his advancements.

He worked alongside the other seamen, doing his chores and perhaps a little more without obviously brown-nosing. While in port, freight was unloaded and new cargo was loaded––a simple feat taking what seemed an extraordinary amount of time as the officers demanded they properly balance and secure their load to prevent shifting in the event they encountered other storms. The crew checked and double-checked the cargo's placement, and the hatches were checked more than once to make sure they were securely covered. When that process was complete, if painting the sides of the ship was scheduled, their hopes for shore leave were dashed. Yoshi felt the disappointment as acutely as the others. Though he did not join the other seamen in off duty activities while onboard the ship, he was considered as good company as anyone while off-duty in ports of call.

The speedy promotions had left gaps in Yoshi's knowledge of basic seamanship, which came to light in unexpected situations. As the ship was nearing Nagasaki, he was told to pick up the signal flags and ask directions on where to dock. He was at a loss; he stood frozen, unable to move. The off-duty quartermaster realized Yoshi did not know the flag semaphore code, so he yelled for him to step back as he took up the two flags and proceeded with the signals. Yoshi was not reprimanded, but he knew he had to learn the signals pronto. Setting aside his usual off-duty activities, Yoshi began memorizing the Japanese semaphore system used by the Japanese navy and their merchant ships instead of the western rotary displays for the Latin alphabet and numbers. Those he would learn after mastering the Japanese system. Each *katakana* character had an arm/flag display based on the brush strokes used to write the kana. Most had two strokes, a few had one, and the others required three strokes for a kana display. Using telegraphy for communication made flag signaling a secondary message system but not an obsolete one. Luckily for Yoshi, other incidents precipitated from his inexperience were minor and soon forgotten.

Events happened just as Minoura had predicted. One of the four quartermasters on board got sick and had to leave the ship. Yoshi was given the opportunity to step into the position. He made quartermaster rank in ten months, a phenomenal achievement. He continued to be mentored by Minoura, and they both made sure there were no gaps in his navigational skills.

Yoshi was feeling like a seasoned quartermaster navigating the ship, making charts, and recording data—duties that soon became routine. During their regular stopovers in Takao, Taiwan, to pick up freight, his shore leaves often became visits to cousin Takeno, Uncle Sutekichi's daughter. She was married to a sugar processing company owner and lived in minor luxury on the island. Always delighted with Yoshi's company, she showered him with attention and treats whenever he visited.

Leaving Taiwan's subtropics climate and heading directly north into Japan's winter freeze had given Yoshi the chills, and he took to bed. No amount of extra bedding helped. His fever climbed, and he could not be roused. When they reached port in Kobe, he was taken off the ship and sent to the hospital, where he spent a month recovering from his bout of influenza. It is doubtful he was a victim of the 1918 flu pandemic since his illness pre-dates the epidemic's spread in the East; however, when the flu did strike Japan, Yoshi escaped that scourge. As soon as he was well enough to leave the hospital, he registered at the placement office for another assignment as a second quartermaster. A job offer came within the month.

The Second Ship

The ship was owned by the same company as the first, the Osaka Shoshen Kabushiki Kaisha. Named Shishen Maru, the ship was a 24,000-ton class freighter with a crew of thirty. Smaller than the first ship, it was newly built, and Yoshi traveled to the Tokyo shipyards to board.

The ship followed a similar route as the first ship, traveling between Japan and Taiwan, which was then a colony. They loaded lumber from Hokkaido and Sakhalin and delivered it to Taiwan, where they picked up raw materials and foodstuffs to take to Japan. In addition, they carried cargo to ports in the South China Seas, going to ports in Java, Borneo, Celebes, Hanoi, Saigon, Singapore, and Hong Kong––a British colony. The variety of the ports of call proved to be interesting and exotic. And a return to Japan every two months was a welcome benefit.

Yoshi no longer had his mentor to guide him through the rough places, but he was confident he could manage on his own. He had been onboard this second ship several months without experiencing any undue problems. The ship was well run, the officers were efficient and solicitous, and the rest of the crew members were little different from those on the first ship, except the names had changed. Yoshi's diligent work habits continued on board this second ship, and he was earning recognition as a valued shipmate.

An early evening departure from Taiwan was a routine procedure, and Yoshi anticipated clear sailing by nightfall. *We'll be sailing north toward Japan when my shift is over. If we turned west instead of north, we'd bump into China, and I'd still be at the helm,* Yoshi mused. *Then I could see those storybook cities of Peking, Shanghai, and more with my own eyes. China is so close.*

"*Oii*, Nomura-*kun*," a voice called out; shattering his reverie. "Any word yet?"

"We're still waiting," Yoshi responded.

It was six o'clock by the time the cargo had been loaded and secured. Yoshi had checked the deck, tested the seawater temperature and wind gauge, and noted them in his notebook. He checked the gauge for distance traveled, and had relayed the information to the duty officer, who entered it into the ship's log. Yoshi was at his station at the helm, just as the rest of the crew were at their stations and ready to depart, but the captain had not returned to the ship, so they waited and waited some more. He finally showed up, delivered by a group of happy partygoers who were reluctant to end the festivities. The captain wasn't quite sober, but he pulled himself together and managed to walk aboard without help.

"Perhaps it would be advisable to delay our departure, sir. We could wait until morning and leave at daybreak," the officer suggested to the captain.

"We'll proceed as scheduled. There are no storms forecast, and it's a clear night. I'll guide you through the channel myself." He proceeded to the wheelhouse and sat down, ready to supervise the ship's departure.

"Sir, we are taking the channel, at night? It would be safer to go around…and…"

"…and lose another four hours, added to the time lost due to our late departure?" The captain's previous assignment had been a smaller, 15,000-ton freighter, which had primarily navigated the seas in and around Taiwan and nearby ports. He did not exaggerate his knowledge of the island's coastal terrain.

"Captain, I have no experience navigating the straits at night. Perhaps we should have the first quartermaster take the helm until we get to open water; he has more experience, sir," Yoshi said. "That's not necessary. I know the waters around Taiwan as well as anyone. As I said, I'll guide you through myself."

Not far out from the main island is another island in the straits, which had to be skirted carefully. The tide was racing out, pulling the ship from the safe course of away from the hidden rock precipices that lay below the shallow sand bed below. Yoshi kept maneuvering the ship in the direction he was told to follow.

"Keep your eye on the moon. Guide the ship by watching the moon."

"The ship keeps shifting; it's difficult to keep the ship on course," Yoshi said. They made slow progress advancing through the strait. They had not cleared the strait after two hours, which normally would have taken less than an hour to pass through.

Then, the unmistakable sound of scraping cut the air. "*Amidala.* We have a problem!" They were grounded. The engine was shut down, they communicated their predicament, and waited in silence. The tide shifted, and the waves began entering the channel. The ship slipped loose and was freed within half an hour. A hole in the bottom began filling the bilge with water, which had to be pumped out as they were towed back to port. Divers found three holes, which they packed. Meanwhile, the crew took two days to unload the ship and put the freight in storage.

The grounding was considered an accident; no one was blamed, and they were not required to appear in court. Without further encumbrances, they sailed to the shipyard in Nagasaki for permanent repairs. The empty ship limped along for seven days, taking two days longer than usual to reach the Japanese port city. The ship was dry-docked for three weeks while the damaged bottom plates were replaced. The crew remained with the ship. They slept onboard and were assigned chores they could undertake under these conditions, including painting and cleaning the engines and other miscellaneous jobs, but they were otherwise free to take shore leave. In private, they hailed Yoshi as a hero for this accidental respite from their real work. With so much unaccustomed liberty, the men spent all their money and tried to borrow from other crew members, only to learn they were broke, too.

Since arriving in port, Yoshi was restricted and had to remain on board without shore leave because he was the errant quartermaster who was at the helm when the accident occurred. There remained little to do onboard, and since an appropriate disciplinary period had passed; a long enough period of time to impress on others that mistakes, even unintended ones, carried penalties. The officers felt it appropriate to end Yoshi's detention and let him take shore leave like the others. He had lent most of his money to other crewmen while he was restricted, and he now had as little money as everyone else.

The repaired ship with a well-rested crew returned to Taiwan to pick up its stored cargo and resumed its scheduled route. No further incidents marked Yoshi's time on the ship. In any event, the accident forced him to take his responsibilities more seriously, and he realized it behooved him to seriously study the waterways in and around Asia. When spring arrived, Yoshi had been aboard a mere six months, but he was reminded his mandatory physical examinations to determine fitness for military service were to take place in May, and he needed to make his way home. He left the Shishen Maru in Kobe.

ANOTHER RETURN HOME

Yoshi's return trip home followed the same route he had taken when he left home two years before, albeit in the opposite direction, but it felt a different, unfamiliar route. He was no longer in awe of the train ride or of the flashing scenery; it was so natural to be speeding to a further destination. And he remembered to get off the train to quickly pick up an obento at the station he had once been told not to miss.

On first sighting his village, the buildings, the paths and roads, everything appeared surreal. During his absence, the scene had become skewed in the mind's eye. But reality soon banished those false images and soon it felt as though he had never left.

Yoshi had promised his father he would return home for his examinations, however, Kakichi had harbored doubts, so when Yoshi appeared before the appointed date, he was relieved and heartened, wondering why his trust had lapsed. "Yoshi, we're glad you're home. *Okaa-san* will be especially happy to see you."

Upon seeing him, his mother wept as if he were her only son. "Yoshi-*yan*, you left without saying good-bye. Your father will be happy to see you, too."

Seinojo insisted he hear all about his younger brother's adventures since leaving home. "Not many changes here. Everyone keeps getting older; everyone stays sober."

Odai was all smiles when she spied the young adventurer. "My little Yoshi-*yan* has become a handsome young man. Am I still your sweetheart?"

The gang-of-three was growing up, too. "Where did you go, big brother? What did you do? What did you see? What did…?

"But where is sister Chisato?" Yoshi asked. "I bought her a special gift."

"Oh, she's gone to be with her sisters, Tameko and Umaye. She must have been lonesome with only brothers, was the answer. "If Kimiko had lived with us all along rather than with her foster parents, things may have been different for Chisato. Who knows?"

"I never understood why *Okaa-san* allowed those people to keep Kimiko. After all, she is our sister, too," Yoshi said.

"Mother remains tight-lipped regarding such things, though she can chatter at length about inconsequential things," Seinojo said on joining the conversation. "The good news is: Kimiko stays with us more often now. You'll like her. She'll have to take Chisato's place. And *Okaa-san* says she's not having any more babies."

Sister Kimiko came around frequently, and Yoshi found her sweet and playful; she did indeed fill the vacancy left by Chisato. She called him *ni-san*, big brother, and followed after him like a girl with her first big crush.

"*Ni-san*, we've just become brother and sister. Can't you stay longer? Must you leave so soon?"

"We can write letters, Kimi-*chan*." Thereafter, she was his beloved sister, the one who survived.

Yoshi made himself useful and helped where he could. The younger boys often followed him around, trying to become acquainted with this older brother they hardly knew. Shiro, more than the others, tagged along after him, constantly plying him for information.

"I want to go to sea on a boat when I grow up, too," Shiro confessed to Yoshi.

"If you study hard, you can attend the naval school and become an officer," Yoshi advised.

"Do you think that's possible? Why didn't you go to school?

Are you going to be an officer?" he asked.

"Maybe I'll become an officer, maybe not. But if you truly want to go to naval school, I'll send money home so you can go," Yoshi said.

"Yes. Oh, yes. I really and truly want to spend my whole life at sea, older brother. Hiromu wants to be a military officer. He can become a general, and I can become an admiral," he said with glee. "Don't you think Father and Mother would be delighted?"

"What does Noboru want to do when he grows up?" Yoshi inquired about the third member of the gang-of-three.

"Oh, he wants to go to Australia and live with kangaroos.

Ha, ha, ha…"

"And, what about baby brother Shitoshi?"

"I don't know what he thinks. He's such a fat, blobby baby. I don't think he'll go anywhere. He'll be too big to even move around when he grows up. Perhaps *Okaa-san's* been feeding him all the treats we never see." He sat silent a while then returned to his original line of thought. "Big brother, will you remember what you said about my attending naval school?"

"I promise you, and I won't forget. How could I let a smart, handsome boy like you wither away in these backwoods?"

"Big brother, they say I look like you."

The small team of examiners, two military men and a doctor, traveled from village to village examining all eighteen-year-old boys to determine if they qualified to serve in the military. They finally arrived in their *mura*, and Yoshi was waiting. They commented on his fine physique. "We can use men like you in the military," said one of the men. However, Yoshi did not qualify. A mere inch over five feet, he was an inch too short for the Japanese army. All the sweets that he had consumed had taken their toll on his teeth, and his sorry dental condition further disqualified him. He was designated "not eligible" to serve in the Imperial Services. The chief examiner commented, "Sorry to lose such a fine physical specimen."

Under different circumstances, Yoshi's rejection would have caused him humiliation and anguish. However, his exploits at sea gave Yoshi self confidence that was never to quit him. He felt his short stature need not be a hindrance and his lack of formal schooling could be overcome with new learning. Now with his physical exam over, Yoshi felt he was free to pursue his goals.

Yoshi planned to leave, but Seinojo once again asked him to stay home for a spell while he took care of business in Nagoya.

"Would that unfinished business be the same business as the last time?" Yoshi asked.

"Never you mind, little brother."

"If you're looking for new business, perhaps I can help."

"All I need is a little of your time. Perhaps two weeks?"

"Since I don't have to sneak away, that will give me time to say my farewells to everyone. You can return whenever your business is done."

Before his departure two years before, Yoshi had a similar "business" problem, and he was sympathetic. His problem's name was Izumi. As classmates growing up in a small village, they had always known each other. Yoshi's attraction to spunky Izumi and her lighthearted spirit never wavered. He had asked her if she would wait for his return. Izumi had given Yoshi a noncommittal reply. Upon his return, Yoshi learned she had gone off to live in Nagoya during his absence, and that was the end of that.

Odai now had a few threads of gray in her hair, and a wrinkle or two creased her face when she smiled. Though she and *Okaa-san* were about the same age, she was aging more slowly than his mother.

When Yoshi had returned from Uncle Shoshun's, there had never seemed to be any time to quietly chat with Odai nor was there much he felt he needed to discuss with her. He did regret leaving without giving her a proper good-bye; he made sure they would have one last chat in private.

The younger boys were still at school, and there was quiet in the sleeping quarters.

"Odai-*san*, what good advice have you been saving for me before I leave this time?" he asked her.

"My *bot-chan* is a grown man now. I don't think he wants any advice from his old nursemaid," she said.

"You once told me to accept my karma as the inevitable. 'What is destined to be shall be,' you said. How did you know everything would work out well when I went to live with Uncle Shoshun? I thought it was the end of my life when I was told of the plan."

"Although your uncle is a rigid sort and you'd be unhappy living with his rules at first, if you were mindful and tried your best, I knew in time you'd discover he was a good man, and you would not be unhappy anymore."

"But how did you know this about him? In the beginning, I was sure he was a messenger of the devil sent to make my life miserable. And all those sutras were to praise the devil."

"You're exaggerating now. It couldn't have been that bad," she said to him, but she realized he was revealing his true feelings, previously unspoken. "About your uncle: since he was Uchida *Ojii-chan's* son and your mother's brother, I felt he, too, was kind and good deep down––only hidden. They did share the same blood."

"When I leave this time, I don't know how long I'll be gone, Odai. I have to go away and make lots of money. Then I can come back and live in Kamisaki," Yoshi said. "Will you still be here waiting for me?"

"Yoshi, I am getting old. Your brothers are all growing up and don't need a nanny anymore. Besides, the time is coming for me to return home and see if my mother is still alive and well. She may need me now."

"But, you can't leave. I'll miss you," Yoshi said. "If I marry you now, will you stay?"

They both laughed at their old private joke.

"They say a child is on loan to his parents until he's grown. Your mother was willing to share her sickly baby boy with me, and she asked me to be your second mother. With two mothers, she felt you had a chance to live and grow up to be a fine man. She is a very generous person," Odai said. "Your mother and I are now releasing you to your own destiny, unfettered by any interference from us."

Honoring Yoshi's adult status, Odai did not embrace him to offer comfort as she had when he was young. Kneeling, facing each other with heads bowed, they remained motionless and silent as their thoughts and emotions transferred one to the other. They clutched each other's hands and wept.

Kakichi's farewell to his son was less formal: a tussle of his hair, a pat on the back, and reminders to write home––the usual father-son discourse, short and succinct.

His mother smiled and told him to sit down next to her on the tatami. "You've grown up to be a strong young man, Yoshi-*yan*," she said, reverting back to the childhood name. "You were the child I thought wouldn't live. You fooled us." She smiled broadly. "You've been a good son. You have a kind heart and loving spirit, which will open opportunities for you. You are honest…except when you pilfered coins from the *mise* cash box to buy yourself sweet treats…"

"*Okaa-san*, I shared with my friends. I didn't eat by myself." "Yes, we all know you're generous. You're bright enough, despite my brother's opinion to the contrary, and you have common sense which he lacks; yet… there's one thing that concerns me."

Whatever is she leading up to now? Yoshi had no idea, so he sat quietly and respectfully listened.

"Yoshi-*yan*, we know you are very attractive to females, both young and old," *Okaa-san* said in measured tones. "And you like the girls as much as your sweet treats."

Yoshi winced on hearing this from his mother. *Oh, please... Not another life-shattering commitment on my behalf.* "*Okaa-san*, what..."

"How many times do I have to tell you? Do not interrupt your mother; I haven't finished."

"*Hai, Okaa-san*," he replied. *Déjà vu, we've been through this scene before. I'm doomed.*

"It is natural to be attracted to the opposite sex. There is no harm in having girlfriends...except a girl who is already married," she said. "Yoshi-*yan*, you must promise me you will never dally with a married woman."

It was a thunderbolt strike. It came out of nowhere so unexpectedly.

"*Nani*? What...?" he stammered. He was completely baffled.

"You heard what I said. Now will you promise me?" she persisted. "It is very important to me that you abide by my request."

She continued to look down at her kimono folds, averting his inquiring eyes. She knew he was curious to know the reason for her exceptional request. She looked up at him and began in a different vein, "I don't know if I've spoken to you before about marriage. As you well know, the custom is for parents to select spouses for their children."

Images of a female Uncle Shoshun began dancing in Yoshi's head. *Woe is me.*

Mother cleared her throat. "Your father and I agree we will not interfere in the choices you children make regarding your marriage partners. You may choose your own spouse."

Even more befuddled and still at a loss for words, all Yoshi could muster was, "Thank you." *How... Why... What modern novels has she been reading?* His parents had always been easygoing about conforming to tradition and custom, abiding by the rules to the extent they avoided being ostracized and ignoring or sidestepping those that brought harm or hurt. Otherwise, their thinking and conduct conformed sufficiently to be considered the norm. So where did this heretical idea of "love marriage" originate?

His mother's speech took on a formal tone. "Yoshi, I have always tried to minimize putting restrictions on my children, thinking it best they have freedoms to experience life and to draw their own conclusions. However, there are actions best avoided as they may lead to disastrous consequences. It's my duty as a parent to keep you out of harm's way even though you are far away. That is why I have asked you to make a vow for what may appear to be a frivolous request."

"I understand, Mother. As you wish, I promise I will not compromise a married woman's reputation or her honor."

Seinoijo returned from Nagoya, and Yoshi wanted to ask his brother if *Okaa-san* had had a similar discussion with him, but he decided against it and asked a set of innocuous questions instead. "Older brother, are you thinking about marriage? Has the family said anything?"

"I haven't decided yet. Marriage is so permanent, and there are two or three sweeties, equally desirable. You understand." What Yoshi understood was that they all, including the *chonan*, were allowed to find their own partners.

For one last time, Yoshi went back to confer with Odai on matters he could not ask his brother. Odai concurred a person's life path could change for better or worse based on one's conduct. "That, after all, is one's karma, but a person should not tempt the gods to withdraw their benevolence." A last lesson given, Odai and Yoshi both knew their life paths had begun heading in different directions. Their heads bowed and lowered close to touching the tatami they sat on; their farewells remained unspoken; good-bye forever.

ANOTHER LEAVE-TAKING

It was time for Yoshi to leave and resume his quest for fortune and adventure and assume self-sufficiency. He knew he was not returning for years nor would he be walking the trail leading away from Kamisaki again.

He was intent on absorbing the images and etching them deep into his memory to last until his eventual return. He walked at a leisurely pace with no pressing schedule. Once he crossed the mountains this second time, he took a detour leading to the village of Noa, where *Okaa-san's* family lived. Uchida *Ojii-san* was long gone. He had concocted his own prescription for his cold and died upon drinking it. The old doctor could have had his physician son prepare him his medicine, but then again, it was karma. Uncle Mototaro carried on the family tradition, and his son Susumu was living in the West for further medical studies.

Yoshi was treated to sweets and endless cups of tea before he finally came around to the subject that had made him take the detour. "Uncle, where is Susumu now?"

"Well, he's in Europe, and he plans to continue his studies in America awhile before returning home."

"I'm hoping my ship visits ports in America. Perhaps I could visit him halfway around the world."

"Nephew, America is a huge country. It's unlikely you'd accidentally meet him on a street there, but I'll give you the name of a doctor to contact if you ever go to New York City; Susumu will be studying with him. And if God is willing, you'll find your cousin there."

Yasue's lineage was one of physicians and priests, groups that fell outside of the four feudal social classifications, and her brothers followed that heritage. They lived purposeful lives in quiet dignity, thought Yoshi. Doctors and priests both administer to and comfort people; doctors treat their patients while they are living, and priests take over when they are dead. That has to be the reason why Uncle Mototaro is so much more congenial than Uncle Shoshun, his brother. Yoshi had time to ponder life's lesser essential questions as he continued on his journey.

Before traveling west to Osaka and Kobe, Yoshi planned to spend a few days of leisure in Ise City; the city where the most sacred Shinto shrine complex in Japan is located and where the Goddess Amaterusu's sacred mirror is kept. Situated in a cypress forest and within a fenced enclosure, the ancient treasure is protected by a structure unlike any other religious edifice in the country. Built as a simple rectangular wood framed building topped by a pitched, reed-thatched roof, it sits elevated by cypress pillars that support the raised platform floor and surrounding decks. Its distinctive sky-reaching forked finials soar above its roofline, and forges the mystique that has become its unique symbol; a symbolism enhanced by the contrast of finials soaring forth from its rustic roots.

The structure is demolished and rebuilt in the same ancient style every twenty years to reflect Shinto belief in death and renewal in nature and all things. Thus, the structure remains new and ancient.

Yoshi scheduled visits to the sacred Shinto *jingu* while in the city, although he had made a pilgrimage there years before with the family. Since the structure had likely been rebuilt since that visit, it was worth another look. Like the train stop when everyone got off the train to buy the stop's famous obento, the rest stop shops leading to the shrine were known for their *zenzai*, the sweet red bean and mochi treat Yoshi was addicted to. And he also intended to look up two classmates who were living and working in the city.

Having checked into the *ryokan*, he had several hours before dinner—enough time to locate the address he had been given. He arrived at the house sometime later in the afternoon, and he was let in when he asked to see his two friends by name. Momoko came sauntering into the main room with a sullen pout as if wakened from a nap. She recognized her guest.

"*Waa,* a it's Yoshi!" she screamed. "How did you come? Did you come to see me? How did you know I was here? Tell me, tell me." "I went home to take my physical. I heard all the village gossip about everyone since I left home, and they mentioned you and Sadako were here in Ise."

"Wait a minute, I'll find Sadako. Don't move. We'll be back in a hurry." She disappeared. From a distance, the patter of feet grew to a clopping gallop, hardly the *tabi*-covered feet gliding on the walkway one expected to hear. In a crescendo, the two girls burst unceremoniously into the sitting area.

"*Ahi-i-i,* it really is Yoshi-*yan.* I thought Momo was joking," said the second girl in her higher-pitched voice. "You look wonderful!"

Yoshi was delighted the two girls seemed as happy to see him as he was to see them. "It's been a long time. Can we go to a private area and talk?" he asked.

"Yoshi, they're very mercenary here. You have to pay to go to a private room," Momoko said in a whisper.

Sadako continued, "We can't crawl out the window like we could back home. There are no sleeping parents here, and there are absolutely no freebies like the old days." The two girls giggled at the thought.

Momoko, whose round face with pink-tinged cheeks resembled the peach she was named for, made one wonder if she was so named because she had such a face or, if given the name, her face transformed to fit the name. She was big-boned and tough, always a tomboy, she still had difficulty playing coy. "Nah...if you had been my boyfriend, things would be different now. Just think..."

"What are you thinking, Momo?" Sada asked sarcastically. "Everyone knew Yoshi liked feisty Izumi the best. Isn't that right?" Sada said, looking directly at him. "I didn't like her much... She went to Nagoya, I hear."

Their meeting had deteriorated to grade school level rivalry; it was time to change the subject. "I actually came here to ask you both if you'd go on an outing and spend the day with me on your day off. I'll take you wherever you want to go. We can just have a good time together. I'm leaving for Kobe in a few days and won't be returning for a long time," Yoshi said.

"Really? You'd take us both on an outing? I think we can arrange to take off on the same day," Momoko said. "You know they're very protective of us. We can't even go shopping or sightseeing alone. They think we'll meet someone in secret. But, if there's two of us and we're escorted by an old friend from the *mura*... OH, WHAT FUN! ...We'll have to ask permission."

"I've already made arrangements and they agreed," he said.

They did? They're usually not so agreeable."

"They welcomed a payment," he confessed.

"Yoshi, you're a sweetheart," Momoko burst out. "And since they have your money, stay and play awhile. Now which one of us do you want to visit first?"

Two days later, on the appointed hour, three girls showed up. "They made us bring Yuriko as a chaperone. Do you mind? They thought we got along too well the other day," Sadako said.

The threesome, now a foursome, went on their outing in Ise City. The girls wore their best kimonos and accessories, fresh hairdos, and makeup that made people take notice. Yoshi wore his *yukata* and brimmed straw hat and a wicked smile. They made quite a parade. The proprietor asked Yoshi as they were leaving to kindly mention where the girls worked if he were asked.

"That was cheap, asking Yoshi to advertise our services as if he were our hustler."

"Yoshi didn't look offended. We'll just have to be extra nice to him and make sure he has a good time."

They were in a party mood, and they strutted about showing the world how they felt that day. Yuriko, their chaperone, initially stayed on the sidelines as the caboose, but soon enough she caught the festive spirit from Momo and Sada and became a willing participant in their frolic. A show, dining, shopping, and play in the park—they teased and laughed, happy for this one-day interlude. They knew there would be no other days quite like this one.

"Perhaps we have time to take Yoshi to the shrine, and we can wake up the gods when we toss in our coins," Yuriko said.

"It's a good suggestion, but what's there to see when they keep us outside the tall wooden fence?" Momo replied. "Besides, Yoshi went there already."

They knew their time together was coming to a close, but they were reluctant to head back just yet.

When Momoko spied a photography studio, she pulled Yoshi in, insisting the foursome have a picture taken to remember their special day. The women were wearing their finest, and they had a willing and handsome escort.

"That *yukata* you're wearing is not right, Yoshi." "We're wearing our best, you should look like…"

"…our rich patron." Sada said.

"It's too hot and humid to wear anything besides my cotton *yukata*," protested Yoshi.

"Well, take it off…" Hands were loosening the obi tie around his waist.

'*Yame-nasai*, stop it. You're embarrassing me…"

"Did you hear that?" When the three women started pulling on his clothes, Yoshi reluctantly agreed to change into the suit provided by the studio for such occasions. Though the suit was much too large for him, no one noticed. What they saw was an intense young man seated amid three well-attired, attentive women.

Yoshi, with former classmates and chaperone in Ise

Upon parting, the grateful chaperone planted a kiss on Yoshi's cheek, explaining, "Western style, *neh*."

Not to be outdone, Momoko stepped between them and planted a kiss on both cheeks. "Yoshi, that's Europe style." Then she smacked him on the lips. With smiles, the three women reverted to Japanese style and bowed; their smiles faded, and they bowed lower.

On the train to Kobe, Yoshi reflected on the changed circumstances of his two classmates. How innocent we were when we were going to school. I never suspected their families were struggling so grievously. Why else would they sell their daughters' services for two years? Thinking about their plight, he choked, and tears welled. No tears here, he thought. He cleared his throat nervously and braced himself to maintain control. They surely had a wonderful carefree day like the times when we were young. He smiled. The excursion had made a large dent in his cash reserves, but it had been worth it. He would limit his future spending, and if he were lucky, the wait to board another ship would be short.

Back at Sea

In Kobe, Yoshi returned to the same familiar boardinghouse owned by Seto-*san* and waited for a new assignment. The jungle neighborhood was no longer intimidating, and he found his way around with few mishaps. He registered at several placement offices with the stipulation that he wanted duty on a ship scheduled to travel the world, as he wished to increase his skills piloting over oceans beyond the Pacific.

"You may have a long wait," he was told. "Openings for a quartermaster aren't as plentiful as seamen positions, but something should turn up eventually."

Yoshi knew his savings would not last a long wait, so he went looking for a job for the duration. He found work in a flour mill. It was a good job—the work was not difficult and the pay adequate, but he ran into a situation he could not tolerate. At the end of the day, he left the mill covered head to toe in flour. It was in his hair, eyebrows, and eyelashes;

every part of his exposed body was white with powder. As he made his way home from work, people stepped aside to avoid passing near him as though he was a pariah. Once he washed and soaked in the *ofuro*, he regained his earthly appearance and composure, but only until the next day when he would go through the experience again. There was only one way to escape the indignity, he quit his job within a week.

Luckily, jobs were plentiful, and Yoshi found another position. His new job was at a tire and rubber tube factory. It was not a clean industry, but a worker did not leave the workplace completely covered with a ghostly residue from his job each day. He learned the public judged others by their appearances, and deviation from the norm meant they were low class or mentally deficient, and to avoid contamination meant no contact with them. Such sub-humans ought to be kept in the shadows. Living life was easier when not encountering such issues daily.

Japan had emerged as a first-tier power in the world arena, and the country's economy was expanding rapidly. While Europe and the United States were involved in a war, Japan busily produced industrial goods. The Western powers had lost many of their naval ships, and Japan picked up the slack by building an armada of new ships; merchant and military fleets. Shortly after the Armistice was declared in November, Japan was contracted to provide transport for released Italian prisoners of war and return them to Italy from areas they had been held in the Far East. A total of ten ships and their crews, with each ship fitted to carry approximately one thousand prisoners of war, were to be provided. The ships would follow one another at designated intervals throughout the journey.

The placement office notified Yoshi there were openings for quartermasters on the ships forming the convoy to Italy. Among the conditions imposed for those who signed on were: a contract for three years of service, and the likelihood that their return to Japan would be at the end of three years. Their pay was to be split three ways: one-third of their monthly pay would be sent to their homes, one-third would be handed over directly to the crewmen for their expenses incurred during the trip, and one-third was to be retained by the company until the end of the three-year voyage when they returned home with the ship. The last payment would be forfeited if the three-year contract term was not fulfilled.

"There are no guarantees any ships will visit the United States," Yoshi was told. "A ship's assignments and travel routes after they off-load their passengers in Italy is an unknown." Yoshi signed the contract, sure this ship was as likely as any other to travel to the Western hemisphere and to the United States, in addition to having prospects for an interesting venture––seeing those faraway lands he had dreamed of visiting.

His assigned ship was scheduled to be commissioned at the end of the year in Kobe. He quit his tire factory job and prepared for the three-year journey. A short visit home was possible, but Yoshi felt it prudent to stay in the city where he could be readily contacted, and reluctantly passed up New Year's festivities at home.

Yoshi boarded the 45,000-ton France Maru owned by the Kokusai Kaisen Kobushiki Kaisha of Kobe in early January. The ship's crew of approximately fifty men spent a month making adjustments on the new ship, and taking trial runs before they embarked on their first voyage. On February 5, 1919, they set sail for the port city of Vladivostok in eastern Russia, west of Hokkaido. They were escorted by icebreakers, making it possible to enter the port in winter. Approximately five hundred Italian prisoners of war were brought on board. The ship then sailed south down the Sea of Japan, past Korea, turned up into the Yellow Sea and headed west to the Gulf of Pohai to Shanhaikwan, China, the city fabled to be the easternmost terminus of the Great Wall. There, another three hundred soldiers were boarded; more than half were wounded and ambulatory. The hospitalized soldiers were accompanied by half a dozen attendant nurses, a medical staff, and the Red Cross. Also on board was the highest-ranking captive, the Far East Generale, who was addressed as Baron. Five other ranking captive officers also boarded the ship. These officers were furnished with quarters similar to those for the ship's officers as well as a private dining room. The France Maru was the only ship among the ten carrying hospitalized wounded and such high-ranked officers; therefore, the ship had been furnished with numerous special provisions not provided on the other ships, and carried fewer passengers.

The France Maru was the fourth ship in the fleet as they sailed south to Hong Kong, where they took on provisions and water. They then proceeded on to Singapore.

Yoshi was one of six quartermasters on board. His shipboard duties were little different from past assignments, and on the first part of their journey, they had sailed through familiar waters. They were now heading for new territories he had not yet seen, and he was excited. The nature of this mission and the human-passenger cargo on board was unique, and for seamen accustomed to isolated lives while at sea, they found this assignment unlike any previous sea journey. Beyond extending usual courtesies, the language barrier discouraged fraternizing with the passengers. The crew found little free time while at sea, and while in port they were kept busy taking on provisions with few shore leaves. The passengers, however, were given opportunities to go on shore and take sightseeing excursions to alleviate the tedium of their long days at sea.

On starting his shift each morning, Yoshi walked the deck to collect data from his gauges and check distance traveled. Each morning, he passed the Italian bakers who were baking bread in special ovens, located as a part of the outside kitchen on deck used by the contingent of cooks from Italy who prepared meals for the Italian passengers. The cooks were not on duty at that early hour when the bakers and Yoshi began their chores, and the aroma of freshly baking bread wafted through the air so enticingly. The bakers knew the sailor who walked by their ovens each morning had not eaten yet, and even an Oriental unfamiliar with bread could not refuse a fresh morsel if offered. Soon they began sharing a fresh sample of their goods whenever he walked by. They waved to him to join them, his nose followed the delicious aroma, and they ate and communicated with hand gestures. Yoshi was hooked on fresh breads and assorted pastries ever after.

From Singapore, the ship traveled north through the narrow Strait of Malacca to the Indian Ocean. They sailed west to Colombo on the southern coast of Ceylon, then north to stop in Bombay before continuing west across the Arabian Sea to Aden, where they entered the Red Sea. Passage through the Suez Canal kept those on the bridge alert and the passengers on deck intrigued with the mechanics of the procedure. Once released from the locks onto the Mediterranean Sea, they stopped in Port Said. One of the ships headed to Venice; the others sailed west away from the isles with their legendary siren calls toward the Island of Malta off the Tunisian coast. The passengers' anxiety escalated as they sensed home was close. They spied Sicily as they passed and then headed north toward their destination, the port of Naples. The trip had taken close to five weeks.

The country was eagerly awaiting the fleet's arrival in Naples. Numerous government officials, the Red Cross, and an array of dignitaries joined in the fanfare and celebrations honoring the returning prisoners of war. It took two days to disembark all the passengers.

Work to convert the ship back to a freighter and wash out and retrofit the interiors took a month. They waited another three weeks for an assignment to pick up cargo. With little to do and a surfeit of free time, the crew was granted liberal amounts of shore leave. Yoshi took in as much sightseeing as possible and joined tours to Pompeii and Mt. Vesuvius, although a port city as notable as Naples provided an abundance of attractions to keep him busy most of his free time.

The France Maru had been transformed, and the second part of Yoshi's journey began. On leaving Naples, the ship sailed north to Marseilles before proceeding south to Algiers and Tunisia, where they picked up cargo. Reversing their earlier route, they proceeded east and left the Mediterranean through the Suez Canal and down the Red Sea. Once up and around the Horn of Africa, they traveled south toward new territories to Durban, South Africa. No storms hampered their journey past the rocky promontories as they rounded the Cape of Good Hope to Cape Town. The ship proceeded north along the West Coast of the African continent, stopping once to obtain water. The water was bad, and everyone on board became sick.

The ship continued north to the top of Africa. When they sighted Cape St. Vincent at the southwest corner of Portugal, the long-standing landmark for mariners heading into the Mediterranean, they turned east, sailed past Gibraltar, and went up the coast of Spain to Barcelona. Taking shore leave, Yoshi joined the group of seamen determined to try their luck at the casino. Yoshi handily lost most of his money along with the others; only the cook was having a hot streak. Laying his money on the cook's bets, he made enough money to break even. Yoshi felt lucky he still had some money for the next port's adventures.

From Barcelona, Spain, they headed east. Glimmer in the distance for miles before anything else was recognizable, the white hilltop church with its bell tower and gilded statue was a visible beacon. The Notre Dame de la Garde Basilica was the landmark that lead them into the port of Marseilles. When their port chores were completed, Yoshi joined four crewmen to visit the prominent landmark so visible out at sea. The five men hailed a taxi for a ride up the hill. Halfway up the steep incline, the vehicle belched and coughed; it stopped, unable to go up any further. Neither could it reverse back down the hill. As good as any Mack Sennett scenario, the five passengers got out and proceeded to push the vehicle up the hill with its driver still steering and shouting instructions and curses in French. All the while, the five Japanese sailors pushed with all their might, grunting and heaving their charge to the top. "BANZAI!" they shouted on reaching the top. The cabbie refused to refund any of their prepaid fare. In spite of their travails, the view was great, and it deserved another hearty, "BANZAI!"

The ship left the Mediterranean with a stopover in Lisbon before proceeding north to London, England, and Glasgow, Scotland. By lucky happenstance, their last port of call in Europe was in the land of Scotch whiskey, where they could stock up on the liquor. News had reached the ship that the United States had banned all alcoholic beverages with the Prohibition Act a few months earlier. The country had gone dry, but doors for illicit smuggled goods opened wide. An opportunity to make some ready cash was too tempting to deny, and the men on board bought as many bottles as they had money to spend. They each squirreled away their cache for their own consumption or for eventual resale.

During the hours of duty at the helm, Yoshi became friends with third officer Saito, whose duties also kept him on the bridge. To while away the hours, they told stories, and as their trust deepened, they exchanged confidences.

"I was still an apprentice on ship. That was many years ago, of course," Saito said. "I left the ship and worked and lived in New York City for two years. When my initial enthusiasm cooled, I realized it was not the life I wanted to live. I managed to return to Japan and attended naval school to become a career officer."

"You probably guessed I intend to leave the ship in New York," Yoshi confessed.

"I wanted you to know it's as difficult to make a fortune in America as anywhere else in the world."

"I'm a second son; you understand the position I'm in. If America is as good or as bad as anywhere else, I'll give New York a try. You said you liked it at first, didn't you?"

"You're young, as I was. At first, it was bewildering: everything was so strange. Then I felt stimulated and alive, but soon the novelty and excitement withered, and I yearned to return to my familiar roots."

"I have a cousin who lives there; another cousin is expected to arrive soon. If I join them, we'll be three."

"I was alone. You're lucky you'll have family."

After crossing the Atlantic, the France Maru arrived in New York City, and the US Customs and Treasury agents boarded the ship immediately and began their search for contraband. With practiced skills searching a ship, the agents located practically all the newly acquired bottles of whiskey and carried the liquor off the ship with them.

The ship sailed to Baltimore, where the crew was finally given shore leave. The two-day leave gave Yoshi time to take a train to New York City and search out cousin Kajuro. Unlike the time he got lost on his first day in Kobe, the taxi driver in New York drove Yoshi directly to the boardinghouse where his cousin lived. The meeting was informative but brief; Cousin had an important engagement to keep. Alone in a city he planned to return to, Yoshi had time to study the location of landmarks and commit to memory street names for future reference before heading back to Baltimore and boarding his ship.

He regretted his earlier lackadaisical attitude about learning the English language. He had not advanced much beyond learning the alphabet and reading a primer or two while in school, but the real puzzle was the language spoken by Americans. It was unlike any he was taught or had heard in Japan; it was completely alien. Studying English aboard the ship was not feasible; it would arouse suspicions among the crew. Yoshi saw no easy resolution to his dilemma. In the beginning, he used his hands and smiled a lot, as he did in other foreign lands, but Yoshi knew a more permanent stay meant additional schooling to learn the language once he landed.

Although he had reached his desired destination, America, he chose to stay aboard and continue the journey to South America. The ship's schedule, he learned, was to return to the United States' East Coast after the journey south. It was his opportunity to see another part of the world before staying grounded on land.

A second reason Yoshi thought it prudent to stay on longer was the threatened strike circulating onboard. The "war bonus," which was added to the crew's pay and had been stipulated on their contracts when they signed on, was to be terminated for the ship's return journey to Japan. Crewmen were angry at the company for reneging on their contract terms, and they began voicing strike threats. Several crewmen decided to follow through on the threat and instigated a work stoppage revolt. They recruited fellow crewmen to join them on the crusade, and most of the lower-ranking seaman and engineers joined.

Yoshi realized escalation of the conflict could jeopardize his plans to leave the ship. There were no hints of forthcoming decisions by the company. In any eventuality, he felt he could not afford to alienate the revolting crewmen or the ship's officers who represented the company. Yoshi said he would remain neutral for personal reasons. As a Quartermaster, he was in a position between the two combatants, and both parties accepted the decision without rancor.

The situation aboard the ship became dangerously volatile. Finally, the company sent a wire back to the ship stating: "In reconsidering the situation, we have decided to continue the bonus payments for the entire contract time."

The crisis over, things returned to normal as the ship sailed south, crossing the equator, bypassing Brazil, and on to Montevideo, Uruguay, and Buenos Aires, Argentina. Yoshi found the climate and ambiance of Argentina, including the customs and hospitality of the people, so amenable, he seriously considered relocating to Buenos Aires instead of the United States. After giving the idea more thought, he decided to stay aboard for the trip back to New York.

Saito advised Yoshi he should stay aboard in New York City and wait until they arrived in Baltimore, where they would be given a longer shore leave.

Yoshi told the second quartermaster, who would be assigned many of his chores, where to find his secreted case of Scotch whiskey, which the Treasury agents had failed to find. It had been hidden under the spare helm, a steering wheel heavy and large enough to keep the illicit goods safely hidden. Perhaps he could gift half of it to the captain and officers for good measure, he suggested. Furthermore, any personal belongings left behind were for him to keep or distribute as he pleased, Yoshi told the man. "I plan to take with me only the clothes I'll wear, some papers, and money." After a short stopover in New York, the ship traveled to Newport News, and the crew was given their shore leave as Saito had predicted. Yoshi wore his suit, new shoes, and hat, and carried with him a small *furoshiki* bundle, a gift package wrapped with a scarf in the traditional Japanese manner. He walked down the gangway and departed the ship. Saito was on deck and watched his departure. Once on the dock, Yoshi stopped, turned and waved to his friend, both with the knowledge it was for the last time. The captain and other officers were also on the deck, so Yoshi waved to them, too. They must have suspected Yoshi was leaving, but nothing was amiss; they said nothing, and as they waved back, Yoshi felt they were wishing him well and good luck.

CHAPTER 4

New York, 1920-1928

THE FRANCE MARU'S SCHEDULED PORT of call after leaving the East Coast was Galveston, Texas, on the Gulf of Mexico. The ship's route beyond that stop was unknown. Also uncertain was whether it would continue transporting goods between North and South America on Atlantic routes for the near future. The only certainty was the ship would eventually pass through the Panama Canal to the Pacific Ocean. The passage through the newly constructed canal, which had been completed six years before, was a journey Yoshi found intriguing. He was not only curious to witness the lock's operation, but he also knew he would be among the few to have passed through both the Suez and Panama canals with a firsthand comparison of the two mechanical marvels. He gave the idea consideration until Saito concurred there was no guarantee their ship would stop in any American ports once they reached the Pacific. Giving up visits to additional exotic destinations and to forgo future bragging rights of sorts was a paltry sacrifice for the chance of living in America to make his fortune; only a fool would jeopardize that dream now that he was so close to his goal.

Yoshi's legal entry into the United States had been dashed when the Mie prefectural officials refused to give him an emigration permit. Unlike the neighboring Wakayama prefecture, whose officials had encouraged their citizens to find work abroad, Mie intended to keep its inhabitants securely in Japan. Meanwhile, the United States was in the process of closing its doors to Asians. It had begun first with the Chinese; now

Japanese nationals with a few exceptions were already excluded from entering the country. A policy of total exclusion was to be in force in 1924. Unauthorized entry into the United States did continue surreptitiously through port cities, although such attempts to leave a ship could be difficult, dangerous, and much less likely to succeed on the West Coast. Illegal entry through the East Coast by Asians was not common nor was the search for illegal Asians as closely monitored as it was in areas bordering the Pacific.

Despite the obstacles, unforeseen delays, and an illegal entry, Yoshi finally landed on United States' soil, and he planned to stay awhile. As Japanese count their birthdays, he had turned twenty-one the week before disembarkation day. He had made his decision as an adult, and he did not look back.

After Yoshi was well out of sight of the ship, he picked up his pace and headed for the train terminal. The trial run made on his previous shore leave enabled him to buy his ticket and arrive at the platform to catch the train to New York City without mishap. Confident he knew the way from the train terminal to the rooming house where his cousin was staying in Brooklyn, he dallied in the city, absorbed by its expanse and pulse. The city was big, noisy, and bustling––an environment Yoshi found stimulating. City streets laid out in a grid were easily deciphered, unlike the maze he encountered in Kobe, and he strolled block after block, stopping to inspect the curiosities. He stayed in Manhattan longer than he intended, and he was further delayed when he made several wrong connections on the subway. When he finally reached his destination, it was late at night, and the doors of the rooming house were locked. He knocked on the door to no avail; he could not rouse anyone from sleep.

The chill in the air gave notice it was overcoat weather, and since Yoshi had none, he kept walking to stay warm. He walked the neighborhood; he then walked further afield and toward the bridge. The spanning structure allowed him to walk across and back without being too conspicuous, and the sights it afforded were worth the time he spent crossing it. At dawn, he went back to the boardinghouse, and an early riser heard his knock and let him in.

Cousin Kajuro finally woke up and came down from the sleeping quarters. He greeted Yoshi enthusiastically, "Cousin, you finally left the ship. Welcome, welcome." He poured coffee into two cups from the breakfast table and handed one to Yoshi. After a loud first sip of morning brew, he continued, "Did you have to come so early in the morning? Where did you sleep last night?"

Yoshi explained the situation.

"Drink, you need the coffee. It'll keep you awake. Better than tea to start the day," Kajuro said as he studied his cousin then scratched his head and asked, "You…walked all night…in THOSE shoes?"

"Oh, they're new. I bought them in Lisbon," Yoshi said. "Ah, ha ha! Yoshi, you're wearing women's shoes!"

"So that's how that salesman found a size to fit me. Everything I tried on was way too big. Finally, he came out with these shoes, and they fit. So I bought them."

Kajuro could not contain himself, and he continued laughing, "Hmm, Europeans are big, and you're small even for Japanese. You'll have trouble buying clothes to fit you. But next time, don't be tempted to buy women's…ha ha ha."

No doubt he's Sutekichi's son; this cousin is from the tactless side of the family, thought Yoshi.

Kajuro was ten years older than Yoshi, and he took his younger cousin under his wing and helped him adjust to his new surroundings in the New World. He and his friend Yoshino had slipped into the US several years before, and he now felt he was a bona fide New Yorker and a bon vivant one at that.

"Get a job for the winter," he advised Yoshi, "and in the summer you can come work for me and Yoshino."

Yoshi made arrangements to stay at the boardinghouse and found his way to Manhattan and the employment office he had been advised to seek. Assisting job seekers was one of the services provided by the association established by a group of early Japanese settlers to provide mutual aid for the benefit of their countrymen living in the area.

"There's an immediate job opening for a dishwasher, Yoshi was told. "The restaurant is small and owned by Japanese. It's the ideal job for someone new to the city."

The restaurant was located in upper Manhattan, a long commute to Brooklyn, and the pay was minimal, but the job required no knowledge of English. Yoshi enrolled in an English language class for foreigners to expand his future job prospects.

His brain was wired for the Japanese grammatical sequence: subject, object, and verb; getting his brain to accept the sequence subject, verb, object, instead, was only one of his difficulties. His mouth and tongue refused to curl around Th, l, r, and v. Yoshi continued to have problems with the new language. He had little spare time for play. Still filled with youthful energy, he was anxious to participate in the enticements surrounding him in the city; for now, he had to be content watching others at play.

SUMMER 1921

In May, Yoshi quit his job and followed Kajuro and his partner Yoshino out to Rockaway Beach along the southern coast of Long Island. The partners made plans to lease two concession stands at the amusement park arcade that year, a cigarette shooting gallery and a Skee-Ball operation. The weeks before the season's opening was spent cleaning their leased premises, refurbishing the concession equipment, and purchasing prizes to be given away. They lived in the back of their stands, eating and sleeping in their makeshift quarters the five months from May through September. Kajuro paid Yoshi a standard one hundred dollars per month salary to be the third man. His presence allowed the two partners to take time off and go into the city for rest and relaxation.

Kajuro often overstayed his designated time in the city, staggering back to sleep off his binge, still too drunk to take over his shift. Kajuro and Yoshi were both Kajiro *Ojii-san's* grandsons; any cravings for alcohol Yoshi could have inherited had been kiboshed by Grandmother Yae's "treatment" a generation before. Kajuro's lineage had not undergone such a cure, and his capacity for and love of booze flowed unimpeded from Grandfather.

Although Yoshi disliked the taste of distilled drinks, preferring sweetened sodas, the easygoing lifestyle around him led him to begin drinking, too. His indulgences were far less frequent and the quantity much less than Kajuro's intake, but he binged on occasion, and he usually passed out and slept it off, or else threw up before falling asleep. And following every miserable hangover, he wondered why he continued to drink.

On one occasion, after a night of partying on bootleg whiskey, Yoshi felt his legs give way while trudging back to his quarters, the sandy stretch of beach underfoot was such a compelling rest stop, Yoshi collapsed and sprawled comfortably on the sand and promptly fell asleep. The sounds of feet, many feet, pounding on the sand resounded in his ears, waking him from his stupor. Men running past him to the water's edge began pulling on ropes. Scores of men pulled and heaved as nets with wooden cases appeared on shore. As they retrieved their sodden catch, the men ran back, carrying or dragging their loot to waiting vehicles. The well-organized operation ended as swiftly as it had started. Yoshi was now wide awake and found he was again alone on the beach with the waves lapping the shore in the moonlight. Only the depressions left on the sand surface gave evidence of what had occurred, and they too disappeared as the sands shifted. His swollen head felt like a taiko drum with a crazed drummer hammering his skull as its reverberations ricocheted endlessly within, and he felt sick. His misery was compounded by his knowing it was self-induced. Why do people exert such herculean efforts to acquire something that only makes you feel so godawful?

The long narrow spit of land and beaches of Rockaway, though further from the city than Coney Island, Brighton, and Manhattan beaches, nonetheless attracted its share of citizens to become known as the "'Playground of New York." The amusement park, now twenty years since opening, sat between the community's developed commercial strip and the beach.

As the strict Victorian ethos of their recent past crumbled, even the Volstead Act could be sidestepped with bootleg whiskey and speakeasies. The populace learned to play and have a good time; such activities were no longer pleasures reserved for the rich. Even a day or two or more away from the sweltering confines of the city to the open expanse of sand and water provided relief followed by good spirits. The visitors were ready to shed their workday personas and enjoy themselves. And the carnival amusements in the playland were there to help make them happy.

Yoshi enjoyed that happy, carefree atmosphere. Also, spending the summer removed from the suffocating city and the menial jobs of winter was a welcome relief, an escape for him as much as an escape taken by hordes of beachgoers on a shorter basis during summer. He learned a few English phrases, but he did not need to speak much English to communicate with the customers. If he smiled and laughed with good humor, people stopped and played at the concession booth. "Hal-lo! Hal-lo! You try? Maybe you lucky! Maybe you win be-goo prize!" A Japanese accent was no detriment to attracting would-be sharpshooters. The concession operators and seasonal workers on-site were generally open, gregarious types who formed a friendly coterie—a surrogate family. Whatever the negative aspects of the work, the positive ones were overwhelming.

The arcade season ended a week after Labor Day. The three men boarded up their galleries, packed their belongings, and returned to the city to look for winter/spring employment.

WINTER 1921

Yoshi took a job as houseboy for a couple living in the lower west side in Greenwich Village. His employer was pompous and overbearing, and he claimed he was a former governor of Virginia. He was also a frugal man. This was Yoshi's first experience working as a servant, and he found the work tolerable though he considered his boss less than agreeable. When he learned there were employers who were generally more considerate and many who paid better salaries, he quit his job of two months. He quickly found another houseboy position with a family in Morristown, New Jersey, for better pay. He stayed until May, when he moved back to Rockaway Beach.

SUMMER 1922

The summer of 1922 was much like the previous year. Yoshino, Kajuro, and Yoshi shared work at the two concession stands and shared quarters in back of their stands again. They cooked their meals on a hot plate when they chose not to eat out. They had no beds; instead, they each had two futons: one served as a mattress and the other one was the cover, which allowed them to sleep on any level surface available. The three venturesome bachelors accepted the arrangement with amicable indifference.

Yoshino was a quiet man, gentle in manner and speech, and truly sweet natured. He never provoked anyone to anger, and only silence marked his displeasure. He was the antithesis of a typical carny, but he was as successful in attracting customers to play at their arcade as any others. Perhaps his aura of goodness radiated and pulled people in. Yoshino worked diligently as much as his partner did the opposite; Kajuro was always trying to weasel out of doing his share of work, and he always sweet-talked his way back into people's good graces for his misdeeds.

"You're such opposites, Yoshino. What brought you and Kajuro together to form a business partnership?" Yoshi asked one day when Cousin was again detained in the city, on another of his vanishing episodes. He and Yoshino had gotten into the habit of keeping each other company with conversation after their long shift of manning the stands.

"Kajuro and I both figured we could make good money running a concession. By working hard four to five months a year, we can make many times over what can be earned working as a houseboy or whatever job comes our way," Yoshino had replied. "But, you can't operate a concession alone. You need a partner or a trusted employee."

"Of all people, why did you choose Kajuro?"

"Well… Kajuro is basically honest, perhaps less so in his dealings with women when he has been drinking. Even at such times, you can trust him when money is involved. So, following the wise Chinese, we entered into a business alliance for profit, not necessarily for social purposes."

"Kajuro must have inherited *Ojii-san's* business acumen as well as his love for drink. I don't think I inherited either."

"There are attributes besides being mercenary, Yoshi. You possess a goodly few. Don't worry about the rest."

"Thank you for the assessment, Yoshino."

"I'm beginning to rethink my own mercenary tendencies."

Yoshi had no idea what lay behind that last remark, so he let it drift. He did know Yoshino had become a friend; he was as good a human being as he would ever come to know. They finished the season in September, ready for a change of venue and time away from each other. They would go their separate ways for seven months.

Winter 1922

Yoshi took on another job as a restaurant dishwasher in midtown Manhattan. When by chance he was offered a better-paying job by a Japanese apartment owner, he switched jobs to do janitorial work and became a general handyman.

The sparsely furnished, closet-sized bedroom provided for him made the summer quarters at the arcade feel like a mansion in comparison, but the closet was rent-free. The majority of tenants were Japanese with few complaints, making it a stressless job. He met a bevy of nationals, more than he had seen since arriving in New York.

The community was small and scattered, easily lost in a city of several million; however, the New York *Kenjin-kai*, a mutual aid society formed early on, provided an expanded social and networking service to the Japanese living in the area. A few stores sold Japanese specialty items catering to the general public, and they, along with a handful of

Japanese-centric establishments, provided a limited selection of foodstuffs and goods from Japan that helped ease their isolation from their homeland. Also, the Japanese Counsel's office in Manhattan was conveniently available in case of dire need.

New York City was booming; it was the Jazz Age. Yoshi was young and free of encumbrances, and he was as caught up in the euphoria of the times as everyone else. His job allowed him leisure time to fraternize with various Japanese he met along the way. They were mostly young adult males who had come to America alone without families. The majority were generally illegal aliens who had jumped ship, much as Kajuro and Yoshi had done, while others had come with proper entry permits to attend school, had dropped out, and stayed on in America. In Japanese society, failure to live up to one's responsibilities is a disgrace taken very seriously. And a failed student having "lost face" was unlikely to return to his family.

There was a scarcity of Japanese women, as well as Asian females of whatever nationality, in and around New York. The disparity in numbers of Japanese men to women led men who wanted female companions into cohabiting and marrying women who were non-Asian.

Though Sessue Hayakawa was overshadowed as to an "exotic" silent pictures matinee star, his successor became phenomenally famous. When Rudolf Valentino appeared in The Four Horsemen of the Apocalypse, fans, especially female fans, found him sexy and irresistible. The craze intensified when "Blood and Sand" was released in theaters that year, and women continued to swoon. A residual of the phenomena was an acceptance of attractive men of different nationalities. That transfer of affection worked to the bachelors' benefit, and Yoshi understood it well.

The Japanese bachelor community Yoshi had joined came from backgrounds as varied as one could find. Koji was an exuberant fellow, hardly typical for Japanese. When Yoshi first met him, he was the trusted first butler for a wealthy stockbroker. His boss had asked Koji if he would allow him to invest one month's salary in the market for a period of two years. At the end of two years, Koji was given a sum of money many times over the original one month's salary. Koji was astonished at the profit, and though he was warned a novice should not play with stocks, he could not resist the possibility of instant riches, and he became addicted. His boss fired him, telling him he had no use for a fool. Thereafter, Koji never had any money, as he continued to invest in one losing get-rich-quick scheme after another. Sadly, his friends, including Yoshi, avoided him to keep from being hit for another loan.

Yoshi was more prudent with his money than his friend. He neither understood the workings of the market nor did he invest his money there, although Koji had tried to teach him the basics on more than one occasion. Instead, Yoshi indulged himself with a set of finely tailored suits and accessories, he felt were a necessary investment for anyone living in New York City. He limited his spending without being parsimonious, and he religiously set aside a sum each month and sent it home to his parents.

It was rare when one of the footloose bachelors had a relative who also lived in the city, but Yoshi and Kajuro had different sets of friends attuned to their individual interests. They did share a number of mutual acquaintances, and there were times during their hiatus from the arcade when they found themselves in each other's company and socialized like family. Generally, Kajuro treated Yoshi much like he treated everyone else and took advantage of him when he could. At other times, when his conscience reigned, he did his best to act like a protective big brother. "You have to live life for yourself, Yoshi. Enjoy the fruits of your own labor. I think Americans have a good philosophy, *neh*."

"Cousin, you did well to move to America. You've adopted a philosophy which would make you an outcast if you lived in Japan," Yoshi said.

Kajuro replied, "And I thought it was rotten luck when I got sick. If I hadn't gotten sick, I'd have stayed on that rusty old freighter. I'd still be there. Now that was karma." Kajuro had attended naval school and was a ship's officer until he was taken off the ship when he fell ill. During his recuperation, Kajuro realized he wasn't suited to living at sea for long periods, and a permanent life on shore was more suited to his talents and needs. When he recovered, he boarded a ship as a regular seaman, and when they reached the United States, he stayed on land when the ship departed. "I'd be in the same sorry state as my brother, always at sea, seeing the world on short shore leaves. It's interesting the first few years, but it becomes a boring routine. It's when you're on land that you really live your life."

"I saw Shozo the last time he came home on leave. He seemed to like his life at sea. In fact, he gave me lots of useful tips about living aboard a ship."

"Like what kind of advice?"

"Humm…like when not to play cards with the crew."

"I'll hear that one when I'm sober someday. Today we ought to drink a toast celebrating our good fortune, you and I. Shozo can have his life at sea. We're here on good solid bedrock, New York City. Banzai!" Kajuro was in a celebratory mood and offered Yoshi a swig of his bootleg whiskey.

Yoshi declined, knowing the precious liquor would be wasted on him. "What's a bottle costing you lately?" he asked.

"Much too much," Kajuro answered. "Which reminds me, I heard a bit of old gossip about our relative Uncle Ryokichi."

"I recall you once said he was still here in New York when you arrived."

"Did I tell you I almost missed him? He was ready to leave for the West Coast to catch a ship back to Japan. He was planning to bring his wife and son back here to live, but he had to do it before they stopped all immigration, even wives and children."

"Why didn't Uncle just send them the money for passage? Why did he have to go back to Japan and fetch them personally?"

"You're asking the wrong person. I have no idea, I barely knew him."

"Same here…"

"Will you let me get on with my story? Well, he was totally inhospitable when we met. I had just arrived in a strange country with nothing, and he didn't offer to treat me to a meal or to share even a dime. What kind of uncle would treat a nephew like that?"

Uncle Ryokichi was the youngest brother of Sutekichi and Yoshi's father, Kakichi. Just as other younger sons had to find a way to support themselves, Ryokichi had to do the same, and his path to fortune was in America. He had entered the United States as a legal immigrant, unlike his nephews, and later he was able to apply for immigrant status for his wife and son.

"How he treated me was so upsetting, I've never acknowledged we were related when others asked. And I've been asked often enough since we share the same surname, Nomura. I remind people it's a common name in Japan," Kajuro said, bristling as he recalled the incident. "A few weeks ago, a group of us got on the subject of miserly people we've encountered. So this guy who I've never met before starts telling us about a guy named Nomura. His boss owned the Madison Square Garden. Yeah, the boss was rich, but he was cheap and didn't pay much. We've all worked for that kind before. Anyway, Nomura worked like a slave and saved practically every penny he made. When you work for a family, they feed you and provide a place to sleep, right? So he has few expenses and gets a dismal salary. Hardly any money changes hands, so there's barely any money for anything. It's a wonder the man was able to scrape up the money to retrieve his wife and son. The guy went on to say Ryokichi's boss was about the same size as Nomura, and he'd give him his old clothes: suits, shirts, even underwear. Hell, Nomura didn't even have to buy the clothes he wore!"

"So was Ryokichi extremely thrifty or just plain cheap?"

"I thought he was the cheapest, most inconsiderate, self-serving person I ever met. I hear the circumstances of how he managed to accumulate enough money to bring his family here and I think maybe he's gotta be the most self-sacrificing person ever. He's a different kind of relation. I don't know whether I should disown him or embrace him."

"I don't have any recollections of him. Why didn't he come back to New York?"

"*Sonna-ga-gun*, Yoshi. Quit asking me such stupid questions. I don't know."

Summer 1923

In May 1923, Yoshi returned to Rockaway Beach for the third year. Yoshino and Kajuro decided to enlarge their popular Skee-Ball concession. They figured they would be so busy, they did not want to be bothered with the shooting gallery and gave it to Yoshi. He welcomed the opportunity to be his own boss and live a life less dependent on the whims of his cousin. His concession was not as popular as the partners' Skee-Ball game, but there was enough work and profit at his gallery to hire Kawachi to help him for the season. The coincidence that his name was the same as the *mise* back home might be an omen, a lucky sign.

Arcade at Rockaway Beach

The crowds were sparse in the early morning when all the concessions had not yet opened. Those hours were Yoshi's most relaxing of the entire day. The chores completed, he opened early hoping to catch a few stray customers on their morning stroll, but most of the time Yoshi just watched the kaleidoscope of people as they passed by his stand. Sachi and her husband were among the throngs of visitors who strolled by that summer day. He noticed them because they were early strollers and they were Oriental.

"Hal-lo, hal-lo! *Ira-shai!*" Yoshi said, beckoning to the couple. With a smile, he continued, "Try win prize! Come try lucky here!"

Stiffly gaited, more pompous than dignified, the dark-suited man obviously had not come down for a romp on the beach nor was he interested in the raucous amusements, but his much younger companion tugged at his sleeve, indicating she wanted to see Yoshi's booth up close. He reluctantly followed her lead toward the stand. He refused to pick up a rifle and try his marksmanship. The woman was not about to leave so soon, she had set her mind on lingering awhile. She picked up a popgun and asked instructions from the young proprietor. "Show me how to hold this gun. Where do I point it? Come show me how," she insisted.

She laughed so hard she missed every shot.

The other stands were still opening up for the day, and few people strolled along the walkway. Yoshi's customer was heralding the start of another carnival day, and she was obviously enjoying herself. The surrounding shopkeepers smiled at her happy countenance, sure she was a good sign for their own days.

Her companion was impatient to leave, and he kept admonishing her. "Sachiko, *ya-me-nasai*, please stop," he said. "It is very undignified…for a Japanese woman. Please stop!" "Husband, I haven't won a prize yet," she replied. "We must go NOW!" he commanded.

Yoshi handed the woman a small stuffed bear. "Here, you won a prize for trying," he said with a smile.

She took the prize and returned his smile.

Sachi started returning to the arcade at regular intervals on her own, and she invariably ended up at Yoshi's gallery. She gave up any pretense she was interested in shooting moving objects for prizes; she was interested in another prize. When she came to the gallery, she hung around and chatted, asking Yoshi to eat lunch with her or just stroll down to the beach together.

"Tell Kawachi you're leaving for a while. Come with me," she said.

Other nearby arcade owners took notice, and they began teasing him. "George, I think she likes you." "She's a sweetie, that friend of yours, Georgie." George was the name suggested to Yoshi when he took up residence in America. Yoshitsugu was too difficult for Americans to pronounce or remember. To everyone except the Japanese, he was now known as George.

Sachi was the rare young Japanese woman living in and around New York City; she was young and attractive, and Yoshi was flattered by her attentions. She shared traits with Izumi, his long-ago girlfriend, especially her impulsive bent for mischief. Yoshi was sorely tempted, but he had made a promise. *Okaa-san*, how could you have known and extended such long-reaching tentacles to keep temptation at bay? Oh, the pleasures lost!

Winter 1923

When they returned to the city that fall, cousin Kajuro had a bit of belated advice for Yoshi, "It was a good thing you did not pursue that woman. A month or so ago while we were working at Rockaway, Kumagai was shot dead by his girlfriend's husband. That girlfriend wasn't pretty or Japanese, but her Japanese husband was one jealous fellow. Too bad for Kumagai; he was a great drinking partner."

"Kajuro, you can tell me the truth now. Did the same thing happen to Torao, your brother?" Yoshi asked.

"I prefer the official version about what happened. Committing suicide is a more honorable way to die, especially if you're Japanese. The police didn't have to look for a murderer here in New York, and no one back in Japan asked any further questions," Kajuro answered. "He wasn't like me at all. He was serious and very smart. No doubt he was the smartest. Had he lived, we'd have started a business, Nomura & Company. We talked about it. It would have prospered, and we'd all be rich." Kajuro scratched his chin as he watched the money fly by in his mind's eye. He continued in a sober vein, "No, maybe he wasn't so smart. He wasn't smart about women."

The employment office greeted Yoshi by name when he arrived. "Nomura-*san*, welcome. When the summer heat cools to tolerable, we knew you'd be stopping in again."

"I was hoping you had something besides dishwashing or houseboy jobs. Are there any janitor jobs? Last year, I did janitorial and handyman work at Tada-*san*'s apartment."

"Those are desirable jobs, Nomura-*san*. We try to place men who want permanent jobs in those positions. You plan to stay in the city only until May, right?"

"Yes, I suppose…"

"Now, here's a job for hotel bellboy in mid-Manhattan. It says the applicant shall be expected to do some cleaning and handyman chores, too."

Yoshi felt he was qualified, and he took the job. A uniform was cut down to fit him, and he beamed as he stood at attention welcoming guests to the hotel. When there was a lull during the day, he busily polished the brass and cleaned the glass, sprucing up the lobby areas, much as a ship is kept spiffy.

The hotel was definitely not first tier; it was a step or two down. Located midblock in from Broadway, the majority of the hotel's clientele were in show business: actors, associates, and their entourages. They were not the marquee headliners; they, too, were a notch or two down on the program listings. Yoshi had never encountered such flamboyance; it was a different breed of people who inhabited a world far removed from the sphere of uptight wealthy families like those previous employers Yoshi had come to know. These hotel guests were egocentric, uninhibited, and usually free with their money. Since Yoshi's wages were minimal, the tips made it worthwhile to stay with the job. Besides, the parade of people coming and going made the day and his job interesting, somewhat like the amusement park in summer. The job was not a routine one.

The length of a guests' stay varied from weeks and months to overnight stopovers. The theatrical crowd who worked evenings and matinees usually kept erratic sleeping and eating schedules. The first floor dining room was usually quite empty since the guests, when not dining out, preferred to order their meals from room service. This kept Yoshi busy delivering and picking up food trays to the guest rooms.

"Manager, would you send your boy here to room 210, PLEASE," came the call.

Yoshi was dispatched to the room, where he was greeted by a young woman who, upon opening the door, stood in front of him stark naked.

"Come in, and take the dirty dishes away like a good boy. Well, don't just stand there. COME IN!" she snapped.

"Yes, ma'am," he answered. He fumbled nervously as he picked up the tray and, in trying to make a quick retreat out of the room, nearly tripped into her.

"Hey, be careful." She noticed he was averting his eyes to avoid looking at her, and she realized the reason for his clumsiness. She stepped directly in front of him and spread her arms wide; a full frontal view. "You've seen this before, haven't you?"

Yoshi grinned and wet his lips with his tongue.

"You're cute! Come back again," she said as he skirted around her, rattling dishes and dinnerware on the stacked tray as he left the room.

When Yoshi returned downstairs to the desk, he was asked by Jim the desk clerk, "George, did she have any clothes on today?"

"Ah, no, sir."

They both spontaneously burst out chortling as visions of her danced in their heads.

Male guests had their eccentricities too; however, the female guests were those Yoshi remembered.

"I'm in room 319. The bathtub is plugged. Send George up to fix it, right away!" was the message. Yoshi had been on the job a few months, and the regular guests now knew him by name. Room 319's occupant was a woman, years beyond young who was still not resigned to being middle-aged. Her bones and bearing indicated she was once quite beautiful, and she remained a commanding presence.

She was attired in her robe, ready for her bath, when she answered the door.

"Bathtub is plugged?" Yoshi asked as he stepped in the room. "Yes, follow me," she said as she led him to the bathroom.

He assessed the situation. The bathtub was full of hot water ready for the bather. "You no pull plug," he said.

"How silly of me," she said as she slid out of her robe and climbed into the tub. "George, don't go yet. You have to scrub my back." She handed him her soap and washcloth and made circular motions so he would understand her request.

Yoshi dutifully squatted down by the tub and started scrubbing her back. Wow wee, gee wee!

When he got back to the desk this time, Jim noticed Yoshi's sleeves were wet. "What was the problem with Room 319's bathtub?" he asked.

"Nah-sing. She wanna scrub," he answered by lifting one arm and making a circular motion in the armpits as she had shown him earlier.

"Jeez, some people have all the luck," Jim whined. "She never asked me to go up and scrub her down. Wow!"

The work was not hard, the guests were full of surprises, and the fun and games never ceased. Yoshi did feel pangs of guilt on occasion. He was spending more than his self-imposed allowance on secondary services, and he had no money to send home.

SUMMER 1924

Returning to Rockaway Beach each May allowed Yoshi to leave behind the menial jobs of the winter months, although giving up his job the winter just past was not without some remorse. It was a serendipitous episode not meant to last. He had the task of preparing the shooting gallery for another summer season and to earn enough money to send home. He hired a new assistant named Yamamoto and hoped his arcade business would continue to do well. Sachi no longer showed up for unplanned visits, and he resigned himself to a routine summer without highlights.

Yoshi received word that cousin Susumu had arrived in New York. His American stopover had been delayed when his studies in Europe were prolonged much longer than originally scheduled. After another year of studying with an eminent Japanese medical researcher in America, he planned to return home to practice medicine. Susumu was carrying on the tradition in medicine of his father and his family history of physicians who served samurai clansmen. They were neither classified samurai nor were they rich, but by association they were among a privileged class and were considered intelligentsia.

His doctor cousin was four years older, and the two were only slightly acquainted, but Yoshi was dismayed by his cousin's unenthusiastic response when Yoshi proposed he visit Susumu at his apartment. His off-putting behavior made Yoshi wonder if a reassessment of this cousin was in order. After all, how often does one meet a cousin halfway around the world from home? He was persistent, and a meeting date was set. He took a day off and returned to the city for the visit. The reason for the cool reception was obvious when he arrived. Susumu did not answer the door; it was a woman. She was young, attractive, and not Japanese.

"Come in. You're expected," she said as she took his hat. "He'll be out in a minute. It's the heat."

She was not a new acquaintance; she was too familiar with Susumu's personal needs. She was obviously accompanying the medical student on his travels.

Susumu appeared with a towel around his neck catching the water running down from his wet hair. "Sorry... I didn't mean to keep you waiting. I haven't acclimatized to this weather yet."

"You've been away so long; you've forgotten how much worse the summers are in Japan," Yoshi said. "Here in America, you can escape the worst by traveling a few miles."

"You're right. I have been away a long time," Susumu chuckled. "Cousin, now you know the reason why I avoided our meeting. She's been my companion since shortly after I started my overseas study.

She arranged this fellowship for me here in New York so we could be together a while longer." He sat back and answered Yoshi's question before it was asked, "Yes, she knows I'm married. Yes, she knows I'll return to Japan alone."

"I won't reveal your secret, Susumu. We all have secrets; most don't ever see the light of day." That piece of business settled, the cousins relaxed to talk amicably about their travels and family. Yoshi was gratified to learn his cousin was as personable as his parents had been to him.

Susumu's friend had not understood a word the two men had spoken, but she understood the gist of their conversation by the tone of their voices. When she saw they were both smiling, she knew it was safe to join in. "Nice to meet you…was that Yoshi? My name is Abigail. Susumu has a difficult time pronouncing my name; you might find it difficult, too. So please call me Abby."

"Abby? Oh yes, Abie Irish Rose, very easy to remember name. I saw show in theater."

They had few opportunities to visit after their first meeting since both cousins had a full schedule of work or study that summer, and Yoshi hated staying in the city longer than necessary when the heat and humidity made city living unbearable. The carnival sphere of Rockaway Beach was crass and noisy, but the refreshing breezes coming from the sea made it all worthwhile in the summer. Kajuro had too many projects of his own to be bothered with this new cousin since they were not blood relatives anyway.

WINTER 1924

Washing dishes was not especially high on his list of favorite jobs, but the selection list was sparse that fall, and Yoshi rationalized the employee meals a restaurant served were a great deal better than the self-cooked meals he had eaten all summer.

The Nikko restaurant, located on Columbus Avenue in the West 80s, was a midsized restaurant with an American menu catering to a middle-class clientele. The establishment was owned by Kobayashi, who was the head cook, and his wife, Faye, the hostess/cashier who managed the front-of-house staff, who were all white like herself.

Two weeks after starting work, the second pantry man took on the fourth position at the stove, leaving his position open for Yoshi to fill. The work was different and far more stimulating than washing dishes, and he got a raise, making the move up better yet. Yoshi learned to make mayonnaise and various dressings for the salads; he prepared appetizers and learned to quickly shuck oysters for the raw half-shell orders, and he sliced and diced whatever his workstation required. He learned the taste and names of the cheeses they served, and he came to love all varieties of cheese, a rather unique palate for an Oriental. It was an acquired taste not always shared by other Asians. And, of course, his lifelong addiction to sugar expanded to all forms of desserts, including both American and European-style pastries.

Faye noticed their new hire worked valiantly to keep up with his orders and only became cranky at someone's crass stupidity or meanness. She took a liking to him, giving him preferential treatment, which did not escape notice by the other workers. "Faye likes you, George." "She never talks sweet to me like she does to you, George." "Where's George, she asks. She yells when she's looking for me," they said. Yoshi maintained his usual friendliness but prudently kept a respectful distance from Faye. He had no desire to antagonize his boss, her husband.

In the back of the restaurant, the kitchen crew was all Japanese, except for the lone African American dishwasher, named Johnson. The restaurant owners provided housing quarters for the bachelor employees in a building close by. Since most of their waking hours were spent at the restaurant, providing such a convenience was a prudent investment.

On his days off, Yoshi managed to visit Susumu, who introduced him to colleagues who were involved in medicine and research. The small, loosely tied fraternity of Japanese students and medical professionals revolved around Dr. Hideyo Noguchi, who was an eminent researcher at the Rockefeller Institute for Medical Research. The group of serious, mostly young, men easily accepted Yoshi's presence; "He's Susumu's cousin" was used in the first introduction. When the men talked earnestly about their medical projects, Yoshi sat in the background listening to their discussions even though most of it escaped his comprehension. They, too, tired of talking shop, and Yoshi joined in when the talk turned to universal and down-to-earth subjects. He felt enriched by his exposure to people involved in endeavors with deep altruistic motives; they were good company, but Yoshi's work schedule limited his visits with them.

There always were friends who happened to have the same days off as Yoshi, and they went to whatever appealed to them that day: a boxing match at Madison Square Garden, a stage play on Broadway, a vaudeville show, a silent movie, and more. In the mornings when the weather was agreeable, Yoshi walked over to Central Park with his clip-on metal roller skates and skated the paved pathways with abandon. The variety of things to do was endless if you were young and lived in New York City.

Summer 1925

May rolled around again, and Yoshi quit his job at the restaurant and returned to Rockaway Beach for another summer season at the arcade concession. Cousin Kajuro was already there and waiting for him.

"Yoshi, I have a proposition for you. This year we can be partners and run the Skee-Ball together. We'll divide the profits fifty-fifty, and you'll make more money than operating the shooting gallery," Kajuro said. "What do you say?"

"What about your partner, Yoshino?"

"About Yoshino… He decided to give it up. He said he's tired of coming here every summer. He's staying with his job in Connecticut somewhere."

"Why would he quit the business? A few summer months here at the beach is more money than years of washing dishes or being a butler. I don't understand."

"I think he's planning to go back to Japan. It won't be any better back there than it is here, God knows."

"Why would Yoshino give it up? Why…?"

"Are we partners? It's fifty-fifty."

Yoshi hated to lose the independence he had as his own boss the past two summers, and he knew problems were inevitable in dealing with his cousin, but the Skee-Ball concession was a winner, and they were bound to make money, so he agreed. He sold his interests in the shooting gallery to his assistant, Yamamoto, and moved in with his cousin. For the rest of the summer, he was located at Stall #27 directly under the Thunderbolt Ride between 102nd Street and Thunderbolt Alley. The earthshaking shudders and the rattling noises were as thunderous as the ride's name. They lived with the racket along with the screams and whoops and hollers most of their waking hours. In time, Yoshi no longer noticed except when the contraption shut down for the night and quiet swept over the park as if the mighty dragon had been slain.

Actually, the location was a gold mine. In the hub of action, the swarming traffic of amusement seekers pumped up with their adrenaline high swirled around them. Often enough, they stopped at the stand to test their strength and skills. With a windup, the baseball-sized wooden ball was rolled up a slightly upward-sloped alley to hit a speed bump and hopefully pop into a circular basket. Different-sized baskets were worth differing points. The wooden alley was still thirty-six feet long at this time but would be shortened by half in a few years. Since strength mattered as well as skill, players were apt to show off to their companions as much as try for a prize.

The cousins shared the quarters behind their concession and became conditioned to the noise. They would relieve each other and take short breaks, either walking inland a few blocks to the commercial center or taking a train to the city for a change of pace, but it was much hotter in the city as the heat radiated off building surfaces, and natural breezes were hijacked to parts unknown. It was always a relief to get back to the seaside.

"There was a letter for you in the package Father sent me," Kajuro said. "It must be important. He's not known for his social graces, including letter writing."

Yoshi had to agree with Kajuro's assessment of the older man. He could still hear his Uncle Sutekichi calling out to "Make way for the rightful *chonan*" as he came to visit the family.

Yoshi opened what appeared to be a mere note and read:

"Nephew, imagine you've just read a half page of obligatory niceties, and let me get on with what I want to tell you. STOP sending your father any more money! Your father is endowed with a goodly share of our family virtues, and we do share the same blood; nevertheless, he is a FOOL. That money you so diligently send is used to promote his STUPID business ventures. He has no aptitude for business, and it's painful to watch him squander away money in one bad venture after another.

I know from my own experiences, it is not easy to work in a foreign country and earn a living. Yoshi, your hard-earned money is not being used to better the family's fortunes, and your sacrifices are being wasted. I strongly urge you to save your money for your own future use.

I will allay any disappointments your father may express when the money stops. I will remind him you are not the *chonan*, and you have to make your own way in this world. Do not worry." Signed: Uncle Sutekichi.

Yoshi knew his uncle was sincerely troubled by what he was witnessing to make such a harsh assessment of Father, and Uncle had felt it his duty to enlighten the victim, his nephew, and provide guidance to him in America as he had in Japan.

Yoshi first sent a letter to his father explaining he could no longer send monies home due to circumstances; he did not elaborate. He also sent a letter to Uncle Sutekichi telling him he was heeding his advice. Yoshi wrote he still had a commitment he was obliged to fulfill, and he included a sum of money. He asked his uncle to be a trustee for the money, which was to be used for his two younger brothers' schooling. Thus, Yoshi's promise to Shiro was fulfilled——ensuring his dream of attending naval school to become an officer, and providing for Hiromu's goal to go to military school.

Kajuro and Yoshi's business agreement was a fifty-fifty split for working the concession and for the profits. Their profits were split according to plan, but Kajuro was a master of indulging his own self-interests. His trips to the city were extensive excursions to eat, drink, and be merry with his girlfriend of the moment. Everyone agreed Kajuro was an all-around good fellow when he was sober. He was smart, a persuasive charmer, and good company––who turned obnoxious and abusive when drunk. His girlfriends often dumped him before he sobered up; once sober, he started the process again with yet another female friend, only to be thrown out again. His old partner Yoshino had finally had enough of Kajuro's antics and had departed. Yoshi was well aware of Kajuro's shortcomings, and yet he chose to become his partner, so when Kajuro overstayed his visit in the city on one of his binges, Yoshi took it in stride. He knew his partner would show up as soon as the girlfriend sobered up. Sure enough, Cousin reappeared with his usual hangover. Within days, he was looking at every attractive and likely eligible female as a potential new conquest. Unfortunately, New York is so big, Kajuro will never run out of victims.

Cousin Susumu finished his studies that summer and returned to Japan alone to resume his life with wife and family and to practice medicine.

Winter 1925

The concession was boarded up and their living quarters padlocked for the winter, Yoshi moved back to the city and found his way to the Nikko Restaurant. Faye was no longer at the desk. "She went back home to Hungary. She said she didn't like America anymore and she told us 'goodbye forever' when she left," the pert little hostess told Yoshi. "Neah, the boss had to go someplace today; he didn't say where. He's trying to sell the restaurant. Oops, I'm not supposed to say that."

"I no tell."

"Say, you wanna sit down at a table and rest your feet awhile?" "No, thank you, Miss. I go now." Yoshi decided not to check the kitchen to see whether his coworkers of the previous year were still there. He was likely to see them soon enough at the employment office if the restaurant was sold.

Faye had the business acumen, and Kobayashi did not have the skills to run the restaurant without her management. He came to the United States as a student, and when he quit school before graduating, he had "lost face" and could not return to Japan, whether he was disowned or not. He had taken on odd jobs to support himself when he met Faye. They worked and lived together, and they eventually saved enough to open the restaurant. They worked hard and long, and their enterprise prospered. They had achieved the American dream; they were independent and comfortable financially. All seemed well the previous year when Yoshi worked there, so he was puzzled why Faye had abandoned it all, including Kobayashi.

Yoshi headed back to the association's offices seeking employment opportunities once again. He asked if there were any available jobs other than work in a restaurant. It was likely The Nikko had job openings, bit Yoshi knew a job there was likely to be temporary due to circumstances the agency was not aware of yet.

"Can you handle a job as second butler? You've worked for a family with a butler, haven't you? Then you have some idea of what they do. As second butler, there will be a first butler to show you your duties. The work shouldn't be too hard."

"Usually, the problem is not the pay..." "The pay here is decent."

"It's the families who can be difficult."

"Nomura-*san*, we can't make guarantees whether the employers are humane or demons, *neh*. We can only hope for the best."

"I understand that, but..."

"Wait, it says here they leave the city for the summer, so the job is not permanent. That sounds ideal for you."

The family lived in a fifteen-room apartment at 270 Park Avenue. The building covered an entire New York City block, and the address at that time was very prestigious. Servants of the families residing in the apartment lived in separate servant quarters in the building's upper levels. The family had seven employees as live-in help: a governess for the children, two maids, a cook and assistant cook, a butler and second butler. The two chauffeurs and the cleaning women did not live on the premises.

Mr. Hofheimer was a stockbroker, and he was Jewish; his wife was Irish Catholic and had been a school teacher. It was well known to friends in their circle that when she agreed to marry her husband, he also agreed to support her widowed mother. For Yoshi, that said much about his employer's character and generosity. The couple had five daughters. The oldest daughter was married, and her inheritance from her grandfather had made her wealthier than her father at one time. By the time Yoshi arrived, Mr. Hofheimer was doing very well with his investments and was many times richer in spite of his lesser inheritance. The four younger daughters still lived at home, and they ranged in age from eighteen-year-old Eileen to ten-year-old Natalie. She and twelve-year-old Joyce often teased the short Japanese second butler, who was not much taller than they were. His imperfect English sometimes set them into gales of laughter.

"George, you must say 'Thank you,' not 'Sank you,'" Natalie instructed.

Joyce added, "Remember, you pronounce my name 'Joyce,' not 'JoySue!'"

"Well, I think JoySue is kind of cute. And being addressed Nah-tah-lee is even more fun."

"Alice just blows smoke at him when he tries to say her name."

"I guess I've gotten so used to whatever it is he calls her, I don't even think about it anymore," Natalie said. "He's not doing it to be mean."

"I speak better French than George speaks English. And I don't even live in France. I bet he speaks better Japanese, and he's not even living in Japan."

"You're impossible, Joy...Sue."

The household was lively with comings and goings of four active girls and the social life of the parents. Special dinner parties, large and small, and a constant parade of friends and visitors flowed through the quarters.

The help was kept busy during the day with a short respite in the afternoon before preparations for the evening began. On party nights, the work continued to the late hours.

In the servants' quarter, Helga, the second maid, thought the second butler, George, should take her on a date on their day off.

"Helga, I too short," George insisted. "You one head taller. Many people think little bit funny, don't you?"

"I don't mind that. Let's go and have some fun, George."

George was finally persuaded, neither the difference in height or the difference in their nationalities should prevent them from going out on a date together. A dark-haired, five-foot-tall Japanese man and a five-foot-eight blond Latvian woman together did turn a few heads, but New York is a big city, and they were not uniquely conspicuous. They went to movies and performances and dined together; only the dancing was a little tricky. The enjoyment was in doing things and going to places one usually did not go alone. Yoshi was content to stay good friends with Helga, but she began to talk about a more serious relationship.

SUMMER 1926

The family began making preparations to leave for their summer retreat, and Yoshi asked to be released from his services early. May had arrived, and he needed to return to Rockaway and do his share to prepare for the new season. Leaving the city early also enabled him to escape further entanglement with Helga. The parting had been stressful, but delaying the split could only make matters worse. He took his leave and found relief in the banal, lighthearted atmosphere of carnival and the roars of the Thunderbolt Ride.

Cousin Kajuro continued his now ingrained lifestyle. His promises to reform were only kept until the next episode. Yoshi was busier than ever with the Skee-Ball concession since his partner's absences were more frequent than before. Yoshi accepted his life of working and living with Kajuro as destined—his karma.

Late at night when the earsplitting racket of articulated cars, filled with screaming thrill-seekers, careening overhead had stopped, random thoughts of tides and temples and things drifted through his head before Yoshi fell into exhausted sleep. Is there to be a different chapter to my life?

EEEE…e..e..kkkkK!!

Why have they started that infernal Thunderbolt so early today?

Winter 1926

In September, Yoshi returned to work for the Hofheimer family for another season. The arrangement worked well for both the family and Yoshi. Helga had taken another job that summer and did not return, giving Yoshi freedom to do as he wished on his days off. He felt at home in New York, and he made his way in the city with few encumbrances, although mastery of English remained a mystery. The city was filled with immigrants who spoke with accents of every sort, and Yoshi put off improving his language skills and relied on providence to ease the way.

Familiarity with his employer's lifestyle allowed Yoshi to smoothly step back into service for a second season. The two younger girls were delighted to see George, their good-natured scapegoat. Joyce and Natalie's teasing enlivened the daily routine. None of it was mean-spirited, just playful. What he found mean spirited were the dinner guests who accepted the host's hospitality and made snide remarks about their host's religion in whispers.

"Welcome back, George. We're happy to see you again," his employer had said.

"Helga's replacement is engaged, George. You'll have to find a different girlfriend," the cook's assistant said with a smile.

"Will you go and buy me a pack of cigarettes, George? Those in the cases are quite stale," Alice said.

"You smoke too much, young lady," said older sister Eileen.

"Kindly mind your own business, sister dear."

"Mother, I think we ought to help George become more Americanized," Natalie announced at the table one evening.

"In what way does a person become Americanized, dear?" her mother asked.

"George Gorge and I were talking about food, and he claimed he had never eaten raw meat…"

"Steak tartare is European, silly girl. In fact, many Americans never eat meat unless it's well-done and overcooked," Alice interrupted.

"…then George said he ate raw fish regularly."

"How awful. We'll have Cook show him how fish should be cooked," Joyce said.

"Your intentions are well-meaning; however, we may be the ones who lack understanding of other cultures, especially Orientals. I have been told the Japanese consider fresh fish eaten raw as a delicacy."

"Lesson learned, Mother."

"Tomorrow Joyce and I will need a chaperone when we go roller skating. Could Georgie Porgie be persuaded? He's quite a competent skater, and we'd manage to keep him in our sights. And could Robert drop us off at the park and pick us up later?"

Mr. Hofheimer died suddenly in February. His wife decided to give up their apartment on Park Avenue and made plans to move the family into a smaller apartment. Most of the staff was dismissed as the family downsized and adjusted to a modified lifestyle. Mrs. Hofheimer asked George if he had plans for his future. Should he agree to continue working for the family as a houseboy for several more years, she promised to back him in a business venture of his choice at the end of a service contract.

"We won't need any butlers, and your chores would involve a variety of things. It would be year-round including summers. I know the girls would be comfortable having you stay on with us."

Yoshi was deeply touched by her generous offer, but he knew he could not accept. This was the first time he regretted having to turn down a very good offer. He told her he had an obligation to work summers with his cousin, and he was reluctant to have her risk monies on any ventures dependent on his business skills; a talent he felt he lacked. With head bowed in the Japanese custom, Yoshi parted, saying, "I will remember your kindness always. Thank you."

Yoshi in New York

He found another job to last until his return to Rockaway Beach. He never forgot his time working for the Hofheimer's, but he soon forgot the name of the millionaire family who lived near the sea in New Haven where he spent the next few months working as second butler.

SUMMER AND WINTER 1927
Another season at the arcade, his seventh, proved to be uneventful. Kajuro was absent regularly, which meant Yoshi worked the Skee-Ball concession

by himself a great deal of the time and lost his time off. September finally rolled around, and the season ended the week after Labor Day. As usual, the two packed up their belongings and went their separate ways––that is, as long as they did not stay at the same boardinghouse in Brooklyn for the winter.

Yoshi's winter job that year was different from his previous jobs. He worked a regular day shift, five days a week, in a shop, drilling holes in Oriental vases to convert them into lamps. The work was not interesting nor was it a challenge, but he was paid well and his nonworking hours were truly his own to explore and do as he pleased. He moved to the Brooklyn boardinghouse which was convenient for work and for his other activities. There was no lack of things to do; there was just a lack of female companions.

One day "she" appeared out of nowhere. She was at the boarding-house, waiting for him to return. "I'm looking for Kajuro," she said.

"Oh, he stay in apartment," Yoshi replied.

"They just told me to wait for you. I want you to take me there," she said with a smile that lit up the room.

He was captivated by the adorable dark-eyed creature who had materialized. Why hadn't Cousin ever mentioned her? He finally managed to stammer, "What's your name?"

"Just call me Botan, the peony flower."

"You are Japanese?" He asked in English before reverting into a more fluent mother tongue. "I thought you were Chinese… that *cheongsam* you're wearing fits you well."

"So you're the cousin Kajuro told me to stay away from." "*Nani?* He's the dangerous one."

"I already know him well, but I appreciate your concern."

Yoshi picked up his hat and coat that he had removed minutes earlier and prepared to leave. "Botan, let's go have dinner together before I turn you over to Cousin Kajuro."

When Yoshi saw his cousin sometime later, he asked if Botan was available to join him for another dinner. Kajuro answered with a sigh, "She disappeared again. I have no idea where she goes or what she does.

And she has never said where she's from or why she came. I never ask, allowing her to keep her secrets. That may be the reason she reappears on my doorsteps from time to time: she remains a free spirit. I never know how long she plans to stay, and once gone, I'm always surprised when she shows up again."

"Kajuro, if you ever find another Peony doll, let me know.

I'd like to have one like her, too."

SUMMER 1928

Summer rolled around too quickly, it seemed. Yoshi was soon working the long hours at the arcade, too busy to be bored. The rhythmic pulse of the ocean waves sounding through the night and morning hours provided the balm for the frenzy of the day that followed.

Cousin arrived back from the city before Yoshi had finished the morning chores.

"Yoshi, you'll never guess who I got a letter from," Kajuro said. He was sober and brimming with energy. "Ho, ho, ho. Uncle Ryokichi's wife is coming to New York for a visit. They've been living in Seattle on the West Coast."

"Is Uncle coming with her? He and his wife lived with us for a while after they married, but I was too young to remember. They moved away so they're strangers to me, though I sometimes heard their names mentioned. I might have missed his visit when I was living with Uncle Shoshun learning the sutra."

"Ha, you would have been a worse Buddhist priest than me a ship's captain. Priests are supposed to give up all worldly things or at least all thoughts of worldly things. No, you love this life with a passion," Kajuro said. "Ryokichi would have made a better priest; he knew how to sacrifice, and now he's dead."

"He died? How did he die?"

"His widow didn't say in the letter. She thought he might have left some things in New York when he left, and she's coming to see for herself."

"Why don't you write her, telling her he didn't own a thing to leave behind? Every cent he made, he saved to bring her and his son back to America. Save her the trip."

"Too late. She's probably on a train on her way here. She sent the letter to the boardinghouse in Brooklyn, and they finally contacted me about it." Kajuro leaned back in his chair. "Hummm. I wonder if the face I remember was hers. She was rather attractive…"

"Let's talk about Ryokichi's wife, the woman we're expecting."

"I am talking about her. Her name is Ito, by the way," Kajuro said. "I think we ought to have her stay at the Brooklyn boardinghouse. I could go down there to keep an eye on those other boarders to make sure they don't get overly friendly with her. Do you agree?"

When Ito arrived, Yoshi could see she had been more than "rather attractive" in her youth. No wonder Uncle Ryokichi was so determined to have her join him in America. She was in early middle age, but she carried herself well. Kajuro was enamored.

"She's the woman of my dreams," Kajuro rhapsodized. He was boyishly attentive to her, and charm oozed from every pore. She was overwhelmed by Kajuro's declarations of love. Yoshi had seen the scenario played out before on too many occasions; he wondered if it was truly different for Kajuro this time. Unlike all the previous paramours, Ito was a Japanese woman, his own kind. Perhaps the others were merely preliminary playmates filling out the empty time until Ito's arrival.

Kajuro busily escorted his new love around the city and was absent from Rockaway a good deal. On one of the infrequent occasions when Yoshi had a day in the city, he arranged to spend a few hours visiting his aunt.

Yoshi learned Ito generally cut the obligatory niceties and spoke her mind, traits suppressed in their culture.

"Kajuro and I want to marry," Ito said.

"Congratulations. When do you plan…?"

"I have a slight problem…"

"A problem? What type of…?"

"Yoshi, you can help me! Come back to Seattle with me. You must convince my son to accept my marriage to my lovable Kajuro," she pleaded. "My son is headstrong like all you Nomura's. Together, you and I, we'll sway him to agree to my leaving him for a new husband. Be a dear nephew, Yoshi."

He agreed to accompany Ito back to Seattle after the end of the arcade season. Yoshi's mission was to talk Ito's son, Yukimasa, into accepting his mother's remarriage. A secondary motive for taking the trip was to sightsee a distant part of America. The train trip would take several days, but viewing such an extensive expanse of America was worth the long excursion.

When the concession stand was closed up in September, Yoshi withdrew enough money for the journey and several weeks of vacationing in Seattle. He packed his suitcase with enough clothes for the trip and filled it to the brim with gifts for his cousin Yukimasa. He left his other belongings with Kajuro with the intent of finding an apartment and a job on his return to New York.

CHAPTER 5

To Seattle, 1928—

IT WAS NOT THE CITIES they passed through that fascinated Yoshi, even Chicago fell short of his expectations. America's second largest city had nowhere as many skyscrapers as his hometown, New York City. Instead it was the vast expanse of land, mile after endless mile of open space, not unlike the open sea between ports, but so different, that fascinated him.

Yoshi sat transfixed, gazing through the window as the scenery evolved. The rolling hills and green valleys stretched on one after another, with small villages interspersed at random intervals and an isolated house, shed, or barn claiming its domain. Gradually the waves of undulating hills joined one another, spreading and stretching until they were flattened plains. The lush green lost its depth and lightened into tawny yellow and browns for more endless miles. Landscapes of a similar hue continued for hours; the panorama changed ever so slowly and seamlessly. It was as if they watched the unfolding in slow motion. What a contrast to the picturesque vignettes that mesmerized him on his initial journey from Ise-*shi* to the port city of Kobe. Scenery viewed from Japanese trains burst in staccato flashes one after another, yielding mere glimpses of the scenic beauty of the land. In America, the focus encompassed a wider range and distance. Admittedly, Yoshi's enthusiasm for sightseeing lapsed from time to time, and he napped as the rhythmic vibrations of the coach and the clatter of the rails became a rocking lullaby inducing sleep.

"Yoshi, my meal didn't agree with me. I should be eating rice, instead of potatoes every day like *gaijin*. Potatoes are indigestible. No wonder they're so ill-humored: they always have bellyaches." She paused two or three seconds, taking in a long deep breath and fortifying her composure before continuing. The interval was not to recoup her thoughts; she never bothered to think what she had to say, the words just rolled out of her mouth one after another. "Yes, a *musubi* with *umeboshi*…the healing pickled plum buried inside a nice plump rice ball wrapped with *nori* would soothe my stomach greatly. Why didn't you warn me they don't serve rice in the diner? I could have made a bento lunch for our journey," Ito complained loudly as she patted her belly, attempting to quell her indigestion.

Yoshi made no reply to Ito's complaints. Whether he made a comment or not, it made no difference. She continued to grouse and complain whether it was a conversation or a soliloquy. Did she complain to anyone on her solitary journey to New York? Or did she manage to keep her mouth shut? Yoshi wondered.

"Ohhh…" Ito moaned audibly as she tried to elicit sympathy from her companion.

"Ito-*san*, it's too bad your dinner didn't agree with you; however, there is something that should agree with you. Since you didn't pay for your meal, it wasn't your money wasted," Yoshi said with a laugh.

"*Atari-mai*, I didn't pay," she snapped. "It's only proper you pay for the meals, good or bad. You're a bachelor and can afford it. I'm a poor widow." Rolling her eyes and twisting her head demurely for effect, she uttered her well-practiced phrase in trembling tones. "*Kawai-so*. Pity me."

Yoshi studied her act. It came straight from the Kabuki stage or the silent movie screens teeming with similar baleful damsels in distress. At the beginning of their journey, Ito had asked him to address her by her name rather than *Oba-san* or Aunt. She had been emphatic that others should think they were contemporaries. If he should absentmindedly forget, an entirely different set of ugly contentions were set loose, he had learned. He wondered, too, what Uncle Ryokichi had really been like. Truly, no man married to Ito could have been ordinary.

Obviously, the discomforts of the trip had squelched whatever good humor Ito possessed, and the ordeal had become an unrelenting irritation alternating with sheer boredom. Yoshi looked past her and through the window, deliberately focusing his thoughts outside his immediate surroundings and turning a deaf ear to her whining whenever possible, and he settled in for the long trip west.

His fidgeting seatmate had the telltale lines of middle age creeping into her face, he noticed, as she bumped her elbows into his ribs. She kept fumbling in her handbag and finally pulled out a compact. After a lengthy and thorough inspection of her face, a procedure involving horrific grimaces and skin pulling of one sort or another, she smothered the entire surface with billowing pats of her powder puff. A slight pass of rouge on her cheeks was followed by another close side-to-side inspection in her small, round mirror. Satisfied, she produced her tube of lipstick and reddened her lips, smacking them as a finale.

She turned to face Yoshi and smiled. "Look young, *neh?*"

He smiled back. Her attempts to hold back the inevitable ravages of four-plus decades gave Ito a vulnerability Yoshi hadn't perceived before. *She has a cherubic cuteness, which undoubtedly attracted suitors in her youth. Assuming Uncle Ryokichi shared the easygoing Nomura characteristics, he too must have been taken in by that look of sweet innocence. No doubt, it was a look that aged well if one took pains to nurture it,* and Ito was doing just that.

Yoshi sat back trying to recollect the stories he had heard about his uncle and his family. Although Ryokichi had brought his bride Ito home to Kamisaki to live in his ancestral home with older brother Kakichi's family, they had moved away. On the rare occasions that Uncle had returned to the village, he always came alone. He had sent a letter informing the family he was leaving for America to seek his fortune. And, his wife and son would continue living with her parents until he returned to take them back to America with him. As promised, he fetched his wife and son and returned to the US while the policy allowing settled Japanese immigrants to have wives and families join them was still in effect, and Ito and Yukimasa came as legal immigrants.

Ito's elaborated versions of the events usually took on a new twist, and Yoshi's attempts to reconcile the variations were impossible.

"People say its karma; I say it's plain and simple bad luck. I married a man who left me twice. First he leaves me with his parents where I'm a virtual servant in their household while he gallivants among the rich and famous in New York. He finally returns for me and our son, and we set off to America with him. Instead of going on to New York, we settle in a god-forsaken, uncultured, uncivilized backwoods called Seattle. Then he up and dies and leaves me penniless in this foreign country." After her pause, she added her usual grace note, "*Honto-ni kawai-so.* Oh, truly pitiful me."

"Ito-*san*, why did the family stop in Seattle, instead of continuing on to New York, a city familiar to Ryokichi?" Yoshi was curious to know.

"I had to recuperate from that grueling, awful sea voyage, so we postponed the transcontinental journey east. One thing led to another, and we found ourselves growing seasonal flowers for a living." Ito continued, "My husband knew nothing about plants. It made no sense. Instead of gentleman's work, he became a farmer."

Ito repeated her tales of woe routinely, interjecting a new twist or detail to her "pity me" fable every now and then. By the time they crossed the plains, Yoshi had heard the repeated reiterations so often he almost believed her story in its entirety. The core events were accurate; it was in the details where half-truths and fabrications abounded and merged.

Yoshi now wondered if she was the same woman Kajuro had talked ceaselessly about since her arrival in New York. He was having second thoughts about his mission to Seattle and whether he should promote the union of Ito to his cousin. He had thought Ito might be the woman capable of taming Kajuro's penchant for drinking and womanizing, and she in turn would gain a husband and worthy companion for her later years. Kajuro was indeed a decent and worthy sort when sober. Ito's prime had been spent waiting for her husband's return; that was unfortunate. There had been little time for leisure for her and Ryokichi in their struggle operating a small-scale business in Seattle, so Ito's short taste of high living in New York had given her hope for a more interesting, richer life at long last, and Yoshi had promoted it.

Yoshi now understood Ito's sweet exterior was merely skin deep, and behind the façade, a fire-breathing dragon waited within. Undoubtedly, it was just a matter of time before their inner demons would reveal themselves and the marriage turn into a stormy battle. Humans cannot control destiny, so they ought not interfere. Sometimes it is possible to see the inevitable in other people's lives, but never your own.

The train's engine pulled its load, heaving mightily as they began climbing and the once-straight passages through wide open country began curving and winding upward on narrow pathways that tapered to mere ledges carved into the mountain slopes. Cut rock abutted one side of the track, and cliffs with undeterminable drops lay on the other side. Rivers often meandered in the valley bottom alongside virulent vegetation and growth. The open side of the train-straddling cliff offered spectacular views of craggy outcroppings among virgin-forested mountainsides, deciduous trees among the profusion of evergreens in endless procession. In the distance, majestic snow-topped mountains presided in their awe-inspiring presence. Yoshi had always felt secure and protected by the mountain ranges abutting Kamisaki. He had deemed them impassable fortresses when he was young; a reassessment was due. In comparison to the voluminous outcroppings he now witnessed, the mountains back home were merely craggy slopes. The towering power and strength of the iconic Rocky Mountain range with its rough and rugged terrain energized his spirit and soul.

Overlooking cliff edges did not suit Ito, so she commanded Yoshi to trade seats so she could sit on the aisle away from the window. He now had an unobstructed view out the window and was able to peer down those slopes that had unnerved his aunt. Her vertigo prevented her from talking, which was a blessing to Yoshi and to every other passenger within hearing distance of her voice. Though they didn't understand the language she spoke; they knew it was incessant. The respite lasted until they reached Seattle.

ARRIVING IN SEATTLE

The pistons hissed and wheels clamored noisily as the truncated passenger cars slowly eased to a stop. Metal wheels screeched in protest, friction resisting the continuing forward motion of its cargo, its mass still inching along the iron rails. The articulated coaches belched and shuttered before reluctantly coming to a halt. The behemoth was reined. Inside the cars, passengers, now assured their conveyance had truly come to rest, began lifting themselves off their seats and awkwardly took their first steps as they learned to balance themselves on motionless footing once more. Their journey across North America had ended.

Ito was full of nervous energy again, nagging Yoshi to get their bags down from the overhead shelf. Yoshi felt there was no reason to rush since they were at the end of the line. If they were to go any further west, they would end up in the Pacific Ocean. He remained silent and followed her. Once off the train and on the platform, she rushed ahead, turning her head to him and shouting, "Yoshi, *ha-ya-ku*! Hurry up!"

She must have brought her whole wardrobe with her, he thought as he lugged her two heavy suitcases in addition to his own valise. She could have left them in New York if she's planning to return there. Then again, Kajuro must have given her a load of gifts.

He found a red-capped porter with a dolly to carry the bags and was surprised to learn he was Japanese, and not Chinese as he had surmised.

They chatted amicably as they walked to the curbside waiting area away from the gang of taxis vying to lure arrivals into their vehicles.

"YOSHI, *kotchi-laaa*," came the unmistakable voice. His train of thought interrupted, he forgot to ask the porter his name as the little man hurried back to catch another customer.

"I'm over here," came the command. "I've been waiting ten minutes for you. Where have you been? Yukimasa is waiting for us in the truck. *Haya-ku*. You move like a turtle. Hurry up!"

The commotion outside the train terminal was still thick and noisy. When Yoshi got to the waiting truck, the cousins, who were strangers, made quick nodding-of-heads introductions to each other. Yoshi insisted

Ito and Yukimasa should leave for home without him so mother and son could be reunited and talk in private. He would take a cab to the hotel. Yoshi had noticed there was no room for him in the truck, and he was not eager to have his aunt sit on his lap in the cab. She was bigger than him. Nor was he eager to ride on the open truck bed in back with the suitcases.

Yoshi stood outside of the terminal building after they drove away. The remaining passengers were scurrying off in separate directions. Before long, the crowd had miraculously dispersed; instead of the bustling hordes, the area was virtually devoid of people. The congestion was a brief interval; there were no other trains on the tracks, no perpetual stream of passengers coming and going as there were at Grand Central and Pennsylvania Station. A breeze swept through the arch where Yoshi was standing, and he caught the faint scent and presence of the ocean nearby. There was no water view where he stood, but the feeling that had momentarily swept past him was unmistakable. That has to be the Pacific close by; I'm only an ocean away from home.

A smattering of Orientals passed by on the street, and he began to wonder what type of American city he had happened upon. More Asian people casually strolled by him in not too great a hurry to get to where they were going, and they were oblivious to his presence. Admittedly, a few studied him a moment or two, wondering if he was an acquaintance worthy of a greeting. Yoshi stood in awe. Since he arrived in Seattle, he had just seen more Asians than he might see in a month in New York City; outside of Chinatown, an Oriental got lost among millions of white people.

The cab driver was reluctant to give Yoshi a ride when he was told the destination. The hotel was just blocks from the station, and he could have walked there easily had he known its location. He gave the cabbie a good tip for the short ride, and he was rewarded by a smile and a word of thanks before speeding off.

Ito had given him the name of the hotel before they parted. Owned and operated by fellow Japanese, she had said, "It is located in Nihonmachi." Ito had not bothered to mention that Japantown bordered the train terminal. The hotel desk clerk conducted the entire checking-in process in Japanese as if the transaction were taking place in Japan. The experience was a trifle unreal and unsettling for Yoshi. After living in America for eight years, he had become accustomed to speaking in his unique English when in public, and he had reverted to Japanese only with friends. In spite of his years in America, Yoshi's English language skills remained rudimentary at best. He had become complacent and had made little effort to improve his English-speaking skills since he managed to communicate, albeit in a limited way. A smile still smoothed most situations.

It felt good to be exchanging casual greetings and information in Japanese. He relished an experience he had taken for granted before. A public Japanese-style bathhouse was around the corner from the hotel, he was told. Also, there were restaurants serving Japanese food nearby or, alternatively, a few blocks south, there were many good authentic Chinese chop suey restaurants where the Chinese dined. "And, if…" the humorless clerk added, "you're interested, the Buddhist church is up the street, not far away." The bath and food were welcome indulgences, but he planned to forgo any religious rites. *I already had a lifetime's worth of chanting the scriptures, thank you.*

The following day, Yoshi walked the neighborhood with the feeling he had been transported to a strange Japanese city. There were eateries, barber shops, grocery and dry goods stores, all operated by Japanese and in close proximity. The sounds of a *shamisen* and *shakuhachi* wafted from an upper-level window where musicians were practicing. He spied a branch of the Sumitomo Bank and, wonder of wonders, there was a Japanese confectionery shop selling freshly made *manju*. Ahhh, manna from heaven!

Nihonmachi has a cadence and lilt lacking in its English translation: Japantown, a word merely designating a location without embodying a panoply of associations and positive experiences for those far from home. Seattle's Nihonmachi perched on the south slopes of First Hill, was settled along Main Street. Its intersection at Sixth Avenue became the focal point from where the community radiated. Down the hill one block, Jackson Street was a busier arterial bordered by a mingling of Japanese and Chinese businesses. The area beyond to the foot of Beacon Hill was the Chinese enclave: Chinatown.

The following morning, with pockets stuffed with sweets to sustain him, Yoshi caught a streetcar to the city's main business and retail core and almost rode beyond it; the central business area was so small compared to New York City's. In the city proper, most of the faces were Caucasian, with few Asians and even fewer black people among them. If he walked west and east, he encountered steep, hilly slopes, some looking like virtual cliffs, that made strolling difficult, so he decided to walk back to his hotel on a level north-south street lined with shops. If he lost his way, he could ask someone the direction to the train depots since he knew his way from there. At street intersections, he could glimpse sparkling light rays bouncing off a body of water beyond. At succeeding intersections, he spied parallel piers lined perpendicular to the shoreline, each supporting a wooden structure of varying size and shape. The requisite boat or two were moored alongside or ferrying about. Yoshi yearned to forge down for a closer look and to soak in the sea air. He sensibly abstained from taking the detour, deciding to save that tour for another time. The route back to the hotel was not far but traversing the hilly terrain had been more strenuous than he had anticipated, and he was anxious to end his sightseeing excursion for the day.

A message was waiting for Yoshi when he returned to the hotel. It was from Ito, telling him to be ready for pickup at two o'clock sharp the following afternoon. She said it was imperative they, the three of them, meet to discuss important matters.

Cousin Yukimasa arrived in his pickup truck at the appointed hour. They headed toward Rainier Valley and drove several miles to the south. During the ride, the cousins' conversation was cordial as they talked about their mutual relatives in Japan. Yukimasa's manner gave no hint of any urgency for their meeting, which made Yoshi uneasy about Ito's latest ploy.

Yukimasa was physically sturdier and taller than Yoshi and five years younger. The cousins shared few facial similarities, and strangers would not recognize them as being related. Like all males of their Nomura clan, they each considered themselves good-looking, and they were in their own way. They were dissimilar in attitudes and experiences, but mostly, it was their personalities that differed. Yukimasa was serious and reserved. He wasn't unfriendly; he was just less effusive than Yoshi in his dealings with others.

They arrived at the small cottage on the hillside above the main arterial. Alongside the wooden structure was a much larger glass building, which housed the flowers and plants. In scattered disarray, all around the grounds were the implements and discards of their trade. Yoshi walked daintily behind his cousin, who trudged along the stone pathway to the house without regard to his footing; he was not wearing dress shoes nor did he care whether he stepped on stone or mud. Inside the door, their muddy shoes were removed.

Ito was waiting for them with treats and tea. She looked a bit disheveled, and her eyes were puffy. She made no excuses for her appearance and started discoursing on the trials and tribulations of being a single mother.

"My son is an ungrateful child. He means to deprive me of any happiness I might find in my old age," Ito wailed.

"*Okaa-san*, I just said you should wait and think about it carefully before rashly making a commitment," Yukimasa responded. It was obvious they had been discussing the subject at length.

"My husband, your father, was a dutiful man. He left us for years to make a better life for us. Finally, when our goals were within reach, he dies!" With clenched teeth, she intoned her epitaph, "Stone-cold dead. How dare he?"

"It was karma, *Kaa-chan*."

She heaved a sigh. "I was hoping he had left something of value in New York. There was nothing. I have nothing. I'm not young anymore. This is my last chance for…for…"

"You're acting like a giddy adolescent girl, not the sensible, mature woman and mother you are, *Okaa-san*."

Ito started sobbing. "An old *baa-san*, he called me! My own son calls me an old woman, a hag."

Yukimasa could only shake his head. All disagreements with his mother followed the same scenario. She would twist the facts or fabricate new ones and accuse him of ingratitude and worse.

As a rule, Yukimasa conceded to his mother's wishes, so much so he had earned praise as the model respectful son imbued with *oya-koko*. Avoiding confrontations appeared to be a family trait from his Nomura father. In addition, the son had inherited a core of steel from his mother, which was unbending when he set his mind to it. And he had set his mind to become a dentist. Yoshi was not enjoying witnessing this family "discussion."

"Yukimasa, so why won't you let your mother leave and live her own life? You're an adult now. You can do as you please and let her do as she pleases," Yoshi said. Solving a problem is always easier when it's someone else's problem.

"It's not so simple," Yukimasa said. "It has complications, Yoshi. The lease to this land is in my name. Father wanted it that way. I agreed to work with him in the business for virtually no pay for five years. In that time, we calculated things would be going well, and there would be money for me to go to school. That was the commitment." He continued talking, deliberately trying to find a resolution to his quandary by talking it through. "It's unfortunate he died when he did. People say it was karma. I don't know whether I believe that any longer. We were desperate, so I reluctantly agreed when Mother said she would go to New York to look for money Father had deposited there."

"What made her think he had put aside a fortune in New York?" Yoshi asked. Uncle Ryokichi's family had no idea he was a legend in the Japanese community, especially among the bachelor immigrants living in and around New York City. The Ryokichi stories circulating related his extreme prudence and sacrifices in his struggle to save money. Yoshi knew that honest household service workers did not amass fortunes, even in freewheeling New York. There were multi-millionnaires with money to burn, and they burned through money before they shared any of it with their domestic help.

"He was in America such a long time, Mother was sure he had accumulated more money than the amount he had when he returned to Japan. There was no hidden money, no bank account accumulating interest." Then, with a bit of sarcasm, he said, "And she just spent a goodly amount going across the country and back."

"Just think of it as your grieving mother's vacation."

Yukimasa ignored Yoshi's lighthearted comment. "Well, I'm stuck with the lease for several more years. I don't know whether the school will accept me then. The costs for long years of schooling to become a physician are out of reach, and I'm already late beginning such studies. But, it is still possible for me to become a dentist. There's a school in Oregon accepting Japanese students. I was hoping to go…to go this fall. Now…"

"About your mother…" Yoshi said before Yukimasa interrupted him.

"I will need her help here now that Father's gone. Besides she just met this cousin. She doesn't know him well enough yet. How…how can she even consider marrying him?" he started to shout as his reserve and composure crumbled.

Ito began wailing at her son's outburst, "You're heartless! You're mean! My own son, an ogre!" Yoshi waited for Ito's punch line.

"*Kawai-so. Hon-toni kawai-so.*" Pitiful. Truly pity me.

While she wallowed in her usual self-pity, real or feigned, Yoshi found a topic to lighten the prevailing mood. "I'm surprised there's such a large Japanese settlement here in Seattle. It feels like you're living in a small Japanese city within a city, *nah.*"

"Full of crude and ignorant people," Ito said. "I prefer New York City. There you associate with a better class of people." "That's only because you met Cousin Kajuro and me. We're the highlights, bright lights," Yoshi said with a laugh.

"You're merely a runty nephew. Now Kajuro, he's a man; he's enlightened, worldly, and has money," Ito proclaimed, "Kajuro said he loved me. It would be a love marriage."

"Please, Mother, you're sounding like a schoolgirl again," her son retorted.

"Kajuro and your mother got along well, as far as I could tell." No progress had been made toward a resolution to the problem and none appeared forthcoming. The conversation then drifted to less immediate matters, and as strangers becoming acquainted, they exchanged stories about their lives in Japan and America.

Considering a New Home

That evening after leaving his aunt and cousin, Yoshi again walked the Nihonmachi neighborhood, soaking in the atmosphere of small-town Japan.

He loved New York: its ambiance, the hustle and bustle, the opportunities available for work and play, its humanity. He had lived there for eight years; perhaps he was ready for a change? He contemplated: Seattle is not large, but it offers a different lifestyle. The Japanese settlement is active and attractive, and family-oriented. Best of all, Seattle is a port city with seagoing activities, and whenever I feel parched, the breath of salt air is close by. The mountain ranges with their snowy peaks surround the city, providing visual strength and a sense of shelter, but they keep their distance, allowing mortals to frolic in their shadows. The plants and foliage reminiscent of Japan are even more abundant and exuberant, filling the soul and spirit to overflowing. Perhaps this initial enthusiasm needs restraining by a notch or two; nevertheless, the basic assessment is sound; life could be as fulfilling here as in Japan, perhaps even better. Yes, I could settle down in Seattle for a spell.

Yoshi proposed an offer to Ito and Yukimasa the next day. If Yoshi were to assume the lease and work the greenhouse business, Yukimasa could go to dental school and become a practicing dentist; Ito could go to New York and marry cousin Kajuro as she wished. It was a splendid solution, they all agreed, and the details were worked out in the following weeks. Yukimasa left for dental school in Oregon, Ito rushed off to New York and married, and Yoshi became a nurseryman.

Since this new trade was wholly alien to his previous experiences, it was a struggle. Yoshi had never had access to a plot of land to grow plants at home in his *mura*. They were busy running a store, and bought their vegetables and plants from vendors. His lone experience was when he helped his aunt, Shoshun's wife, nurture a small vegetable garden, which had offered welcome relief from his sutra memorizing lessons. Yukimasa had given him detailed instructions on the culture of the plants to be grown, but remembering everything and applying the specifics to growing the plants was not simple. Luckily, the transfer occurred at the end of the major growing season. Yoshi began reading books on horticulture, meeting other Japanese in the trade, and joining their organizations. Had his roots been in farming rather than the sea, the process would have been easier.

Yoshi believed if he applied himself to this new task, things would work out. He had made the decision himself. There was no blaming karma.

Since arriving in America, his routine was working summers at the Rockaway Beach arcade and at season's end working odd jobs in the city. Now his life revolved around a plant's growing season. Even in winter, there were chores to prepare for the planting season ahead. In the spring and summer, there were never enough hours to do what needed to be done. The plants would continue to grow he hoped, but they needed a balance of heat, light, water, and nourishment. Not too much and not too little. Then the plants were carted out and sold to the wholesaler, who Yoshi hoped would pay a sum over the costs so he could make a profit. Easter lilies were the trickiest flowers to produce: the spring holiday does not fall on the same day every year nonetheless, the lilies had to bloom for Easter whatever the month and day. There was no money to be made for too early or too late blooming specimens.

The on-site cottage was more than adequate for Yoshi's needs. Since neither Ito nor Yukimasa had an immediate need for furnishings and household goods, they took only their personal belongings, leaving him with a furnished house. When Yoshi's own steamer trunk packed with his personal belongings arrived, Yoshi knew his ties to New York were severed. He did, however, return there in his thoughts, remembering his youthful exuberance and his unfettered life there. He left his ship with a few belongings tied in a *furoshiki*, disguised to look like an intended gift. In eight years, the only tangible things he had accumulated were a trunk and one suitcase full of clothes and papers. He never retrieved the bank account he had left there for his return.

Seattle greenhouse before Easter

Yoshi bought a truck and learned to drive——a necessity to deliver his products. It also gave him mobility. On weekends, he usually found his way to Nihonmachi and joined the laborers and farmers who came into town to participate in the activities and cultural amenities to be found there. He was soon making friends with the locals, and he began to feel Seattle was his home.

As one of the four major port cities on the opposite side of the Pacific Ocean from Japan, Seattle had been a major entry point for Japanese immigrants to the United States in the first two decades of the twentieth century. Desperate for work and opportunities, those who grasped the possibilities available in a faraway and strange environment and were willing to make sacrifices, seized that chance. When the Chinese were barred from entry into the US, the market for contract laborers shifted to hiring Japanese. These new immigrants began arriving in the 1890s. Glowing stories from earlier emigrant laborers filtered back to Japan with tales of riches to be made in America. Then, as the emigrants prospered, they began sending monies back home to their families still in Japan, thereby elevating the prosperity of those areas and helping to mitigate the dire conditions and economy of the region. Emigration was encouraged in prefectures experiencing great economic distress, and officials encouraged their citizens to follow. Exit permits were liberally distributed in prefectures such as Yamaguchi, Okayama, Wakayama, and especially Hiroshima-ken.

The emigrants were generally son's other than the *chonan*, first son. They had to find their own way, and working overseas provided opportunities. Emigrant older siblings often persuaded younger family members and relatives to join them. Many laborers returned to Japan at the fulfillment of their contracts, while others stayed and joined the immigrant pioneers, whose numbers increased each year.

In the Northwest, jobs were plentiful in the logging and railroad companies, in agriculture, and later in fish canneries. The laborers lived in isolated communities far removed from urban centers; their shifts were long, the work grueling, and their pay small. Settlers who remained in

Seattle and Tacoma found work as domestics and in the service industry. In time, early entrepreneurs began operating hotels, opened restaurants, barber shops, and other personal services shops catering primarily to their countrymen.

The percentage of women immigrants was fractional in the beginning. As the men became financially stable, they sent for their wives and children and often siblings to join them. Unmarried men had marriages arranged by proxy, and the brides traveled to America to join new husbands. The majority of Japanese immigrants settled on the West Coast, and their concentration in and around the port cities promoted the growth of Japanese districts, which were convenient and beneficial for the new immigrants. Widespread discriminatory real estate practices and exclusionary restrictive covenants adopted by the nonminority populace forced Asians to reside in enclaves, ghettos where they were allowed to dwell. Removed from the general public, they could live their lives with minimal assimilation and more easily maintain their cultural ties to their motherland. To others, such ethnic concentrations were worrisome and garnered increasing animosity.

The racial mistrust and hatred prevalent during those years precipitated governmental policy decisions initiated and vigorously endorsed by anti-Asian proponents, which greatly affected the immigrants' lives. The Gentleman's Agreement of 1908 between America and Japan significantly reduced immigration of Japanese laborers, while parents, wives, and children of settled residents were still allowed to enter the US to reunite families. Eligible relatives arrived in great numbers until the loophole was closed with enactment of the 1924 Immigration Act. By this time, there was a larger presence of women and children: a group whose numbers kept increasing as children were born in America. Their presence not only expanded and enriched the community, its focus was redirected toward promoting permanent settlement.

The growth and prosperity of the Japanese community was symbolized by Nihonmachi's vitality at the time of Yoshi's arrival in Seattle. The "city within a city" had grown from businesses catering to the needs of contract laborers to the full-blown gamut of services required by a population of eight thousand-plus Nikkei residents living in Seattle and its environs in 1930.

The Furuya Company was the largest and most successful multiservice business catering to the Japanese in Seattle. Masajiro Furuya had arrived in Seattle from Yokohama by way of St. Louis. In 1892, he initially opened a tailor shop, then added a grocery store with imported foodstuffs favored by the immigrants. As the business prospered, it began selling Japanese art products and provided a postal service along with other incidental convenience services. The company branched into labor contracting, vying with other established contractors to hire Japanese men to work for American railroads. Opening offices in Yokohama and Kobe facilitated recruiting. The company also opened branches in Tacoma, Portland, and Vancouver, British Columbia. Their salesmen were sent throughout the Northwest where Japanese worked and lived, taking orders for goods not otherwise available to them. Their venture into banking, begun in 1907, was enlarged by the purchase and merging of several other banks that were then consolidated into a holding company. This became a major source of money for business owners and farmers in the Japanese communities where the company operated.

The heady optimism and energy evidenced by the community's continued growth and expanded activities were highlighted by Nihonmachi's lively annual Bon Odori festival in mid-summer. The taiko drumming and traditional folk music with dances on the street reflected their exuberance as they participated in the prosperity America was experiencing.

The Economy Falters

The stock market crashed a year after Yoshi left New York. Like a missile shattering the water's surface, the splash transforms into a ripple, then more ripples of ever-widening spheres; the effects of a depressed economy reached the West Coast and Seattle.

As the economy faltered, so did many small businesses. Jobs became scarce and wages minimal. Workers left the area looking for more lucrative opportunities elsewhere, while others returned to Japan as their pursuit of becoming rich turned into failure. In 1932, the Furuya Company declared bankruptcy, investors lost their money, land, and businesses, and a ready money source for investments disappeared. Optimism died as the reality of hard times returned.

Cousin Kajuro wrote from New York saying he had given up running the Skee-Ball concession. He and Ito were now running a boardinghouse in Brooklyn. Exchanging bachelorhood for marriage and a wife had changed his life completely, and the collapse of the stock market had altered everything else around them. "You would never recognize our old haunts. Those carefree, spirited days are gone. It's depressing to think about it. But, guess who I ran into the other day? Sweet Botan. She heard I was married, so she had kept her distance. This chance meeting really cheered me up. We had a great time talking stories about the good old days. She remembered you. She was that peony doll; I'm sure you haven't forgotten."

Yoshi had not forgotten, but his present life was so far removed from his freewheeling years in New York, he could only chuckle at the memory.

On the occasions when cousin Yukimasa came into Seattle during his years of study in Oregon, he usually contacted Yoshi and stayed at the house. They remained connected, knowing they shared an ancestral bond. They had different enthusiasms and a separate circle of close friends, and generally went about their affairs independently.

One mutual friend had managed to coerce them both into accompanying him to the Christian fellowship of his church. Attending Sunday service was a new experience, like so much else they had encountered in America. The rites observed were mystifying, and the continual references to the Bible were completely alien to both of them. They sat and politely listened, all the while trying to connect the words of the minister's sermon with the teachings of Buddha, which were more familiar to them. The church members were friendly and welcoming, and they charged no fee to attend; they merely asked for a donation. One Sunday, they were asked to join other parishioners at the altar, and both innocently complied, thinking they had been asked to come forward and *ogamu*, respectfully pay homage. The words spoken were in Japanese, but they tuned out the mumbo jumbo from habit, just as they did to the chanted Sanskrit sutras of a Buddhist ritual.

"I baptize thee in the name of the Father, the Son, and the Holy Ghost."

The two men were baptized as Christians at the Japanese Congregational Church.

"Hallelujah!"

Yoshi admitted his own naiveté was instrumental in his being baptized a Christian. The deed was done, and it was something he could not undo, but he could and did disassociate himself from further commitments by staying away from the church henceforth.

Kenjin-kai

There were numerous Japanese associations Yoshi could not join. They were the various *Kenjinkai*. In America, wherever there were large concentrations of Japanese immigrants, the settlers banded into groups based on their home prefectures. The vast majority of immigrants came from rural areas, and they tended to converse in their own dialects with unique speech patterns rather than the standardized Japanese taught in schools since the Meiji reforms. Speaking the same dialect and sharing regional customs promoted easier bonding and trust among strangers. Earlier arrivals assisted newcomers in adjusting to their new surroundings, and they provided housing and employment advice, and credit if necessary. It was easier to form a *tanomi-moshi*, pooling money and rotating credit, within such groups. In addition to mutual aid, the *Kenjinkai* promoted networking by holding social functions, such as the celebratory New Year's gathering and an annual picnic in the summer. Hiroshima and Yamaguchi prefectures, with the greatest numbers of immigrants, had the largest *Kenjinkai* in the area. So few immigrants came from Mie prefecture, no one ever organized a Mie *Kenjinkai*. From time to time, Yoshi met someone from Mie only to have his initial enthusiasm dampened when he learned the person's home village was so far removed from his *mura* that he felt greater kinship with people from neighboring prefecture, Wakayama-ken, than with fellow Mie expats.

The Japanese living in New York had arrived in America independently, and their backgrounds and experiences differed greatly from the general Japanese immigrant experience of settlers living on the West Coast and Hawaii. The New York *Nihonjinkai* was a group that embraced Japanese nationals from any part of Japan, rather than limiting its memberships to people from one prefecture. Yoshi's participating in the New York organization gave him a chance to meet a broad spectrum of fellow countrymen, but without a *Kenjinkai* he was eligible to join in Seattle, Yoshi felt isolated an outsider in the community.

The worsening economy took its toll on Yoshi's greenhouse endeavors, too. He had survived his early ignorance of the business, and each year he felt more confident he knew what he was doing or should do to grow and nurture his plants. This understanding was not instinctive; he had no green thumb like farmers' sons who had the knack, but Yoshi was learning, and he was willing to work hard. Unfortunately, flowers are not a basic staple people need to survive in hard times. Consequently, the orders for his flowers plummeted. He aggressively pursued wholesalers and retailer alike to buy from him and succeeded often enough to stay afloat. He reduced his flower production to levels he estimated he could realistically sell, and filled the now-empty spaces with tomato plants to augment his income.

PIKE PLACE MARKET

Sitting on the ridge of the steep hillside between the downtown business core and the waterfront roads serving the maritime industries and activities in and around the jutting wooden wharves, the amorphous market structure clings to the incline supported by concrete, blocks, stilts, brackets, and the grace of God. The building's structural elements as well as its surface elements––its floors, walls, windows, and ceilings––follow no coherent plan or plane; they exist in random space. The maze of spaces housed permanent shops with shelves selling an assortment of wares, packaged, canned, and bottled foods, spices and more. There were cheese and meat vendors, fishmongers, and bakeries. Along long tables, individual farmers and vendors displayed their fresh products for sale. Whether neatly piled or casually grouped, the fruits, berries, and vegetables radiated their freshly picked glow. Alongside the food, flower vendors competed for customers' attention, pitting each glorious floral bouquet against the next even-more-glorious arrangement of floribunda.

The market opened in 1907 when the City Council passed an ordinance allowing farmers to set up their carts to sell their products directly to customers and bypass the dishonest practices being perpetrated by commission houses and middlemen at the time. The original wood-planked site west of Pike Place soon acquired a covered arcade and was joined by an extension, and more extensions, plus additions, and the joining of adjacent buildings as well as the construction of new buildings. It continued to grow exponentially into the amorphous market shelter.

One story said a Japanese farmer was among a small, brave group who brought vegetables to sell on that rainy opening day. Like the others, his cart was swamped by buyers, who tore into his merchandise, helping themselves and leaving without paying. Other peddlers were luckier and later found coins left behind on their carts as payment for goods taken. Perhaps the farmer's ghost is still looking for reimbursement for his taken goods and has joined the roster of fabled spirits still haunting the crooked passageways and dark corners of the market.

The market's never-ending expansion was evidence of its success. Japanese truck farmers who labored on their small acreages in the Shirakawa, White River, area and surrounding environs south of Seattle began bidding for tables to sell their produce at the market. As their numbers kept increasing, resentment surfaced among other, non-Japanese sellers. They tried to regulate the Japanese by requiring them to sell only goods that they had grown, a restriction not applied to non-Japanese. And, as the Japanese were a people ineligible for citizenship––and ineligible (as non-citizens) to own land, the antagonists attempted to extend those restrictive legislative policies to exclude the Japanese from the right to lease space at the market. The Japanese Pike Place Market Corporation was organized in 1927 to counter such attempts, and it succeeded. By blocking racial restrictions, the presence of Japanese in the market kept increasing in the next decade. In the days before supermarkets, the Pike Place Market sold fresh goods at a better price than the small neighborhood shops prevalent at that time. Even during the Depression, the public market thrived.

The long rows of tables that bordered the main aisle were apportioned into separate lease sections, each manned by a different farmer selling his goods, each displayed in his own way and huckstered in his own style to attract the roaming crowds of shoppers and non-shoppers. Serious shoppers meandered, stopping at various stalls examining goods, and moving on to check competitors' samples before making a purchase. Others walked with purpose, seeking specific items penciled on their grocery lists. Melting ice sloshed under the seafood-laden bins of the fishmongers, often Sephardic Jews who hawked their products noisily and successfully. The butchers sold their meat with less shouting, although consummating a sale required a booming repartee of sorts to overcome the reverberating clatter of the active market. Under the sweeping arcade roof, the voices and accents of different nationalities, all speaking English unlike the King's, managed to communicate without embarrassment, whether they were immigrant Japanese, Italian, or any other. The boisterous crowds, the frenzied activity, the interaction between shoppers and vendors, the hubbub, and, most of all, the positive mood of the people as they wandered in and about the market, were reminiscent of the boardwalk in Rockaway. Yoshi was comforted by the similar ambiance.

On Saturdays when his hothouse tomatoes were ripe, he joined the hardworking, gregarious vendors and went to the market to sell his product. He joined other vendors on the lower level who sold smaller quantities of goods, and by sharing space, they kept their rents to a minimum. He had joined an affable fellowship of market venders. Over 50 percent of the total leased tables were rented by Japanese, and Yoshi had also unknowingly joined their "club." Yoshi could not claim he met all the Japanese vendors, but he felt a general kinship with them all and made lasting friendships, which had been denied to him previously as a *kenjin* outsider. That sense of connectivity was extended to the entire fraternity of market merchants.

Yoshi usually sold out his less-than-bountiful supply of hothouse tomatoes well before the market's closing, which allowed him to wander through the market and visit. He met a group of second generation Nisei who were coming of age; many helped their parents at the market. He usually gravitated to certain stalls to chat. He had never been shy talking with strangers, Japanese or non-Japanese, male or female, and at the market he met Nisei who were usually conversant in Japanese.

"Hello, Yoshi. You sold out your tomatoes early today," said Ken, as he rearranged his table of vegetables.

"Not make much money. Lotsa time to visit," Yoshi replied with a smile. "Any luck finding a job yet?"

"It's the same old thing. They all tell me they don't hire Japanese."

"You went to the university. You graduated in engineering."

"It makes no difference to them; I'm not *haku-jin*, a white man. I've just about decided to go to Japan to find an engineering job. I can't stay here helping Pop at the market. I should have a real job and contribute to the family."

"You're American. You were born here."

"If I had a choice, of course I'd stay in America. If you don't see me here someday, you'll know where I've gone."

Yoshi stopped in at the Golden Flower Shoppe, where Kazuko tended the store. Their business was not brisk, but their array of bouquets was enticing, and enough customers bought their florals allowing them to stay in business.

"Have you talked to Ken lately? He is thinking of going to Japan to find a real job."

"I think that's terrible. He's a Nisei. He would have a hard time adjusting in Japan"

"I think so too. He speaks only little bit Japanese. But, he is desperate."

"Perhaps he could find a job back East? Andy says there are more opportunities there for Japanese than in Seattle."

"Does Andy plan to stay there?"

"Well, I hope not. We're getting married when he comes back from school."

"Congratulations, Kazuko. But about Ken, maybe you can talk to him?"

"Nomura-*san*, Nomura-*san*. I'm glad you came to the market today," Kimiko-*chan* gushed as she approached. She was one of Yoshi's younger lady friends. "Mama says I can go to nursing school when I graduate from high school. Isn't that good news?"

"Yes, Kimiko, it is good to help sick people, but you no marry when you grow up?"

"Nomura-*san*, this is Modern Age. I'll do both, become a nurse and get married, too."

Yoshi welcomed the optimism of youth.

CHAPTER 6

Bachelor Days, 1928-1933

IN SEATTLE, YOSHI'S ASSOCIATION WITH the white populace was generally limited to contacts for business and later at the workplace; his social
activities centered on the Japanese community. Nihonmachi was where
he landed on his arrival from New York, and though he no longer lived
there, he continued to spend a good part of his non-working hours there.
The mom-and-pop grocery stores sold the type of foods he preferred; the
varieties of produce and imported specialty foodstuffs were readily available in abundance such as Yoshi had not seen on the East Coast. An affordable mainstay of Japanese diets, tofu, was made fresh by more than
one purveyor and sold by the block. Customers usually brought their own
containers to carry home the wobbly soybean loafs.

The open fish markets displayed their products on tables laden with
shaved ice. Big fish cut and sold by the pound, medium-sized fish sold
whole, and small fish sold by the basketful shared the ice beds with local
Dungeness crab, clams, oysters, and large tentacle octopus caught in the
outlying Puget Sound waters.

"Our octopus here is so overwhelming we can only buy one tentacle
or a portion of one. Back home, the *tako* is petite, and we can buy one
whole."

Another customer instructed her daughter, "When you buy fish, look
at the eye for clarity. Cloudy eyes mean not so fresh, *neh*." "*Chot-to*…wait
a minute, I want one pound cut from that big piece. The one you try sell
me, only my cat would eat."

Melting ice continually dripped from the tables, and clerks wearing rubber boots and rubber aprons replenished the ice beds often to keep their fish clear-eyed for as long as possible. In Yoshi's *mura*, their daily staple of fish was never more than several hours from having been caught, and they never had to check the eye of any fish for freshness. The often-long droughts of fishless meals in New York made Yoshi appreciate whatever was available in Seattle's fish markets, whether they were located in Nihonmachi or the Pike Place Market.

Yoshi's bank was the local branch of the Sumitomo Bank, where the cashiers all spoke Japanese. His barber was located on a convenient and accessible side street, one of many in the district where the Asian clientele could get a haircut, since they would be refused service from non-Asian barbers elsewhere. When Yoshi needed a relaxing soak, he found his way to the *sento*, the Japanese-style public bath where a person washed himself and rinsed before entering the hot-water pool to soak and release the aches and pains piercing his tired sore body.

A clothier carried sizes to fit smaller-statured men. A few alterations, and the clothes fit almost as well as the tailor-made outfits Yoshi once owned. Not that he needed such a wardrobe any longer——he just never forgot the feel of a good fit and a good suit. Better yet were the shoe stores selling footwear sized for Asian customers. Other Asian men besides Yoshi wore small shoes, and the shops carried many styles from which to choose, as long as they were black or a shade of brown. Yoshi's choices were still limited, he learned. Others had short and wide feet; his small and narrow feet were still sized like women's feet. The shoe repair shop handily resoled his treasured "perfect fit" shoes for a second life.

There were a number of shops he bypassed. The jewelry store sold merchandise he had little use for and could ill afford, but he entered the premises periodically because his once-reliable pocketwatch occasionally came down with the hiccups, requiring the services of the watch repairman who worked at the back of the store. Regretfully, he rarely had enough time to browse the bookstores that were teeming with Japanese-language books and periodicals shipped direct from Japan. Yoshi further regretted not having more time to read. A choice of several daily Japanese-language newspapers published locally kept residents of the city and surrounding area informed about community events and happenings. The papers reported headline news appearing in Japan, and a smattering of stories in the US and Seattle pertaining to Japanese or Asians. Including more general news was deemed unnecessary since Seattle's three local newspapers provided coverage, although many of the Issei, the immigrant/first generation, could barely read English.

News from Relatives

While in New York, Yoshi had fairly predictable earnings from running his concession during summers. It had afforded him indulgences and extra monies to send home and then some. His winter jobs kept him in funds adequate for a bachelor. He had always had money in his pockets, but after eight years of living as a transitory sojourner, he was ready to exchange it all for intangibles: the promise of a more wholesome and settled life available in small town Seattle. The work operating a greenhouse was no worse than most of the winter jobs he had held in New York; work was work. As his own boss, Yoshi was not beholden to anyone, and success depended on his skills and luck. He eked out a living. The days of fancy suits and easy indulgences were over; money was scarce. He no longer sent money home. Money for his two younger brothers schooling had been forwarded as promised, and he felt no further monetary obligations were due.

Letters from home kept him in touch. Brothers Shiro and Hiromu had gone on to their respective schools. Noboru never made it to Australia. He came down with pneumonia and died at home. Youngest brother Shitoshi never joined his riotous "gang of three" brothers. Instead, he basked in his privileged position as the baby of the family until he died at the age of seven. Of a total of twelve births, only five of Yasue's children lived to adulthood.

A letter arrived from New York; to Yoshi's surprise, it was from Ito. Previous transcontinental communiqué had been with cousin Kajuro, and Ito had remained uncharacteristically silent. She had never bothered to write one note to him since her departure from Seattle.

What crisis has shattered her peaceful existence, prompting her to contact me? Yoshi wondered. Prickly with curiosity, he methodically sawed the envelope's sealed flap with his metal file, his go-to apparatus whenever his scissors disappeared. It's time for a new pair of scissors. He opened the letter and began reading, straining to decipher her sloppy penmanship. All the elaborate preliminary niceties were eliminated. Why is it that I have more than my quota of relatives who dismiss the usual letter writing formalities? Ito got to the point immediately. "Nephew, you knew Kajuro's shortcomings and said nothing. How could you have remained silent, knowing he is an ingrained alcoholic and lecherous debaucher? You knowingly led me into this deception, you miserable worm…" Obviously the honeymoon is over, Yoshi mumbled to himself. As he ruminated, he fell into a fit of giggles. Perhaps Cousin found solace with the bottle and sweet, blooming Botan. Could anyone blame him?

Roiling with anger, Ito had set pen to paper venting her frustrations and unhappiness. After diffusing her immediate anger, she proceeded to drag every remembered hurt she had experienced at the hands of her present and past husbands, their families, and the entire extended clan. "You Nomura men are all the same, strutting like peacocks thinking we females find you irresistible. You're merely egocentric boors, a bunch of delusional skirt-chasing drones, every single one of you. You're so spineless; you cower and kowtow to a matriarch who lords over the household behind a mask of demure and kind solicitude. She revealed her true self to me, expecting me to work like a lowly servant rather than treating me like a valued sister-in-law. No one, absolutely no one, had the fortitude to defend me from her treachery."

Yoshi's face flushed as he continued reading.

"She sashays around like a queen bee, wresting flattery and homage from the villagers; it's a sham! She's a fake! Her alluded connections to samurai are forbears who merely treated wounded warriors, a blood-and-gore business."

What? Screamed through Yoshi's head. *Kichi-gai.* She's crazy.

The letter continued: "As for a female who wantonly produces passels of babies is no better than those four-legged she-animals commonly known as…"

"That's it! She's gone too far!" Yoshi hollered; he was livid. Ito in a rage had cursed and insulted his mother to the core. Her putdown of Nomura men, two of whom she married, was the ravings of a disillusioned woman, but heaping poisoned insults on *Okaa-san* was vicious and unforgivable. He tore the letter into shreds, and he cussed some more.

"*BAKA-NAaaa*…" Fool? "*KUSA-TAaa*…" Rotten? Never mind spewing grossly inadequate Japanese curses. He spat out, "SON- NAGA BEE-CHI!" in full fury, followed in rapid succession by, "LA- TEN SON-NAGA BEE-CHI!" which he bellowed repeatedly. Then Yoshi added, "*MAGA-HAI!*" to the American curse; his hot, angry reaction eased to a seething simmer. He had no idea what that last alien vindictive meant. It was something he had picked up somewhere along the way, a mere curse evoked by millions of Chinese. He would shout it, too. At least it's got more venom than "fool" and "rotten."

Yoshi wrote a terse note to Ito severing all future contact with her—that Dragon Lady *Oni-baba!*

Although the feud did not involve cousin Yukimasa, he sided with his mother and broke off any further contact with Yoshi. The severed ties with his cousin were painful to Yoshi, but he respected his cousin's loyalty to Ito, just as his defense of his own mother had fueled the feud. Mutual friends dropped news of Yukimasa's progress from time to time, of his passing the dental exams and starting a dental practice. It was others who later told him Yukimasa had married. The ties remained severed.

SOCIAL LIFE

A noticeable number of Yoshi's acquaintances in Seattle remained tacitly silent about their lives before arriving in America and of their families in Japan. Their backgrounds remained guarded even under the most relaxed situations. Whatever it was they preferred to keep hidden, others politely provided them the privacy they sought. It was altogether unlike the open and easy camaraderie Yoshi had shared with his bachelor friends in New York when they reminisced and exchanged stories of growing up in Japan. The ex- students among them had usually come from the privileged class, for who else could send sons overseas to be educated? They admittedly had lost their way, and they harbored few secrets of their past misadventures that prevented them from returning home.

In Seattle, even the raconteurs who feigned memory loss of their Japanese pasts never regained those memories even when they were inebriated. They curiously remembered every incident of their lives after leaving Japan, and they talked away the night with their innocuous blabber.

Yoshi was befriended by a number of longtime sojourners who were still playing the bachelor game. Prohibition was still in effect, but speakeasies and places where one could buy a drink were not hard to find. Yoshi rarely indulged now that Grandmother Yae's curse had clenched tight. He still preferred drinking a soda over liquor, and his friends accepted his sobriety because it was not rooted in either religious or moral taboos. Besides, he proved useful as a designated driver.

On the occasions when Yoshi went out to eat at a restaurant, he found himself sipping tea while other men drank their bootleg whiskey in teacups and told their stories. When their liquor addled brains erased the memory of an earlier telling, the stories repeated themselves and the cycle replayed the rest of the evening.

"In the old days, everything was more centralized, I tell you. Now the businesses are spread out all the way to Dearborn Street. Good thing Beacon Hill starts there and blocks Nihonmachi from spreading further south, otherwise it would reach to Renton," said the imbiber as he swatted away an imagined fly.

"Hey, the important places are still close enough to walk to," argued his companion.

"It's the inconvenience I'm talking about. Hell, in those days I would roll out of my bed into the arms of my sweetheart, she was so close."

"He practically lived at the *jolo-kai*, he did," mumbled the companion.

"When did they form a club? You said *kai*," Yoshi asked. "Who cares…a club, a house? It weren't a shed."

"What I meant was 'nowadays, you gotta walk down the hill to Chinatown for the same favors.' Psssssh."

It was time for Yoshi to leave. He had had enough soda for the evening and more than enough ramblings of two inebriated oldtimers. "I go now…"

"*Mada, mada…* Don't go yet. Sit down and have another…"

In the early 1890s, when Japanese immigration had barely begun and settlement was still sparse, a survey conducted by the Japanese counselor office recorded: ten restaurants and one grocery store owned by and employing Japanese were located in Seattle. The majority of settlers, the report stated, were engaged in illicit endeavors such as gambling, pimping, prostitution, and ownership of brothels. The women were brought from Japan, often under false pretenses. Lured to the ships, agents in collusion with sailors smuggled them into America, and, once delivered, they were set to work. Those engaged in such endeavors recognized the opportunities presented by the hordes of male laborers traveling overseas who were alone and far from home without companionship and recreation. By offering services not undertaken by legitimate operatives, these erstwhile entrepreneurs made their illicit profits and were among the earliest Japanese settlers. Within a decade, as the immigrant population expanded and settlers increased their business base, the proportion of legitimate enterprises overtook the old. The brothels within Nihonmachi were forced to move away from the family-oriented core and relocated south across Jackson Street to King Street. There they were housed and grouped separately by the clientele they served: Japanese, Chinese, or non-Asians. The demographics of the community kept evolving, but many remembered the way things were, and they talked about those "good old days" often.

Those imbibers Yoshi met were among the large surfeit of unmarried Japanese men still working and living in Seattle and its vicinity. The men were generally older by a dozen years or more, having arrived in the first decade of the century as young men. These men were no longer young. Mindless of the passing years, they languished in unfulfilled middle age. They had lost their vigor and ambitions, often living day-to-day in pursuit of immediate pleasures and gratification, unaware they had become the embodiment of youth long past. Of course, there were others who were less self-destructive and led purposeful lives. They were busy pursuing goals elsewhere.

Yoshi's friend Min didn't follow the usual pattern; he was a married man who went about like a bachelor. He never got sloppy drunk or acted like a lout; he was just the opposite. Always considerate and sensible even after his customary two drinks, his conversation remained rational. He was a worthy friend and good company. Yoshi wondered if it was the customary Japanese macho bravura that induced Min to stay out and drink and gamble instead of going home to his wife. Their meetings were rarely planned. Customers tended to migrate toward a favorite haunt, and in a small village like Nihonmachi, even infrequent visitors knew where the gallery of nightly habitués roosted. In that way, Yoshi could find Min.

"Come with me to the Club tonight. I feel lucky," Min said.

The Club was private, and promoted gambling––not exactly dens of infamy, the usual denizens were a different sort than those who consorted in polite society. Chinatown housed an array of such establishments, which were owned by different nationals and generally patronized by their own ethnic group. The Toyo Club was the largest Japanese-operated gambling club in Seattle and was said to be the second-largest such establishment on the West Coast. It was the one Yoshi had visited with his companions. Obviously, there was no open-door policy at the Club; however, his friends were acquainted with procedures for entry, and they were quickly allowed in. After passing the scrutiny of the lobby clerks, they had climbed the stairs to the second-floor gaming area, where cards and Chinese gambling games held sway. The clacking of tiles and stones generated a different tonal pitch as they were expertly mixed on their individual tables. Dice and other Western games of chance were available, though they were less popular and drew fewer players. The volume of noise generated by the gamers rose to a rumble and fell to a murmur with no discernible pattern. Without warning, the room might come alive with anguished shouts from a player or two or their entourage of friends, acquaintances, or sympathetic bystanders as they cursed or cheered as money changed hands in the smoke-filled chambers.

Yoshi had visited smaller, less elaborate Chinese-operated establishments in New York when he was footloose and had money in his pockets. Even in those carefree circumstances, he had decided such games of chance were a pastime that did not particularly engage him, much as the card games he had avoided aboard the ships.

"If we go together, I may be twice as lucky," Min said.

Yoshi usually declined such invitations, but that night he decided to tag along, knowing full well he would lose money. "Only the Chinese," he said, "could figure out a way to take your money by merely counting beans. What an ingenious people."

"I never thought about Fan-tan in such a clinical way.

Those beans usually produce a lot of emotion."

"Gambling is like depositing your money in a bank. The difference is, they won't let you withdraw the money once you deposit it," Yoshi said as the two men made their way down the hill to cross Jackson Street.

"You're too pessimistic. That's why you don't win. Believe you'll beat the odds, and you'll win."

"Actually, I think I've been very lucky. I must have been born under an auspicious sign. Only, my auspicious sign has a few holes where I'm not lucky."

"Auspicious signs with holes? That's a unique concept. So, what are your unlucky holes?"

"Hummm…business and gambling."

"Business is like gambling. How well you do or don't do in business, that's karma. Maybe gambling, whether you win or lose one game, is short-term karma. Now name something where you've been lucky."

"Hmmm…" Yoshi rubbed his chin. He smiled broadly when the answer crossed his mind. "I've been lucky…with women."

"You're incorrigible!"

"Any man would be jealous," he said in jest as he laughed in delight at his own audacity.

Min didn't notice the lighthearted humor. His mind was searching for the applicable theory befitting their musings. "Lucky with women and unlucky in gambling; that has to be a yin and yang dichotomy somehow…"

"You're probably right. Yin and Yang sounds more plausible than Holes." The two men had reached the Club. Instead of entering, they stood outside to continue their conversation. The glow from the Chinese restaurant across the street lit the sidewalk as passersby walked briskly past other darkened storefronts closed for the business day. There was enough traffic on the street and pedestrians on the walkways to indicate not everyone had called it the end of their day.

Min took a last drag of his cigarette. "Perhaps my lucky and unlucky Yin Yang Holes are opposite to yours. That means I should be a big winner tonight."

"That doesn't follow. You're not unlucky with women; you have a fine wife, so…"

"No, not true," Min interrupted. "Miyo and I are getting divorced. I didn't know how to tell you."

"What? But why?"

"She wants to marry her boyfriend. He's rich and will become richer; it's inevitable. She became enamored with all the nice things he can buy for her. For a while, I was gambling hoping to win something really big, hoping that might help me keep her." Min avoided looking at Yoshi. He turned his face upward, his eyes searching the skies for his lost star.

"When she told me she was pregnant with his baby, I knew it was over for me. She wants to marry him as quickly as possible——foolishly, she says to avoid gossip."

A century before electronic devices made instant communication commonplace, ripe juicy gossip sped as fast and as unimpeded as it does now.

"There are few secrets that can be safely hidden. Miyo should know that," Min said. "The rich and prominent are apt to be victimized more vigorously by wagging tongues than the rest of us who live on the sidelines. Perhaps the scrutiny may be unjust, or then again, they might be guilty of greater lapses and transgressions, and exposure is the great equalizer."

"Even on a broader scope, resolutions remain complex. If the seed money for your present legitimate operations originally came from illegal sources, say drugs dropped from ships off the coast decades ago, doesn't that dirty money still tinge the present business operations and profiteers?" Yoshi asked.

"So, you've heard that story, too. The skeletons in that closet keep resurfacing. Let's save this *mukashi* rumor for another day." Min and Yoshi entered the Club that night and silently climbed the stairs toward the smoke-filled gaming room, each for the last time. Within weeks, Min slipped out of Seattle and resettled in southern California to start life anew.

PONDERING MARRIAGE

Like the Chinese workers who came seeking their fortunes in Gold Mountain, and the Japanese sojourners who followed, though they never identified America as golden or a mountain, Yoshi and Min also had come to America in pursuit of the same goals. For most, the riches they hoped to take home with them never materialized. Yoshi came to realize he, too, had joined their ranks, and great riches would elude him. That was karma. Now, neither Japan nor New York City was a place of refuge from the worsening worldwide financial depression. Things had changed everywhere, a recovered economy and good times were years off. In spite of such gloomy forecasts, Yoshi felt there were still more opportunities for him in America than in Japan. Seattle possessed the attributes that had originally enticed him to stay, and after considering the alternatives, Yoshi decided to jettison any plans of returning to Japan for the present. Now that he accepted his status as an immigrant settler, albeit one without official papers, he acquired aspirations common to settlers: a comfortable home life with a wife and family.

In the decade preceding Yoshi's arrival in America unmarried Japanese settlers had found wives by exchanging photographs with women willing to marry them by proxy; willing to leave Japan and come to live in America. The practice of "picture bride" marriages had ended, and had such arrangements still been available, Yoshi was unlikely to have used the service. His ego persuaded him he was quite capable of finding his own wife. Furthermore, he had been released from any arranged marriage compacts or of pre-approvals of his choice when his mother, with fortuitous foresight, had given him the freedom to wed a woman of his own choosing. That he intended to do.

Marrying someone who was not Japanese had always been unacceptable. Yoshi's intention to return to Japan had not been forsaken; it was merely postponed. It was wholly unrealistic to expect a non-Japanese wife to adjust to life in a small Japanese village with no knowledge of the language and customs; such a marriage could not survive. Since a native Japanese woman could not immigrate to America, that possibility was also closed. Yoshi was limited to two options.

A distinct stratification of generations had occurred in the Japanese community in America. Male immigrants arrived in the United States' mainland in the decades before and after the turn of the century, but few wives had accompanied their husbands. As the men settled, the wives followed in the following decade until new legislation shut them out as the men had been shut out earlier. Children appeared on the scene in great numbers after the first decade of the century. The second-generation children, the Nisei, born to immigrant parents, the Issei, were coming of age around the time Yoshi started looking for a wife. A young Nisei woman for a wife was one of his options.

Early on, many Issei parents had sent their young born- in-America Nisei children back to Japan to be raised by their own parents to ease the burden of caring for them while the immigrant parents struggled to make a living in America. More importantly, they wanted the children to receive a Japanese education and exposure to Japanese culture and traditions. These offspring became assimilated Japanese more closely resembling their parents in thought, manner, and identity than their siblings who had remained in America and believed they were Americans. To differentiate the two types of Nisei, the term Kibei identified the Japan-educated second-generation offspring. As older Kibei finished their education in Japan, they began returning to America, the land of their birth. Marriageable young ladies were among them and provided a second option.

Yoshi thought he was a good marriage candidate. As a self- employed bachelor in his early thirties, he was not nearly as old as his many competitors, and he believed the image looking back at him in the mirror could still attract the ladies. He did not drink, gamble, or smoke, and by most testimonials, he was a decent man. To his dismay, there was one glaring factor that worked against him. His illegal status disqualified him as a marriage partner to many potential bride choices. When parents learned he had entered the country illegally, they were unwilling to risk their daughter's future to a possible deportation. Such a handicap made finding a wife a difficult task. Yoshi scaled back his pursuit since new candidates would continually be reaching marriageable age every year, and with luck, he would eventually meet a woman he wanted to be his wife, and who was willing to take the risk of marriage to an illegal.

Actually, there were other comely candidates on the sidelines willing to marry him, but he disqualified them for his own personal reasons. "Hurrummf. Her mother is a bar hostess," he said with disdain about one woman. His low opinion of women working such jobs had formed when he had worked in a restaurant, and it stayed with him. "Her crooked teeth, she's too dangerous to kiss." "*Ah ii- mini-kui*. Hard on the eyes, *nah*." He felt he was entitled to be picky––after all, marriage was a lifelong commitment, and he expected that to be a long time.

Yoshi had grown weary of haunting his usual bachelor hangouts on his nights out. Nihonmachi was a less vibrant place since the economic slump deepened and businesses in the area became leaner and scarcer. His best friend had moved away, leaving a void, and, for all purposes, he had no kin. He began visiting married friends with children, visits with an erstwhile surrogate family. In the beginning, the friendships were with neighbors involved with plants and gardening. They welcomed his company and mentored his progress as a flower grower, and also guided him through the intricate ethos of their community.

Down the hill from his little homestead, Noji-*san*, who operated a larger-scale greenhouse operation, befriended Yoshi without any qualms of competition. Always available with good advice on plant care and its propagation, he and his bride provided hospitality and home-cooked food along with their friendship.

Another neighbor living on the eastern slopes of Beacon Hill not far from the Nomura greenhouse was an older couple, Yamazaki-*san* and his wife, and their two sons.

A stranger, a large Asian man, appeared on Yoshi's doorstep shortly after Yoshi moved in. "Hal-lo, I'm a friend of Yukimasa. I came to introduce myself," the visitor bellowed.

Yoshi had no time for visitors, but he noticed the stranger's Goliath size, and he knew he best make a friend than an enemy. "Welcome." Their introduction was nothing special, but the contact was to be important for Yoshi.

Yamazaki was initially curious to meet Yukimasa's cousin who was taking over the nursery business. Intending to assess the man's character and abilities, the experienced Yamazaki saw immediately the newcomer was a fish out of water regarding plants and agriculture. Knowing the circumstances why Yoshi had taken on such a task, Yamazaki felt compelled to take him under his wing and become his mentor. He provided the novice with useful hard gained tips for plant propagation and care especially suited to the area's environment. Most useful was his providing English names to identify the popular varieties of vegetation grown in the region. In addition to plants, Yamazaki knew Yoshi should be aware of the social intricacies at play within the community and advised him how to conduct himself and his business within it.

Yoshi's circle of acquaintances expanded beyond plant-oriented mentors and bar-stool-straddling bachelors.

The Atlas Hotel was situated a half block south of Jackson Street in Chinatown where the terrain was a friendlier gradual slope. One of many Japanese-owned and operated in the area, the hotel served the ethnic community surrounding it. Yoshi had become friends with the owners and manager, and he often socialized with them. The hotel's entrance was one shop removed from one of the confectionery shops that sold his beloved Japanese sweet treats. He could not pass the store without stepping inside and buying a confection to satisfy his sweet cravings. Selecting a delectable sweet morsel from the enticing array had lost none of its appeal since his youth, only now Yoshi could afford to purchase as many as he pleased without raiding the till. "Me see. I want two pink and two green and...four with *kinako*. And add an assortment of four baked *manju* for an even dozen in the box. I want one *ohagi* on the side to eat now."

They were his favorite treats to bring when he visited friends. It served two purposes: they were the obligatory *omiyage* accompanying his visit, and since the treats were more special than anything stored in his host's cabinet for such occasions, the recipient hosts almost always opened and served the treats with tea, thus he could eat his cake, too.

Yoshi often stopped by Terada-*san's* home in a fourplex located conveniently up the hill from Nihonmachi on Yesler Way. Terada was a great talker who expounded on practically any subject with gusto and self-styled expertise. Yoshi was a good listener and managed to insert just the right amount of approving comments to make him a welcome guest. Besides the "men talk," the Terada family often invited Yoshi to stay and share a meal. On one such visit, a young female friend of theirs was also visiting.

She appeared to be on familiar terms with the family, and Yoshi wondered why they had never met before.

Yoshi was making mental assessments of the woman. She was small—not likely over five feet tall—and there were no clues to her age.

Noticing Yoshi's eyes were following her around the room with a quizzical expression, Terada laughed and explained, "Yoshi, haven't you met Aiko before? She's Hayame's daughter."

"You mean Michihira-*san*, who owns the grocery store across the street?" he asked. "She's too young to have such a grown daughter."

"I forget you're not from around here. Aiko is Hayame's husband's daughter by his first marriage. There's only about ten years' difference in their ages, so they act more like sisters than mother and stepdaughter," Terada explained.

Aiko had disappeared into the kitchen to help Mrs. Terada with dinner.

"*Ah iii...* She might be a wife candidate for you, Yoshi," Terada said as the idea struck; he stroked his chin, letting the thought blossom. He was momentarily distracted as his thumb ran over his smoothly shaved cheek, and he noted no stubble or evidence of a five o'clock shadow marred its surface like his guest, who sat across from him. Once assured he was clean-shaven, Terada's mind quickly returned to the interrupted subject of Aiko as a prospective wife. "Aiko-*chan* doesn't have a father, and Hayame-*san* would be relieved to relinquish responsibility for her. She probably wouldn't ask the questions about immigration that others feel are so important. By the way, I do know it has hindered your efforts."

He continued in a confidential tone, "I've been meaning to discuss something with you for some time, Yoshi. I strongly recommend you keep quiet about your illegal status. You're not obnoxious or loud, which is good, so continue to keep a low profile. There are people in this community who prey on that type of information. It's best kept secret. When they learn a person is an illegal, they're known to blackmail such people for money, lots of money. They threaten to report the ship jumper to immigration officials or else." He shook his head. "There are all kinds of people living here mostly good people, but we also have some rotten fish."

Actually, Min had warned Yoshi earlier to be discreet about discussing his illegal status. A second friend, Terada, reinforced the warning more colorfully.

Japanese girls, upon finishing high school, generally worked helping parents and relatives on the farm or in the family business or trade. Government agencies, public schools, industry, and businesses in general did not hire minorities. A small number of girls went to college. Often, the female children were passed over, and the monies were spent on educating sons, who were given the opportunity to further their education. The route many girls took to earn their keep was to enter domestic service. The Japanese came to be known for their hardworking ethics and their quiet and obedient unassuming manners, which white clients valued. The housewife employers had their help scrub floors, wash windows, dust and clean house, change bed linens and make the beds, wash, and iron. The rich hired an array of help, who worked on specialized tasks; the middle-class housewife could afford to hire one house girl. The employer was relieved from the drudgeries of housework, but she was obliged to mentor her domestic help and teach the Asian girl how to be an American: how to properly set the table, how to serve meals, how to cook foods the American way. The girls were encouraged to attend sewing or enrichment classes, and they learned American customs and traditions. Since the Japanese had a tradition of sending daughters to finishing school to learn the womanly arts of tea ceremony, flower arranging, and the like, they considered their experience working in an American household a continuation of that practice.

Aiko had been living with a Caucasian family in Bellingham as a live-in domestic worker. She was not unhappy about her immersion in Americana. The work was far from strenuous compared to life on a farm, and her employer was considerate. When her stepmother, Hayame, asked her to return to Seattle, she was even happier to be back in the big city and in close proximity to the sights, sounds, and attractions of Nihonmachi and the community.

Hayame had taken a lease on a small grocery store on Yesler Hill, which had living quarters in back and bedrooms on the second level. The store supported her and her children, and the arrangement allowed her to quit her chambermaid job making beds at the Atlas Hotel and stay home. By having Aiko return to Seattle, she had help in the shop and help in navigating transactions in English. As convenient as it was to have Aiko assisting her, Hayame understood it was for a year or two at the longest. Her stepdaughter had turned twenty, and Hayame's responsibility was to see Aiko married and starting a family of her own. Aiko needed exposure to meet the eligible men available in Seattle. If she remained in Bellingham, where few Japanese lived, Aiko would surely end up a spinster.

With a surplus of males, there was absolutely no scarcity of men desperate for a wife, men who felt any female would do. Hayame knew a good many of those eligible bachelors were not suitable husband material. They were too old with too many bad habits, indigent, or down-and-out unworthy. She wanted Aiko to have a share of the good life due her and to find happiness with a good husband. Had she and Aiko switched personalities, the pursuit of finding that husband would have been easy, but dour, sensible Aiko got lost in the woodwork. As self-effacing and quiet as Aiko was, she had a stubborn streak, and she could be as unyielding as a brick wall. She harbored modern ideas, too, and she claimed she would never be forced into an arranged marriage without love.

"You've been reading too many romance stories. Be realistic, Aiko. In a good marriage, love can develop; you don't need love in the beginning, believe me."

"I want both; a good marriage and a husband I love, Mama," Aiko replied.

"All these modern ideas girls have nowadays," Hayame commented, and wondered how such a simple process had evolved into such a complicated ordeal. She remembered her own marriage arrangements to a man she had never seen; the marriage worked, but unfortunately it ended too soon.

The Teradas, their two children, and the two dinner guests were well into their dinner of sukiyaki with condiments and rice and soup.

"We consider both of you like family, so I didn't make anything fancy I cooked something simple, *Neh.*"

Everyone at the table knew the meal was not an ordinary, tossed-together affair. Special ingredients had been purchased and added, including the mushroom most prized by the Japanese.

"It must be the first Matsutake mushrooms of the season.

It's a rare treat."

"The market had only a few specimen mushrooms, not enough to add to the sukiyaki. Diced small and put into the soup, everyone could have a morsel for taste." Indeed, everyone was sipping the soup, savoring the delicacy floating in the clear broth.

"The subtle favor of the Matsutake is so delicious, *oi-shi*," Yoshi swooned.

"The first taste of the season is usually the most memorable," Terada said. "In a couple of weeks, the markets will be flooded with them."

"That's one of the things so amazing about Seattle. I never saw one matsutake all the years I lived on the East Coast."

"Gee, I thought a mushroom is a mushroom except the poison kind," piped up the boy.

"You're both excused from the table if you've finished," their father said.

The children left the adults and scampered off. Daughter began her piano practice in the next room, her fingers falling on enough wrong keys to be jarring to listeners.

"Wife, couldn't you have persuaded your daughter to take up another instrument that wasn't so loud? Perhaps the *koto?*"

"You'll remember, we bought the piano at a distress sale. A decent *koto* would be an expensive investment."

"Nevertheless, if she played a little better…" "Give her time, she only began taking lessons." The women got up to clear the table.

"Aiko, have you thought about getting married?" Terada bluntly asked.

She answered him with a sigh, "Mama wants me to start looking for a husband. She's worried I'm becoming an old maid. I told her she shouldn't rush it. When I marry, she will become an *Obaa-san*. She's too young to be a grandmother."

"Haaa, ha, ha. Hayame, a grandmother! I like that. Some of her men friends might get scared away...consorting with an *Obaa-san*," Terada roared as he pictured Hayame as a staid grandmother.

"Husband, that's unkind. Hayame-*san* is a very nice person," his wife scolded.

"I agree with you on that point, wife. But, she wouldn't be offended. She would think it was funny, and she'd laugh about being a thirty-one-year-old grandmother, too!"

The dishes removed, the two men were served tea as they picked their teeth.

Chores completed, the women returned to the table to sip their own tea. The conversation reverted back to the subject of marriage. "Yoshi is a bachelor, and he's looking for a wife, Aiko. Why don't you two get to know each other? You might like each other, *neh*," Terada said. "In America, young people go on a date and get acquainted. In Japan, your parents tell you who you're going to marry. Sometimes you're lucky and you like your spouse right away. Mostly you learn to care for your spouse through years of shared experiences. There are an unfortunate few who hate each other from the first day and never overcome their initial displeasure. They stay married for the sake of others, their children or parents or people's good opinion. They are doomed to be miserable until they die."

Terada was on a roll. He rambled on, "A Buddhist, when he dies, awaits a new reincarnation. He gets to live a new and different life. He can forget everything about his nasty old spouse that made his life miserable. A Christian might not be quite that lucky. When they die, they go to heaven. That's somewhere in the sky where everyone who was good goes forever after. The bad ones go somewhere in the middle of a fire for eternity. Now if a couple splits up and they go to different places, that's fine. They won't be seeing each other again."

"How do you know...?" Yoshi began to say.

"We'll get to that later; I'm not finished. So, in those religions providing a heaven where the married couple is united together forever, that's all right if you really liked each other, I suppose. But, if you couldn't stand each other and you see each other forever in heaven, that's terrible; that would be unendurable punishment," he proclaimed with absolute certainty.

Neither Yoshi nor Aiko were about to countermand Terada's words or his suggestion they get to know each other. They made arrangements to have dinner together the following week. The initial meeting had been a lucky happenstance; it was coincidence they were at the Terada's at the same time. They probably would have been formally introduced to each other eventually since they shared a friendship with Terada-*san* and it was known the two shared a common goal to find a marriage partner.

Definitely, Aiko was not the prettiest skirt Yoshi had seen in Seattle. She was not homely, or *mini-kui*, as he would have said. He decided she was best described as plain and quite ordinary looking––the kind of woman no one bothered to look at twice nor remember her in passing. Part of that assessment could be attributed to her dowdy wardrobe of drab, loose-fitting clothes favored by women twice her age.

Yoshi asked Aiko early in their meeting how old she was. She told him she was twenty years old. He could not believe she was so young, but she was too candid not to believe. Her composure and restraint belied her youth. Aiko appeared to be unassuming, always eager to please; she would never try to dominate in a relationship. He saw qualities in Aiko that appealed to him, qualities deemed desirable in a spouse. Everything pointed to conscientious and frugal habits, and she knew how to keep house and to cook, too.

Yoshi began to imagine his days spent as a married man, a man married to Aiko. He thought he could be content and happy.

When Aiko was told the stranger she had just met might be a husband prospect, she could not believe it. She had always been on the sidelines where boys were concerned. Boys liked the cute girls with sassy personalities. Older boys liked the come-hither, playful ones. She was always so far down on anyone's list that no one looked to the bottom to see her there looking up. The only boys who talked to her were the sons of family friends who came to visit. They were trapped on such occasions and were politely sociable. Needless to say, she had never been invited on a date before. She was well aware there were a disproportionate number of men in the community compared to eligible women and a husband would eventually be found for her. The available men ranged in age from senior-citizen old all the way down to boys of her age. Those contemporaries were the ones who had never expressed any interest in her. As for the older men who desperately wanted a spouse, Hayame could read them like a book, and she was determined to keep any lecherous louts at bay.

Aiko had learned to accept her karma with good grace a long time ago, but she hoped against all odds for one bit of good luck. As teenagers, when she and her friends had whispered confidences and shared their yearnings for the future, she had held back one most cherished dream that she never revealed to anyone. If her secret wish were to be exposed to the light of day, it most surely would vanish and never come true. Preposterous dreams and reality exist in two different worlds, but she had prayed to the gods––Buddhist, Christian, rabbit-foot, four-leafed clover, and more––to gift her a husband she could love and live with in harmony for a lifetime. Oh, please… Please.

Aiko had betrayed her secret to Mama only because she was afraid her stepmother might be persuaded by others to arrange an inappropriate marriage just to be done with it. Now that Hayame had been told she was not going to be a pushover concerning husband choices, Aiko knew Mama would honor her decision.

Have the gods heard my prayers? Aiko wondered. Had they arranged my chance meeting with Yoshi? He was older, but not too old, and he was more handsome than the man of her dreams. He was easygoing, not arrogantly demanding as many men were prone to be, the kind who cocked their feathers like a peacock and honked rudely for attention. Yoshi wasn't that way at all. Aiko knew she already liked him; she liked him a lot.

Yoshi plunged into his new mission; as a benevolent Svengali, he took Aiko in hand and introduced her to the world beyond Shirakawa and Nihonmachi.

"But, I don't feel I've been constricted. I journeyed to Japan and back, and I lived in Bellingham among *haku-jin*, white people, for two years," Aiko said in self-defense.

"And where did you go in Japan?" Yoshi asked.

"We landed in Kobe, took a train to Hiroshima, then we went to Mama's family home, where we stayed for two years. I was supposed to go sightseeing to Miyajima once, but the trip was canceled, so I never saw the shrine. Everyone who has been there say it's very beautiful."

"You've always lived so close, yet you never traveled the few extra miles to see and visit a destination. I still can't believe you've never been to Tacoma. For sixteen years, you must have lived no more than twenty miles away."

"*To-san* didn't have as many connections there, so he usually went up to Seattle. Most people don't travel the world like you, Yoshi."

"It was my karma to see the world while I was young and impressionable. By witnessing different lands, people, and customs, I'm doomed to view life with those impressions in mind. I also have to be mindful and accept what my karma has in store for me in the future."

"Am I to share in your karma?"

"Only if you will be happy married to a poor man like me, someone who can only afford a one-day honeymoon trip visiting Mt Rainier, but on our return, we could detour through the city of Tacoma."

"What? We're not going to San Francisco? Hummm?" Aiko asked jokingly. "Seriously, Mt. Rainier and Tacoma were always places I wanted to visit since I was little. That would be a nice honeymoon." Yoshi was heartened when Aiko shook off her usual serious demeanor even for a mere minute or two.

Yoshi was candid about his finances when he said he could not offer much, but Aiko had had so little her whole life, he felt she was being truthful when she replied her happiness was whatever he could share with her. Aiko had the traditional values he sought in a spouse, and she was eligible and eager.

Hayame was delighted to learn her stepdaughter had met a prospective husband, a person Aiko professed she could love. The Nisei children who were coming into marriageable age were insisting on love marriages, the type portrayed in American novels and movies; proponents insisted love should be the basis for marriage. Hayame had no problem with the concept. She also believed there was merit in the custom and tradition of arranged marriages that need not be discarded as love could grow in such marriages. And, unspoken was the fact that there could always be love without marriage.

In no way would Hayame, who had had a good marriage, set up a roadblock toward her stepdaughter's future happiness. She could overlook the details of the suitor's illegal entry into the country. If problems should arise, they could be handled at that time. Also, Hayame harbored no pretenses about wealth or family lineage and expected no inflated credentials from the groom-to-be. By all indications, the prospective groom appeared to be decent and hard- working, and he was undeniably likable. The fact that her future son-by-marriage was a year older than Hayame the future mother-in-law, was a constant source for good-humored laughter, and it especially tickled Hayame's funny bone. She knew others saw the incongruity; after all, she was just beginning her third decade and in full womanly bloom and was easily attracting a passel of attentive males herself.

CHAPTER 7

The Valley, 1900-1931

Aiko's father had arrived in America at the turn of the century with the great wave of Japanese immigration to the West Coast. The family had descended into genteel poverty, and although he was the first son, he felt he could best contribute to the family's welfare by seeking work overseas, enabling him to send money home to sustain them. He left his home in rural Hiroshima-*ken* at age sixteen with the knowledge any return to Japan would be in the remote future. His brothers were too young to join him on this journey; they had to assume the responsibilities of the absent *chonan* until his return. Masaichi intended to become a settler for the long haul rather than a short-time sojourner, but he did not reveal that information to his siblings.

The earliest Japanese laborers recruited to work in America had been urbanites from the Tokyo and Yokohama areas. They were sons of the emerging middle class, they were not farmers' sons accustomed to hard manual labor. These early exports proved to be such unsatisfactory farm laborers that they cast a shameful image of the Japanese character and their work ethic. To avoid further embarrassment and to reverse those first opinions formed by Americans, the Japanese government changed its policy and began sending only men from rural areas to be contract laborers. Hawaii was the destination for the earliest group of workers. When their contract terms were fulfilled, many returned to Japan, while others chose to stay and become settlers in the islands. A smaller number left Hawaii and moved on to the mainland West Coast, where job opportunities were numerous and varied. In addition to the contract laborers who left home and family, thinking their time away was to be temporary, another segment of immigrants intended to stay on and become settlers to stake their futures in America.

Masaichi caught his ship in Kobe and journeyed to Vancouver, British Columbia, from where he made his way down to Washington State. Upon leaving Canada, his trek was a series of bewildering and frustrating mishaps caused by his ignorance; similar episodes he intended to avoid in the future. He resolved to learn the speech and customs of this new land and not remain a stranger. Stopping briefly in Seattle, he was surprised to find a small, burgeoning area of Japanese businesses. Access to a Japanese settlement where he could communicate readily with others and where familiar goods were available was a godsend. His contract stipulated work as a farmhand in an area between Seattle and Tacoma. His assimilation not yet started, he needed help. Upon inquiring at a general goods store, Masaichi was led to a clerk who knew the valley, and he was given detailed directions to locate his contact.

When he finally trudged up the dirt road leading to a tilting wood shack in the midst of weeds and scattered debris, a welcoming party of five Japanese men and their boss, who were members of the "labor gang" he had joined, met Masaichi. After setting his bag down next to the covered straw matting assigned to him, he rejoined the others at the table, where the men were preparing to eat their evening meal, *dango jiru*, broth with flour dumplings and greens.

They introduced themselves each in turn and gave the name of the villages and prefecture from where they came. The men spoke the language with accents the newcomer understood.

"I don't know where any of your villages are located, but, thank goodness, you all speak understandable Hiroshima-*ken* dialect," Masaichi said. "On the boat…well, actually, since leaving home, I've met people claiming to be Japanese who speak an alien form of our language."

"One correction needed––there's one person in our midst who passes himself off as a Hiroshima-*kenjin*. Listen carefully, and he'll come up with an odd word once in a while, nothing an honest- to-goodness Hiroshima-*kenjin* lets loose," one of the men said.

"Hiroshima-*ken*, Yamaguchi-*ken*, we speak same dialect. Once in a while, 'odd' word slips out," said the pretender. "Maybe my word is good Japanese word, your Hiroshima word is the strange one."

"You speak good, understandable Japanese like the rest of us, Zentaro," he was assured. "You are not a problem. It's those Kumamoto-*kenjin* from Kyushu who speak strangely. They hardly speak Japanese at all."

"To them, everything is *But-ten*. this and *but-ten* that. Nobody tells me what *but-ten* means," another man added.

"They're OK people; they just talk funny. It's those hoity-toity guys from Kyoto area who irritate me. They use that high-tone dialect to let everyone know they didn't come from the hinterlands like the rest of us. Just because they were born near the old royal capital doesn't mean they're high-class."

Regional dialects and customs sharply differentiated the settlers in those times before mass communication rendered individuals into larger stereotype groupings. Where possible, the labor gangs were formed with men from the same geographical areas to promote easy communication and camaraderie within the group.

As day laborers, they were sent to jobs where white farmers and land-owners needed them in the valley. They knew how to farm and how to work hard, and their employers observed that they appeared to live on nothing. They took on projects others refused, and they often worked for less pay. It worked to their benefit to be known as good employees; however, other residents harbored resentments, feeling they were being squeezed out of jobs that should rightfully be theirs.

The rich alluvial soil in the valley between Seattle and Tacoma was ideal for farming, but as lowlands, the area flooded often. Served by two rivers and their tributaries, their surrounding lands blend-ed into one valley. Fed by separate glaciers of Mt. Rainier and the Puyallup River, the valley lay south of the White and Green Rivers, which coursed through a more northerly area before merging into one.

Japanese who settled there came to know the valley as Shirakawa, literally "White River." The Native Americans who originally inhabited the area had been scattered by the settlement of white pioneers early on, well before the Japanese arrived. Much of the area was forested, and the land had to be cleared of trees and stumps. The swamps and marshes had to be drained and ditched before the land was usable for agriculture. The Japanese laborers were hired to do that work during the winter months when the inclement weather allowed little agricultural work to be done on the farms.

Joining a handful of earlier pioneer settlers, the entrepreneurial Japanese laborers who managed to save their money or otherwise found access to sufficient amounts of money or credit, began to lease land, enabling them to start farmsteads of their own in the following years. The ubiquitous Furuya Company, having started a commercial bank in Seattle in 1907, was one source for loans. Another favored source for start-up money was the traditional practice of pooling money commonly utilized in Japan and the Far East. A *tano-moshi* was formed by a group of people who each agreed to contribute a set sum of money to the pool at regular intervals with the purpose of lending the pooled sum to the members in turn.

The lease lands made available to the Japanese were areas considered less desirable either due to unfavorable geographic features or location. Most often, the parcels were undeveloped areas requiring clearing or draining. The new settler's felled trees, dynamited stumps, and cleared the land in preparation for cultivation. Having come from a land with minimal arable land, these settlers who had long practiced intensive farming methods in their considerably smaller plots in Japan carried over their methods to their farms in America. They labored long hours, as they were accustomed, and they managed to eke out a sustainable living. It was a living. It was a hardscrabble life, but for most, the opportunities available to them in America were far greater than if they had stayed in Japan. Luck played a role in a person's success in farming as it does in all endeavors; some families prospered, others did not.

The native Indian inhabitants were now relegated to designated reservations, and there were practically no Chinese laborers living in the valley by this time; they had left the area. The Chinese presence and their experiences in America were as different in as many ways as they were similar to the Japanese experience. As Asians, both were victims of blatant racial hostility and discrimination in different times and ways. The experiences, events, legislative acts——each a distinct strand joined and interwoven—— became the fabric of Asian history in America.

As the first Asians in America, the Chinese pioneers endured the initial brunt of hardships and abuse heaped on the laborers brought in from across the Pacific. The major Chinese migration to America preceded Japanese arrivals by decades. Beginning as a trickle after the Gold Rush of 1848, the upheaval of China's economy following its defeat in the Opium Wars prompted men to sign on for contract work in America. They came primarily from the southern provinces of Guangdong and Fujian, where access to ocean-going ships was available. Enduring a month in transit, these men from the provinces began arriving in San Francisco to fill the labor shortage in the western territories. They worked in mining and at timber mills and for the railroads. They came as sojourners to make their fortune in Gold Mountain and planned to return home to their families with their riches as soon as possible.

Chinese laborers were scattered throughout the West. Their numbers in Seattle increased greatly when the city became a direct route port from the Orient in 1874. Newly arrived immigrants joined countrymen who had already spent long years as contract laborers in America. When the project jobs were finished, such as the completion of a rail line or after the end of their contracts, these men headed for the major cities. In Washington, they flocked to Tacoma and Seattle to find jobs. These men were "strangers from a different shore" who were dissimilar racially and culturally from the white, European-rooted populace.

Public animosity was so great, the Washington territorial government passed anti-Chinese legislation even before the appearance of Chinese in the area. Discriminatory regulations continued to be enacted regularly.

The antagonism toward the Chinese continued to escalate and erupted into acts of mob and gang violence with assaults, beatings, and murder committed against these strangers, the Chinese. It was a time now labeled as the Anti-Chinese Riots of 1885-1886. Many Chinese fled the area, and vigilante gangs rounded up most of those remaining aliens and forced them to board ships returning to the Orient. Only a few were left in Seattle until after the Great Seattle Fire of 1889.

The Federal government enacted the 1882 Chinese Exclusion Act, which prohibited the entry of Chinese laborers into the United States. In 1888, the act was broadened to exclude "all persons of the Chinese race," and in 1902, the law was extended to continue indefinitely. When entry was shut to all Chinese, Japanese immigrant laborers were brought in to fill the job shortage.

As the presence of Japanese increased, the same types of racial animosities and discriminatory tirades increased and were now directed at them. As the forerunners, the Chinese suffered the brunt of public hatred during those times. The Japanese were not subjected to the same abuse initially, but in time, legislation was enacted that put the Japanese in the same category as the Chinese; they were also denied eligibility for citizenship and denied other rights based on their race.

The Japanese immigrants presented additional irritations to the general populace, problems different from the Chinese. Although both immigrant groups initially came to America as contract laborers, sojourners who would return to their homes in Asia, many Japanese intended to stay as permanent residents. They were joined by the sojourners who had changed their minds and decided to become settlers, too. Those settlers who farmed in the valley were scattered among non-Asian neighbors, where there was greater interaction and communication between people as neighbors. Nevertheless, hostilities existed, and periodic outcries for enactment of discriminatory regulations continued. The closer ties between the US and Japanese governments prevented the type of mob violence perpetrated on the Chinese in an earlier era, and these new Asians could not be so easily herded onto boats and sent back to their homes in Asia.

The greatest concentration of Japanese immigrants outside of Hawaii was in California, where the majority of settlers were involved in agriculture. As important and dominant as they were in that endeavor, the levels of hostility directed toward them by non-Japanese farmers and the white populace in general was proportionately greater and acrimonious compared to other states. In 1913, the State of California passed an alien land law, making it unlawful for an alien ineligible for citizenship to own real property, which in effect limited them to land leases, usually of three years' duration. These laws were aimed primarily toward Japanese, and many states throughout the West enacted similar laws. Washington State passed an alien land law in 1921.

Statutes existed in Washington State that prevented Japanese from buying land prior to the passage of the alien land law, however, the new law clarified the ban.

The majority of Japanese immigrants in the area were joined by their wives and picture brides after the first decade of the century, and the second generation, born-in-America children followed. There was a fallow period until these born-in-America children came of age and, as citizens by birth, were eligible to purchase land. At maturity, these children became available for parents to buy land in their names. Until such time, the settlers leased land from landlords who were often absentee owners.

Luck, good and bad, always hovered. The unlucky tenant was the one who, after clearing the leased land and having developed the acreage with hopes for years of bountiful harvest, was told the lease was terminated and was kicked off the property by a greedy landlord. A farmer with a rotten karma could repeat this process over and over, hoping each time his luck had changed and the next landlord would be a fair and decent person. On occasion, someone did find a true Caucasian friend who agreed to buy the desired land in his name until it could be transferred legally to the Japanese farmer.

Masaichi knew he could never improve his lot if he remained a "for-hire" laborer. He decided to lease land and try his luck as an independent farmer. As a relatively early arrival to the valley, he had accumulated years of working knowledge regarding the lay of the land, the soils, the weather, and conditions peculiar to the area. He avoided problems that newcomers were likely to make. In addition, he was still young and willing to take risks.

He chose a parcel of land out of the floodplains with good soil and sun exposure. It was forested and needed to be cleared. Because the site was not readily accessible, clearing the land was difficult, but it made the terms of the lease more favorable. Masaichi started on a small scale, and by methodically clearing cultivatable space, he kept enlarging the productive acreage.

Masaichi determined his land was not suited to growing strawberries, raspberries, and blackberries, which were becoming popular crops among Japanese farmers around Auburn and outside the White River Valley in areas such as Bellevue and Bainbridge Island. Instead, Masaichi decided to follow the example of others who were succeeding with an even more popular crop of that time: potatoes. He did well, but as the number of Japanese settlers joined the ranks of independent farmers, they too took up growing potatoes as their cash crop, and the market became saturated. Masaichi switched to growing cabbage and head lettuce. Initially grown for the local market, they were later shipped east by produce distribution companies located in the valley.

Masaichi had made smart choices about the land he leased and the crops he planted. He worked hard, and he was rewarded. As his sense of well-being grew, he decided it was time to find a wife and start a family. He could not afford to leave his farm fallow and return to Japan to look for a suitable wife. Besides, finding a woman willing to leave Japan and everything familiar to live in America indefinitely was like looking for an oasis in a desert.

Masaichi was one of the immigrant men who sought a picture bride. He sent back word to his family in Hiroshima that he was looking for a spouse to share life with him in America. A woman living in a neighboring village with acceptable credentials was found, and the message was forwarded to the prospective groom. There was no deception in their exchange of personal information, and the photo sent to Japan pictured a rugged, sculpted face topped by short-cropped hair. Masaichi was not handsome, but his bony features conveyed a sense of strength, which worked in his favor. An ever-present hint of a smile and twinkle in his eyes were the less obvious clues of his warmth and good nature.

The woman's name was Itono Sasaki. She was twenty-two years old and had been married previously. She was a victim of an oft-used practice peculiar to people living in the Hiroshima-ken area in that era. For whatever reasons, her husband divorced her after she bore their first child. He kept the son, since the mother could not legally claim the child, and Itono was sent back home to her family. She had no prospects for the future; she was looked upon as a rejected commodity. When the family received inquiries whether there were any marriageable females willing to marry a settler, emigrate and live in America; Itono was persuaded to accept the proposal. She could leave the baggage of a failed first marriage behind, and in a new land, she could seek a better life for herself. Her brother Kanjiro, who had once dreamed of emigrating, had seen his hopes fade as government restrictions closed the flow. He realized this was his opportunity, too. His sister, as a wife of a settler, made him a relative of a settler, the qualifying relationship needed. The loophole in the Gentleman's Agreement let both Itono and Kanjiro to immigrate to America. She married Masaichi by proxy in a simple ceremony with her brother standing in for the absent groom.

Travel and expense money that was sufficient for both her and her brother was sent, and they set sail for Seattle as soon as possible.

The brother and sister took their leave of the family with the formal stoic farewells that rules of etiquette required. As well- mannered, civilized adults, the siblings kowtowed with their perfected bows and checked their emotions, although they each had broken hearts knowing the parting was likely forever. The formalities over, they boarded the train for Kobe with mixed feelings: truly sad yet happy to be traveling together on their new adventure.

The ship had dozens of other picture bride passengers. They would be meeting their husbands for the first time, and they were anxious and apprehensive. They endured the wretched conditions in the hold of the ship during the nearly three weeks of transit crossing the oceans to reach America, and they each had time to wonder: Who's the man waiting for me? What does the future have in store for me?

After what felt like endless hours of standing and waiting in lines to answer questions and to be examined, Itono completed the immigration procedures and walked out the door into the open. A throng of mostly men milled around the doors and waited. Wearing their Sunday best or funeral-going black suits—undoubtedly one and the same—they were as uncomfortable in their starched collars as they were standing around waiting... Waiting in prolonged agony to see, to meet, their new wives.

Itono was dismayed that the waiting crowd was so large. How would she ever find her husband, if he were in the group? She stepped to the side and systematically began checking the faces. Standing outside of the crowd not far from her, she recognized the face; her husband was among the throng of strangers. Masaichi was there to meet her. Smart man. He waited where he could be found. Itono walked up behind him and asked, "Michihira Masaichi, gozonji desu ka? (Do you know the man?)" She was smiling when he turned to face her. He had never heard her voice before nor had he seen her likeness wearing a smile. Her eyes told him she was Itono.

"Ha ha haa," he roared. "I think I saw him leaving with a beautiful *musume-san*, a gorgeous girl, maybe five minutes ago."

Itono faked a frown. "He slipped away, you said. And I've come all the way from Japan to meet him."

The two strangers smiled broadly; the ice was broken. They stepped back from the milling crowd, where they exchanged formal introductions followed by the expected mundane pleasantries. The mood had changed; they fell silent. They were strangers again, unable to find a topic of conversation. They stood stiffly, and to avoid curious inspections of the other, they both looked straight ahead into the crowd pretending to be totally engrossed in their search for Itono's brother Kanjiro. They knew it was all a sham since Masaichi had no idea what her brother looked like. They stood and watched the mini-dramas taking place in the congestion as people looked for their mates or witnessed the initial reactions of couples having found each other.

A woman suddenly darted behind them, and she grabbed Itono's skirt and tried to wrap it around herself. "Hide me! Please hide me!" she pleaded. "I made a mistake, a bad mistake."

"What do you mean? What kind of mistake?" Itono asked as she turned to look at the intruder. She was a young girl who barely looked of marriageable age. Her eyes were wild, and desperation marked her features.

"I can't be married to that old cadger. He's ancient. They sent me a picture of a young, handsome man. They lied to me!" she hissed. "I want to go back on the boat. I want to go back home." Then in a long, forlorn wail, she called for her mother, "Okaaaa-*chan*."

Itono sympathized with the young girl's distress. She, too, had called for her mother when she was ousted from her first husband's home. She knew she was in no position to offer any real assistance at the moment, but she would give it a try.

"Take hold of my husband's arms and hide your face in his sleeves. You will be hidden between us, and the three of us will slowly walk toward that building. Then go inside the building and try to find an authority to help you."

Masaichi was flustered by the young girl's unexpected interruption, but he stood in wonder as his bride had quickly come up with a solution that satisfied the girl. He had said nothing and walked along with the females as Itono had outlined. At the building's entrance, the girl ran from view into the building and away from the reprehensive old fart.

"It's unfortunate some people use a ruse to get something they want. I think that is dishonest and worse when someone else is hurt," said Masaichi.

Itono realized she was lucky. She had married a man she could respect. "I agree with you, husband," she said with a smile.

"That young girl was deceived as she claimed. Her husband had submitted someone else's picture, no doubt. I've heard of such incidents before. If she wasn't exaggerating and he is very old, he knew his chances of catching a wife of childbearing age were remote had he submitted his own picture." He continued, "I feel sorry for the young girl. She deserves a nice young husband."

Itono knew then she was twice lucky. She had married a man she liked as well as respected.

Masaichi, in turn, had learned his bride was quick-witted with a kind heart.

"Over this way!" Itono shouted to be heard while waving her hands wildly. Her actions were hardly proper etiquette for a Japanese woman in public, but she was willing to forgo such proprieties in this situation; she needed results. "What took you so long?" she asked Kanjiro when he reached her.

"A man in the crowd grabbed my sleeves and cornered me.

He said he was looking for his wife who was lost." "Was the man young or old?"

"*Nani?* What? He... he was obviously well past middle age. I guess that makes him old." Getting past his sister's interruption, he continued, "Well, he wouldn't let go of my sleeve. He acted as if I had something to do with his wife's disappearance. He was rude and thoroughly obnoxious. Why do you ask about his age?"

"*Alla maa...gomen-kudasai-mase*, Masaichi-*san*. I didn't introduce you to my brother," Itono said as she bowed low, then lower as her head nodded with emphasis.

Thereupon, Kanjiro bowed to his brother-in-law. "Please forgive my sister's thoughtless rudeness. She's too candid and gets carried away with her enthusiasms. Unfortunately, she tends to forget her manners at those times."

Masaichi had been so engrossed in watching the siblings' free-wheeling exchange, he, too, had forgotten the proper introductions had not been made. "We're family now. Let's forget all this formality," he said to them both.

Itono smiled with relief.

The house was a ramshackle wooden shack. "This is our home," Masaichi had said. Itono studied her crude surroundings as images of the home she left in Japan came to mind. Her parents' house was small and plain with few amenities, which reflected their meager circumstances. In comparison to her new home, it was a gemlike palace.

"*Don-na*," Itono addressed Masaichi politely. "Husband, this American house is so different and strange. Do you give me permission to add things that will make it more familiar to me?"

Masaichi assured her the house was her area to make changes as she pleased. It had been a bachelor's pad, finished and furnished with bare essentials, with little thought given to amenities. It was little different from the first house he had stayed in with the labor gang ten years before. Using that structure as a pattern, he had added few creature comforts when he built his own abode.

In the winter, the cold and wind blew in through the cracks and holes in and between the planks that made-up the exterior wall; a single layer of siding separated the inhabitants from the elements. The floorboards––where they existed––were as full of cracks and knotholes as the walls. The futon mats were laid on those boarded areas raised above the dirt floors. Whether boards or bare soil, the floors were cold all the time. A dwelling cruder than a humbler man's home in Japan, it followed in principle their tradition of providing summer comfort over winter warmth.

Itono found little time to make the improvements to their living quarters as she had originally envisioned. She did diligently stuff wads of paper in the cracks between the wooden boards to reduce the airflow, but it was an endless task and offered minimal resistance to the cold. Endless, too, was the daily work that had to be done. In addition to the cleaning, laundry, and cooking chores performed exclusively by females, she was also expected to help her husband by working in the fields. Itono was no stranger to such labor having participated during labor-intensive seasons in the planting cycle at home in Japan. But, the labor she and other immigrant wives were expected to undertake was far greater than she had anticipated. She persevered.

"*Gam-batte*" was the rallying cry on the tip of their tongues, a mot to the Japanese all shared: "Endure. Persist."'

Itono was not unhappy; she only wished for periods when she was not so bone tired. Thoughts of her brother Kanjiro popped into her head at odd times, and she was reminded of shared moments when they were growing up, unaware of what life had in store for them. A momentary flush of remorse for their separation was inevitably followed by feelings of guilt for not writing to him as often as she should. He had traveled on to California to meet his contacts shortly after their arrival in Seattle. Since that time, she occasionally found a scribbled note from him in her mailbox. The brief letters were always filled with as many apologies for his lapses in communication as there was information about him. His demon was the relentless heat and sun, inescapable in the California desert farming communities where he found work. "Sister, you found haven in a cooler temperate climate; How I envy you," he wrote.

All the more, Itono missed his counsel and company and wished he could have stayed north with her. It was not to be; it was not her karma.

Masaichi felt truly settled with a companionable wife and with the beginnings of a baby on the way. He felt he needed to escape the uncertainties ever present in plant cultivation, and switching to dairy farming offered the opportunity of steady, year-round work. A contract laborer had learned the trade working for white dairy owners in the area and had started his own dairy and shared his expertise with others. A handful of settlers had already made the change, and Masaichi decided to join them. Other Japanese settlers became interested and joined them; the valley landscape became dotted with numerous dairy farms alongside the increasing numbers of produce farms. In time, a Japanese dairy cooperative was formed, and the milk their dairies produced was delivered to all parts of the region.

Masaichi found himself clearing land once again, this time for pasture. On a site closer to Auburn in the township of Christopher, he started his new endeavor. In addition to a barn for the cows, his priority was to build a more substantial house for Itono, who thanked her gods for finding her such a considerate husband. The requisite outhouse was placed some distance from the house, and a second little hut was built to house the *ofuro*. The deep, water tight wooden tub with a fireproof metal plate bottom was constructed atop a fire pit. The water-filled tub was heated by the wood fire Itono lit and stoked, before returning to the house to prepare dinner for the family and any laborers they had hired that day. The water in the *ofuro* tub was ready for soaking by the time Masaichi came in from his chores, and he bathed and soaked before dinner, as did their hired help. Only after her chores were completed late at night could Itono take her turn in the hot, soothing water, where her weary body found relief and the burdens of the day melted away. It was a luxury that made life tolerable, and even the god-awful odors of the dairy seemed less noxious. Admittedly, their noses became desensitized to it in time.

The cows needed to be milked twice a day, every day, without any holiday or vacation breaks, and a dairy farmer, unlike a produce farmer, had no slack months in the winter. Such a daily year-round operation leaves little open time, but Masaichi managed his chores and still participated in all manner of organizations: the Hiroshima *Kenjin- kai*, the dairy farmers' cooperative, the Valley Buddhist Church, and other sundry activities. He was a joiner and an active member who was sought by others for his enthusiasm and generosity.

A BABY IS BORN

The numbers of Japanese contract laborers diminished as the supply of new recruits was cut off. Those who did not return home stayed as landed immigrants and became settlers who were joined by family and relatives. The population of Japanese living in the White River Valley and its surroundings grew exponentially from the turn of the century. The total number of Japanese living in the state of Washington was actually a small fraction compared to the total state population, but their concentration in a few locales, especially in Seattle, Tacoma, and the valley between, made it appear they were much greater in number. As children were born and the settlers became family oriented, a Buddhist church had been established, and social organizations were formed in the valley much like in the two neighboring cities. The Christian presence among the farmers was an Episcopal mission and a group of Methodists, a small fraction compared with the "born in the church" Buddhist majority. Whatever their religious or prefectural affiliations, there were events encompassing the entire valley settlement, unifying and identifying them as a community.

Daughter Aiko was born in March 1912. Masaichi was delighted to be a father, and though he wanted a son, he was happy a daughter meant Itono would eventually have a helper with the chores. Itono was delighted with her baby daughter for reasons that went beyond a future chore-sharer. She poured her affections on the child, remembering how she had been denied the privilege with her firstborn. Her husband made no comment about his wife's lavish pampering of the child, a girl child at that, and he marveled how well behaved and sweet-tempered their daughter was in spite of the spoiling. The child followed after her mother, mimicking her routines, and after learning them, she took on less strenuous chores as soon as she could manage, then assumed them as her responsibility. Aiko was cooking the rice for their meals by the age of five. However, when she started primary school, her knowledge and ability to perform household chores meant nothing. Aiko entered school with no knowledge of English. She spoke and understood only Japanese. It was her only language. She felt utterly humiliated by this experience, which remained a thorn in her side and influenced many of her future decisions. This predicament was not uncommon among the early Nisei children whose exposure to spoken

English was extremely limited until they attended school. They lived in Japanese-centric homes and communities.

Itono and Masaichi with daughter Aiko

Aiko understood she needed to study diligently to learn the language and stay on par with her classmates academically. She believed one way to accomplish this goal was to attend school every day and never be absent; each school year she received her "perfect attendance" certificate. The schoolwork was not difficult, and as soon as Aiko overcame her initial language handicap, she was accepted as an equal member of the class. She was physically small and retreated into the background with shyness, but she was sweet and forever helpful, with a good head of common sense. She was an introverted version of her extroverted father; there was little to dislike. Little to no homework was assigned to the students since they all had chores to perform once they returned home from school.

The jobs to be done were endless, but even the most hardworking knew to avoid "all work and no play." Churchgoing every Sunday was a Christian ritual, though services for the dead––whether the long-dead or funerals for newly deceased brought them to church regularly; they were gatherings, not happy socializing events. It was the holiday celebrations, American and Japanese, that lightened their lives, and the Emperor's Birthday picnic was the grandest. Besides the Japanese finger foods every family prepared, the sponsoring committee purchased snacks and beverages to overflowing. Games were organized, and races for all age groups were held. Aiko was never to forget how, riding piggyback on older Masae's back, they had come within in a hair after the winner, and were relegated to second place, missing the prize. A picnic was a time and place where exuberance dispelled gloom, and chores were forgotten for a few hours.

Mother Itono felt her strength ebbing away. She relied on Aiko's help, and the six-year-old performed whatever tasks were asked of her. Itono's constant bouts of ill health were worrisome to Masaichi, and he made concessions when she felt too weak to work, and asking him to remain silent about her condition. When Itono became pregnant again, her health deteriorated even further. The son and heir Masaichi so wanted died soon after birth. Itono never regained her strength, and she, too, died not long after.

Masaichi intended no disrespect, but the time of the funeral and every subsequent seven-day service was squeezed in-between chores and milking the cows. Masaichi curtailed any superfluous activities during this period of mourning, mindful not to agitate Itono's spirit while it still wrestled with more profound resolutions about itself in nether space. After the forty-ninth-day service, when her spirit was freed, even a devout Buddhist like Masaichi was relieved that services for the deceased had ended until the one-year anniversary.

"*To-san*, why is a service on the forty-ninth day? Why not on the fiftieth day?" Six-year-old Aiko asked.

Curse the day Itono taught her to count, thought Masaichi before he patiently began the explanation. "The service is the seventh one in a series of seven-day services. If you count to seven, then add another seven, and another seven again, then continue adding sevens seven times in all, you will end-up with the number forty-nine."

Aiko sat bent over, eyes focused on her fingers as they wiggled in sequence as she counted. "*Ah-yah*. I lost count!" she said as she vigorously shook her hands to erase the calculation. "I have to start all over."

"She's lonely with no one to *ai-te* her, no one to keep her company," he said to himself.

She dropped her hands when she dropped her interest in counting sevens. She posed another question: "Why? *To-san*, why is the forty-ninth day important?"

Another cursed day for Itono for always explaining everything to her. How to explain this?

She watched him, waiting expectantly for an answer.

"On the forty-ninth day, when the soul…" He pointed to his chest. "A person's soul is invisible, and it lives in the body. The soul is the real essence; the body is only a temporary covering." She remained silent as she listened. He continued, "After a person dies, the soul must come to terms with its new bodiless state. It passes through seven different stages and finally after the seventh stage on the forty-ninth day, the soul is released and doesn't have to hover around anymore. It's free to go into a new body, to be reincarnated for another try toward ultimately achieving nirvana."

"Huh? Oh…" Subsequent explanations, though simplified, always varied in the details, which confused Aiko more than before. She decided it was all beyond her grasp.

Masaichi and Itono had had a warm relationship, and her illness had been the only major negative aspect to their marriage. He felt he owed her spirit peace and tranquility, which the burial of her ashes in Japan would afford. Itono's ashes were placed in an ornate brass urn where they could rest comfortably. The urn and contents were deposited at the Buddhist temple for safekeeping until the time Masaichi could retrieve them to take back to Japan and fulfill his obligation.

Aiko was motherless at age six, and Masaichi was without a wife/helper again. Aiko did the best she could to assume the chores and help her father before and after school, but a farmer needs a wife and sons to share the workload. Masaichi loved Aiko, and she adored him. She was as mindful as any parent could wish for in a child. Her life, he knew, would not become any easier when he remarried. To mitigate the distress Aiko was bound to encounter, Masaichi promised Aiko he would never relegate her to less than a much-loved child with equal status as any future siblings. Aiko was pragmatic; that was her strength. Whatever course her life should take, she understood her survival depended on remaining flexible.

The forty-nine days well past, Masaichi felt he, too, was freed to resume a normal life, and that included plans for the future. Absolutely no marriage should take place before the one-year anniversary of Itono's passing, but he felt he should begin the process of seeking a new wife quickly since entry into the United States was scheduled to end for all Japanese nationals in a few years, and his age could be a hindrance in attracting a suitable spouse. He wrote and asked relatives in Japan to look for a bride for him once again. This time around, he specifically requested the candidate be an able-bodied woman of childbearing age; someone who was strong and healthy. His own personal information was expanded to include his age as approaching forty, a farmer operating a dairy south of Seattle in the White River Valley, and a widower with one young daughter.

Hayame's family and kin were not strangers to Masaichi's family since they lived in close proximity to each other in Hiroshima-*ken*. She and two sisters had actually been born in Hawaii when the parents lived in the islands as contract workers. The girls were sent back to Japan to be reared by grandparents when the parents transferred to the mainland to work. Additional children were born while they were in America, and though they had spent many years abroad, they chose not to become settlers. They returned to Japan, where they were reunited as a family——a family that continued to increase in number as more children were born. When the inquiry seeking a wife for Masaichi reached Hayame's family, immigrating to America was not an alien concept.

Hayame was the oldest child and at the age of eighteen was considered an eligible candidate for the marriage. Although the prospective husband was twice her age, he was not too old, and the likelihood of his maturity squelching her often unrestrained exuberance was considered a positive attribute. The two families conferred and decided the marriage was amenable. She fulfilled his request for a healthy young woman, and the prospective husband's financial prospects were better than promising. That fact was confirmed by mutual acquaintances living in the valley.

The designated wife had grown up believing an arranged marriage was an arrangement negotiated by parents whose motives were to create or enhance familial bonds; love was not part of the pact. Hayame docilely accepted the marriage arrangements made for her and became a picture bride to a man she had never met. She felt a tinge of trepidation when told the husband chosen for her was a much older man, a man twice her age. In her private dreams, she had hoped for a husband like the young bucks she favored for those sporting frolics far from censoring eyes. She had an enviable array of willing suitors, but they had been rejected by her parents. By arranging Hayame's marriage to a settler, the way was eased for her siblings to gain entry to America and to maintain useful connections for the future.

A Remarriage

In the years since his first marriage, Masaichi had been exposed to bits and pieces of American customs in the past dozen years, and he wisely incorporated those benefiting him and his causes. When his young bride arrived in Seattle, he was there to whisk her away on a weekend honeymoon in the big city. They ate at a different restaurant for each meal, shopped for an American-style wardrobe for her, and extravagantly loaded up on preserved foodstuffs for their pantry to last until their next foray into Nihonmachi. Hired help had milked the cows during Masaichi's short absence, but he could never stay away long in his business, so they wistfully started their journey home traveling south through the valley. Hayame was wide-eyed looking at the sweep of her new environment. The hills to the east and west were spread so far apart, and the horizon to the south rambled on until it ran into a mountain.

"*Anata*, husband, what is the name of the mountain? It looks like our Fujiyama's brother."

"It's known as *Tacoma-no-Fuji*," Masaichi answered. "American name is harder to pronounce: Re-ni-a."

Hayame continued inspecting the landscape. "The plants and scenery are like Japan except everything is stretched with lots of space between. So much open space, so many trees, everything is much larger, and…"

"Over there is Orillia. I had first farm there," Masaichi said. "On the other side in the house over there, that's Otoshi-*san*'s place. They're Hori-*san*'s relatives."

The names of Japanese settlers were rattled off one after another once they passed Tukwila. Easy-on-the-ear Japanese names were interspersed with strange-sounding names of nearby communities such as Thomas, O'Brien, Kent, and Auburn. Later there were names like Sumner, Fife, and Puyallup to learn.

Remembering those strange sounding area names were apt to be a struggle, but the fact that so many Japanese lived in the valley and were known to her husband reassured Hayame. She knew she was not alone, and she would have new friends in short order.

Aiko was waiting for their arrival when they finally got home. As the newlyweds reached the door, she called out, "*To-san*, you're supposed to carry your bride into the house."

"*Nani*? What are you talking about?" her father asked. "It's American custom."

"I'm too old for this kind American custom. She weighs more than a sack of rice."

"Of course I weigh more than a sack of rice. You've been feeding me ever since I got to Seattle," Hayame said before bursting with laughter.

Bride and groom entered the house in a jolly mood, each walking in on their own. They kicked off their shoes as soon as they passed through the door and slipped into awaiting zori.

Aiko bowed politely to Hayame. "Welcome to your new home," she said.

"Our home, Aiko-*chan*. This is also your home, *neh*," she said matter-of-factly as she glanced around looking for a strategically placed cushion on the rough-hewn wooden floor. Spying a single *zabuton*, gracing a chair, she plopped herself on it without ceremony. "That was a long ride from Seattle. I need something soft to sit on."

Masaichi slid onto the well-worn picnic table bench, having been displaced from his usual head-of-the-table cushioned chair. "Aiko, we'll have to get ourselves some new cushions. This new mistress needs a soft seat, and so do I."

"Why didn't you say this was your throne?" Hayame said.

Trying to get beyond her first impressions, Aiko, still serious, looked up and inquired, "How would you like me to address you? For me to call you by your given name is disrespectful. Oba-*san* is inappropriate. Would you prefer Okaa-*san*, Kaa-*san*, Ka-*chan*, or maybe Mother or Mama?"

"You can address me any way most comfortable to you, Aiko-*chan*. Just don't call me *Obaa-san* yet. Let me be a mother before I'm called grandmother," she answered with a chuckle.

"I will send you back home to Japan if you're an old *Obaa-san*. They told me you were young, they did," Masaichi said in joining the fray. He had watched his bride and daughter's banter and knew everything bode well.

"Since I'm allowed to choose, I'll call you…Mama." Aiko announced. She had always called her mother *Ka-chan*, and she was relieved it could be reserved for her birth mother. Calling her new mother Mama seemed so new and Americanized. Additionally, it let others know their relationship immediately. "I'll boil the water for tea now. To-*san*, did you buy some *okashi* treats we can nibble on with our tea?"

The young bride was extroverted and exuberant, as Masaichi had been told. She brought life and a breath of fresh air with her, and though her chatty irrelevancies were merely noise at times, it contrasted sharply with Itono's disposition, which had turned somber and cheerless as her health deteriorated. The pall that had descended on their home vanished, and the sun shone through brighter than before. The household took on a spirited air, and Masaichi smiled and laughed often, happy with the positive turn in his life. Hayame realized she had not landed on a bed of roses, but her situation was not as bad as she had feared. She needed to make a few adjustments, which could be accomplished in time.

Hayame's youthful disappointments were soon tempered as she realized she had been lucky in her marriage. Her husband was indeed older than the man of her youthful dreams, but he was not too old nor was he an ogre. A second-time husband also had advantages. The first wife had softened the rougher edges of an essentially good man who had learned to be a considerate spouse. And an uncomplaining and willing assistant in the form of a stepdaughter had been bequeathed to her by her predecessor.

She was delighted with the little bonus who came with her new husband; she was an endearing, ready-made daughter who assumed responsibilities beyond the usual eight-year-old. She was a little sister, only better. They had no rivalries, and they each accepted the other without reservations.

Hayame also experienced what she had been told happens: love grows between partners in a marriage. She understood, too, that love could exist just as likely outside of a marriage; love was not necessarily an exclusive entity.

Masaichi could not have asked for a more willing and hardworking helpmate of a wife. With boundless energy, she did what was required outside the house in addition to her domestic chores inside the house. The valley community readily accepted her cheerful participation as she accompanied her husband to functions and actively involved herself in the *Fujin-kai*, the local Buddhist ladies' auxiliary. Her role was the willing and able assistant who rolled up her sleeves to get the job done; she was not the boss who gave the orders without getting her hands dirty. She was a gem.

His new wife's absences from gatherings were usually no longer than a couple of months following the birth of a baby. Daughter Masaye was followed by daughters Kimiye and Hamayo. Aiko was the ever-present assistant to help Hayame with the growing family, which was increasing by one every other year. She felt she had little time to nurture outside interests of her own, but with so many babies to keep an eye on and with the comings and goings of hired help working in the dairy, the household was always bustling: *nigi-yaka*, noisy. With constant distractions, there was no time for contemplation or to even think about the lack of such time.

Modern conveniences taken for granted by later generations were not yet available or even invented. Household chores were a time-consuming drudgery in those "good old days," but there was one convenient service, now gone, that was available to housewives stuck on the farm. It was the peddler who traveled the countryside from one Japanese house to another selling his wares. The store came to them. Especially welcome were the food vendors and fishmongers selling fish and tofu products and the grocers with myriad Japanese specialty items. Salesmen from Furuya came and took orders in addition to independents with their trucks loaded with goods to sell. The valley families, and especially the wives, welcomed their stops for the convenience and for the brief social interactions when they could collect news and gossip along with making purchases. Hayame had her own garden where she grew vegetables for the family's needs, but she usually bought something from the produce vendor as well as the others to make sure they made a stop; especially that nice, accommodating young hunk good for a chat and a smile.

A Little Leisure Time

As the settlers became comfortable with their lot, there were more opportunities to relax and indulge in play. Baseball had been introduced into Japan in the latter nineteenth century, and the Japanese embraced it as their favorite team sport. The game had a particular appeal to the Japanese, and this was true for the settlers as well. Japanese immigrant groups along the West Coast with sizable populations organized local club teams. The teams were initially formed by Issei; later, as Nisei boys began graduating from high schools, they joined the sports clubs, enabling them to continue their involvement in the sport. The valley produced its share of athletes in sufficient numbers to form several teams who competed against each other and with teams from Tacoma and Seattle. Seattle's Asahi team was semipro caliber, and they occasionally played against Caucasian teams.

Masaichi with brother, wife Hayame and daughters

Baseball was the one pastime Masaichi loved above all others, but organized sports did not interest Hayame at all. Masaichi was never a player himself, even as a youth, but he was an active supportive spectator: the noisy fanatic fan. An unofficial cheerleader for the local teams, he rallied the spectators without the acrobatics. He did jump and stomp his feet and wave his arms and hands, but he was best shouting encouragement whether his favored team was winning or losing. He questioned the umpires' calls noisily when such calls went against his team. He cupped his hands to be heard, yelling: "Bring the eyeglasses! Lend him your *megane*!" "Yuhhhh… Go! Go! Go! Ayah, pop ball!" "This umpire has a crooked eye!" "Ohhh, ala, ala! That NO strike. Missed the plate by mile!" "Atta boy… Strike him OUT!!" His cajoling and commentaries from the sidelines were loud and uninhibited; his enthusiasm for the game was contagious, and it ignited the other fans to join in the verbal fracas. Everyone had a good time, especially Masaichi.

He began taking Aiko with him to watch games regularly after Itono's death in hopes of distracting her. Since he was unable to persuade Hayame of the game's merits, he continued to take Aiko along to have a sounding board at home to talk through the finer points of the game. She became a true and ardent fan. Baseball fever had bitten her, too, although she kept her commentaries at a civilized pitch.

Valley farmers supported other sports, such as sumo and two judo dojos, as well as basketball and football teams. Those sports had their adherents, but baseball remained everyone's favorite and the most popular.

For those with less interest in sports, local dance/drama schools, generally attended by second-generation Nisei students, periodically put on theatrical performances locally. Traditional odori dances and *shibai* dramas were their ties to their culture and the local shows were as welcomed by the valley settlers as any show put on in Seattle's Nippon Kan Hall. These shows were Hayame's favorites, and she never missed a performance. Masaichi ceded to his wife's enthusiasm and became an active supporter of the dance/drama troupe, too. He learned entertainers not only performed make-believe, but they inhabited a different world that was entertaining itself.

When the announcement was made in early summer of 1927, the news traveled through the community like wildfire. The sponsoring Osaka Mainichi newspaper was planning to send Japan's high school baseball tournament's winning team on its first goodwill tour of North America, and the White River Valley had been selected as the first stop on their tour before they headed south to California. Shirakawa had been selected over Tacoma and Seattle. Masaichi was ecstatic when word reached him. Life couldn't get any better than this.

Preparations were made for the August 24 event. A team of star Nisei players from local high schools and recent graduates was formed to play against the visitors. An after-game banquet and festivities were planned by the Nihonjin-kai, monies were collected for the fete and for gifts to be presented to the touring guests.

Masaichi managed to find hired help for the day, freeing him to witness the greatly anticipated game. By all accounts, it was a well-played game witnessed by three thousand spectators. The champion Wakayama-ken team won over the locals by a score of two to zero. The commemorating banquet that followed in Auburn was an all-out affair, the likes of which had not been seen before.

The heyday for local Nikkei baseball and championship teams was yet to come.

Hayame's fourth child was a boy. Masaichi loved his daughters, all four of them; however, a son carries on a name for generations, and he was happy. He cooed and teased the baby like a first-time father. He expanded his dreams, incorporating his son and heir in his future endeavors.

"I made an appointment with the photographer for next week, Saturday morning, eight o'clock. Everyone dressed and ready so we can leave by seven o'clock," Masaichi announced as though he were an officer giving orders to his troops. Actually, the room was empty; his only audience was Hayame, and she frowned at the announcement.

"Husband, what's the occasion? We had a family picture taken a few years ago. Why do we need to take another picture?"

"That was before son Katsumi was born. We need a picture of the whole family," he said with pride. "I want everyone to see and know what fine children I have…and what a pretty young wife." He uncharacteristically patted her lap as she pouted on the bench next to him.

"Even your young wife won't look her best at that hour." She was annoyed, knowing the ordeal involved finishing breakfast and the chores plus getting the children dressed in their party best, all completed before such an early departure. It'll be a wild scramble. Like all men, he doesn't think about such things. It wasn't the extra work she minded; Hayame just didn't like to be unduly rushed.

"It's the time after milking the cows."

"Nobody dresses up in their best clothes at seven in the morning."

"Aiko will help with the children."

"Ai-*chan*, please come," she called loudly to be heard in the bedrooms. "Come here a minute. Your father has something to tell you."

Whenever Mama was displeased with To-*san*, she disclaimed him, and he became Aiko's father until the parents made up. She decided to take her time before stepping in the arena between them.

"Hayame, when we're finished taking picture, we'll have time to eat chop suey at that Chinese restaurant."

"The Chinese have more sense than we do. They wait until a sensible hour to open for business."

"If they're still closed, we can go to that American-style diner. Where was it located?"

"It's too expensive to pay for food the children don't eat." "Then you can make some *musubi* to take with us for lunch." "That's a terrible idea. I already have too many things to do to get ready, making lunch…"

"After lunch, we can go shopping at Natsuhara's Store." He had said the magic word: shopping.

His wife beamed, and she was suddenly recharged with energy. The magic potion was powerful, indeed. She was hardly a child bride at this point. Charged with five youngsters, she was as responsible and hard-working as any wife in the valley. Her husband, who had no qualms saying how lucky he had been with his second wife, was still taken aback when one of her unexpected bouts of annoyance surfaced. It had taken a while, but he had learned she could be quickly converted to smiles by using a little guile. Those girlish swings in mood, he was convinced, just enhanced her charm.

Instead of walking to the stove to make a pot of tea as Masaichi expected, Hayame walked directly to a spot behind his chair and began massaging his shoulders with her strong, dimpled hands. "We need so many things. I should make a list, *neh*," she mumbled as she squeezed and released his taut sinews and muscles.

When Aiko entered the scene, her father was groaning from pain and pleasure as the massage escalated to sharp raps with the sides of Hayame's hands on his shoulders.

"*Ii-tai, iitai*. That hurts… Ahhh…that feels good…" He said as he continued moaning.

Aiko knew they had made up while she had dawdled in the bedroom after being called.

WIDOWHOOD

Not long after the picture-taking appointment, Masaichi drove into Seattle to attend a friend's wake service. It was a journey to the city he made several times a year. He was unusually tired that evening and friends tried to persuade him to spend the night and get some sleep; he could drive home in the morning. He deferred, saying the cows needed to be milked in the early morning, and he set off for home that night. The drive home was long, especially over poorly lit streets. His mangled body was found the next day in his overturned truck in a ditch along the side of a road.

The valley farmers rallied around the young widow, and a funeral worthy of Masaichi's standing in the community was held. Businesses, associations, and friends sent flower wreaths; the abundant display was a testimony to the man's wide-ranging influence and friendships. "Pull in closer together, *mina-san*. I'm trying to get you all in the picture," the photographer said to the crowd attending the funeral.

The dairy and its implements were sold, and Hayame moved to Seattle with her children. With her husband's soul at peace, his business affairs settled, and the double-indemnity proceeds from his life insurance policy safely in her possession, she found herself unencumbered and a relatively rich widow for those times. She gathered up all five children, including stepdaughter Aiko, and sailed to Japan with her husband's ashes in tow.

Her children were young, and they adjusted to their new environment easily; Aiko was not as lucky. Her knowledge of Japanese customs and traditions were bastardized versions. They had been adapted to fit the immigrant environment in America. She had not been made aware of the differences, and she felt as alien in Japan as she had felt when she first entered elementary school without any knowledge of the English language. She was a teenager living in Japan with rudimentary reading and writing skills in Japanese, which prompted taunts and insults from less-than-sympathetic classmates. She was the nail that stood out and had to be pounded down to be like the others.

"*America-jin, America-jin,*" the girls spit out from a distance. When she innocently neglected to add subtle linguistic and cultural niceties so deeply rooted in their inclusive society, she was also snubbed by the adults who called her ill-mannered and crude.

In America, everyone considers me Japanese, Aiko reflected. Here in Japan, they're calling me an American. Yes, I was born in the United States. I guess they're right after all; I am American, and my children born in America will grow up knowing they're American. They'll never have doubts of their own identity.

Meanwhile, Hayame, with her indomitable spirit and insurance riches, found diversions suitable for a young woman not yet thirty years old.

Hayame was no longer a youth in the eyes of society. She was a widow with children and responsibilities, and she should behave accordingly, she was told. The creeping austerities of the Depression made a frivolous and unproductive lifestyle inappropriate for such dire times, and Japan was enforcing militaristic and rigid policies in ordinary lives now. Hayame's ideas had changed while living in America, too. The strict rules of conduct imposed on a mature widowed woman in Japan felt restrictive, and she yearned for the independence she had experienced living abroad.

She decided to leave her two younger daughters with their grandparents and relatives to be raised in Japan, much as she had spent her own youth. She packed up her other two children older daughter Masaye and young son Katsumi, along with Aiko, and headed back to Seattle. Hayame lost some money in an unfavorable money exchange, and she had also been persuaded to invest in several parcels of land by weary relatives in an attempt to stem her free-spending ways. Upon her return, she was not quite the rich widow she had been on her departure.

Hayame sent Aiko off to work for a white family in Bellingham. She, through connections with friends, found a job working as a chambermaid in the Atlas Hotel to support herself and her children.

Before long, with savvy advice and by using her still-remaining cash reserves, Hayame was able to lease a small grocery store up the hill from Nihonmachi on Yesler Way. The stand-alone wood building conveniently had living quarters in back of the retail area with bedrooms on the second level. Across the street on Eighth Avenue lived her friends, the Terada family, where Aiko met Yoshi.

CHAPTER 8

Marriage and Family, 1933-1940

IT HAD NOT TAKEN MANY visits for Yoshi to learn Aiko's life story. Precocious about accepting responsibility, she was that obedient, self-effacing, five-year-old elf grown to adulthood who had garnered little acknowledgment and few rewards. Consummately serious, she was bereft of carefree light-heartedness common to one so young, that is, except when it involved baseball. She sang not a note; a grade school reprimand had forever squelched her songs. Aiko's usual dour countenance was further accentuated by the unstylish clothes she preferred to wear. A typical last girl sought out to step onto a dance floor, she escaped the wallflower tag only by missing her last two years of high school while spending those years in Japan. On her return, she rekindled her friendship with several close girlfriends from the valley, but she was the outsider who eagerly listened to others' adventures, not having participated in any of her own.

When Yoshi assumed the role of Aiko's Prince Charming and mentor extraordinaire, he presented her with small gifts in addition to showing her a larger world beyond Nihonmachi with promises of travel and experiences further afield. The gifts were incidental things that more privileged women would have considered trivial, but they were what a poor man could afford, and they were given with a generous spirit. The engagement ring Yoshi bought for Aiko was set with a diamond, best described as smallish, and set in dull platinum, not gold. Aiko was overwhelmed by his giving spirit. It was more than she had ever expected, and she always wondered how she had become so lucky.

To placate the noisy advocates of tradition, Yoshi agreed to designate a *baishaku-nin*, a go-between whose duties of marriage broker were not necessary in this case, and the title was to be an honorary role in name only. Yoshi had reluctantly accepted certain customs of the community without chafing at what he considered unwarranted controls on his life. Occasionally he vented a little steam then prudently resumed his cover of an anonymous local resident.

Plans for a Buddhist ceremony were made. Arrangements to rent tuxedos for the groom and his attendants, rental arrangements for the bride's gown and her attendant's apparel were discussed with the clothier in Nihonmachi, and an appropriate dark kimono was borrowed from friends for Aiko. Just as the final plans were being completed, Aiko's cousin died suddenly. The wedding date had to be postponed, and all plans were put on hold. To ignore the mourning period of such a close relative was crass and disrespectful and likely to invoke bad luck upon the irreverent kin. The wedding was to be rescheduled for a day as soon as it was prudent to celebrate.

"Nomura-*san*, shall we reserve the chapel for a Saturday or Sunday wedding, one year hence?" the priest asked.

"We're not planning to postpone our marriage for a year.

Why such a long delay?" Yoshi asked.

"The one-year death anniversary…"

"After the forty-nine days, the spirit of my wife's dear deceased cousin can come to the wedding and help us celebrate."

"But…but…"

"Could we reschedule the wedding in eight weeks? That will give everyone time…"

Who is this whipper-snapper? I've never seen him at our services. What does he know…?

Aiko wore the traditional white gown during the wedding ceremony and pre-ceremony photo session. The bride then set aside the white and changed into a traditional black kimono for the celebratory dinner, which was held at the Nihonmachi Chinese restaurant popular in the community. The restaurant, owned and operated by Japanese, employed Japanese cooks whose menu of Chinese-style foods were infused by Japanese flavors. There was scant resemblance between the "Chinese" foods served there and the more authentic Chinese meals one found several blocks to the south in Chinatown presided by Chinese cooks and patronized by Chinese customers. However, the authenticity of those meals could sometimes be questioned, too, for where in China is chop suey ever served? In any event, the pseudo-Chinese banquet food the guests enjoyed was several times removed from any original recipes.

The wedding guest list was relatively small, but the wedding ceremony and banquet displayed all the standard flourishes. The groom bore the full expenses for the wedding as was the custom, and Yoshi could have kept the nuptials simple and less costly, but he indulged Aiko and let her have a wedding fulfilling her girlish dreams.

The newlyweds settled into the little cottage on the hillside next to the greenhouses. Yoshi tended to the fall flowers, which had to be readied for market, and his bride set about making the bachelor pad into a tidy home. As work for the season eased, Aiko realized she was pregnant. Happily, the two set about preparing for parenthood as they waited out the pregnancy.

Aiko's contractions began in mid-May. The midwife was summoned to assist during birth. Yoshi was in a dilemma; it was Saturday, his day to go into town to the Pike Place Market to sell his hothouse tomatoes. The sale brought in a few precious dollars, and there would be no profit if the ripe tomatoes were turned over to someone else to sell. The midwife who had also acted as their go-between, assured Yoshi his wife was in good hands and that he should leave for the market, because a nervous expectant father would only be in the way.

The birth was unexpectedly difficult, and Aiko was physically drained. The baby girl had survived the ordeal better than her mother and thrived. Aiko was advised not to have any more children. Her recovery took an achingly long time, and she forever lost her youthful reserves of energy. Had he had a clue that Aiko's labor was to be so difficult, Yoshi would have taken Aiko to a hospital with proper facilities and an attending physician for the delivery. This precaution was not taken, and Yoshi lived with that regret. The demands of parenthood merely added to their chores, but the new parents were happy.

The Family Moves

The lease on the nursery property was ending at the end of summer, and Yoshi decided not to renew it. Operating such a small greenhouse facility had become a losing battle as the country's economy worsened. There was little demand for his product in economic hard times; to continue growing such perishable ornamentals ensured a mean survival for himself and his family. Another factor that worked against his successful operation of the nursery was its location. Built on a clearing on the eastern slope of Beacon Hill and surrounded by thickets of trees, there was never an abundance of sun for his blooms. It was an unlikely and unwise location for a greenhouse where the elements were working against the flower grower. Yoshi was ready to give up this struggle.

Job listings were scarce, and when Yoshi learned a gardener/handyman position was available, he felt his six years of growing plants and his various work experiences in New York made him ideally suited for the job. Since the elderly couple also requested housekeeping help, Yoshi and Aiko easily qualified and they were hired. The childless couple assured them an accompanying infant was not a problem. As soon as the plants were sold and the business operation was closed, Yoshi and Aiko packed their belongings, rented a trailer to haul their possessions, and headed to their new job and home in Brinnon, Washington.

Moving to a small hamlet on the eastern shores of the Olympic Peninsula bordering a long captive waterway of Puget Sound was not what Yoshi had in mind when he told Aiko he would show her distant places. She had no reservations about moving away from Seattle as long as she was accompanying her husband. With baby in tow, she was a willing companion on whatever adventures he took.

J.T. Beam had been the supervising engineer during construction of one of New York City's bridges, and on retiring he had moved west. He found a waterfront site on Hood Canal suited for a house of his design. The structure was uncomplicated: a simple rectangle devoid of nonfunctional elements or fussy filigree. It was a starkly practical concept like an engineer is apt to design. He relished utilizing the readily available timbers to clear-span long lengths between supporting walls to create the unobstructed, open interior spaces he desired. Calculating the required beam sizes was a simple task compared to the complex dynamics of bridge structures he had worked on in the past, and he oversized the structural members with a hefty safety factor, as engineers are also prone to do. His plans included storefront-sized windows with a vast panorama of the distant shore, and the waterway ebbing and flowing in the foreground. The display was ever changing; it was the beauty of the environment that had captivated the builder. Tidal currents lapped at the shore then receded in endlessly repeated cycles. Far more timid than the ocean's billowing waves and thunderous roars, mellower breezes usually prevailed, and the water's changing patterns moved in harmony with the gentler rhythms. During the occasional storms, wild winds kicked up waves in spitting anger. Nature was always close and in view from their window.

The perimeter road closely followed the coastline of the canal as it wandered north from the town of Shelton at the canal's elbow toward Port Townsend at the far north tip of the peninsula. Sometimes the paving hugged the land as it skirted the water, and in other stretches the road turned further inland, allowing sited structures to sit closer to the water's edge. This was the case with the Beam property, where sufficient buildable land existed for the construction of the house. The original cottage on the waterfront property was situated a short distance up the slope from the new main house, and it was now designated the caretaker's cottage. Aiko and Yoshi found the house cozy and better maintained than their previous abode, and they readily settled in with their infant daughter for a long stay.

The young family now lived practically a day's drive away from Seattle and its distractions. Taking a ferry from Seattle, west to Bremerton shortened the time, but pulling a trailer filled with household goods meant taking the roundabout route, driving south to Olympia and north again. In spite of its distance from major cities, it was not a truly remote location, since the arterial ran conveniently west of the property making it possible to see people by driving to the general store several miles down the road. The pockets of human habitation were scattered throughout the area though mostly along the waterways. There were neighbors to the north and south of the Beam's house, but they were beyond talking distance.

Trees surrounding the site offered the sense of isolation the Beams sought. The sun-blocking canopy of old-growth forests still covered the peninsula, reaching from the canal to the Pacific Ocean. Although the timber of milling interests was working full bore cutting down trees, the resource was so vast, the supply appeared endless. The largest sawmill on the West Coast was in Port Blakely on the shores of Puget Sound on the southern tip of Bainbridge Island across from Seattle. The mill had a history of hiring Japanese immigrants from before the turn of the century when they had first arrived as contract laborers. Japanese still worked for the mill, and they lived with their families well entrenched in the company camp. The Port Blakely mill was an indelible part of the early history of Japanese living in the Northwest.

The shoreline not only provided the sweeping vistas, but Hood Canal itself provided an abundance of seafood from which to feast. During low tide, oyster beds were exposed to allow easy picking, clams could be dug in the sand, and mussels could be picked off rocky protrusions. Further out on the waterways, traps could be set and later retrieved, full of Dungeness crabs as well as spiny shrimp; a pole with bait yielded fish catches of all sorts, including salmon in season. Yoshi had never seen such a varied seafood bounty even in the seas next to his village. Here, even an unskilled fisherman such as he could bring in great specimens of fish, and he felt empowered.

Yoshi began his duties in earnest, tidying the overgrown shrubs and laying in batches of autumn flowers before the rains started. The inside work was not demanding, and Aiko was able to perform her duties without exhausting herself. The elderly couple was more than satisfied with their new caretakers, both with their work and their easy, accommodating ways. They had been apprehensive about hiring a couple with an infant; since they were childless themselves, their life had always been a children-free adult world. Since the accompanying infant was so young, they easily acceded her presence and allowed Aiko to set the baby on a mat while she worked. Before long, the couple took delight in watching the baby's responses and began acting like doting grandparents. They returned from errands with small gifts for the baby each time they were near a store.

J.T. and Mrs. Beam routinely scheduled weeklong trips to Seattle to visit acquaintances and attend to business matters as well as take in a social function or two. In early October, the couple left to begin their weeklong participation in the hustle and bustle of the city, leaving their caretakers with instructions to consider the time as their vacation, too.

A few days before their expected return, Yoshi was notified J.T. had suddenly collapsed and died of a heart attack and that Mrs. Beam's return home was to be delayed several days. Both Aiko and Yoshi were deeply saddened by the death. J.T. had been genuinely kind and generous to them. It was the second time an untimely death of a benevolent employer darkened Yoshi's own fate. He knew how lucky Aiko and he had been to have met such caring people who had provided them friendship, a sense of security and comfort, and a relationship they had hoped would last a long while.

Upon the widow's return, she presented her caretakers with boxes of infant clothing and baby paraphernalia in abundance. Shopping for the infant wardrobe had been high on her to-do list, and the couple had plunged into a shopping spree upon arriving in the city. J.T. and his wife had reverted to a less frenzied schedule the following days before it ended so unexpectedly. The staff of the club where they had been staying assisted the new widow with the necessary arrangements and details, which were discreetly and efficiently executed as though such services were a routine part of their job. Within the week, she was driven home to Brinnon in a hired car.

Along with the luggage and boxes of gifts that Mrs. Beam brought home, she had carried an unwrapped box containing the urn filled with J.T.'s ashes. The unadorned urn, befitting a man of mathematics and engineering, was placed on the mantel of the centerpiece stone fireplace.

Mrs. Beam assured the two solemn Japanese attendants who watched, "It's a temporary resting place." She continued as calmly as before, "I must ask another favor, Yoshi. Would you do one last thing for JT.? Will you scatter his ashes out in the canal? That was his wish."

Mrs. Beam's stoic composure since the death of her husband surprised both Aiko and Yoshi; that such a kind, open hearted woman could contain her emotions so well. A short while later, seeing the vase of late-blooming garden flowers Aiko had nestled on the mantel next to the urn, the widow stopped to contemplate the tender tribute. As her thoughts turned inward, a collage of memories flashed through her mind, and the long-suppressed tears began coursing down her cheeks.

Early in the morning of the designated day, a few hours after daybreak, Yoshi got into the skiff and rowed out toward the middle of the canal. Setting the oars to rest, he clapped his hands two times and looked heavenward before picking up the open urn. He slowly poured the ashes alongside the boat as it drifted on the waves. Bits of ash wafted in the breeze before hitting the water, but mostly they floated on the surface, spreading in broadening patterns before sinking into the dark abyss of the sea. Mrs. Beam watched from inside her view windows, seated on her pillowed couch with a blanket on her lap and binoculars held steady as she witnessed the unrehearsed ritual. She watched Yoshi drop the upturned urn into the sea as he had been directed. She could not see how quickly the metal urn disappeared from sight. Then, curiously, Yoshi clapped twice again then, hands pressed together as if in prayer, he mouthed "Amen" before taking up the oars to row back to shore.

Yoshi had been too preoccupied to notice that the previously calm waters had turned choppy and he was rocking in the boat. Yoshi put muscle to his oars and rowed toward shore, realizing he had no time to lose; he had to get back to shore as soon as possible. All the signs of an impending storm gave clear warning, and he wondered how he had not noticed them earlier. He managed to shove the small craft up on shore, and he dragged it into the boathouse along with other loose implements and tools. When Yoshi went into the house, he warned his wife to prepare for a windy day.

Invited to stay in the big house for the duration of the storm, the couple, along with the widow, felt secure that J.T. had built a shelter equipped to withstand any raging winds. Trees were less stable, and their limbs snapped or were uprooted in their entirety. When they fell on the power lines along the highway, all electricity was cut, Yoshi quickly found and lit the candles that were stored in easily accessed locations for such emergencies. The waves crashed the seawall with thunderous crashes, and the white-painted pergola sitting at the end of the dock bust apart, sending shattered pieces into the raging sea. The wind and water kept battering the dock until it, too, crumbled section by section. The storm was not yet finished and found targets for destruction throughout the area before dissipating. The three-some had sadly watched as J.T.'s handiwork was devastated by the forces of nature.

Yoshi was not particularly superstitious, and he refused to attribute any connection between the onset of the storm following so closely after he scattered J.T.'s ashes. It was a coincidence, he said. However, before the winds began gusting in full fury, the interval that allowed him to return to shore was karma. He was lucky; this he believed fervently. Of course, he had added a bit of insurance by clapping twice to wake the sleeping gods in the Shinto manner, chanted a remembered segment of Buddhist sutra, and had wrapped it all up with a Christian amen.

The storm was no ordinary, run-of-the-mill storm. The Pacific coast is seldom battered by severe hurricane storms common on the East Coast, and fall short in comparison, but the October 21 Storm of 1934 was the biggest storm to hit the region recorded at that time. The record remained unchallenged for more than fifty years before another October storm with greater severity and destruction passed through the canal.

The weeks following the storm were spent packing the Beams' belongings in preparation for the widow's move to California to be closer to relatives. The house and grounds were put up for sale, with the dock left in its damaged condition. Aiko and Yoshi packed up their own belongings, and with their infant daughter moved back to Seattle.

Less than three months had elapsed since they distanced themselves from the hustle and bustle of the city, and in that short time, they had lived a quiet, focused life with warm, loving individuals. It had all vanished as if in an instant, but they felt blessed they had had the experience.

New Home and Job

They were back where they started; they had neither a home nor a job. It was worrisome, but Yoshi was an optimist, and he felt it was a temporary predicament. He knew good jobs would be scarce when he checked in with the Japanese employment agency, only to learn a job similar to their previous one was available. The housekeeper/cook position had not been filled because it was not permanent; the job was for six months. It was ideal for them. Yoshi and Aiko as a couple were qualified and experienced, and the six months gave them time to find an apartment and a more permanent job.

Mr. and Mrs. Ujimoto, the Japanese couple who were housekeeper and cook for a surgeon and his wife, had planned a trip to Japan to visit family and needed a couple to fill in during their six-month absence. Aiko and Yoshi left their larger belongings with Hayame and moved into the servants' basement quarters of Dr. H.T. and Mrs. Buckner's Spanish-style house with red-tiled roof, a style definitely more fitting in California and the Southwest. The mansion stood well above the rock-laden shores of the Sound with defiant hauteur. Originally constructed by a timber baron, upon its completion, the owner decided to build a larger, grander mansion for his family in an area north of Seattle. Perhaps he, too, saw the incongruity of a hacienda set in Seattle and started anew.

Since there was a full-time gardener responsible for the expansive premises with formally landscaped terraces and a cleaning woman who came regularly during the week, Yoshi's duties were to help Aiko with kitchen chores, act as a sometime butler, and serve dinner, which Aiko cooked. Since Mrs. Buckner was in frail health, the owners seldom entertained. They had no children, and the out-of-the-way location of their home prompted few visitors to drop in.

The multi-guest bedrooms each with private, tiled bath-room were rarely occupied, and the upstairs ballroom remained unused and, sadly, quiet and empty. The long living room with ivory-colored stucco walls stood in sharp contrast to the heavy carved beams, exposed and dark like the doors and woodwork within. The voluminous room was filled with comfortable overstuffed couches and dark, weighty wood furniture well suited for unhurried conversations and languorous lounging. The covered veranda running alongside the room blunted the sun's penetration, and each window was gauzed, further filtering the light. Weighty, dark drapery panels embellished the sides of each window, absorbing extraneous light and sounds.

The ponderous décor of the living room was not evident in other parts of the house, and daylight streamed through the widows, leaving not a hint of gravity. On entering the house through the oversized front doors, family and guests found themselves in a cavernous two-story lobby with an ornate chandelier overhead. The main entry was not for servants' use; a back door through the kitchen was designated for them. On the opposite wall from the entry, the grand staircase followed the contours of the curved walls up to the second level in a glamorous and luxuriant way;

similar stairways were used to showcase headlining stars in Hollywood movies of the thirties.

Work at the Buckners' house was more formal than the casual ease of the Beams' home, and Aiko wore a black dress uniform during working hours. His busy practice kept the doctor away a good part of the day, and anytime he was home on evenings and weekends, the possibility of emergency calls always hung in the air. Mrs. Buckner pursued quiet interests of her own; she rested a great deal and made few demands. This allowed Aiko time to keep an eye on the baby, who was becoming physically active.

When the Ujimotos returned from Japan, they resumed their roles at the Buckners' home. Grateful to Yoshi and Aiko for having taken on the job during their absence, they asked the younger couple to assist them on special functions from time to time or again fill in while the older couple took a vacation. They were all well aware that Yoshi and Aiko appreciated earning the extra spending money. The two couples formed a friendship that lasted to the ends of their lives.

Yoshi was hired for the summer by his friend and mentor Yamazaki-*san* to do gardening work with the team of men who mowed and cared for the lawns and gardens of folks who could afford the services provided. Gardening as a trade is a seasonal business in wet, temperate Seattle. In the summer months, plants and grass grow in profusion, and in other seasons, there is not sufficient work to hire help. The temporary summer job had given Yoshi time to settle his family into an apartment, but now he needed to find a permanent job.

Yoshi had worked jobs of manual labor from time to time when he had no other choice. His aversion was not the physical exertion itself; what he abhorred was the grime and dirt associated with it. His sensibilities led him to look for indoor jobs he felt were better suited for him, albeit effete by macho perceptions.

In September, Yoshi found an inside job as graveyard-shift janitor/handyman at the New Washington Hotel, which was the second-largest hotel in Seattle at the time. His job was to vacuum and clean the lobby and other main-level public areas, dining rooms, and the kitchen. There was little staff and customer traffic during those hours, and he was able to work unhampered with minimal distractions, so Yoshi found time to do unassigned tasks to fill his time. The first to arrive for work in the early morning was the pastry chef, Kitty, who appreciated the extra help Yoshi often extended. In return, she offered him freshly baked offerings of sweet pastries: the best reward, over any other, for Yoshi. The freshly baked goods reminded him of the aroma of bread baking on the ship returning prisoners of war to Italy. That had led to his addiction. There is nothing like those baked breads in Japanese cuisine, and Kitty's sweet treats reinforced that fact with every bite.

Yoshi arrived home shortly after eight in the morning and slept until dinnertime. The apartment they rented was small and without a separate bedroom, made undisturbed sleep difficult. The once-easy-to-care-for baby had grown into a toddler who ran, jumped, and climbed. Weather permitting, Aiko walked with her pent-up child much as a dog owner walks her pet for exercise. Their destination was nearby Collins Playfield, the double-block-sized park with a fieldhouse, open spaces of lawn, manicured shade trees a sturdy swing set, and a rarely functioning wading pool. Conceived as part of the Olmsted Brothers' plan for Seattle parks and linking greenbelt, the landscape designers had also proposed locating playgrounds and playfields the size of a small block or two within a half mile of all residential neighborhoods throughout the city. The playfield's green oasis in their midst was welcome and much used, fulfilling the planners' egalitarian visions.

When the chance to manage a Japanese-owned apartment became available, Yoshi decided to give it a try. Responsibilities were minimal, and Aiko felt she could handle the daily cleanup chores without assistance. Their managers' living quarters was a three-room unit with a separate bedroom, and it was rent-free. Aiko and Yoshi were now caretakers of the small apartment on Yesler Way, approximately five long blocks east and down the hill from Hayame's grocery store.

Aiko and Yoshi with daughter Midori

During this time, I not only ran around like a wild banshee driving my parents crazy, but also my conscious memory started to function in brief and random spurts. I remember standing by a south-facing window as the sun streamed in, watching anxiously to catch sight of an expected visitor to cross the street to our apartment. That insignificant incident was to beam through that primordial fog clouding my conscious memory since birth. The shroud covering was lifting, and I became aware of me.

"Up, up, up in the air so high," Mother had read to me. I pumped my legs on the upswing and swung ever higher. "Look at me, Mommy," I called down to her. "I can go higher." Being aware was so exhilarating.

My second-earliest memory occurred when we were living in that same apartment. My parents surely had huddled before calling forth that family meeting. I sat straight-backed on a chair with my short legs pointing toward them. I was too high up to squirm away. Mother and Father faced me with stern faces. "The toy iron must NEVER ever be plugged into an electric socket like a grown-up's iron!" they each warned. They had never ganged up on me before, and the warning was duly stamped on my consciousness.

The two random incidents were etched on my previously blank memory slate, scenes that launched the hodgepodge collection of life incidents now cluttering my memory bank.

To my parents, I was their precious little daughter, and their attention flowed in my direction. Although I had outgrown the cuddly, bouncy stage, I remained the focus of their lives, and I thrived in the cocoon of warmth and security they provided. I lived among adults, had no contemporary playmates, and, like my mother, I was extremely shy away from family. I rarely got into mischief and was never harshly disciplined. Only once did my mother tell me to stand in a corner for doing something naughty. I stood there for five minutes with no clue it was meant as punishment.

Aiko and Yoshi's relationship followed the course set early in their courtship. Yoshi was the benevolent benefactor, and Aiko was his unassuming, pragmatic mate. The marriage had quickly settled into a comfortable alliance similar to long-married couples, which suited them both. They spoke Japanese at home, though Aiko felt at a disadvantage due to her limited vocabulary. She spoke to me in English; it was a part of her plan to impart modern American ideas and customs on me. Yoshi did not impinge her freedom regarding household matters or my indoctrination.

I do not remember when we moved to the fourplex on 8th Avenue, though that's where my sense of home emerged. Our family, Daddy,

Mommy, and me, Midori, shared the second floor of the fourplex. The elderly Hashimotos lived in the southerly unit, and we lived in the northerly half, sharing a front door and set of stairs. Mrs. Hashimoto gave private shamisen lessons in her living room, and the plucking and accent vocals and cues were familiar sounds that transferred through the walls to our unit. I had less contact with the two downstairs tenants.

The building was located two blocks north and up the steep hill from Hayame's store. We lived close enough to the store that we could see it upon stepping outside our front door onto the walkway. Since Daddy slept during the day in the bedroom area situated between the living room and the kitchen, Mommy and I tried to keep as quiet as possible. After the chores were done, Mother and I routinely made the trip down to the store.

Obaa-san's Store

As we walked the steep slope down to the store, we kept hoping no car passed while we were still on our way. The roadway was not paved, and any vehicle traversing the roadway kicked up billows of choking dust. The dust not only beset unwary pedestrians, but it also blew further afield and eventually settled on everything inside a house as well as outside. There was no curb defining the edge of the road either so what kept vehicles and humans in their own lanes separating the two, was the linear patch of long-stemmed wild grasses and assorted weeds rooted there. Bright colored dandelions and tendrilous purple sweet peas mingled with hordes of wily weeds that grew in profusion everywhere on the hill. The one area of respite from the invasive weeds was the well-manicured garden surrounding the Kubotas' house further up the hill to the north. Even further up, where the hill crested, loomed the stepped profile of Harborview Hospital. Below the crest to the south where we lived, the land sloped precipitously; there was no level land to speak of... well, almost. Situated on the irregular terrain, vintage houses and two-to-three-story buildings stood scattered about in no particular order in different stages of disrepair. There was no question the ramshackle structures were lived in. The colorful array of laundry hanging in the breeze always changed. Sundry items pinned to pulley-guided ropes with cables crisscrossed above the backyards were sun-bleached and dried the "green" way. Open plots of land sprouted weeds in abundant flurry as overgrown scrubs sprawled and tangled to claim their share of light and space. An abandoned rosebush full of delicate blooms flourished behind arching cascades of blackberry tentacles lined with honed spikes. Nature's beauty existed; it was not manicured or tidy here.

The cable car operating on counterbalances rattled and clanked on its scheduled run on Yesler Way past *Obaa-san's* store. The residents living along the street no longer noticed the noise; it became a part of urban living. Our trips to the store meant crossing the cable car's steel rails. The strange gurgling and clanking noises within gave off ominous warnings of chained ghouls in a netherworld below, clanking, clanking to be set free. The challenge was to cross the tracks before one of the noisy ghouls grabbed me from below. So, every crossing over the demon tracks forced me to quit my usual hippity-hop prancing and ready…set…go run like a flash over the rails to the safety of the other side.

The Japanese word for "old woman" and "grandmother" are one and the same, and though Hayame was only in her thirties, she was not bothered by having a little twerp following after her calling her *Obaa-san*. What's in a name after all?

Obaa-san ran her grocery business in a leisurely fashion in spite of the competition. On Yesler Way, a few blocks to the east and equidistant to the west, were two other Japanese-operated grocery stores, making *Obaa-san's* easily identified as "the one in the middle." She had sufficient traffic to generate enough income to support her family, and she was uninterested in aggressively expanding her customer base. When she felt she could manage the expense, she sent for daughters Kimiye and Hamayo to rejoin her in America. Their seven-year sojourn living with grandparents and relatives in Japan was best ended. When she learned a friend from the valley was returning to America after a visit with kin, the girls were entrusted in his care during the return voyage. The girls returned as teenagers with a need to relearn English. Still young, they quickly made the lifestyle adjustments and joined older sister Masaye and younger brother Katsumi to form Hayame's united family.

Customers came to *Obaa-san*'s store to shop for groceries. Friends, neighbors, and relatives did a little shopping, but they came primarily to visit. Hayame's easygoing "open-door policy" meant her visitors, upon entering the store proper, should walk straightaway past the counter, through the connecting open doorway into the "great room" of the family quarters where they were greeted. To provide visual screening between public and private at the open doorway, they hung a *noren*, the short fabric curtain with slits traditionally suspended at the top of doorways to a kitchen.

The kitchen occupied one side of the multipurpose room. The sink, stove, and cabinets, with doors above and below, lined the wall. A cloth on a string covered the opening under the sink, hiding the metal can storing the one hundred-pound sack of rice and the ceramic crocks filled with vegetables soaking in their pickling brine. Along the opposite wall was the well-worn sofa whose bedspread cover hid its fraying bald spots. The bulky easy chair was set wherever the sitter felt inclined to push it. The rocking chair was also a nomadic piece of furniture, more easily pulled than pushed. Perpendicular to the two described walls stood the wall separating the family space from the store and where in a corner the heater gloated ever popular in winter and sat ignored in the summer. The two windows on the exterior wall opened onto a view of unruly, overgrown brambles and the ubiquitous hearty blackberry limbs cascading over an urban forest. The southern exposure let in the welcome warmth of sunlight and also highlighted the clutter within. On the wall were two calendars, each with a single-month display to be torn off at month's end. A photo on the top half of each calendar showed a pretty, kimono-clad girl smiling demurely. One wore pink and carried a parasol; the other wore purple and held a fan. I decided there were two nearly identical calendars because Grandma could not decide which one was the prettier girl who deserved to be displayed. On the same wall, closer to the sofa, hung the real calendar everyone referred to; the large twelve-month wall calendar with the railroad's yin and yang logo was far more eye-catching than the nondescript view from the window. High on the wall above the sofa was the framed horizontal "picture" that consisted of a single line of calligraphy. Every well-appointed Japanese family had at least one such work in their living room. The stylized kanji brushwork was as admired for its beauty as a pictorial scene. No large framed photos were displayed, not even one of the emperor.

No one bothered to notice how worn the linoleum on the floor was, or its need for a replacement. Although it was swept and mopped daily, the prominent bald spots never looked it. The pile of spent magazines shifted about the floor as readers, after perusing the contents, threw them onto a second pile. Usually the Japanese magazines were kept in a different pile, which dwindled as visitors borrowed issues to read at home. The copies of Esquire, which male visitors left behind, were my favorites to look through for their colorful full-page cartoons of cute, skimpily clad chorus girls and lecherous goggle-eyed men. I made it my job to straighten the piles when I found them in disarray.

The large oval table with claw like legs occupied the center of the room. It was once round before the table extensions were permanently installed. The red-and-white checked oilcloth table covering would have better fitted an Italian restaurant setting than as a backdrop for the Japanese comfort food that *Obaa-san* could whip up in a jiffy. A main dish of chopped vegetable with miniscule bits of meat, the *okazu* entrée, was served with rice and pickled vegetables; thus, dinner was served on *Obaa-san's* centerpiece table. The meals were simple, although the menu could be augmented by products from the store. Hayame prudently limited using store items as a private pantry to avoid consuming her profits; instead, she pickled an assortment of vegetables in brine, *nuka*, or *kasu* to cure in covered ceramic jars. The tsukemono pickles augmented with cooked rice meant there was always food to eat. Just as she was able to routinely feed the dairy workers during her years as a young wife, she was able to offer her hospitality to visitors even as a single parent of four.

The acquaintances who regularly dropped in and visited were a varied lot. Terada-*san* often crossed the street from his home hoping to find a pliant ear for his discourses on his currently favorite subjects. The length of his stays usually corresponded with the affinity of his audience on any given day. The kitchen was short on glamour, but it was roomy, comfortable, and full of good cheer. Neighbors taking a respite from their own chores came to socialize over a cup of tea. Old friends from the valley who, on making the journey to the city with a stop in Nihonmachi or the Buddhist church, knew they would find a welcoming oasis a few short blocks away in Hayame's kitchen, where they regularly extended their trek to make one more stop before starting for home. Their hostess was kept up to date on the latest Shirakawa happenings and gossip as if she were still an active participant in their community.

"Our Nikkei baseball team is so good now, if they had played that high school team from Japan, we'd have won for sure," the visitor from the valley said.

"I recall they were the Japan high school champions." "Even when the teams weren't so...hummm... In those days it did not matter, the baseball games were always interesting, win or lose, when Masaichi-*san* came to watch. He shouted and cheered, getting the crowd to hoot and holler with him. We all went wild and had a great time," he reflected. "Baseball in the valley has never been the same since he died."

Another old friend from those early valley days was the little gnarled old man in overalls who came often and made himself at home in the kitchen. Upon his arrival, he was greeted as casually as any member of the immediate family. Without further ado, he gathered up loose zabuton cushions and cushy pillows and, in a well-practiced ritual, he carefully placed each item to properly cushion the wooden rocking chair before setting his bony buttocks down on the seat. Once comfortable, he started rocking himself to and fro with toes touching the floor only as the rocker swung forward in its pendulum swoop. When the conversation lagged, his head drooped; with chin nestled on his chest, he lapsed into his raspy slumber. Visitors came and went while he slept. Frequent drop-ins, on seeing the rocker occupied, made note of his presence, "I see Mat-*san's* here taking his usual nap," after which they felt free to ignore his presence completely. Other visitors were curious to learn how the old-timer had gained such a cozy role in Hayame's family circle.

"He has a home where he sleeps, but during the day, Jit-*san* spends his day in the kitchens of old friends. He finds his way here often too."

He was neither neighbor nor family. And few bothered to address him or refer to him by his real name though custom dictated such courtesy be extended to such an old man. The convention of adding an honorific to a person's name was also ignored. Instead, his surname was abbreviated, and he became known as Mat-*san*. Most acquaintances, even old-time friends, struggled to remember his surname. Was it Matsumura, Matsumoto, Matsuyama, Matsui, or something similar? He was often alternatively called Jit-*san* a derivative of *Ojii-san*, meaning grandfather or elderly man. He answered to both names.

Mat-*san* had been a for hire farmhand in the valley from before anyone could remember. No one knew when he had come to America initially, because he did not volunteer the information, and it was unforgivably bad manners to ask personal questions of that sort. Through the years, he had worked for many Japanese farmers at one time or another, and he knew practically everyone connected to the valley. Masaichi had hired him often from the time he began operating a farm. Though Mat-*san* was shorter than most men, short even in comparison to the turn-of-the-century Japanese male, he was a bundle of muscles and energy who could handle tasks as well as men twice his size. He had practically no schooling, nor did he possess the traits and skills to do other types of work; he was a dependable, much-in-demand manual laborer for hire.

Even in the early days, people noticed Mat-*san* had a phenomenal memory for names, places, and goings-on within the valley community. He was a walking repository about things Shirakawa from the decade before the turn of the century until he left the valley and moved to Seattle, when he became too old for regular farm labor. Since he knew all the stories, in time Hayame heard the history of the valley, of the tragedies, celebrations, and even the scandals that took place prior to her arrival, including stories of her husband's first wife.

"Hayame-san, did you save me the *ko-ge* from last night's dinner?" he asked, grinning mischievously.

"We never know when you're popping in for dinner. I'm sure we ate it," Hayame answered.

In the days before automatic rice cookers, a thin layer of slightly burnt rice crusted the bottom of the rice pot, much like the socarrat crust of perfectly made paella. That toasted crusted layer is favored over the perfectly cooked, moist white rice kernels by *ko-ge* devotees, which Mat-*san* was one of. Hot tea poured over the hard crust of rice softens then separates it into kernels and infuses the tea with flavor. The tea with floating rice granules is slurped from the rice bowl much like noodles are sucked up, as both acts create the same slurping sounds. This slurp is not polite company etiquette; this, a person only partakes in the privacy of their home or among non-uptight friends. Advocates believe no meal is complete without a bowl of *ocha-zuke* infused with *ko-ge* along with a side of tsukemono. And topping it all off with a resounding after-dinner burp.

"*Ko-ge ocha-zuke*, sooo good. Aiko-*chan* could cook a pot of rice with no overly burnt *ko-ge* when she was five years old, she could," Mat-*san* said. He was prone to repeat the long-ago incident as old folks tend to do, and it fell on deaf ears. "If you're staying for dinner, Jit-*san*, you can have the *ko-ge* tonight."

He smiled his toothless grin, animating the long, deep crevices that ran across and down his face. The crinkles around his twinkling eyes and the smiley creases surrounding his upturned lips danced in delight. Actually, Mat-*san* always appeared to be smiling because those folds on his face had aligned themselves that way. He was never ill-tempered or mean-spirited even when he relayed the foibles of others. "Well, neither of them expected her husband to return home so early. Why else would a man jump out the window and break his leg? Poor man, he lost many days of wages. And he forgot to take his pants with him when he jumped."

"Have another cup of tea, Jit-*san*." The old man sipped it with his customary gurgling slurp, caused by his missing front teeth. "Now the woman, you said her name was…?"

"Can't say. She still lives among us."

Mat-*san* came and went without a schedule. He had a wife somewhere, though no one knew exactly where. He had a grown son, married with his own family, who was also on his impromptu visit list, just like all his other friends. The hardworking days over, he was content to indulge in the hospitality of old acquaintances. A host of people felt affection for the wizened old-timer who preceded them in the harrows of old age.

Also in regular attendance at *Obaa-san's* kitchen was an assortment of bachelor men; unattached men who usually lived in small rooms alone and with few comforts. To relax in comfortable surroundings and network with a variety of people who gathered there in friendship, was ample reason to drop in and visit. In addition, their hostess was not only good-natured and generous, but she was also a woman without guile or pretension, and her perpetual positive outlook never faltered. She was charming, and like bees to honey, men were attracted to her.

Mommy teased Grandma, asking who her favorite boyfriend of the moment happened to be, as they giggled like teenagers. My favorite was tall Hiyama-*san*, who always found time to chat with me and sometimes gave me a present.

Hayame's children were an integral part of the activities, and they accepted without question having visitors traipsing in and out of the kitchen. When they felt a need for privacy, they retreated into the parlor or to their upstairs sleeping quarters. The parlor was adjacent to the kitchen and was reached through an open doorway whose door had gone AWOL years before. Other residents might have furnished the room to receive their guests; for Hayame, the room became a repository for furnishings and items that did not fit elsewhere. The sewing machine was usually piled high with an assortment of clothes, including washed and dried clothes that needed to be folded were thrown over those that needed repairs. A collection of mismatched wood chairs that were deployed when guests in the kitchen outnumbered the available seats huddled together on the side waiting for their call up. A friend's cast-off sofa with broken springs making it too uncomfortable to sit on, collected all manner of junk and treasure that could have otherwise been deposited on the floor; or, more likely, on the table holding pots of spiky Mother-in-Law plants and the unwieldy jade plant which never bloomed. On the floor near the stairs was the small mattress that had been placed there for my afternoon naps. I no longer used it, but the mattress stayed. Extra futons and zabutons were scattered on top of the pad, which made it a cushy nest to curl up in and listen to the radio conveniently placed nearby. Mommy often maneuvered one of the wooden chairs close to the radio and sat upright with embroidery hoop in hand, adding a few more colorful stitches to her handiwork while listening to a ball game. Leo Lasson's play-by-play baseball broadcasts made his voice as familiar to me as the Japanese conversations that prevailed in the kitchen. I understood neither; just the sounds were familiar.

Mommy and I spent many hours in *Obaa-san's* kitchen too, but when other guests were present, we were peripheral participants in the social interplay that took place. Mommy assumed her old role as Hayame's assistant, though in a lesser way now that she had a family of her own. She remained in the background, present but not counted.

Doctor Moon treated my eczema flare-ups, but he was unsuccessful in getting me to gain any weight. I was little and skinny. As an obstinate picky eater, none of the healthy foods advocated by nutritionists interested me in the least; however, there were two items in *Obaa-san's* store I yearned to have.

In a rare instance of tough love, Mother withheld the soda pop I wanted, and she was even more adamant I not have any Chinese preserved ginger, a savory treat among Asian youngsters. "It's bad for children. It'll make you *ba-ka*, dumb, she said.

Instead, Mother handed me a slice of white cheese riddled with large holes that smelled worse than an old dish rag. She said to me, "THIS is good for you." It tasted worse than the smell. When the coast was clear, I crept into the bathroom and flushed it down the toilet. The knob at the end of the hanging flush chain swayed and bounced on the back wall; tapping away. The noise was troublesome; it might give away my secret,

Mother prepared a menu of Japanese or American-style dinners, but I was not exposed to many different ethnic foods. I loved spaghetti, although the version I was served was Italian in name only. The occasional Chinese-style dinners I remember were large, celebratory gatherings held in Japanese-owned restaurants, the ones where the Chinese-style foods had been adjusted to placate Japanese tastes. Sometimes the "Chinese" foods were brought home as take-out for a family gathering. *Obaa-san* insisted on ordering Egg Foo Yung. As long as I had sweet and sour spare-ribs, my meal was complete. As for cheese, it was a food item never used in Japanese or Chinese cuisine.

Obaa-san knew I dumped that slice of Swiss cheese: "I tell Mommy you no eat *chee-zu*," she said.

How dare she tattle on me! I gave my antagonist a swift kick to her heels and called her *Ohni-baba*, ogre.

"Ah-ya," she yelped. "*Bachi ga ataru yo*! The gods will punish you!," she warned. Whether she said it in Japanese or English, I understood the message.

Although Mother spoke to me in English, as did my aunts, I was surrounded by Japanese-speaking people who congregated in *Obaa-san's* backroom kitchen, and I gained some understanding of the language along the way. I knew that *Ohni-baba* had the right nuance that its English version lacked. Even a kid figures that out.

The upturned bananas still clinging to their stems hung from their ceiling anchor near the store's entry. The edible chandelier of circular clumps of plump green-yellow-tinged petals was displayed. Much like a barber displays a red-and-white-spiral barber's pole, the stalk of bananas identified the premises as a food store. Actually, anyone looking at the building knew immediately it was a grocery. The exterior walls bordering the streets were plastered with product names and logos, and advertising placards were placed on the windows, too. It was an advertiser's bonanza, and "Drink *Coca-Cola*" was the most prominent.

Hayame's daughters were now able to offer more help in the store. They stocked merchandise, swept and tidied, served customers, and even made deliveries to those in the neighborhood. Those services were usually limited to their regular customers, but once in a while, requests for packs of cigarettes, gum, or incidental snacks were delivered to the painted-face ladies whose presence was preceded by the scent of the heavy perfume which lingered well after their departure. They lived a block or two to the south and west of the store, near the shortcut path to Nihonmachi and Jackson Street. They were friendly and always paid promptly.

On weekdays, Hayame tended the store alone. The bell devised to ring whenever the door to the store was opened, rang out a pleasant ding-ding, and Hayame appeared to attend to her customer. When the store was empty, she tended to her household chores or visited with her drop-in guests at leisure.

When their regular school was over, my aunts, along with other Nisei classmates, walked to Nihon Gakko, the Japanese- language school, for another two hours of Japanese language studies. Attending the privately sponsored school was mandatory for many Nisei children, whose parents were determined their offspring learn the Japanese language and culture. For some Issei parents, it was an attempt to close the generational gap between themselves and their children, a chasm without a common language and shared cultural values. Others were wary of exclusionists' loud threats to deport back to Japan the "not eligible for citizenship" Issei parents and their families, and those parents were taking precautionary measures to ensure the children were prepared for such an eventuality. Whatever the motives, Nisei youngsters were sent to learn the language of their parents wherever there were communities with sufficiently large Japanese populations to support the language schools.

The language school in Seattle opened shortly after immigrants began arriving in the area. Originally housed on the second floor of the Furuya building, the school moved to the Buddhist church until a permanent facility was specially designed and constructed on Weller Street in 1913. The school's two nearly identical wooden buildings, plain by design, displayed no distinctly Japanese idioms or fenestrations, thereby visually supporting their claims of being secular and nonreligious. Japanese-language schools in other regions were often affiliated with the Buddhist church. This was not the case in Seattle, where the school remained independent. Teaching their Nisei student's the Japanese language was the primary goal, but knowledge was meted out in the strict, disciplined system practiced in Japan.

A Younger Generation Grows Up

We were living in a Japanese-centric ghetto world where the Issei still ran the show, but the demographics of the community were evolving. The Issei were aging, their womenfolk nearing the end of their childbearing years. This middle-aged generation was inching toward old age, joining early settlers like Mat-*san*, who was already elderly. The earlier-born Nisei, now young adults, were the front runners for the hordes of later-born Nisei, who were still underage. Statistically, the born-in-America second generation now outnumbered the Issei's. The Nisei were coming into their own; pushed to excel academically, they were aiming for university educations and degrees, and they were beginning to flex their muscles. New organizations were formed or existing groups merged to create a unified platform to address common concerns on a national level. The Japanese American Citizens League, with roots in Seattle, was to play a prominent role in the years to come.

American values gained over old-country Japanese ways; the focus was shifting toward the younger generation. The *Kenjin-kai's* continued functioning for Issei's, but a younger generation of newly established Nisei associations serving different age groups were proliferating, including church-affiliated youth programs promoting religious and social fellowships. Church-sponsored Boy Scout and Girl Scout units were also flourishing.

James Sakamoto, founder of the English-language newspaper, the Japanese American Courier, also initiated a series of community leagues for basketball, football, and baseball. Nisei youngsters were thus able to participate in team sports, with local businesses and organizations willingly sponsoring the clubs. The enthusiasm of participating players was matched by their faithful and boisterous fans.

Japanese sports, with early support from the Issei's, still flourished, and adherents of the martial arts had built their own practice halls in the neighborhood. Uncle Katsumi took up kendo, the modern-era version of sword play, and "the way of the sword."

Historically, during the period of Japan's isolation, there were no battles for the samurai warriors to fight, yet they were expected to improve their warrior skills. Training in sword skills included another component: mental discipline, thereby making it a body/mind exercise. Warrior principles, ideal values, and ethics were compiled into a code of conduct, the Bushido, "the way of the warrior." Training groups began holding matches using wood swords for practice sessions at a time when civilians were prohibited from wearing swords in the Meiji era.

Wielding a wooden katana sword, the *kendo* students aimed to strike their opponents in three different body parts before the final thrust to the throat. With participants wearing masks, breastplates, and gloves, Japanese fencing was a sport with robust props compared to fencing with foils.

I usually remained scarce whenever Uncle chose to practice his thrusts with a bamboo pole on the sidewalk next to the store, but my curiosity sometimes emboldened me to watch him from the sidelines. He was all seriousness as he raised his pole high.

"O-men!" Whack down the head. "O-do!" Whack from the side. "O-kote!" Off with the wrist.

"O-baa-a-a-san!" I screamed as I ran for cover before he made the last thrust to the throat.

Aunts Hamayo and Kimiye both took private lessons learning to play traditional Japanese instruments; one studied the *koto*, an instrument that rested on the floor and whose strings were plucked with finger picks, and the other aunt played the shamisen, which rested on the lap and was plucked with a single ivory pick. Since we never turned on the radio at home while Daddey slept, my aunts practicing their lessons and our next-door neighbor's shamisen lessons were the only music I generally heard. Whenever my aunts participated in a recital at Nippon Kan, it was our chance to dress up and go to the theater. After less than a half hour of listening to plucked strings and bamboo blowing, I was ready to go home, but Mommy insisted we stay until both aunts had made their appearances.

Since its construction in 1909, the Nippon Kan Hall was the gathering place where meetings, rallies, matches, competitions, movies, recitals, variety shows, and theatricals of all types were held. Japanese dramas performed by theatrical clubs were especially popular, much as they had been in the valley. Performed by amateurs, many were Nisei with limited fluency in Japanese. memorizing their lines phonically. Their fumbled lines and missed cues added to the entertainment. The authentic-looking costumes and kimonos, along with painted settings and crafted props, played their part in disguising the less-than-professional caliber of the actors and of the performance. From the clapping wood blocks accompanying the curtain's opening to the actors' strutting appearances along the Hana Michi walkway to the stage, I could see the drama unfold from my post in the balcony. I could not understand a word they spoke, along with many Issei in the audience who were unable to decipher the archaic dialogue. The inflections in speech and the actors' stylized body movements told the story. These thespians overacted shamelessly, well beyond the already exaggerated gestures of Kabuki. Here, grown-ups playing "let's pretend" produced their own magic. Magical, too, was going to a downtown theater to see Walt Disney's Snow White and the Seven Dwarfs. We had choices whether to partake of Japanese or American, be it language, food, or entertainment. We never confused the two.

Family Days

Sunday afternoon was family day, when we often visited family friends. They seldom had children my age, so I sat wishing I was home with toys to play with. Occasionally, we just drove out to the countryside for a change of scenery. On our family-day Sundays in the summer, we went on picnics. Mother always made my favorite deviled egg sandwiches with cut-off crusts. Sometimes, she also made rice balls with umeboshi in the middle, but the pickled plums were too sour for my taste, so I got a special rice-only onigiri. She packed the goza mat for sitting on the grass and a blanket to protect us from the chill. We then climbed into the Model A, and I sat on Mother's lap since the car was a two-seater with the gearshift in the middle. The motor would crank over with angry fits, then jerk to a start with gusts of dust billowing behind us, we roared down the hill onto the intersection with paved streets. Daddey had not outgrown his characteristic *ga-sa, ga-sa* nervous energy of a kid, in whatever activities he undertook. Behind the wheel of a car, Daddey drove like a maniac let loose. He sped up on the stretches and braked hard at the stops. Mommy did not seem to notice the herky-jerky ride as I bounced on her lap for the duration of the trip. She delighted in watching the changing scenery and for the opportunity to leave the routine of home for a few short hours.

After making the turn onto Yesler Way by *Obaa-san's* store and reaching the top of First Hill, we zoomed down heading due east toward Lake Washington. We encountered another hill, and no matter how much Daddey pushed the gas pedal, the car crept up the slope at its own pace, grunting all the while. On reaching the apex of Cherry Hill, we were soon coasting down the incline like a roller coaster, and with that forward momentum, the car zoomed halfway up another hill. Once over the top of this third hill, we could see the lake far below us stretching all the way over to the far eastern shores of the lake. The road stopped at the top of an embankment, as the ground was too steep for vehicular travel. Even the cable car stopped well short of water level with its turn-around situated on the level ground before turning into a cliff. We took a turn onto the road leading south and followed the winding roadway through the trees and natural vegetation, part of the greenbelt feature of the Olmstead Brothers' comprehensive park design. As we approached the lake level, we once again passed houses as we reached Lake Washington Boulevard. The grassy tree-lined strip of land bordering the lake runs continuously from Madrona Park all the way south to Seward Park, offering endless areas for picnicking on the grass. Once Mommy and Daddey decided on the sunniest, most likely to be private location along the long stretch, he parked the car. We unloaded our gear, and unfolded ourselves to spend an afternoon outdoors in the sun. Sometimes we could see the new floating bridge in the distance, and speculated when the span would be completed. If activity is associated with picnic, I suppose ours was not a picnic. There was practically no activity on our outings. Daddey usually napped or read a book, Mommy, who seemed to need more rest than ever, rested, and I entertained myself as usual. I could look at my books, color in my coloring book, or look for the elusive four-leaf clover. Additionally, I could run around like a wild banshee, or just lie on the grass and dream.

The real picnics were the *Kenjin-kai* picnics held annually at a local park. Mother, *Obaa-san*, and all their kin were from Hiroshima, and they belonged to the Hiroshima *Kenjin-kai*, the largest prefectural club in the community. Each family prepared its own obento of assorted Japanese foods, including American favorites such as potato salad, fried chicken, and hot dogs. These were occasions for fancier fare than the usual meals, and the women spent hours preparing sushi and *tsumami-mono*, the finger foods so appropriate for these occasions. Watermelon and beverages were provided by the sponsoring group, and participatory games were organized for the day. These picnics were not much changed from the picnics of earlier years in the valley; the glaring difference was the addition of American picnic foods and snacks. While the entertainment and games varied little from year to year, the participants kept getting older.

Daddey usually stayed home to catch up on his sleep, but these annual picnics were special, so Mother would forgo listening to a baseball game broadcast; the portable radio was still a luxury, and we did not own one. For me, these picnics meant I could drink soda pop the entire day without restrictions. Picnics were wonderful!

Once, a special community picnic for all Japanese was held when the Japanese naval training ship visited Seattle. The entire community participated, and attending families each adopted a trainee seaman to host and to share their obento with. The women took greater pains than usual to prepare their foods, and they dressed more stylishly than for the usual picnic, all to impress their young guests from Japan. There were speeches, entertainment, and games and races for all ages, with prizes worth the effort to participate and to win. Best of all, the picnic-goers were able to visit with friends from different *Kenjin-kai's* in this casual and festive setting; when protocol was waived, women's voices escalated above a whisper, and the child in every adult was set free for those few hours. People with box cameras kept snapping the keepsake photo to be included in their picture albums.

We usually walked down Yesler Way whether east or west away from *Obaa-san's* store, situated near the crest of that segment of Yesler Way. It was steep either way, but West downhill toward the sea was the route logs were sent sliding down the slope in olden days. It remained an energy-sapping trek to walk it, so we all hopped onto a cable car on our way to a big tent circus that day. It was a noisy, jerky cable car ride down the hill with clanking and ringing bells, and the babble of passengers' voices. As often as I had watched from the sidelines the trolley's passing, the thrill was to actually ride in one. We transferred onto another rattling streetcar with its own set of noises to get to the circus tent. I have no memory of the circus acts; it was the journey that was memorable.

Japan Day was an annual event at the Playland Amusement Park on the shores of Bitter Lake in north Seattle, where my aunts took me, perhaps reluctantly babysitting me. We rode the Ferris Wheel, and they bought me cotton candy, but were steadfast in refusing to let me take on the bumper cars. I had visions of driving like Daddey: step on the gas and bump to a stop. Alas, it was not to be. Nor would they take me on the Big Dipper, saying, "You're too little. It's too dangerous."

It is unlikely I was ever told me exactly where we were going before we got there, being told instead, "Too many explanations. She won't understand." I tagged along with Daddey, mindful not to wander and get lost in the traffic jam of people walking in the same direction. Stopping, we were standing on the pier at Smith Cove to see family friends depart for Japan on the huge ocean liner in front of us. As the ship set sail, everyone on the ship's deck and those on the dock threw a zillion streamers in happy celebration. I thought it sad they were leaving, so I pocketed my streamers instead of throwing them and saved them for another occasion when I put on my own bon voyage event.

Mother brought me with her on downtown shopping excursions. We mostly window-shopped at Frederick & Nelson and the Bon Marche department stores; without going to Rhodes, MacDougall's and the JC Penney stores, which were located off our route. We made a stop at Woolworth or the Kress ten-cent store to buy me a trinket to cool my complaints on our walk home. This day, rather than the usual trivial gadget, Mother bought me a wonderful metal lunchbox painted with frolicking penguins, all black and white with an eye-catching orange-red background. It was the handsomest lunchbox in the world.

In the morning, Mother filled my new lunchbox with a sandwich and cookies; I could live without fruits or vegetables, but I inherited Daddey's sweet tooth, and I needed that sugar high. Lunchbox in hand, Mother and I walked to the Japanese Baptist Church Nursery School, which was perhaps five blocks away. Voices of children in another part of the building penetrated the lobby where Mother concluded her conversation with the woman who had answered the door. The woman took my hand.

"We'll meet the other children, shall we?" she said. I looked back at Mommy.

"Go and meet the other children, Midori. I'll come to take you home when school is over," she said.

I was abandoned. I was totally lost in this kids' zone surrounded by nasty little monsters, and I was miserable. The other children had been enrolled at the beginning of the year, and they knew the routine: what to do at lunchtime, nap time, toilet time, and go home time. Worst of all, a she-devil tried to swipe my new lunchbox. Luckily, Mommy had etched my full name on the side, and I was able to reclaim it.

As we walked home, Mommy asked, "What wonderful things did you do at nursery school?"

I refused to answer her question. "I'm NOT going back!" I blurted and proceeded to bawl as loudly as I could. Mother gave up; her attempt to have me break out of my shell and mingle with other children had failed.

We began taking weekly trips to the library to check out books Mother would read to me. The children's book section was thoughtfully located in the basement and could be reached through an unobtrusive side door at street level. Luckily, we did not have to climb the series of stone stairs leading to the main library entrance of the monumental Carnegie-donated library. There were few readers in our part of the building, so Mommy and I leisurely browsed through the books before making our selections.

Sick's Stadium had opened down on Rainier Avenue where the Dugdale Baseball Park had stood until it burned down. Mother was anxious to see the new facility and watch the Seattle Rainiers play. On a sunny afternoon, we took a streetcar to the stadium to watch a game. The afternoon game was not very well attended, and the cheap seats where we sat were virtually empty. She watched the game like a true fan, and I fussed and fussed. There was no play-by-play by Leo Lasson coming over the airwaves, and I found it all incredibly boring. Mother usually gave in to my whining, but she was undeterred that day, and we stayed for all nine innings.

Daddey was not a particularly keen baseball fan, and he managed to learn the barest rudiments of the game in order to keep Aiko happy. Though he maintained an interest in boxing from his New York City days watching bouts at the Garden, he really got hooked on horse racing. The Seattle Star newspaper had a weekly contest to pick winners of three races. One week he got lucky and won twenty-five dollars. It was the proverbial beginner's luck to win a jackpot and he became addicted to play. Thereafter, he could be found reading the horse racing pages. Daddey did not have the money to place many wagers, and went to Longacres only a few times a year, but he liked the ponies almost as much as Mother liked baseball. How adults could find such boring pastimes interesting was a mystery.

We left Mother at home while Daddey and I went fishing for shiners. We drove down to a waterfront pier. Daddey let down his line and hooks and caught tiny little fish. The fish continued to wiggle in the pail, but they proved to be awful playthings. Daddey was having a great time, and kept ignoring my pleas to go home, even when I said I had to go to the bathroom. Maybe he knew that it was a fib.

I do not recall whether we ate his catch. Anyway, no fish ever tasted as good as pork chops, especially the fatty part. That was one of the few foods I liked and ate without coaxing. Watching Mother make sushi was interesting; it was an OK food. Once in a great while, we ate dinner out. We almost always went to one of two downtown cafeterias with line service where food choices were displayed. Those ventures were a real treat, since Daddey preferred eating home cooked meals.

Daddey's work and sleep schedule precluded doing many things on days other than Sunday, and his promise to Mother to show her the world was put on hold. She did not mind; she was comfortable and content in our constricted routine. She had a husband and child she loved dearly. Yoshi was a kind and considerate husband with an adoring wife and child. He accepted their circumscribed life, which he was sure was only temporary, and he felt his karma held a brighter future.

News from Japan

As did most immigrants, Yoshi read the local Japanese language newspaper, and also had access to the magazines published in Japan circulating through *Obaa-san's* informal magazine library——usually located on her kitchen floor. He felt he was up to date on what was happening in Asia.

The letters from family in Japan were rare, though they did relate brief highlights of their lives. Older brother Seinojo had remarried, and his daughter Shizuka from his first marriage remained with the family. Sister Kimiko had married a village boy, and they now had children. Younger brother Hiromu, upon graduating from military academy, had been sent to Manchuria, which was now a possession of Japan.

Most of all, Yoshi wanted to know what progress Shiro was making toward his goal to become a ship's captain. Yoshi felt the monies he sent for him to attend naval school had engendered a special bond with him. As a cadet, Shiro traveled on a training ship much like the one that came to Seattle and had occasioned that special picnic. Bypassing the rigors of seamen that Yoshi experienced, Shiro, as a ship's junior officer, was on his way toward his goal. On a routine voyage in the Japan seas, the ship encountered a storm, floundered in the rough waters, and sank. Thankfully, Shiro was among the crew members to be rescued. Dismissing the misadventure, he soon boarded another ship. Sometime later, while near the Aleutian Islands, this second ship encountered a storm, not uncommon in the area; freight on board the tossing ship shifted, and an SOS was sent out as the ship began to list. Shiro was miraculously picked up before the ship sank. He was one of less than a handful who survived; all other crewmen perished. When he went home to recuperate, the family pleaded with him to give up the sea.

"You've been lucky twice. Please, please stay home."

"Superstitious people can put you in harm's way, Shiro."

"Reconsider your choices."

"Become a teacher; stay on land, and stay safe."

Shiro could not be deterred from his goal. He was assigned to another ship, and he went back out to sea. His dark omen followed him aboard, and one night he disappeared while the ship glided through calm and balmy waters. They found no trace of him; he had vanished.

The letter from Japan contained a postscript "I may have forgotten to mention before that Odai returned to her village now that you children have all grown up. She felt she was no longer needed. She remembered you as her favorite, and always inquired about your health and welfare."

The letter brought back thoughts of home, the family, and what divergent paths Odai's charges had taken. Yoshi understood Shiro's reluctance to stay on land and to "stay safe." Doing so meant giving up the freedom and exhilaration that comes while floating through an ocean with an endless horizon.

Shiro's luck had run out. Yoshi knew he had been luckier.

School Begins

I started school in the fall, and Mother enrolled me by my American name, Sylvia. I answered to Midori, my middle name in our *Obaa-san*-centric world. In those days, the majority of children who were my age were given an American name and a Japanese name. My parents agreed their choices in naming me were appropriate; for a greenhouse operator to name a child Midori, the color green, was perfect. The American names given to girls were usually the simple and popular ones of the time. Mother had fallen in love with the name Sylvia, meaning "of the forest," which was related sufficiently to green and plantings, so I was named. It, however, contains three syllables that Japanese have difficulty negotiating, especially Daddey, so I was known as Midori at home to simplify things.

I was assigned to Miss Waterhouse's morning kindergarten class of approximately two dozen youngsters. I was not the only bewildered student lacking the social skills to navigate among these strangers. We found each other as we stood on the sidelines, happy for a few hours of friendship and a sense of belonging––all wallflowers, we. Many of the other students had formed friendships in nursery school or had older siblings who had prepared them with stories of what to expect at school. Eventually, we all made the necessary adjustments, and before long, every one of us loved our teacher and our school.

Located east of Chinatown's business district, Bailey Gatzert School was within the community, and most of my classmates were Japanese or Chinese born-in-America children. The exclusionary legislations had affected the patterns of migration differently in the two communities, and there were far fewer Chinese families compared to Japanese, who provided the overwhelming majority of students at the school.

Miss Mahan, the principal, had years of experience working with children of Asian immigrants. She respected her students' ethnicity in a time when it was not a popular tenet. And by understanding the parents' respect for education, she had embarked on a strict program to foster learning. It all started in kindergarten with a soft approach. Not only did we memorize the Pledge of Allegiance and salute the flag each morning, but Miss Waterhouse also managed to instill hygiene practices and more. She said, "From tomorrow, everyone must bring a handkerchief to school. The boys will carry theirs in their pockets, and the girls shall attach theirs to their petticoats near the hem of their dresses with a safety pin."

"Miss Waterhouse, the boys can see my panties when I pull my dress up to wipe my nose!"

"My dear, you must first unpin…"

"But it's a lot easier to wipe my nose on my sleeves…" "That is what you must NOT do."

When we were in the classroom, we assumed our American personas, and everyone spoke English, even the few who struggled with their limited English vocabulary. Actually, all of us were less than proficient, but we were also bilingual to a degree. Miss Waterhouse was there to enrich our lives by introducing us to all manner of things American. We played games, made things, painted, cut and pasted, and we listened to stories. My favorite story above all others was The Little Engine That Could. "I think I can…I think I can…I think I can!"

Well after the school year started, a new boy recently arrived from Japan joined the class. He spoke no English, and the students most adept in Japanese were enlisted to translate. Yozo was undoubtedly frustrated in his new environment, and he found comfort in drawing pictures rather than joining the rest of us in group activities. He stood at the easel and painted large drawings of airplanes flying over gardens and houses. We five-year-old innocents asked him what the dotted lines were doing in the middle of his otherwise bucolic scenes.

"*Sore wa bakudan*…ack, ack, boom, boom… Boom!" His pictures and his explanations made no sense except to the boys who had seen the current events newsreels of Japan's invasion and occupation of Manchuria and their incursion into China proper. Miss Waterhouse tried to persuade Yozo to draw pictures without the airplanes and bombs. America was not a country at war.

The students understood other expectations were in store for them the following year when they reached first grade. Their classes would not only last into midafternoon, but when regular school was dismissed, the Chinese children would go to Chinese school in Chinatown, and the Japanese children who were enrolled in Nihon Gakko would walk east in the opposite direction to Japanese school for language classes. I was too young for that yet.

No one was walking home in my direction after we reached Jackson Street. Now walking alone, I took a diagonal path to Main Street toward the old Buddhist church and climbed another dirt path to reach the sidewalk next to *Obaa-san's* store. The sunny-day shortcut reduced my eight-block walk to school, although, I had to stay on paved sidewalks on rainy days, prolonging my exposure to the wet. Mother was usually waiting for me at the store when I arrived from school, but as time went on, she stayed home and ventured down the hill to *Obaa-san's* less frequently. She was tired and began to stay in bed even during the day.

Daddey switched to a new job and worked mostly during the day. We were still adjusting to his new schedule.

I spent a good part of my time hanging around *Obaa-san's* store, where there was more company and activity than at home. Mother did not seem to mind as long as I was not a total pest. Mat-*san* came frequently, and I automatically gave up the rocking chair so he could take his nap. The Buddhist church now held regular Sunday morning services like the Christian churches, and also provided classes for children. Periodically, my aunts took me to Sunday school. We walked the few blocks to the church, and they unceremoniously dropped me off in the basement, where the children's classes were held, before they rushed upstairs, giving them ample time to mingle with their peers before the adult services started.

"Don't just stand there––sit down," I was told by Miss Smarty-pants, as she pointed in the direction of miniature chairs set in a circle. "This one's saved for my friend. Find another one," a pint-sized pissant snarled as I attempted to sit down. I found a seat far away from the snarly one and waited. A plump young woman hurried toward us, dragging a chair behind her. Once she and chair had joined our circle, she greeted us enthusiastically. "Hal-lo, hal-lo, *minasama*. It's nice to see you all today!" After everyone was handed a printed handout, the children, led by the smiling leader, began a group chant in a language that was neither English nor Japanese. One or two of the children may have actually been reading the kana print written on the card; the others were reciting the sounds from memory. I sat there bewildered until the chanting came to an end, and I joined the rest as we clasped our hands together circled by our, *jizu*, the Buddhist equivalent of the Catholics' rosary. *Obaa-san*, an ardent believer, had given me a child-sized *jizu* with tiny orange-red beads. She had promised to exchange it for a beautiful adult-sized one with crystal beads and purple tassel someday; someday, meaning when I became a faithful Buddhist.

"Nami ami-da butsu, nami ami-da butsu," we kept repeating. Our leader had reverted to speaking Japanese for the rest of the session. The story was told in Japanese as well as the game we played. I had no idea what it was all about. When you're a kid, no one ever bothers to explain anything. I observed without comprehending, and I was too timid to ask an adult for an explanation.

I didn't have to kick up my heels and refuse to go to Sunday school after a second try because other forces at work soon ended further attendance at those Sunday sessions.

Looking for a New Home

Living on Yesler Hill, our concerns centered on our immediate surroundings and we took little notice of the territorial vistas on view for us to see, and did not hear its rich history of place. In Seattle's pioneer days, from somewhere close to where *Obaa-san's* grocery store later stood, the felled logs brought from the forested interior was skidded down the steep Yesler slope to the mill near the waters' edge; the area was called: Skid Road. From Yesler up the steep slope where we lived, north to the top of the hill where the old King County Courthouse once sat, was also known as Profanity Hill. It was a label coined by early attorneys and their clients, who cursed climbing the steep incline from downtown to have their cases heard. Later, Harborview Hospital was constructed on the approximate site of the demolished courthouse on a promontory overlooking the city. This was the neighborhood where I lived, my home.

The city of Seattle created a separate agency, the Seattle Housing Authority, to plan, organize, construct, and operate a public housing development for low-income residents that would be racially integrated. To augment its own budget, the City took advantage of a New Deal funding program, and they started the process. The Seattle Housing Authority then identified approximately twenty-two acres of land on Yesler Hill to be cleared.

The Authority's selected development site incorporated parts of the slope south of the hospital, terminating on Main Street with Nihonmachi as the southerly border. A portion of Yesler Way fell within those boundaries including *Obaa-san's* grocery store site. The proposed redevelopment area encompassed our neighborhood. Plans called for the removal of existing inhabitants from the area before beginning the demolition of dilapidating buildings and residences. In redesigning the site to work with the topography, streets were best eliminated or realigned, and the steep terrain graded into terraces to accommodate the low, two-story residential structures envisioned for the revamped development.

Plans crystallized; work began. Properties and businesses were bought out, and residents were told to vacate the premises. Landlords told their tenants to find new quarters and move out. Hayame searched for another grocery store location and found a suitable site north of the downtown retail core in the old Regrade Area. It was on the other side of town far from Nihonmachi where few Japanese wandered, but she had a family to support, and this was her opportunity. A three-level apartment above the store was included as part of the lease. The apartments were rented, so Hayame's efforts went into preparing the street-level space into a store with a small living area in back for her and son Katsumi. She kept the landlord's apartment for her three daughters. Her two older daughters were able to assist and manage the apartment units while she tended to the store.

Apartments were scarce in the area, and Hayame's retail business was even more leisurely than on Yesler Way. There were few walk-in visitors to fill the time; everyone had to make adjustments.

The Buddhist church agreed to sell its property, and plans were started to build a new, larger facility several blocks east; two other congregations were also relocating. Families were finding new homes, and people were moving away. The exodus was slow and evolving. A house occupied last week became vacant the following week, and its windows were shattered then shuttered.

Our neighbors, the Hashimoto's, were old and reluctant to move, but when the ceiling plaster above their bed began flaking down on them in sizable chunks, they made a hurried decision to find new quarters.

One Sunday, instead of heading toward Lake Washington and the picnic grounds, Daddey drove toward my school, passed it, crossed the bridge to Beacon Hill, drove down a couple side streets, and stopped at a small house. A woman waiting there for us, showed us the interior. There were four rooms and bathroom; a kitchen with an eating space, a living area, and two bedrooms.

"Midori, this will be your bedroom," Daddey said as we reached the little room next to the bathroom. That was the key that opened my imagination to the wondrous possibilities of living in a house with my own bedroom. I immediately began mentally arranging my toys within "my" bedroom. I barely noticed Daddey was still talking to me. "It's close to school, and you can have a garden."

Mommy thought the house was fine, and I loved it. Daddey made arrangements to lease the house, and we left thinking we would be moving in soon. The landlord decided to lease the house to someone else, and that was the end of that dream.

MOTHER IS SICK

The walk home from school was lonelier than ever as I headed up the hill from Jackson Street. There was far less traffic, and few people ambled along the sidewalks where their random voices could be heard. Dusty paths sprouted more weeds. The abandoned buildings grew in number and became more decrepit as their neglect was prolonged. It looked like the slum neighborhood that others had labeled it. The Terada's had moved to the hotel in Chinatown that he managed, leaving their once-bright and cheerful corner unit empty and dark. Across the street, the array of battered advertising signs still plastered on walls and windows were useless remnants of *Obaa-san's* lifeless and forlorn store. There was no mistaking our once-viable, inhabited neighborhood was no more.

I turned six years old a few weeks before the end of school. I had the flu and missed the last week of classes which worried me, since Mother had been insistent it was important I not miss school. She'd never told me she had a handful of "perfect attendance" certificates from her school days, which she prided and had stored away. She wanted me to follow in her footsteps, no doubt. In spite of my furlough at year's end, I was promoted to the first grade.

The long-anticipated summer vacation was a dud. Everybody who counted had moved away; even strangers were scarce. Daddey worked days, and Mommy was tired all the time. One day I climbed the counter to reach the stash of hidden candy and made a tray presentation with three different candies: foil-wrapped kisses, candy corn, and an assortment that Daddey preferred. It was my surprise for Mommy when she woke up from her nap. She did not eat the candy, and I understood she was very sick.

That summer, Mother took to bed and pretty much stayed there unless she had to cook or wash. She must have recognized her symptoms as similar to her mother's, which she had observed many years before: the gradual fatigue that became all-consuming and coughs that she suppressed as much as possible. She was reaching the age Itono had been when she became seriously ill. The coincidence of similar symptoms, similar age, and a much-treasured young daughter only six years old——it was all too dark for Aiko to dismiss, and it frightened her. If she could dispel those thoughts from her mind, she might escape the same inevitable fate as her mother, so she had to deny her illness. She never shared her fears with another soul, and she tried to hide her symptoms, even from Yoshi. By early summer, she could no longer make excuses and went to see a doctor. No definitive diagnosis was made.

As the summer wore on, Mother's cough became persistent, and she started to cough up blood. A doctor and nurse came to the house to examine her. Before leaving, they talked to Daddey. The next day, Mommy stayed home in bed. Daddey and I went down Yesler Hill to the public health clinic and had X-rays taken.

Aiko had joined that group of pariahs who had contracted tuberculosis. The devastating illness struck random victims, but more often it struck members of the same family. That pattern of spreading through families led the Japanese to believe the disease was hereditary. During the traditional background investigations to determine suitability of eligible marriage partners, a practice the Japanese continued to employ, prospective candidates from families with a history of mental illness and *hai-byo,* as the disease was known in Japan, were eliminated to avoid introducing undesirable hereditary traits into their lineage.

Yoshi had not bothered with such formalities. Besides, Aiko's mother had died from the effects of childbirth, he had been told, and her father had died in an automobile accident. He was to learn after Aiko was diagnosed with TB that perhaps the mother's illness had been the same, but old-timers were reluctant to say so except in whispers. The disease consumed the lives of many more immigrants than they were willing to admit, and Aiko had close friends who had succumbed to the illness well before she had her own symptoms.

The absentee landlord of our fourplex notified her tenants dutifully for months that they had to leave, vacate the premises, and move out. "Please, please go!" she said. The city was demanding everyone be cleared out——no more stragglers. The landlord appeared in person one day. She was a most unlikely slum landlord. She was a sweet, gray-haired lady who came to plead with the squatters to please find other housing before we were forcefully evicted. The Public Health Department prevailed over Public Housing in our case, and further harassment to move ceased. The tubercular patient was on her way to a hospital as soon as admission could be arranged. She was not to be moved to other temporary quarters, and demolition of the building had to wait.

The brown paper bag safety-pinned to the bed sheet on the side of the bed filled up ever more quickly with Mother's wads of coughed-up blood. It was one gauge telling us her illness was getting worse.

Daddey began packing away the knickknacks that had graced the living room cabinet, the crocheted embroidered doilies and headrests, linens that Aiko had decorated with colorful embroidery, along with the Christmas ornaments and baby's first shoe that were already stored in Aiko's metal trunk. Also added were personal papers along with a portion of my dolls to fill the trunk to the brim. An upright steamer trunk was filled with Yoshi's own small collection of belongings, and they were brought to the back of Hayame's store for the duration. Clothing and kitchen items were also sent there since Daddey planned to rent a unit in the apartment above the store.

The handsome bedroom set that had been lovingly selected and presented to Aiko as a wedding present, although oversized for every residence they had rented, was sold to a secondhand dealer, as well as other furniture that had become dispensable. The sale stipulated the furniture movers could take possession of the furniture only after we moved out. Daddey told Mother all the furniture and household items were being stored until her return from the hospital He did not have the heart to tell her the truth: the bedroom set was sold.

At the end of August, we vacated the premises. I was going with my mother to stay at the hospital, too. Our household was essentially dismantled in August 1940.

CHAPTER 9

The Hospital, 1940-1942

THE CHALLENGE WAS THERE: A set of stairs. I ran up the wide, covered stairway as fast as I could. I reached the top panting for breath and full of expectations. This was my favorite restaurant. We had not eaten here in a long time. I could barely contain myself. I knew better than to dash in by myself, so I danced my "hurry up" two-step while waiting for my parents to climb the stairs. They were still near the bottom, making their way up the stairs very slowly. Daddey was supporting Mommy all the while as she took a hesitant step then stopped for breath before lifting her foot to take another step. She had been bedridden and had not walked or exercised for a while, so she was out of shape, I figured. At that pace, I had time to run down to the street, run back up to the top and still beat them to the entrance door. I was huffing and puffing from the extra round of stair climbing when they finally reached the top landing and joined me.

They found a booth along the window near the door. Mommy sat and waited while Daddey and I walked to the beginning of the cafeteria line to make our selections from the dishes of food displayed. I walked quickly past all the plates of different green salads with their assortment of sliced eggs, cucumbers, tomatoes, and colorful bits of cut-up vegetables. That's rabbit food, I thought. I knew better than to be fooled into choosing jelled tomato aspic. Finally, I spied what I was seeking, the group of molded gelatin salads: yellow, green, orange, and red, each sitting enticingly on a bed of lettuce.

"Daddey, I want a red strawberry Jell-O. It's my favorite." At the steam tables, I searched until I found the pan of spaghetti. I pointed. "Daddey, that's my very, very favorite." He placed a dish of red-sauced noodles on my tray.

Besides adding dishes to his own tray, Daddey put a glass of milk on mine. I protested, "I want a strawberry soda pop. I don't want to drink milk today."

"Mommy say Midori drink milk today."

Why argue? My eyes were already fixated on the grand finale waiting up ahead, in the glorious, yummy dessert display. I could taste the tiny sugar crystals in my mouth already: white or yellow cake, brown and dark chocolate cake with nuts, apple, cherry, berry, and cream pies, custards, and more... How to decide? The banana cream pie with its whipped cream topping sprinkled with toasted, shredded coconut strands was my choice that day.

We got to the end of the line with two trays of food. Daddey paid the cashier, and I was told to stand guard and watch our tray while he brought the first tray to our booth where Mommy was sitting. Hurry, hurry back for this second tray, Daddey. I moaned, bursting with anticipation. I'm gonna roll that Jell-O around my mouth a couple of times then squeeze it between the top of my mouth and my tongue and force it to slither down my throat, never bothering to chew. Jell-O is such a fun food!

Mommy ate little; she mostly just sat there watching us and trying not to cough. I figured she was conserving her energy to get down the stairs. When she saw me looking at her, she smiled. She knew a smile would keep the gloom away from our little party. I finished my Jell-O, and after a mere taste of my favorite spaghetti and pie, I was done eating. Daddey ate the rest of my meal for me. I sat and fidgeted and looked out the window.

"Midori, that's the Frederick & Nelson department store across the street. We went shopping there to buy your dress. Do you remember?" Mommy said.

"Oh, um," I mumbled. I wish she was well again so we could go shopping together.

She spoke to Daddey in Japanese, the favored language when she wanted a private conversation with him in my presence. She then turned to me, "I told Daddey it'd be a good idea if everyone at the hospital called you Sylvia, your American name, and not Midori. Wouldn't you like that, Sylvia?"

"Ah, umm." Sure, Sylvia and Mommy could go shopping again... someday.

After our lunch, we got into the car, and it almost felt like we were going on one of our Sunday picnics to the lake. We never went after Mommy got really sick. She had to stay in bed, but she did not get better like people are supposed to after they rest so much. That's the reason why we were going to the hospital where they would take care of her, and she could get well. They found I had a spot in my X-ray, so I was going with her to keep her company.

Daddey drove out of downtown and headed north into unfamiliar territory. There were no more tall buildings; they were replaced by block upon block of neat houses with lawns and trees and an occasional cluster of small neighborhood stores. The further we drove, the houses became sparser and interceding wooded thickets more dense. Daddey made numerous turns, and was confronted by detours that took us around steep hills or creeks. He reversed the car out of more than one dead-end street before confessing he was lost.

Mommy dozed in her seat, head resting on the door. I shared her seat, with my bottom barely touching the edge, and watched the scenery pass by. I noticed we passed the same prominent markers more than once. We came to a large park-like clearing where a man was busy shoveling. Daddey stopped the car and got out.

"Hal-lo, hal-lo," Daddey said as he walked toward the stranger. The man with the shovel stopped working.

"I am lost," Daddey said. "I try to find the big hospital, Firland Sanitarium. Which way I go?"

"Well, this is the wrong place, mister. When they die over there, they bring them down here. Ha, ha. Ho, ho, ho. This here is a cemetery."

"I take my wife to hospital. Which way I go?" Daddey said quietly.

"Sorry, mister, I just couldn't pass that one up. I meant no harm. Actually, you're not too far away. A dozen blocks maybe. You have a map? I'll show you where you are and how to get there."

From a distance, the three-story clay-brick building posturing at the end of the central driveway looked like a glossy cover photo from a New England college recruiting brochure. Tall, mature poplars lining the main entry road cast long fluttery shadows with alternating streaks of late afternoon sun as we drove to the building's main entrance. A second three-story brick building with far less ornamentation stood perpendicular to the main building and parallel to the row of poplars. The well-manicured shrubbery and the expanse of lawn surrounding the visible buildings enhanced the college campus image. Such a photo shoot would have been taken during semester break when the campus was empty.

The hospital grounds were devoid of people. We did not see a single sole wandering around the vast complex when we arrived; it was inanimate and ghostly. I lost my bounce and bravado and stuck close to my parents as the three of us walked hesitantly toward the ornate entrance and into the voluminous lobby. It felt like the anteroom of a cathedral, and no one was in sight to greet us. Mommy rested on a chair, and I stayed as close to her as I could. I wanted to suck my fingers. I resisted. Daddey, in his usual fashion, went skittering about looking for someone in charge. He reappeared with a tall, uniformed nurse in tow.

"You understand you're very late. Your wife and daughter were scheduled to be here at three o'clock, Mr. ahh… What was the name?" the pinched-nosed nurse said curtly.

"My name is Nomura," he said. "We get lost for long time. The hospital is so far."

A second nurse arrived pushing a wheelchair.

"Agnes, would you take Mrs. No-muura upstairs to her room, please," said the first no-nonsense, pinched-nosed nurse.

Mommy transferred herself from the waiting-room chair to the wheelchair. She reached for my hands, "Mommy will be here near you.

Be a good girl, *neh*." She continued, "When we get well, we'll both go home with Daddey."

Nurse Agnes was in a hurry and began pushing the wheelchair away. Daddey ran up and grabbed Mommy's hand in his and whispered, "Aiko...*gam-batte, neh*." He said nothing more. He turned away, allowing Agnes to proceed.

"You understand we're very late. We have..." Agnes was saying as they went down the hall. Their backs were turned to me, and I knew Mommy could not see me, but I stood there and waved goodbye until Mommy was out of sight.

"Mr. No-muura, I just need to have you sign these two papers now. Your wife and daughter will officially be our patients. And you may leave as soon as that is done," said the first nurse very officiously. "We'll be taking your daughter to the children's ward. There will be other children for her to play with." She saw the worry crease Daddey's brow, and she softened. "Do not worry. We'll take good care of her. She will like it here at the hospital."

"I come on visiting day, Midori. Be a good girl, *neh*." "Bye, Daddey."

I followed Nurse No-Nonsense down another hall in the opposite direction of the one where Nurse Agnes had taken Mommy. We went through a pair of swinging doors, down a concrete ramp, and into a long underground tunnel. She walked briskly, and I had to pedal my legs quickly to stay abreast. We did not speak, and our footsteps were the only sounds to be heard. When we passed the open doors of a kitchen, the clatter of metal utensils was the first indication we were among other humans. We climbed up a series of ramps, then through a sequence of empty rooms to a small room at the corner of the building.

"My dear, this will be your room," the nurse said. "You will stay here by yourself for two weeks. You may NOT leave this room by yourself. Do you understand?"

"Ah-hum."

"That is not a proper answer. Here you answer either yes or no. If you meant to say yes, say yes. Do you understand?"

"Yes."

"Now take off all your clothes except your underpants. If you're cold, get under the bedcovers. We'll be bringing your meals on a tray, and when you need to use the bathroom, the bedpan is here inside the bed stand." She opened the door of the bed stand, which revealed an oddly shaped metal pan, something I had never seen before, then closed the door with no further instructions. She busily gathered up my clothes, including my purse filled with gum, a roll of Life Savers, and my favorite charms. I had carried the charms to protect me. They were all swooped out of the room along with the nurse.

I crawled under the covers as Nurse had suggested. The single thin blanket provided little warmth, and the cold, stiff starched sheets scratched my exposed skin whenever I moved. I curled up into a ball, but my shivering continued. My thoughts were to get warm. I was still struggling with the cold when someone entered my room.

"Here, we brought you some dinner," said the cheerful voice. She placed the tray on the bed stand. "It looks like our little patient is hiding under the covers."

She pulled back the covers from my head and saw me trembling. She rushed out, and after a few minutes, returned and wrapped me in an oversized hospital gown and placed a second blanket on my bed. She took my feet and rubbed them in her hands, "You need time to acclimatize, sweetie. All those heavy coats and blankets you're accustomed to made you weak. You need lots of sunshine and fresh air to make you well. We'll just have to wean you from those old habits more slowly; otherwise, you'll catch pneumonia. God forbid."

I did not understand what she was saying. I just knew she was a nice nurse with red hair bouncing under her nurse's cap. My shivering stopped, and I was finally warming up. The food on the tray wasn't appealing, so I left it untouched, but I managed to drink my milk. I made a mess with that strange curved metal contraption; its proper use no one had adequately explained. I fell asleep before they discovered it. The next day, the nurse told me I would be taken to a real toilet at regular intervals during the day. Aside from those bathroom trips, I was a prisoner in my unlocked room.

The room was in a remote corner of the building where new patients were first put in isolation, separated from the other building occupants. A window facing a group of tall fir trees dominated one wall. On the adjacent wall, a pair of french doors opened onto a small, private deck. My view of the outside was greatly enhanced from that viewpoint, but I rarely ventured out because the late summer sun was low on the horizon by the time it shone on the balcony, and it was much too chilly to stand there wearing only my underpants. The rest of the walls were painted a light institutional green, and the ceiling color was the standard institutional ivory hue. The glossy, painted surfaces offered no patterns, no weird or fanciful shadows to interpret. I languished without physical activity or mental stimulation as I lay in my bed passing each endless hour, day after day.

The white-painted metal bedframe did not even have chipped spots that could inspire an imaginary tale or two. My room was much too small to kick the wall and send my bed rolling around the floor. If my bed moved more than a few feet, it would bump into the metal bed stand with its hidden bedpan, knock over its cargo onto the radiator, and I would really be in hot water.

The nurse had said there were other children to play with when we arrived at the hospital. I never saw them. I could hear them playing outside on the lawn and hear their muffled voices in areas close to my room from time to time, but I could not join them. I had to stay shut away by myself for two weeks.

When Mommy and I get well, we can move into a house, just the three of us. The house will be like the one we went to see before Mommy got sick. There will be two bedrooms, one for Mommy and Daddey, and the second one for me. It must be oh-so- much larger than this tiny room I'm in, a bedroom big enough to put all my toys in it and ...and... I lay there and visualized room configurations, and furniture placement, and the garden and lawn that surrounded the house. Our future house provided the setting for a wonderful life for the three of us. The room layouts kept evolving endlessly as new inspirations popped in my head. Boredom was replaced by those "dream house" schemes, making time pass, and I no longer thought about being lonely.

"Here, I brought you your shoes and stockings, Sylvia. Put them on. You may leave isolation today; your quarantine is over," Miss Ahern said. She had been the most frequent attending nurse while I was restricted to my room, and I was comfortable in her presence. She was handsome rather than pretty, medium-tall with dark brunette hair crowned by her nurse's cap. It was her soft and melodic voice that smoothed her brusque, highly efficient manner. "Come with me. I will show you your new bed."

I tagged along after her, wearing my underpants, shoes, and stockings, which were to be my official uniform henceforth. I felt uneasy walking about with bare skin exposed; under normal circumstances, underpants were not exposed, so they did not count as clothing. If *Obaa-san* saw me now, she'd have let out a loud whoop and thrown a blanket on me.

I was promoted out of isolation and felt emboldened. So I peeped, "Nurse, they forgot to give me a pillow."

"We don't use pillows here. They're bad for young postures.

Come along, Sylvia."

We walked through two large rooms, each room bare of any furniture, through a pair of swinging doors to a huge outside deck. The deck was only partially covered, and the semicircular portion at the end was open to the sky above. There were perhaps eight or ten beds out in the open. The nurse said, "Here we are. This is your bed. You'll take your nap here this afternoon, and you will sleep on this bed from now on. You must learn to recognize your name so you will know which items belong to you. Now we'll walk down to the dining room. Follow me."

We walked back inside to the core of the building to the dominant central circulation ramp, that I had climbed up two weeks earlier. Miss Ahern led the way, and I trailed behind, holding onto the handrail as we walked down one level then down another. We arrived at the ground level and entered the enormous dining room, in which the cluster of tables and chairs were dwarfed by the empty spaces. Children of various ages, all naked like me, were already seated four to a table. They were grouped according to age but not by sex. Boys and girls, young and older, all turned and looked at Miss Ahern and me when we entered.

"Attention, everyone. Sylvia is joining us today. Please say hello and welcome her. Also, you'll all promise to help her learn our rules, won't you?" Miss Ahern said.

I was now a full-fledged resident of Josef House, the children's ward of Firland Sanitarium. As ill patients, we children were prohibited from straying beyond the grounds surrounding our building. There was a tall chain link fence on three sides of our vast, well-groomed lawn. The fence separated us from dense, undeveloped woods on two sides of the property. On the third side, a group of low, nondescript structures sat hidden among trees and bush on the south. They were a unit of the hospital complex, it was said, but as usual, the nurses, like all other adults, never explained precisely what the facility was used for. There was no enclosing fence on the fourth side; instead, a curbed concrete access road was the boundary. We children were not allowed to set foot beyond the curb and were told, "Don't even think about crossing the road."

The borders of my new world were sacrosanct, but the area it encompassed was vast compared to my corner-room prison. I was elated to be released from isolation, but soon enough my apprehensions took over. I had just entered a whole new strange world, and I had to face the unknown alone.

"Hi, new girl, I'm Ethel, and she's Estelle. What is your name?" she said after I was seated at their table.

"My name's Sylvia," I said as I stared at the food placed in front of me.

"I never knew anyone with that name before."

"It's American. I have a Japanese name, too. Midori."

"Oh...ah, new girl, drink that stuff in that little cup first."

"What is it? I never drank it when I was in isolation."

"Well, you gotta drink it now. You don't have to eat anything if you don't want to, except you gotta drink your cod liver oil and finish your milk or they won't excuse you from the table." She tilted her head back, gulped twice, swallowed the contents of the small paper cup, and was done with it.

"What's the red thing in the bottom?"

"It's tomato juice so it won't taste so bad. You gotta drink it real fast—— fast as you can. Then you eat some food right away so you won't taste it anymore," Estelle seconded Ethel's instructions.

I picked up the cup with cod liver oil, tilted my head, and gulped just as Ethel had done. "It doesn't taste good," I said as I reached for my glass of milk and drank.

"Don't drink milk right after the cod liver oil. It makes the milk taste bad. You gotta eat something."

Our cod liver oil cocktail appeared every morning and I practiced Ethel's ritual for drinking it for the duration of my stay at Josef House.

Ethel took it upon herself to be my primary guide and teach me the rules that Miss Ahern had alluded to. Though she was my age, she was bigger than me and relatively husky, much more so than the rest of us, who looked more like TB poster children. She was self-confident and cocky in an easygoing, matter of fact way. Though their interests were dissimilar, quiet, dark-haired Estelle tagged along after Ethel because there was no one else her age at the hospital. She was a year younger than me, but I was smaller and shorter.

After lunch, Ethel and Estelle led me from the ground floor up the ramp to the first floor. "This is the boys' floor. We can't go there without a nurse. Girls can only go to the waiting room and office," Ethel offered as explanation. We continued walking up the ramp to the second floor. "This is the girls' floor, where we stay."

"What's that door for?" I asked as I pointed to a door adjacent to the ramp we had just climbed.

"We can't go there, either. Some nurses live upstairs in the attic. It's private."

We went to our beds out in the open deck and rested for two hours. Nap time meant shoes and stockings off, lying on the bed, not sitting or standing, and no talking allowed. I had outgrown taking afternoon naps years before, and the enforced quiet time became my uninterrupted thinking time. My thoughts expanded beyond a future house to encompass the world of new ideas to which I was being exposed.

The adult oriented world I had lived in was replaced by a child-centric one ruled by nurses. The hour we were roused out of sleep in the morning, the time we were expected to be in the dining room for our meals, nap time, and the time we had to be in bed each night, were set. Periods when we were not sleeping or eating, were in theory our treatment time: exposure to fresh air and sunshine. We could run and frolic as we pleased on the lawn, invent games and play, or waste our time to our hearts content, undertaken outdoors.

Daddey brought most of my clothes and a good many of my toys to the hospital and had asked the nurses to forward them to me. The clothes, except for a few dresses and one sweater, were returned to him since I would not be wearing them.

The following day I was told to go to the reception room, where Estelle was already waiting. She was as bewildered as I was to be called into the office. She stood off to the corner, her eyes the color of her black, wavy tresses. The attending nurse, who was new to Josef House and whose name I did not yet know, was holding up my two yellow dresses that Daddey must have brought to the hospital.

"Let's see. This one fits Estelle, so it must be hers. This other one is a size smaller, so it must belong to Sylvia," the nurse said. "But...but...the dresses are both MINE. You can't give her MY dress," I said. The nurse was putting my favorite yellow dress on Estelle, the one that Mommy had bought for me at the big department store. The dress was purchased one size larger so I would have another pretty yellow dress for backup when I outgrew the much-worn one the nurse said belonged to me. The pretty dress had also been an incentive for me to "Eat and grow big and strong so you can wear your new yellow dress."

"My mommy sewed the pretty flowers on the dress just for me. That's MY dress!"

She studied the small hand-embroidered flowers decorating the dress; they were not machine sewn. It was obvious the handiwork had been added to the store-bought dress. Her face flushed, and her mouth twisted.

"I said this dress belongs to ESTELLE, you selfish brat. This other one is yours. You don't have two dresses. That's final. Now LEAVE!"

The tears flowed. A virtual river ran down my face; my sobbing turned into hiccups. Everything I knew and loved had slipped away. Now they had taken my new yellow dress, and I was powerless to do anything about it all.

Later that same week, Deanna and Agnes (the latter resembling the nurse with the same name who had so hastily wheeled away Mommy on our arrival to the hospital), invited me to visit their den. The two girls were older than the rest of us and rarely bothered to associate with us younger girls except to taunt us and boss us around. Why were they being so congenial?

The two led me to a small room formed under the stairs that led to the attic nurses' quarters above.

"Come in, Sylvia. Come in. We thought you would like to borrow a toy from our toy lending store," Agnes said. Inside the room, a huge array of toys was displayed. They were all my toys, toys that Daddey had deposited with the nurses. I recognized doll after doll, stuffed animals, miniature stove and icebox, boxes of ceramic dishes and tea sets, and more. I had rarely played with my collection of toys; our apartment was too small for me to spread them out, so they had been stored away in a closet. As an only child, I was lavished with toys by my parents, relatives and friends, and the collection had grown without the usual attrition wrought by wear and tear of oft handled toys.

"Those are MY toys. What are you doing with my toys?" I asked. "They're not your toys. They came to the hospital, and we get to keep them," Deanna interjected.

"We got first dibs. So they belong to us now. Ha."

"Now, do you want to borrow one? You can check out a toy like you check out a library book," Agnes chortled.

"They're my toys," I whispered. I grabbed the scruffy stuffed animal that was lying within reach. I turned and left the room more angry than sad. I hugged the battered stuffed toy whose resemblance to a cat defied even wild imaginations. "They took all my toys… Everything, KittyKat."

The head nurse learned about the toy store. The items were collected, and Daddey was told to take the toys back home for safekeeping.

When Daddey came to visit, I did not bother to tell him my new yellow dress had been given to someone else. I was wearing the well-worn one, which I was beginning to outgrow. I noticed Estelle was not wearing the contested yellow dress. The dress had disappeared.

I was busy making up my list of things I needed: things the hospital was not providing. "Daddey, next week can you bring me some Life Saver candy, Juicy Fruit gum, a coloring book and crayons, and two bottles of strawberry soda pop, and..."

"So many things... I not remember, Midori." "Dad-deee, you can't forget."

"I try."

Josef House

"And… You should call me Sylvia now. Remember, like Mommy said?"

"Hummm, you are always Midori to me. It issoooo hard to say… Su-ru-bi-a… Surubia?"

Daddey could not pronounce my American name without mangling it. It was just as well he continued calling me Midori. It was much better than having people make fun of him for mispronouncing my name, his own daughter's name.

Visiting days were on Thursday and Sunday for two hours. For decency's sake, we were required to wear clothes to cover our underpants. Boys wore pants and shirts, and girls wore dresses that our parents had sent from home. Daddey came faithfully every Sunday. He first visited Mommy in her ward; then afterward he visited me. He always carried a bag with a welcome treat and often a small "Made in Japan" toy, too. None of the other children had parents who visited them as diligently or with such bountiful gifts. I was lucky. Occasionally, *Obaa-san* made the trip with Daddey, and always remembering to bring Japanese treats, which were welcome too. At Josef House, we were a community of less than twenty children ranging in age from around four to twelve years. All of us had been diagnosed with tuberculosis in an early or mild form, and we were not bedridden. We were expected to be self-reliant regarding our personal habits, and the small core of nurses assigned to our ward looked after our general well-being. Our daily schedule was regimented, but we had the freedom to do nothing most of each day to replenished our energy and spirits without worry or stress. A child's stay at the hospital could not be predicted. The healthy regimen imposed on us was the only treatment available in the days before antibiotic drugs were discovered. A stay at Josef House was usually a matter of months rather than years, and there was a constant turnover of patients.

As I became familiar with the hospital routine and joined the ranks of the long-stay patients, traumas of the sort I had experienced early on diminished. Mrs. Morris had arrived and taken charge of Josef House as the permanent head nurse of the children's ward a few months after I came. Initially, her graying hair and matronly features belied an authoritative persona, but in short order, there were no doubts she was the person in charge. She ran a tight ship; she was fair, and never unkind. There was little rancor in the ranks, and Josef House ran smoothly. That environment permeated down to us children. We knew Mrs. Morris was strict, and as long as we followed the rules and did not act up, it was smooth sailing. In time, I became her favorite; even then, I was not spared all of life's reverses.

My nemesis was Miss Finke. She was a blonde with brunette roots, whose squat nurse's cap accented her puffy face. She was bulgingly plump, and the uniforms she wore looked like they had shrunk out of fit, with buttonholes pulled taut like Blimpy's. She never smiled; she snarled.

She hated me. It had been she who gave away my yellow dress. She left shortly after that incident, only to return to taunt us all. None of us liked her, but no one hated her as much as I did.

The air was turning cold and nippy, so our beds had been moved to the roofed area of the deck. My bed was next to the ramp wall, where the low angle of the winter sun cast its light and warmth. It was nap time, and as I lay awake on my bed daydreaming as usual, I heard the clump, clump of footsteps on the ramp. Curious to know who was walking up the ramp, I stood on my bed and peeked through the window. It was Nurse Fatso Finke! She was by my bedside in a flash; she must have flown in on her broom. Ordinarily she swaggered like a shoulder-padded line blocker looking for the next tackle.

"You come with me, missy. And don't deny you were standing and looking through the window." she huffed as she forcefully dragged me away. She slapped the swinging double doors open, and charged through before they bounced back on us. She had such a tight grip on my wrist I thought my arms were going to pop their sockets. We got to the ramp and started down; she stopped. "You broke the rules, you miserable brat! You were playing during nap time!" she screamed. Then she paused, taking a breath. Her voice took on a sinister tone. "You stood up to spy, to see if anyone was coming. Didn't think you'd get caught, did you? And you think you'll get away with it, don't you? Miss Smarty-pants. Well, not with me, you won't," she hissed. "You broke the rules!"

She grabbed my shoulders and shook me violently. Tears rolled onto my cheek, but I gritted my teeth and glared at her. She then loosened her grip and swung, slapping me across my face. My cheeks were stinging and hot.

"Well, what are you standing here for? This is nap time! Get back to your bed. Now!"

How I hated her! I knew I had broken the rules by standing up on my bed during nap time, but I was not playing, and I was not spying on anyone. But how had she seen me? I wondered. The same low-angle sun that warmed my bed had projected a shadow of my head on the inside wall of the ramp.

No nurse, including Mrs. Morris, ever mentioned the incident within our hearing. A few of the children who were awake and had stood on their beds peeking through the windows to witness the event, secretly reported the scene to the other nurses. My swollen face and half-shut eyes were evidence that the stories were true. They treated my face with cold compresses, told me to be more careful and not walk into any more doors in the future.

"Gee, Sylvia, we haven't seen Miss Fatso for a while. Do you think she went someplace else?" Ethel asked. The others noticed her absence before I did.

"I hope she's gone forever." I said. "Yeah, me too," the others said in unison.

Winter at the Hospital

As winter set in and the weather became colder and wetter, our beds were rolled indoors more frequently——a necessary precaution to keep from finding our frozen little bodies lying in frost-covered beds in the morning. We were now allowed to wear sweaters for protection from the elements. When the staff decided we lacked sufficient exposure to the healing rays of the sun, we had sessions with a tanning lamp of sorts. We hated it because it was boring to lie still in the artificial light with goggles protecting our eyes and nothing to do.

Cathy had no one else her age to hang around with, so she divided her time between the two older girls, Deanna and Agnes, and we younger ones. She did not really fit in either group, but she spent more time with us since she could boss us around.

Cathy and I were the only two not permitted to go to the movie that Saturday night. A movie was generally shown once a week in the basement of Josef House. Adult patients from the other buildings walked through the tunnel to the large basement viewing room, set up with chairs and equipment. Viewing a movie was a privilege we children were told. If we gained weight during the week, we were allowed to go down and watch the show. If we had not gained any weight at the Saturday morning weigh-in, we had to stay upstairs. Alas, I could never gain any weight, and I usually found myself the only one upstairs in bed. I had company that night.

The on-duty nurse, red-headed Miss Palmer, had accompanied the movie going group and had switched the PA system to a radio broadcast to keep the rest of us entertained.

"I'm hungry. Do you have anything to eat, Sylvia?" Cathy asked. "I think I still have some animal crackers."

I found the half-full box of treats. We sat on our beds and ate a few. I was biting off one limb at a time, first the legs, then the head, and the body last.

"I like the frosted kind better. I can lick the frosting," Cathy said as she licked her lips. "It's so good and sugary."

"Yeah, I like them a lot more, too."

"Hey, maybe we can put our own frosting on the crackers." She slid off the bed and skipped away. She returned with a tube of Pepsodent toothpaste. She squeezed a glob on a cracker and handed it to me. "Here, eat it."

She piped the paste on another cracker and threw it into her mouth. "That's pretty good," she said. "What's wrong? Don't you like it?"

"It tastes awful. I don't feel so good." I wanted to sleep off the experience. "You can have the rest of the crackers," I told Cathy.

A large Christmas tree was brought into the dining room, and the front reception room was decorated for the holidays. Christmas carols rang out from the radio, and we drew celebratory pictures of the season: evergreen wreaths, jingle bells, Santa, and the like. One evening, the Sunshine Boys and Girls, wearing their Christmas costumes and smiling good cheer, came and put on a program for us "unfortunate children." On behalf of Santa, they passed out a present to each of us. Ethel received a doll that cried when placed on its stomach. The following day, Ethel performed a bit of crude surgery and removed the crying mechanism from the doll's stomach; the poor thing never fully recovered. I donated my picture book to the schoolroom bookshelf after the first look over. Daddey appeared with a stuffed panda bear present for me.

He did not realize I was growing up, and I was not particularly partial to stuffed animal toys anymore, but the bear was cute and it was good company for KittyKat, the one I had rescued from the clutches of those two enterprising toy hustlers. Daddey also brought an armful of presents for the hospital staff. He gave the regular nurses and the cook, Miss Eyers, each a pair of silk stockings for "taking such good care of Sylvia." For Mrs. Morris, in addition to the silk hosiery, he brought a box of chocolates. Needless to say, Daddey was a most welcome visitor to Josef House.

Mother was located in the main building where the seriously ill patients were housed. A second building on the spacious campus housed the less ill patients, who were not bedridden and were allowed to attend the movie screenings in the JH basement. The large freestanding building across the access street which had smoke or steam continually streaming from its chimney towers was the laundry building. There was always activity inside that building, in contrast to the mysterious set of low buildings situated south of our fence. Thick, unkempt brushes effectively hid the buildings from our inquisitive eyes. "It's a quarantine ward," we were told, but curiously, it never appeared to be inhabited. For want of something better to do, we once shouted and banged on the fence to fetch attention; it was to no avail.

Once a month, I was allowed to wear a dress other than for the twice-weekly visiting hours. A nurse escorted me to the adults' Ward to visit my mother. Not only was I allowed to wear a dress, but it was also the only time I ever left the grounds of Josef House. We rarely walked through the tunnel passage to the main building. Properly clothed and looking less like a beggar's child, I followed closely behind Nurse, mainly because I did not know my way around the grounds. We cut across the mowed lawns to a side entrance to the building. Before entering Mother's room, I was reminded I had to stay away from her bed. She would be propped up in her bed, and I had to stand by the wall at the foot of her bed. We talked to each other across the room. I was not allowed to get any closer, nor was I allowed to touch her. I would tell her the things we did at Josef House and about Daddey's visits, and I was prompted to sing a song or two. With each passing month, I found it more difficult to find things to say during the visits. They became performances without a script. We no longer had common experiences to share, and the absence of physical contact and emotional bonding with my mother took its toll. She was becoming a stranger to me. She looked frail and weaker, and her responses were made with greater effort, too. She was not getting well.

A VISIT

As the worst of winter passed and the weather warmed, our beds were rolled out onto the deck more frequently. We knew we had to give up our sweaters soon. Our routine remained basically the same. Every Saturday morning, the nurses measured our height and weight, and every day a nurse took our temperatures, our pulse rates, and recorded the readings. We were fed a plentiful, healthy diet, including the daily elixir cod liver oil concoction. We napped and slept in the open, surrounded by fresh air to spend endless hours basking in the sun.

Our beds were scattered on the deck in no particular order, and mine was pushed up against the wall one morning. It was still early morning, and the light was barely making inroads in the night sky. I was roused from my sleep. I twisted in my bed. It was still dark out, too early to wake up.

"Midori…listen…" the voice murmured.

Too cold to get out of bed, I looked toward the doorway where the voice came from.

"Who's there?" I muttered groggily. "Who's calling me?" "Be a good girl, *neh*."

"Mommy?" Before I could interject, "Where are you?" the voice trailed off, "I love you…. Daddey…remember…"

I could barely hear the words. I tried focusing my eyes toward the shadows in the doorway; it was too dark to see clearly. There were only faint, hazy outlines; perhaps it was a figure, but then again, maybe not.

"Mommy…talk to me. Don't go." There was only silence. The spectral show was over.

My mother was Nisei, a second-generation Japanese, born and educated for the most part in the United States. English was her first language, the books she read were written in English, and she knew and understood American culture, but she was also a product of her Japanese heritage. Following custom, she never outwardly showed physical signs or verbalized words of love or affection in public, not even toward husband and child. That did not mean such love did not exist, nor was it any less intense or less sincere than showy demonstrations. The feelings were held deep within, not on the surface, and those feelings were transferred nonverbally.

When she asked me to be good, I understood the layers of unspoken concern, affection, love that lay beneath the innocuous spoken words: "Be good."

After breakfast, Miss Ahern sat me in the bathtub and scrubbed off the grime and the top layer of my skin. I felt like a skinny peeled banana.

"Why did I have to take a bath, Miss Ahern? Today isn't bath day," I said in protest. She ignored my question. She was helping me dress. I was quite capable of dressing myself. The nurses helped the little kids get dressed. We were expected to dress ourselves. So, what was happening? There was something fishy going on. And it wasn't Sunday.

"Why do I have to wear a dress? It's not visiting day. Today is Saturday, not Sunday."

"Today you're going home for a visit, Sylvia. Isn't that nice?" "Home? A visit? Do I have to come back?"

"Yes, your father will bring you back tomorrow." "That means I won't be here tonight?"

"That's right. You'll be home with your father."

"But Miss Ahern, I gained weight this week. I get to go to the movie tonight. Now I'll miss it!"

"Perhaps you can see the movie next week." "Oh, I hope so."

I was still sitting on the dressing table used for the little kids. Miss Ahern was buckling my shoes. It was all confusing my getting special attention and going home for a visit. No one had ever mentioned home visits before. "Do you think my mommy could come home and visit, too?" I asked.

Miss Ahern turned abruptly and bolted out of the room.

I buckled my other shoe, and I eased myself off the table. I found my purse in my locker and stuffed it with a few treasures and went downstairs to the reception room and waited for Daddey.

It felt strange to be leaving the Josef House premises. The only times I had stepped out of the boundary was during my monthly fifteen-minute visits with Mother. It was my home the past six months, and memories of life before my hospital stay had dimmed. On the ride into Seattle, I told Daddey about Mommy's early morning visit.

"Mommy is thinking about you all za time, Midori."

I was looking out the window at the houses we passed, trying to select a suitable dwelling we could move into when Mommy and I no longer stayed at the hospital. Oh, I wish Mommy could have joined us. Without any nurses around, I could hold her hands and...

"I'm home," I said to no one in particular, upon entering the apartment.

"Midori, you grow so big. You're a big girl now," *Obaa-san* said in greeting me. She spoke to me in Japanese, but she always kept her words simple so I understood. "Maybe you're tired? You sit down and rest over here, OK? *Obaa-san* and Daddey are busy now." The two went out, and I was left alone.

The living room displayed the usual clutter characteristic of *Obaa-san's* living quarters. Old magazines were stacked in a disheveled pile; the sewing kit was open on a side table with different colored spools of thread tossed about, and the vacuum cleaner stood erect in the middle of the floor with its cord snaking around on the floor beside it. *Obaa-san's* clutter was never stagnant; any particular disarray was always temporary, as new and different arrangements of clutter replaced the old in short order. Her home was never sterile; it was always warm and comfortable and welcoming, best described as a livable shambles.

I was engulfed by the overstuffed sofa that I had curled into. The sun shone in through the window and radiated warmth throughout the room. It was so cozy. The sun's rays focused directly on my exposed arms, and I noticed for the first time the mass of hair growing through the skin. My arm was covered with hair: black and long. I was turning into a fuzzy, furred animal!

The pair of embroidery scissors I found in *Obaa-san's* sewing kit was the tool of choice. I began to snip the hair on my left arm from the wrist on up to the elbow in a narrow band then I snipped back down my arm to the wrist. My fingers got tired, so I switched hands. I could not maneuver the scissors as well with my left fingers. In frustration, I decided to quit such a time-consuming task and looked about for something more interesting to do.

The magazines I could look at later. I walked around exploring through the main room, knowing *Obaa-san's* clutter hid a treasure trove of things to inspect. In a partially hidden alcove, I spied the Butsudan, the elaborate little altar that devout Buddhist families own and display in their homes. Housed in a carved wood enclosure finished in black lacquer, the pair of hinged folding panels, when opened, revealed the ornate filigreed gilt altar. It had always fascinated me. Every day or nearly every day or perhaps just often enough, *Obaa-san* placed a fresh mound of rice in a small ceremonial bowl as offering so the departed would not go hungry. The small, framed picture of a man, her husband, my grandfather, I had been told, was set inside in memoriam. I decided to check to see if she had placed fresh rice there today or if it was shriveled dry and hard as rock from the day before or earlier. I walked toward the altar, noting the front panel was folded open. A fresh, mounded rice offering had been made, and behind it was a second framed photo. I stared at the picture, my eyes glued to my mother's image. I understood; Mommy had died. The fresh rice offering was meant for her.

I stood there paralyzed as the tears flowed in an unending stream. Why didn't they tell me? Grown-ups always keep secrets. They never tell kids anything. My tears were unstoppable.

Obaa-san and Daddey returned and found me crying. They knew immediately I had somehow learned my mother was dead.

"Why didn't you tell me?" I wailed at Daddey.

"Everybody is so sad and unhappy. Nobody want to tell you because you will be unhappy and sad, too, Midori."

"Mommy in heaven," *Obaa-san* interjected. "Buddha said heaven is filled with flowers. They cascade down like rain from the sky. Aiko no sick anymore; she is very happy in heaven. She want you to be happy too, not sad and crying, *neh.*"

Daddey opened a box and pulled out a new dress. The dress was navy blue crepe. I changed into it immediately. The style, fit, and fabric were ill suited for my bony frame, but the somber color was appropriate. My coat, a piece of clothing not allowed at the hospital, had been stored away and was now too short; it was inches shorter than my new dress. Buying a new coat was out of the question. I could toss the coat on my shoulders and wear it like a cape, everyone agreed.

Auntie Hamayo and Uncle Katsumi were enlisted to take me to Volunteer Park in the afternoon to distract me from thinking about my mother. The afternoon was unseasonably warm, and the cherry trees were in full bloom. It was a glorious spring day in Seattle, but the three of us were not particularly engaged, and though they tried, we did not really have a good time. In the evening, we all set out for the funeral home where the services were to be held.

Daddey and I sat in the secluded alcove to the side of the main hall curtained off from view, but with a sight line to the opened casket and the wreaths surrounding it. Though screened from those assembled to pay their last respects, I could hear them shuffling to their seats and hear the creaking chairs as they shifted their weight from one bun to the other. In addition, a sniffle sounded every now and then.

I sat quietly on my chair, alert to the proceedings except when the rough seams of my ill-fitting new funeral dress scraped against my skin, and the urge to scratch had to be suppressed. This was not a time to fidget. Daddey sat stoically, giving his *jizu* a twist from time to time, or alternately patting my hand. The solemn tones from the organ set the requisite somber mood, and I sat quietly, contemplating random life events. When an especially poignant memory came to mind, the tears followed. Sometimes I inspected the new *jizu Obaa-san* had given me for the occasion. It was a smaller version of an adult one and much more handsome than the red beaded set I used in Sunday school. I examined the purple tassel and the clear-cut crystal beads I had once so dearly coveted. The chanted sutra droned on and on in monotone along with the intermittent bell tapping, interspersed with speeches and a sermon of sorts spoken entirely in Japanese. What it all meant was a mystery; it was just another one of those things adults never bothered to explain.

Father and I were the first ones to light our incense in front of the coffin, and the other attendees followed in a procession, paying their respects. The service ended, and chairs near the front were unceremoniously pushed out of view. A few chairs were placed on both sides of the casket, and Mat-san claimed one and sat down.

Others were reluctant to take a seat placed so prominently in front; gathering around the back of the casket, preferring less exposure in the keepsake funeral picture. A photo of the event was still customary. Daddey lifted me up so my head showed above the bouquet of flowers on top of the coffin, whose lid had now been closed. We were positioned front and center, while everyone gathered around displaying their somber, tight-lipped faces, eyes downcast, or grimly staring straight ahead, as appropriate for the occasion. After the photographer finished and waved everyone away, people again gathered and milled around, greeting and chatting with each other. It was a modest funeral, and most of the attendees knew each other. They were discreetly socializing before leaving for home.

"OOOOoo…" a woman shrieked.

"She's fainted," a man called out. Mrs. Nakamura lay collapsed on the floor. A group of people surrounded her, trying to revive her.

"Oh… I was so overcome by Aiko's death…leaving her baby…" she sobbed as she came to. They led her away for some fresh air.

As the various attendees stopped to give Yoshi their condolences before leaving, Yukimasa stepped forward and took his hand. It was the first time the cousins had met since the raucous letter exchange between Yoshi and Ito. He introduced his wife, Kiyomi, and said it was unfortunate their wives had not had a chance to become acquainted. Yoshi was gratified their rift was on the mend, as he sincerely offered his blessings on his cousin's marriage, though somewhat belatedly.

People appeared to be going every which way, and I lost sight of Daddey. I looked among the groups of people still chatting. He was gone, and I began to panic, rushing from one person to another.

"Are you looking for your daddy? He went downstairs. Come with me," the man said.

Other people were downstairs, too. I heard Daddey's voice in the distance. I was relieved.

"There's Midori. She hasn't said good-bye to Mama yet!" I was scooped off the floor and cradled in the stranger's arms, eye level to the small window. Gas jets shooting thrusts of fire were fueling the conflagration within. Whoosh, whoosh, whoosh, flames continually fed by more fuel: blinding, searing, intense. Whoosh, whoosh, whoosh sounded as blowtorch-piercing blasts erupted into blazing chaos. These were not graceful undulating tapers morphing into vapors. The fires raging in this furnace were fierce, roaring all-consuming: an inferno. "Say good-bye to Mama," the man said as he took my wrist, shaking it, making my limp hands wave. Bye-bye Mama. He put me down, satisfied I had given Mother a proper send-off to nether land. I ran off to find Daddey. Where, oh where is he?

It had been a long, eventful day, and I dozed on *Obaa-san's* lap as Daddey drove home from the funeral. The car came to a screeching halt, and I was jolted awake. It was dark, and the roadway was ill lit. Daddey saw the outline of a body lying in the middle of the road. Our car had stopped barely a foot or two away. Daddey stepped out of the car to check on the man's condition.

"Hey, what's a-matta?" Daddey shouted as he stood over the prone object. It twisted. Daddey leaned over and shook him.

"Whoaaaa…" the man groaned as he shook himself awake. He sat up and squinted toward the car's headlights beaming on him. He turned and looked at Daddey, who was still standing beside him. "Whoaaaa. I need a drink. Say, buddy, you got a dime?" he asked as he rolled his eyes, trying to focus on his surroundings.

"You almost die; get run over. No sleep on street," Daddey said as he helped the drunk walk to the sidewalk. He fumbled in his pocket and came up with a couple of quarters and gave it to him. "You go sleep in hotel."

"Almost a second death," *Obaa-san* said. "We all have our *jizu* tonight. That saved him."

RETURN TO THE HOSPITAL

Daddey drove me back to the hospital the next day. The other children had been told my visit home was to attend my mother's funeral. And henceforth it was not a matter for discussion, especially with me. When I returned to Josef House, no one asked me about my visit home, neither the children nor the nurses. Without questions to answer about the funeral, I was not reminded of the events of my visit home, and I resumed the familiar hospital routine. Things returned to normal except at nap time.

My usual nap time daydreams went on holiday. As I lay on my bed absent of sleep, an overwhelming sense of loss would envelope me. It was the total emptiness I felt when I first found my mother's picture sitting in the Butsudan. I cried and cried. Death was so final. The fierce, roaring fire incinerated everything... Mommy was vaporized into nothingness...poor, poor Mommy. I sobbed and continued crying. The nurses left me alone even past nap time. They let me cry until I stopped, allowing me to rejoin the others on my own. As the week wore on, the river of tears I shed diminished; the well of tears was running dry. My crying became intermittent.

Mommy will never come home anymore. She'll never go with us to the lake and feed the ducks. She'll never walk downtown with me to buy me a yellow dress. She'll never ever go with us to my favorite restaurant to eat spaghetti and Jell-O. She'll never... when you die, it's the end of everything, I said to myself. Everybody will die someday. Then they'll burn you up in a hot, hot furnace. People get old and die...even Daddey and me. We'll get old and die.

Whaaaat? Me? Die? One day I have to die, too? And someday I'll be vaporized into nothingness? My whole body shook in anguish. NO! NO! I love being alive! I love me! I love the world and all the wonderful things in it! I want always to be able to think thoughts and be conscious and daydream and feel the warm sun and see the sky and...to be alive. I don't want to die ever! I agonized in silence, and the sobs erupted again. I had become aware of my own mortality.

My crying continued in torrents. When I die, I'll have no memory again. I won't know me! Those around me had no idea my grief for my mother's death had transformed to a despair that I, too, would die one day; it was inevitable and inescapable. The nurses waited patiently for my crying to abate. Even Ethel stood apart and watched wordlessly and with great sympathy.

On visiting day in mid-May, Daddey was accompanied by *Obaa-san* and teenaged aunties Kimiye and Hamayo, and Uncle Katsumi. They came to help me celebrate my seventh birthday. They gave me little gifts to open and a huge sheet cake to be shared later with the other children at dinner. Though my aunts and uncle were not adults, for this special occasion, they were allowed to enter the grounds, and we visited together on the expansive lawn. On an ordinary visit, my aunts and uncle would have been relegated to the large gazebo across the road from Josef House, limiting contact to waving at each other.

Estelle was allowed to go home before summer's arrival, and a few months later, Ethel went home, too. Deanna and Agnes, who had both been allowed to wear dresses to cover their blossoming upper torsos, left Josef House, too. Whether they returned home or to another part of the hospital complex with more age-appropriate activities was never explained. Other children arrived to take their places. Sisters Sue and Millie were not my age. Older Millie was shy and reclusive, and younger Sue was outgoing, energetic and participated in our little adventures. Newcomer June was very thin like me. She had blondish hair, which hung drooping alongside a long, narrow face that seldom smiled. Maybe she smiled with just the least bit of a curl at the end of her mouth like a comma, so one had to look hard to detect it. She was older than me by a year, but she was quiet and reserved, quite the opposite of Ethel. Now that I was an old-timer at Josef House, I was no longer intimidated by older girls, so June and I got along well. Cathy tagged along with us now that she had lost her two older companions. We usually ignored the younger children, who played their baby games and needed more supervision from the nurses.

There were changes in the boys' ward, too, but I was not particularly attentive to their doings. Handsome Paul had come and gone, and Victor, the other Japanese at Josef House, was a short-timer. Sonny, a Filipino boy my age, arrived at the end of summer, and we became good friends. I did have a hard time forgiving him for one despicable thing that happened, involuntary though it was. He vomited in my face at lunch one day. I was sitting at the table to his right when, without warning, the godawful projectile splashed directly on my face. Agh! Double agh!

The first anniversary day of my arrival to Firland was approaching, and the seasonal changes I was witnessing reminded me of that time. It was all so very long ago; much had happened and changed, and I was not the same scared little girl. Now I was comfortable in the familiar confines of Josef House, the schedules and rules that governed my life offered a sense of security. I had to take care of myself and my belongings. I had learned to cope. I felt I had grown up.

"This year we have a teacher who will be coming to Josef House. On Wednesday afternoon each week, you children will go to school." Mrs. Morris announced at breakfast.

I gulped down my cod liver oil without second thoughts. Done with the disagreeable chore first, I began chattering to my table companions about the announcement.

"Sylvia, you are talking instead of eating your cereal. You know the rules."

I could hardly contain myself: We were going to school! Gobbling up my food, I asked to be excused, and ran up the ramp to wait for the others. There, we could talk about school.

We school-aged children were gathered in the large ground level classroom well before our new teacher's arrival. There were two rows of typical schoolroom desk/seats that increased in size as they went toward the back. Low shelves filled with books and toys were augmented by several child-sized tables and chairs. Half of the room was open for non-sedentary activities. The blackboard on the wall verified the rooms status as a classroom.

Mrs. Engle wore her hair in a bun on the back of her head, which made her look elderly. Her glasses sat on the middle of her nose, emphasizing the granny look when she peered over the rim. She was soft-spoken and kind, and obviously overwhelmed by her new assignment.

Actually, there were only about nine of us who were eligible to attend school. There was no kindergarten. We students represented four different grades and nine levels of learning skills. It was an impossible undertaking; in reality, we each needed a tutor. Other than a spelling exercise we were required to finish, we were allowed to leave our desks, to go to a table to draw pictures or play with toys. The one imposed rule: only one toy at a time. Setting up dominos to topple was everyone's favorite. I found the realistic three-dimensional images rendered by a handheld Biograph great fun. Many of the other toys appeared to be almost as old.

Before the end of class, Mrs. Engle read us a story. For me, story time was the best part of our school day. Best remembered, was the story of the proud tree that refused to shed its beautiful leaves one autumn. During the winter, the once lovely leaves became torn and tattered by winds and storms. When spring arrived, the other trees sprouted beautiful new leaves. The moral of the story was elusive, but I am reminded of the sorry tree every spring when the bare limbs of winter sprout fresh growth, and a new crown of shimmering leaves inevitably follow.

Not much learning took place at our school, but it kept us occupied, and I heard one keepsake story.

One afternoon, June and I found Sue with her mother in one of our empty winter bedrooms.

"I'm going home with my mother today," Sue said. "They're getting my things now. I'll miss you both."

"What about Millie? Is she going home, too?" I asked.

June piped up, "They're putting her in isolation. She's been really sick. She has to stay in bed." We were all little medical specialists by now. Our hospital environment and exposure to medical jargon and wellness lectures made us well versed in treatment procedures. Bed rest was the basic treatment to cure an illness.

"My mother said they already took Millie to the quarantine ward." Sue and Millie's mother was a small woman with jet-black hair tied to hang behind her back. She stood by the window with her back toward us the entire time we chatted with Sue. She pretended she was lost in her own thoughts to avoid talking to us.

"I'll send you some shells and special beads. The beads have magic power to make you well. Then you can go home, too."

"Gee, will they be Indian beads? I never had a real Indian bead bracelet. I have a kind of Buddha bracelet at home." I said. "If you put it on your wrist and pray real hard, maybe your wish will come true."

"Did you ever have any wishes come true when you prayed with your bracelet?" Sue asked.

"Nope, nothing happened. That's why I really need a real Indian one."

"And if you made it for us, it'd be a real Indian bracelet," June said.

June and I were shooed out of the room, and we never saw our Indian friends again.

June, Cathy, and I were a threesome now. Having become the older girls at Josef House, the nurses had become more lenient, by giving us small privileges. We were allowed to play quietly in the reception room, which was our parlor except during visiting hours. It was the only room in the entire building with cushioned chairs. It was our "temperature-taking" area, too. We put the thermometers in our mouths and waited for Nurse to take the readings and check our pulses each day. We sat on the sofa, looking through magazines or the wonderful Sears and Roebuck catalogue that appeared one day. The vast number of pages devoted to toys kept us busy for long periods. When there were more than one ogling the catalogue, we played "Mine". On each page, we studied each item in depth before making a decision, then slap our hand on the item we liked best.

Slap, slap, slap. Our hands went down on the page and covered the photo of a coveted toy. We played the game endlessly. We never bothered to look at the little girls' clothing section since that was pointless.

In the evening, Mrs. Morris sometimes allowed us to play Chinese checkers on the Josef House office table. We usually wanted the same marble color and argued. I tried to teach the other girls rock-paper-scissors to easily resolve such issues, but their rock-heads could not grasp the concept, and we argued some more. Once the game started, we were amicable and became company for Mrs. Morris while she went about her office chores.

"Oh, yes. My husband died in the war, a long time ago." She meant the Great War, of course. "I wanted to be near him. They needed nurses, so I went to Europe."

"Where is Europe, Mrs. Morris?"

"It's on the other side of the Atlantic Ocean. There are many countries there, and they are at war again." She rested and reflected, "War is a terrible thing. There is so much destruction, and people are killed, even children. Soldiers die, and many more are wounded. They're inflicted with such horrible wounds. The doctors do the best they can, but too many brave young men suffer indescribable pain before they die. We couldn't help them enough." She had not intended to say these things to her young audience. We three sat in silence.

"Believe me, war is terrible."

CHAPTER 10

The War, 1941

THE COLLEGE CLUB WAS AN ivy-covered brick building in the center of town, a private men's club with a smaller and younger membership than several others in the city. Its location was convenient, and the club was well attended, especially during the day. The service staff was mostly Japanese, and staff openings were rare. Yoshi's working experience in restaurants, as a janitor, and a second butler qualified him for the job; nevertheless, he felt lucky he had been hired. He gladly left his midnight shift to work days and sleep at night as most people do. He had begun the job in April before Aiko and Midori's admission to Firland Sanatorium. During this turbulent time for Yoshi, he'd weathered the Housing Authority's threats of eviction, Aiko's undiagnosed illness (whose symptoms kept getting worse by the week), all the while, adjusting to his new job. When wife and daughter were hospitalized, and he in essence, reverted to living a bachelor's life, the meals provided at work were a godsend. His Sunday work hours were adjusted, allowing several hours off in the afternoon to make his visiting day appointments.

The employees were addressed by their American names or a short-ened version of their native names. When a multiple-syllable foreign name was difficult to pronounce, an easier one was substituted. Yoshi again became known as George, as he had been called in New York.

Dr. Rembe was a lunchtime regular at the club. He was a physician versed on public health matters and he was well aware of Yoshi's situa-tion. They exchanged greetings, and one day shortly after Aiko had been admitted to the hospital, Yoshi asked the doctor for an honest prognosis and chances of her recovery.

"Are you sure you want to know, George?" He searched Yoshi's face, trying to determine if it was an impromptu or a deeply pondered inquiry.

"Yes, please."

"Well… George… The truth is, your wife's illness is so advanced, she will not recover. We don't have any miracle drugs to cure TB yet." He answered with precision then slowly shook his head from side to side. Softly, he added, "I'm sorry."

"Thank you, Doctor."

"Take heart, George. Your daughter is fine. She'll be able to come home soon."

The doctor had confirmed Yoshi's premonitions; Aiko's illness was terminal.

He grieved alone and in silence. There was so much he had wanted to do for her, places he wanted to take her to… She had led such a constricted life. He thought there was a lifetime to deliver his promises, a long lifetime. Instead, her lifetime was destined to be incredibly short with no future of better times together.

There was little Yoshi could do for Aiko now. The handsome new wristwatch he bought to cheer her spirits hung so loose on her thin, bony wrist, it was best stored away. Yoshi tried to be chatty and optimistic during his Sunday visits, but it was obvious she was weaker each week; she was failing. When he was called to the hospital unexpectedly, he understood the end was near.

Friends commented on Yoshi's stoicism at the funeral and how well he had adjusted to Aiko's death in the following weeks. Others did not know his grief had played out in the preceding months when he had watched helplessly as his wife's life ebbed away.

Yoshi sought Dr. Rembe's advice again after Aiko's passing. "Yes, that's a big problem if there's no one at home to take care of your daughter. How old did you say she is?" "Midori is six year old, pretty soon seven year."

"Six years old… We definitely don't want to send her home where there's no supervision while you're working. It's not a safe or healthy environment. We don't want her to have a relapse after all the months it's taken for her to become well and cured," the doctor said. "Let me think this over."

Several days later, Dr. Rembe took Yoshi aside to talk to him. "Sit down here, George." Seeing his discomfort, he continued, "It's all right for you to sit down for a few minutes. I told Joe I had something important to discuss with you. What I have to say won't take long." Preliminaries over, he began, "You were told your daughter is well and that she can leave the hospital. That is true. I discussed your situation with members of the department. They decided your daughter could stay at Josef House, if you agreed. She can continue to live there where she will be well taken care of. Everything can continue the same as it has the past six months. Let me know what you decide, will you, George?"

His personal life was in a state of limbo. He was a widower, not a bachelor, though he had the freedoms of a single man. His role as parent intruded on his life for a mere few hours once a week now that Midori was being cared for at the hospital. His aversion to card playing took a holiday, and he found himself engrossed in late-night sessions weekly. Occasionally he visited family friends, but he found the visits constrained without a wife to accompany him. These and other activities were distractions that kept him from dwelling on his predicament; however, periods of introspection were unavoidable.

Yoshi realized Aiko had kept fears that her fate was repeating that of her mother: she would die young, leaving her husband with a young daughter. That was her karma, as it was her mother's karma. Would it be repeated in the third generation? There was no clue, but the possibility existed that Aiko had considered these things. "One's karma is not controlled by humans, one must just accept it." Yoshi remembered he had been told. If that were the case, then could the years before an inevitable early death be made into a happy experience? Odai was not there to counsel him. Yoshi decided that was his new mission: to accept the responsibility to make Midori's life as happy as possible, whether it be a long or short one. Not long before, Yoshi had been full of doom as life's reverses tested him. Karma, Smarma, he thought as often as not. The gloom lifted, and Yoshi was sure his karma was once again on a positive track.

CRASH! The sound of falling dishes breaking on the floor sounded from the hallway.

"It sounds like Kay did it again."

"It sounded like a loaded tray today."

"He breaks so many things; the club must be suffering a huge loss on his account," the third waiter said.

"If he was working anywhere else, he'd have been fired by now," the first waiter replied.

Yoshi joined the other three men. He shook his head. Kay was a long-time friend, and the fumbling accidents were distressful. Not only could he lose his job, but the accidents also prompted derision.

"You're right. Kay's lucky they let him keep his job," Yoshi interjected. He knew his own record for dumb-headed mistakes and accidents were minimal compared to his clumsy friend's record. Although Yoshi was a comparative newcomer on the job and had low seniority, he had become a worthy team member, and his good humor was welcomed by staff and members alike. Yoshi was not unhappy with his job.

Getting up so early on that Sunday morning was the last thing he wanted to do, especially since his two younger brothers had been allowed to sleep in. Eleven-year-old David was accompanying his father to a church on the other side of Honolulu where his father taught Sunday school. When their bus reached the end of the line, they had to transfer onto a second bus. On a bluff overlooking the city, they saw the columns of black smoke rising into the clouds. They were coming from the harbor. "It must be more maneuvers," they both thought. No transfer bus arrived. instead, military vehicles commandeered the roads. Few planes roared overhead, but sporadic ack ack and blasts in the distance signaled the exercise was not over, nor was the commotion. Shining and shimmering in the early morning sun, the cluster of previously barely perceptible airplanes was exposed as they left the scene. They each bore a red circle insignia. These planes were not American.

"The dirty Japs bombed Hawaii. We're going to war and fight those Japs!"

The news reverberated throughout the building. America had been attacked by the Japs, and they were our enemies. As patriotic Americans, young though we were, our fervor of patriotism was boisterous and loud: "Kill those bad Japs!"

I was disappointed when Mrs. Morris told me Daddey had called to say he was not able to visit me that afternoon. Daddey always came on Sunday to visit me. I was especially disappointed because I was anxious to tell him how we were going to "fight those dirty Japs."

"Sylvia, don't you know? Jap is short for Japanese?" Sonny said to me incredulously.

"I'm Japanese-American. Nobody ever called me Jap. I'm not a dirty, bad Jap!" I stormed and stomped angrily. I began to cry. Others gathered around us, and Sonny told them my predicament.

"Sylvia's our friend." "Yeah, she's not a Jap!"

"I'm an American," I said vehemently.

"We know you're American, Sylvia. But you're Japanese, too." "It's too bad you're Japanese."

"I can't help it, I was just born that way," I said.

"You can split yourself down the middle, and one side can be Japanese and one side can be American," someone snickered.

"We know all Americans are good. Sylvia is American. So Sylvia is a GOOD Japanese and not a BAD Jap," Sonny declared. "And she's our friend."

Everybody agreed with that logic. I was accepted as an American and a friend once more.

Japanese planes bombed Pearl Harbor!

Reports blasting from the radio are not true. Tell me it's a bad dream. Why? Raced through Yoshi's head. It was all incomprehensible: Japan bombing an America territory. It was an act of war: Japan against the United States. Why? His beloved homeland had attacked the country where he had sought his future and had lived half his life.

He had an emotional investment in Japan, his family, the culture, the language, its history; it was home, and he planned to return someday and live out the rest of his life there. As a second son, he had to make his own way. He left to seek his fortune; America offered greater opportunities and he had benefited. The fortune eluded him, and a worldwide economic depression persuaded the intended sojourner to stay put. He married a Nisei and fathered a Sansei child whose loyalties were to America. Yoshi had to admit he had become accustomed to the freer, less restricted life possible in America, where he now felt like a settler.

There were negative aspects of being an alien, legal or illegal, living in a foreign land. Yoshi could never master the English language, and as a nonwhite, he was relegated to second-class status. A Japanese settler is not welcomed with open arms.

In New York City, where the immigrant population was immense and the diversity of peoples included those from all parts of the world, rudeness and insults were commonplace as customs and cultures clashed; it was general and less personal. It took a different turn in Seattle, where the newest immigrants were mostly from Asia, not from Europe as on the East Coast. The public felt mistrust when dealing with people who looked different, and they made them prey for their abuse.

Yoshi was initially taken aback when racial and personal insults were flung at him unexpectedly and for no apparent reason, abuses many long-suffering Orientals in the West had long endured. He had rarely encountered such animosity and discrimination and he came West without the bitterness and resentments many long-term immigrants had acquired.

Yoshi was unafraid of mingling with the white majority, his interactions with *gaijin* were open and sincere, and a friendly smile eased tensions.

Yoshi might have been conflicted had he been asked to choose a country earlier; now it was moot. The hatred against him and everything Japanese would only escalate. *Shikata-ga-nai.* It's something one cannot do anything about.

The immediate reality was that he had just turned forty-one, and was an illegal immigrant from an enemy country residing in America with a US-born seven-year-old daughter staying in a TB sanitarium. He called the hospital, letting them know he would miss visiting day, and he walked to work.

The boarder from room 208 was raving and shouting as he banged his fist along the wall as he walked down the corridor. "I'm leaving if you don't get rid of those slant-eyed yellow bastards. Get the Japs out of here." He slammed his door for emphasis and disappeared into his room.

"He's been acting like that since he heard the news on the radio," Kay told Yoshi. "Mr. Joe's having a meeting at four o'clock for the crew. It's posted on the board."

The meeting began promptly at four.

"We want to assure you men that, despite the Japanese attack on the United States, we consider all our employees to be loyal to our country and to the club. That includes our Japanese employees without exception. As friends, we will…" began the manager's speech. As an employer, the club treated its immigrant service staff with a paternalistic hand, kindly and tolerant. Yoshi felt truly lucky to be working for the club.

Many other Japanese were not so lucky, and covert hostilities were exposed that eventful day or soon afterward as employers abruptly rid their staff of Japanese by firing them from their jobs.

Federal government agencies took steps to regulate Japanese aliens immediately. FBI agents directly rounded up men from their homes, arrested and detained them, and later sent them to Justice Department detention centers located in states removed from the West Coast. These men were mainly the community leaders who were on an FBI list of possible subversives; Buddhist priests and Japanese-language school teachers were included in the list as persons with strong ties to Japan. Along the West Coast, contraband such as radios with shortwave bands, cameras, binoculars, and guns owned by enemy aliens had to be surrendered. From time to time, the FBI made spot searches in Japanese homes looking for such items. Individuals found it prudent to get rid of items that could be construed as unpatriotic, including Japanese flags, photos of the emperor, and similar items rendered subversive. More than one backyard bonfire were lit to destroy such items.

The attack on America was as much a surprise to those in the Japanese community as to the nation as a whole, with exceptions. A small percentage who had strong premonitions of an impending conflict or were thus warned, took actions to be living in the right country in that eventuality. Mr. Hiyama, one of the regular bachelor visitors to *Obaa-san's* store on Yesler, returned to Japan when his employer called him back months before the attack. Plucky Vicky, attending a finishing school in Japan, was advised to return to Hawaii, and she managed to catch the next-to-last ship to set sail to America. Shizuyo and her ill brother were refused boarding on the filled to capacity ship despite their pleading. When the siblings' relationship to a professor who once mentored the ship's doctor became known, they were given passage. They were put in the only open beds on the ship: in the ship's hospital.

University graduate Ted, spending a year in Japan honing his Japanese-language skills, lived in a Buddhist monks abode with cold showers and other aesthete treats. "For your own safety," he was told, "leave at once." He spent days cooling his heels while officials officiously procrastinated stamping required approvals for him to return to America. After his return, he spent the war years in Ann Arbor teaching advanced Japanese-language classes to military personnel for the war effort. The lucky ones boarded the last ships crossing the Pacific. Many others found themselves stuck in a country not of their choice. Yoshi's Nisei friend Ken, who sold vegetables at the market, had gone to Japan to find a job in his profession, was later inducted into the Japanese army.

On December 8, the United States officially declared war on Japan. As the country united against an enemy, the Japanese, few bothered to distinguish between those living in Japan and those living in the US; whether they were "ineligible-for-citizenship" aliens or their "born-in-America citizen" offspring. Radio newscasts and the written media, especially the Hearst newspapers, continually and blatantly inflamed existing hostile sentiments of the populace. Animosity toward the Japanese living in America escalated with each day. The anti-Japanese sentiments raged over the land, but the loud and most vicious were on the West Coast, where the majority of Japanese lived. There, deep-rooted resentments had existed since the immigrants first arrived in America. The newest settlers had taken on the least desirable, dirty, and difficult jobs others refused, just as earlier immigrant groups had taken on before, and later immigrant groups would continue to do. As farmers, they had taken unwanted scrubland and, through hard work, sacrifices, and perseverance, had succeeded in making the land produce, and had prospered. The Japanese in America were making inroads in other occupations as well, with diligence and patience. There were people, however, who coveted what these Japanese settlers had achieved, thereby creating an alliance with scaremongers who aimed their invectives and escalating the hysteria against all Japanese. From every corner, their outcry was to ouster the Japs: round them up, and herd them into interior wastelands. To remove them from the West Coast where they cannot aid and abet the enemy in an invasion; and intimating the sentiments of Lieutenant General John L. DeWitt, "A Jap is a Jap."

Daily Life Continues

Yoshi continued to make his Sunday visits to Firland, and for Christmas. He brought the customary Christmas gifts for the nurses: silk stockings, which may have been their last pair until war's end, and for Midori there was a special new doll. New Year's was not celebrated with its customary abundance of traditional foods and activities, especially in households with absent patriarchs. A gloom prevailed throughout the community.

The atmosphere was ugly on the streets. The club was an oasis where the Japanese employees were treated decently and with dignity. Aside from going to work, Yoshi limited his social activities, keeping an unobtrusive presence. The world had changed, and it was unwise to provoke an incident no matter how unintended the offense might be. Even while walking along a sidewalk, a stranger might suddenly call out a hateful racial slur, turn to spit on a person, or worse.

There always exists a small minority who will swim against the tide, and there were people who spoke up for the civil rights of Japanese Americans when the government, the media, and the general public were vilifying them, and clamoring for them to be subjugated without a trial. Not everyone branded the Japanese in their midst as spies or enemies to be despised and degraded. The Woodwards, who edited the Bainbridge Review, were a singular defending voice in the sweeping bias and hate-fraught journalism of that era. The stand they took was extremely unpopular, and unfortunately, they were victims of reprisals.

There were also individuals who continued to hearten the Japanese with kindness in many ways.

"Hello, George. How is your daughter these days?" Dr. Rembe asked after the holidays. He continued to take a special interest in Yoshi's predicament.

"Daughter is fine, thank you, Doctor." He then quietly added, "Sometime it is dangerous to drive to Firland. It so far away. One time, police stop me and say go home."

"Humm…maybe we can ask a couple of my friends to help us." The doctor walked over to two men who had entered the club a short time before, and the three of them sat down at a table together. "Come over here, George," he called as he waved Yoshi toward them. "George, I want you to meet agents Bob Pringle and Ron McHugh. They're FBI agents. Perhaps they'll be able to advise us."

"Hello, nice to meet you, George," they said in unison.

"Hal-lo," George answered and bowed his head, a reflex action acknowledging the greeting.

Doctor Rembe began, "Let me give you a little background first. George's wife and daughter had tuberculosis, and they were both sent to Firland Sanitarium more than a year ago. His wife died about nine months ago. His six-year-old daughter is still out there."

"Daughter seven-year-old now," Yoshi interjected.

"Right, she's now seven years old." The doctor collected his thoughts and continued, "George drives out to Firland every Sunday to visit her. He was stopped by the police once and told to go home. I believe he's a bit fearful that in the future the authorities might not be so friendly, shall we say."

"Where's the sanitarium located?"

"In an area known as Richmond Highlands. It's approximately ten, perhaps a dozen, miles north of us here."

"Would he drive on Aurora Avenue to get there?"

"That would be the best route. It's a few blocks east of the highway on approximately 190th Street"

"You say she has TB? That would preclude moving her to another hospital closer to the city, is that right?"

"Yes," Dr. Rembe said. He decided to forgo further explanations regarding the status of the daughter's health.

"It seems to me all George needs is a travel permit. What do you say, Ron?" Agent Pringle said.

"He shouldn't have any problems getting a travel permit. We don't think George is a subversive. If he had been on our list, we'd have picked him up last month," Agent McHugh assured the doctor.

"George, just come up to our offices. You've probably heard by now, we're in the Federal Courthouse building. Come in and get an application, fill it out, and submit it. The permit itself usually takes a week to be issued."

"If you have any further questions, just see either Agent Pringle or myself, will you, George?"

"Thank you. Thank you very much," Yoshi said as he nodded his head in gratitude and eased himself away.

"I'm ready to order some lunch. We still have time for a couple of sets. Will you two gentlemen join me today?"

As predicted, Yoshi had no problem getting a travel permit. Mr. Joe had readily agreed to sign the application as a reference. When either of the two agents saw George in their offices, they were as courteous and helpful as they had been at the club.

Evacuations Begin

In early February, the army defined twelve "restricted areas" on the West Coast. German, Italian, and Japanese enemy aliens living within those areas were imposed with a curfew, between 8 p.m. and 6 a.m.; the hours when they were required to be in their homes. Additionally, any travel was restricted to an area within a five-mile radius of their homes.

On February 19, President Roosevelt, using his war powers, signed Executive Order #9066. Authority over civilians was transferred from the government to the military. The Secretary of War or any military commander he might so designate was authorized to define areas that would exclude "any and all persons…as deemed necessary or desirable…" Copies of the order were published, distributed, and posted on bulletin boards and telephone poles in areas densely populated by Japanese.

General DeWitt, the secretary's appointee, began issuing public proclamations designating various military areas—areas where the Japs would be excluded. Another executive order created the War Relocation Authority (WRA) to implement the orderly evacuation of "undesirables" from designated military areas. A few days later, Congress enacted a law which penalized persons who violated orders to leave or enter those military areas. Less than a week later, all voluntary migration in or out of Military Area #1 by Japanese was prohibited. The five-mile travel radius and evening curfew were extended to all persons of Japanese ancestry, whether alien or US-born citizen. New laws were enacted, and orders and proclamations came one after another.

On March 24, all Japanese living on Bainbridge Island were notified they would be evacuated from the island by March 30. They were given less than one week to put their affairs and properties in order and be ready to vacate and moved to parts unknown. They were escorted off the island, taken by ferry to Seattle, put on trains and shipped to Manzanar Relocation Center in east-central California. This action served as a warning of what was in store for all other Japanese living in the designated military areas. No one was in denial any longer.

In February, Hayame married Shigeichi Hori. He was a long-time friend from the valley who had known her late husband Masaichi even longer. The two men came from neighboring villages in Japan, and after arriving in America, both had engaged in vegetable and dairy farming. They had also been active participants in the close-knit White River Valley communities. It was Hori who had accompanied Hamayo and Kimiye back from Japan, and the families had kept close contact through the years. Hori had become a widower recently, and at a time when new restrictive regulations were continually being imposed on them, he could not follow courtship convention too long. They needed to act fast. He proposed, and she accepted. Hayame closed the store, and she and her children moved to his home in Kent. The blended family, her four children and his four, would be together wherever they might be sent.

Yoshi felt his problem might not be as easily resolved.

"Of course, George. Whenever I can help..." Dr. Rembe answered when Yoshi once again sought his advice.

"I think the army will make all Japanese evacuate—me, too. I don't know if daughter can evacuate, too."

"George, I understand patients in hospitals are excluded from that order. All our Japanese patients who are in the hospital now will remain at Firland. Your daughter will be safe at Josef House if you are evacuated."

"She is little girl, Doctor. If I go away, no one will visit her. She will be very lonely," Yoshi said. "Maybe I be gone many years."

"Do you want to take your daughter with you?"

"I think so. I feel very sad if she stay all alone and I cannot visit." "We have no idea what the conditions will be like where they're sending you. They may not be very healthy or sanitary, in which case we don't want to expose your daughter to more germs and potential illness."

"I will take good care. She will become strong and healthy and not so lonely with her daddy."

"I agree, ultimately she'll be better off with you, no matter what the conditions. She is well, and there is no reason for us to keep her. I'll initiate the papers to have your daughter released from Josef House," he said. "Don't worry, George."

"Thank you, Dr. Rembe," Yoshi said, his head nodding in abbreviated bows.

Yoshi got one last extension of the travel permit for this trip to Firland. I was waiting in the reception room saying my goodbyes to the other children. Mrs. Morris kissed my cheeks and hugged me farewell; it was a first and last time. A small suitcase easily accommodated my meager wardrobe of underpants, socks, Panda Bear and KittyKat who had endured the tribulations of my long stay. I wore my visitor's day dress and cold weather sweater. Daddey thanked Mrs. Morris profusely for taking such good care of his daughter the past year and a half. He handed her a small, wrapped package and apologized for the meagerness of the gift. He carried the suitcase filled with my possessions, and we were on our way.

"Good-bye, everyone. Good-bye, Mrs. Morris. Good-bye, Josef House," I whispered as I waved through the window. Soon the hospital and its spacious grounds were replaced by unfamiliar landscapes, but I continued my good-byes.

"Daddey, do I have to go back to Firland again?" "No, you have no more sickness."

Daddey kept the car on its familiar, well-traveled route back to the city. The springs on the car were old and stiff, and we bounced along accompanied by creaks and thumps. The journey home was taking much longer than I had remembered from the trip I had taken a year earlier.

"I can stay home with you from now on?" "Yes, Midori."

I sat and ruminated, then decided to reveal my recent nightmare to Daddey; I could now confide in him. "Daddey, I had a dream. I was all alone by myself so I went looking for you. I looked all over, but I couldn't find you. So I just kept running and looking, looking everywhere for you. I got so tired and so scared. Finally, I found you inside an old falling-down house near *Obaa-san's* grocery store. Everything was falling down all around. You were looking in a mirror, and you were shaving."

"Oh, maybe is morning time. Daddey shave every morning."

I ignored his flippant comment. "I was so happy I finally found you. I wasn't lost and by myself anymore."

RETURN TO SCHOOL

The tall downtown buildings loomed in the distance when we reached our destination. Standing four stories high beside an overgrown weed-ed lot, the wooden structure looked forlorn and out of place. It looked shabby, somewhat like the rundown shack of my dreams, in comparison to the dignified brick apartment building that graced the corner of the opposite block.

As soon as Daddey parked the car, I ran out toward the remembered storefront. There was no grocery store! Behind the locked door and un-washed windows, I could see empty store fixtures in disarray, and bits of dried macaroni distinguishable from the spilled flour, paper, and general rubbish strewn on the floor. Dust clung to everything.

"Where's *Obaa san?* What happened to the store?" I asked. Daddey was fetching the suitcase stuffed with my possessions. I ran to him and pointed to the empty store. "What happened?!"

"No more store. *Obaa-san,* she marry nice man, Mr. Hori.

Everybody move to Kent."

"When? You didn't tell me." It was my usual lament: "They never tell us kids anything."

We walked up the stairs to Daddey's two-room unit. It was a Spartan bachelor's pad. A hot plate and sink with drainboard constituted the kitchen, which was minimally equipped. A table and two wood chairs sat in the middle of the room, and on the bureau pushed up against the wall sat the single luxury item within. It was a handsome Zenith tabletop radio/record player. We would have to share the bed in the second room, which barely accommodated the dresser. My toys had all been packed away, and there was nothing to interest a kid in the two-room apartment until I discovered the Life magazines strewn on the floor.

On Monday, Daddey was enrolling me at Bailey Gatzert. I had walked to my kindergarten classes there, but we now lived on the other side of downtown. Daddey figured there was no point in enrolling me in a strange school, though it might be closer and more convenient. It was much too far away for me to walk to school so Daddey had to drive me there and back.

I was finally going to a real school again after an almost two-year hiatus.

Pedestrians on the sidewalks walked purposefully that time of the morning, presumably to their jobs in the buildings bordering our route. Most office workers had made their way to their jobs by that hour. A few raced with newspapers often tucked under their arms as they dashed in or out of little eateries or tobacco shops along the way. Retail stores selling merchandise other than sundry items were not yet open, and the legions of leisurely strolling shoppers were not yet up and about. The workday hum, and hustle and bustle on the streets had barely begun as Daddey drove down Second Avenue, past the multistoried buildings, toward the older stone and brick structures displaying gaudier signs in their storefronts. We were headed toward the clock-towered train station, where taxis queued in front and waited patiently for fares, while other vehicles wove in and out of the loading zone picking up or dropping off passengers. Travelers scurried about carrying boxes and suitcases, some accompanied by red-capped porters who carted their luggage for them. The porters looked like my friend Sonny, and I smiled. Only much later, I learned they were relatively new hires replacing the Japanese red caps, who had been fired at the onset of war. On the corner, a woman stood alone, lost or confused, wondering what to do next.

At the intersection, our car veered left, and we headed east on Jackson Street toward the morning sun. The buildings grew shorter, and the shops lining the street had American names, though Asian-scripted signs were displayed in the windows and the pedestrians along the sidewalk were primarily Oriental. Continuing on, we drove past the loan shop, Higo's Variety store, an assortment of small shops, and a slumping clay hillside to another enclave of small shops and eateries. We turned right before reaching the open-sided vegetable stand. The Marine hospital sat grandly in the distance; I knew we were close. In the past, I had walked the two blocks between that intersection and my school twice each school day. The low-profiled brick school building looked just as I remembered it. And, there was Miss Waterhouse's kindergarten classroom on the southeast corner of the building with its prominent view of the hillside hospital. It felt good to be back in a familiar neighborhood.

I followed Daddey as we entered the deserted entrance corridor. It was eerily quiet, making me believe we had come on a school holiday. The office was to the side, and light streamed through the door window. As we walked inside, we saw two clerks rushing about filing folders in cabinets while two student assistants busily sorted papers, performing their chores with perfunctory efficiency.

"Hal-lo, Miss," Daddey addressed the clerk and began explaining the reason for our visit.

"Let me have you talk to the principal," said the clerk and disappeared into a second office.

The student assistants were obviously curious about me, the new student, but they kept to their tasks, making only piercing glances in my direction. I moved to the other side of Daddey to escape their eyes. They were appraising me as fodder for their recess gossip. Little did I know, they had concluded I was a twerp for trying to hide from them.

The clerk led us into the principal's office. It was not exactly a Spartan cell; in the inner sanctum, several select Japanese ornaments were displayed.

"How do you do? I'm Miss Mahon," she said as she extended her hand.

"How do you do," Daddey replied as he shook her hand. "It is very nice Japanese picture."

"Yes, isn't it lovely? I received the scroll when I visited Japan."

"Oh, you visit Japan?"

"Yes, quite a number of years ago. The parents of our Japanese students made it possible for me to make the trip. I enjoyed it thoroughly. And yes, the war is most distressing."

Miss Ada Mahon was well beyond middle age. She had supervised the old Main Street School in the heart of Chinatown/Nihonmachi for many years before moving on to Bailey Gatzert when it was constructed in 1921. Old-timers said that on the first day, she and the entire student body had marched the eight blocks through the rain to the new building. Not until other children of ethnic backgrounds moved into the low-income Yesler Terrace Project development, which had replaced my old neighborhood, at both the old and new school her students had been almost exclusively Japanese and Chinese. Miss Mahon's students, generally bilingual, were taught correct English in the classroom. But outside of its confines, the students easily reverted to conversing in their hybrid English mixed with their parents' language.

In China and Japan, both cultures shared a tradition of great respect for education. Historically, in China, the exceptionally bright child was sponsored by the entire village and sent out to pursue an education. The educated adult, upon attaining an exalted position, then rewarded the village and its peoples with largess, thus benefiting all. In Japan, the Meiji Reformation adopted a form of universal education for its people. Only a minority could afford schooling past the mandatory grades, so those who continued on to upper-level schools were highly respected as persons with knowledge. They were teachers, *sensei*. The immigrant parents who worked under great adversity and discrimination understood it was possible for their children to escape a similar repressive fate by acquiring an education and moving on toward a better life. There were few parents who did not make sacrifices for those goals. Their children took to heart their parents' dreams; they studied and learned, and excelled academically.

Miss Mahon and the other teachers at Bailey Gatzert understood the school's unique characteristics and pursued their work with a sense of missionary zeal. In addition to teaching the required basic curriculum to their diverse and generally pliant and well-behaved students, the staff made it their challenge to instill their charges with American traditions and values. It was not only to be aware and understand them, but also to pledge an unequivocal loyalty to those ideals. Miss Mahon approached her task with authority and laid a foundation of discipline—perhaps more accurately described as militaristic control with benign motives. The parents of her students appreciated her stance and supported her completely. She was a legend in the community.

She was well aware of the trauma the Japanese living in the area were experiencing. Every Japanese family was undergoing major disruptions as they prepared to leave their homes all along the West Coast. The mass relocation of all Japanese from Seattle was to begin soon, just as those Japanese from nearby Bainbridge Island had already been taken south to a desert in California. Miss Mahon was well aware this relocation would reduce the student enrollment at her school by more than 50 percent.

Daddey left me at the school and went to work as soon as the paperwork was complete. I followed the clerk out of the office as she waddled briskly and with great resolve down the hall. From one side to the other, her body bounced as her short legs propelled her forward. We passed closed classroom doors, each door restraining the collective energy of youngsters within. The corridor in this part of the building no longer felt deserted, though there was no one in sight.

We stopped at a door. The clerk knocked, opened it, and quickly stepped inside. "Come quickly," she said and waved me in.

"Why are you interrupting my class, Misa?" the woman scolded.

"I'm bringing you a new student, Mrs. Lewis," she said almost apologetically as her voice trailed off. She took a few backward steps toward the door and eased herself unobtrusively out of the room, avoiding further notice. Hers was a well-perfected exit.

Mrs. Lewis heaved a heavy sigh, rolled her eyes skyward then back down and focused them on me. She squinted at me good and hard, reading me like a book without her glasses. I squirmed.

"What is your name, my dear?" she asked in a not-unfriendly way. "Sylvia Nomura," I barely squeaked out.

"A little louder, dear, the class cannot hear you."

After a second try, I was formally introduced to the class, and they were told she expected them to remember it henceforth. "Now we'll find a desk for you, Sylvia. Let me see. Yes, the empty one behind Kathleen." She led me to the back of the room as all eyes followed me to note where I would be sitting. "You may just watch us today," she said. Then as an afterthought, "By the way, I am Mrs. Lewis."

Oh, heaven help me! I gasped in silence. The dreaded Mrs. Lewis. I had hit the jackpot! Cannons exploded in my head then continued bouncing back and forth in my cranium like a pinball zinging in a machine. Ding, ping, zap, boing, boing, boing. When we were in kindergarten, Marian had conspiringly confided to those of us gathered around, "My sister told me Mrs. Lewis is the strictest, meanest teacher at Bailey Gatzert! Just hope you never land in her class." I had been carrying this warning around with me like a soldier's dog tag for almost two years.

I sat there in the back of the room, the silent observer, trying to make myself invisible. Among the thirty or so students, there were only two heads without black hair. I wanted to see my classmates' faces, wondering if I recognized any, but students in this class did not wander about; they stayed put. They did not toss and turn in their seats or try to catch a friend's attention on the other side of the room. Definitely, no one talked out of turn: speak up and speak distinctly when it's your turn; otherwise, remain silent. The class sessions flowed smoothly as long as everyone followed the rules, and everyone knew the rules by now. I did not, and I could not decipher what was going on. I had no clue.

The bell rang out its incessant high-pitched clamor with a startle and continued to reverberate through the halls outside the classroom. Books closed, students sat erect in their seats with all eyes focused on Mrs. Lewis.

She gave a nod, signaling permission to stand and walk––not run––toward the door. The students moved quickly and formed a queue in pairs alongside the wall by the door. The boys indulged in a bit of jostling for position or to avoid being paired up with a girl. When they settled down, they stood at attention and waited like little soldiers. Kathleen motioned for me to get up from my seat and follow her. We were the last to join the queue. Not a word had been spoken since the bell rang.

"Straighten up the line," Mrs. Lewis barked. "Show the new girl a straight line. Now!" The precision of the lineup would have made a drill sergeant smile. She started the cadence: "Left, right, Left, right..." and legs were lifted in a standing march. The door was opened, and the troop marched out in double file down the hallway to the restrooms. Every class marched in formation down the school halls at recess and to the lunchroom or auditorium, but none could match Mrs. Lewis's classes for precision or discipline. Even when the lineup was broken in the restroom, monitors kept order and quiet, or else! Teachers were not reluctant to use the paddle or a ruler for punishment for any student's infractions of school rules. They knew parents supported them, and the reprimand would often be reinforced with even harsher punishment when the student went home. Once outside the school building and a safe distance away, all hell broke loose. There were no regimens or restrictions. Everyone could run and shout and play like the children they were. Back inside the school building, they were transformed into robots again, and quiet reigned.

Mrs. Lewis soon discovered I was illiterate. Lucky for me, there was a second student who also could not read, so I was not alone. Richard enrolled at the school and was assigned to Mrs. Lewis's class shortly before my arrival. His family had moved to Seattle from another state. He talked sort of funny. My ears were accustomed to English spoken with accents, but his English was entirely alien. At times, I studied him intently to decipher what he was trying to communicate. He never gave a reason for having missed the first grade. I wondered how he had spent the missing two years he had not gone to school. We never had an opportunity to exchange those stories.

"Richard and Sylvia, please follow me to the back of the room," Mrs. Lewis commanded. "Whenever the class starts their reading lessons, both of you are to come back here to study independently from the class." We were relegated to the very back of the classroom where there were no bolted-down desks, only loose tables and chairs. There, the two of us could study on our own by staring at our primers without disturbing the class. We wore no visible dunce caps; they were invisible, but we all knew they sat atop our heads.

Richard had a head start and had already started the first-grade reader, the Dick and Jane Primer, and had progressed to the fictional siblings' dog, Spot. He was overjoyed to find I was less skilled in reading than he.

"You-all's dumber than me," he said when he learned I could not read, not even the first page of the primer. He didn't say it maliciously, so I chose to ignore his frank assessment. He was probably right; I did not want to believe it.

I scooted up next to Richard and pointed to the first line of my book and shrugged my shoulders and looked at him quizzically. He whispered, "See Dick." When I pointed to the new word in the next line, he said, "Run."

Oh, now it says, "See Dick run." I could even read the next line myself: "Run, Dick, run." Easy enough so far, but practically every new line added a new word. Not easy at all; it was frustrating.

At the end of the week, Richard told me he was being sent down to the first grade the following Monday. It would be easier for him to start fresh at the beginning, he was told. He looked so sad. I guessed part of the reason was that I was about the only person he talked to at school, although our communication was mostly shrugs and quizzical looks during our private reading sessions. If the other students bothered to acknowledge his existence at all, they taunted him for his strange grammar. Otherwise he was just ignored for being different, for not being a black-haired Asian kid like the rest of us.

Somehow it hurt less when there were two of us relegated to the back of the room. And Richard had been my tutor. I was going to miss him.

As my stomach churned and gurgled from overeating at lunch, I knew my immediate misery was the consequence of another school rule: "You have to get permission to leave the table. You have to eat all the food on your lunch tray, or the lunchroom monitors won't let you leave until you do." "Children in China are starving. You here in America should never leave a kernel of rice in your bowl." I had forced myself to comply, and ate every morsel in order to leave the table to go outside into the sunshine and breathe fresh air that did not smell like floor polish. I hated this lunchroom rule above all the others. I dreaded sitting in back of the room and being conspicuous as the only nincompoop who could not read. And I found the conventions and ethos of my Oriental classmates different and often confusing. I was Oriental, but I was an outsider.

I decided to quit Bailey Gatzert. I was not coming back to school next week! No. No. No!

After the initial euphoria of coming home from the hospital had worn off, I found myself alone without friends or family, and my long-held dreams of attending school had disintegrated because I could not adjust. I was miserable, in a morass I knew not how to escape. I morphed into an obnoxious hellion. I was obstinate, I threw tantrums, and I was uncontrollable in my misery.

PREPARING TO MOVE

Yoshi had no idea how to handle the problematic behavior. He had not been active in childrearing, letting Aiko handle it; then he had ceded the responsibility to the nurses at Josef House. At the hospital, Midori had become self-reliant and independent. The once timid little girl, who hid behind Aiko's skirt and sucked her fingers, still resembled the comely iconic creature of Japanese art, but in an instant the mask of cherubic innocence, once flung aside, revealed the monster with horns and demon eyes, not unlike an old Noh mask. A demure Butterfly garners an audience's sympathy with a poignant aria and her diffident demeanor, but long-suffering Cho-Cho-*san* was not Midori's model; it never would be.

Yoshi grieved in silence for that amiable sweet daughter Midori once was. Going to the hospital was fate, but her stay was extended a year for his convenience. He felt complicity in the dreadful turn her behavior had taken, and he vowed to atone for it. Without a partner to shoulder the burden of child-rearing the child had no mother's skirt to shield and protect her. Neither did she have an Odai who would always be there when needed. The responsibility was now his alone; he could not abandon, ignore, or delegate it to others. Yoshi renewed his commitment to make Midori's life a happy one. He was ready for the new challenges facing him; he had a mission. It was his karma.

On Monday morning, Yoshi went back to the school and explained to Miss Mahon he was taking Sylvia out of school early because he would be among the first to be evacuated from Seattle. They hastily made out a report card for her one-week enrollment at the school with no mention of her academic prowess or lack of. She was officially excused from attending any more classes. He continued on to the club and gave notice, that he would be quitting his job at the end of the week.

Rampant rumors regarding the imminent evacuation of Japanese from Seattle played everywhere, but without any official notice, the Japanese community was stuck in limbo; waiting and wondering in apprehension. With his savings account at Sumitomo Bank frozen, Yoshi's cash was running low. Unanticipated expenses had been greater than usual, and he knew there were more to come.

The following day, notices were posted that said Japanese persons living in Exclusion Zones #1 and #2 (areas within the exclusion area of the Western Command and the Fourth Army) would be evacuated the following week. The first contingent of evacuees was to be workers, such as cooks and others, needed to assist those who would follow starting on Thursday and Friday. The apartment in Belltown was located in Zone #1, which was essentially northwest Seattle, including most of downtown north of Jackson Street and west of 5th Avenue. Zone #2 was all of South Seattle to the city limits.

Yoshi had known it was prudent to prepare for an eventual evacuation after the Bainbridge Islanders were shipped out. The following week, he had packed away photo albums and the two boxes of letters Aiko had collected for her daughter to read in the future; words to refresh faded memories. Wool blankets, linens with hand-embroidered fancies, a set of dishes and tableware, and favorite knickknack mementos were packed into two steamer trunks along with Midori's dolls and whatever toys fit. Excess clothes that could be squeezed into the trunks were included. Less-fragile kitchenware was crated, and the entire lot was taken away by the busy transfer company to be put into storage in the Buddhist church basement, joining other members' belongings in rooms crammed to capacity. Business owners of shops and hotels who owned their own buildings, generously took in storage items from friends and acquaintances, filling their facilities for the duration. Homeowners stored their own belongings in locked closets or basements, taking the chance that they would remain secure.

In many ways, Yoshi was luckier than most. He was spared the trauma of liquidating a business and inventory, achieved after a lifetime's struggle to become established, only to lose everything. Some unloaded their merchandise at less than fire-sale prices; a few luckier merchants made arrangements to lease their shops to non-Japanese or were able to entrust their possessions to trustworthy friends. But such friends were in short supply in contrast to the hordes who took advantage of the Japanese in their desperate plight. For most, the financial losses were staggering.

Every Japanese family was scrambling to dismantle their homes and sort through personal belongings very quickly. Everything they owned had to be sold, given away, thrown out, or, if kept, packed and stored in a safe place. The number of things they were allowed to take with them on their forced journey was only "what they could carry."

The mercenary vultures hovered then swarmed, feasting on others' misfortunes, stripping the wounded clean of everything except memories.

It was now a long year and a half ago when Yoshi had had to send his wife and child to Firland and move out of the Yesler redevelopment area. He had sold his furnishings at a time when there was still a market for used furniture. He remembered the fine bedroom set he had reluctantly sold on consignment to a Japanese dealer. He was sure the family who had purchased the set was now wondering what to do with it. He had gone through the process of giving away or throwing out the household goods not needed by a bachelor; it had not been easy. His trauma had preceded what others were now undergoing.

Yoshi had come to terms with the disintegration of his family. Now he had to concentrate on myriad details to prepare for the evacuation.

"Midori have no winter coat. We go buy coat today," Daddey said. Indeed, the coat I wore as a cape on the day of my mother's funeral was way too small.

"I don't need a winter coat, Daddey, winter is over," I announced.

"Maybe we go to cold place. Maybe no store to buy winter coat." I had visions of going to the big department stores downtown like I had with Mommy. We always did a lot of window shopping and ate lunch, too. When we started our shopping excursion, Daddey drove through and past downtown where the department stores stood and continued onto Jackson Street and Nihonmachi.

"Why did we come here?" I asked. "We buy coat for Midori."

"We went past the department stores." Everything was topsy-turvy now. There was no logic or order.

The Japanese shopkeepers were frantically reducing their inventory, clearing up their wares, and packing dry goods for long-term storage before their own forced moves. The quantity of available goods had been drastically reduced due to "the war effort scarcity." The general public avoided Japanese stores in order to be patriotic and buy American. The usual Japanese customers were buying only the essentials to take with them on their upcoming journeys, the less the better.

The stores we patronized were almost deserted. Shelves were flaked with dust. Debris scattered about was merchandise no longer arranged as an organized display. There were no promotional flags to grab our attention. We were met with disarray and clutter, and clerks who were more intent on putting away merchandise rather than making a sale.

The sales clerk who was reaching for the top-shelved suitcases got off his ladder and finally came to greet us.

"We sold most of our winter coats. This is all we have left *neh*. You should have come in earlier," the clerk said.

"Yes, yes," Daddey replied. It was useless giving explanations for our shortsightedness.

"Here, try on the coats, see which one fits best," he said as he handed me a light, unlined cotton coat.

I took off my sweater and put on the lightweight coat. I began to shiver. It offered no protection from the chill.

"Not warm. Need wool coat."

"A nice coat for warmer days, I agree. Here, try this other coat," he handed me a gorgeous wool coat. It was a deep maroon color with a black velvet collar; it was a princess style. Fit for a princess like me. I loved it.

"This coat is prettier than my old one," I said happily. I put the coat on, and my wrists were an inch too long at the sleeves. It fit so snugly I could barely button the coat. Alas, it was too small.

Daddey pulled off the coat and hurriedly started putting my arms into the third coat. I got it on, and it fit, sort of. There was two years of growth factored in the fit. That was just what I needed.

"Oh, nice coat, Midori," Daddey said enthusiastically.

I stood there and gawked. It was the ugliest coat I had ever seen. In fact, it didn't resemble anything I had seen before. The coat was navy blue with a rusty red tinge, similar to postwar cars painted navy blue that began oxidizing into ugly, rusty blue. The coat was not a beautiful midnight blue. It was made of tightly woven, boiled wool with a gnarled, lumpy surface. Its basic utilitarian style had no fitted darts to give the coat shape. It had a plain rounded collar, a front opening with plain round buttons, and pockets at the side seams; it had no ornamentation. Worn, it made me look like a little round bear ready to hibernate—a not-too-cuddly one at that.

Yoshi and Midori before Camp

Daddey bought the awful bear coat over my vehement protests. I would not be a princess without a princess coat. I did not feel like Goldilocks, either. Instead, I felt like baby bear that lost its porridge whenever I wore the coat, the scowl on my face stayed on, too.

After our shopping excursion, we walked up the street and joined a line of people. The queue wound through the hallway and entered another door to the doctor's office, where people were getting their typhoid vaccinations.

"Why are we standing in line for?" I asked Daddey.

"Everybody get *ti-foi chu-sha*. The government say so."

"I don't want to get a shot."

"Everybody get *chu-sha*. No more sickness."

"I don't wanna shot!" My bad humor had not worn off; it had escalated. When we finally got to the doctor, I put on a wild tantrum. Daddey was embarrassed and exasperated. Undoubtedly, my yelling and screaming put the fear of God in a few of those waiting in line; others thought I needed a spanking. That was probably true. I was actually a veteran in getting vaccinations. At the hospital, we were poked with needles like we were pincushions; it bothered me not at all. I was just being extremely ornery, expressing my disappointment in a highly unsocial way.

We got two more typhoid shots later without incident.

Following instructions of the official Civilian Exclusion Order No. 17, Daddey went to the Civil Control Station on the weekend to receive our relocation instructions. He received tags for the luggage we were bringing and a family identification number, which we would retain until the end of the war. Our evacuation from Seattle was scheduled for Thursday, April 30. We would be in the first group to evacuate.

"Midori, remember family number, *neh*. Won, zeh-lo, eh-to, fa-e-vu, won."

"OK… One, zero, eight, five, one."

CHAPTER 11

Puyallup, 1942

THE BULGING DUFFLE BAG YOSHI called his seabag, and two suitcases, one large and a small, black one sized for me to carry–– the same one that had handily fit all my belongings upon leaving Josef House––now stuffed to the brim, were set near the doorway of *Obaa-san's* abandoned grocery store. We were early, but there was no point in waiting in our bare apartment, so Daddey and I had come downstairs early to wait for our ride. My stay in the apartment above the old store was so temporary I felt no qualms about leaving. Each day living away from the rigid schedules of the hospital had felt like living a different movie; there was no routine, and new experiences kept unfolding. I was learning to navigate through the unfamiliar. I felt safe and secure with Daddey, and trauma was an alien word. Those earlier tantrums, I reluctantly decided, were counter-productive, and I discarded them. I remained stubborn and uncoopera-tive whenever I itched, but the hysterics were a thing of the past. "This is a special day and journey," I had been told; I was curious and anxious for the day to unfold.

Yoshi was going on another prolonged journey with minimal bag-gage. On leaving home to go to sea, and when he boarded the train in New York bound for Seattle on a cross-continent sightseeing excursion, he had carried little more than a change of clothes and a shaving kit. The intended vacation had stretched into a fourteen-year stay. He had little to show for those years; a marriage and wife were gone, and his acquisi-tions amounted to sentimental keepsakes of little monetary value. The remnants of a household were a wooden crate packed with a collection of miscellaneous kitchen utensils, sparsely used bedding, and whatever fit into two trunks were the bulk of his possessions; he owned little else.

An intangible burden that had weighed on him, especially since arriving in Seattle——keeping secret his illegal entry status had been revealed when complying with the 1940 Alien Registration Act. A section of the legislation, also known as the Smith Act, made advocating the overthrow of the US government a criminal act with consequences. Concerns of possible sedition became pre-eminent, greatly overshadowing the government's pursuit and persecution of illegal aliens. It was never abandoned; it was downplayed. Now that Japan and America were at war, Yoshi felt the chances of being singled out for deportation was unlikely in the near future and he would be treated like all the other Japanese being rounded up on the West Coast.

Daddey had sold his well-traveled, black Ford Model A coupe to Kitty for a pittance. She had been a generous and a true friend since their days working together at the New Washington Hotel. Daddey was pleased he could return her past kindnesses in this way. She was thrilled with the "gift" and had readily agreed to let Daddey use the car until the day before our departure.

At the agreed-upon time, Kitty arrived to pick up Daddey, me, and our luggage to drive us to the departure area. Our two suitcases and bursting-at-the-seams duffel bag overwhelmed the car's trunk, and no attempt was made to close the lid. Daddey and I squeezed into the passenger side for the five-block ride. The route included a steep downhill descent; otherwise, it was a relatively level stroll, and without our luggage, we could have navigated the distance from the apartment to our departure area at Virginia Street and Elliot Avenue on foot. However, it would have been a struggle if we had to tote the "only what you can carry" luggage crammed with necessities for a journey to an unknown place for an unknown length of time.

Thursday was a regular work or school day for most residents, the streets and sidewalks we passed showed no signs the day was anything other than ordinary. As we rounded the corner, we saw the chaotic assemblage of Japanese and a jumbled assortment of luggage bearing government issued tags in the clearing. We had arrived at the departure station. Daddey got me and our luggage quickly off the car before the backed-up cars began honking their horns. He only had time to wave his good-bye as Kitty blew him a kiss and drove away with angry drivers behind her cursing the day. "What's the problem?" "Dumb female driver!" "Gitta movin.' Them's only Japs." "Good riddance."

An armed soldier walked toward us. "Hey, you… Yeah, you!" He told us to move off the street and motioned with his rifle for us to get in the meandering queue.

Daddey slung the seabag on his shoulder and picked up a suitcase. I carried the small black case packed with my precious belongings and clung tightly to his jacket hem with my free hand as we joined the crowd. The street was now utterly congested with vehicles as others arrived, off-loaded their luggage and wandered, puzzled at what to do next. The noise escalated as people tried to talk above the din as newcomers trying to cozy their way to the front of the line were brusquely directed to the back. Feigning ignorance, they gathered their bags and trotted to the end of the snaking line, where they set claim to their space. As the crowd grew in size and disarray, the soldiers standing guard scurried around like herd dogs in their attempt to maintain order and keep the streets open for traffic. The earlier arrivals, with their anxieties now at bay, were feeling tired and sleepy, and they wearily watched the commotion raised by the adrenaline-pumped newcomers. This was the first day of the roundup, and we at the Port Area departure station were the early contingent of evacuees from areas north of downtown. The process was untidy. In any case, removal of the Japanese from Seattle had begun.

Vans arrived, and our bags were thrown in. People watched helplessly as their possessions were so roughly handled. And they worried their precious baggage might get lost, accidentally left behind, or worse. The words were not always spoken, yet their faces reflected their concern.

"Each piece of luggage has a tag with the owner's family number. Don't worry," the Nisei baggage handlers said reassuringly. "Shimpai-nai."

What else could one do but follow orders? *Shikata-ga-nai.* We boarded the buses, and as they filled, each drove off to a collection area and waited. From there, the assembled vehicles filled with evacuees caravanned to the assembly camp. The large contingent of evacuees who waited at the Eighth Avenue and Dearborn Street departure area were picked up after us. We were leaving Seattle.

"Welcome to Camp Harmony!" a voice called out on our arrival in Puyallup. There were a few audible groans. The irony was beyond my comprehension. The majority ignored the greeting.

The volunteers who had arrived on Tuesday were on hand to help the hundreds of new evacuees get settled. We were given instructions and shown our quarters. Our unit was near the middle of a very long building––a barrack, they called it, and our barrack was one of an endless row of identical buildings. All barracks positioned in parallel rows like blocks of bricks laid side by side in stack formation. Each two rows of barracks faced each other with their entry door sides facing the common pathway between. The back side of the barracks faced the back sides of the next pair of barracks, with an alley between. The buildings looked so alike in the beginning. We counted down from the end to make sure we were on the right path to our unit. It was a long detour if we mistakenly walked down the wrong "street."

Daddey set out to retrieve our bags at the central baggage drop-off point. The open area not far from the gate was the temporary repository for the massive pile of suitcases, duffel bags, boxes, and the like, which were thrown into a pile helter-skelter. An unruly crowd rummaged through the pile, each individual searching for his or her own possessions. The luggage the evacuees searched for represented their entire wealth, and in their attempts to find and retrieve, they abandoned their long-practiced courtesy to others. Their reserve vanished; there was no *enryo*. The pile was in a constant flux as items were shoved about. Once bags were located, people removed them quickly and carried them back to their units. The regulations limiting luggage size was loosely defined and broadly interpreted, and more than a few struggled to carry their heavily loaded luggage away.

"Midori, you stay inside and wait. OK?" Daddey said when he left. I sat on the bare mattress and waited anxiously for Daddey's return. There was not much else to do except take inventory of my new surroundings. The room was bare except for two cots with mattresses, and two blankets. The floorboards were rough wooden planks nailed to 2x dimensioned lumber laid directly on the ground, an unacceptable construction practice under normal circumstances. Similar planks made up the exterior walls and the exposed under sides of the sloped roof. The wood door was in the middle of the front wall and opposite to the small window on the back wall facing the alley. That arrangement was probably good feng shui, allowing evil spirits to run straight through our apartment and out the window. No one needed any additional bad fortune lingering on their premises, real or ethereal. That door-to-window arrangement is not a good one when good luck enters a home since it should linger, but good fortune was in short supply during this time.

The sidewalls that separated us from our neighbors were made with the same wooden planks used throughout; they were hung side by side vertically and nailed to supporting studs. These separation walls were only as high as the rear exterior wall, which supported the low side of the sloped roof. The front wall with door was several feet higher, thereby allowing rain to drain from the top of our roof into the alley, but inside, underneath the sloped roof, a triangular opening was created. That triangular opening ran through the entire length of the barrack, giving sound transmission free reign from one end to the other. I tried to unscramble the muffled conversations I heard from other parts of the building without success. I did know I was not alone.

I heard Daddey's voice. He was talking to someone outside our door. He came in shortly after and dropped the seabag and our suitcases to the floor.

"Daddey, who were you talking to?" I asked.

"Oh, I meet nice people in building across road. They are very old people, so I help them carry heavy bags."

"Is that why it took you so long?"

After lunch, we evacuees were ordered to show up for physical examinations. Men and women were to go to their examinations in different buildings. Daddey explained the situation to me, and before he left me at the door of the women's examination area, he asked the two women entering the building if they would keep an eye on me because I was alone.

"Oh, yes. Of course we'll watch your little girl. *Shin-pai naku.*" Not to worry, they both assured Daddey.

"*Domo…tanomi-masu.*" He bowed to the ladies and was on his way to the men's examination entrance.

"Ga-ru-*san*, you no scare doctor, *neh?*" I was asked by one of the ladies as we began our wait in line.

"Scared? No," I replied, puzzled by the question. She smiled, and I assumed I had given her the right answer. I suppose Daddey's not the only person who jumbles up his words, I thought.

The physical followed standard military procedures: Hurry up and wait.

The exam was broken up into segments with long waits in line between each. Examinations were routine in the hospital, and I had no fear of doctors or of being examined. The two women who so graciously said they would keep an eye on me were solicitous initially, but they became distracted, and I silently followed after them from one station to another without further communication. I sensed it was they, the two ladies, who were apprehensive about the entire examination ordeal, and when we got to the chest examination station, they told me to go on ahead of them in line since I did not have the buttons that they had to undo. In the process, the two ladies and I separated, and I no longer saw them in line. After finishing the last exam, I walked to the exit door to leave, and darkness and pouring rain greeted me.

What shall I do? I don't know how to get back to our apartment in the dark.

As I stepped outside, Daddey came rushing toward me with an open umbrella.

"Daddey, I'm so glad you're waiting for me." I was truly relieved to see him.

"You take long time. I think maybe I miss you. I do not see two ladies."

"They got lost. I think they were afraid of the doctor and they told me to go first."

The pathway between the barracks had turned to gushy putty with pools of water everywhere. Those braving the rain were scurrying in any way other than a straight line trying to dodge the worst mud puddles. On our way back to our unit, we followed the lead of others and zigzagged our way through the mire. Everyone was familiar with the rainy patterns of spring; we were just not prepared to deal with it yet.

Our task was to get settled and adjust to the routines at Camp Harmony. We earlier evacuees had a few days' advantage familiarizing ourselves to our new environment while others continued to arrive. Area A, where we were located, was the first compound to be occupied, with approximately two thousand residents. Areas B and C were filled with another combined two thousand people. The three areas had been nearby parking lots used to augment the Puyallup Fair compound, the site of the annual Western Washington State Fair. The large open areas of level grounds provided ideal sites for the speedy erection of temporary structures within a short time frame. Instead of the proposed one-month construction deadline, by employing a thousand workers, the building project was completed in seventeen days. The town's residents had watched in disbelief at the speedy progress made in the erection of the camp in their midst.

Since the compounds were not contiguous, each compound was self-contained. Barbed wire fences surrounded each, which were guarded by armed soldiers. Residents living inside could not move about freely from one area to the other; special permits were required to do so.

Area D, the fourth and lastly occupied compound, was located on the Puyallup fairgrounds proper. In addition to new barracks built in open areas within the compound, existing fairground structures were also utilized, including permanent facilities such as restrooms and kitchens. More than 7,600 evacuees were housed within the four compounds of the Puyallup Assembly Center by mid-May. Puyallup was only one of seventeen assembly centers hastily erected to evacuate the Japanese from restricted zones all along the western regions of Washington, Oregon, California, and parts of Arizona. To expedite construction, open, level sites close to rails, arterials, and urban settlements with access to utilities were selected for the centers. Nine centers were located on fairgrounds, two at racetracks, another two at migrant workers' camps, an old CCC camp, and a livestock exposition hall. The Manzanar and Poston reception areas morphed into permanent camps.

Built simultaneously with the same deadline and basic specifications, each center was required to provide living units for families; be they situated in existing buildings once used as livestock halls, horse stables, or in newly constructed barracks, regardless of how crude the structure, as long as they were functional. Mess halls to feed the masses, restrooms, showers, and laundry facilities were to be provided. All compounds were enclosed and guarded to make sure no enemy aliens escaped. Beyond the basic requirements, each center varied in layout with flexibility in the details.

The assembly centers were ready within a month, and they were opened to receive the over 110,000 Japanese, born in America and alien, evacuees who had lived in the designated exclusion areas in the western United States.

LIFE AT CAMP HARMONY

Yoshi had lived in the apartment over Hayame's grocery store north of downtown for a year and a half. The area was sparsely occupied by Japanese, and he knew no one who lived even remotely close by. At the departure area, he had seen no one he knew, except a few men with whom he had a nodding acquaintance, though they were preoccupied at the time and no nodding exchanges took place. Walking down the pathway between the barracks, he still saw no one he recognized. He was living among strangers who were long time Seattle residents from the northwest sector. Yoshi had thought this was the beginning of a new life; he had not expected to be so isolated and friendless.

The elderly Mukai's living across the walkway, whose bags he had helped carry after their arrival, took a liking to Yoshi and invited him over for conversation in the evenings.

"*Hazuka-shi, neh.* I'm so embarrassed I can't offer you any tea and refreshments," Mrs. Mukai said each evening as Daddey and I arrived for our visit. The lack of small comforts was dismaying and added to their immediate discomfort. They had no means to be hospitable hosts; they had no simple refreshments to offer nor a comfortable chair to sit on. But, the friendship they offered was warm and gracious. The couple's two young adult daughters would join in when they were not busy elsewhere.

They had brought a set of *karuta* cards, the *Iro-ha*, kata- kana syllabary version popular with children in Japan especially during the New Year's holiday. The Mukai's taught me the game. One set of "reading cards," each with a proverb or saying is read aloud by the dealer, one card at a time. The players searched for the matching picture card from the set scattered about on the playing surface. Making a matching pair was very difficult because Japanese was still a foreign language to me. With repetition, I honed my memory skills and began to win games and I also learned a bit of the Japanese language. The evenings were no longer dreary when spent with friends.

During the day, I walked around the pathways to watch the go-ings-on. Weather permitting, everyone stayed outside. It was dark and gloomy in the units. A couple of kids were playing tiddlywinks, and when they made no offers to let me join, I wandered off to watch two older men who sat studying a square wooden board lined with squares, and flattened round stones of white and black placed at various line intersections. The men contemplated each move so long, I concluded it was a boring game to watch and moved on. One day, a man was sitting outside on a crude bench carving a wood object, that upon inspection, turned out to be a *geta*. Daddey had once owned a pair of wood slippers that he liked to wear after a bath. I could see no nails in the pair the man was working on, and I surmised he had carved each from a single block of wood. The supporting wood slats were much higher than others I had seen, and the carver explained it was to walk above the mud and puddles. I never did see the *geta's* worn, and wonder if the wearer ever managed to balance on the stilts.

I had wandered beyond my usual haunts when I happened on a couple of teenaged girls running to catch oranges flying in over the fence from the outside. The missiles were sent by a young woman named Billie. Billie, a Broadway High School student from Seattle who, with a couple of friends caught the bus, involving several transfers and several hours, to journey to Puyallup to visit interned classmates in the camp. The meetings took place on opposite sides of the barbed wire fence, and when armed guards at the ready had warned the visitors away, Billie had tossed her gift of fresh oranges over the fence to her friends on the inside. An independent spirit, she always remained true to her ideals.

The community of strangers was reduced by one when Daddey ran into Mat-*san* one day. He insisted Daddey and I come to visit him. His legs were less inclined to take long walks, he said. He lived in a barrack on the other side of Area A, and it felt odd for us to be visiting him instead of him popping in to see us. The camp address system was no longer a mystery, and we found Mat-*san's* unit without difficulty.

The two men sat on the bed catching up on news. The old man had collected an incredible amount of information regarding the whereabout of city and Valley acquaintances. The roundup was still in progress, and with less-than-able legs, how did he access the goings-on? I assumed he was a magnet and the information beamed in to him.

"Hayame was smart to marry before evacuation. Otherwise, she and Hori-*san* would be separated to different camps," Mat-*san* said.

"Why? Aren't the valley people coming here? They live only a few miles away from here."

"They and the Tacoma people go down to California." "Oh, to Manzanar where the Bainbridge Island people were sent?"

"No, not so far. You know California maybe?"

"Mat-*san*, how do you know all this?"

Mat-*san* and Daddey chattered happily like two gossiping old crones, and they ignored me and the elderly woman who sat at the table playing cards by herself. She played solitaire intently, one game after another, oblivious to all around her. I had never watched anyone play the game before, and I was fascinated. I began to understand the game, and when she hesitated on an obvious move, I thought to help her by pointing my finger on the right card. She slapped my hand, and without saying a word, she continued her play. When the game was over, she shuffled the cards and started a new game. She never spoke a word nor did she ever bother to look away from her cards the whole time we visited with them.

"That's all she does, play cards. *Komaru*…it's a problem," he said to Daddey as we took our leave.

"We'll come visit again in a few days."

When we left Mat-*san*, Daddey answered my question before I asked, "Mat-*san*'s wife was in hospital. She go back to hospital ban-by."

When I became tired of strolling around my new neighborhood, I just hid in the tall grass by the open area near our barrack and watched the parade of people pass; it was such a pleasure to be sedentary and have the action roll on in front of me without being seen. The parader's were all Japanese; they varied in size, shape, and age, and they moved to their own rhythm.

I was indulging in the lazy inactivity of watching people again when I spied in the background across the field, a big, almost adult-sized, girl curiously railing and flinging her arms about like a baby demanding attention. The mother came, lifted the long-limbed "baby" girl onto her back and carried her in the customary way Japanese mothers carry their infants. The mother struggled under her unwieldy and heavy burden, yet there was a bounce in the mother's steps as she rocked her big baby. The body grew up, but the mind remained an infant. It made no sense to me; something was scrambled, askew. In our society, such disabilities had previously been hidden from public sight, but privacy was lost in camp. A different "real" world opened up, and it was on view in Camp Harmony.

When I was not people watching, I just looked up to the heavens as the clouds rolled by. The cloud formations in camp were as varied and wondrous as they had been when I watched them during my rest periods at the hospital. I made friends with Bette, who thought cloud watching was as interesting and relaxing as I did. We planned to meet the following day and explore for more active adventures.

SICK AGAIN

That evening, less than three weeks into our confinement, I came down with a fever and threw up my supper. I was feeling weak and delirious, and put in bed, where I alternately shivered and perspired under my covers. Daddey cleaned up the mess and made his way to the restrooms to rinse out the towels and bucket, and fetch some fresh water for me to reduce my fever. Because it was late at night, past lights out, he ran the water and rinsed up in a darkened men's room. The door was kicked open, and the beam of light searched the room for the source of noise. The light beam found Yoshi and flashed his face. The patrolling guard pointed his gun straight at him. Daddey had broken curfew. He tried to explain the circumstances. There were no exceptions.

"It's CURFEW! You DUMB-ASS STUPID JAP!" the soldier shouted. "Sick baby, no sick baby. No damn excuses. Now GIT THE HELL OUTTA HERE and back to your room!" He fingered the trigger nervously. "GO NOW, or I'll SHOOT!"

Daddey managed to get back to our apartment, thoroughly shaken by the encounter. He tried to dismiss the sight of the rifle aimed at him. Fumbling in the dark, he wiped me down, and when the cold compresses reduced my fever, he fell asleep.

My sleep was fitful as my "fever nightmare" returned. I kept struggling to break out of my confining box, breaking through, another box, again and again. All night long, I struggled to break out of boxes, one after another, in my delirium. I was too tired to wake up.

In the morning, red spots began appearing on my face and body. Neighbors that Daddey consulted for a diagnosis unanimously agreed Midori had the measles.

The authorities said I had to be quarantined.

Two men came in a truck and loaded our beds, mattresses, and bedding into the back, then unceremoniously threw our luggage on top. Since I was delirious, they let Daddey sit in the cab with me bundled on his lap, and the second mover rode with the cargo.

I woke up in a dark, cavernous room. There was a window next to the door, but only a small amount of light filtered in through the window panes. Dust and grime on the glass was not what was blocking out the sunlight. What was coming through was secondary light; our barrack of sorts was actually built within a huge exhibition barn. The single incandescent lightbulb hanging from its cord down the middle of the room was woefully inadequate. Its wattage so low that only the space around the lightbulb was illuminated. Not only were the corners of our room dark, the entire space toward the back of our spacious room was inhabited by shadows

My hands reached and touched the pillow my head rested on. No, this is not a dream. I have the luxury of a soft, warm pillow. But, where am I?

"It's so dark in here, Daddey."

"You wake up. You feeling better?" he asked.

"Daddey, why is it so dark?"

"Your eyes have sickness, too. They should rest to get well. When everything dark, they can rest."

With that bit of folk advice, my body as well as my eyes went into rest mode, and I fell asleep again. When I woke up, I was feeling better and willing to eat a bite or two of the dinner Daddey had brought for me on a tray.

"I have surprise for you, Midori." He went into the shadows and came back to my bed with a large, flat box, setting it beside me. "Happy birthday!"

The sheet cake was large enough to feed dozens. It displayed a rainbow assortment of sugary pastel flowers with leaves made of icing swirled in fanciful shapes. "Happy Birthday, Sylvia," was lettered in red.

What a wonderful surprise. I had been thinking about my upcoming birthday for weeks, but the delirium of the last few days had wiped it out of my mind.

"The cake is so pretty, I don't want to cut it up."

The two Mukai daughters had made arrangements with friends on the outside to purchase and deliver the cake to them in camp. It was a complicated undertaking, intended to be a special treat for everyone: cake from a real bakery. When I came down with the measles and we were sent to isolation, the cake-eating party was called off, and the entire cake was sent over to us by way of friendly personnel. Daddey and I ended up with a cake just for ourselves. Each day, "Sweet Tooth" Daddey and Birthday Girl had a good-sized piece of cake for dessert.

"Daddey, save the flowers for last." He cut the cake into a checkerboard pattern, and we ate the less decorated pieces first. We savored each mouthful. The cake made my eighth birthday special, and my measles made it unforgettable.

After he ate his own meal, Daddey brought me a tray of food from the special commissary, and I had room service while quarantined. I wasn't allowed to leave our room except to use the facilities. Daddey seated me in a stall, and when I was done, we would walk out past the urinal trough as a row of men dropped their jaws in disbelief on seeing an eight-year-old female walking past them as they stood with unzipped trousers. They were in such a state of shock, no one ever made a commotion. Their gaping lower jaws took a while to close. Later, when I was better and steadier on my feet, I was able to make my way to a small private restroom Daddey serendipitously found not far from our quarters. It was not marked and may have been provided for maintenance workers during civilian times.

As I began my recovery, though my face and other body parts still retained those red polka dots, I slept less. With longer bouts of consciousness, I became restless and bored staying in bed in our dark hole. How depressing. It was then when Daddey began telling me stories to keep me in good spirits. We had no books with stories for children with us, and I missed hearing the tale of The Beauty and the Beast, which Mother had read to me often, as I never tired of hearing the story. Daddey's repertoire of fairy tales was limited, especially non-Japanese kinds, so he repeated the same ones he remembered over and over. After a while, I could follow the flow of the Japanese words and they were not so alien any more.

"*Mukashi, mukashi*…a very long time ago…"

To maintain my interest, Daddey began augmenting his small trove of tales by telling me true stories. The stories were sometimes about mother's relatives, people populating our photo album. He told me how Mommy's own mother had died when she was little, just like me, how her father had remarried a young woman only ten years older than she. *Obaa-san* was not Mommy's real mother? She was my step-grandmother? The complicated relationships were revealed, and I did mental acrobats to place the pieces in their proper loops.

"Daddey, if you marry again, I'll have a stepmother like Mommy had?"

"Hmm…"

"And I'll have stepsisters and stepbrothers, too?"

"Mommy was lucky. She had nice stepmother and sisters and brother."

"Daddey, I don't want a stepmother and stepsisters and stepbrother."

"You are thinking story. Sometime stepmother and stepsisters are not so kind, same like Cindalala. Daddey no want Midori to have mean stepmother, *neh*. Midori, no worry. Daddey no marry."

To pass the time, Daddey started making a set of cards. It wasn't the type with hearts, clubs, spades, and diamonds; it was a *karuta* card set. He cut up the white birthday cake box into same-sized rectangular cards and began writing a memorized proverb on separate cards. When he could not remember a proverb, he made something up. Then he began drawing pictures on a second set of cards. Using my tin of watercolors, he went to work. The task was completed before the end of my quarantine, and Daddey and I played the "pick up the cards" game to my delight. The card set was crude, but like the wood *geta* I had watched being made, the people were resourceful and creative to fill their time. There were true craftsmen among them who made items of beauty and ingenuity from found objects and scraps of wood. An exhibit of their handiwork was collected and shown. We internees marveled at the skill of artists in our midst.

Mrs. Morris would have been appalled if she had seen the dank, sunless room where I spent my three weeks of quarantine. Had she known, she would have had me snatched up and dumped back into Josef House. At the hospital, sunshine and fresh air were the prescription to health. I had not been exposed to any sunshine for three weeks, and I wore clothes, not just a sweater, to keep warm. Our room did not stink, although the air quality inside was questionable. The dim lighting was likely a blessing, making it impossible to inspect the premises. Were those spooky shapes slithering around in the dark regions related to those underground ghouls clanking along Yesler Way? It was just as well we did not know exactly what the dark splotches marking the walls were. Who knew what had been lodged in the stall before us? It was best not to inspect too rigorously.

Leaving Quarantine

Daddey got permission for us to move to Area D instead of returning to Area A, "To be closer to relatives for the sake of my motherless daughter," he had told the administration. After our three weeks' quarantine, our beds, mattresses, blankets, and luggage were piled in the back of a truck once again, and we were moved out of isolation. When the movers came, Daddey and I climbed onto the open bed of the truck with our possessions and plopped down on the mattress for lack of any seats. Outside the barn, the sun was bright and shining, giving warmth to the early June day. The air was free of recycled musty odors as the breeze swept through, leaving a lingering scent of flowers in bloom. It felt great to be outdoors again, and riding on the open bed of the army truck allowed us to survey the route to our new home in Area D.

As soon as we boarded the movers' truck, it jolted into gear and began bouncing around in a double-jointed twist as it negotiated the rutted ground. The truck took several sharp turns and entered into a curved and bordered roadway before turning off onto the pitted walkway between two barracks and then stopping abruptly. The driver and his assistant wasted no time opening the tailgate and helping us off the back. "Folks, this is your new home. It's a lot better than the one you just left, *neh*?" he said as he guffawed loudly, amused at the understatement.

Our barracks looked like those in Area A, with each pair of identical buildings facing each other row upon row, but the buildings were not all the same length. Our barrack was longer than the one in front and shorter than the one in back. Our new compound was set into the center grounds of a racetrack, which determined the length of each building within. The large, covered grandstand sat as the prominent focus of the raceway. The track was bordered by a whitewashed fence on two sides and rimmed with marigolds planted well before the fairground's conversion into an assembly center. The profusion of orange and yellow blooms lasted the entire summer of our stay and provided a bounty of cheerful color in sharp contrast to our bleak quarters and the circumstances of our presence. The flowers were a welcome antidote to our stark, man-made environs.

I was busy helping Daddey unpack our bedding while offering him unsolicited opinions regarding furniture arrangement, namely deciding the best locations for our two bed cots. With only two in our family, we had much more flexibility on cot placement than larger families because all the units were the same size. We had heard a child's whimpering off and on all the while, without paying it much attention. The child began to cry loudly nonstop. Since the open gap above the common wall with our neighbor transmitted the sound as if we were in the same room, we could no longer ignore it. The crying continued, and no one tried to ease the child's discomfort. Daddey was concerned, and he went to the neighbor's door. The door was padlocked on the outside. It was a dilemma. To be sure there was no adult in the room, he knocked politely; there was no response. He banged on the door to rouse any inhabitants; it was unsuccessful. Daddey went to the neighbors on the other side of our unit and knocked on the door. "Hal-lo, hal-lo. I'm your new neighbor," he said and introduced himself to the woman who came to the door.

"Yes, I have to admit I've been wondering why no one has tended to the child and has allowed her to cry so long," she said. "Their name is Esaki, but we don't know them well. We have no idea where the parents have gone. Sorry I'm not much help to you."

Our close open quarters required the residents to extend a form of courtesy much as they did in Japan. The Issei's reactivated their practice of allowing others privacy and had switched to selective listening by "not hearing" talk not intended for their ears. They had learned the polite etiquette in the thinly partitioned homes of their youth. In situations outside their immediate family circles, they now only heard conversations directed to them. Other extraneous talk, whether hushed or loudly broadcast, blended with annoying noises and indiscreet sounds, and fell on deaf ears. Others in the building did not hear the neighbor's crying child.

Daddey moved a bed over to the wall separating us and the crying baby and attempted to scale it, but he failed. With his youthful gymnastics prowess on the bars still vivid in his mind, he was sure he would succeed by giving it another try. He tilted our still-unmade cot on end against the wall and managed to climb it using our still stuffed seabag as a prop. He stretched, got a grip of the top, pulled himself up until he could swing one leg over the wall, and straddled it. With his other leg over the top, he released his grip and dropped to the floor on the other side. He crawled out the window with the child, who had stopped crying after her rescue.

"Midori, we go and find Esaki-*san*."

Daddey carried the young girl in his arms, and I followed. We walked toward the central complex of permanent buildings, where people were gathered. Daddey asked all the passersby we came across if they knew the child or her parents. Everyone politely said, "*Iie*, no, sorry," or shook their heads, all the while looking at us quizzically, too polite to ask for an explanation. Others passed us by, but no one knew the child. A man came toward us, walking jauntily along the path, and Daddey asked the stranger the same question.

"Oh, my… Yes, she's my Zumiko. She's supposed to be sleeping at home," he said.

"She's been crying for an hour. We've been looking for her parents."

"She was sleeping so soundly, I thought I'd go watch the sumo tournament for a while." He took his daughter from Daddey's arm and thanked him for his intervention. "Nice to have you as our new neighbor, aAh… Your name was…?"

We turned back toward our units while the two men amicably exchanged stories. "We lived on Yesler Hill until…"

"That was a wicked hill to walk up; riding up on the cable car was worth every cent."

"To drive down Yesler hill, we needed good brakes for our car."

The little girl had fallen asleep again cradled in her father's arm, and I tagged along after the two men, curious to know what a sumo tournament might be. I'll have to go see for myself, I decided. Mrs. Esaki came over the following morning to thank Daddey. She was away visiting her son in the hospital she explained, and she apologized for the commotion her daughter had caused during her absence. She appreciated his kind gesture, and she bowed and thanked Yoshi sincerely. The woman, Yoshi noticed, was youngish, about Aiko's age. She had a sweet voice and disarming demeanor, and she spoke Japanese more fluently than his wife had. She looked nothing at all like the dark image he had conjured in his mind yesterday, and she certainly did not look or behave like a careless mother. They exchanged the usual pleasantries before parting and the mandatory bows.

Ready to explore our new surroundings, Daddey and I took the path we had taken the day before in our search for our neighbor. We were on our way to find the sumo tournament, so we continued our walk along the marigold-lined track until we reached the central complex. Inside the largest building, we found a virtual fair with people engaged in all sorts of activities, either as participants or as spectators. There were small and large groups scattered about here and there, and hordes of people walking and browsing the goings-on. I followed Daddey, who walked past all the interesting things without stopping until we reached a small arena with stepped seating on the side. We found seats higher up for a good view of the proceedings. Men made up most of the audience, and they enthusiastically cheered the combatants and the show. Two fat men, who were basically naked except for the thing-a-ma-bobs covering their private parts, crouched on opposite sides of the ring. After a spell of staring at each other, they began shoving and jostling each other around the circular mat. Usually within the blink of an eye, one man took the advantage and got his opponent to step off the mat. With that, the round was over. To my dismay, there were long intervals of unfathomable ceremonial rituals between the bouts. Why did the combatants alternately lift one beefy leg up sideways, like a dog peeing on a fire hydrant, then bringing it down with a loud thud and repeating it with his other leg? THUD. The subtleties of sumo escaped me: not enough rough-and-tumble action.

"Daddey, watching sumo isn't any fun," I said. "I want to go look at something else. Can I go by myself? I won't get lost. I'll come back here. I promise."

Daddey stayed and watched the sumo tournament of amateur wrestlers who had trained in the dojo's in the valley. It was a men's sport; I went exploring to find something more interesting. I stood and watched a ping-pong tournament for a while before moving on to watch a seated circle of ladies knitting. One woman was showing a novice who had just joined the circle how to hold the knitting needles and begin the first row of stitches. I watched on the sidelines and absorbed her instructions; when I got up to go, I was confident that I could knit if I had the proper tools. The crocheting group met a ways off, and their lessons were more complicated. I then happened upon a group of mostly younger people seated facing a storyboard on an easel. The storyteller was pointing to a wooden boat cutout attached to her board. I sat down in one of the empty chairs and joined her audience.

"Noah had built an ark as God had instructed," she said.

Whoa, that looks like a big rowboat. What's this ark thing? "While he and his sons worked to finish the ark, the people laughed and ridiculed him, saying… And all the animal species came on the ark, two by two… For forty days and forty nights it rained, flooding the earth." Finally, at the end of her story, she said, "…you must believe in God the Father, the Son, and the Holy Ghost to be saved as Noah was saved."

That was a wonderful story. But who is God the Father, the Son, and Holy Ghost? I wondered.

CAMP FOOD

The dining hall was a much longer walk from our quarters than it had been in Area A. It was housed in one of the huge permanent fairground buildings. We had to stand in long lines to get to the chow, and when we saw what was being served, another unappealing and ugly-tasting meal, the disappointment was real. The menu made no accommodations to Japanese diets, and everyone hated the food. Stories of food poisoning were rampant. I liked the wieners when they were served, but I had so little interest in food it hardly mattered what they served. After picking up our plates, Daddey and I had to find a place to sit down among the long rows of picnic tables. I stared at the unappetizing glob of food, trying to decide whether I was hungry enough to taste it.

"You should eat, *garu-san*. People in China have NO food. They are starving," said the diner sitting next to me as he pointed at my plate with his fork.

"Even starving Chinese wouldn't eat this stuff; they know better," said another diner sitting across from us.

"Starvation is no laughing matter. I avoided starvation in my early years in America eating a diet of rice and *tsukemono*."

"That's a royal diet for a Nihon-*jin*. Even the Chinese would eat it. They'd probably add some different spices and call it fried rice."

"If you fed *haku-jin* only *tsukemono* and rice, they'd think you were starving them. That's not white man's food."

"What are you all talking about? As long as you have rice to eat, no one is starving."

"If that's the case, we're all being starved here. We haven't seen any rice since we got here."

They continued their banter, and the small group of strangers became a fellowship for the duration of the meal as they laughed and made light of their plight.

The mass-produced meals were not much different from those of most large quantity kitchen facilities, where quantity rules. Admittedly, the impersonal communal dining was a new and unappealing experience for most evacuees. The cavernous building echoed and magnified the noise generated in the kitchen and the dining hall proper, making a negative experience worse.

Daddey was not a fussy eater. He ate what was put on his plate without complaint and without discussion. Nor was he known to compliment or give praise for a meal meriting such kudos. It was a matter of eating for sustenance. He no longer bothered to finish my uneaten portions, I noticed.

"I'm not hungry today," I said after scrutinizing my platter, looking for those miniscule bits of pork sometimes tossed into the bean mix, therein complying with any "truth in labeling" edicts in effect at that time. As soon as my search for meat was completed, I pushed my plate aside and waited for Daddey to finish eating. I was ready to scrape the rest of my dinner in the garbage and be on my way.

"Drink your milk, Midori."

"It tastes bad. I don't want it. It's yucky." I had no idea I was drinking reconstituted powdered milk.

Daddey was concerned I was not eating properly; and without proper nourishment, he was afraid the TB might return. The problem was solved when he learned there was a special children's dining room. The foods Daddey had picked up in a separate commissary while I was quarantined, were specially prepared healthy menus for patients. These nutritious meals were also available in the small, comfortable dining room in a separate building on the fringes of the central complex. It was a welcome oasis, a quiet, civilized place to dine removed from the masses and noise of the main mess hall. The tables and chairs were not standard government-issue furniture, and the bright, cheery décor suggested the facility was used as a specialized restaurant during the fairs. It was an alternate dining room open to children accompanied by a parent, where the carefully prepared meals were served using real butter, dairy milk, and the like. Pork and beans were not on the menu. The food and its preparation were similar to my meals at Josef House. I readily ate without my usual complaints, and when I finished, I did not need to be excused from the table. Happily, this dining room did not serve the mandatory cod liver oil.

A slice of fresh bread with a pat of butter was always served with dinner. Daddey began bringing a small metal cup containing a scant tablespoon of jam with him to our evening meals. He and I spread our bread with jam very carefully with the knowledge our supply was limited. Daddey had included a large tin of real strawberry jam among the necessities he had packed in the seabag he carried to camp. He stoically accepted camp food, but it did not mean he had no food preferences. His sugar habit went underground due to circumstances beyond his control.

Besides the tin of good-quality strawberry jam, Daddey had carried a five-pound sack of sugar in his seabag, too. Had he known sugar rationing would make the sweet crystals a scarce commodity through the war, his stash would likely have been twice as much or more, adding weight and value to our baggage.

For whatever reasons, the children's dining room was underused. Less than two dozen families ate there on a regular basis, and it was never filled to capacity. Each family generally had a table to themselves. One mother and her two daughters were among the regulars. I learned later that the girls had a Chinese father, and although they were only half Japanese, they had to be interned with their Japanese mother. I was to meet the older daughter when we were third-grade classmates.

A New Social Structure

The relatives Daddey had thought we would live closer to in Area D were housed outside the racetrack grounds where we lived. The distance made visiting an infrequent outing. Actually, the relatives were Hayame's siblings and their families, and Daddey and I were a branch related through marriage and not by blood. With Hayame, her children, and her new family interned elsewhere, and with my mother gone from the scene, there was no focus for maintaining our close bonds as in the past. When the communities were uprooted and dispersed, the social networking fractured, and any once-strong familial or kinship bonds that may have existed, crumbled, and family unity fragmented.

In Camp Harmony, our neighbors and the people living near us were strangers, and this was generally true for others; living units had been assigned without input from the evacuees. Daddey began making friends, first with our nextdoor neighbors, then with others living nearby, gradually initiating a network of acquaintances.

The usual rains and cool temperatures departed, and warmth dispelled the chill from the early morning air as the sun beat down on the single-ply tarpaper roofing of our barracks. The black absorbed the sun's heat, and transferred it indoors. With the onslaught of summer, when the sun shines for two months, the sun-starved residents took to the outdoors to bask and delight in the welcome warmness and light. With greater visibility, the circle of communication widened, and strangers became neighbors with names, and others became friends.

The novelty of sunny days wore off as we began to feel the effects of the constant sun, the heat making our living quarters stifling and unbearable as it got hot and hotter. Hardly a breeze flowed through open door and window. The best relief was to sit outside; the backyard was best. The backyard alley we shared with the barrack facing away from us was narrow, covered with grass, and never used as a roadway. It was a place for contemplation and relaxation.

The evacuees had endured the anxiety-filled months since the start of the war, and its resolution was our present reality. We lost our freedom;

we were wards of the US government. Housed, albeit in structures some called coops. We were fed food most described as godawful chow, and we had few opportunities to work and be useful.

Shikata-ga-nai, abide by the inevitable; we were powerless to do anything except accept our present fate.

Of course, the degree to which each individual accepted his or her present fate varied. Whatever angst or resentments an individual harbored was generally internalized. As in any society, there were hotheads too; they were usually the younger folks. The majority of older internees realized they had leisure time they had never known before. They had the time and opportunity to pursue or indulge their inner interests; to while away their time doing nothing, or maybe just sit and contemplate.

Arai-*san* lived in the barrack behind and opposite our unit. On hot summer afternoons, he could be seen seated on the grass, legs sprawled in front, with his back propped up against the wall. His round-rimmed glasses sitting halfway down his nose, he read his book intently, or just stared blankly into space oblivious of all else. His books appeared to be his one leisurely indulgence, as he sat day after day consumed by his reading. He was not unfriendly; he was totally absorbed by his own private thoughts. The neighbors understood this and never disturbed his privacy at such times.

Yoshi still loved reading books of historical events, an avocation he had had little time to indulge. He realized, to his regret, he'd not included any books in his luggage; no history books or fairy tale collections. He was curious to know what subject could so fascinate his neighbor to sit alone and read for hours. He had to satisfy his curiosity. Yoshi also thought to use a politer form of Japanese to address him, since he appeared to be an educated man.

"Arai-*san*, you always have your head buried in a book. What, may I ask, do you read? It must be very precious to you. How else to explain your including such a weighty tome as part of 'only what you can carry'?" Yoshi said to him one afternoon.

"It was really an indulgence for me to bring a few of my books, but I couldn't leave them behind. My wife reluctantly agreed and allowed me to put them in my luggage."

"*Gomen-nasai*, excuse me. I don't mean to be rude or impolite, but what is the subject of your book which keeps you so entranced?"

Arai-*san* smiled broadly. "Only a fool like me treasures a book of poems."

"Ah, haiku poetry?"

"*Iie*. No, they're *tanka* poems. My hobby is to write *tanka* poetry. Unfortunately, inspiration is only a small part of the process. I have to read and study to give my inspiration its proper voice."

Yoshi listened attentively. Arai-*san*'s conversation was interesting, more so than the gossip he had been listening to lately. "You're a scholar, then."

"Yo ho ho. I worked at the sawmill doing physical work like everyone else. I became interested in poetry back when I was in school, but there was little time to concentrate on poetry since then." He continued, "The irony is now that I don't have to work, my housing is free, as are my meals, and my entire day is filled with leisure to do as I please, my brain has dried up. The inspiration and poems are gone. That's why I sit blankly—— hoping some idea will drift into my head."

"Perhaps you'll be kind enough to let me borrow one of your books. I've read some *tanka* poetry, as we all have when we attended school, but I'm intrigued to learn what it is that has the power to mesmerize a man such as you for so many hours." Arai-*san* encouraged Yoshi's interest and welcomed the opportunity to share his knowledge of the art form. Perhaps talking about poetry might shake off his writer's block.

"Should you decide to write poetry, you'll study harder than a more-schooled man for sure Nomura-san, but one's level of formal schooling isn't the main criteria for writing poems. Your neighbor, Mrs. Esaki, writes *tanka* also. She has written some very good poems."

"And I thought she was so busy being a wife and mother. She's so often visiting a sick son in the hospital, I rarely see her. How does she find time to think about poetry?" Yoshi suddenly felt new respect for his neighbor with the crying daughter.

"*Yoi-sho, yoi-sho*," a man repeated as he trotted by. He had a lumpy, misshapen mattress drooping over his shoulders. Other people in our neighborhood also passed by lugging their oddly shaped mattresses toward the tracks to a drop-off area in the distance. Later, these same people passed our unit again going in the opposite direction as they returned to their homes. They were still loaded down with their mattresses. I watched the parade quizzically through our open door. All the while, Daddey quietly read his borrowed poetry book.

"Daddey, what is everyone doing? Why are they carrying their mattresses outside? Don't we have to take our mattress somewhere, too?"

"It is time to change the hay in their mattress. They throw away the old hay and get new hay for the mattress. It will be very fresh."

"I thought horses eat hay. Is it the same kind of hay?" "I guess so."

"We don't have hay in our mattress. Why does everyone else have a hay mattress?"

"You have many questions, *neh*." He obviously wanted to get back to his reading; instead, he put his book aside and answered, "Daddey and Midori come to Puyallup early, we live in Area A. People live in Area D, they come last. In the beginning, administration have many good mattress just like mattress we sleep on. Pretty soon, too many people, no more mattress. People need mattress to sleep on, so they make hay mattress."

"The Kondo's across the road aren't changing their hay."

"They say they have hay fever sickness, so they get real mattress, no hay mattress."

"Daddey, we must be lucky. We got the good mattresses in Area A, and they came with us to isolation and to Area D."

Yup, we were lucky.

"*Yoi-sho, yoi-sho, yoi-sho.*" The man was returning home. He trotted in rhythm with his chanting, his load weighted on one shoulder much as a carrier balanced his weighted pole. His dash of élan distinguished him from all the others, who took on their chore like beasts of burden. I continued to watch him as he trotted away.

We always carried some squares of toilet paper with us when we went to the toilet. I don't know if early on, real toilet paper was provided or not. Much as administration had run out of cotton-wadded mattresses and had made a substitution, boxes full of brightly colored squares of tissue paper appeared in the women's restroom as a substitute for real toilet paper. The tissue papers were the size and type used to individually wrap fruits, such as apples and pears, in those days. It felt really weird picking up a sheet or two of deep purple or rose-red paper to wipe my butt. Those colorful substitute sheets did a better job than old catalogue pages or cut-up newspapers no matter how much they were crinkled, so nobody complained.

It very well may have started with a lady with time on her hands and a craft project in mind. The bounty of beautiful colored sheets of "substitute toilet paper" were ideal; by carefully folding each sheet and connecting one to the next, they could be braided then wound into fanciful coils for display. The braided origami craze took off. Women and children raided the boxes of colored tissue and began making braided coils. The tissues disappeared from the restrooms, and the resulting inconvenience was of our own making.

Camp Harmony was populated by people of all ages; but, my daily contacts were other children and old folks like our parents. There was a whole spectrum of others I took little notice of since we rarely interacted with each other. The teenagers and young adults were well aware of their predicament and the constraints put upon their life, their future. They were young and energetic, and doing things to ease the boredom. At night, while we innocents slept, there were dance socials they could attend. "The Harmonaires", a popular Nisei swing band, played in a different area compound each night, providing the familiar music of the big bands of that time.

For us younger kids, we were well occupied with simpler activities. Daddey had fetched a bucket full of tepid water at the communal sink some distance from our barrack and brought it to our backyard.

"What's the water for?" I asked.

"You feel not so hot when feet cool. Water is for feet. Try."

I stripped off my shoes and socks and stepped into the bucket. "That feels good, Daddey." He was barefooted by then, and he took his turn.

The barest sound of water must have traveled. Other children in the neighborhood were soon waiting their turn to cool off their feet. Daddey left, letting us kids play with the water. Everything was orderly, and we were having fun until Big Bertha came and hoarded our bucket by sitting in it. She was a bully, and instead of confronting her, the rest of us left and found something else to do without her.

Every day brought a new experience; there were lots of children to play with from morning to night. In addition, I had no nap times and no nurses keeping an eye on me.

"Ets-lay o-gay hopping-say," Gloria called out to us.

"Good idea. Maybe they'll still have some good chocolate candy bars," Molly replied.

"What did Gloria say?" I asked. "I didn't understand what she said."

"You didn't get it? Are you stupid or something?" Molly asked. "Don't you know Pig Latin?"

"What's Pig Latin?"

"Hey, guys, she doesn't know Pig Latin." They all laughed. Thenceforth, they talked in their gibberish Pig Latin whenever I was around, and they laughed uproariously when they saw my distress. In time, I was able to decipher what they were saying, but I didn't bother to let them know I had broken the code.

Mrs. Hidaka, our other neighbor, waved me over one day and said to me, "*Otoo-san ga kairu made, uchi de asobinasai, neh.*"

I hung my head and looked at her blankly. I did not understand a word she said. She had spoken to me entirely in Japanese.

"Gloria, what did your mother say to me?" I asked.

She stared at me intently and realized I was serious. "Don't you understand ANY Japanese? Gee, you're really stupid!" she spat out her words as she shook her head. "My mom said you could play at our house till your dad comes home."

During the year and a half I spent in the hospital, I had heard only English spoken. I lost what little comprehension I once had of the Japanese language. My skills had never developed beyond basic children's level, but my exposure to the language at *Obaa-san's* kitchen had been a subliminal learning experience, and I often got the gist of overheard conversations; that ability had disappeared. Daddey understood that and spoke to me in his ungrammatical English. Most parents of children my age were Issei, or they were schooled-in-Japan Kibei who generally communicated with their born-in-America children in a hybrid English and Japanese. They navigated between the two languages using crucial words understood by both, mixed with words and grammar of their first language. Thus, both generations had a rudimentary understanding of both languages. I was not one of them. I was an anomaly.

The fact that I had no Japanese-language skills traveled fast. My playmates dropped their Pig Latin and openly spoke Japanese to each other whenever they did not want me to know what they were up to. Their own Japanese was sufficient to communicate with peers. Passing on secrets is fun, but doing so out loud without whispering was a novelty, and they took great joy in flaunting it in front of me. I was their scapegoat.

I'll have to figure out what they're saying in Japanese. Fast! I told myself.

We bought our candy bars at the canteen. I groused the selection was too small on learning my favorites were not available. I chose a Butterfinger rather than a Snickers bar. Not knowing at that time the candy we bought were to be the last ones available to us until after war's end. Had we known, we could have savored every sweet morsel of chocolate; instead we gobbled up our candy with our usual gusto and regretted that hasty consumption for years.

Having spent our money at the canteen, we decided to prolong our outing and took a detour back to our barracks. Our candy eaten, we were walking under the grandstands when Molly invited us to visit her family's apartment, which was close by. Built in an enclosed area under the grandstand seating area were units that looked similar to the isolation units of my quarantine stay. Clerestory windows served the voluminous areas where the units were located, providing a natural light source, but the light barely penetrated into the apartment, and the interior remained dark and dank. It was too gloomy for a long visit. On stepping into the enclosure's walkway outside the units, the sun's rays streaked through the windows above, and I spied in the light millions of tiny particulates now made visible. Shining and twinkling in suspension, the dust could not escape and disperse as occurs in the open air.

No wonder Molly keeps coming down to our barracks. How lucky I am to live in a barrack built outdoors with lots of fresh air and sunshine. Mrs. Morris would approve.

With time on their hands, boys will be boys, and their projects were often mischievous. One notorious scheme involved knots. The boys easily popped out large eye-level knots in our wood plank walls, providing "I spy" peepholes. Unwary inhabitants were the victims. The grown-ups did not think the prank funny. Early on, a group of boys in Area D found their windfall, and try as they might, they never found another adventure to top it. The boys managed to sneak inside the fun house, which was a permanent feature on the fairgrounds. The admission was free; however, there were no lights, so they crawled through the convoluted passageways, prolonging their merrymaking tour and having the time of their lives. They tried to keep their exploit a secret, but it was too good to be contained, and as the news spread, every fearless kid in the compound wanted to sneak in and have a look. The boys banned girls from participating, saying it was too dangerous an obstacle course for dress wearing females. The real objection to girls was they talk too much.

The secret leaked, and the adults found out about the break-in. Subsequently, the fun house and all the surrounding gallery structures were securely boarded up and the area enclosed with fencing. Henceforth, absolutely no trespassing was allowed in the amusement area.

Whatever curiosity Yoshi may have had to revisit an arcade and boardwalk galleries, he never mentioned it to others. The off-limits area was deader than Rockaway in winter, and even the ghost had fled the scene.

The wooden rollercoaster trestle supporting the undulating tracks of swooping arches with its careening twists and turns stood silent, towering incongruously above our shanty barracks, ignored during its long hibernation. Blockaded and fenced into isolation, the structure waited to be liberated, to be activated. Wait, summer's heat still burns, though shadows grow longer by the day, autumn and the rains are still kept at bay. When will the interlopers be tossed out? How much longer to wait for the fair's festivities to commence?

Of course, there would be no Western Washington Fair that year.

Move to Internment Camp

We temporary dwellers on the fairgrounds were also becoming restless, ready to move to permanent quarters with accommodations more fitting for human habitation. The move from Camp Harmony began before autumn.

Daddey and I sat side by side in the railcar filled with people who lived in our vicinity in Area D. Since most of the passengers had a nodding recognition with the others, they had a degree of comfort knowing they were not among complete strangers. They relaxed and settled in for the long train ride ahead. The early polite conversations dropped off as the rhythmic clatter of the wheels droned on mile after mile, while the riders sat in trance-like states for long periods of time.

The train stopped without any announcements. "They must be loading on water," someone spoke out.

Mrs. Arai, who had been silently sitting near the front of the car, stood up and faced the passengers. "*Mina-san*, don't drink the water on the train," she said. "I've been told by others who left before us that many became sick after drinking water while on the train." She made the same announcement two more times as she walked to the end of the car. Rumors, negative stories often unverified, spread and mingled with reiterations of true events and precautions.

Passengers began discussing the situation informally in small groups. "No, they're not trying to poison us."

"Perhaps the water they're taking on isn't pure drinking water."

"I think the water container on this train is old and rusty; it hasn't been used in years."

"It's obvious this is an old railroad car brought back into service to take us to our new camp," Yoshi said. "This car is older than the one I rode from New York to Seattle in 1928." He didn't bother to bring up his experiences about taking bad drinking water onboard their ship; that was West Africa twenty-two years before. It was still wise to stay away from water from questionable sources while in transit.

The air was stuffy, and the seats were hard. The older people complained of their bony bottoms getting sore, about their need for fresh air, and about being thirsty. The passengers in our compartment stayed thirsty, and no one got sick.

The rhythmic rocking and clackity lullaby of the train lulled me to sleep whenever I tired of my mental grab bag of mind games or listening to others' conversations. It was impossible to read on the swaying train, so Daddy set aside his book and sat silently exploring his own grab bag of thoughts.

Our train left behind the trees and lush green of coastal Washington. As the view of mountainous peaks receded, our train continued on a flat, featureless landscape of fine yellow sand, pocked with low-lying sagebrush for mile upon mile. I had never before seen land without greenery, and neither had many of the others.

Minidoka under construction

CHAPTER 12

Minidoka, the First Year, 1942-1943

AFTER ALL PERSONS OF JAPANESE ancestry living within designated Military Area #1 in the western states had been uprooted from their homes and forced into hastily constructed assembly centers in the spring of 1942, a few months later, they were moved again as the second phase of their exodus commenced. In late summer and early autumn, evacuees were transported out of Military Zone #2, where the temporary assembly areas had been located, and resettled further inland, away from the Pacific Coast, into permanent camps.

The move from Camp Harmony began in mid-August 1942. Five hundred residents a day were put on trains in Puyallup, Washington, and sent eastward into the remote wastelands of South Central Idaho. There, the Morrison Knutson Company, under contract, had constructed and were still in the process of completing Minidoka Relocation Center when the evacuees began arriving. In early September, evacuees from the Portland, Oregon area joined the move to Minidoka, as well as Japanese residents from Alaska. When the move-in was complete, more than nine thousand internees were housed in Camp Minidoka.

The evacuees found themselves in an environment far different from the Pacific Northwest. No geologic distortions intruded on the plain: it was a landscape bereft of trees, vegetation, and greenery cover; there was sky, sand, and the ubiquitous scraggly sagebrush. We had been collected there not to be disciplined––we were put there to be controlled.

"QUIET! EVERYONE QUIET! We know you're tired and you wanna get back to your units, but there's a lotta things we need to tell you today. You'll have lotta time to visit later. Let's get started."

The volume of chatter continued unabated. The free-reigning noise diminished only slightly. Latecomers to the assembly darted about seeking seating on the benches. The cacophony of voices swelled as each attendee talked ever more loudly, each trying to be heard above the din.

"There's some seats over here."

"Boy-*san*, don't SIT on the table!"

"Whaaaat?"

"Don't put your ass on the tabletop, is what she said."

"Who she think she…"

BAM, BAM, BAM. The speaker banged his cup on the table to quiet the inattentive crowd. Startled, people stopped their conversations in midsentence. Heads turned toward the source of banging. With arms waving above his head, the speaker changed his tactics and clapped his hands to attract attention. Finally, the noise receded, and the gathered crowd focused its attention on the speaker. He was one of them––a young Nisei. He worked in administration, and his present assignment was to disseminate information and provide instructions to the new residents. Still new to his job and unaccustomed to public speaking, he hesitated and braced himself. The crowd watched him expectantly. He took in a deep breath and came forth with a baritone rumble. "*Mina-san*," projected from his mouth. He smiled broadly, proud he had started his address in Japanese.

"*Mina-san*, ahh, everyone," he stumbled. His Japanese vocabulary lapsed, and he reverted to his mother tongue, English. "Welcome to Minidoka Relocation Camp on your first day to your new permanent home. You'll find Minidoka is a tremendous improvement over the temporary assembly center facilities you just came from. We want you to be comfortable and happy here. After all, you may be here a looooong time, maybe two, three, or five years, maybe ten years. Nobody knows." The room fell silent.

"Maybe we will be here for ten years?"

Many in the audience gasped. "Ten years?"

"What did he say? What did he say?" buzzed through the crowd. The inattentive and those who did not understand the language questioned others around them. They sensed they had missed something important.

"*Nani? Nani?* What did he say?"

The speaker was sure he now had everyone's attention. He cleared his throat and began, "Let me start this orientation with a brief summary of the camp. We're located in Hunt, Idaho, on 950 acres of land. There are thirty-five Blocks. All the Blocks look like this one. The first Block is Block 1, and the last numbered Block is Block 44. Some Blocks are missing. I don't know the reason for the missing Blocks." The speaker picked up his glass of water and drank a mouthful before he continued, "Blocks 1 and 2 start at the west and continue east in pairs to Block 19. That's this Block. You live in Block 19, Area A."

"Block 19. *Ju-kyu bura-ku,*" a man repeated loudly into his cupped hands wrapped around the ear of his spouse.

"*Bura-ku* na-in ten," she repeated.

"There's a long road separating this Block and Blocks 21 and 22, the start of Area B. It continues East and South and ends with Block 44," he elaborated. "You'll understand the layout in time. It'll all make sense after a while."

Someone in the audience raised a question.

"No, there is no fence and gate between Areas A and B. Minidoka is a single compound," came the answer. "Yes, it's a very long walk from Block 1 to Block 44."

"No, I don't know why they planned it this way. Your guess is as good as mine."

"Yes, it'll take a longer walk to visit friends in other Blocks. Even you folks living in Block 19 won't visit Block 44 too often unless you have a sweetheart living over there."

Bad joke. Silence. No laughs.

He continued on, "There is one advantage to this expansive layout. You'll feel less confined. There's a lotta open space all around us."

From the crowd, a voice rang out, "Lots of open space all right, yeah, all on the other side of the fence. Inside, no trees, no plants––just sand. That's why it looks big and open. They drop us in the middle of a desert!"

Loud murmurs of agreement swelled in the hall.

"Hell, they wanted a clear sightline to shoot you if you tried to escape," pierced a voice through the rumbling crowd.

"Hey, that's not funny!" someone interjected; others gasped.

"What? What he say?"

"Nothing. He said nothing."

"The WRA just thought you wanted a change of scenery; they traded your ocean view for this vast sea of sand." It fell on deaf ears; it was another dud. "OK, OK," the speaker said, then, enunciating each word distinctly, continued, "Back to the subject. This is your mess hall, where they'll serve your meals. Each Block has a kitchen and dining hall. It's much better than that big old barn at Puyallup, yeah?" Those who were listening nodded their heads. "Each Block has its own core buildings, and all the Blocks are built the same––they're carbon copies. The other building in the center of the Block, which you passed to get here, has a laundry area with washtubs for washing clothes and space to set up your ironing boards. In the other half of the building, there are separate bathrooms for men and women. A third building is located on the side of the Block; it's called a recreation hall."

The audience was becoming restless again. The speaker picked up a handful of printed papers. Waving them above his head, he continued in a higher pitch, "These handouts. You will all receive handouts outlining the major camp regulations, but let me go over a few of them now, in case you have any questions." The seated audience members shifted about on the wooden benches, each wishing he or she had a something soft to sit on. Those who had been standing to better view the proceedings decided to find seats still within hearing range. Everyone settled down for a long afternoon.

"The sign-up sheets for various jobs in the mess hall and laundry/ boiler room are located on the… Later you will vote for a Block manager and a representative to the council…"

After the speaker read the list of prerequisites, the question and answer period finally arrived.

"Yes, we're allowed to send and receive mail. We do live in the United States of America. The Block manager will act as your mailman… Censorship? Hmm…let's not forget we're at war. There may be spies lurking about."

"The guards are also here to protect you." Quickly he took another question. "Yes. Yes, the water is safe to drink."

"The laundry sinks and showers are ready to be used. Unfortunately, the sewer plant isn't finished, so it's not hooked up, and the bathtubs and toilet fixtures haven't been delivered yet. You'll have to use the toilets in those two little wooden buildings near the road."

"Oh, you found them already? Yes, there's one for men and one for women. It's clearly marked."

"Yes, we'll tell the sign maker to add another sign written in Japanese. Big signs, so there'll be no mistake. OK, painted in white so, you can read them in the dark."

"Real toilet paper should be provided. Yes, sir-ee, each and every out-hou… ah…restroom."

"I don't think you should worry. I'm sure they'll relocate them once in a while. They won't get filled up."

"I won't forget, I promise to let administration know that buzzing, shiny, blue-green monster flies mean it's time to move the shacks."

"Oh––ah, ah… Can we move on and discuss something else besides the latrines? We still have a lotta things to talk about, *Neh*."

Another major concern for those gathered at this initial meeting was the subject of food. It was everyone's favorite topic; a sure distraction from annoying subjects. "Your mess hall will provide three meals a day. They'll clang an iron triangle like they do in those cowboy movies to let everyone know when it's dinnertime. That's when the food is ready."

"Hey, don't we get room service?" someone spoke out.

"Sorry, there's no food service to your units here. You're living in Camp Minidoka, not the Olympic Hotel." The crowd bellowed out in laughter. This is a good sign, thought the speaker. They're relaxed; now if only the other Blocks where I have yet to visit act accordingly. He continued, "You should eat in your own mess hall. Each Block is allocated an amount of food according to how many people live there. Every Block gets the same rations, and the head cook for each Block was chosen based on experience. I'm sure the cooks in this Block are excellent chefs." The doubter's in the crowd moaned audibly.

The questions that followed lost their audience appeal. The speaker knew it was time to end the session. "Thank you all very much. *Domo, domo,*" he said while vigorously nodding his head in the requisite Japanese manner. "Don't forget to sign up for Block jobs…"

Only a few clinging young children, me being one of them, had accompanied their parents to the meeting. Finding myself alone, I stood on the sidelines while people weaved through the picnic tables in various directions to pick up handouts, to check out the sign-up sheets, or to stand around socializing. Acquaintances greeted each other, bowing and acknowledging their good fortune to be more permanent neighbors, and smiled in fellowship with strangers, who had become neighbors for the long haul. I noticed many of the attendees were neighbors from Camp Harmony, or people I recognized as having lived close by. The Esaki's, Hidaka's, and Arai's were among them. The crowd dispersed slowly.

Daddey finally found his way to where I was standing.

"I sign up for dishwasher job, Midori. I be in kitchen to work every day." He patted me on the shoulder. "You are big girl now so you can eat in mess hall with everybody, that OK, *neh*? Always I be not so far away."

"Maybe they won't give you the job, Daddey."

"I have experience. I will get job."

I got in step with my father, and we trudged back to our unit to begin the task of unpacking for the long stay. Maybe even ten years? Ten years is almost forever.

None of the ten relocation centers built by the War Relocation Authority were identical. Differences in site configurations, sizes and topography contributed to the variations, some were due to bureaucracy. Basic to all ten camps was the Block concept of a mess hall, a laundry/restroom building, and twelve equal-sized residential barracks, In Minidoka, the two core buildings were sandwiched by half a dozen barracks on each side, standing in formation one in front of the other, and all facing forward. The design, construction, and relative placement of the buildings within the Block were consistent; one Block identical to the others, except the recreation hall, whose location followed no format. The varied placements, broke the symmetry of the rigid plan and introduced some flexibility. Door and window positions on our barracks showed no such flexibility.

A camp's administrative facilities, including military police offices and separate residences for the non-Japanese staff, as well as a hospital were usually located nearby. The standard Blocks were set in a rigid grid pattern, concentrated and grouped into an orderly, compact configuration in the other nine centers. For reasons unknown—though the smoothly undulating topography may have forced the variation; Minidoka's site layout was unlike the other camps' rigid grid. Instead, it was free-flowing and meandering as if the site engineer had followed a dream rather than a rule book.

The long main arterial ran between paired Blocks, connecting them consecutively though not always strung out in a straight line. As the road angled, so did the paired Blocks' angle. Past Block 19, the last Block of Area A, the road veered sharply at a near 90-degree angle, then proceeded straight through open, undeveloped space until it reached a second group of Blocks, where it turned and twisted to the end of Block 44, the last numbered Block. Adding to the unpredictability of the Block layout was the absence of nine Blocks and its random location. The unique sprawling layout meant no Block was hemmed in on all four sides. Our Block was not a paired Block since Block 20 was a missing one, and we were adjacent to only one other; Block 17.

Our Block was located near the middle of camp, but everything important was a long walk away. Five miles of security fencing was erected at Minidoka, reads the statistics. Residents describe it as obtrusive, and they reviled its presence. I have no memory of it.

When I lived at the hospital, the fencing along three sides of the Josef House grounds were primarily a deterrent to keep others out to prevent contact with tubercular patients. There was no fence on the fourth side of the property. It was open to the roadway serving the sanatorium complex; the demarcation line that I, as a patient, was forbidden to cross. There were no physical barriers keeping me hostage, but the transparent barrier had been impressed on my mind, and I never violated those limits during my stay there. In Puyallup, the barbed fencing enclosing Area A was a stark, ever-present barrier, both physical and visual. The fencing in Area D was less visible, especially to those of us living in the winners' circle within the racecourse. Surrounded by the white fence defining the track and its continuous border of blooming perennials, our barracks and the areas I traveled were far removed from the perimeter fencing, but we knew it was there.

Each move had placed me into a larger compound: all were enclosed and each had restrictions, but I felt more liberated as we progressed. When we arrived in the great expanses of Minidoka, I knew there was space enough to roam with expectations for new experiences.

That is not how most of the internees felt about the fences erected in the desert; their constrictions had not been so visible in the past.

DAILY LIFE IN CAMP
One of the camp's five sentry guard towers stood outside of Block 17, our neighbor Block. It looked like a typical prison guard tower, and no

one questioned its function. The tower's presence was a constant visible reminder we were under guard. Sentries were stationed at the tower when we first arrived. Their elevated stations bombarded by the sun's direct and reflected rays; with minimal shelter and comforts provided, it undoubtedly made the duty unrewarding. Given the responsibility to watch for suspicious activities or imminent escape attempts, the guards were relegated to watching the menial day-to-day chores undertaken by well-behaved inmates who went about their own business and were blithely unconcerned at the discomfort and boredom being inflicted on the sentry guards watching them. The guards disappeared from the towers when they were given less tedious, more productive duties elsewhere. It was obvious to all sensible people, especially to the internees, that no one intent on staying alive would leave the camp and walk for endless miles in a bleak, hostile, godforsaken desert full of rattlesnakes and worse. On foot and unarmed, who in their right mind believed odds favored their survival on encountering a vigilante with itchy fingers? Food, shelter, and protection were being provided merely for relinquishing one's freedom.

The tower, though empty, stood arrogantly within easy viewing distance, still projecting its power to intimidate. That is, until a few adventurous youngsters in the neighborhood found a use for the abandoned structure. The tower, they reasoned, was the perfect hideaway for secret smokes far removed from disapproving adult eyes. Their innovative sagebrush cigarettes were readily assembled but volatile. Nor were the concoctions "so free and easy on the draw."

One afternoon, the horns and clanging bells of the fire truck came louder and louder, then stopped. Those of us who were outdoors ran toward the area where the sirens had abruptly ceased. We looked for signs of smoke. A crowd of curious bystanders had already formed to watch the fire brigade maneuver the fire hoses toward the smoke escaping from the smoldering watchtower. The fire was quickly extinguished––well before the structure was engulfed in flames. What a disappointing, anticlimactic end to the brief excitement. A second disappointment for those watching the show was that the structure remained; it had not burned to the ground. The charred tower was off-limits to all further adventures, and it remained standing, neglected and ignored. It had lost its iconic significance.

Our address was 19-6-F. Daddey and I lived in Block 19, Barrack 6, Unit F. Since there were only two of us in the family, we were assigned to one of the small units. The small units at both ends of a barrack each accommodated a family of two or three. Our room was approximately twelve feet wide by twenty feet deep. Next to the small end units were the larger units, which were twice as large, while the two middle units were 50 percent larger. Each unit had a potbellied stove sitting in a sandbox, and a closet with no door or clothes rod. Our unit had three windows, one in front and a pair in back. The door led to an entry vestibule shared with the adjacent unit.

We moved the metal frame beds together to conserve space. Actually, Daddey had brought only double-bed-sized sheets. Having the beds joined together to form a double bed solved the bed linen problem and eliminated a space-consuming aisle. We were also able to share the khaki-colored wool blankets issued to each person; valued items much needed for the cold winter nights ahead. Daddey never hogged the blankets. It was his habit to sleep straight as a board like a mummy. He maintained the same exact position all night long. He may have acquired the habit while sleeping in cramped quarters aboard ships, and he never changed. The rigors of sleeping outside were long past, and I needed the layered warmth of many blankets to stave off the cold at night. No matter how many logs were jammed into our potbellied stove before we went to sleep, and no matter how red-hot it glowed, the fire was long gone with barely a nugget still smoldering deep within heaping ashes when we woke up in the morning.

Soon after our move in, Daddey salvaged lumber from the scrap heaps leftover from construction and borrowed tools to construct two desks and two benches; storage units were made from wooden crates. The largest crate held our kitchen utensils, which consisted of a pot, a few dishes, dinnerware, and whatever treats we might have put away. Later, he made a small box to house the chamber pot, a necessary item saving night walks outside in the dark and cold. He hung an old bedspread to hide the clutter in the closet. And every horizontal stud was utilized as a ready-made shelf.

The building was basic two-by-four wood stud framing with exterior walls of wood plank sheathing covered with tarpaper. Slender vertical batten strips stretched from roof to floor level and were distanced at precise intervals along the sides of the building, providing the barracks with their cookie-cutter uniformity.

Inside the single-wall construction, the two-by-four studs were exposed; however, interior partitions between units were finished on both sides with manufactured fiberboard, which provided a semblance of fire protection near the stove and enhanced privacy between neighbors. The same board was attached to ceiling joists, thus hiding the gabled attic space. Sound transmission was greatly reduced between the apartments compared to units at Camp Harmony, but the lack of insulation between adjoining walls did not block all sounds traveling through the walls. The residents discreetly lowered their own voices and turned a deaf ear to their neighbors' talk. Unfortunately, not everyone did so, and private conversations sometimes boomeranged and returned as gossip.

We were settling into our rent-free government-issued unit, trying to make it feel comfortable, and were adjusting to desert living. Further away in Area B, other internees continued to arrive.

When planners hastily drew up the comprehensive plan for the camp, the priority was to provide long-term housing for the internees. The uniform, self-contained Block concept advanced speedy construction; the intricacies of utility systems were engineered. Guard towers and enclosure fencing were all considered and constructed. However, they forgot to include school buildings for the children in their plans. Well after the initial move-in had begun in mid-August, residents in half of Block 10 and Block 32 had to be relocated, and the barracks were hurriedly converted to classrooms for the two grade schools. All buildings in Block 23 were converted into classrooms for grades seven through twelve, and was to be identified as Hunt High School.

Back to School

Notices for school enrollment were posted. Registration for all school-aged youngsters, it read, was taking place in the mess hall the following week. The announcement set off a wave of anticipation. Parents of school-aged children were heartened their offspring could proceed with their education, other adults were happy knowing children were to be confined and out of sight for hours each weekday. At the same time, the children held a range of opinions about going back to school. Good scholars anxiously waited for school to begin, others hated having their free-range playtime impinged, but most felt a little of both.

The much-anticipated day arrived, and a staff of Nisei registrars came with notefiles and their papers. Daddey and I, along with all the other parents with eligible school-aged children living in our Block, showed up. Whatever personal information they deemed pertinent was recorded that day, and each student was assigned to his or her appropriate grade at the end of the interview. Since few families had included their children's report cards among the precious essential papers they had carried with them to camp, Administration had decided the student's age should be the criteria to determine the applicant's grade level, unless a report card verified a different grade assignment was appropriate. The families living in each Block came from divergent communities, and the children had attended dozens of different schools with varied academic standards. The simplified grade assignment process did not take such subtleties into consideration.

The administrators asked their questions, then consulted their charts and made their decisions. The sign-up lines moved quickly. The registrar interviewed us and wrote down the information we gave her.

"Hmmm… This report card is from Bailey Gatzert." She looked up and smiled. "I attended Bailey Gatzert, too. It's a fine school." As she looked over my report card, she mumbled as if to herself, "It says second grade here." She studied the card quizzically for a moment then asked, "You're eight years old, is that right?"

"Yes, I'm eight years old," I replied.

"Fine, that puts you in the third grade when school starts. Lucky your parents brought this report card with you when you came to camp. There's no question what grade you belong in."

I looked at her wide-eyed and blinked. Yes, I was lucky. She had not asked why my report card showed my second-grade attendance had lasted only five days, and she did not test my reading ability, or rather, my reading inability. Despite those disastrous five days at Bailey Gatzert School in early April, I was anxious to give school another try. I was convinced the root of my problem had been my unfamiliarity with the strict rules and procedures enforced at Bailey Gatzert. How do you follow rules when nobody tells you what the rules are in the first place?

My playmates had an endless supply of "Before the war..." school stories. I longed to share such experiences. They never asked me to contribute my school experiences during those story sessions, and I did not volunteer any. My school vacation, not counting the five-day episode at Bailey Gatzert, had lasted more than two years, not the five-month vacation everyone else had. Going to school meant I would really be like everyone else now––one of them, and not an unschooled dodo.

Elementary school finally started in mid-October, and we all trudged off to our barracks school. We didn't have new back-to-school finery or supplies. We just showed up for school knowing our lives were now assuming some normalcy. Though everyone felt a bit apprehensive going to a new, unfamiliar school with unknown teachers and unknown expectations; I felt I was on an even playing field now.

Miss Queen was our Third Grade Teacher. She was the youngest and most attractive teacher at our grade school, and we were delighted to have her for our teacher. We marveled at her peaches-and-cream complexion, and her imperturbable demeanor. She was neither too strict nor too lenient, and she controlled the class with minimal signs of effort or distress. We all adored her. Even the usual show-off bullies restrained themselves in class, reserving most of their unsocial antics for after school.

I recognized a few faces in my classroom from kindergarten, but most were strangers. I sat down beside Kinu, whose round, sweet face and gentle disposition I remembered from the past, although she showed no signs of recognizing me. Sadaye, whose mother ran the vegetable stand on Jackson Street, was also present, and so was Marian. Additionally, I identified the diner who ate with her mother and sister in the children's dining room. Her name was Hazel, and she wore glasses. She must be smart.

All went well the first day, but on the second day I got my first rude awakening. We were given an arithmetic test to assess our individual skills. The first row of problems had two sets of digits, one on top of the other, with a plus sign. Easy. I had learned to add using my fingers. But the second row showed a hyphen instead of a plus sign. Whoa, what does that mean?

"Remember, class: NO talking. Do NOT look at other people's work, and do NOT count with your fingers!" Miss Queen repeated more than once.

I'm sure that hyphen means something, but what? I was stymied. Since I could not look at anyone else's paper for help–– children who knew what they were doing covered their work. I proceeded to add that second row of numbers, too. I got the lowest grade in the class, only 50 percent correct! I had never learned to subtract.

Reading period was worse. Besides the first few pages of the Dick and Jane Reader that Richard had coached me on in the back of Mrs. Lewis's classroom, the only words I could read were the articles, a, an, the, a few consonants and pronouns, and the word "ring." To my dismay, no stories we were told to read contained the word ring. Even when the half dozen or so slow readers gathered for extra tutoring sessions, I was obviously the worst reader of the group. Miss Queen skipped calling me to recite and relieved me from that humiliation. I knew I was the dummy of the entire class!

Children establish a hierarchy based on physical attractiveness, prowess and talents, and also intelligence. Being an extrovert helps, too. Needless to say, I held a very low rank among my peers. There were three of us, two boys and me, who were glaringly unprepared for the third grade. We were put on probation, and our skills were evaluated. Only one boy was put back into second grade; two of us were not. I was allowed to stay in the third grade by the grace of God. How else to explain Miss Queen's opinion that I had the capacity to learn and the potential to catch up some day? When our third-grade readers finally arrived, there were two versions. Two-thirds of the students were given the standard Streets and Roads reader and workbook, and the more advanced third got the More Streets and Roads edition, which was more challenging than the standard reader. Those students were also moved to the left side of the classroom, an elite group. Ever so slowly, I learned to read, though never well enough to join the More Street and Roads group. As I progressed, I passed up a few of the slower readers, and school became less intimidating overall, and more interesting.

I sat next to "*Hana-tare*" Homer most of the year. Our skill level must have been comparable at that time. If he wasn't trying to copy my work, I was copying his. We had a "mutual assistance" pact of sorts regarding our academic assignments, but when the others teased me that we were a pair, I did not find it flattering at all. I had my eye on a few really cute boys––boys who didn't have a constant runny nose like Homer.

The walk to school could be challenging as winds scooped-up sand into its turbulence blender, tossing and swirling the grit every which way. When trudging through a blinding dust mist, the sand granules pelted our faces and exposed flesh, bombarding us like multiple needles stabbing a pincushion. Squinting offered some protection for our eyes. Walking backward against the wind was an alternative, but not practical except for short stretches. The dust comingled in our hair, coated our brows and seeped into our mouths. It tasted like what it was: gritty sand.

In the winter, it was bitterly cold at times with temperatures falling below zero. My detested "bear" coat served me well, but I still envied every other classmate who showed up wearing a "princess" coat. They looked so fine in their velvet-collared fitted finery compared to the shapeless knobby outfit I wore. Why aren't you hibernating little bear? Grrrrr. Since I had quickly reacclimated to bundling up in clothes, I fared no better than everyone else in the fearsome bitter cold.

Perhaps the worst weather to endure while walking to school was the rain. Our customary walking paths became obstacle courses when it rained. Water was not sucked up by the soil; it did not penetrate and disappear. It stayed on the surface, forming smooth, flowing rivulets and swirling eddies. Ponds and puddles appeared everywhere, and as the rains continued, they merged and grew into lakes. The "land of a thousand lakes" stretched from building to building, and Block to Block. On such days, it was wise to walk along the central road, whose gravel paving elevated it above the surrounding muck. As the camp's main road, it was built and maintained to be negotiable at all times. Pedestrians did not have the right-of-way; we jumped out of the way and off the road when a vehicle approached or passed. Undoubtedly, we inevitably stepped into some potholes. We considered ourselves lucky if it was a water-filled hole, but usually the puddle was a muddy morass. The gushy mud oozed into our shoes, slithered into our stockings and curled around our toes. Adding insult to our discomfort, we had to free our feet from entrapment. We pulled and tugged to overcome the restraining suction in order to release our feet from the quagmire. Once in a while, we had to rescue a wayward shoe still caught in the muck. Glub glub glub turned to slush slosh as water drained from our shoes as we trudged on. When we were allowed into the classroom, our shoes still mud-covered, and our legs splattered and dotted with mud spots to our knees. The mud dried and flaked off during class, leaving a dusty residue for the janitor to sweep up at the end of the day. On a good day, our shoes dried and were wearable the following day; only to repeat the routine until the rains stopped.

School lunches were not provided, and we had to walk back to our own mess halls for lunch each day. Since Block 19 was the furthest away from our school in Area A, we walked home briskly, ate, and wandered back. We made the trip to school two times each day. When the weather cooperated, it was not an unpleasant walk. During times of inclement weather, I was battered by wet, mud, or dust two round trips a day, giving rise to snide taunts from students who lived closer to school, about the disheveled appearance of certain classmates who should limit their exposure to the elements and stay clean and tidy like civilized people.

As the holidays approached, Miss Queen included numerous arts and crafts projects to celebrate the seasons, and we relished the change of pace. We were making progress academically, and both teacher and students settled into a comfortable routine.

The Holidays

On Thanksgiving, we were served the traditional turkey with all the trimmings. Our plates were loaded with cranberry sauce, mashed potatoes and gravy, giblet stuffing, green vegetables, and a slice of turkey. Dinner rolls were on the side, and there was pumpkin pie for dessert. Our meal resembled those luscious advertising photos in Good Housekeeping and Better Homes and Gardens magazines. Norman Rockwell could have painted our meal as true Americana. It's not a typical Thanksgiving meal tradition, but almost everyone would have traded the rolls or mashed potatoes for a nice steaming serving of rice. There's nothing better than rice with gravy, turkey, and trimmings on the side.

Our chief cook and his assistants were all cooks by profession and had worked in restaurants and other quantity food service establishments before camp. This was true for the cooking crew of each Block. For many cooks, cooking was just a job with long hours. But there were cooks who truly loved to cook, and took great pride in the meals they served. A few lucky Blocks had such truly talented chefs who, provided with the same basic ingredients distributed to each mess hall and a menu to follow, produced delicious meals; their reputations spread throughout the camp. Residents from other Blocks tried to finagle meals there, although we were supposed to eat in our own Block mess halls. The cooks in our Block were average cooks. They did what they could with what was given––not terrible meals nor epicurean delights.

In early December, the camp newspaper, The Minidoka Irrigator, announced a contest for the mess hall with the best Christmas decorations.

Crepe paper streamers and bows with red foldout bells were strung along the ceiling of the dining room. A decorated fir tree was placed in a corner of the dining room along with a fake fireplace. Someone's discarded stockings hung on the fake mantle, and a couple of fake candles made with corrugated cardboard painted red sat on top. Our Block 19 entry was ordinary and lacked the creative flair and effort of the prizewinners; ho-hum efforts were not even contenders for an honorable mention. No prize, but it hardly mattered; the festive décor of our gussied-up mess hall promoted a holiday focus and seasonal good cheer for everyone. The majority of internees were Buddhist, and the celebration of Jesus' birth and Christian religious aspects of Christmas were alien to their faith, but being a pragmatic people and recognizing the positive value of good cheer, they went along with the spirit of the season. There was no good reason to upset the status quo; all could have a good time as long as there was no active proselytizing.

I retained few memories of celebrating Christmas when we lived up the hill from *Obaa-san's* grocery store on Yesler. Random snapshots of those past holidays preserved scenes lost to me: a foil-icicle draped tree, a pile of wrapped presents under the tree, and a family dinner with a table set up in our parlor. Putting on a Christmas party would have been one of Mother's tactics to Americanize her family by involving us in an American custom. Other non-Christian Japanese did the same whatever their motives. We also colored eggs for Easter, and Mother made sure I had a new bonnet whether I was taken to the Buddhist service that Sunday or not.

The first Christmas I did remember was the one at the hospital when the Sunshine Boys and Girls handed out gifts after their musical program. The war started shortly before my second Christmas at Josef House, and most festivities were canceled. This wartime Christmas in camp felt like a first Christmas to me. The music and songs, the festivities and decorations were wondrous. My playmates had memories of Christmases past filled with abundance, and they complained they were shortchanged this year. I paid them little heed to avoid catching their discontent and darken my blissful state of mind.

"Daddey, can we have a Christmas tree? We should have a Christmas tree," I announced.

"We have nice big Christmas tree in mess hall."

"That Christmas tree is Block 19's. That's not our tree."

He studied my face to see if I was serious. I was. He said, "The canteen no sell Christmas tree. No Christmas tree for sale in Sears & Roebuck catalogue. Nobody sell Christmas tree in camp, Midori."

"But Daddey, it won't be a real Christmas without a Christmas tree."

"Room is too small for Christmas tree. Where you put tree?"

All that logic persuaded me I could not have a Christmas tree this year. It was fate. I could not stop the tears. "I just never had a Christmas tree for a long time."

He looked away, saying nothing. I found his soft spot.

"Maybe I can find nice Christmas tree, we see. We look for special Christmas tree for Midori."

I said nothing further. I knew he would find me a tree because he said he would.

A few days later, Daddey came trudging back from a walk in the desert with a handsaw in one hand and an unwieldy sagebrush limb in the other. He brought it into the room along with its pungent aroma. With a couple of well-placed spikes, Daddey attached the trunk of the bush to the exposed vertical two-by-four framing stud above our makeshift shelf unit. The side of the bush against the wall was relatively flat, but the side branches arched and flowed out in both directions toward the adjacent studs. Two relatively short branches in front added a third dimension without protruding too far into the room.

I stood on the sidelines and watched silently until Daddey had finished. "Thank you. Thank you, Daddey. It's a wonderful Christmas tree!"

Daddey smiled at his handiwork and acknowledged it was indeed, a fine choice.

I spent days making decorations for my tree. There were construction paper rings to be glued together into long chains, then strung from branch to branch. I drew multicolored objects and cut pictures from magazines and hung them with thread from the branches on the tree, so they could dangle or twirl in a breeze. And whatever ribbons I found, were also tied as bows to the limbs. My Christmas tree was beautiful!

O, Christmas tree. O, Christmas tree. How lovely are your sagebrush branches…?

On Christmas Eve, after the program and sing-along of Christmas carols, we children each received a bag of candies and nuts, and a wrapped gift. Organizations on the outside collected gifts for charitable giving to "those less fortunate," and we were the recipients. I received a book about Hans Brinker. It was too advanced for me to read at the time, so I set it aside for a long while.

Christmas dinner was a repeat of Thanksgiving dinner, except chocolate cake with white frosting was served for dessert instead of pie. And rice was an option instead of potatoes.

Thanksgiving is an American celebration, and Christmas's origins are Christian. New Year's is celebrated the world over. For Americans, the festivities take place on the eve, and hangovers are nursed on the first day of the year. For the Japanese, New Year's Day is the main holiday when family and friends meet and share specially prepared commemorative foods and fellowship that lasts for days in Japan, but often cut short in America when the following are work days. It could have been worse if Japan had not adopted the Western calendar and continued to use the lunar New Year's date which changes each year and falls on a day closer to Presidents Day.

"*Shin-nen Omedeto*! New Year's greetings!"

The immigrant settlers brought with them their New Year's traditions from Japan. They kept their traditions intact as best they could and passed on to their descendants the spirit of the holiday; generous hospitality and amiable social interactions. The younger generation especially savored the special foods prepared and served in abundance.

Nostalgic memories of New Years' past reminded the evacuees of the wartime scarcities and how circumscribed their lives were.

The announcement said mochi rice was being distributed to each Block kitchen before New Year's. Having the glutinous rice patties that are as synonymous with Japanese New Year's as Christmas cookies in Scandinavia was a wondrous, unexpected treat. Few pondered the logistics of how and why such a unique Japanese food item, totally alien to Americans, was being made available to them. It was best not to question––just accept the miracle.

The mochi rice and the special implements needed for the *mochi-tsuki* arrived in our mess kitchen. Large quantities of mochi rice were washed, steamed, and when ready, turned onto a special carved-out wood stump. Two men alternately pounded the rice with special wood mallets as a third person turned the rice as it congealed into a glob. Wielding the mallets back, over, and down, the two men took their turns then waited as the third person leaned in to pick up the glutinous mass, turn, and drop it with the same count as the pounders. Pound, pound, turn...pound, pound, turn. I sat and watched, mesmerized by the rhythm. The synchronized beat had to be maintained for the rice turner's benefit, lest his hand be left a smashed mass of bones. When the rice was pounded to a fine, gooey texture, it was removed from the pounding bowl and turned over to the waiting women at the tables. They then pinched the mochi into appropriate sizes and flattened each into round patties which were dusted with a starch to keep them from sticking. Each family received a share of this communal effort allowing us all to savor a true tradition.

The mochi had no flavor of its own, and the gummy patty turned to rock within days. If sealed and stored to prolong its flexibility, mold grew on the patties and had to be scraped off prior to ingesting.

"I eat my mochi with *shoyu* and sugar," I said.

"It tastes better when you eat it with sweetened *kinako*," my friend Mae said.

"Where do you get it?"

"At a store, but you gotta wait till after the war 'cause it comes from Japan."

Then Kiyomi added her two cents' worth; "We eat our mochi in *ozoni*. It gets real soft and you can sorta slurp it down."

"That's dangerous. You might eat too many and get plugged up."
"Aaahuggg…"

"Geez, double aaahuggg…"

There were countless other New Year's traditions the internees were unable to follow. They reminisced about past festivities and hoped for a future when they could celebrate the holiday again in proper style and abundance. I was learning about all sorts of traditions I had somehow missed. I needed to catch up.

FRIENDS AND NEIGHBORS

Yoshi reported to the kitchen three times a day prior to mealtimes, joining the dishwashing crew in their sudsy cleanup tasks. The men were sometimes raucous, and the noise of clanging, banging pots and pans vibrated through the dining room during the dinner hour. Getting the job done fast meant more leisure time––and hang the noise. Their job had none of a cook's responsibilities nor the longer hours required to accomplish their tasks, yet they were paid a mere three dollars less a month. They were not an unhappy lot.

When the dinner bell clanged––actually, our bell was a large hanging strip of iron hit by a hammer––it produced a sound lacking any tonal merit. It just let us know the mess hall was open for business. The chow line formed along the dining room wall from the entry door toward the serving counter that divided the kitchen and the seating space. We picked up our food-laden dishes, then sought a congenial spot among the long rows of picnic-style tables with integral benches. The furniture was the same ones used in the cavernous barnlike eating area in Puyallup, but the ambience of the hall was much improved. Sized to accommodate no more than three hundred diners at one seating, windows lined two walls to provide natural light, and a ceiling absorbed the worse clatter generated within. The space was cozy in comparison.

Few families sat together as a group to eat. Most diners sat where it was convenient or next to friends or acquaintances. I could usually find a group of children sitting away from parents to socialize with during meals. Even when I sat with adults, I was comfortable since no one in the Block was a stranger any longer.

"*O-cha, ko-hi...* Tea, coffee?" Mrs. Watanabe, one of the waitresses, usually called out while walking up and down the aisles with pots in her hand. When carrying pitchers, she called out, "*Mi-ru-ku*, boo-boo... Milk, water." She would pour out whatever we requested. For her adult audience, she called out *mi-zu* instead of baby talk "boo-boo." The other ladies dispensing beverages were not in the same league of hucksters as Mrs. Watanabe. She was one of the fearless mochi turners who plunged her hand into the mochi mass, turning it before the mallets slammed down during *mochi-tsuki* sessions, and we gave her respect, which was her due.

My friend Lily's mother was one of the exceptions who insisted her family eat together. Lily and her two sisters dutifully sat with their parents at every meal. Friends could join them, but not vice versa. Usually younger Nisei mothers, like Mrs. Yamagishi adhered to personal guidelines and enforced stricter discipline on their children. She had definite rules for her daughters; a good many of us had few. I sometimes wondered if, I too, would have had my unfettered wanderings curbed if my mother was still alive and well.

Mrs. Yamagishi was close to my mother's age, and her husband was Issei like Daddey. He was a small man, physically built like my father, mild-mannered, and he puttered, too. But he had achieved a skill as a photographer, and found a job in the trade in remote America far from the West Coast. His employer agreed to sponsor him, enabling him to leave camp. Mrs. Yamagishi was soft spoken with a quiet demeanor; relatively tall for Japanese, and she had a few interests not too common among the evacuees; she read books and played the piano. She encouraged her daughters toward similar pursuits. Also, a set of encyclopedias sat on a shelf in their apartment.

The Yamagishi family joined their father and left camp as soon as he was settled into his new job in Oklahoma. My friend's departure from camp left me untethered.

My peers, I noticed, were the youngest children of Issei parents, the oldest children of Nisei parents, or, like Lily and me, had one Issei and one Nisei parent. We were a transitional group between Nisei and Sansei, or half second and third generations.

Children with mostly Japanese-speaking Issei parents had a greater command of Japanese, its language, culture, and naturally assimilated via greater exposure. Those elderly old-fashioned parents may have been strict at one time, but now as seasoned child rearing veterans, they had loosened their apron strings for their youngest children, allowing them greater liberties.

Since my Sansei friends' parents were English speaking, those friends' ability to speak or comprehend Japanese was often abysmal. They were being raised American and had limited Japanese influences. The Nisei parent, usually the mother, was often strict and controlling, and I had my problems with them.

When classmate Janis invited me to eat lunch with her in their mess hall, I accepted. Not only would I have company at the table, it would save me a couple blocks walking back to school. Her mother asked me, "Did your parents give you permission? Do they know you're here with us?"

I looked at her quizzically. No one had ever before said or implied my father should be told my whereabouts except at night. We children lived within a gated, secure and safe environment without fear of criminal elements or intent. Antisocial acts in a closed society such as ours could not be concealed long, and once discovered, the perpetrator was made an outcast, unable to hide or escape. Most parents understood this and relaxed their restrictions. "Oh, my father doesn't care where I eat; he's busy washing dishes in the mess hall."

"Your mother certainly wants to know where you are." "I don't have one. She died."

"Very well. Next time, you must first tell your father where you're eating lunch."

The Nisei mother was applying her standards on someone who had free rein.

Those of us whose parents were a mix of generations, were brought up with an ambiguous mix of influences and expectations; we were a hybrid generation. I was one of them and could best relate to them.

Residents of Block 19 were content to let others live their lives without interference. We had no rabble-rousers, influence peddlers, or power seekers in our midst, nor any take-charge leaders to gather a team and create a fabulous prizewinning Christmas scene. Yes, there were busy-body women, and men, who had nothing better to do than gossip. There just was so little funny business going on in our Block to gossip about, they remained frustrated crones.

Hana was my only female classmate who also lived in Block 19, but we were not close. She rarely had time to play. She was the only daughter among eight brothers, half of them younger than her and the other half older. Her mother depended on her help almost constantly. We didn't often walk to school together, either. She couldn't predict when she could leave her chores and usually ended up making a run to class to be on time. I preferred a more leisurely walk to school even if that meant walking alone.

In February, we in Miss Queen's class were given a dandy project. In preparation for St. Valentine's Day, we were busily making elaborate cards decorated with paper doilies and artwork. Inside, we added the syrupy sentiments of third graders. Our finished cards were to be sent to classmates via the ornately decorated cardboard mailbox that had been placed in the front of the classroom. On the fourteenth, the designated postman opened the mailbox and delivered all the cards in the box. We were innocently introduced to a popularity contest. As the mailman delivered the cards, we all noted the most popular students received mounds of cards from fellow classmates. The rest of us escaped the ignoble fate of receiving nothing at all, only because classmate Kazu had bought a book of printed cutout cards and had generously sent a card to each person in the class. Every person opened at least one envelope containing a card with a silly sentiment. That one card was precious, a truly kind gesture.

The weather had warmed up slightly since the record twelve degrees below zero three weeks before, but the ever-familiar oozing mud was now frozen rock hard. The rigid walking surface was not smooth or walkable; it was a virtual minefield of dips and ragged protrusions waiting to twist ankles of the unwary. Walking a convoluted path through the frozen firmament, Hana and I walked home together that day. At intervals, we blew our warmed breath into our cupped hands to protect our exposed noses from frostbite in the frigid air. Mostly we commiserated about our fate; we had both received only one card from the Valentine box, and our cards happened to be identical.

THE QUESTIONNAIRE

Little did we third graders know or care about the central topic besieging the adults at the time: The Questionnaire.

Almost as soon as the 110,000-plus Japanese were settled into the more permanent relocation camps, the WRA in October 1942 began a campaign of encouraging the evacuees to seek employment outside the camps in an effort to disperse them throughout the United States. "We do not want to be responsible," Dillon Myer, director of the agency, said, "for fostering a new set of reservations in the United States akin to the Indian reservations." To eliminate the lengthy investigations that were required before evacuees were allowed to leave the camps on "indefinite leave," a questionnaire was devised to replace the time-consuming process.

Also, at this time, the army was planning to organize an all-Nisei combat unit, and a loyalty oath would be required of all volunteers. They felt by adding the loyalty oaths within the questionnaire, it could serve both the army and the WRA as security clearances for individuals.

In February 1943, the WRA began administering the "loyalty questionnaire" to all evacuees over seventeen years of age. Simply titled "Application for Leave Clearance," the questionnaire became an unintended benchmark of the evacuation. Two key questions requiring either yes or no answers were pivotal.

Question #27 asked: "Are you willing to serve in the armed services of the United States, in combat duty, wherever ordered?"

Question #28 read: "Will you swear unqualified allegiance to the United States of America and faithfully defend the United States from any and all attack by foreign or domestic forces, and foreswear any form of allegiance or obedience to the Japanese emperor, or any other foreign government, power, or organization?"

Many citizen evacuees unquestioningly affirmed their loyalty. Women were baffled why they should be asked to serve in combat when that was not US policy. Others were angered by the demand to affirm their loyalty after being unjustly denied their rights, held against their will, and forced into camps. The poorly titled and worded questions contributed to confusion and were especially treacherous for the Issei.

The original law of the United States of America allowed citizenship to "free white persons," but later amendments permitted Africans and some Asians to become naturalized citizens too––but the Japanese were excluded. As a people specifically denied US citizenship, the Issei continued to be Japanese citizens. By answering yes, they were being asked to renounce that citizenship and possibly become a people without a country. Or they envisioned a possibility of being denied visits to relatives and friends in Japan when the war ended if they answered yes. Tremendous controversy surfaced. Question #28 was later changed to read: "Will you swear to abide by the laws of the United States and to take no action which would in any way interfere with the war effort of the United States?"

The ambiguities in the original question that led to unintended interpretations were clarified, but the damage was done. The questionnaire caused widespread dissension among the evacuees, it devastated families and split friendships when people disagreed on their answers. Boisterous hotheads in other camps, mainly Manzanar and Tule Lake, instigated protests and turmoil at their camps during this time. The administration in Minidoka had quickly begun a campaign to explain the intent of the questionnaire when the ambiguities emerged, and mistrust was minimized.

A "yes, yes" answer was needed for clearance; a "no, no" answer branded a person as disloyal and ineligible to leave camp. In Minidoka, the majority signed: "yes, yes." Many were weary of the conflict, and in the end, they signed what they thought was expected of them in order to avoid future problems with the authorities. The controversy hung in the air, and no one remained entirely oblivious of that negative cloud.

The three available bathtubs in the women's bathroom were reserved for the very old and the very young. At age eight going on nine I did not qualify, but I still hated showers. I had selected a stall at the far end, where I was struggling to twist the metal knob to turn on the hot water. The knobs were unwieldy like a cranky garden hose faucet handle. The water preferred to stay shut off.

Two women entered the dressing area deeply engrossed in conversation. They continued talking while they disrobed, and stepped onto the concrete shower area, taking the stalls next to mine. A small side panel separated each shower from the adjacent one, but without doors, the stalls were otherwise open and lacked privacy.

Water splashed from the adjacent stall. "Ah, Shigeno-*san*," the bather next to me said to a woman showering in a nearby stall, "my boy Jimmy says he is going to join the army as soon as the all-Nisei group…"

My water came on, and it was ice-cold! I was turning into an icicle. I quickly twisted the other knob for the hot water.

"My husband disagrees, and they fight every day. I don't want him to go off to war and get killed, but what can a parent do?"

You can come and help me adjust the water, I thought. I finally got the desired water combination and started to scrub.

"Our children haven't been instilled with *oya-koko*, parental piety, that's what," said the companion woman. "They have no sense of duty to their parents."

I kept turning from front to back, having the water splash and warm me alternately. I could never feel warm all over at the same time.

"How about your two boys, Shigeno-*san*?" Usually questions are not so bluntly posed. Perhaps the circumstances of standing naked and exposed prompted such an unadorned inquiry.

"My sons obeyed their father, and I suspect they will be taken away. I would rather they fight and die in battle than rot in a prison in dishonor." She turned off her water and quickly walked out to the dressing area.

My water suddenly turned scalding, and my skin was turning beet-red.

"I had no idea...*kawai-so, neh*." It is so sad.

I managed to shut off the water and started past the two chatty ladies.

"Midori-*san*, you're red as a lobster. You are supposed to stand under cold water at the end of your shower. It will wake up your body." No, thanks, I thought. I still had to negotiate the walk back to our unit in the frigid cold.

CHAPTER 13

Minidoka, the Middle Year, 1943-1944

"Mɪ-ɴᴇ-ᴅᴏ-ᴋᴀ *wa*... ʜᴍᴍᴍ, ꜰɪᴠᴇ *On*... Mi-ne-do-ka *no.*"

Tap, tap, tap, tap, tap, from thumb to baby finger, he tapped each sound on the tabletop.

Daddey sat at his desk counting syllables on his fingers just as I solved my simple addition problems by counting on my fingers. Only I managed to be more discreet about it now. Miss Queen frowned on finger counting.

Why do you count only to five or seven, Daddey? You never count to six or eight or four. How come?"

I had invaded his mind-world of poetry in the making. He realized he had been performing to an audience, and he chuckled. It was now question-and-answer time.

"*Mukashi, mukashi*, a long time ago, people who write poems decide *tanka* poem must be five, seven, five, seven, seven *On*. Total thirty-one *On.*"

"Why didn't they use four, six, four, eight, and eight? Total thirty?"

"Those numbers are not so good; everything is even number. In Japan, even number is not so beautiful like odd number. Five and seven are odd numbers, and they make poem very beautiful."

I had to give that bit of information time to digest.

The poetic form Yoshi was interested in was the *tanka*, also identified as *waka* or Japanese song/poetry. The label distinguished the form from the Chinese poems known as *kanshi*, that were familiar to the learned aristocrats of earlier times. The Chinese writings provided inspiration, but the development of the native *waka* followed its own course. The term encompassed a broad range of poetic forms that gained popularity and later fell into disuse, leaving *tanka* the major *waka* form prevailing through thirteen centuries.

The thirty-one *On* poems became the vehicle used when letters were exchanged between friends and notably between lovers in earlier historical eras. In the classic *Tale of Genji*, the author included hundreds of *waka* supposedly exchanged by her fictional characters. The custom was that on the morning after a tryst, good manners required a freshly composed *tanka* thank-you expressing the writer's feelings regarding the rendezvous of the previous evening. The verse was carefully scripted on selectively crafted paper or a fan, placed in a container, and tied together with an ornamental branch or single blossom to create a total aesthetic presentation, and enhance the composed missive inside. It was then delivered by messenger to the lover's residence. Upon receipt of the poem, a reply poem was written and given to the waiting messenger to return to the initial writer. The level of skill in composing and scripting the poems went a long way toward the success of the engagement and enhanced the popularity of the lover. This was especially true in the court, and among nobles who availed themselves to amorous indulgences. They were educated with leisure and the wherewithal to embrace writing poetry as a social gesture. The *tanka* poem as a celebratory tribute was broadened to include events of many types.

The early eighth-century chronicles of ancient Japanese history and mythologies included songs attributed to ancient eras; however, the first anthology of poems was the twenty-volume *Manyoshu*. Included in the volumes were primitive early poems, recognizable as *tanka*, along with poems by emperors, known and well-regarded practitioners writing in the time the collection was being compiled, as well as the poems of the past. Compositions by women and unnamed commoners were included along with those by nobles. *Waka* anthologies continued to be compiled, often under the auspices of the emperor, and the collection of poems flourished to modern times.

Unlike Western poetry, *waka* poems are not rhymed. Most words in the Japanese language end in a vowel, and achieving a rhyme can occur without effort 20 percent of the time. Nor do Japanese poems have a metered structure. The language lacks the accented syllable within words so necessary to create the meter employed in Western poetry. Similarly, accented ending vowels of Japanese words provide no tools for emphasis. The tool used in Japanese poetry is the sound unit *On*, similar to a syllable, which provides a cadence or rhythm to the phrase.

The traditional *tanka* is a thirty-one-syllable poem separated into five phrases, or lines when written in *romaji*, the Romanized spelling of Japanese. The phrases contain a sequence of five, seven, five, and seven, seven *On*. Each phrase, or line, consists of an image or idea. The first two or three phrases present the image using a *kigo*, the nature or seasonal word, a word that implies a season by association. A pivot word or phrase then shifts the poem to a personal response or commentary to the imagery phrases. The later developed haiku form maintains the first three phrases of five, seven, five syllables for a total of seventeen *On* and omits the personal response.

With its roots in aristocratic culture, the elevated tone and language of that patronage remained. The *tanka* form's popularity waned at times, but it was revived by reducing creative restrictions that had become stifling. Earlier emphasis on passion and heartache was expanded to include a broader spectrum of subjects and emotions. Strict definitions and rules that accumulated through the centuries were loosened, promoting greater flexibility and a more viable composition. The Japanese language possesses a surfeit of allegory and metaphor, and along with all manner of allusive devices common to the culture, there is a wellspring of possibilities in composing a *tanka* poem.

Yoshi was engrossed in those possibilities, and he took up the study and writing of *tanka* poetry with a passion. When he wasn't working in the mess hall or doing the necessary domestic chores, Yoshi sat at his desk and read those precious borrowed books on Japanese poetry. He struggled and lip-read the *Manyoshu*, whose poems, scripted in archaic Japanese, proved challenging.

A Kanji script dictionary and a hastily compiled Kanji- English dictionary were printed by the Harvard University Press, and their availability at that time was a godsend. The two weighty tomes were delivered to him in Minidoka, and a gleeful Yoshi could hardly contain himself while opening the package. The spirits of his ancestral language and the eminent university were to circle and hover above, beaming down enlightenment on the books' owner, and he was to keep the books close to him thereafter.

Mr. Arai, our poetry-reading neighbor in Puyallup, was assigned to a unit a short walk from ours on the other side of the laundry building. The proximity was convenient for Yoshi to drop in for frequent consultations. Since Arai-*san* had not signed up for a job, he was available at all times. He had more leisure time to pursue his interests.

"If I had the time to study poetry when I was younger… the time I have now, I'd have thought I was in paradise," he said to his new pupil. "Unfortunately, my mind is on its downward trajectory and doesn't function as it once did. My thoughts wander, avoiding focus, and the phrases elude me. It's a sad fate."

They sat at the small table in the Arai's apartment, drinking tea. Mrs. Arai sat off to the side busily sewing small pieces of leather, making accessories to sell for pin money. The setting was as comfortable and welcoming as Hayame's informal back-of-store kitchen had once been. To gather with friends, to communicate in Japanese, their mother tongue, rather than using halting English, made everything ever more pleasant. Hayame's guests had been a varied lot and so was the chatter that was usually laced with a good amount of gossip. The conversation initiated by Arai-*san* was varied, too, without the gossip. Yoshi relished being a part of his teacher's conversational topics and esoteric thought processes, and he was inspired to learn more.

"We spend our whole lives working at menial jobs to support our families in order to survive. Artists, writers, poets struggle, too. Their art doesn't support them. No wonder poetry was the pastime for royalty and the court," Yoshi mused.

"Nevertheless, with access to education and books, even common folk can indulge their spare moments studying and composing poems. It keeps your mind active and enriches your everyday existence."

"Since I've never had the aptitude for business or the skills for accumulating wealth, perhaps it was karma that I should be introduced to an alternative mind-and-life-consuming interest which I can pursue."

"While you're in camp, you have the leisure time to study *tanka*, Nomura-*san*. I can guide you, but you must read and study the old anthology collections. You'll begin to discover the riches hidden within for yourself. This will help you in your own compositions."

Yoshi gratefully thanked Arai-*sensei*, his teacher. He was overwhelmed by Arai-*san*'s generosity to take him on as his pupil, to be his mentor. His karma had taken a positive turn for sure.

The other *tanka* poetry enthusiast living in our block, Mrs. Esaki, provided a second ear willing to listen to Yoshi's attempts at composing those thirty-one *On* poems. He began consulting with her often.

"I'm having a problem with the *kigo*, the seasonal word," Yoshi said to Mineko during one of his consultations.

"Here in this desert where sagebrush never undergoes seasonal changes through the year, it's a problem finding the multi-layered word."

"It'd be so much easier in four-seasoned Seattle, *nah*."

"Nomura-*san*, you're using a dialect: '*nah*'."

"Hmm, I guess I've lived with people from Hiroshima-ken so long now, I've picked up their way of saying *neh*, except on occasion when I revert back to old habits. Growing up, everyone where I come from in Mie said *nah*. Ours was an isolated village, and our speech contained some local quirks, but we spoke a gentler, dialect-free version of the language. We're relatively close to the old Imperial capitals, Kyoto and Nara, and well within their sphere of influence. Those from provinces further removed from those historical centers have the distinct dialects."

"I wish my husband could drop his dialect. I still can't get used to it," Mineko said. "He's from the far north, of course."

"His '*zuu-zuu ben*' dialect is famous throughout Japan. It's fascinating. Those people can't get their tongue around *su* and pronounce it *zu* instead."

"But I didn't name our daughter Zuumiko, as he calls her. Sumiko is the lovely name I chose."

The two poets' conversation ranged on subjects not limited to *tanka* poems.

Following the advice given him by Arai-*sensei*, Yoshi began his studies by reading the recommended books in earnest. Arai-*san* and other poetry-loving internees, who had their books returned to them the past November, willingly shared them with Yoshi. The *tanka* enthusiasts who were loosely acquainted with each other began meeting regularly and soon banded together to form their *utakai*, a *tanka* poetry club, in remote Minidoka.

At the monthly meeting, each participant submitted one of his or her own poems to be critiqued by the others in attendance. In turn, each submitted poem was read aloud by its author, followed by an open discussion of the poem's merits and shortcomings. Suggested changes for improving the poem were flung into the fray. At times, there were uncharacteristically honest assessments voiced, but on the whole, discussions were clothed with polite cover. Tea and refreshments followed along with amicable socializing to soothe any ruffled feathers. Yoshi was overjoyed when he was invited to join the club.

"Midori, I have new name," Daddey announced. "Huh?"

"I write poems. People who write poems are same like people who write stories, so I need the pen name."

"What's wrong with Yoshitsugu? It's sort of long and hard to pronounce, but your mother and father gave you that name when you were born. They thought it was a nice name."

"Oh, it is very good name."

"Then why do you want to change your name?"

"I keep Yoshitsugu name, too. Not so many people have same name, so it is special. People read my name and think it is pronounced something different. Always in the beginning they call me wrong name. I have to tell everyone it is pronounce Yo-shi-tsu-gu."

"They pronounce your name wrong in Japan just like they do in America?"

"No, no. It is different mistake. Americans cannot say 'tsugu,' so they give me name George."

"But Japanese can say '*tsu-gu*' easy…"

Daddey interrupted, "When Japanese write word, it can be pronounce different way and have many different meaning. So people read za word Yoshitsugu and say, 'Your name is Kaji? No, cannot be right. How do you pronounce your name? They ask me."

"What's wrong with Kaji?"

"*Kaji* mean 'fire' in Japanese," he said and continued the explanation in English, juxtaposing Japanese words and phrases here and there. "A son with name 'fire' sure to bring very bad luck. No family is so stupid to ask for bad luck, so they ask me how to pronounce my name. All my life, only two or three people see the word and guess my name is pronounced Yoshitsugu. They are very educated and know old archaic words and meanings and how to pronounce."

"I never knew people's names could be so complicated."

"I find a good name. Name is short and easy to say. I will sign all my poems with my new pen name: Osei Nomura." He was tickled, contemplating a new identity that would forever be associated with all his wonderful future compositions.

"Oh say, oh say…gee, Daddey, the Star Spangled Banner starts like that. 'Oh-o say can you see…'"

He frowned, annoyed at my irreverence, but then he grasped a connection.

"Osei mean 'spirit fly high.' American eagle fly high, too. American flag, too."

Daddey was obviously delighted with his new nom de plume.

Resettlement Begins

At the end of the school year, Miss Queen announced she was leaving Minidoka. We third graders were sad to hear that bit of news since we liked her; she was, without exception, everyone's favorite teacher. We had been ready to plead our cause to have her assigned to be our teacher for fourth grade, too, but she was moving on.

Minidoka's population was in flux, too. Almost as soon as they had stepped foot into camp, qualified, able-bodied workers had been recruited to work on farms on a temporary basis as seasonal workers to help bring in the harvest. As seasoned and experienced agricultural workers, it was logical they be hired to help alleviate the manpower shortage created as American men were drafted into the military. These laborers generally decided to continue working on the outside since resettlement was now the official policy. The young adults whose lives had been derailed by the evacuation were eager to resume a semblance of normal life, albeit a wartime life, and pursue opportunities to becoming contributing citizens instead of languishing away their time, unproductively idle on the inside. Those who found sponsors and were offered jobs on the outside and those who found colleges willing to enroll them as students began to leave the camps.

The West Coast from where they came was still off-limits. They re-located to other parts of the country wherever they were accepted. Many found themselves in communities with scant exposure to Asian people, resulting in unintended misunderstandings. There was less anxiety and a sense of safety by moving to areas where other Japanese Americans had re-located. A large number migrated to Chicago, where they found work and comfort in a burgeoning resettlement community of ex-internees from the camps.

After the attack on Pearl Harbor, Japanese Americans were no longer accepted to serve in the United States military except to aid intelligence services. Those men who were already in the service at the start of the war were often relegated to maintenance duties or were discharged. Government officials by mid-1942 were reconsidering their stance and backed the formation of an all-Nisei combat unit. Barely a year after Executive Order #9066 was signed, President Roosevelt on February 1, 1943, declared, "No loyal citizen of the United States should be denied the democratic right to exercise the responsibilities of his citizenship, regardless of his ancestry." Tacit approval had been given, allowing Nisei to serve in the military.

The 442nd Regimental Combat Team was formed with Japanese American volunteers from Hawaii, recruited volunteers from the internment camps, and those Nisei already in the army. They were sent to Camp Shelby, Mississippi for combat training, as were the all-Nisei 100th Infantry Battalion, which had been a Nisei Hawaiian National Guard unit federalized after Pearl Harbor. This group of men joined not only "to exercise the responsibilities of their citizenship," but they also fought to prove their loyalty to America, the land of their birth, and dispel any suspicions to the contrary. Their motto, "Go for Broke," became emblematic of their deeds in combats that were to follow.

Recruiting for volunteers did not go smoothly in the camps, as the issues raised by the loyalty questionnaires were still a divisive topic that smoldered among camp inmates. In Minidoka, the concerted interventions to explain and interpret the ambiguously phrased questions had mitigated much anger and hostility; however, authorities in the other camps had been less forthcoming, and the internees' frustrations and prevailing hostility initially worked against recruitment while Minidoka's relatively temperate and less contentious populace produced the most volunteers to enlist.

Young adults were not the only residents moving out of camp; entire families left to live life beyond a fenced compound. My friend Lily's family had been early resettlers. Usually the patriarch, a Nisei or younger Issei, left to find work and later sent for his family to join him. The majority of people, however, stayed behind and made camp their home.

The demographics of the camp changed as the young-adult population diminished. Camp was a secure refuge for youngsters and the old who remained; The Issei generation were generally in their fifties and older. Past their prime physically, few had the energy or eager motivation to start anew once again. They had worked and endured, only to be up-rooted, causing them to lose much of what had been gained. *Shikata-ga nai.* What happened was beyond their control; they would acquiesce and take a vacation for the duration.

Those community leaders, Buddhist priests, Japanese school teachers, and others on the government surveillance lists who had been rounded up so unceremoniously by the FBI on or immediately after Pearl Harbor Day were still detained in separate camps. Considered suspicious aliens, they had been taken to immigration or army detention centers and interrogat-ed. They were then handed over to the Department of Justice and moved from time to time to various locations; often into centers holding German and Italian aliens. Inmates later deemed less dangerous were released to rejoin their families in the relocation camps while others were held for the duration of the war. Thus, there were families in the camps who struggled without the support of husbands and others throughout their camp years. Another, smaller group was sent back to Japan.

The pain of separations and the conflicts within families were en-dured. *Gam-batte.* Keep a tight upper lip. One's suffering is not broad-cast. Beyond the obvious physical dislocation of internment, the majority of settlers internalized the psychological misalignments and stresses ac-companying those events. The all-encompassing *Shikata-ga-nai* was the verbalized rationale.

Yoshi, who was now in his early forties, fell into the category of young-er Issei. Their numbers were relatively small since they would have entered the United States as youngsters prior to the Exclusion Acts. Issei who ar-rived after enactment of the restrictive policies had generally entered the US illegally as young men. The contingencies of war deferred chances of deportation to this group for the short term, but they had not been given amnesty nor were they guaranteed permanent residency. Nevertheless, Yoshi, who belonged to this latter group, was no longer muzzled as he had been since arriving in Seattle. He felt he was free to express his thoughts and opinions openly as long as he remained silent about politics, policies, and the war itself. It was still best to avoid controversy; besides, that better suited his temperament.

He was no longer young; he was a mature adult content to pursue his personal interests. Yoshi found that writing poems within the restrictive, arbitrary rules of *tanka* gave him an outlet to express sentiments and feelings in a socially acceptable format. Most themes for his poems were the innocuous odes of an amiable nice guy, suitable for posterity should his poems outlast him. Once in a while he vented an aggravation and released it in that same thirty-one *On* structure. A less popular idea he held, he never wrote down on paper.

"Here are some books for you, Midori."

"Goody!" I loved presents, and they were rare commodities these days.

"Maybe you can learn Japanese." He handed me two workbooks for learning Kana strokes. I flipped through the books, and the practice lessons looked easy enough. The individual Kana looked familiar from the Puyallup days when I had learned to play the karuta card game.

"It looks interesting, but why do you want me to learn Japanese?" I asked. "Mommy said I didn't have to learn Japanese."

"When we go Japan, it is necessary to know how to read and write the language where you live."

"Who says we're going to live in Japan?"

"When Japan wins the war, we go back to Japan." "Whaaat? Who said Japan's going to win the war?"

"Japan win every war since Sino-Russian War. Japan is a powerful country. It has number-one navy and best soldiers in the world."

"I say America is going to win the war. We're going to beat the Japs to smithereens!" I shouted. "And everyone says so: the radio and newspapers––everyone!"

"It is American propaganda. They hide truth. Japan is winning the war."

"Daddey, you're wrong! Wrong! Wrong! Wrong! I'm an American, and I'm staying in America. Besides, America will win, and Japan will lose."

One of Mother's conscious decisions about my upbringing was that I was never to have doubts I was an America-born American and my loyalties were to America; the indoctrination had started early. She never forgot her humiliation on her first day of school because she spoke no English and how she was taunted in Japan for being an America-*jin*. Daddey rarely argued with me, just as he almost never scolded me. He dropped the subject. We had been indoctrinated on the superiority of two opposing nations. Father and daughter, our views clashed.

When did Daddey become so dumb? I wondered.

I buried the two Japanese-language workbooks under my pile of comic books and never retrieved them.

SUMMER ACTIVITIES

I signed up to attend the Buddhist summer school program, while others went to a Christian Bible program. Those children less interested in organized activities spent the long, hot summer vacation in self-directed activities. There was still plenty of time to play jacks, jump rope, and when enough kids from several blocks gathered, we joined in on a rousing game of Gin-tori or Kick-the-Can. The latter game was best played at night when you could hide and stay unseen. The game sometimes continued to the wee hours of the night, ending when the Keeper of the Can realized all the other participants had sneaked home to bed and were no longer hiding. Gin-tori was our version of "Capture the Flag," played without a flag. Only a large open area was required. It was probably everyone's favorite, but it was most fun with a lot of participants, and rounding up a whole gang of kids from several blocks was the problem.

The older, more adventurous kids went down to the swimming hole at the crook in the canal that meandered south of the blocks in Area B. Located well beyond that long, straight arterial and a distance beyond Blocks 23 and 24, the water spa became famous as the unsupervised mecca for kids. Due to distance and the spurious nature of the enterprise, none of my friends ventured there, although we were all hoping to get there eventually. "Yeah, let's go next week after lunch, even if we don't go in the water. The guys say we're missing a lot of fun." Then word that a boy drowned while with friends down at the canal spread throughout the camp and curtailed most water activities.

It was hot every day, with few places to find relief. The trees planted since our arrival, if they had not already died in the desert environment, were still saplings. We usually gathered in the shade of buildings, trying to decide what to do. If staying indoors was tolerable, those picnic tables placed in the bare back half of the laundry area became the gathering place to play board games or cards for whoever showed up. Sometimes the junior high school kids joined in, but the older high school kids stayed out of sight. They had different interests and activities to occupy their time other than the perpetual pursuit of "fun things to do" that preoccupied us younger kids.

The adults were busy with various projects, too––definitely less fun and more constructive. The internees' number-one priority item was to build a pathway system within each block. The administration did not share the same sense of urgency for the project and agreed to provide materials if the residents in each block organized, supervised, provided the labor, and did the necessary work in their own blocks.

The fine-grained sand that turned into a sandstorm with the wimpiest breeze during the dry season transformed into globby glue with the onset of rain, making travel between buildings an ordeal. Residents had resorted to a "quick fix" amorphous pedestrian walkway for the short term. A network of wood planks was strung on the ground in front of each barrack, with shorter boards joining doorways to it like disjointed ribs. Those walkways had then joined broader pathway spines of mismatched lumber to connect to the communal mess hall and laundry/bathroom doorways. The crude maze of lumber trails facilitated our moving about the block without wading through ponds and getting stuck in the mud, but the walkways were a stopgap remedy that turned hazardous when the mud dried. It had been built in desperation, not by design. A resident's ingenuity in finding long, wide planks ensured a more walkable path than others that used short scraps for pavers. It was the haphazard wooden sidewalks that had to be replaced.

The walkway system the residents cobbled together was a gravel pathway edged with stone borders. It was filled and raised several inches above the summer sand and winter mud. Although less than expertly constructed, the new paths were a great improvement over the wooden ones, and praise greeted its completion. Each pathway joined the next in rigid ninety-degree angles, but no one walks in a straight line and takes a precise right angle turn at intersections except soldiers on parade, so convenient diagonal footpaths off the raised walkways began to appear as pedestrians took the shortest route to their destination, weather permitting.

The camp's sewage treatment plant was in full operation now, and shiny new water closets plumbed in neat rows gleamed, immodestly exposed, awaiting privacy screens in the restrooms. The outhouses were a distant memory. In the services complex, the camp hospital and infirmary, staffed by internee doctors, nurses and aides, was functioning. I never once used their services the years I lived in Minidoka. Daddey was sure the dry desert air contributed to my good health.

With the basic services systems up and running and a walkway in place, residents began their own outdoor projects. The plot of land between two barracks was considered the front yard of the unit with its door facing it. The land was public and could not be fenced, and the walkway passed through it, but the space could be used and developed as the yard's "owner" wished. Though many households put up a clothesline for their own personal use, many never bothered to lay claim to any sort of yard. Occasionally, miniature Japanese gardens utilizing desert plants were constructed, becoming attractions to be admired. Our block had no landscape artist.

Daddey put up our clotheslines and prepared a small area for his flower garden. He ordered flower seeds from a catalog and planted them without my supervision. I never took much notice of what he did until I saw a finished product. Tall-stemmed cosmos, bachelor buttons that looked like baby carnations, sweet peas with their curly tentacles, and red-purple snapdragons began to bloom in his small garden. It was an incongruous but happy sight.

A New Teacher

When school started in September, it was a relief returning to a routine and to cooler weather that followed. We were not smiling after we met our fourth-grade teacher. We had idolized and loved Miss Queen; our new teacher, Miss Keck, was a great disappointment.

She looked twice as old as Miss Queen despite the camouflage of her thickly powdered face with inexpertly applied rouge and lipstick. She looked like the Wicked Witch of the East's older sister. As she stood in front of the class by the blackboard, we began noticing her idiosyncrasies. She appeared to get taller and shorter throughout her lessons. She slowly lifted her heels off the floor, resting her weight on the balls and toes of her foot; gently she brought her heels down. Slowly up and down, up and down. It was hypnotic; our eyes and heads automatically followed her up-and- down movements, requiring us to give our heads a shake or two to break the trance her movement cast. The pencil held by her curled pinky finger waved about like a conductor's baton as she moved her hands. A couple of rapid blinks were needed to dispel that magician's spell. Her ever-ready powder puff appeared at the oddest moments. A lesson was often interrupted as she clicked open her mirrored compact and proceeded to powder her cheek or nose. Even we innocents understood it was a weird show.

Her lessons did not deviate from our textbooks, and everyone soon understood the "fill in the blanks" assignments were also word-for- word sentences from our textbooks. It became a race for the brighter students to see who found the question sentence in the text first.

"Pssst…page thirty-five, second-to-the-last paragraph."

"I got that one. Where do you find the answer to number five?"

"You're leading me on. Everyone finds that one. Look at the name of the chapter."

"Oh, it's so obvious. Sorry…*gomen, gomen*."

"Shhh…keep your voice down. I wanna look at your comic book when you're done."

Passing answers around the room, if done discreetly, did not bother Miss Keck. As long as assignments were completed, she cared not what methods had been used to find the answers. Most important, she asked that we maintain general quiet and order. What we students did in the quiet and orderly room was limitless, and the students whiled away the enforced school hours engrossed in their own projects. Students read magazines and comic books hidden inside academic book jackets, boys drew airplane pictures, and girls whispered together behind open books; gossiping and note-passing prevailed unabated the whole school day. Even the usually boisterous, unruly students understood the unspoken truce between teacher and students, and they minimized their disruptive behavior while in the classroom.

"Teacher, I gotta go *shi-shi!*" the sky-pointing pupil said as he gestured.

"She doesn't understand. Speak English," MacArthur hissed. "I gotta go pee, pretty please," he pleaded.

"Hey, Robert, she's Miss Keck to you, and watch your language," Arthur said.

"OK, OK. Miss Keck, can I go to the bathroom, please?" "Did anyone warn her about 'Little Bladder Robert?'"

Third-Arthur asked.

We had three Arthur's in our class, and two of them also shared the same last name. We distinguished them by allowing Taisho to be known as Arthur, the second Arthur was called MacArthur like the general, and the third guy was hardly ever called.

Miss Keck was grossly ineffective as a teacher, but she was not unkind, and we learned the packaging was deceptive; it hid a very decent human being. Both teacher and students made adjustments to each other, and a harmonious façade prevailed. This laissez-faire environment gave me time to catch up academically while the others stagnated without intellectual stimulation.

New Residents

The agitation and violence that had erupted in several other relocation camps, especially after the loyalty questionnaires episode, prompted the

WRA to designate Tule Lake Camp in northern California a segregation camp. Potential troublemakers in the system, evacuees who wanted to return to Japan, and many who had answered "no, no" on the questionnaire, including their families who chose to stay with them, were moved and concentrated in a camp where they could be better watched and supervised. Our neighbors in Unit E, who had asked to be repatriated to Japan, were sent to Tule Lake before they were placed on board the Swedish prisoner-of-war exchange ship, the MS Gripsholm. In the neutral waters of Goa on the western coast of India on the Arabian Sea, they were transferred to a Japanese ship for their return to Japan. The now-empty unit next to ours sat quiet and housed no eavesdroppers, but I missed my friend Dickie after their departure. I never much noticed the others who moved away in our block.

To make room for all those detainees from various camps being sent to Tule Lake, the loyal non-security-risk residents already living in Tule Lake were allowed to select another camp to be transferred to. Close to 1,500 people chose Minidoka. In late September, the new families from the northern California center began moving into empty units throughout camp. Most were from the Northwest and were reuniting with friends and relatives, and many just wanted to be closer to home. Prior to relocation, the Japanese who lived south of Seattle on farms and rural towns in the White River Valley, including Tacoma residents, had been sent to Tule Lake. There they were mingled with Californians, who constituted the majority of residents. Geographic distance and dissimilar life experiences had created attitudinal differences between the northerners and the California residents, which caused aggravations. Just as the Bainbridge Islanders chose to be moved out of predominately California-populated Manzanar, northerners who had been sent to Tule Lake generally chose to relocate to Minidoka. There were exceptions; one family who moved into the barrack in front of ours was originally from rural California. They came with a son who was to be a classmate and a year-younger daughter who became my friend.

I was sitting at my desk, staring blankly at the arithmetic assignment. I had not mastered addition or subtraction, and my calculations still progressed at a snail's pace when Miss Keck had the audacity to introduce multiplication to our mathematical mix. I had no greater aptitude for solving multiplication problems than I had for addition and subtraction. Furthermore, multiplication could not be readily solved by counting on my fingers——fingers that were often swollen and painted with Mercurochrome.

Swollen fingers. I often snagged splinters on my hand and fingers while practicing to improve my skills playing jacks. No one in fourth grade could ever beat Gladys, our champion player, who never missed a trick, and who ended up playing solo through recess while the rest of us girls watched in awe. She systematically threw the ball up, snapped up the requisite jacks, then caught the ball after the first bounce. First one jack at a time, then two at a time, and on and on until the last pickup, when she scooped up all the jacks at once. After completing the first easy set, she went onto the second "Under the Bridge" set, followed by "Over the Fence," as each set became more challenging than the last. Her hand adroitly wove through the pile of metal; her long fingers curled to pick up the required number of jacks and quickly deposited them in a second, spent pile. Watching her skill was like watching a flawless pool player clearing the table solo. I sometimes had to give up my turn by clumsily dropping a jack or two on the initial toss-up, which was totally embarrassing. I needed to practice.

The wood floor planks of our units were rough-hewn and prone to shedding pointed splinters directly into the unwary. Kids were especially vulnerable to sliver wounds when playing on the floor. A few days before, the nastiest sliver had lodged itself just under my fingernail, the most painful and dreaded penetration. Luckily, the splinter was long enough for a sewing needle to maneuver it out. Tending to my still healing wounds thoroughly distracted me from my multiplication tables. I began swabbing the days' old wounds on my hands and arms with another coat of pink antiseptic and gave old scabs on my knees a dab of color. At first barely perceptible, then dimly from a distance, I could hear the rumble of a slow-moving truck coming closer to our apartment.

The truck's wheels had managed to skirt the new raised gravel pathway in front of our barrack, but it plowed right over the minefield of adjacent potholes. The truck groaned, bemoaning having traversed such bumpy terrain with its heavy, shifting load. When it reached our end of the barrack, the shelves laden with pots and dishware, as well as the makeshift table and stools in our unit, vibrated and rattled from the vehicle's motor until the engine was turned off. A man was shouting orders, the truck's tailgate slammed and rattled, and I heard footsteps. Metal screeched on metal, then thudded as objects hit the ground.

I sat quietly, listening to the commotion going on outside our door. The movers were bumping into the walls of the cramped entry as they maneuvered metal bed frames through the small hallway. Unwieldy mattresses scraped the same surfaces as they were pulled through the same pinched space. Footsteps came and went; boxes and luggage were dropped on the wooden floor with resounding thuds, then the noise stopped.

"That's it, we're finished," someone barked.

The truck doors slammed shut, and the movers, now in an empty vehicle, roared away in their customary swirl of sand and dust.

Shortly after the movers had gone, new sounds of heavy shoes thumped up the stairs, through the entry hallway into the adjacent apartment. The first set of footsteps shuffled slowly on their journey, accompanied by a second set of slow but deliberate steps. Next were the quick taps of a woman wearing loafers, perhaps? Lastly, someone skipped up the stairs.

"Remember to close the…" The door banged shut.

Goldilocks had arrived with the three walking bears.

I sat there itching with curiosity and wondered what our new neighbors were like. About ten minutes later, the neighbors' door opened, and footsteps came directly to our door.

Three staccato knocks were followed by another set of three.

"Hello. Hello. Is anyone home?" came the voice outside my door.

I opened the door and saw a scowling middle-aged woman squinting at me.

"I'm your new neighbor," said the woman as she forced a crooked smile. "Look, someone made a big mistake."

"Huh?" I responded.

My reply irritated her. "Where are your parents, anyway? They left you all alone, by yourself? When are they coming back?" she demanded. Without waiting for me to answer, she continued in a higher pitch. "They put our name next to your door. George Y. Nomura is my brother's name. That sign belongs on our side, next to our door!"

"No, no. George Y. Nomura is my daddy." I beamed back at her. "You can't take our sign."

The housing specialists in administration had perpetrated a mischievous prank on us when they assigned two heads of household with the same name to be housed in the same block, in the same barrack, in units next to each other. Actually, their Japanese given names differed. Yoichiro and Yoshitsugu were not exactly the easiest names for Americans to spell, pronounce, or remember, and they had decided independently, but for the same reasons, to use George Y. Nomura to avoid confusion and problems. That is, until they became neighbors.

The new neighbors were an extended family of five, therefore entitled to the larger unit. Grandfather, with the shuffling feet, was very old and overweight. He had relegated his position as family patriarch to his son George Y. Having relinquished his responsibilities along with his title, the old man preferred spending his days nodding off in his chair or napping on his bed. His wife, many years younger than her somnolent husband, spent her energies being the Good Wife. Their daughter Yoko, in her forties and unmarried, was now duty bound to care for her elderly parents in their old age. This was *giri,* to serve one's superiors with a self-sacrificing devotion; however, she had a second responsibility. She was also raising her young niece, Marie, her brother George Y's daughter. Yoko was determined her young charge be raised properly even if that required raising her voice loudly.

The playful housing specialists could not have known the two men with the same name who they assigned to be neighbors shared other similarities––although there were important differences. Neighbor George Y. was almost ten years younger than Daddey, and he was a Nisei. Facially, they were both quite handsome in their own way, and women were attracted to their good looks and to their marriageable status. The two men shared easygoing attitudes and gentle temperaments. The confusions arising from their similar names amused them both, and they sometimes sat and laughed as they exchanged details of the latest snafu. Ironically, both George's had a single child, a daughter, and each had lost his wife to tuberculosis before the onset of the war.

I was 2-1/2 years older than my counterpart, Marie, and free to do as I pleased. I was not encumbered by a maiden aunt who made me toe the line as was Marie: "Marie, do this or that. Marie, you may not do that today or any day." Her world was full of restrictions.

Ah, but Marie had the advantage of a rare gift. She was born with a beautiful, gorgeous face. She was not cute; pretty did not really describe it, either. Think Ava Gardner embellished with a slight Asian twist: no cleft chin, nose a tad shorter with the slightest slant to deep dark eyes accented with perfect eyebrows. And dark, dark black hair accentuated the fair complexion. Something got mixed up in heaven when they bestowed such extraordinary features on a not-yet seven-year-old.

Not a person could look upon her for the first time without exclaiming, "*Bep-pin*," "*Hon-to-ni bep-pin*," or "*Su-goi bep-pin*!" "Beautiful," "Really beautiful," or "Absolutely beautiful!"

Miss Absolutely Gorgeous had moved in next door when I was nine. Forever thereafter, my own mirror reflected a less than stellar image no matter how hard I looked to find one; it always fell far short of the enchanting image that walked through my neighbor's doorway. Life was unfair. Then again, *shikata-ga nai.*

Why the big buckteeth an' beady little slant eyes? What is your answer?

Mirror, mirror on the wall. Oh, give me a pretty face!

"That's five, seven, five, seven, seven," I said aloud to myself. I had counted syllables with my fingers, copying Daddey. So I cheated a little.

SLANT doesn't have to be two *On*, the T can go with eyes. Slan'teyes sounds OK.

Marie and I gravitated to playmates our own ages rather than to each other. I could more easily shelter my bruised ego by staying clear of the lavish compliments constantly heaped on my young neighbor. She in turn would not be contaminated by my freewheeling, undisciplined ways, which pleased Auntie Yoko to no end.

RECREATION

The empty units housed families again, and the boost in population energized progress on civic projects. A year of concerted effort had brought about organization and order to the camp. There was a camp newspaper, the Irrigator, a community council was formed, the farm supplementing our food supply kept expanding, and moreover, a swimming pool was being planned. We had settled in.

The recreational halls, one located in each block, were shorter than a barrack, and they were always sited on the desert-facing side of the block. Originally, they had no specific function, but in time they acquired specialized usages. The building in Block 8 was set up with chairs and showed a first-run movie every Saturday. Block 16 housed the stand-up piano where piano lessons were given. Judo was taught at Block 17, and when Block 14's rec hall was converted into a canteen, it became the destination if one had money to spend. The big-time spenders in Area B had their own store.

With the wartime scarcity of nonessential goods, and sugar rationing in effect, popular candy bars like Hershey's with or without almonds, Mound bars, and Butterfingers were not available. Convenience items like bobby pins and paper clips, too, were gone for the war effort. The so-called gum had no elasticity and crumbled in our mouths. How we dreamed of a mouthful of Double Bubble gum. Once in a great while, the canteen had a small brown bag of pine nuts for sale. If it was available, and you somehow had thirty-five cents to spend, it was the ultimate treat.

The canteen was our source for comic books from Superman, Batman, Plastic Man, and the whole gamut of crime fighting heroes popular at that time. Current issues of magazines were available for adults, along with dry goods, fabrics and bedding, in addition to small household goods and tools. Items unavailable at the canteen, included most apparel, which were ordered through Spiegel's or Sears' catalogs; although ladies who were skilled seamstresses sewed custom clothing for a fee. It was not a flourishing business since dressing fashionably was not on everyone's list of priorities. Older teenagers were the exception, and set the trend for us younger wannabes. When the wooden shoes with leather uppers became the craze, I convinced Daddy to buy me a pair. They were great to wear in the rain and mud, but a bad idea to wear when jumping rope.

My walks to Block 16's rec hall for piano lessons were short-lived. When the finger exercises progressed to both hands, my brain went into stall mode. I was not ambidextrous. The short-circuiting synapses in my brain were sparking wayward impulses causing lost communication. I was also no good as a one-hand pianist. I considered a switch to the violin after my piano lesson fiasco; the lack of practice instruments curtailed that ambition before I could embarrass myself further.

Actually, I had better luck with knitting and crocheting. No one was willing to teach me sequences beyond the basic stitches that I had learned earlier. I ran out of yarn before my knitted scarf reached its requisite length, and since I had only one ball of yarn, I unraveled it and started again. When there was absolutely nothing else to do, a single loop of string provided a distraction until something better turned up. My fingers adroitly maneuvered the string, dropping loops and picking up select strands to play Cat's Cradle by myself. The challenge was to move from one sequence to another without creating a knot.

As an only child, I had no built-in-playmate siblings, and I had learned to occupy my solo hours at an early age, but in camp and at the hospital, playmates were readily available. Occasionally, we traveled further afield to visit classmates who might suggest different fun things to do. Playing hopscotch was popular in other Blocks, and when the school library opened, we visited during story time. I added another favorite tale to my collection after hearing the story about "the house that became bigger and bigger one room at a time." As family members living in the house acquired new interests, they built a new room to accommodate that new interest. The concept of a house with rooms each designed for a specific function was wonderful, and by applying that idea, I could expand plans of the house we might have moved to before going to the hospital. And a new house would have even more possibilities. Yes, a place where a family did not have to live in a single room. Then I remembered Dr. Buckner's Spanish-style manse with multiple rooms. A breakfast room was used for the morning meal; all others were eaten in the dining room. A desk and shelves full of books were located in the doctor's study. There was also a ballroom used for parties, which had a private passageway to the kitchen. I stored away those ideas for future reference.

Soon after, there came a day I met another Nomura girl.

Admittedly, the name is not uncommon, but she, too, was an only child. She was a few years older than me, and luckily did not live next door, yet I had known about her. She had remained the unseen phantom for quite some time.

"You are Nomura-*san*'s daughter? I see your papa at Sears Roebuck store before the war, *neh*," the stranger greeted me cordially.

"Oh, my father didn't work at Sears Roebuck. We're a different Nomura," I replied.

"No work Sears Roebuck? Hummmph…I not know your papa." She turned and sailed away, leaving me a nonentity once more. I was a victim of mistaken identity more than once through the years. Then there she was, being introduced to me.

"Hi, I'm really glad to meet you," I said to the other Nomura girl. "I've wanted to see what you looked like, for a long time. I thought maybe you looked like Shirley Temple."

"What?"

"I'm really glad you don't look like a movie star, too." Since I had so rarely attended the movie screenings at Josef House, I was not yet addicted to movies and only rarely went to the Saturday matinees. After watching The Pride of the Yankees, the Lou Gehrig story, I cried and understood tragedies could strike Americans as well as the Japanese.

The mess hall was the focal point for each Block just as it had been on our day of arrival. It was the one sufficiently large space able to accommodate all Block residents and then some for special projects and activities. The occasional talent show, with internee participants, toured select mess halls, as well as performances by traditional dance and drama groups. They were all amateur productions, but they provided the same welcome escape from the humdrum for a few entertaining hours.

Our site at the remote edge of the core blocks was not a favored location for presentations, and only a limited number of shows of any kind made a stop in Block 19. When the announcement was made that our mess hall was selected to show a Japanese movie, it was such a rarity, a scurry of excitement circulated among the Issei residents; it was an event not to be missed. The film reel had been taken hostage when the war started, and it was made available to various blocks for viewing. It was a recently issued movie that no one recalled viewing previously in Japantown theaters before the war. Since I had no memory of watching any Japanese movies, it felt like a premiere event for me, and I was curious to know how movie productions in Japanese compared with Hollywood's.

Do the actors kiss? I never saw any Japanese kiss before; Issei's don't even hold hands. Are they all so up-tight, even when they're young? I had many questions.

The regular mess hall furniture was pushed to the side, opening up an area for folding chairs. We kids sat on the floor practically under the screen, and the adults crowded in behind us, vying for a spot with an unobstructed view.

The film's opening segments, showing the daily routines of a city-dwelling Japanese family, elicited little nostalgia for the Issei's in the audience; they were not city folk, and they had left Japan long before the story's time line. Our seats became uncomfortable, and our attention to the movie waned. We youngsters tried to follow the dialogue in the unadulterated Japanese spoken by the actors; it was not the watered-down version familiar to us.

Starting with a shudder, the tremors grew increasingly violent; it was the 1923 Kanto Earthquake. The young boy's teacher shields him from falling debris, and he miraculously survives. The selfless sacrifice elicits muffled gasps and moans at first and turns into tears. The earthquake's devastation and the cataclysmic fires that followed lead to chaos, and the boy and his family are separated. More sobbing in the audience. Their search for each other fails as fate denies them a chance meeting, more than once. The audience's tears flowed in unrestrained streams as they watched the tragedies unfold. Handkerchiefs wiped away tears of grief. Mother and son are finally reunited at her deathbed, a happy/sad ending––their perseverance was rewarded. Everyone loved the movie and loved crying buckets of tears at each negative twist of the plot.

The themes of loss, sacrifice, separation, *giri*, perseverance, and a whole gamut of touted Japanese values had been incorporated in the plot, and they resonated with the audience. Such themes dominated much of the popular entertainment that was sent to immigrant communities from Japan in that era. The story lines differed, but the messages were recurrent. Circumstances stemming from a natural disaster, illness, death, or unrelenting poverty and oppression fueled the misfortunes and suffering to be borne.

Shikata-ga-nai: Abide by the inevitable; be resigned to fate.

Gam-batte: With a stiff upper lip, carry on in thick and thin; persevere.

They were all elements of the Japanese psyche that had been tapped. And this audience could sympathize; they had experienced their own reverses. Perhaps these stoic adults who'd had to *ga-man*, endure their own fate, perceived there were no restrictions in sympathizing with others' adversities, and weeping so unabashedly was permitted. Daddey came back to our unit sniffling and teary-eyed, and clearing his throat the way he did when he was uncomfortable and nervous.

Happily, the second movie shown in our mess hall was a samurai fairy tale whose intrepid hero meets up with predestined companions who together avenge their princess's misfortune with the aid of a magical sword. It was a great precursor to the samurai *chan-bara* movies produced after the war, movies that offered a respite from popular American westerns. Before the introduction of guns and aside from bows and arrows, the weapons used by Japanese were swords or long poles, requiring a whole different set of techniques and skills unfamiliar to us kids. The hairstyles were alien, the women's kimono's were stunning, the men's wardrobe strange, and their customs often unfathomable. Archaic dialects made the language spoken even more incomprehensible, but who cared——it was an action movie, with lots of swordplay and magic along with the exotica.

The movie was a robust *mukashi*, *mukashi* tale even better than the ones Daddey once told me. Subliminally, I was gaining an appreciation of Japanese culture and traditions. The samurai "good guys," by their honorable codes and deeds, explained why Japanese wanted to claim them among their ancestors.

The two Japanese movies, shamelessly riddled with clichés, were engrossing. A picture is said to be worth a thousand words, and the stories illustrated intrinsic Japanese values in a way kids could comprehend. Along with the folklore I was exposed to, I realized being Japanese was a heritage I need not reject. When the war began, I thought all things American were best, and I shunned my Japanese-ness. Shipped off to the desert for being ethnic Japanese, I was told to show my loyalty to America, to act and be American. Ironically, I was inundated with a heavy dose of things Japanese while in camp, and I learned there is much to accept and admire of things Japanese.

Ghost Stories

One morning, Old Man Shibata did not wake up; he had died in his sleep. We knew him as the oldest resident in our Block; the old man resembling Father Time with his long white hair and scraggly beard. He, the stooped over man weighted down by his invisible load. Shibata-*san* was older than ancient, and people no longer sought his advice or counsel. And he spent his days contemplating his navel. He was worn out.

His demise did not come as a great surprise, but news of the event flashed like wildfire providing a meaty topic for diners to chew on at lunch that day.

"Tamura claims he saw one last night," the diner said to his companions at the lunch table. He lifted his last spoonful of dessert deliberately to his mouth, knowing the others were mentally ingesting his words.

Wada interjected, "It was rolling away from the Shibata apartment toward Block 17...they say."

"He followed it?" blathered the first speaker as he tried to swallow.

"A short distance. Then it faded away." The talking became a free-for-all.

"I heard it was glowing like a fireball and rolling as it bounced away."

"Who told you that?"

"Can't remember exactly who..."

We kids sat wide-eyed, barely touching our food; we were so engrossed eavesdropping on the adults' conversation. The grown-ups were similarly caught up in their subject, and didn't notice how we were hanging on to their every word.

"There are plenty of witnesses to those *hino-tama*, so they must be real."

"In Nihon, there's a lotta stories about them rolling in the fields at night."

"I would rather follow one than have one chase me."

"*Yame-na-sai*. Stop all this talk. It's creepy. I don't like talking about dead things when I'm eating."

"You're too sensitive." He cut into what resembled meat on his plate, stuck it into his mouth and chewed with exaggeration.

"Maybe the dead person's spirit is in the fireball."

"Does the spirit wander around in the fireball for forty-five days until it's allowed to go to heaven?"

"Not to heaven. It's to be born again. The word is reincarnation."
"And that's forty-nine days, seven times seven, not forty-five."

"Maybe...Shibata-*san*'s *hino-tama* is still rolling around in..."

Wada turned to face us kids and continued in a conspiring whisper, "If the fireball is still wandering around, it just might follow you! Be very watchful from now, *neh*."

We didn't want to believe him, but doubts lingered. There just might be some truth to it. Wada turned his attention back to his companions and nonchalantly picked at his teeth. Gullible kids, heh, heh.

Japanese ghost stories and tales of the supernatural were infinitely scarier than those told in English, though the Gothic tales of the American South bear a resemblance, with all the Spanish moss surroundings. America is expansive, open, and transparent. Ethereal ghosts cannot dwell and spook around in the bright light and lively energy of loud, noisy, forthright Americans. They are haunted by ugly, misshapen demons who sneak around looking for bloody revenge, and their spooks can be challenged. The Europeans favor ghouls and vampires and the devil in different disguises. In Japan, otherworldly creatures delight in transforming themselves to entrap innocents as well as those deserving harsh reprisals. They materialize, slither about, and evaporate to haunt the unwary in a land of shadows and innuendoes. We did not walk alone at night with the same abandon as we did before we learned about *hino-tama* rolling fire balls.

A typical Block in Minidoka after tree planting project

SUMMER RETURNS

With Summer came the blazing sun and long hours of daylight, shoving ghosts and ghouls into dark, deep crevasses and out of mind. We had survived fourth grade, and I realized I had spent a whole school year never getting to know the new kids in our class who had joined us from Tule Lake. I kept the tiny photo of the whole class standing with the Nisei Air Force hero Ben Kuroki, when he visited all the classrooms as part of his tour of Minidoka. Like the celebrity he was, they hustled him from one group snapshot session to the next, and we barely had a chance to say hello. The photograph was evidence of his visit, and it captured the faces of my fourth-grade classmates whose names I remembered, and all the other nameless ones. The small keep-*sake* photo remains one of a few taken of us during our time in camp. Images of our growing up were never recorded because cameras had been confiscated.

Schoolwork was still a personal challenge, although I was no longer the bonehead in our class. I had somehow moved up closer to average in my grades, albeit mostly due to Miss Keck's less-than-challenging academic standards. My inflated grades buoyed my self-confidence, and I began to believe I was not so dumb a scholar after all. I decided to abandon all tedious self-imposed catch-up studies and cruise through the Summer Break doing only fun things. My earlier ambitions to join the More Streets and Roads smart bunch had vaporized much like the rainy day mud puddles which had turned to dust when the sun and fair weather arrived. School vacation meant we escaped the oppressive, airless classroom only to find the great outdoors dry, hot, and unbearable, too. We spent an inordinate time looking for shade and the wisp of a cooling breeze.

As the inevitable dust storms whipped up, we bemoaned our circumstances as we remembered another time and a better place we had been forced to leave.

RELIGIOUS QUESTIONS

I planned to sign up for Bible school rather than the Buddhist summer classes I had attended the previous summer.

All year long, my friends had talked glowingly about the variety of activities offered at last year's Christian summer program, and I was determined not to pass it up this year. To gain a little familiarity as to what Christian folks said and did, I occasionally tagged along with enthusiastic Bible-toting friends on Sundays, and attended Sunday school, which was led by Reverend Andrews. Christians sang hymns instead of chanting sutras like the Buddhists; either way I could only watch the others and wonder where they had learned the score.

Most every former Seattleite living in Minidoka would have heard the name Reverend Andrews. Andy was the pastor at the Seattle Japanese Baptist Church since 1929. He had also served as Scoutmaster for the church-sponsored Boy Scout Troop #53, and his assistance was forthcoming wherever it was needed. When his congregation was interned to Minidoka, he uprooted his own family and moved to Twin Falls, Idaho, the closest town to camp. This move enabled him to commute and to minister to his flock. He generously encompassed the entire community in his service and dedication to them without questioning their church affiliation. He undertook more than fifty trips back to Seattle to retrieve stored items requested by the internees. His home outside of camp often served as a hostel or a meeting place, for which he and his family suffered threats and humiliation from the townspeople. His ultimate compensation was the respect and love of the entire community.

I spent the early weeks of summer vacation in the Summer Christian Bible program that proved to be as interesting as I was led to believe. It was not like ordinary school. Without tests and grades, we found "the smart ones" were not necessarily the most adept in every activity. The well-organized program involved us in arts and crafts projects, singing folk songs as well as religious hymns, and fun interactive games. We heard a different Bible story every session from the book that was a treasure trove of stories. Since the program was led by Nisei laypeople, everything was spoken or sung in English, in contrast to the previous year when the Buddhist texts, songs and sermons were in Japanese. English was a second language to those priests and their assistants who were born and educated in Japan.

The fellowship I found, and the Bible stories were worth making the switch. Also, no one asked whether I was a believer; it was soft-sell proselytizing. My religious education had taken an ecumenical turn.

I sat through Father Tibersaw's conversations at the Arais' apartment on more than one occasion, and though the subject matter went way over my head, the priest's earnest demeanor and sincerity convinced me he spoke truths; Catholicism was the one and true church, he said. A gift booklet from the priest about the Virgin Mary and a second book identifying the saints prompted me to think I might one day become a Catholic like the Father.

To an innocent straying from the Buddhist fold, the more I learned, the more confused I became. The Christians and Catholics said sinners were condemned to be punished in a Hell full of fire and brimstone, and burn in a vast crematorium-like furnace forever for their sins. Everyone is born with sin, the Catholics said. What's a sin? I wondered. So, is it inevitable we are all doomed to end up in Hell? Not so, said the Christians. Jesus was crucified on the cross so our sins could be forgiven. You have to be baptized. You must believe in the true Church. A Buddhist, *Obaa-san* had said to me when Mommy died, goes to a heaven filled with flowers. That destiny is certainly better than burning in Hell; however, I would be miserable with my hay fever in the midst of a vast flower patch where it rains flowers forever.

"Buddhist is good, Christian is good, Catholic is good. They all teach people to be good, to be kind to everybody, and lead good life," Daddey said. But that was not the response I wanted to hear.

"You have to choose one only, Daddey. They say you have to be a Buddhist, a Christian, or a Catholic. I want to know which one is best."

"I try to tell you only one is not the best, they are all good. In America, people can decide any religion. In Japan, most people are born Buddhist, and they are always Buddhist. They do not decide. When Japanese come to America, they learn about other religions. Sometimes they decide to change, and they join Christian churches."

"You don't go to any church. If you were born Buddhist, then you must be a Buddhist."

"Maybe yes and maybe no."

Discussing religion with Daddey was frustrating. Whatever religious beliefs Yoshi may have held as a youth, as well as the Buddhist sutras and rituals he was made to memorize, they had become distant memories, and his ties to Buddhism had waned in the years since his departure from Uncle Shoshun's tutelage.

The Shin and Nichiren Buddhist sects had set out to expand to America. They organized congregations and founded temples, becoming predominant among the immigrant settlers while other sects remained a lesser presence; that included the Zen sect. The Shin Buddhist rituals were not the familiar ones Yoshi had endured. He felt as much a stranger in those temples with ornate altars as he did in the simpler Protestant churches and missions founded for the Japanese converts. Not all could be counted as true converts, for among them were less-than-true believers who merely followed the flock. Yoshi knew better than to bring up the subject of his baptism.

"I don't want you to burn in Hell when you die, Daddey." "Nani? Why I go to Hell?"

"If you're not Buddhist, and not a baptized Christian, you will go to Hell.

Yoshi stopped to appraise his chances for avoiding Hell. Hmm... Yes, I am Zen, and I am baptized; I go to heaven. Next week I give Father Tibersaw donation for extra good luck. Increase odds for win, show, and place. A satisfied smile crept over his face before he returned his attention to his young inquisitor.

"I have many friends who go to different churches and they all tell me to join them. Maybe they want to save me so I no go to Hell. If I go to church with one, my other friends will not be happy with me. So, I stay away from all churches, and everybody stay friends with me."

"That excuse isn't good enough."

"That is bad news. I like to stay friends with everybody."

"People have to decide one way or the other while they're still alive, and you're getting old."

"I am old? I no look old; mirror tell me I am still…"

"You're getting a little bald."

"Hmm. Maybe so, but all hair is black, no white." His antagonist was frowning, obviously dissatisfied at the turn their discussion had taken. Yoshi's thoughts shifted, Aiko had been such a giving, compliant wife, never argumentative. How could such an obstinate, self-willed creature have been a product of her womb? It was time to appease his daughter. "Maybe before I die, I can be Buddhist again and go to same heaven as Mommy. That OK?"

"Maybe. I'll have to think about it."

Finally, subject closed, he thought. What's next if she hears about Shinto or Muhammad?

"Daddey, I have to decide. You're no help to me at all!"

"You are very young girl. You have lotta time to think about these things. Everyone makes own decision."

"Thanks a lot for nothing."

"In church, they don't talk about Heaven and Hell only. They tell people to be good and kind when they are living. I say so again, because that is most important."

"Hmmm…"

Decision making became more complicated when a friend signed me on for a correspondence course sponsored by the Seventh-day Adventists. Go to church on Saturday? Why?

Summer Bible School had ended too soon, and we were adrift with a surfeit of free time; time we had looked forward to the entire school year. Now that vacation was upon us, I was at loose ends trying to fill the directionless days with interesting and time-consuming projects.

The backside of the laundry area was still our favorite meeting place and we gravitated there looking for company.

"Bites! Ban bites, ban bites! Bites! Bites! Bites!" Everyone was shouting one or the other.

"Who has the treat?"

"Yuri has an apple, and I said 'Bites' before she said 'Ban bites.'"

"OK, you're the only one who gets a bite 'cuz I said 'Ban bites before the rest of you guys," Yuri said. "Make sure you only take a small bite."

Who knows how it all started? The rules avoided real problems.

Some stupid kid starts punching you on the arm, and you say, "PM, PM, C, C, K," as fast as possible, and he quits punching you. The letters stood for "Pall Malls, Philip Morris, Camels, Chesterfields, and Kools," all popular cigarettes at the time. Why? No one ever explained. You said it anyway to avoid a black-and-blue arm.

The owner of the Monopoly board game set was absent, so we were playing cards. Everyone owned one or two decks, and no one was dependent on others to start a game.

"Now all you kids come to practice in the mess hall tonight, OK? We want a lotta participation," the organizer said to us kids playing team solitaire.

"What kind of practice?" I asked Mae.

"*Bon Odori* practice."

"So what's *Bon Odori*?"

"Sometimes I think you came from outer space. Didn't your folks ever take you to watch the *Bon Odori* in Nihonmachi before the war?"

"No, not ever."

"I guess they don't have that kinda stuff on Mars," Mae said. "People wear their kimonos or happi coats, they form a big circle, and they dance to different folk songs. It's real easy, and it's fun."

As Mae said, joining the practice sessions and learning the various repetitive dances was a lot of fun. With the phonograph at high volume, children and adults joined the ring of participants, and we did as Mrs. Mori, our leader, commanded and demonstrated. We gestured and swayed in unison and clapped hands in time with the drums. Dip to the left, plant the rice, dip to the right, plant the rice, now step, step, clap, and clap.

"*Ah yoi, yoi!*"

What a way to greet visiting dead ancestors. Never mind if you were converted, the ancestors were all Buddhist, and they would surely take the opportunity to revisit those of us still living during *Obon*. These spirits were not the scary kind; they liked a good celebration like the rest of us.

"*Ah yoi, yoi…*all together."

CHAPTER 14

Minidoka, the Third Year, 1944‑1945

WORLD WAR II WAS RAGING on, and we were living in a desert in Idaho due to that fact, yet the realities of blood, gore, and deaths remained remote. News of the actual fighting and battles being waged were taking place in unfamiliar locales: Saipan, Guadalcanal, and others; we kids heard news headlines, and they barely intruded on our everyday lives. Those older than us with a greater perspective of world events were not as blasé, and they shook their heads at our ignorance. We were innocents. We did notice the hanging banners that began appearing in windows displaying a star or two or three indicating the number of sons in the family serving in the armed services. Servicemen sons and a few daughters still wearing their uniforms began visiting their families in camp before being sent overseas. They were our heroes, and we listened to their every word.

"The Hawaiians can be short-tempered; they're always ready to get into a fight," our hero said.

"Hawaiian? Hey, I thought you guys were in an all-Nisei unit," quipped a pint-sized hero worshipper.

"We are. They're Nisei from Hawaii, commonly called Buddha-Heads."

"Oh, I get it. Cuz they're mostly Buddhist."

"And they call us from the mainland Ko-tonks."

"Whoa, you got me stumped. What's it mean?"

"They claim our head makes that sound when it gets busted. Ko-tonk. Ko-tonk."

"Isn't that kinda insulting?"

"Them Hawaii guys are OK. They talk funny and sometimes it's hard to understand them, but in a fight I'd rather have them hotheads fighting on my side than on the other side against me. They're "go for broke" kind of guys."

"Soldier, you can explain that one, too, while you're on the subject."

"In card playing, when you think you have a winning hand, you bet your whole pot, everything you've got: you Go-for-broke."

"I'll remember that."

Another pip-squeak joined the questioning, "I heard there's a lotta Negros living in the South. You see them?"

"We see them when we're off the base. They don't mix with the *haku-jin* whites much. They even have separate drinking fountains and restrooms for them to use."

"Was there a separate one for yellow people like us?"

"No, there wasn't. That's why we were confused in the beginning. We didn't know which one to use; we weren't colored, and we weren't white."

"Geez, so…"

"We weren't colored, they said, so go ahead and use the one for whites."

"No shit. They said white?"

"Seems to me there's all kinds of prejudice people have to put up with. It's not just against Japanese."

RECLAIMING POSSESSIONS

It was not only the length of time we had lived in Minidoka that made us feel at home; another factor was the sense of permanence. A policy change was made to allow families to retrieve stored items at government expense. As families reclaimed boxes and crates crammed with possessions they had packed away at the onset of evacuation, apartment interiors lost much of their Spartan sameness as the added clutter of stuff individualized ones living spaces.

The amount of things families retrieved from storage varied, as did the contents. Daddy had filled one trunk with my dolls and toys. Each had been wrapped with the hope chest linens Mommy had collected. The steamer trunk Daddey had had since his bachelor days was filled with clothes, once-important papers, and memorabilia, along with two albums of photographs. A wood crate was packed with our dishes and flatware protected by two wool blankets. It was everything Daddey owned, and most of it stayed packed away except my dolls and toys, and the two wool blankets, which were immediately put to use.

My extensive collection of dolls had been stored for nearly four years, and taking them out of the trunk was like going to a toy store. They were placed neatly on the shelf Daddey made for me, and I gave each a name except the Shirley Temple doll who already had a name. For the most part, they sat on their perch untouched; I had outgrown my interest in dolls during the time they were inaccessible. Another toy I retrieved from the trunk was the toy iron. It was the same little iron my parents warned me never ever to plug into a socket. "Oh, it works good," Daddey said to me. He had completely forgotten his dire warnings. The miniature electric iron was just the right size for me to manipulate, and I managed to iron my own clothes, which Daddey washed for me.

A washing machine appeared alongside one of the double sinks in the public laundry room one day. The white enameled tub with attached rubber wringers used to squeeze the water out of wet clothes, was set on metal legs with wheels, making it conveniently portable. It was all so modern and high-toned. Everyone understood it was personal property, an appliance for use by the owners only. As the owners had run a furnishings store, everyone felt *atari-mae*––it was right that they own such an appliance––and did not begrudge them their good fortune.

All the other resident families continued to scrub clothes on a washboard and squeeze out the water by hand in much the same way they had washed clothes in the years before the war. Now, at least, they were provided a two-compartment sink, which made the work much easier than leaning into a bathtub to do the family's laundry. If they had a complaint, it was the poor quality of soap available. The mechanized washer was a reminder they had once dreamed about the luxury such a machine afforded. After the novelty of its appearance wore off and the initial pangs of envy were contained, no one bothered to give the lone washing machine a second thought.

We had arrived in camp with only what we could carry. Bereft of extraneous material possessions, we had lived in assigned living quarters resembling chicken coops. Our reduced circumstances had made us equals in a Communist-ideal sort of way. We assessed people by their actions, and not by what they owned. With the appearance of material possessions, that sense of equality diminished, and pride of ownership and status-enhancing attitudes crept back into our lives, preparing us for life in the real world again someday in the future.

Fifth Grade Begins

When school started in the fall, we were all hoping for a fifth-grade teacher who would make attending school intellectually stimulating again. Mrs. Sampson had a completely different personality than Miss Queen and Miss Keck. Somewhere between the two in age, she was hip and energetic, and she was attractive in a different way from our peaches-and-cream third grade teacher. Her commanding approach to teaching and class discipline was not subtle, but on those occasions when she was not provoked and had a semblance of cooperation from the class, she was an effective teacher, and she was basically fair. The girls accepted this different rule. They agreed she was an improvement over Miss Laissez-Faire. The boys were less accepting of Mrs. Bossy. This was not going to be a peaceful school year, and an undeclared war ensued between a few of the boys and Mrs. Sampson.

A few weeks after school started, Mrs. Sampson read the announcement affecting students living in Block 17 and Block 19. It said: upper-grade students, namely fourth, fifth, and sixth graders living in those two blocks, would be transferred to Stafford School beginning the following week. Huntsville School in Block 10 had only one class per grade, while Stafford School in Block 32 had two classes per grade. This transfer was an attempt to equalize the number of students in each class.

I quivered in disbelief. I don't want to go to a different school…without familiar classmates to provide a security net, and to be dropped in the midst of strangers who don't particularly want a Huntsville in their area. Woe is me.

There were no protests from parents demanding a hearing. They shushed their complaining children with their usual reply: *Shikata-ga-nai*. We obediently followed the new regulation and hoped our fears were overblown. Besides, there could be a benefit in leaving Mrs. Sampson's war zone for a peaceable classroom.

There was one obvious advantage to the transfer: we got a ride to school, since the distance from our homes to the new school was deemed too far for grade schoolers to commute on foot.

We waited alongside the main road near the mess hall, the boys in one group, ignoring the girls in another group. Finally, the transport vehicle roared into view with its canvas top wildly flapping in the wind. The truck stopped as it kicked up a sheet of gravel and the usual choking particulates of dust. This was the camp's version of school busing circa 1944. The driver jumped out and dropped the tailgate. The boys clamored in and grabbed a sideboard seat, while the Block 17 boys who were already in the truck wholeheartedly greeted their Block 19 classmates. We girls climbed aboard a bit more sedately, ever careful not to expose our underpants.

"Is that everyone now?" the driver asked.

"Kewpie-*chan's* not here yet," one of the girls called out.

The tardy student was nowhere in sight. She was rarely on time, and the other passengers had lost patience with her constant tardiness. Those delays often caused everyone on the "bus" to get to their classes after the starting bell.

"I see her turning the corner," said sixth-grader Tai. "Now watch this," he said to those onboard. He bellowed loudly to the pudgy young girl waddling hurriedly toward the truck, "Run faster, Piggy! We're all going to be late! Faster, Piggy, faster!"

She picked up her speed and got to our waiting truck panting and puffing. Tai and one of his cohorts grabbed her arms and pulled up as the driver gave her a shove from below. She plopped unceremoniously on the truck deck, belly first.

"Geez, you gotta quit eating. You weigh a ton," Tai said as she picked herself up and sat down daintily in the space made for her on the bench, ignoring the scrawls on the faces of girls sitting around her. The boys sat on the sidelines curled up with laughter watching the show unravel.

"Don't be late anymore, Kewpie-*chan*," scolded one of the girls. "You have to tell your mama, too."

"I second that and third it!" growled an irritated rider.

Kewpie-*chan* sported her toothy, stretched Cheshire cat grin. With puffed-up cheeks red and round as a ball, they squeezed her eyes nearly shut, leaving two narrow black bands to peer through. Settling herself primly on the wood bench and smoothing the wrinkles from her skirt, she was oblivious to the admonishments hurled at her. It was common knowledge she lived in her own sheltered world of smothering mother love; she was the baby cub who never left her mother's protection, except to attend school. Reality rarely intruded into her world, and the recriminations fell on deaf ears.

"There's no standing when we're moving. Got that, boys?" the driver said, repeating his routine safety speech though he knew no one ever bothered to listen.

The driver slammed the tailgate shut with a bang. Within seconds, he revved his engine, set it into gear, and with a jerk we roared down the unencumbered straightaway toward Area B. Decades before the advent of mandatory seat belts, we in the back of the truck knew to hold on for dear life. We were tossed and bounced to and fro like popcorn in a hot skillet. Our driver was not averse to slamming on the brakes occasionally.

He figured the boys enjoyed the wild ride; the girls had to bear with it. Collecting ourselves from that final, abrupt stop, we all scrambled off the bus with rubbery legs. The wobble of the first steps soon wore off, and we dashed to our classrooms when we were late. Our classmates thought we were a privileged lot getting a ride to school instead of struggling through the mud like the rest of them.

Mrs. Sparks had welcomed us warmly to her fifth-grade class on our first day––a good sign. The students were a cautious bunch, obviously suspicious of the trucked-in strangers from Huntsville School. The teacher had coached her class to be friendly to us newcomers, but they kept their distance nevertheless. Betty from Block 17 and Keiij, Frank, Hana, and me from Block 19 were the fifth-grade transfers. As students, we were all middling scholastically. No high achievers. The five of us were average, and none were "a nail too high" students.

I searched through the faces of my new classmates, but no one in the class looked familiar. Later, Betsy and Kate said they had attended Bailey Gatzert, but they did not remember me. Many of the students were from Portland, Oregon, and other areas remote from Nihonmachi. They had formed friendships in the two previous years they had been together, and they did not feel the need to alter the status quo. They were not hostile nor were they embracing. In self-defense, Betty, Hana, and I stuck together outside of the classroom, forming our own clique of three. We strutted about and acted superior to hide our own anxieties. The boys had to make their own way among their new peers as well.

Another room of fifth graders was located in the barrack classroom behind ours, but there was no communication between them.

We usually kept our distance from upperclassmen, not only because they acted superior, but also because their cliques were hierarchal, with a leader and lieutenants who ruled those under their control. Leaving Huntsville meant adding distance away from them, only to learn Stafford had its own girl Amazon who needed no lieutenants.

The boys had their own cliques and pecking order, and when fellow bus passenger Tai, an upperclassman, was transferred to Stafford School, he managed to create his usual waves in a new venue. Flamboyant and fast-talking, he made himself known wherever his whirlwind landed. There was no sixth grader in all of Minidoka who had not heard of him or at least one of his exploits.

I definitely regretted being lazy and complacent during the summer months. My assessment about my improved reading skills had been inflated, and I was barely keeping up with the class. It didn't take long to figure out my new classmates' scholastic status; I was near the low end as before. Instead of being motivated to study harder as I had once been, I blamed my ennui on lack of stimulation, and declared schoolwork was both a chore and a bore.

Mrs. Sparks piled her brunette curls atop her head with a scarf band; she made no other fashion statement. She did wear a smile often. And her usual good cheer made her a likable package. Perhaps neutral best describes her position in the pantheon of teachers we encountered. We plodded through our tedious lessons, and when we were introduced to division, I found it was a mechanical procedure as long as I was up to speed on my multiplication table. Somehow, all the tedium of our school day vanished during the story time sessions that engaged the attention of the entire class, even the smart-alecky ones. We were too old for the usual story time readings: our stories were swashbuckling types, whetting our appetites for more classics later. She did not read a book to the class word for word. Even as fifth graders, our attention span was short. She read a chapter or two the night before, and the following day she skillfully summarized the story and read us pertinent sections best not abbreviated. In her reprised version, she used words we understood and infused enthusiasm into the plot. We all eagerly waited to hear the next chapter. The stories always contained words or terms that were beyond our experiences, requiring explanations.

"Rebecca and her father were Jewish, and they were being…"

"Mrs. Sparks, what means Jewish if they live in England and he doesn't come from a country named Jew? People from Japan are Japanese; Chinese come from China."

"A Jewish person is so defined by the religion he practices.

It's not…" Mrs. Sparks tried to explain.

"You mean like when a guy is called Buddhist, even if he's really Japanese and never goes to church and never does his *Okyo*?"

"I suppose it's something like that."

"Why didn't you say so in the first place?"

"What about Indians?" another student questioned. "Why are they called Indians when they don't come from India?"

"They're Americans because they live in America," a third voice chimed in.

"That didn't answer my question. People who live in India are Indians. So why do we call some people living in America: Indians?"

"Look, you live in America, you're American, and they still call you a Jap––same difference."

"Geez, that still doesn't…"

"Will you guys shut up? Quit asking dumb questions. I wanna hear the rest of the story!"

Sick Again

I had had the measles already, and the spots didn't look like warts. They were itchy, and they sprouted all over my body. I was diagnosed with chicken pox and had to stay in isolation for three weeks. Missing school and staying inside our apartment for three weeks suited me fine. It was luxury compared to dark stalls in the exhibition barns at Puyallup's quarantine area. Things were so cushy now.

Our small, brown plastic radio sat perched on the horizontal stud at the head of our beds. The radio's range was short, and it was better at receiving static than music or voices. When it buzzed and the static pierced the airwaves, it could be fixed with a couple of sharp slaps to its side. On Saturday mornings, a Salt Lake City station airing Let's Pretend came through distinctly enough for me to hear its weekly, dramatized fairy tale. The commercials always came through loud and clear, and I sang along: "Cream of Wheat is so good to eat, we have it every day. We sing this song…" I had no idea what the cereal tasted like. It was not served in the mess hall.

Weekdays offered adult fare, and a station from Twin Falls generally came through with better reception. Their afternoon broadcasts were devoted to soap operas, and I became addicted to them during my isolation. Stella Dallas, Backstage Wife was my favorite daytime soap. Evenings were filled with programs like The Shadow, and other crime-fighting programs all the kids listened to and discussed with friends the next day. They all had a moral——absolutely no ambiguities for our young, impressionable minds.

My pox spots diminished, as did the itching, and I needed other distractions.

In order to keep me entertained and to minimize my complaints, Daddy went to the canteen and bought me a few magazines to supplement my collection of comic books, which I was tired of rereading. I may have been the only kid in camp with a subscription to two comics. Looney Tunes and Merrie Melodies, and Bugs Bunny comics arrived regularly every month in the mailbox. I was graduating into adventure comics like Captain Marvel and Wonder Woman, and was expecting to get the latest issues of my current favorites. I was bitterly disappointed when he came back and presented me with the Saturday Evening Post and Liberty magazines.

My reading skills had not advanced to the level of general interest adult magazines yet, so I flipped through the magazines, giving them a fast, initial perusal. The stories contained too many hard words, and the articles I attempted to read were far too long and boring. I realized the advertisements were definitely more interesting than the articles. A couple of picture ads caught my eye. I cut them out and added the pictures to the special heart-shaped box I filled with precious favorite things. These advertisements were not the splashy, full-page type. They were printed in black and white, no larger than three inches square, with minimal copy; in fact, the picture shown was not the advertiser's product. The small Honeywell advertisement was a picture of a house. It was a Bauhaus modernist-style two-story, flat-roofed house with glass-brick features and a smooth, finished, curved wall. The second advertisement I saved showed a pristine U-shaped kitchen with unembellished white cabinets and appliances. The ads depicted a glimpse of the future that whetted my desire to share in that American dream someday when I grew up. I started envisioning possible floor plans for the Honeywell house that always incorporated that U-shaped kitchen with white cabinets. I resurrected my long-neglected interest in designing my ideal house, a pastime that had lapsed when we moved to camp.

SAME COMPLAINT

Daddey learned I was skipping breakfasts in the mess hall soon after our arrival in camp. Worried that malnutrition might precipitate a relapse and a recurrence of my TB, he had begun taking a few minutes from his job each morning to pick up a platter of food and bring it home for me to eat in leisure. I had to eat scrambled eggs, real or made from powder, to keep Daddey from nagging me. I argued that cornflakes tasted different from Wheaties, or toast without jam did not taste good, and the syrup on the pancakes had no sweetness; I refused to eat any of it. I ate very little of whatever was served; food did not interest me. I continued to look like a starved poster child from the Third World.

Whatever foods we were served, the quality of the meals continued to be a topic with unanimous consensus: godawful. Large volume cooking does not often translate to quality dining, but there were other justified reasons for the internees' complaints. Initially, the menus and food items were not foodstuffs familiar to the Japanese diet. Potatoes eventually gave way to rice as the staple, and tsukemono became a table condiment that could be eaten with the rice when the entree item was too unappealing.

"Aaggg, they give us Columbia River smelt again!"

"When you no can eat the bones of such small fish, it's wasted effort."

"When I lived in Hawaii before I move to Seattle, I eat a small fish with strong, large bones which you had to pick at to get the flesh. I found it was worth the effort," an elderly man said as he diligently picked his fish for tidbits of eatables.

"I like to eat my fried smelt whole, bones and all. If it's cooked right, I eat the head and tail, too."

"That's the best way to eat them, but you have to get smelt from the Sound."

"You're right. First time I eat this kind smelt, I try to eat bones. It stick in my throat, and I almost go to hospital."

The men laughed, making their disappointing entrée a tad more palatable.

We kids had no long memories of tasty eatable smelt, so we left our fish untouched. We picked up our slices of bread and slathered them with the ever-present apple butter jam to ease our hunger.

"Double aaggggg! We hate apple butter, too!"

On other days, our cooks had even less appealing menus to cook and serve. Few residents could stomach mutton. It was completely alien in taste and smell to the residents.

"Why did I complain about the smelt the other day? This meat is worse."

"Look, when the sheep is young, lamb can taste good."

"Then this sheep they feed us must be old––as old as Shibata-*san,* and died of old age, too."

"It stinks all right, but I remember *haku-jin* complained our takuwan smelled bad."

"How can it? It's only a vegetable, not old meat."

"Nevertheless."

"Just eat your dessert. They're giving us canned pears today."

"Do you remember getting canned pears when Suzuki was head cook?"

"Don't remember. Anyway, he's gone."

"I just wonder how much food he stole from the kitchen. I bet all the good stuff."

"Needed to keep feeding his fat wife, is what I think."

"Yeah, and he must have sold a lot of stuff." "Anyways, he got caught, and we're eating better."

"If the cooks could only get rid of the smell… Make it smell like beef stew is OK."

"Keep dreaming, like the man says."

Another Christmas and New Year

The voice over the radio was "dreaming of a White Christmas," which was the signal for me to start making new chains and tree ornaments for my neglected sagebrush Christmas tree. The knurled bush still clung to the studs on our wall, collecting dust and spider webs during the months between Christmases. My preference was to put up a new bush, but I did not want Daddey going out in the desert to find me another one. Besides, the time required and difficulty of finding another "tree" as comely and fitting was likely impossible as well. New was not that important. In one of the trunks we had retrieved, Daddey had put away two blown-glass bird ornaments that I was anxious to display. I doubted there was anyone else in camp with such a handsome Christmas bird on their tree.

Daddey often walked out away from the barracks and meandered alone, lost in his thoughts. The sagebrush-covered desert could not compare to the open sea for inspiration, but its wide deserted expanse also provided a setting for introspection. Alone, he could recite aloud the new *tanka* poem he was composing, giving sound to his unfinished or just-completed poem in private, away from curious ears. He had killed a few rattlesnakes among the sagebrush and had brought them home and skinned them. He saved the rattles at the ends of their tails and stored them for show-and-tell. It still frightened me that he should be wandering out alone in such precarious surroundings. I didn't want any harm to come to him.

The Block organizers were putting together a children's Nativity pageant as part of the holiday program for our Block. To no one's surprise, neighbor Marie was chosen to be Mary, mother of baby Jesus. She got to wear a white sheet wrap and a make-believe halo around her head. She looked radiant.

I was crushed when they told me to wear my bathrobe as my costume. My role as shepherd was to stand in the background holding a long pole. Hoping to be supplied with a better costume, I lied and told the organizers I owned no bathrobe. A donor came through with an Indian-motif wool blanket as a loaner. It was a quick lesson on the consequences of lying. Now I looked like Chief Sitting Bull straight from Little Big Horn (no disrespect intended); even without the ceremonial headdress, I looked like an extra from a cowboy movie dropped in the midst of a Biblical pageant. I felt like crawling into a hole. The kids in the audience tried to distract us from our poses, while the mostly Buddhist adults sat bemused, watching the goings-on without a clue to the scene's significance, although their exposure occurred every December. They knew the pageant was a Christmas ritual, so they applauded politely when it was over. We participants threw off our costumes and lined up to receive our bags of sweet goodies.

I enthusiastically joined in on the Christmas carols sing-along, and Santa passed out gifts to all the children. They were donated gifts, as in past years. I hoped Santa's bag held something other than a book I could not read. It turned out to be a board game, backgammon, which no one knew how to play. At the end of the program, we were told Block 19 had been passed over again; our entry missed an honorable mention in the Christmas decoration contest a third time.

The period following Christmas was always such a letdown, even when the decorations and Christmas tree were left in place for another week. Christmas songs are shelved, and the hype filed away for another year. Although a second holiday followed within a week, giving us another celebration to extend our school break; for me, it meant little more than an opportunity to eat mochi. Too young for New Year's Eve parties and dances the teenagers and young adults attended, I wondered what all the hoopla was about, since my eyes refused to stay open until midnight, and I was fast asleep as others noisily greeted the New Year.

The adults, glad Christmas was over and done, looked forward to New Year's Day, their traditional big holiday. The size and scope of the festivities, especially those involving food, remained crimped, but they did what they could to make it a special time. The women vigorously cleaned their apartments, though they knew the next big windstorm's residue was likely to leave as much sand as they had just swept out.

"I'm reminded of how we had to scrub and clean the entire house before the New Year. What an ordeal to change the tatami. So much work," reminisced Mineko Esaki, Yoshi's friend. She refilled both cups with hot tea, leaving empty her husband's cup, seeing he had slumped in his chair and dozing.

"After the cleaning, special New Year foods were prepared by all the womenfolk and household servants and…" Yoshi said as memories of his youth rolled out of his mouth in the language of his youth. "…*kanashi, neh.*"

"You must be joking. Who had household servants? When you're the one who labors, there's nothing nostalgic or *kanashi* about it."

"We were merchants, and our family had hired help."

"That sounds plausible that your family had household help, Nomura-*san*, but few among us were that fortunate. Most of us came to America because we were destitute. We did not have the luxury of servants; we did all the work ourselves. We were proud farmers experiencing dire times."

"In the old feudal class system, merchants were lower than farmers for the value of work they engaged in. In reality, though elevated in rank, farmers led very hardscrabble lives. As merchants, even in a small village, we hired help for the business and for household work to ease the burden. Social rank didn't correspond to one's quality of life."

"Think about it: a person's social status had everything to do with how they were treated, addressed, etc. It's important for one's sense of self-worth even if you wore rags," Mineko said.

"But worthiness shouldn't be based on such an arbitrary scale, one that's now archaic in these modern times. The tenets of your religion have more validity. You're told to lead exemplary lives by doing good deeds and treat others equally well…"

"Yes, I know Christianity teaches us all that, but it doesn't address my intrinsic Japanese-ness. My immediate ancestors were farmers; however, must I remind you, I am a descendent of Samurai!" Mineko said.

"Ah-yah!" Yoshi exclaimed as he suppressed his laughter. "Mineko-*san*, you and practically every Nikkei living in Minidoka are descended from Samurai stock. Now that's hard to believe. Don't you think so?"

With no material wealth to show off or bragging rights to past exploits gone hollow, the Issei found a means of overcoming a loss of status by acquiring a Samurai ancestry and elevating the family's status in the old country. Only a fool would presume to be royalty or from the nobility, but next up were the Samurai. Bound to the mystique of strict codes of conduct and honor, they inhabited a rarified position in the hierarchal society the populace held dear. The immigrant could banish his past and acquire a new persona in America. Far removed from family registries to be readily inspected and to verify lineage, no one could easily refute inflated kinships. Without fear of possible exposure, the proud descendants promoted their ancestors up the class ladder.

Mineko sat back in her chair and sipped her tea considering her options: How to best answer her inquisitor. She began slowly, "What do I think, you ask me. Of course they're stretching the truth. It's human nature, wanting to feel and act superior to others, and not have to kowtow, especially to those who deserve no such respect. A remote Samurai ancestor is much more convenient than being saintly and performing good deeds."

"What you say is true. Now I will ask you another question. How did so many Samurai become farmers?"

"They became *Ronin* when the lords had to disband their armies. Even rogue warriors have to eat; they became farmers. You know your history. Why do you ask me?"

"Only testing you, Mineko." He said with a smile.

"Nomura-*san*, don't judge too harshly. We all need to believe in our own self-worth, even when it's based on a made-up ancestry."

However skeptical Yoshi felt about claimants' facts, he remained silent.

In America, the immigrants had changed, adapted, and assimilated to survive and prosper in the new world, so what harm was there in a bit of lineage chicanery?

Mineko and Yoshi had become good friends since the days we were neighbors in Puyallup.

MINEKO

Mineko was born in the US and had gone to Japan with her parents and siblings. She had spent her childhood in Japan, was educated there, and returned to America as a young adult. She was a Kibei. She could read, write, and speak English, but they were her second language.

She radiated a positive attitude that transformed her ordinary features into a pleasing face, and her agreeable disposition made her a pleasant companion. She was spunky, albeit in a brainy sort of way. She was not interested in the young man who declared he wanted her for a bride. She resisted, but she was finally forced to marry him when her father demanded she do so and gave her no choice. Her father had accumulated a large debt to the suitor's father, who promised to void the debt if the marriage took place. The young couple returned to America, and two children were born. Mineko's husband drank, was irresponsible, and physically abusive. To escape this nightmare, she ran away with the two young children and sought a divorce. Divorce carried an enormous negative stigma in the ethos of the community, and she struggled to support herself and her two children. Acquaintances persuaded her she should remarry.

Rumors had circulated that a fellow had gotten lucky and won a large pool of money while holed up in a hotel hiding from immigration officials. The amount of money was substantial; enough to support a family, and he was eager to have a wife. Mineko was in no position to bargain.

To sweeten the deal for the prospective groom, her go-betweens insisted she give up her daughter and allow her childless brother and his wife to adopt her. She entered the marriage with just one child. No one told her the groom had lost his fortune as quickly as he had won it, and he entered the marriage without a bankroll. To escape the inevitable immigration raids, her new husband found work at a distant, far from the city, sawmill, where they settled in a worker's camp.

Esaki was a simple man who accepted his responsibilities by working diligently to support his new family. Gambling and playing cards was a bachelor's activity, he said, and abandoned those vices now that he was a married man. He never bothered to take up any new interests to replace those activities. He made few demands and was content with his lot. Mineko was grateful the physical and verbal abuses of her earlier marriage were just a bad memory, and she was determined to be a good wife to her new husband. Initially, she welcomed the quiet and routine of life in the small community isolated in the forest, but in time, she could not deny she was starved for intellectual stimulation. Her salvation had been Mr. Arai. He, too, worked at the sawmill, and helped her to renew her lapsed interest in *tanka*. She began composing the five-line poems under his guidance.

Yoshi and Mineko talked poetry and wandered through the realm of Japanese history, culture, and language, exploring and finding word associations integral to their poetry. The mere name of a place with a significant event adds volumes of meaning, much as a word like Gettysburg holds reams of associative meanings for an American. The double or triple meanings of a single-sounded word, the adopted Chinese ideographs that can be pronounced many ways in Japanese, all contribute to the subtly layered facets of the outwardly simple thirty-one *On* poem. The two poetry enthusiasts relished having a partner for these discussions of shared interests, thus, increasing the scope of possibilities by incorporating the subtle references into their own compositions. Mr. Arai was their sensei, their teacher; he was too elevated to banter with as equals.

For the sake of propriety, Yoshi went to the Esaki unit to visit; it was never the other way around. They addressed the other by last name in public, though Yoshi often called Mineko by her given name in private. When Yoshi visited, Mineko's husband sat on the sidelines, bored with the esoteric subject matter the two poets discussed. He was brought into the conversation for the sake of being polite, and he responded with ambiguous feelings, neither happy nor unhappy to be included. I occasionally accompanied Daddey on a visit, but I found the conversations as boring as Mr. Esaki did, so I usually stayed home.

It was obvious Mineko and Daddey liked each other; that they had become very good friends was known to all living in our Block. On passing a neighbor in the compound, the parties usually exchanged polite but brief pleasantries and continued on their way; the two poets could be seen chatting at length, mindless of the time, though mindfully scrupulous in maintaining the propriety of a merely friendly relationship. There were no signs that theirs was anything other than an intellectual and platonic friendship, and Mineko's husband never felt he was a cuckold spouse. The gossipmongers in the Block thought otherwise. To their credit, they were not on a witch hunt and kept their scandalous musings to a murmur. Mineko ignored the gossip, and Yoshi, secure in the knowledge his promise to keep the vow he had given to his mother, harbored no feelings of guilt, and nourished the friendship unabated. Under different circumstances, the friendship may have taken a different turn.

DANCE LESSONS

Our recreation hall in Block 19 was underutilized; it sat vacant and dark most of the time due to its inconvenient location for most camp residents. Earlier that year, without any fanfare, the Nakamura dance group decided to locate its second studio in our rec hall. Lessons in traditional Japanese dance were scheduled every Tuesday afternoon. Like other traditional art forms, young Nisei and Sansei were not flocking to take lessons, choosing instead more popular activities like baton twirling. Truly serious *odori* students had started taking lessons at the age of four or five, but Sensei was willing to take on less serious students of any age.

Even a sow's ear thinks it can be transformed into a silk purse, and this was my golden opportunity to indulge my recent enthusiasm for Japanese culture and learn the classical Japanese dance. I was almost ten years old when my lessons began. Daddey had immediately agreed to my proposal and willingly paid the tuition fee. The two of us had gone to the canteen to select the fabric for my practice *yukata*, the cotton kimono, which Mrs. Esaki sewed for me. We also purchased a pair of tabi, the Japanese footwear, and I was on my way.

Lesson One was learning the proper kneeling bow given as a sign of respect to Sensei at the beginning of the lesson. It was all a game, and I willingly made my proper bows in a show of conciliation. Everything that followed was more difficult than I had imagined. I learned how to stand and move properly, how to take a step and turn in the artificial way of the *odori*. It did not feel natural; every movement was stylized, but when perfected, it was fluid grace.

Each week, a new, short dance segment was added to the previous lessons. So much to remember: Lean back, slight circle step, and Pigeon Toe leading foot. Stop. Fold arm gracefully; make each movement meaningful. Stop. Turn head slowly.

Now what? Mind blank…

O-shisho-san, the name we called Mrs. Nakamura, laid down her shamisen, put one leg down, then the other from her squatted position, and got off her chair to patiently demonstrate the forgotten sequence. The problem was: she demonstrated a revised sequence that was not exactly like the previous week. Those dance sequences were not written in stone, and every week I was learning a new variation. It was utterly confusing, but, I loved it all. Several students were worse than me, and they quit in short order. The majority of students had started training prior to the war; they were dedicated and skilled with no trace of memory problems. Their lessons came after we newcomers had fumbled through the basics. I sat and watched them, enthralled at their skills and grace. The fan manipulations performed by older, longtime students were my favorites.

The Nakamura group was one of three in Minidoka. The Yayoi-kai was headed by a Portland dance teacher, the Hatsune-kai group specialized in dances performed by geishas, and the group I joined was named Mimasu-kai, and we concentrated on Kabuki theatricals and their accessory dances.

There were many versions of Mrs. Nakamura's history. My favorite was, that as a child born into a theatrical family, her dancing lessons had begun at a very early age, as well as training in all aspects of the family's profession. She showed great talent and skill, but she stopped growing, and she remained exceptionally small. Realizing she was too delicate for the rigors of the theater, the family decided she should practice her skills and teach the immigrants who lived in America. She was married off to a Nisei born in Port Blakeley, where Japanese had settled from before the end of the 19th century. With a husband to support and care for her needs, the transition was made. She taught dance, and put on theatricals in Seattle and the Valley before the war.

The Mimasu-kai group was putting on a show in the spring. It was the Minidoka edition of a traveling Kabuki troop. The performances were to be held in several mess halls in Blocks willing to set up a stage and provide other necessary accoutrements. The evening program, starting with the traditional opening dance, followed by different dance sequences, ended after the two featured plays. The first, a lighter-themed play preceded the heavy drama that ended the show. Madame Nakamura reluctantly took on the heroine's role in the drama since her best, experienced students had already left camp.

Wonder of wonders, Sensei chose me to be one of seven in the chorus. I had been a pupil for a little over a year by that time, but my prowess in *odori* was still nonexistent. Any other student with properly functioning synapses would have progressed with mind/body coordination by that time. Mercifully, the sequence was short, so short there was barely time to embarrass anyone, including myself. Or, Sensei may have intentionally included one klutz to mess up the chorus for its comic value. I refused to read such subversive intentions in her decision, because I was overjoyed to be participating in a real live theatrical.

After lunch on performance days, a truck came by, picking up everyone connected with the production: dancers, musicians, stagehands, dressers, parents, and assorted assistants. We were dropped off at units made available by the Block hosting the show, while those in charge organized the necessary preparations. Makeup was applied on dancers in midafternoon. The traditional white chalky base was applied with a wide, handle-less brush, much like a first coat of primer. After the face was painted ghostly white, the entire neck, extending to a portion of the back to be exposed by the kimono's low-slung back collar, was treated with the same whitewash application. Each girl had a pink-hued tint applied to the upper eyelids, then a sweep down on each side of the nose. The tops of noses had a straight streak of white, making our Oriental noses appear long and narrow. A little rouge and painted eyebrows with thin, deep-red lips completed our makeup. We lesser significant dancers were made up first and told to keep our makeup undisturbed until the performance. Of course, that was when our noses became itchy and triggering cries to be scratched. "*Gam-batte*, resist the urge (to scratch)," we were told. The experienced dancers with significant roles were made up with stylized and dramatic expressions painted over the same chalky base.

The elaborate kimonos and costumes required dressers to properly clothe the participants so they would stay snug and proper throughout the performance. Women with previous experience, usually parents who were familiar with the costumes, took on the role of dressers. We minor participants were again dressed first and told not to fidget until after the performance, although it was still hours until the start of the show. I came to understand why Japanese females had learned to walk in little baby steps with toes pointed in. The kimonos did not allow us to walk any other way without hobbling about or stepping on our hems. I learned, too, the low collar in the back did facilitate moving our heads from side to side; doing so in a circular motion and sashaying about with the long kimono sleeves made me feel like a delicious Japanese doll.

Kimonos, along with their under linings are not custom cut and sewn; they are "one size fits all" apparel, a situation where each garment is shaped to fit the wearer by using ties. Since each kimono wearer required lots of ties, old sheets shredded into strips worked well because they achieved their magic hidden from view. The length, folds, pleats, and front openings of the garments were held in place with ties all pulled tightly around the torso. The process was repeated, beginning with the undergarments, to the exposed outer garment. The wide obi tie was then wound around the upper waist a couple times, hiding the excess folds, pleats, and ties. The obi was cinched tight, compressing the hidden patchwork, and cinched even more––tighter than tight––ensuring the ensemble stayed tidy throughout the rigors of performance. The cinched obi also flattened breasts like pancakes; it was the nape of the neck that mattered.

The Nakamura's had retrieved their large collection of costumes, kimonos, and wigs, which added visual authenticity to the programs. Craftspeople made props and painted sets for the shows. The rapidly struck wooden clappers signaled the curtains to open and the show was on.

When they finished their set, a few young performers took out their books and diligently studied their homework assignments. The rest of us novices were not so inclined; after we finished our act and were allowed to change out of our imprisoning kimonos, we rushed back to watch the rest of the show with our whitewashed makeup still masking our faces. We sat in anticipation for the last act to watch Madam Nakamura, the real pro. She was all grace and so convincing in her role, the audience was crying nonstop at the finale. I was convinced nothing in school could compare to this exposure to theater and a uniquely Japanese art form; it was intoxicating.

There was a bonus after the performance. The host Block treated the entire troupe to a specially prepared dinner or a bento box treat because we had not eaten since lunch. A few host Blocks provided a party almost as good as New Year's Day, with lots of soda pop for us kids. Soda was a rare commodity in those days, and we drank to our good fortune.

The Kabukizaya it was not, but the end result was an amazing and wonderful theatrical production in a remote sagebrush desert of Idaho in 1945.

The practices, rehearsals, and theatrical performances were a welcome distraction that spring. The other was my kitten, Cookie, who was waiting for me at home every day. Classmates Kate and Betsy had walked from their home in Area B to our apartment one Saturday carrying the tiny kitty cat, hoping I could adopt it. I had never owned a live pet, and once I saw the white and tawny bundle of fur, I accepted the gift gladly. Daddy disliked cats and was unhappy with my decision, but Cookie easily endeared itself to him, and he even ended up changing the kitty litter without complaint.

Leaving Camp

After the festivities of the holidays had passed that year came the realization that after spending three Christmases in camp, much of the novelty and excitement of earlier years had faded, and even the special days had become routine. Yet nothing remains static, and our teacher, Mrs. Sparks, announced she was leaving Minidoka with her husband. The Caucasian teachers originally recruited to teach at the camps were leaving for better opportunities on the outside, and no new replacements from the outside were hired now. Young Nisei with college degrees were stepping in to fill the void. Few had previous teaching experience in those years when public school districts did not hire Japanese Americans no matter how qualified their credentials.

Two young Nisei were hired to jointly take over the responsibilities upon Mrs. Sparks's departure. One, a female teacher handled all academics, while a male assistant supported by handling the discipline. The pair were greenhorn teachers, and we were veteran students often taking advantage of the situation. A few classmates went further, managing to ingratiate themselves into their good graces. Our mentors were not immune to favors; impartiality left our classroom with Mrs. Sparks. *Shikata-ga-nai*. Perhaps we will have better teachers next year.

On a broader level with camp-wide consequences was an edict that become effective after the New Year. Public Proclamation #21 had officially restored evacuees their right to return to their former homes. Their reappearance into their communities was rarely popular with the local populace, yet the lure of familiar home towns was strong, and the desire to return home was undiminished. At first, only a trickle of fearless souls ventured back, then others joined them, and the exodus from camp gained momentum.

The departure of young energy drained the vibrancy that once permeated our camp. And as the social dynamics waned, a quietude descended and spread gloom with each newly vacant and lifeless apartment. Camp Jerome in Arkansas had been closed back in 1944, the first camp to close. Entire families were moving away. The food lines in the mess hall became shorter and shorter, then food services were consolidated. Block 17's kitchen closed, and their remaining residents walked over to join us at meal time. Other services were drastically reduced, and inconveniences abounded. The authorities wanted to close the camp, and they wanted us out. The notion of a long incarceration had changed almost as soon as it had begun. Our stay would not be for ten years.

"Daddey, we have to leave camp," I pleaded again and again. "We'll be the only people left in camp!"

"OK, bum-by."

"Why don't you listen? We have to hurry and leave like everyone else, Daddey."

My father made no move to acquiesce to my demands; he did not budge.

I was reminded of another place and time when my neighborhood underwent a similar fate. The same foreboding black clouds settled in and my nightmares began. Empty barracks row after row. Sand blizzards with relentless blistering winds. Daddey and I brave through the storm toward sounds of pounding hammers.

"Where is everyone?" We shout to be heard.

"They all left. The camp is closing." The hammering man shouted to us from his ladder.

"When did they go?"

"Don't know. We're leaving too. Our work is almost done."

Daddey decided I needed a change of scenery, and he needed, peace and quiet from a pestering daughter. He arranged with *Obaa-san* for me to visit her for a month.

She and her husband were farming sugar beets in Payette, Idaho, close to Ontario, Oregon, in an area with a thriving Japanese community of former internees. Aunt Masaye had died and gone on to the Buddhist heaven full of flowers. Aunts Hamayo and Kimiye had not made career plans yet. Uncle Katsumi and stepbrother Teru, had just graduated from high school and were waiting to be drafted. They lived with their parents on the farm and were helping in the fields. I brought Cookie along with me, so I had company to help keep me occupied when the others went out to work. When it became too hot for outside activities, I stayed indoors and played variations of solitaire without having anyone telling me I was wasting my time.

Obaa-san was the same hardworking, good-natured person I remembered, and I followed her around as she did her chores. She collected eggs in the morning, walked across the road to pick asparagus growing wild in a neighboring orchard, and killed and prepared the chicken later served for Sunday Dinner. She started the fire for the *ofuro*, so the water was ready for a hot bath and soak after dinner. Her energy was boundless.

Obaa-san was never enthusiastic about my cat since she was a dog person, and she was not very sympathetic when Cookie mysteriously disappeared one day. I was devastated, and I continued to cry day and night. *Obaa-san* decided I should return to camp a week before the month was up. She had heard through the grapevine that a young man was willing to accept another passenger for his trip to Minidoka to visit family. *Obaa-san* kept the extra sugar and other ration coupons I had brought, and she sent me on my way. I figured my otherwise kind grandmother was the culprit who had taken Cookie for her last ride, and she realized she had best get rid of me before I openly confronted her. She may have remembered my calling her *oni-baba* and that I was apt to morph into a real monster.

I sat in the backseat of the sedan while the driver and the smart young woman who was his other passenger sat in front. The two chatted without taking a break the entire trip, and I listened, engrossed with their grown-up chatter.

THE BOMB

An atomic bomb was dropped on Hiroshima on August 6. News of the bomb's devastation hit the Issei especially hard because so many immigrants had come from that prefecture, including Hayame and Aiko's family. Yoshi was from a different prefecture, but to learn such a destructive device existed and had been dropped on his homeland with horrendous consequences––physically in its devastation and psychologically to Japan's core values––was mind-blowing. Yoshi's belief Japan was winning the war was not based on an ideology where either side was morally right or wrong. The indoctrination was so ingrained, that he felt Japan could never be defeated or lose. He finally understood America had been winning all along, and the war was soon ending with the aid of such a powerful weapon. How could he have been so wrong? How could he have believed the Japanese propaganda that Japan was invincible? He now knew the truth, and he knew he must accept it or remain a perpetual fool.

He went directly to administration and asked permission to leave Minidoka. There is the matter of wanting to return to Japan, he was told.

"I want to see my parents, especially my mother. When I left them, I didn't think I would stay away so long."

"How do you feel about it now?"

"The war will be over soon. I don't know what conditions will be like in Japan if America drops more horrific bombs of the sort dropped on Hiroshima."

"Why do you want to leave camp?"

"If I go outside, I can earn more money. If my parents need help to survive the aftermath of the war, I can help more easily."

"Your illegal entry may disqualify you from returning to your home on the West Coast," Yoshi was told. "We'll process your application and let you know our decision."

He returned home and began organizing our belongings for a return to the outside. He withheld any mention of his intentions until he received confirmation we could leave.

Yoshi was apprehensive about unforeseeable difficulties he was bound to encounter: raising a daughter alone in the outside world removed from the sheltered confines of camp. Never a pessimist, he believed his good karma would continue to serve him well in the future. I was positive there could only be a bright future awaiting us on the outside now that Daddey and I were moving out of camp––leaving someone else to be the last person left in Minidoka.

Somehow those dreams of our being abandoned never died; they went into remission to reappear on those occasions when I was mired with anxiety. Deja vu––the winds still howl, blowing up swirling blizzards of sand as we strain to reach safety along the silent, deserted barracks; we are alone. "Everyone's gone. They all left. Hurry, Daddey, hurry. We have to leave, too."

CHAPTER 15

Spokane Interval,
1945‒1947

No need to dodge potholes when concrete sidewalks paved the way. Traffic lights signaled us to stop or walk at street intersections––all reminders of things I had not dealt with the past three years. My observations of our urban surroundings were perceived with a sharper focus now that I was a grown-up of eleven, and could read signage along our route. The street scenes we passed were lively and full of curiosities worth investigating on another day. "Oh what fun it'll be!"

We turned right at Main Street and passed another tavern with a "No Minors Allowed" sign hanging inside the open door. No loud raucous voices sounded forth from the establishment; only a single man stood behind the counter, leisurely wiping its surface as the long row of empty stools languished in the dark waiting for customers. Why is a minor so unwelcome? Is there something wrong for a person to work in a mine? Like the soldier said, there are different kinds of prejudice. I wonder if Daddey knows about minors. There are a lot of things, American things, he doesn't know lately.

The shoe repair shop next door was a cacophony of loud, shrill grindings and whirling belts, as machines were pressed into service. They don't have a "No Minors" sign on their door, and they appear to be busy. Daddey and I walked quickly past the noise, then slowed to inspect the large storefront display of cameras, small appliances, flatware, silverware, watches, jewelry, jewelry boxes, suitcases, and more. Everything was arranged in a hodgepodge, with varying levels of dust coating the window arrangement. The merchandise did not look new; their age and previous uses varied as much as the selection. Clothes hung from the ceiling and on racks and were overflowing from steamer trunk drawers. Ornamentals and curios of all sorts cluttered the pathway into the depth of the shop. I wanted to go inside and have a better look at the things for sale, but Daddey pressed on. Next door was an empty shop with dirty storefront windows. A couple of workmen were sawing and busily hammering, preparing the vacant space for a new enterprise. I went skipping along the sidewalk looking for other interesting fare, hoping to find a store selling comics or sweets; the possibilities were endless.

"Midori. Come back," Daddey called out.

He stood in front of an open doorway I had hastily skipped past. I looked up in the direction he was looking and saw the two-sided sign protruding above the opening. "Square Deal Hotel," it read with a squiggly arrow pointing down toward the entrance. The sign was old and faded and easily dismissed in the company of boldly painted and fancy-shaped signs, some with glowing neon tubes, all clamoring for attention as they lined the street.

"This is the hotel. Lucky I find it so soon."

I turned to walk back, wondering how I had missed the hotel. A pair of tall wood frame doors with etched glass panels was held open with wood stoppers. "Welcome" was painted in neat block letters on the glass of one door. The other door displayed a cardboard sign: "NO GIRLS." When I looked beyond the open doorway, all I could see were the scuffed and battered stair treads and bruised risers mounting steeply up the narrow, dimly lit stairway. I could only see dark at the top.

"Are we going to stay here, Daddey? It looks spooky," I said.

"Don't worry, Midori. Everything be oh-lite."

Without further hesitation, Daddey led the way up the narrow stairway. He carried our two suitcases, holding them high off the treads, and scooted rapidly up while I straggled behind. I was reluctant to enter that dark abyss at the top, but I was too scared to be left behind by myself, so I grabbed the handrails and slowly pulled myself up, one slow step at a time.

When I got to the top of the stairs, Daddey was resting on a wood chair a few feet in from the landing.

"Climbing steps is good exercise, *neh?*" he said. It had been a number of years since he had climbed a whole flight of stairs, and he was winded.

I looked around, not happy with what I saw.

There was no one in sight to greet us. Daddey repeatedly tapped the button on the metal bell, ringing for attention. The bell sat on a large wood desk, rolling slats pulled up, exposing the owner's papers. A single lamp illuminated the desk and chair where Daddey sat, but its sphere of light was limited. Daylight filtered through the obscure glass in a door facing the street. "Manager" was painted on the glass. There was enough light to define the open area where we waited. I spied an overstuffed black davenport with a stretched out of shape leather covering, and a small table with magazines in disarray ready to spill over onto the floor. Why aren't magazines ever piled neatly? On the opposite side of the hotel lobby was a U-shaped staircase with an overhead skylight intended to splash the interior with light. Instead, thick layers of grime covered the unwashed, wired glass, filtering any sunlight with an overcast cloud. A corridor running the length of the building from front to back was lined on each side with painted wooden doors. The operable glass transoms above each door were the only windows serving most of the rooms. I stopped my exploring when I heard a muffled hum. A short, hunchbacked man not much taller than me appeared from the dark corridor, shuffling toward us, arms akimbo and swinging loosely at his sides. Daddey stood up, and I quickly disappeared behind him.

"Hal-lo. Nomura *desu*," Daddey introduced himself and he followed it up with the usual polite formalities.

The hotel manager/owner insisted Daddey keep his Japanese formalities to a minimum in the future. "I live in America so long, and I almost never see other Japanese. I forget my curtsies. I don't want to offend you with my rusty manners," he said. "Now let me show you to your room. By the way, my name is Ijima."

He resumed his interrupted guttural humming and led us up the stairway to the second floor of the hotel and down a corridor to the very rear of the building. "It's the only room with a window to the light shaft, Nomura-*san*," he said. "The two rooms in the front have windows facing the street, but they are both occupied now. All the other rooms have no window."

The bare bulb hanging naked from the middle of the ceiling, having lost its decorative shade eons ago, came to life with the twist of a knob. The lightbulb's wattage was so minimal that patterns on the faded wall-paper were barely discernible. Dominating the room was a double bed. There was a nightstand with a pitcher and bowl, and a chair. Nothing else cluttered the chipped and worn linoleum floor. Mr. Ijima lifted the shade covering the window to half-mast, and dim daylight managed to filter through layers of dirt and dust. "No view," he said. "Pretty soon, front-room people will move out. You can move in after." His head bobbed up and down in agreement as he turned to leave the room.

This is a new experience; I never stayed in a hotel before. Outside are adventures waiting, shops galore to be explored. This is fun! I thought.

I promptly got sick and stayed in bed for the better part of a week and survived on Campbell's chicken noodle soup warmed up on a hot plate. Daddey had to start his job as dishwasher at the Quality Café, and I had to spend the day alone in our dingy room. He bought me comic books and movie magazines to keep me entertained since he could not stay and tell me stories as he had done when I had the measles in Camp Harmony. These comic books were not the Bugs Bunny and Looney Tunes variety I had in camp; they were Archie comics about teenage antics. My interests were maturing.

School on the Outside

School was about a mile's walk from our hotel home. On leaving the commercial hubbub of Main Street, storefront businesses along my route diminished and ended entirely before I reached the gaping arched tunnel supporting the train tracks above. My path continued past smaller industrial shops and older apartment buildings, before changing to a residential area of small homes. Nestled in its block-sized site in the midst of clapboard-sided homes with picket fences, stood Lincoln School. The handsome two-story brick building with plaster filigree accents was built from the same pattern book as other public schools built in the same era, but I thought it sparkled in its landscaped surroundings, and I loved it on first sight. It was a real school, and it looked like one.

The students inside the building did not resemble the student bodies of other prototype brick school buildings located in more picturesque residential communities far from industry and commerce. Lincoln School's proximity to the inner city provided a socioeconomically diverse student population. The white student majority ranged from comfortable and settled middle class to transient poor. Japanese students constituted the racial minority, and like their white counterparts, they too were divided into a group of settled residents living in neat houses in the immediate neighborhood, and the group of recent arrivals from internment camps living in apartments and hotels. For many, their stay in Spokane was a temporary stopover before returning to the coast and their prewar homes. The school was a good fit for me. My ragtag wardrobe that followed me from camp was no cause for derision nor was my lack of academic proficiency unusual.

Miss Donovan was our teacher: the archetypal dedicated spinster teacher of earlier eras. She had the straight-back stature and stately proportions of a Gibson Girl well past her prime. A corset undoubtedly propelled her robust chest up and forward beyond her flat stomach, and all was supported by thin Babe Ruth legs and ankles. Her gray hair was rolled into a neat bun at the back of her neck, and her reading glasses hung by a ribbon from her neck. She exuded the aura of a grande dame who expected and extracted due respect. Her reputation as a tough teacher extended well beyond Lincoln School's enrollment boundaries, as word-of-mouth fables about her had spread through the decades.

I had heard no stories about Miss Donovan's reputation, unlike the warnings I had carried with me about Mrs. Lewis. Perhaps, fate had sent me to her class to teach me a lesson. Beware of heresy?

I was completely lost again. Lessons I had learned in fifth grade were a blur and a bore, especially after Mrs. Spark's departure. Like a criminal who's sorry for committing misdeeds only after they are caught, I once again regretted my recent lackadaisical scholastic efforts, only because I knew the inevitable consequences waiting for me in the classroom, a dunce cap.

In the waning months of summer when we all knew leaving camp was sooner than eventually, stories about schools on the outside flourished. I had been forewarned.

"My friend said she was really behind in English and history," Dorothy had said.

"What about arithmetic?" Marian asked.

"Arithmetic and PE were the only classes she didn't have trouble with. She thought we were at least one grade behind the outside schools."

"That's bad," we listeners said in unison. Having finished our *odori* lessons, I had stayed to socialize with the experienced dancers.

"Yeah, we really have to study hard when we leave camp or get demoted. Then *haku-jin*, white people, will feel they were right all along, thinking Japanese are dumb." Thereupon Dorothy resumed juggling her three beanbags while adding a fourth mid-air, eyes and hands in perfect coordination.

If brainy Dorothy has to study hard, I'm doomed.

The stories proved to be exaggerated in most cases, and after the initial adjustment period, the internee students had few problems. Margaret had preceded me at Lincoln the year before. She stayed a short time, and having returned to Seattle had left a legacy nevertheless. She had been in the other fifth grade class at Stafford School. I had never met her, but had heard she was exceptionally smart, and her abilities along with the diligence and scholarship she had exhibited, eased the way for us who followed. And as for me, I was not singled out as a black sheep.

With renewed diligence, I caught on in time and kept up with the class academically. Initially, I had no close friends to distract me from studying. Miss Donovan was not a terror, despite her reputation. As long as everyone maintained strict discipline in the classroom and persevered with their lessons, the class time flowed quickly as we covered one subject after another to the end of the school day.

Miss Donovan pulled down the rolled wall map brusquely, like rolling down a window shade at night. Displayed was the world map printed as a flat surface with the inevitable distortions: Greenland looming so large. With her oft-used pointer, she pinpointed a spot in Asia. We knew from previous lessons that it was somewhere on the opposite side of the Pacific Ocean.

"When the Japanese soldiers were systematically invading all parts of East Asia, the British who then governed Singapore, decided they could protect the city by directing their fortifications to repulse any and all attack from the sea surrounding them." She swept her pointer in a semi-circle on the blue ocean and continued, "All their guns were aimed facing the sea, and their armies were stationed to repel a naval invasion. The Japanese realized they could not overtake the British with so much gunpowder aimed at the sea, so the Japanese army came by land into Singapore from the north, where the British had practically no fortifications. They had considered an enemy attack by land over such treacherous terrain and conditions as highly improbable."

"Miss Donovan, that's really interesting," Billy blurted out without being called, "but why do we have to hear these war stories? It's all history now; it's about dead people and old stuff."

"I don't believe any of you will ever be confronted with military strategy. If you were, you would avoid a similar miscalculation like the British made. Now the lesson you can learn from this story is that you should not base your decisions on a single assumption. You should consider all factors before you make a final decision."

Billy spoke out again, "Why didn't you just talk about making decisions? You didn't have to tell us all about the British and Singapore, wherever it is."

In the same unhurried tone, she continued, "You needed a story so you'd remember the decision lesson. You learned a little geography, and you learned a little history about the war, which was until very recently a current event."

Billy, the fair-skinned, blond teaser, was not afraid of Miss Donovan. He was the only student who spoke up and asked questions. His freckled, red-haired buddy, Keith, was less vocal and a model student in the classroom, but he joined his pal in riotous play and laughter outside of the classroom. They were the high-spirited ones. On the opposite end of the energy spectrum was Raymond, who often dozed off in class despite Miss Donovan's reprimands. He confessed, one day, he spent his evenings in movie houses, watching showing after showing until they closed. His whole life was movies, and his ambition was to become a movie projectionist in a theater as soon as they gave him a job.

Brothers Joe and Russell joined us later in the school year. They both addressed Miss Donovan as "ma'am," a term I had only heard spoken in movies. Their everyday speech took odd twists, and they were very polite at school. Obviously, they were far from their birthplace. They kept to themselves, too ill at ease to mingle with the rest of us. Another boy from distant parts, Texas perhaps, joined our class, too. He was older than his years and truly out of place in our part of the world. Strange, too, was his name. "TJ's my name; it doesn't stand for anything. Geez, NO, it sure isn't no Tom James or any other sissy name," he explained to inquiries more than once. "Don't you ask me again, you smartass kid."

Students also left our class and our school. Quiet Roderick, who we called Ronnie because the name suited him better, was fairer complexioned than Billy and so reticent he was almost part of the woodwork. He left our rough-and-tumble ways to concentrate on his ballet studies. And at the end of the year, we learned Keith's parents were enrolling him in a different school in another part of town to be better prepared for college in the future.

I became friends with Shirley, whose perky bundle-of-energy ways made her particularly accessible. Her dark hair was naturally curly, unlike my straight, black Asian hair, and the curlicues framed large blue eyes. A sea of freckles surrounded a pert, upturned nose and full, puffy lips, that never ceased moving––that is, except in Miss Donovan's class. She was greatly admired by the boys, who pestered her for attention. She reciprocated by teasing them. She talked the talk of grown-ups, and the boys could not stay away.

Then Melody moved to Spokane with her mother. They lived in an apartment on my route to school, so I often waited for her outside their building, and we walked to school together. She was very self-assured for her age, and she gave the impression of being much older than she was. Her light brunette hair fell straight to her shoulders as if she had just run a brush through her freshly shampooed hair. No facial feature dominated; they all contributed and blended into a very pretty face. She was reserved, while Shirley was loud. When the boys got tired of playing games with Shirley, they noticed lovely Melody.

"Well, are you my friend or Melody's?" Shirley bellowed at me. Since the boys had shifted their attention from her, she considered Melody a threat and rival. As far as she was concerned, there were two sides, either hers or Melody's.

"But, Shirley, I like you both. I'm your friend, and I'm Melody's friend," I countered.

"No, you can't be my friend and Melody's friend at the same time. Now, you choose one of us."

"No, I won't," I said. I was moving onto neutral ground. It was time to find another friend.

There were other Japanese girls in the class who were cordial and we got along during school, but went our separate ways after school. Their families were rebuilding their lives and settling in to pursue the postwar

American dream. They were permanent residents. Daddey and I were from Seattle and suspect transients whose stay in Spokane was likely to be temporary. By any measure, I led an unconventional and unsupervised life, that well-meaning parents found suspect, too.

Life at the Hotel

No kids lived in and around our hotel. There was no one to explore the neighborhood with me, and I found it tedious covering the same ground day after day. I spied someone with roller skates one day, and I knew it was the means to venture further afield. To my surprise, Daddy readily agreed to buy me a pair of skates when I asked. He even showed me how to clamp them onto my shoes.

"Yes, I skate in New York when I was young," he said. "So many places in Central Park, I roller skate."

My metal rollers rumbled along the concrete sidewalks, churning out gnashing groans, changing their pitch as the road surfaces changed. I was soon scooting past pedestrians and swerving around obstacles with abandon. The food market across the street was a regular destination, although I merely walked on my skates while in the store. My business there was to buy bread and baloney for my lunch, and a Twinkie for dessert.

No wonder everyone always talked about what they would do after leaving camp. There is so much to see and do on the outside.

I wrangled my shoes out of the clamps, and with hands clutching the straps, I hoisted my skates onto my back. My ritual was to run up the hotel entry stairs and scoot through the lobby to the stairs leading upstairs, hoping all the while that Mr. Ijima was out of sight. He was at his post at the desk as often as he was absent. When he was bent over writing entries in his workbook or shuffling his daily newspaper, I quietly crept past him. When he was just sitting daydreaming, or looked to be snoozing with half-shut eyes, I ran past him as fast as possible to be out of his sight.

"Why you run in the hotel, Midori? You should run outside, walk inside, *neh*," Daddey said as I came in panting for breath.

"He is so scary."

"Who is scary?"

"Mr. Ijima," I said.

"He is very nice man. He is not scary."

"He is too, scary. He peeks at me like a monkey all the time."

"Ohhh, me see. Hmm. He is not so handsome," Daddey agreed. "In Japan, there was very famous, very smart ruler who people say looked like monkey. He was very good ruler in Japanese history. Men think it is OK if man is not handsome, but women like handsome men."

Daddey and I were on different wavelengths. Monkey ruler, not handsome, not scary?

He continued, "Midori, you should be kind to Mr. Ijima. He has very sad story. When he come to America, he worked on the railroads. Those days, it was very hard work and dangerous. He no gamble or drink whiskey like lotsa men. He saved his money. He wanted wife and family, so he paid for picture bride from Japan. He went to Seattle to meet her boat. When she see Mr. Ijima, her new husband, for first time, she run away. He looked and looked for her, but never could find."

"That's awful. Didn't his picture bride have a picture of him, too? She could have said no if she didn't want to marry a man who looked like Mr. Ijima. And she didn't have to come to America."

"Maybe he borrow somebody picture. Maybe he send picture of za handsome, young man. She find out he trick her, and she disappear."

"Then it was his fault, after all."

"No, it was not his fault. He was not lucky. It was his karma to be born not so handsome. Girls no like boyfriend or husband to look like monkey. He never say he borrow picture of good-looking man. I guess it is his secret." Daddey never had such a problem, but his heart ached for a man so unlucky.

I tried to think of our landlord in a more kindly light, and I no longer ran away from him. I remembered ancient Mat-*san* as a small man bent over with age whose personality and animated face kind of resembled a chimpanzee. He was endearing and approachable. In contrast, Mr. Ijima was far less sociable and lumbered along like a solitary little gorilla. He almost never said a word to me, and I didn't have the social skills to initiate polite salutations, so we acknowledged each other's presence with nods of our heads. I came to realize that what I had thought were creepy glances were actually his way of watching to keep me from harm's way when I was in his establishment. In his own benign way, he had befriended me.

Outside the door to Mr. Ijima's living quarters was a side table with a jumble of newspapers and a few magazines, much like the fluctuating pile in *Obaa-san*'s kitchen. Only these were not Japanese or girlie magazines—there were two especially thick commemorative issues of the MGM studios. For a movie magazine aficionado, the booklets were far better than the Photoplay and Silver Screen copies I bought and studied. Now that Mr. Ijima was no longer my nemesis, I sat on the lobby couch and pored through the two issues, putting names to faces in the large group photo of the studio's actors and actresses. I noticed Mr. Ijima clicking his tongue in his mouth as he passed. Was he smiling? I wondered.

As he had promised, within a month of our arrival, Daddey and I had moved into a larger front room with windows letting in sunlight and the noises of the street below. Once all our luggage arrived, we felt we were settled in. Daddy cooked my meals on the hot plate between his shifts washing dishes, and there was space to set up the clothes rack to dry our laundered clothes. Our room was much cozier than our unit in camp, along with a number of other inconveniences, but the amenities of living on the outside made it tolerable.

A single unisex restroom located on each level of the hotel proved adequate, as there was never a line of people waiting their turn outside the door. A separate room on the first level next to the U-shaped stairs housed a lone bathtub for the hotel's guests. There were never conflicts about its use among the hotel residents, either; the "uninvited" roomers were the problem.

I put on my new chenille bathrobe; it was an item I convinced Daddey I needed, though I had been hankering for it since that blanket trauma during the Christmas tableau. Discreetly wrapped and tied, I scooted down the corridor, peeking down the stairwell to see if the coast was clear, then dashing to the bathtub room and locking the door.

Click. I turned on the light and promptly shut my eyes to avoid witnessing the traffic jam playing out below. I sensed the rustling vibrations as the battalion of leaderless critters scattered, this way and that, seeking cover. Little ones, medium-sized ones, and big ones raced crazily on the floor, the walls, the door, and the bathtub. I saw the wild scramble if I opened my eyes too soon. I shivered and cringed with closed eyes until I felt the rush was really over. A small colony would still be skittering about, undecided about which dark corner offered the best place to hide. I walked to the tub, taking care not to step on any. It was not Buddhist teachings to not kill any living creatures that kept me from stomping on them; it was to avoid any gruesome crunching or squishing sounds, and the dead bug goop getting stuck to the undersides of my slippers. I thumped the side of the tub to scare any foolhardy ones still up and about before setting the plug and turning on the water.

"Hurry up and get out of my tub, you stupid cockroach… this is not a swimming pool!" I screamed. Usually the pinhead-sized ones did not know their directions and were unpredictable. They were still itsy-bitsy and the last ones to find cover, but they would all grow up to be ugly like the others; with undulating antennas and squat, icky, greasy bodies set on perpetual motion legs. I might have tolerated the cockroaches if they had all made a beeline to a dark hidden crevice and stayed out of sight for the duration of my bath, but no, the dimwitted ones zigzagged endlessly before disappearing. Miraculously, the entire army would finally disappear into its trenches while the light was on. A straggler or two might sometimes risk drowning, so I kept a close eye on stray frolickers. In addition, there were adventurers that had to be whip-snapped and sent airborne for having hid in my towel or robe. I shook them vigorously. Up. Down. Snap. Up, down, snap. "Arrrrgh! I hate you, ugly cockroaches."

I later learned the procedure was to stick a hand inside to turn on the bathroom light and wait five minutes by the doorway before entering. The wayward army was usually under cover with a mere handful still on patrol.

A New Friend

Another Japanese girl joined Miss Donovan's class. I had never seen her before. She was obviously not from Minidoka. I had shared classes with two-thirds of those in my grade and had seen the other third in proximity during our last school year in camp. There was no mistake.

She sat quietly at a desk on the blackboard side of the classroom. Loose black curls ringed the bold features of her face. Thick eyebrows projected over alert, darting eyes, and a far from dainty set of lips betrayed its initial quietude. She was neither friendly nor unfriendly. She just preferred to be left alone. But no one could ignore her grossly scarred left leg, nor was anyone so brash to question her about it. Curiosity fed whispered conjectures, always behind her back.

"Frances, my dear," Miss Donovan said as she called on the new girl. "Could you do the class a big favor? Everyone is absolutely enchanted with the unique scar engraved on your leg. Would you show them the scar and tell everyone how you happened to get it?"

She walked to the front of the class with head bowed; she looked back to Miss Donovan, who smiled and nodded her head.

"When I was about four years old, my dad backed up his truck and accidentally ran over my leg," she said. "I was playing on the driveway, and he didn't see me when he started up the motor. My broken bone mended, but they couldn't fix up the flesh and skin like it was before. The doctors said maybe when I'm older, they can operate and make it look better, more normal."

She twisted her left leg, revealing the oftentimes obscured inner side, and exposed the scar in full view for us all to see. The scar ran the length of her inner calves from knees to her ankles. The skin was shiny and taut in areas surrounding bundled scar tissue. It was grotesque. The students, who had gathered around the front-row desks for a better look, quietly turned and went back to their desks without comment.

The exhibit had exhausted our curiosity, and Frances's scar was no longer a topic of whispered gossip.

It took a whole week before I noticed Frances walking home from school in the same direction as me. She was headed toward the concrete tunnel, the passageway for both cars and pedestrians and our connection to downtown and home.

"Wait for me. Can I walk home with you?" I called out.

She said nothing. She just stopped and waited for me to catch up.

"How do you like our school?" I asked, trying to make conversation.

"It's OK, I guess," she replied without elaboration.

We walked in silence. We were almost at the end of the tunnel when she chirped, "I hate it when this place smells like *shi-shi*. Pee-ewe!"

I burst out laughing. "Lucky it doesn't smell so bad all the time, cause we have to walk through this tunnel every single day to go to school."

"Maybe on Saturday, I'll look for a different way to walk to school so I won't have to smell it." The ice was broken, and we could not stop talking after that.

We reached Main Street, and I turned left and Frances turned right. She lived at the Barnard Hotel a few blocks away, making it that much further away from the noise and congestion of the city center than the hotel I called home. Her hotel was a four-story brick building surrounded by single-story shops, which permitted window placement in all the hotel units. The interior was brighter, roomier, and nary a cockroach was spied there. The hotel was owned and operated by a Japanese family, and the clientele were mostly Japanese living there by the month. On our arrival to Spokane, Daddey and I had visited Mr. and Mrs. Ujimoto, who had lived there since leaving Minidoka. They were the housekeepers at the Spanish-style mansion in Seattle I remembered so well. The couple's residence in Spokane was, in fact, instrumental in persuading Yoshi to move to the city when we had to leave camp. He was not allowed to move back to Seattle and the West Coast initially, and that is how our sojourn to Spokane came to be.

Frances shared a room with her older sister, Margaret, while her mother and second husband shared another. While the adults worked, Margaret kept a wary eye on her younger sister, but Frances was almost as unsupervised as I was. We became constant companions.

When Lincoln School held a fundraising paper drive, it was Frances who decided she and I should canvass the smaller businesses around town.

"You want me to ask strangers to donate their old newspapers and magazines? I'm too scared to talk to strangers. Let's not do it," I whined.

"What a coward! What's there to be afraid of?" Frances said;

"They might be mean and nasty to us, that's what!"

"Then we'll just walk away, that's what."

She would walk jauntily into a shop, leading the way, while I shuffled along behind her. "Hi. Our school is having a paper drive. Do you have any old newspapers or magazines?" We collected a few items, a magazine or a newspaper or two, from time to time; more often we left empty-handed.

The entrance to the hotel showed little promise. The small lobby was bright and clean, old and a bit straggly in a genteel way. Frances gave her usual spiel anyway. The elderly desk clerk smiled. "Indeed, we have some old magazines. We were planning to have them removed, but you girls are welcome to take them for your paper drive." We were led down a narrow stairway to the elevator pit, which was strewn with piles and piles of old LIFE magazines. We had hit the mother lode.

Since neither of us had many restrictions placed on us, we spent our time away from school browsing through downtown stores, and often just walked to different parts of the city, as far away as we had time and energy. Frances was resourceful, too, and we found the downtown library, the ice skating rink, and later the outdoor amusement park. But our favorite pastime remained window-shopping, an activity that consumed hours going from one store to another, as girls are wont to do. Sundays, however, were reserved for the movie matinee. We consulted with Raymond, the movie addict, on the best movie showing in Spokane that week. We never ran into him in any theater, though we believed him when he claimed he saw them all, good and bad movies alike.

The Fox Theater was the poshest in town; the Art Deco decor made watching a show there twice as good.

"I can understand why the heroine in a movie has to be the most beautiful, but why is the heroine in every book always the prettiest, too?" I asked as we walked home from our show.

"Why should that bother you?" Frances asked in return.

"Because there are more unbeautiful people in the world, and we don't ever get the breaks or the good-looking guys."

"Regular people have to work harder. Think Abraham Lincoln."

"He's special. I mean normal people."

"I wish I were a normal person without a scar."

"Sorry, Frances, I'll try to remember how lucky I am."

At the end of the school year, we were all promoted to the seventh grade. With no separate junior high school in our area, Lincoln included seventh and eighth grades. Conveniently, we students would return to the same building in the fall. Miss Donovan announced she planned to teach one more year then retire at the end of the term in June. And, she had decided to move up one grade to teach the seventh grade. That meant Miss Donovan was to be our teacher a second year. She never explained what prompted her decision to take us on again. Perhaps she was tired and wanted to avoid the challenge of breaking in another batch of raw students. We were not her brightest or her best; we were accommodating and tried our best to please her, and she understood.

Daddey and I moved out of the Square Deal Hotel and into the Savoy Apartments. The three-story walk-up building was on the other side of the arched tunnel that supported the railroad tracks. We were further removed from the commercial core, making it less convenient to downtown stores and markets, but, it was closer to school for me. We were located in a transitional zone marked by scattered empty lots of dirt and weeds. Within a block or two, small single-family residences replaced the open, weed-choked sites. We had moved to the other side of the tracks, although it was sometimes hard to know which side was the better side of the tracks. The brick building belonging to the Sunshine Baking Company, manufacturer of crackers similar to the famous Ritz Crackers, loomed large directly across the street, obstructing sight lines to the north, including the trains chugging past on their elevated rails, and filled the fresher up-town air with the aroma of baking crackers. There was no escape from the sounds of rattling trains with their piercing whistles, although we never saw them through our windows.

Our third-level unit was reached by a wide set of stairs with daylight streaming through windows without filters of dust or grime. From the corridor, we entered our unit directly into the cozy kitchen, which housed a gas stove, sink, and icebox, along with a table and two chairs. Later, a wooden apple crate was nailed to the outside window frame of our unit, which proved to be more efficient in the winter than the insulated contraption sitting in the kitchen, which required blocks of ice. Practically every unit was fitted with the makeshift food cooler hanging outside the window. From the exterior, these appendages resembled air-conditioner units fitted into window openings of buildings without central air-conditioning. Our food cooler was perfect for congealing Jell-O in the winter, except during the coldest nights, when the gelatin froze solid.

The larger second room with wood sash windows was large enough to accommodate the double bed for Daddey and a twin-sized bed for me. The potbelly stove in the corner sat closest to my bed. Daddey set a large scavenged wood tabletop on the trunk, and we shared it as a desk. The weight of our dictionaries stabilized our writing platform from moving about. I sat there doing homework, and Daddey wrote out his poems.

Next to the stairs and at the end of the hall at each level were two sets of restrooms, one for men and one for women. Installed in each restroom were two water closets and a bathtub, each with its own enclosure. And there was not one cockroach in sight. What a luxury to soak in a tubful of warm water without little critters crawling around looking to test my bathwater. I knew we had risen one notch closer to Dick and Jane's typical American dwelling. Yoshi was called George at work. Since the only acquaintances who had known him prior to our move to Spokane were the Ujimoto's, there was no confusion with the name switch. The couple was invited to return to Seattle by their prewar employer, Dr. Buckner, and they left Spokane to resume their lives as trusted housekeeper and cook for the physician and his new wife. Yoshi now had no ties to former friends in his new environs; his isolation was unintended but complete.

Yoshi had little time in his day to cultivate new friendships or spend much time on his poetry. He worked breakfast, lunch, and dinner shifts, and rushed home between shifts to perform necessary chores and cook dinners for a daughter, before walking back to begin his next shift. His walks were his free time to count the *On* of his budding new poems. Before their departure, Ujimoto-*san* had passed on a tip about a dishwashing job at a different restaurant.

Calling Joe's Café a restaurant was a misnomer. It was a true hole-in-the-wall diner. It was a storefront with a door opening into a narrow aisle that accommodated two walking, not abreast, but sideways, crab style. The aisle was bordered on one side by an oft-painted plaster wall and on the opposite side by a single row of plastic-covered stools bolted to the floor. The counter extended nearly the length of the aisle but was cut short by the swinging gate at the far end to access the service side aisle. The cooking grill and ovens sat along the sidewall next to the front window displaying the cooked roasts under heat lamps ready to be sliced to order. The simple menu was printed on a large painted board hung on the wall near the entry. A back room housed the dishwashing sinks, larger utensils, and other kitchen paraphernalia best kept out of sight. Yoshi spent his working hours in that back room.

Joe was not the owner's name either. It was Bill. His wife was called Min, to the merriment of their customers who thought they were the Asian version of Wallace Beery and Marie Dressler in the movie with those names. Bill, the owner/cook, was neither gruff nor grouchy; he was a kind-natured man with a ready smile. Min more closely resembled her movie counterpart. She was the no-nonsense assistant whose bark was worse than her bite. They were both beyond middle age and beyond caring about youth long gone. Their life centered on the diner; they worked long hours together, and they were comfortable and content.

By all appearances, Min and Bill looked and acted like a well-matched couple long past celebrating a silver wedding anniversary. Yet, this was not the case. Bill's first wife of many years left him shortly after the war began. She no longer wanted to be married to a Jap. She packed her bags and was gone. Min had endured a miserable early marriage without children or solicitude. Her husband died, leaving her money and insurance benefits. The once friendly townspeople where she lived turned hostile at the onset of war, so Min packed up and moved to a less hostile locale. She found work waiting on tables to supplement her benefits. Bill, who had drifted to Spokane, was cooking in the same establishment. They got together, decided Joe's Café was a viable business venture, and they prospered.

The cafe offered a limited menu of roast beef, pork, and ham, either in a sandwich or plated with sides. They also served a Denver sandwich and a daily special. The food was simple, ample and tasty, and served with jolly good humor. Though they were not open for breakfast, Bill started the day early to roast the meats in time for lunch. Min arrived before the lunch opening, and Daddey started his shift at that time, too. They understood Daddey's responsibilities at home, and accepted his afternoon break without question. Later, they hired a waitress to work part time to help Min, though their business did not warrant more help. Pretty Amie was young, married, and the mother of two.

Her husband, Kazuo, was young and handsome. Together they looked like an Asian movie-star couple; the reality belied the appearances. His bad temper and tantrums got him fired from the jobs he managed to find. He often drifted away for indefinite periods and, on his reappearance, returned to his abusive ways. Min hired Amie during one of Kazuo's disappearances, when the young woman was desperate for money. Min hoped the job might help alleviate the young woman's situation at home, and she also excused Amie's unpredictable absences from work. When she showed up, she often sported a discolored bruise or two still visible through her pancake makeup. When all was right, Amie just had to stand behind the counter and smile. The customers, even the grouchy ones, took notice and were happy to gaze on such a pretty countenance. When she laughed and teased the men, each beamed and glowed at the attention and scheduled a return visit.

She was great for a business whose customers were unattached men wanting a simple meal.

"Amie, now you go straight home tonight for sure. OK, honey?" Min said.

Amie swung her coat nonchalantly on her back and strode down the aisle, her high heels clicking. She turned to Min and flashed her a smile with eyes twinkling.

"Yes, Min, mommy," she said before disappearing through the door.

Min watched her leave, and she shook her head. The day of reckoning came sooner than Min anticipated.

"Oh, Min.... what can I do-o-o?" she sobbed on the phone.

"What's the matter, Amie? What happened?" Min asked.

"He's crazy. He's gone berserk. I don't know what to do!"

"What's that husband of yours done now?" Min demanded. "What did he do? Did he hit you?"

When the crying subsided, Amie replied, "Hits me all the time, that's not new. This time he took all my clothes and burned them! I have no clothes to wear!" she wailed. "He said I can't leave the house; he made sure I can't run away! Oh, what'll I do, Min?"

The movie magazines I had become addicted to buying promoted the glamorous lifestyles of the stars, but they also exposed their woes. Beautiful people have their problems in real life, the same as in Hollywood, I learned. In those days, I lived closer to the high dramas, some trivial and others worse, being played out in our part of town. The scenarios had more variety than the soap operas I heard on the radio, and they were real-life events. In comparison, the settled residents appeared to lead predictable, staid lives like the residents of my dream house. We had moved up all right; we were in a transitional sphere, a sort of permanently settled transients.

A Funeral in Seattle

"Daddey. What are you doing? Why are you packing?" I asked. I had come home late for dinner, but he had not gone back to work yet.

"You eat, Midori. I am busy."

"You bought a new suitcase. Are we going someplace? So, where are we going?"

He was folding a set of underwear into a corner of the new suitcase. "I go to Seattle tomorrow. You stay in Spokane. Daddey be gone maybe four, five days."

"How come you're going to Seattle? How come I can't go, too?"

"You go to school. You stay here." He said as explanation, "I go to funeral in Seattle. Cousin Yukimasa, he die."

No one had to tell me a funeral was no entertainment for a kid.

I had a week's supply of baloney and bread, some leftover rice, and a dozen eggs to stave off hunger. Daddey asked the landlord to keep an eye on me, and Daddey went on his mission assured everything was under control. Five uneventful days later, he returned. He brought back a shopping bag full of *omiyage* for me: Japanese sweets, a vast array of trinkets, and a stuffed teddy bear. A stuffed teddy bear? Sometimes he thought I was still a kid.

After his return, I noticed he sometimes gritted his teeth and bristled with anger at unexpected moments and muttered to himself, "*Oni.*"

Such a display of ill humor was uncharacteristic. There were rare explosions when he got really mad at me when I had knowingly pushed him over the limit, but this was different, and his anger was not directed at me.

"Gosh, Daddey, why are you so mad?"

"So selfish woman. All the time, money, money, money, money for herself!"

Daddey and his aunt had another argument while in Seattle. It was the first time they had met since she had left to live permanently in New York City. They managed to be civil to each other at first, then shortly after the funeral, Aunt Ito approached him.

"Nephew, will you tell those people the insurance money is rightfully mine."

"What do you mean? His wife's name is on insurance paper."

"That's just paper. All the money from the greenhouse, including the rent you paid, went to Yukimasa for his dental school expenses and to set up his dental business. I didn't get a penny in return."

"Your son inherited the business from his father, and he worked it until he went to dental school. Aunt, you went to New York and got yourself a new husband."

"My present husband, your cousin, whose father was the first *chonan*, and... Look here, you should have warned me he was a drunk with an ever-roaming eye for women. You knew that––you're responsible. I blame you for the miserable life I've led since I left Seattle."

"What? You're crazy. Everyone warned you to be prudent and stay in Seattle instead of running off to New York."

"Nevertheless, that insurance is rightfully mine."

"You selfish old witch..."

"*Nani?*"

Yoshi's face flashed red-hot, and the words tumbled out of his mouth. "Your son died, leaving a wife and two young sons, one a mere infant. She needs the money for support. How is she going to live?"

"That is her problem."

"You mean-hearted demon, bloodsucking monster of the first order..."

"Quit calling me insulting names, nephew of my first husband." She returned to her original premise and hissed, "It's payment for an old debt owed me. Get that through your thick head."

"You heartless witch, you're worse than I ever imagined."

"You disrespectful offal, offspring of that self-serving, sniveling shrew, I hope I never see you again! Now do as I said."

ANOTHER SCHOOL YEAR

Variety was added to our usual school subjects in seventh grade; the girls were offered Beginning Cooking. What a surprise to find a basement room in the school furnished with three sets of model kitchens. They resembled those models pictured in magazines that activated my dreams.

There is a proper way to wash dishes, we were told; glassware first, flatware next, followed by dishes, and lastly pots and pans. Separate soapy wash water, then rinse and dry. So many items to wash; it was four times more than everything we had in our kitchen. And everything was immaculate. We spent half the session scrubbing and polishing to maintain the look of perfection.

We started our cooking lessons with a breakfast menu: fruit cocktail assembled from scratch. Wonders of wonders, it did not come from a can. Scrambled eggs with bits of vegetables became an omelet, and fried eggs which began as sunny-side-up, when flipped, was an "over-easy." My favorite was the Eggs Benedict. Daddey already knew all the menu items I told him we had learned to make. He had somehow failed to pass on that bit of information before.

"In New York, I worked in restaurant and for very rich family. I watch the cooks. Sometime they give us sample to taste."

"Is that why you like cheese? In camp, nobody else liked cheese"

"In Japan, we no have cheese. Japanese country people don't like cheese smell. American-style restaurant have many cheese, so I taste. I like cheese very much."

Daddey was sure dumb about a lot of things, it seemed to me; his spoken English was awful, and there were fewer and fewer things he could enlighten me about when I had questions, but he sometimes surprised me at the number of things he did know.

At school, Miss Donovan was slowly preparing for her retirement. Her accumulation of personal memorabilia was being dispersed. The potted palm and creeping vines were entrusted to Mr. Wilcox, the school janitor. She was giving away her collection of old National Geographic magazines to the library. Her collection of books, long stored in the small bookshelf in the back of our classroom, was being given away, too. A student could keep any book he or she wanted on one condition; he or she had to give an oral report on the book in front of the class. Extra credits were included with the report

By the time I got to the bookcase, it was nearly depleted. Everyone had zeroed in on the easy reading or picture books. I studied the titles that were left. It was like going to the wrong section in a library and finding only books on arctic entomology or advanced astrophysical theories. The books I saw had zilch appeal. I finally picked up a volume with a red cover. It had twice as many pages as the others. I flipped through the pages; it had no photos to reduce the text, and the subject was not one I wanted to tackle: The History of China. I was ready to put it back on the shelf.

"I'm so glad you chose that book, Sylvia," I heard her say. "What?"

"I thought for a while no one would select it. That would have been a disappointment." She continued, "It is not an easy book, for sure, but it will be very rewarding, my dear."

I was stuck with the book. I was not going to disappoint Miss Donovan.

The book was a greater challenge than I expected. The first chapter exploring theories of the Chinese people's origin; was incomprehensible. The second chapter about the different ethnics was boring. Then as aspects of Chinese culture were explored, being it was so different from European history and Western experiences, I found it fascinating. I wanted to share my new enthusiasm with the class in my oral report. Miss Donovan, who was already a China buff, loved my report. Everyone else in the class was bored to death.

It was easier for Billy to sidetrack Miss Donovan now, and when she got off the subject, we sat back and listened to her stories. We were happy to delay our lessons, until recess if possible.

"We once had a Jewish neighbor who on Saturdays came running out of his house and shouted at us to be quiet because he and his family were observing their Sabbath. As Catholics, Sunday is our Sabbath. Well, on Sundays, that same neighbor ran his machines and made a racket. We on our side of the fence called out to him and told him to stop the noise, 'This is our Sabbath!'" Her lips would curl with pleasure as she recalled the long-ago dispute. "Do unto others what you would have others do unto you. Isn't that right?"

I wonder if Saturday was Rebecca's Sabbath, too. She was Jewish. Interesting their Sunday is on Saturday just like the Seventh-day Adventists, but I don't think they're related. I'll have to meet someone Jewish someday and ask them.

"Miss Donovan?"

"Yes, Billy, do you disagree?" our teacher asked.

"Well… They say to turn your other cheek."

"Splendid. You've learned your Sunday school lesson well."

Finding Adventures

Frances and I elected ourselves to be the committee to buy Miss Donovan's farewell gift. We collected money from everyone in the class, and we began our search for the appropriate gift. We went to Woolworth's lunch counter to discuss our mission.

"I finally saved enough from my allowance. I'm splurging today, and I'm ordering my favorites: a clubhouse sandwich and a chocolate milkshake," I announced to no one in particular.

"Nah, I like malts better any day," Frances said. "I'll just have a tuna sandwich and water. I spent most of my allowance already."

At thirty-five cents, a clubhouse sandwich was my rare treat. I had to save part of my allowance for weeks to afford it. "We could buy her a nice fountain pen," I said between bites of my rare treat.

"She won't use a fountain pen very much when she's retired. She won't have to grade papers and all that kind of stuff."

"How about getting some really nice stationery? She'll still write letters to her friends."

"That's not a very good idea," Frances said. "When she uses it all up, there won't be any reminder we gave her a present."

"This is going to be hard. I thought it'd be fun to look and shop.

By the way, do you want to finish my shake? It's too much for me."

We crisscrossed downtown in our search. We eventually settled on a wooden music box. Whenever she lifted the lid and the music played, we hoped she would think of our class. Tears came to her eyes when we presented it to her, so she must have liked it.

Frances's mother had suggested she sign up for sewing classes at the Singer Sewing Machine Store, so I joined her, and we kept busy for a while being little seamstresses––but what else to do? We took the long ride out to the amusement park, but we needed to conserve our coins because the rides quickly depleted my piggy bank.

"I like the roller coaster the best. Only the first hump is the scariest. The other ones aren't. Besides, the ride is too short. I wish I could ride on a really long, scary one," I said to Frances. "When we reach the top of the first hump, we're so high up, up above the telephone poles and everything. When I fly in my dreams, I have to work really hard to get above the telephone poles and wires so I won't go crashing into them."

"People do not fly, silly. They don't fly in their dreams, either. All you have to do is to get on an airplane, and it will fly you wherever you want to go."

"Well, I can too fly in my dreams. But I can't fly as high as I want." I wanted to soar. Frances was not a believer. "Don't you ever dream about something that's not true, but you wish could happen?"

"Of course I do." "Well, what then?"

"I dream I was with my dad."

"You said my dream is impossible. Is your dream impossible or possible?" I asked.

"If you think about it that way, my dream is possible. But yours is still impossible," Frances said.

"If yours is possible and you want it to happen, why don't you make it happen?"

"You mean I should go to California and see my dad?"

"I'll go with you. There should be some really big roller coasters in California. The movie stars live in Hollywood, too." My enthusiasm bubbled. "It'll be a fun adventure!"

By giving up my dream Schwinn bicycle, I had just enough money to buy a bus ticket to Los Angeles. Then I could stay with Frances and her father in California before returning to Spokane. I needed to borrow some money from Daddey for the return trip.

"Daddey, I'm going to go to California with Frances. She's going to visit her father in Los Angeles. I need to borrow some money from you."

"How you go to California?"

"By bus. I have enough money for my ticket."

"You stay in hotel? Where you eat?"

"That's why I need to borrow some money."

"We see," he said and dropped the subject.

Frances was busy persuading her mother to allow her to go. Their encounters were more traumatic than mine with Daddey. She became more determined the more her mother resisted.

Daddey realized we had made up our minds that we were going to California no matter how impractical our plans. Frances and I were both too headstrong to be dissuaded from our new mission. To head off a long, protracted battle and to assure our safety, Daddey said he would join us. "I need vacation, too. I think I like to see California."

Daddey went to visit Frances's mother, telling her his plan to go on the trip and be our chaperone. During their conversation, she acknowledged Frances was unhappy about her present situation and perhaps a visit to California would do her some good.

Frances's mother finally agreed Frances could go.

Daddey notified Bill he was going on vacation.

We packed our suitcases, and we were on our way. The trip was hot and uncomfortable. The network of freeways had not been constructed yet, making the trip a long one as we passed through every little burg along the route. At regular intervals, the bus stopped at a roadside diner/ gas station, where we all took our restroom break, and on longer stops we got a bite to eat. Luckily, Daddey accompanied us and paid for our meals—I had not included the cost of meals in my earlier budget calculations. The long spells between stops were monotonous. The bus swayed and rumbled along, and hiccupped when it hit a patch of rough road. Our train ride to camp had been more comfortable, but our destination now was to a place of our choosing.

At the beginning of the trip, we could not stop chattering. Soon our initial excitement wore off, and we spent the time dozing, mostly in a hazy state of consciousness. Without air-conditioning, our passage through central California was miserably hot. The suffocating heat subsided at night, and we were able to sleep.

Our bus slowed to a stop for our first morning break that day. The stop was a good-sized diner in an isolated stretch of highway, an oasis without another man-made structure as far as we could see. Above the deserted desert, the entire sky for miles to the horizon glowed a royal rose-purple splendor, infusing our spirits with wonder and awe. We must surely be close to heaven to witness such overwhelming grandeur, I felt. Slowly, the solemnity receded as sun streaks breached the eastern horizon, bleaching away the royal rose to reveal the eternal blue sky. In that short time before daybreak, I witnessed a glorious sunrise in the desert that was so awesome, I was convinced it had to be the handiwork of a god. There surely is a God of heaven and earth.

Eventually, familiar vegetation began appearing in the landscape, and although I searched the hills and valleys we passed, the land was not a jungle of palm trees nor did it look like an exotic wonderland as I had imagined. The rigors of the ride faded as we neared our destination.

We arrived at the bus station happy the trip was finally over. The congestion at the depot was maddening. Daddey was getting our bags, and I was following Frances as she searched the crowd.

"Daddy, Daddy," she shouted. She ran to a tousled-haired, well-built man who then swooped her up into his arms. They were talking and crying at the same time. He was still carrying Frances in his arms as he made his way to Daddey and me.

"I'm Frances's father. Thank you very much for bringing her down to Los Angeles. You are very kind," he said as he tried to reach out his hand to Daddey. Frances was too heavy to hold with one arm, so he nodded instead.

"My dad is taking me home to his house. Maybe we can get together sometime before you go back to Spokane, OK?" Frances said.

"Yeah, that's swell," I answered. I waved to her as she and her father disappeared through the depot doors. I never saw her again. We corresponded for a while, but that ended in time, too.

I spent an activity-filled two weeks in Los Angeles, although I never saw any movie stars during the entire time. I asked, and Daddey took me to the amusement parks in the area so I could test the roller coasters. I was seeking more thrills than I could get from the one in Spokane. Indeed, they were longer and went higher, dropping us for a few weightless seconds before climbing up again to repeat the fall. The best ride swerved way out toward the ocean before careening back to safety. Daddey appeared to be enjoying these excursions in a different way. Since we scheduled our amusement park visits early when they were still opening up for business, Daddey usually strolled through the still deserted arcade alleys and chatted with a friendly proprietor or two. After several rides, I was ready for other adventures. Santa Anita was closed for the season, but we managed to ride the streetcar to Hollywood Park, and Daddey played the horses without much luck. I browsed the downtown department stores, then went to an afternoon matinee or two. In the meantime, my father managed to track down the widow of Aiko's uncle, her mother Itono's brother who had gone to California shortly after their arrival in America. He had married and died before he and Aiko could meet. Auntie Kimiye had relocated to Los Angeles, and we contacted her, too. Perhaps Daddey's most rewarding times were visiting fellow tanka poets living in the area. He was finding the trip a great source of inspiration for new poems. Our vacation over, we returned to Spokane by way of San Francisco. Like one of his shore leaves when he was a seaman, Daddey decided we should go sightseeing. He signed us up for a tour of the Bay Area on our one-day stopover. From Union Square, we crossed the Bay Bridge to Berkeley and ate lunch at the Claremont Hotel before going to look at the redwood trees in Muir Park, then crossing the Golden Gate Bridge back to the city. Daddey was satisfied, and we also had more memories to take home with us. I was not only sad the vacation was over, but I also knew I wanted new experiences. Frances was no longer around to show me where to find them. It was time to return home to Seattle and venture out on my own.

"Daddey, we should move back to Seattle. Everybody we know lives in Seattle. I don't want to stay in Spokane anymore."

"Me see," he said.

Later I reminded him again, "I really, really want to move to Seattle, Daddey. Don't you think about Seattle?" I had heard him talk longingly about Seattle's physical features, which he had compared favorably with Japan. "Seattle has mountains and the ocean, and the pretty plants and flowers, just like Japan, that's what you said."

It did not take much persuasion. Bill had offered to teach Daddey how to cook his specialties with the idea of selling him the diner when he decided to retire. The offer was enticing, and Yoshi had been toying with the prospect. It meant being permanently tied to Spokane and keeping him isolated from old friends and other poetry enthusiasts. His visits with fellow poets in Los Angeles reminded him that direct contact and exchanges were essential to honing one's creative skills, that would stagnate without such stimuli. Once again, Yoshi decided to forgo an opportunity to become an entrepreneur. He said he had no head for business, and he longed to pursue his art more actively.

Time in the Valley

Daddey decided to fly us to Seattle for the experience. He opted to pay the expense in order to forgo another long bus trip with a testy, nagging daughter. I was deposited with *Obaa-san* for the rest of the summer while Daddey looked for a job in Seattle, and also to find us an apartment.

Obaa-san and her husband, Shigeichi, had left Idaho earlier and were living in the parish of the old Buddhist church in Thomas, a rural village in the White River Valley. They had returned to the area once largely populated by Japanese immigrant families, and where Aiko had been born. Like other former residents, they had returned after the war to familiar land and a familiar livelihood; however, many other Japanese never returned. A good many Issei were too old and tired to farm actively. Nisei children had moved on to city jobs and professions, and other former residents who had moved to other parts of the country temporarily for the duration, decided to stay put and did not return. Meanwhile, other nationalities had moved in, and previously available leaseholds were no longer available; commercial developments were also creeping into the fertile valley, displacing farms.

The number of parishioners had dwindled at the Thomas church, and the wartime neglect to the building and grounds had taken its toll. Church services were held infrequently and were held only when a visiting priest could be found to conduct one. Until the members made a decision regarding the building and site, *Obaa-san* and Shigeichi were entrusted as church caretakers and allowed to farm the land surrounding the building complex.

Green beans were their only cash crop, and they were sold directly to commercial packing plants for freezing or canning. Their acreage was relatively small, and hired help assisted in the labors. Pickers were needed when the beans ripened, and I had come in time to be a bean picker.

Agriculture was a mainstay in my heritage, from my mother and her father all the way back––far, far, far back to a proverbial samurai ancestor, perhaps. To *Obaa-san's* dismay, she learned this born-to-the-soil step-granddaughter had hay fever. As soon as I walked into the rows of tall, staked bean plants, my eyes itched and watered until they were swollen almost shut. When leaves scratched my exposed arms or face, I flushed, then blistered with rashes of every size and shade of red. The runny nose and sneezing never stopped. I looked and felt like I was ready for the emergency ward. "Midori must have inherited a weak strain from her mother and grandmother. Midori is sickly like them. I think we should keep her out of the fields. I could never forgive myself if she became sick again. She can help me inside the house instead," *Obaa-san* decided. And so, banished from the bean fields, I was the princess who stayed indoors.

Obaa-san was made of sterner stuff, like most of the other pioneer women. After finishing her morning household chores, she joined the others in the field. She was the first to leave the fields to begin her second round of chores. Even before reaching the house, she stopped at the freestanding little hut, the *furo-ba*, to start the fire under the bathtub. The bathwater was sufficiently heated by the time others finished their work and came in for the day. When he returned from the fields each day, Shigeichi, as head of household, was the first person to wash up and soak in the *ofuro*. The others followed the parade to the *furo-ba* after him.

In the summer, dinner was always a variation of freshly picked string beans cooked with bits of meat, with or without other vegetables, a limitless amount of rice, and a variety of homemade *tsukemono*. The menu was monotonous though filling. The head of household was also served an *okan* decanter or two of warmed *sake* with his evening meal. The *ofuro* and *sake* numbed the aches and stress of work

Shigeichi was no longer young, and working the fields was much harder now than he remembered. Upon his arrival in America shortly after the turn of the century, he had worked as a house-boy for a Caucasian family in Tacoma and had learned English. He gained greater fluency in the language than many other immigrants, and his ability to communicate with both the white and Japanese settlers proved providential. He later worked as a buyer, a middleman coordinating the flow of produce from the farmer to the wholesaler. He knew just about every Japanese family in the White River Valley during that era.

"I'm sure it wasn't from husband Masaichi's side of the family. He was strong and energetic; he'd still be alive today if he hadn't fallen asleep while driving home alone late at night," Hayame said to Shigeichi.

"Hmm, that was karma, his dying so soon," her husband said. "There was a lot of bad karma those days…"

"Masaichi's wife… Hmmm…what was her…hmmm…? Ahh… Her name was Itono," Shigeichi said. "Yes, Itono wasn't like you at all. She was respectful and reserved."

"So you've told me a hundred times, and a hundred times I tell you: my first husband did not prefer quiet and reserve. He was like all other men; men prefer a woman with energy and spice," she said. "Isn't that true, Papa?"

"What? What did you ask?"

"Men like lively women with lots of life, *neh*."

"Well, husbands really need a wife with some reserve. Then the husband doesn't have to waste time worrying whether other men are sharing a little life with his full-of-life wife! Ho, ho, ho."

"Papa! You had too much *sake* tonight."

"Mama, come with me, my full-of-life wife. We had a full day."

"First I take my bath. It's finally my turn," she said as she wrapped up her kitchen chores. "Midori, come, we take bath."

I was old enough to take my own bath, but she did not trust me. Stripped and sitting outside of the wooden tub filled with hot, steaming water, I waited for *Obaa-san* to splash me with hot water. "You wash with soap and rinse. No make water soapy, *neh*." She gave me the same instructions with every bath. After scrubbing ourselves and rinsing, we gingerly stepped into the deep tub. *Obaa-san* sat down on the wood screen lying on top of the metal bottom. The water reached to her throat, and she moaned in bliss. "Feel so good, *neh*."

I finally managed to crouch to the same depth and felt my flesh boiling. I stood up to stop my skin from cooking off my bones. "Why you stand up?" she asked.

"It's too hot. I'm getting out," I said as I dried myself and prepared to leave.

"Crazy youngster doesn't appreciate a heavenly soak."

I was almost as useless helping inside the house as I was outside in the bean fields. I didn't know how to cook. I didn't clean house, especially *Obaa-san*'s full-of-clutter manse. And I couldn't keep a fire going under the *ofuro*. I did string a lot of beans for *Obaa-san*'s dinners.

My summer stay with *Obaa-san* had convinced me and my hosts that I was unsuited for farm work. "Alas, Midori is a city girl. I never heard of anyone having hay fever before. It must be a newfangled sickness for city people," *Obaa-san*'s husband said.

It was still a few weeks before the start of school, and the bean harvesting was not yet complete, but to everyone's relief, Daddey sent word that I should leave the farm and join him in Seattle.

It was time for me to leave the farm for the city.

CHAPTER 16

Back in Seattle, 1947-1949

IN EARLY 1945, LESS THAN three years had passed since the Japanese were evacuated from the West Coast. At a time when the war was still raging, the restrictions banning them from coastal areas were lifted, and those screened and deemed eligible were allowed to return to their homes. The WRA opened resettlement offices in several Pacific coast cities, including an office in Seattle. By coordinating and assisting returning evacuees in readjusting to their changed communities, and in facilitating the process, the agency felt it would hasten camp closings. The first Japanese Americans who returned, did so with much trepidation. Instead of welcomes, they often encountered hostility, including attacks to their person and properties; racial discrimination was still raw and rampant. Young adults had led the return in trickles at first, followed by older adults and then the families.

Those who still owned homes had to reclaim their properties. The fortunate returnees were those with non-Japanese friends or associates who had been diligent caretakers of properties entrusted to them; other less fortunate found their properties neglected and their stored possessions ransacked or gone. There were tenants who had paid rent, but others had not, and the freeloading squatters had to be removed. The majority of returnees owned no property and needed to find rental housing. Covenants placed restrictions on where they could live and buy homes. Their old neighborhoods now housed a different minority, who had moved in during the war––African Americans.

Former business owners and tradespeople suffered the greatest financial losses. They had to start all over again. Due to the Evacuation Order, they had closed their operations quickly, selling inventory at a loss or having to abandon it all, knowing opportunists were hovering like vultures waiting to pick clean the remnants. On their return, some were able to pick up the pieces and thought to try again, however, many felt they were too old; they no longer had the energy or time needed to start a business again. Most Issei men were into their fifties, sixties, and older. Nisei, in increasing numbers, were in their thirties and twenties; the children of Nisei, the third-generation Sansei, were arriving on the scene. This stratified generational division continued to be a factor in the economic and social dynamics of the community. That the generational groupings were the same for all Japanese settlers on the mainland was a phenomena different from other Asian communities in America.

Younger adults started small businesses, filling the void left by Issei who were content to retire. Returning veterans now armed with GI Bill benefits joined the entrepreneurs or went to college, married, and started families

Most everyone needed a job of some sort, and finding work was all the more difficult when union shops were still closed to Japs…er, Japanese.

Other opportunities were also opening up, and the Nisei were prepared. They were citizens born in America who spoke the language and were educated. Many had earned college degrees before the war despite the meager chances of finding jobs open to them in their fields of study. In addition, this younger generation had acquired a gritty work ethic adopted from their parents. Government agencies no longer barred the hiring of Asians, while large and small companies loosened their restrictive hiring practices. The Boeing Company, the industrial giant in Seattle, who had previously banned all persons of Japanese ancestry from stepping foot on its property, was now an employer.

The true heroics and sacrifices made by young men in the 442nd Regimental Combat Team and other Nisei who served so honorably during the war, endowed Japanese Americans with an honored legacy that eased old hostilities and doubts about Japanese American loyalties and their contribution to the country as citizens. In the post-World War era, the community came to believe they would share in the nation's greater prosperity, and the promise for an equitable and better future.

Issei were still dominant players in community organizations, especially in those initiated by the immigrants in prewar years, but Nisei were taking over the leadership reins. They, the second generation, were also promoting programs addressing their own needs and interests, including those of the younger generation following them. The fabric of Japanese American society as it existed before the war had a new pattern.

When Daddey and I belatedly straggled back to Seattle and to our roots in mid-1947, the community was already deep into its rehabilitation, settling in and reconnecting with disrupted social networks. My personal travails had begun before the others when I went to live in a sanatorium; Camp and Spokane. Now our odyssey was finally over, and Daddey and I were eager to join the others. We would adjust and glance backward only to reconstruct our bearings; we were starting a fresh, new chapter of our lives.

Housing was still in short supply. Although public housing developments had been erected during the war to house defense workers, available units were insufficient for the numbers requesting housing. The bare classrooms of the Nihon Gakko were rented to families who accepted living in a one-room unit not much different than their barrack accommodations in camp. They called it the Hunt Hotel.

Daddey found a real house for us to live in——albeit shared with two other families. It was not the Honeywell dream house whose interior layout I had been conceptualizing and designing since my bout with chicken pox, but our new quarters were a great improvement over our previous dwellings.

The large two-story structure sat secure and grand on a corner lot. The land sloped steeply to the south and west, which kept the rooftops of downhill houses well below our windows and sight line. The grand corner entrance to the house served the family who lived on the first floor. A set of steep wooden stairs, resembling a fire escape added as an afterthought, was attached to the east side of the house to serve the two families living on the second floor. Within a few feet of our stairs was an even larger neighboring structure, a fourplex serving as many families. The building loomed large, managing to block our morning sunlight and kept us in its shadow.

Our apartment on the second floor faced north and west. We now had the luxury of three rooms with a private bathroom, which for some quirk in design was accessible from the joint-use front corridor. It was an inconvenient technical glitch, but we no longer had to share with any others, human or roaches, which were a bad dream now long gone. The bedroom was Daddey's. I slept on a newly purchased studio couch in the main room.

The kitchen was large enough to accommodate a table with four chairs, and the brand-new Philco refrigerator Daddey bought. It was not an icebox; it was an electrical appliance! A light came on when the door opened, and food placed inside stayed cold winter and summer, all the time. What a marvel! I made Jell-O desserts all summer long. Daddey also purchased a used and reconditioned Singer sewing machine for me, after much persuasion that he would save money if I sewed my own clothes.

Our living standards had advanced, evidenced by two rooms designated for specific uses: a separate bedroom for sleeping, and a kitchen for cooking and eating. Since the living room also served as a sleeping area, sewing space, etc., we were closer, but had not yet achieved that dream house with a separate room for different functions. Like that ever-expanding house tale I'd heard about in camp, my ultimate dream house was acquiring a long list of specifications.

From our kitchen window, we looked west over rooftops for blocks and blocks, past the commerce-lined valley below, toward the steep slopes of Beacon Hill to the southwest. The view of the hill was different from our kindergarten windows at Bailey Gatzert, but there was no mistaking the red brick structure with a staggered profile was the Marine Hospital propped atop the crest of the hill. A deep gap separates Beacon Hill from First Hill to the north. They say the cut through the hill was made when the city's forefathers came up with the idea to route a passage from Puget Sound to Lake Washington at that location, but the plan was abandoned. Later, a proposed passage from sea to lake was built further north by building a canal and using existing Lake Union as part of the passageway. The excavated gap I saw provided a convenient level traffic connection to the waterfront and to industrial flatlands to the west. The steel grid 12th Avenue Bridge that spans the man-made cut and connects the two hills when viewed in silhouette against a spectacular sunset, always provided a picture postcard scene. The train track and depot were a dozen long blocks west toward the Sound, but the train whistles could be heard in the distance. We had moved further away from train tracks, but we had not escaped them entirely.

At *Obaa-san*'s farm in the valley, the railroad right-of-way bordered the building's property line. The train tracks were closer than close. First the clatter and chugging got louder and louder until it reached thunderous and mind-numbing proportions. The earth quivered and shook as the behemoth passed along the tracks within yards of the Thomas Church and the connected parish housing *Obaa-san*'s living quarters. As the train approached, the shrill whistles were ear-shattering; once past, the noise receded to a din, drumming into our heads the principles of the Doppler Effect with each train passing. A second set of railroad tracks ran parallel to the one rumbling along next to us. Thankfully, this set of tracks was laid half a mile away to the west. Trains running on that track were also loud, but they were too distant to shake the ground under us. Sociologists may grapple with issues based on which side of the tracks one lived on; without question, living between two active train tracks was a noisy proposition.

Our neighborhood in the city was much quieter, with the sounds of traffic a mere rumble reminding us we lived close to the urban core. It was a great location with a bountiful Japanese populace living all around us. Many families owned their own homes, having purchased them before the war, though most were renters who chose to live in an area with their own kind, in an area where they were not discriminated against renting or buying housing. The neighborhood was a diverse mix, and alongside us Japanese lived white, Chinese, Filipino, and black families who rarely mixed with each other socially.

St. Mary's church was located up the block to the east, and on the corner was the small Gai's bakery, where we bought delicious frosted banana cupcakes, as many as we could afford—which was usually one. They advertised their bread products early on when television started broadcasting locally, and the bakery grew and expanded. They quit making those cupcakes; for selling them one at a time to us local kids was not profitable.

The Jewish residents were moving further out, building synagogues in their relocated neighborhoods and selling the old ones. The Italian neighborhood, identified as Garlic Gulch by some, flowed south down the Rainier Valley. Even among Japanese, many sought to buy homes and live further away; away from the ghettos.

Nihonmachi was still a viable Japanese-centric area, though the social center had moved eastward toward the new Buddhist church location. The old wooden building that had once provided dormitory quarters for single men and living quarters for the priest, and where I had endured Sunday school sessions years earlier, had been demolished for the city's redevelopment project. A new, larger facility was built several blocks east between 14th and 16th on Main, a site across from Collins Playfield, where my mother had taken me on outings. The new church was designed by a native son Nisei architect. The handsome, sedate brick structure was western in concept and construction, while incorporating Japanese stylistic embellishments in simple and subtle ways. In addition to the Hondo worship chapel and its ancillary offices, classrooms/meeting rooms, and a service kitchen, the building included a large social hall with a stage, providing a focal point for community-wide functions.

Since the hall would be made available to the community, Japanese residents, regardless of their religious affiliations, were solicited to donate funds to the capital campaign to construct the building. The structure was completed just prior to the war. The US military occupied it during the evacuation; thus, damage to the building was contained during the war years. Since most Japanese are born Buddhist, the temple's congregation was large and dominant. The Nichiren, a different Buddhist sect with a smaller congregation, owned a building several blocks away.

The Christians in the community had been introduced to their religion by different Protestant sects that had provided charitable assistance to the immigrants in conjunction with their mission to proselytize their beliefs; they had opened branches of their churches for Japanese settlers earlier in the century. These Protestant congregations included the Japanese Methodist church, the Congregational church, and the Episcopal mission that were located within a five-block radius from the Buddhist temple. The Japanese Presbyterian church was closer to Chinatown and the Baptist church was still on the hill where my old neighborhood was once located, and where Reverend Andrews continued his work for his congregation and the community.

The Japanese Catholic converts worshiped in a church that was not segregated; they were part of the larger Catholic congregation, and they were prone to socialize with other Catholics. However, churches of smaller denominations, like the Shinto temple, were interspersed in smaller buildings as well as a few dojos serving their disciples. Surrounded by commercial establishments and residences of many sorts, they all contributed to a viable mix.

Organizations owning buildings to return to had provided a presence and a place for Japanese to rebuild their disrupted social networks, and the churches had been among the first to reactivate their social programs.

CHANGES

Daddey and I had moved back into the Japanese-centric area in the vicinity where my prewar memories were based. Now our home was within easy walking distance of the Buddhist church, although our former home up the hill from Yesler Way had been an equal distance from the old wooden church. I now lived no closer or further from the social center than I had before going to the hospital. We had only moved sideways.

Those years when we lived up on Yesler Hill were a whole different time and era. The places I remembered were gone, including the dusty street in front of our fourplex. Now a short, paved connector outlet, the steep, curb less roadway billowing with dust had been given a facelift. The entire hillside was now scraped smooth, regraded, and redeveloped. Streets were realigned; the land was terraced and landscaped with manicured lawns and plantings. Identical multifamily housing units stood in orderly repose on the sloping terrain where the ramshackle mishmash of my old neighborhood once bustled with life. Gone were the bulging, slumping dirt hillsides spilling over onto pathways made impassable, and gone were the deep cuts, ruts, and gullies with wild brush, weeds, and nettles sprouting hither and beyond. Yesler Way still runs east and west, but the side street next to the grocery store disappeared, and so had the grassy knoll we walked through, our shortcut to reach Nihonmachi.

Years later, I was enrolled in a required American Housing sociology class, which unfortunately started at noon. Our professor, Mr. Burns, had a knack for making the subject insufferably boring. Since I had another class immediately following, I usually ate my sandwich at the beginning of this lunch-hour class. By sitting behind the broad-shouldered boys who populated the class, I could eat without being detected. Mr. Burns was oblivious to everyone's boredom as he droned on and on about housing conditions then existing in Washington, DC.

"There are squatters' huts right next to the Mall. Deplorable," he said. Few of us had been east of the Mississippi, and even fewer, if any, had been to DC.

"To give you a better idea of the situation, I have some slides to show you a comparable area that existed right here in Seattle."

This is great, I thought. Maybe I can rest my eyes while the room is dark.

The lights were turned off, and the first slide was projected on the screen.

"This is what the area looks like today. Quite attractive, don't you agree?" He flipped on several other slides.

Those buildings look familiar. Where?

"The public housing project you're looking at replaced a notorious section of the city just a few blocks up the hill from Smith Tower."

Gee, he's talking about Yesler Hill. I sat up.

Professor Burns mustered up a bit of enthusiasm. "Between weed and debris-strewn empty lots stood ramshackle houses and crowded, run-down tenements. The conditions inside the buildings were worse than what showed from the outside." Professor Burns flashed slide after slide of miserable, squalid, dirty quarters unfit for human habitation.

I swear I never saw anyone's house look like that. The pictures must have been taken after it had been abandoned for some time.

I was sitting straight up and paying attention. Well, those aren't pictures of our old house, although our upstairs neighbors, the Hashimoto's, did have a large chunk of ceiling plaster fall on them one night while they slept in their bed. I didn't see it, but they said it was a mess.

"Such conditions breed social aberrations, the worst kind. This area was a notorious red-light district."

WHAT? I lived and grew up in a red-light district? Oh, my God. I never knew. No one ever told me. My face flushed, and I groaned silently as I sank into my chair thinking everyone in the room now knew I had lived in a red-light district. Woe is me.

"These ladies of the night plied their trade night and day. No man could walk through the area without hearing their tap, tap on their window, or more brazenly…"

He's got this all wrong. I NEVER heard any tapping on windows. I had to admit my memories of our life in the old neighborhood had faded some and were indistinct. Humm, I wonder… those buildings on our walk down to Nihonmachi. Hmmm, those ladies who always smelled like flowers…their faces powdered white, with lots of red lipstick and rouge. They bought cigarettes or chewing gum when they came to *Obaa-san*'s store.

The junior high school was three blocks away. When the dismissal bell rang at the end of the school day, students dispersed in that jubilant, haphazard way, radiating in all directions away from the building. The student body was as diverse as our neighborhood, and although we were a blended mix during class hours, we chose to separate and socialize with our own kind after hours. It was a place where we could be comfortable with our ethnicity.

Shortly after the beginning of school in September, the Jewish students took an entire week off from school for their New Year and Yom Kippur holiday. Mrs. Sparks, who had introduced us to Rebecca and her father in fifth grade, had obviously bypassed a ream of information about their religion. My Chinese classmate Mary, upon her return to school after her father's funeral, described rituals and ceremonies far different from the Buddhist services I had witnessed. The mixture of cultural backgrounds and races was stimulating; it enhanced our experiences and instilled not only tolerance but imbued an appreciation of others different from ourselves. The enrollment mix was different compared to Spokane, as was the total experience.

It is doubtful many on the teaching staff held such a favorable opinion of the student body and of the school plant itself. A series of one-room portable buildings surrounded the original three-story structure, reducing the open sports fields into holding pens. The staff was in transition. Longtime teachers continued using their ancient lesson plans, knowing their retirements lay a few years hence. Another group of teachers barely hid their distaste at being assigned to such a dilapidated school with a ragtag student body. They impatiently waited to be reassigned to schools outside the central core with a homogenous population more like themselves. And the newly graduated first-assignment teachers who lacked experience handling such street-smart youngsters were overwhelmed. They usually lasted one school year. A few left sooner.

The old, longtime teachers were imperturbable. They had experienced much, and a smart aleck or two was easily put in his or her place. They were frustrated more by the changes they noticed in their postwar wards, and they occasionally let us know.

"You Japanese students have changed," our language arts teacher groused as she shook her head. "Before the war, I had a well-mannered

Japanese boy eager to learn and please. He came to school with a clean, starched shirt every day. His mother washed the shirt in the evening and ironed it for him in the morning. When he arrived to class, his assignments were complete and perfect. Now what's your excuse?"

"I'd feel guilty, a first-class ingrate, making my mother slave 'n wash 'n iron every day just so I could show off in my clean white shirt. She's got plenty other work to do."

We were a younger, less stigmatized generation. Our Japanese ancestry was no longer publicly vilified, and our heritage was not identified as "of the enemy and evil." We were accepted as Americans, and we aimed to live our lives as mainstream and au courant as possible.

I was happy to be back in Seattle; Seattle was home, but I was lonesome. My homeroom class was "the other" class––all the Japanese girls were in a different homeroom, and I envied their shared camaraderie. Just as students from one fifth grade class did not mix with those in the other classroom in camp, neither did eighth grade classes mix at the school. Luckily, I lived nearby, and the walk home alone was mercifully short.

An only child has long-standing tactics to dispel boredom, and I resumed involving myself in solo activities. The summer sewing classes Frances and I had taken together now allowed me to sew a cotton dress or two for myself. My magazine subscriptions had advanced from comic books and movie magazines to Look and LIFE.

I usually went further afield in my solitary search for interesting things to do. A three-block walk to a bus stop and a short ride took me through Chinatown and past Nihonmachi to the central business district with its array of shops, theaters, and a variety of businesses awaiting a visit from me. My once-a-week movie habit continued and I carefully studied movie reviews to select the best movie showing. The two large department stores on Pine Street were my favorite window-shopping destinations with their different departments allowing me to pick and choose an area of interest to investigate. The really high-toned ladies' apparel shops were too snooty to browse without suspicious, upturned-nosed salesladies following me around making sure I was not a shoplifter. The specialty shoe shop on Pine was not to browse—not because they did not allow it, it just was the place to buy the shoe "everyone is wearing." The "in" shoe was purchased straightaway, because to wear a knockoff of the shoe in style was a gross faux pas.

A block or so off my usual beaten path, I found a used books store that also sold an assortment of unused books. Among them was a copy of *Gone with the Wind*. I remembered Lily's mother had made a favorable comment after reading the story. I bought the book and read all 1,037 pages, and loved it all. Coincidently, the movie was rereleased at that time, and I sat through two screenings at a time. The spunky heroine was a woman after my own heart. Clark Gable was my favorite hero, too, even though he was about the same age as Daddey.

Frances had reacquainted me with library basics, and when window browsing held no interest, and purchasing books proved too expensive, I climbed the massive stone stairway to browse books. I never returned to the basement children's section, which I had visited with my mother. Instead, the volumes on the main level held more interest. I found a few popular historical down-South romance novels; they lacked Scarlett and Rhett, and I quit reading them. I turned to the classics in an attempt to improve my mind. I decided I should systematically read through the Modern Library collection. That went by the wayside very quickly. The books were too difficult and their contents too weighty for my junior high school mentality. Henceforth, I chose to find books on whatever subject I fancied, and my tastes were eclectic. I found and read *Pride and Prejudice*, and the short stories of Maupassant, but on a remote shelf off the main aisle, I found condensed movie scripts bound into books. They were from motion pictures released in an earlier decade, but they reinforced my interest in movies of all eras. A few illustrated books on historical clothing piqued my interest too, though the gorgeous contemporary gowns presented in movies were more inspiring. The picture books of houses did not show the modern types I preferred. When I later found a photo of the proposed Guggenheim Museum in one of my magazines at home, I cut out the picture and added it to my Valentine box collection of special things that I still treasured. Sadly, Better Homes and Gardens and cook-books were not among the favored subjects.

Work and Poetry

Yoshi found a service job at the Benjamin Franklin Hotel in midtown, not far from the New Washington, where he had worked the graveyard shift before the war. At his new job, he was the janitor who kept the public areas vacuumed and the lobby looking spotless. His diligence and accommodating attitude continued to win over his employers and fellow workers, and charmed the guests. The work was not demanding; it was a comfortable situation. His work hours allowed him to be home to prepare dinner meals, and his evenings and weekends were free time.

When the manager of the hotel was shifted to another hotel in their chain, he asked Yoshi if he would switch to the new hotel and work for him there. This he did.

On his days off, Yoshi was busy visiting his poetry group friends from camp. They had already reorganized themselves as the Seattle Tanka-kai. Although Yoshi had kept in contact with members of the group by mail, he quickly became a dues-paying member and joined them in their monthly meetings. He spent a good deal of his free time preparing for those monthly poetry critiques––writing a new tanka poem or reworking an earlier piece to be submitted.

Missing from their group was Arai sensei, who had moved to Michigan to work for the church when he converted to Catholicism. Yoshi continued to seek his counsel by sending his teacher copies of his work for comment. Without input from the senior practitioner during the monthly critiques, Yoshi jumped into the fray with his own comments about the others' poems. Osei had to be reminded he was the most junior practitioner and ought to defer to more experienced members.

Bruising criticisms were allayed by the end of their meetings when refreshments were served; treats were provided by the host at whose home they were meeting. The array of foods provided were once again presented without generating embarrassment that wartime constrictions had produced in the past. Those social ties formed in camp were to continue for a lifetime. The Seattle Japanese-language newspaper periodically published a number of the members' poems, and Osei contributed as many as the others.

He found time to pursue self-indulgent interests, and he joined various community organizations. The Shigin club, whose members vocalize in stylistic song, was one of his favorites. It was obvious to others, but Yoshi did not realize he sang off-key. He was virtually tone deaf, and the serious hearing impairment in his right ear resulting from a childhood incident exacerbated his problem. He had more bravado than skill, and since he was not the only talentless singer, he was encouraged to continue on the chance he might someday improve. To the unfamiliar ear, it all sounded like wailing.

Yoshi managed to dodge all attempts by his friends to coerce him into joining a church. His refusal remained adamant. He felt he had paid his dues many times over and nothing more was due. He continued to spend his Sundays as he pleased.

NINTH GRADE BEGINS

Ninth grade was still a part of nearby Washington Junior High's three-year program; however, students in the Franklin High School district departed to enroll in their four-year program. I had signed up for algebra rather than business math since I was intent on going to college. I was undecided on a future college major since I was still in the process of eliminating a few of my wannabe career objectives. I found myself in the same classes with the group of girls who had been in the other homeroom. Their friendships had solidified in the three years since leaving camp, and they had no reason to be more than cordial to me. We were in the same classes; however, I was still an outsider yearning to be a friend of theirs and share in their activities.

A few of our ninth-grade teachers were several notches above others we endured, and Mrs. Kendell was one such teacher. She did not fall into the old-timer or new-hire categories; she was that exceptional educator who felt she could make a difference. A rather handsome woman who was intelligent, stylish, and self-assured; it was obvious she was born, raised, and schooled somewhere far removed from Washington Junior High. The fact that our school building was dilapidated, and the economic and ethnic diversity of the neighborhood and students were totally unlike her world and experiences, only increased the challenge she felt. She treated us with respect, and we returned the favor.

Our class assignments were original and stimulating, not the staid old hash we were usually given. We got into the spirit of expanding our sphere of interests and intellect.

A handful of girls were asked to stay after school, but I was not among them. Mrs. Kendell had a new project she wanted to initiate. Were they interested?

"Girls, do you think you can enter into an experiment with me?" Mrs. Kendell posed the question to the girls.

"Of course, we have to know what the experiment is about before we can make a commitment," analytical Margaret replied. She spoke for the group, who had relegated the task to her without comment: a voice vote was not necessary.

"In the 'I Wish...' essay that the class turned in last week, I received a paper with a wish you might undertake as a project."

"That was a hard assignment..." Kate whispered in the background.

"Yeah, I couldn't think of anything without being foolish..." Betsy whispered in return.

"Mrs. Kendell, I thought you said it was an experiment."

"Let's call it an experimental project."

"Mrs. Kendell, don't keep us in the dark. What was the wish, and how do we fit in?" Marian chirped up.

"This student wrote her wish was to have friends with whom she could join in on activities. And I was hoping you'd all like to take this on as a project and make it happen."

"Will you give us a few minutes to talk this over?" Margaret asked and turned to her friends. "Well, what do you girls say?"

"Of course we'd welcome another girl."

"I never thought we were unfriendly. Do you?" "Gee, we're not exclusive."

"And we need more girls to join our basketball team."

They were all talking at once, a chaotic, dissonant scene.

Margaret interjected, "The consensus is affirmative ever though you haven't told us about the experiment part."

"Will you two ladies quit giggling over there in the corner and come join us?" The two stopped their private chatter and moved in toward the teacher.

"Popular opinion says girls can't keep a secret. Let's prove them wrong. No one will ever mention this little discussion took place. And no one will broadcast other students' essays," Mrs. Kendell said with a smile. "I'm sure you all understand."

As they left the building, Marian broke the silence and spoke the name, which hadn't been spoken before. "Sylvia was in my class in Huntsville. She was always kinda quiet and standoffish; I never really got to know her."

"She wasn't so quiet when she came to Stafford School," corrected Kate.

"In fact, she was rather bossy," Betsy said, affirming her friend's comment.

"Maybe she was quiet when you knew her, Marian, because there was someone else in the class who was bossy. Hmmm?"

"Are you implying…?"

"Forget it. It's just a joke."

"The rest of us don't know her from camp, so we'll start a new slate. All of us."

The girls started greeting me as though I had just dropped into their midst, although I had been sitting on the sidelines watching them since school started. Betsy and Kate refreshed our lapsed friendship from fifth grade, and the others, who I had never met before, introduced themselves and invited me to join their gatherings. Marian, who I had known since Miss Waterhouse's kindergarten class, two grades in Minidoka, and as one of Mrs. Nakamura's longtime *odori* students, hardly remembered me though she was the girl I had known the longest. I was the nebbish people never notice in their presence. I was heartened when that changed.

We all had a heavy academic load with no-nonsense algebra and science classes. Language arts and social studies, the usually easy subjects, were taught by experienced teachers who continued to rule with a tight rein. Ninth-grade Spanish was the only foreign language offered, and we were all in the same class again. Our teacher was Miss Purdy; she was young and a first-year teacher who had not yet acquired the skills to control the class. Students took advantage of her in experience and vented their cooped-up energy in her class. It was also a good time to coordinate plans for our after-school activities. Actually, there were a handful of students who studied and learned the language; they remained silent and never made the fact known. The conduct of these college-bound students was far from elitist; the class was unruly and in constant chaos.

"Don't bother me now. I'm trying to read this stuff." Elaine spent less time acting up with moronic stunts than the majority of students in the class, and she actually learned something. Margaret made getting perfect grades look effortless. She never appeared to be spending any more time with her books than the rest of us, yet she nailed the top grade time and again. Studious or not, everyone took advantage of the free-for-all hour in one way or another.

Missing one year of rudimentary Spanish before taking ninth grade Spanish put me at a disadvantage again. The only thing I had committed to memory was "*el puerro e la gato*," which was as bad as "Dick and Jane" in the second grade. Now they were rolling their Rs and repeating unpronounceable place names like *Popocatepetl*.

Miss Purdy shushed the class to introduce the new girl. A round of shouted greetings rang out.

"Hey, what took you so long to find your way back to Seattle?"

"Wouldn't they let you out of camp?"

"Never mind those guys. They haven't changed any since you last saw them."

"Yeah, long time no see."

"Obviously a good many of you already know our new student," Miss Purdy said.

Alice had been in the other fifth grade class at Stafford School so she was rejoining former classmates. I hadn't met her then, although I knew who she was. She returned to Seattle later than the rest of us. Since our Spanish class was her introduction to the language, she too struggled in the class.

"Miss Purdy, was that your boyfriend I saw you with down at the Club 300 diner? Huh?"

Her face flushed with her sense of invaded privacy. She quickly recovered and asked, "Shouldn't you have been in school that hour of the day?"

"Would you believe I had a hangover and overslept?" "Then you should have joined us for a cup of coffee." "You really mean it? I'll remember to do that next time."

In the meantime, the class was gathering a head of steam as the noise and commotion increased.

"*SIENTE SI USTED!*" commanded Miss Purdy. Heads turned to see who she was addressing this time. She called a name and told the student to sit down through the hour. The guilty culprit would do as told while the others continued to do what they were doing until they were called by name.

"Class, I really need your attention," Miss Purdy said in desperation.

"Ho, Miss Purdy, *en Espanol, por favor,*" a voice rang out.

"I'll say it in English so everyone in the room can understand. Since your comprehension of Spanish is next to nonexistent, it'd be pointless."

"Ah, Teacher, is it our fault we haven't learned any Spanish?"

"I've tried to teach you, but you haven't tried very hard to learn."

"Have pity, Miss Purdy, have pity."

"What I wanted you all to hear is that this class has been reported to the principal's office. Mr. Perry said our class was so loud he could hear the noise from half a block away."

"With the windows open or shut, Miss Purdy?"

"They didn't say. We're accused of being out of control, and they are now considering putting this class on probation and reassigning me."

"This sounds serious."

"It does get loud in here. What if we all just whisper? We don't want Miss Purdy to get into any more trouble, do we?"

"No…never. We like Miss Purdy. It'd be different if Teacher was someone we didn't like."

"Yeah, you guys. No more crawling out the window during class. Got that?"

"Geez, that takes all the fun out of Spanish class."

"Just use ze door, you day crawlers."

"Whoa, speaking of the devil. Here comes Mr. Perry, sucking on his cigarette. He must have worked late last night."

"Harold. Please get away from that window and sit down. The rest of you, *siente si.*"

No one could resist a peek at the protagonist, and heads throughout the room bobbed up and down like meerkats on patrol.

"What a jerk. I thought he was a cool dude; I guess not…"

"Say, Harold, you ever been to the China Doll?" a buddy whispered over to him.

"Nope, they won't let me in. No minors…"

"I'd sure like to see Mr. Perry blowing his trumpet in that dive some night."

"It'd be easier to get into the Black and Tan. And it'd be a heck of a lot closer than the China Doll."

"I just wanna see the snitch blowing his brains out. Besides, I'm the wrong color to get in the Black and Tan. I'm not black, and there's not enough sun around here for me to get a tan."

"Now that's too bad cause this guy Lester who used to be in my class last year said the music at that club was really first-rate. Cool, he says."

"How would he know?"

"He plays the saxophone and hangs out down there whenever he can. He says he'll quit school someday and play his sax night and day. That's all he ever thinks about: music."

"Have you seen him here in school lately?"

"Humm… Don't think I have. Maybe you and I can walk down to that record store on Jackson after school. It's a short walk, maybe four blocks. We just might run into him down there."

"No, thanks. I don't go to that part of town."

Mr. Perry was actually a dedicated teacher. He chose to work in our school where he, too, hoped he could make a difference. He worked evenings as a musician to augment his teacher's salary. He practiced a form of tough love, which was not always reciprocated.

Forming a club

The parks department offered after-school activities at Collins Playfield for the diverse neighborhood youths, but the Buddhist temple two blocks down the hill from school was a more amenable facility providing a variety of programs sponsored by Japanese organizations and businesses for the benefit of young and old, and for Buddhist and non-Buddhist alike.

The Japanese Christian churches were not only grappling with rebuilding their memberships and their organization, they were also struggling with the generational divide. In the past, Japanese speaking ministers had served their immigrant Issei parishioners well, however, the younger Nisei needed English speaking ministers to get their message across.

The nearby Methodists solved the problem as the Baptist had done, by hiring a second priest. A newly ordained veteran arrived with enthusiasm and a fresh outlook. A like-minded university graduate student who had recently joined the church promoted an agenda to involve high school and college age young adults in stimulating and fun projects along with service programs. A revitalization was occurring on many fronts everywhere.

Helen May Smith had appeared on the scene just prior to this time. With a forgettable title and duties, church officialdom had assigned her to the Japanese Methodist church in Seattle. Whatever her official church responsibilities may have been, she unofficially took in our little group for special attention.

"We're meeting at 10 a.m. in the church kitchen. And remember to bring your cup of sugar," said Helen May. "We're having a taffy pull."

"What's a taffy pull?"

"Come and find out. It's fun."

We were introduced to bits of Americana in unexpected ways.

Living in a strange city and working with an immigrant congregation no doubt was the missionary phase of Helen May's life. She immersed herself in her work for the Christian ministry as a dedicated layman. In a line-up to identify the missionary zealot, she would have been spotted in a flash. She was a poster model for that breed.

Of average height, she was built a little heavier, perhaps better described as having a boxy profile. Her chestnut-hued hair was done up in a nondescript no-fuss hairdo. She wore sensible shoes with laces and flat squared heels, the type favored by grandmas. Her uniform of comfortable suits was dressed up or down with the different blouses she wore. Had she been a Roman Catholic, she would have worn a habit with a cross hanging from a rosary. She, too, wore a cross; it hung as a pendent from a chain around her neck. A pale pink lipstick was the only makeup she wore, but it highlighted the natural pink in her cheeks in her otherwise "plain Jane" face. In addition, her bubbling good cheer and animated enthusiasms made her glasses dance on her nose. That was the package that had come to do God's work.

She and her little sedan could be seen careening around corners throughout the neighborhood as she provided taxi service to parishioners in an era when a car was not yet parked in every family garage.

"Everyone, come get in the car."

"But there are seven of us, Helen May. The car might break down if we all get in."

"Well, we'll never know if that'll happen if we don't try it, will we."

We all piled in three deep to the roof, and arriving at our destination without a hiccup. Helen May could be an old fuddy-duddy at times, and then again, she was young in spirit.

The other girls had joined the Baptist church Girl Scouts upon their return from camp, but now as ninth graders, they had outgrown those activities and were currently unaffiliated. Those of us with no strong ties to the Buddhist church began attending Methodist Sunday school with Margaret and company. We missed eligibility to join the hip college-age and high school teens' programs at the church by a year. A one-year wait was too long. Since the friendships of our little group were beyond church affiliations, we joined together after services at either the Methodist or Buddhist church to decide how to spend the free afternoon.

Utilizing a slack period in Spanish class, we agreed to form a club. We also decided the smallish parlor adjacent to the entry lobby at the Methodist church, furnished with donated wooden chairs, a sofa, plus a rocking chair, was an ideal meeting room for us. Plus, the space was rarely occupied except on Sundays. We asked Helen May to be our advisor.

By unanimous vote, Margaret was selected president. She was the natural leader, "The brain." She had all the right attributes: common sense, fairness toward everyone, and was likeable; we all acknowledged that. And Joyce became vice president of our club. Joyce, "Miss Personality" was a sweetheart to everyone, in addition to her "sweetheart". Sensible, hardworking Marian was the secretary/treasurer overseeing the details. I was accepted as a bona fide member by that time, and I happily joined the non-officers group who were relieved from onerous duties. We were free to voice any comments or complaints during discussions; adding our two cents or two bits worth. We were also prone to wander off the subject in question at any time. Robert's Rules procedures for our meetings were dropped early on; they were too cumbersome for our freewheeling get-togethers.

"Among the submitted group name proposals, I like Reginas the best," Margaret said.

"Regina means queen. That fits us, don't you all agree?" Joyce was saying.

Elaine had something to say and interrupted, "Other people will consider us presumptuous. Queens, no less."

"Would empress be any better?" Kate asked.

Betsy followed up, "What do they call a female Mikado? A Mikadress?"

Gale: "This is getting silly."

"We can be 'Japanese American Princesses,' 'JAPS' for short."

Alice: "Throw her out!"

Fumi: "I second it."

"You can't second anything yet. We're still in discussion."

We adopted the queenly name Reginas after we each had our say. We were a group of twelve friends, all Japanese Americans girls in the ninth grade. I was included as a charter member: a Reginas.

The original impetus to organize had been to form a basketball team. That idea was soon squelched; only a few girls showed any athletic talent or sustained much interest. Betsy preferred taking piano lessons, Gale and Marta had responsibilities at home, and me being not only a klutz, but I also had the specter of TB hanging over my head. "Don't exhaust yourself, Midori. Don't get sick like Mommy." That was a warning I heeded.

The Reginas' group photo

As Reginas, our focus was directed to promote social activities; we planned parties, socials, and get-togethers with various boy groups. Helen May stepped in on occasion, reminding us service projects ought to be included in our program. We found ourselves each sewing and putting together stuffed toy animals to be donated to the Children's Orthopedic Hospital on Queen Anne Hill. We rode the bus to the hospital on that occasion rather than piling into Helen May's car for transport. Admittedly, our charitable projects were few compared to our social agenda.

At a time in our lives when being included was important, I was lucky to have such congenial friends.

HOME LIFE

I managed to be home for dinner every day because everyone else was sensible enough to head for home in time to eat supper. Eating and food still held little interest for me, and I was still a skinny kid.

Daddey thought malnourishment contributed to TB, and he aimed to keep me healthy by fattening me up. He could now provide good foods to make sure I stayed well. He shopped on his way home from work before taking the bus home. His workplace was an easy walk to the Pike Place Market, where he shopped for fresh produce and renewed friendships with the old-time vendors still hawking their wares. Located a half block east of the larger emporium was Oliver's, a choice source for meats. Also nearby was Manning's, and Van de Kamp's Bakery which sold a full line of pastries that were impossible to resist. On any given day, he bought pecan rolls, butterhorns, éclairs, cream puffs, or whatever sweet pastry struck our fancy. When the sweets were depleted, another variety arrived on our table. He even remembered to return the metal pie tins later... The best Napoleon pastry was sold on Pine Street, either at the Frederick & Nelson department store bakery or at the restaurant across the street where the street clock stood.

Frying pork chops or an occasional filet mignon served with rice and a boiled vegetable was the easy meal; as was spaghetti, when the noodles only needed ketchup for saucing. Daddey asked his women friends how to cook specific items in order to broaden our menu. For someone who ate whatever was placed in front of him without complaint, Daddey had a memory of the fancy foods he had previously been exposed to, and he introduced me to them from time to time. He was most successful when he indulged his sweet tooth.

My interest in cooking remained minimal. An expanded schedule of social activities and my studies kept me extremely busy, and I felt there was little point in learning to cook when a tasty, filling meal always appeared on the table at dinnertime.

"Did you eat leftover sukiyaki and *gohan* I left on table?" Daddey said after taking off his coat and hat upon returning home. It was one of those rare occasions when he had not come home to prepare dinner.

"I ate," I said as I put down the magazine I was reading. "Where did you go? You're all dressed up, and you smell like aftershave lotion. Funerals don't start so early. They're usually held at night."

He didn't answer. He went into the kitchen to make himself some tea. I could hear him doing his throat-clearing gig. That nervous tic bolstered my curiosity. I was suspicious. He was being evasive, not his usual open, transparent self. He came back with his tea and sat down.

"I go with a friend and meet lady," he said, rather giggly.

"Oh, you went on a date?"

"My friend thinks I am lonely, so he wants me to meet with widow. She is lonely, and she is rich, my friend says. She wants to meet you, too."

"You mean your friend is a *bai-shaku-nin*, a marriage broker?" This was beginning to sound ominous

"No worry, Midori, I no marry this woman. I told her I still have responsibility to raise you. I tell people you come first, and she be second. I have to tell her in beginning, so no misunderstanding later. I know she always think she is number one, never number two. So she pretends she is sad we will not make match."

Now that I was reassured a remarriage was not in the near future, I wanted more details.

Daddey continued, "This widow is rich because she has very good business head, and everybody know she loves money and making money is number-one interest. She boss her husband, tell him do this, do that until he die, poor man."

"What kind of a friend is your friend? Why would he want to see you stuck with someone like that?"

"Because some people love money so much, they do anything to have more money. My friend no can find bachelor like that, but widow keep telling him to find good man for her. I just go to meeting for my friend."

"You weren't interested from the very beginning?"

"Not for marry. I want to meet her and see myself if she is like woman other people say. She no have very good reputation."

"But Daddey, you're the one who once told me not to be overly concerned about what other people say about you. Why are you making her reputation so important to you?"

"Me see… We talk…" He reverted to Japanese to finish his thought, "…about status based on a person's ancestry. I said I did not believe a person's true worth should be based on connections whether by birth, relationships, job, wealth, etc. A reputation is usually based on a person's own accomplishments and deeds, not by association on someone else's accomplishments."

Daddey's complicated Japanese went over my head, but I got the gist.

"When we were in camp, people were so proud to be from samurai family. Now everyone talks about how rich they are, and they buy cars, and talk about things they own. In camp, nobody had much. It was a truly equalizing experience as far as money and material wealth were concerned. For a few years, you and I were able to live with few anxieties." He said quietly, "Most people lost many material things and opportunities, and some lost precious sons. We had already lost practically everything we had before the war started. We had very little to lose. Our pain preceded the majority's loss and pain."

Daddey had become too reflective. I needed to change the subject. "So was this a final meeting with the rich widow?"

"I think so. She is very bossy. I don't need two females to boss me around all the time. She doesn't like children, so she would be a terrible stepmother. And she never spends a penny except to make another penny. Making money is all she thinks about. We, you and me, would be very unhappy." He sipped his tea, contemplating the consequences of such a union. "You betcha. It is last meeting."

I let him drink his tea without comment even though he was sucking loudly. And where did he pick up 'betcha'? Was he playing the ponies again?

We hardly ever talked with each other anymore. I had out grown his mukashi, mukashi stories, and I was looking to the future, not back when the ancestors lived. Daddy was no longer the source of all knowledge, and besides, his pronunciation of words and places was unreliable. There was no problem with Pompeii and Suez, but I was told by others there was nothing clever about Cleveland as Daddey pronounced it, and Philadelphia did not end with "fair."

Considering a Future

Choices for a future career had been flitting through my mind during my quiet moments from early on. With high school looming ominously close, the urgency to make a decision weighed on me. In high school, I would need to select classes that are prerequisites for my major of choice in college. I never considered nursing; spending time in a hospital taking patients' temperatures held no appeal. A classroom of unruly children nixed teaching. Something other than the traditional women's career had to be found. Psychiatry was a particularly topical subject after the war, and I thought understanding my own and other people's psyche's could be a fascinating lifelong study. Reality spoke and told me I was not a doctoral candidate, and my interest was not an all-consuming one, a career as a psychiatrist had been crossed off my list early.

Clothes are a high-priority interest for girls, and I was no exception. The books on native costumes and historical clothing styles I had found in the library during my summer reading were among my favorites. Adding fashion design to my future career list was a realistic choice, with costume design for the theater as an ultimate goal. I began my focus reading about contemporary styles in the pages of Vogue and Harper's Bazaar, and browsing through women's apparel in department stores. Each season, a bevy of beautiful clothes appeared on the scene only to be regarded as passé and supplanted the next season when another batch of beautiful creations were introduced. Fashion apparel was ruled by the whim of the moment; it was impermanent and fleeting. The continuous cycle of new styles could easily become a rat race instead of a fulfilling turn on a merry-go-round. It lost its appeal as a permanent career. Interior decoration, as it was identified in those years, shared many of the same characteristics as apparel design, except the cycle of change progresses at a slower pace. Another difference was the presence of those who accepted no change and regressed to old stuff. No one wears fashions of a century or two ago, but some think living in homes furnished like replicas of past centuries is chic. I did not have that history, and it did not appeal to me, either.

All my earlier career choices had been eliminated except one: Architecture. Like the Honeywell advertisement showing the house with glass blocks that I kept as a memento, I had later found another house photo worth keeping: it was the Falling Waters residence designed by Frank Lloyd Wright. I was awestruck: the house was so wondrous and beautiful as it hovers over the rippling creek; its mystique was unshakable. I wanted to be part of that world of houses and buildings, designing and creating. My career decision to tackle such a male-dominated profession as architecture did not intimidate me, but it did reinforce others' opinion of me as being "different" because normal Japanese American girls did not dream of becoming an architect. I had matured sufficiently to ignore their opinions and proceeded with my plans. Daddey accepted my announcement without comment. He did not consider it a subject requiring his approval, nor did I.

Summer Vacation

Our graduation from ninth grade lacked ceremony, and no one felt remorse or shed a tear to be leaving the school behind. Our tenancy at Washington Junior High School had ended, and we looked forward to a new start at Garfield High School in the fall. We were ready to abandon the adolescent pranks and distance ourselves from the mechanical drawing teacher who kept a ping-pong paddle on the ready in his hip pocket. And we bid a silent farewell to Miss Lamont, whose fat thighs, though stuffed in fashionable hosiery, scraped against each other as she walked, sending swish-swash, swish-swash signals that she was creeping up the aisle behind us checking for slouchers to chastise. We were moving on to grown-up privileges and scholarly endeavors.

It is unlikely much nostalgia was felt for the worn-out building, and no alumnus was saddened to find only empty space and memories where our old school once stood. The school building was torn down a few years after our departure. The bakery had expanded its plant onto the school site and had erected its gigantic elevated "WONDER BREAD" sign far above the rooftops at the site for all to see. In the old days, no student needed an identifying sign telling us the bakery was located across the street. We only had to follow our noses to the source of those wondrous aromas of freshly baked bread that whetted our appetites and drove us to distraction with thoughts of yummy, scrumptious food food food. On Yesler, two blocks north of the behemoth enterprise, another smaller baker, Brenner Brothers Bakery, was making divine challah.

The summer vacation that I looked forward to with so much anticipation during the school year turned out to be a conflicted time. I had always welcomed the respite from study and freedom from schedules; it was a time for indulgences and leisurely pursuits. Now that I was a teenager, I needed to augment the allowance Daddey gave me and find a summer job like the other girls my age. My expenses for items I considered essentials increased incrementally the older I became. Membership dues were a legitimate expense, along with myriads of incidentals. Making choices was no longer so simple. The only lipstick to touch our lips was a Revlon product and not the cheaper ones sold at the drugstore. A sweater was not any wool knit; it had to be cashmere. The girls with rich parents wore cashmeres with specific labels and argyle patterns; the rest of us wore those with a lesser label. No one could see a label, we reasoned. And our shoes were the genuine name-brand article, not a copy.

Minorities were not yet hired for outside jobs. Outside did not mean outdoors; it meant where an employee could be seen by the public. Salespeople in all retail stores, large and small, were white. Minorities, be they black, yellow, red, or shades in between, stayed hidden. The only exceptions were in establishments owned and operated by minorities. Our favored specialty shoe store, along with a few other local retailers, hired minority secretaries and clerks, janitors and backroom merchandise stockers––all personnel well out of view. Such positions were coveted by the adults; we summer hires had no chance of landing those jobs.

Teenage girls could sometimes find work as a mother's assistant. Nisei women had found similar positions working for individual families before the war. Their diligent work ethics and honesty had established a positive reference for the younger Nisei who followed. The duties encompassed a wide range of tasks from babysitting to housecleaning. Mother's helper duties might include assisting in cooking and serving the meals, besides washing dishes. There were no set standards for pay or workloads. The lucky job seeker was one who found a kind and considerate boss. The unlucky ones ended up with an employer who did not know slavery had been abolished in the US.

For others work meant harvesting farm crops. There were fewer Japanese farmers in the valley after the war and *Obaa-san* and her husband left too. Moving to California after injuring his back, they felt the warmer climate would hasten his recovery. My job source was gone.

Living in the city away from potent plant pollens, I foolishly signed up for a season of berry picking work. My allergies returned in full force and I was back home within a week. Hence forth, never to forget I am a city girl.

The Reginas suspended most activities for the summer due to scheduling conflicts and summer jobs. With my prospects of finding another job nil, I spent the rest of summer doing what I had done the summer before: going to the library and beginning my reading program. My ambitions to read the classics fizzled a second time, and rather than make reading a dreaded chore, I switched to contemporary subjects which were easier reading and a lot more interesting. I discovered self-improvement books, along with biographies and a different batch of architecture picture books.

My giving up fashion design as a career did not mean I had lost all interest in clothes. I continued to search through magazines to find inspiration for a gown to sew for a future prom. The research was premature planning, but I had a lot of time.

The buzz making the rounds was Tami's party. She was an upperclassman; although we were not invited, we'd all heard about the event. She had invited three good-looking brothers who had moved to town from Hawaii. New exotic imports in our resource pool was good news indeed.

CHAPTER 17

High School and Beyond, 1949-1957

WHEN SEATTLE SCHOOLS START IN September the Wednesday after Labor Day, the summer sun has lost its vigorous luster and the morning air is brisk and likely heavy with dew. If a blanket of fog has descended, the sun's rays fight long and hard dispelling the filter to give us a glowing Indian summer day. The crisp autumn mornings sharpen our wits, and we reach for our wraps as we realize the new school year has begun.

Our walk to Garfield High School was more than a mile. We usually walked up Jackson Street and looked through shop windows along the way. Yesler was an alternative route, with steeper slopes and sparser storefronts along the street to distract us on our journey. On reaching 23rd Avenue, we turned north and continued another six blocks to where the buses unloaded students who rode to school. Those students lived further afield and usually in plushier neighborhoods.

Each morning, I joined Betsy and Gladys, and like typical teenagers, we never ran out of things to talk about during our walk. Gladys, my third and fourth grade classmate in camp so proficient playing jacks, was not a Reginas. She was deeply involved in a different church and organizations with less frivolous pursuits; she had a separate set of friends for after school. Betsy and I managed to find subjects not involving our club while we were with Gladys.

"Sylvia is always in a hurry to get to school. Have you noticed that, Gladys?" Betsy said. "When we were in the fifth grade, she was always coming to the classroom in a run."

"That was Kewpie-*chan*'s fault. She always held up the bus by being late," I said.

"What bus?" Gladys asked. "I don't remember any school buses in camp."

"It was just a truck that picked us up and took us Block 17 and Block 19 kids to Stafford School."

"Oh… I never made the connection of why I never saw you anymore. I assumed you left camp."

"Heh heh heh," Betsy burst out laughing from a tickled funny bone. "She came over to my school; that is, she came to school whenever she couldn't find a good excuse to stay home."

"Those teachers we had after Mrs. Sparks left didn't inspire me. They had a knack for making our studies so boring, I thought school was a big waste of time those days."

A great deal of conversation inevitably reverted to the evacuation years. It was a shared experience, and there were as many different stories as there were people; the variations were endless. When we were together, it was the common bond, and we talked about it a lot. However, when we were in the company of non-Japanese, we talked about other things, things they had knowledge of.

When the old Broadway School where my aunts and their peers had attended high school was converted to a technical school shortly after war's end, Garfield's enrollment boundaries were enlarged to incorporate Broadway-area undergraduates. The expanded Garfield enrollment area encompassed the geographic and historic central core of the city with its wide range of neighborhoods. There were rich folks living in a gated community and in mansions along the waterfronts and on hillsides with a view. There were poor folks trying to survive in decrepit hovels, while others managed to score, a unit in one of the public housing projects. If it was Yesler Terrace they, too, had a commanding territorial view. The rest fell into categories somewhere between the extremes. Restrictive covenant clauses common in newer neighborhoods outside the area and the widespread discriminatory housing practices still in effect had effectively kept the majority of minorities in housing within and near the central core.

When the colorful mix from Washington Junior High and the substantially better-off white students from the other junior high were joined together in our high school, there was a truly diverse mix of students, economically, socially, and racially. At that time, practically all minority students living in Seattle attended Garfield, a handful attended Franklin, and a few other schools claimed a token minority or two. As diverse as we were, and despite a white brain drain of sorts perpetrated by wealthier parents sending their offspring to private schools, white student enrollment still constituted more than half of the student body. They were rich white, poor white, middle-class white, and Jewish students. African-American, Chinese, and Japanese students constituted the racial minority. Koreans and Southeast Asians had not begun their mass migration to America, and the Latinos had not moved so far north yet. Filipino youngsters generally attended Catholic schools and seldom ventured to our sphere of activities.

In the classrooms and during school hours, the diversity was scrambled much as it had been in junior high school. Lunchtime was the exception, and voluntary segregation was the norm, especially on the girls' side of the lunchroom. Girls gathered together along social and ethnic lines and ate lunch with their own kind by choice. Socialite white girls sat with their sorority sisters. The Chinese girls ate at one long table, the Jewish girls at another. We Japanese girls were too many for one table, so we separated into subgroups. This self-imposed segregation had a few advantages; no one was embarrassed to bring foods alien to typical American diets.

I never had anything worthy enough to share with the others at lunchtime. I still threw a slice of baloney between two slices of bread, smeared on some mayonnaise, and considered it lunch.

"There are a few slices of salmon Satsuma-age left. Have some," Marta said.

I put a slice of the homemade fish cake in my mouth, relishing its flavor. "They're so good. You're really generous to be sharing with the rest of us."

"Not really. No, no. I don't mean it's not good, it is. I mean I'm not really being generous. My dad catches so much fish, he makes it all the time."

"But no one else makes the fish cake with salmon. That's special."

Marta's father was TT, the best fisherman in these parts. His renown extended beyond the Japanese community as he garnered prizes by catching sizable salmon in one fishing derby after another. He came from a fishing village bordering the Pacific Ocean in Mie, close to the border of Wakayama and a long distance from Yoshi's village. He ran a small hotel in the Pioneer Square district, which allowed him time to fish and hone his expertise, further committing to memory the good fishing holes throughout the Sound.

In the fall, Margaret brought each of us a *nashi*, an Asian pear, from the tree in their backyard. Only years later would this fruit be grown commercially and widely sold in stores. Another treat she shared with us whenever her mother made the Japanese side dish, was *kinpira gobo*.

"I love your mom's *gobo*, but…"

"But what? Say it."

"I don't want to be critical."

"Just blurt it out."

"The *gobo* tastes a little funny today."

She tasted a few strands, as did the others at the table.

"Ahugg… What makes it taste so different today?"

"Yup, it's cinnamon. Your mom accidently used cinnamon instead of black pepper! It tastes a bit like cinnamon toast, don't you think?"

Diners unfamiliar with diced burdock root flavored with sugar and soy would be puzzled at all the fuss, because to the uninitiated it tastes like chewy teriyaki wood chips.

"Talking about cinnamon makes me hungry for a cinnamon roll today. Hope they haven't sold out."

"You'd better hurry over there. I saw a long line of buyers earlier."

"I swear, our cooks make the best cinnamon rolls in the world. They're better than the ones my dad buys at Van de Kamp's."

The other lunchroom tables were occupied by unaffiliated students who sat with their own groups and friends, unconcerned about the obvious cliques who insisted on sitting at the same table every school day. We were just as ambivalent about these "natural preferences." After school, we again separated along similar lines.

During our stint at Garfield, our basketball teams did well, but the powerhouse football teams were yet to come. When outsiders took issue with our mixed palette, and when adversaries with underlying prejudices wrongfully accused Garfield students of misdeeds, we were as fiercely united as any. We had pride in our diversity and loyalty to our school.

"For the umpteenth time, our students have been accused of smearing paint on Chief Sealth's statue following last night's football game."

"Not true. We're Bulldogs, not vandals!"

"Go, Bulldogs. Purple, white. Fight, fight!"

High school was a great improvement over junior high school in every respect except physical education. Showing athletic prowess was not limited to boys; girls also aimed to be sporty and fit, as they were well aware such skills were an adjunct to popularity. I could not hit a ball coming toward me, whether it was a baseball, tennis ball, or volleyball. Sports by whatever name were not my métier. Instead, I utilized every legitimate excuse to cut my gym classes with their energy-sapping exercises.

My friends were sports and exercise buffs and they increased their participation in sports activities by busily taking part in after-school sports programs, earning badges and chevrons to sew onto their regulation sweaters. I had enough sense to recognize a few of my limitations, and passed on joining them. That meant walking home from school alone; walking solo always took twice as long, a fact I well-remembered. I learned Elaine had also passed up after-school sports, and we began walking home together.

Elaine had skipped past the rest of us along the way and was more mature by years. She had outgrown the peer pressures the rest of us were still wallowing in; she was pursuing her own interests and goals independent from us. It was refreshing to talk with someone who was beyond the "upcoming Saturday dance at the Buddhist church" chatter. She was as smart as Margaret, and the scope of her readings and reasoning easily overwhelmed me. I was the sponge trying to absorb her rarefied treatises. We talked about our wartime experiences, too.

"Elaine, I don't remember seeing you in camp. Were you in Tule Lake?"

"Only for a while, then we joined my father in Crystal City."

"You left camp early."

"On the contrary, our camp closed after the others."

"I know there was a Camp Manzanar, Topaz, Heart Mountain, and others, but I never heard about your camp. Where were you located?"

"Crystal City was in Texas, and it wasn't a WRA camp like the others; it was a Justice Department camp, and the setup was different."

"How different?"

"Our camp housed German and Italian nationals besides Japanese."

"I really want to hear more. Can we continue next time?" She was good company, making the walks home way too short, and cutting our talks too short too.

HIGH SCHOOL STUDIES

My friends and I were all taking the college preparatory curriculum, but I rarely found myself in a class with my Reginas friends except one; she was Alice.

Her late entry to junior high school meant she was in the same predicament I was in; we both lacked a second year of Spanish studies to meet a two-year foreign language requirement for college. We learned so little in our ninth grade Spanish class, it was folly to continue for a second year in high school. We decided independently to switch to French for the required two years' credit.

We found ourselves in the same Beginning French class, which was also our homeroom. Our teacher Mrs. Olmstead, was what we imagined to be the iconic French woman, but she was American. She taught with real knowledge of the language and love of the country, and we had to respect her for that. She played Edith Piaf records for us as a treat, knowing it would enhance our enthusiasm for the language and promote the latent Francophile within us. Alice and I were on par scholastically, so the competition for the better grades varied from test to test. I crammed for the exams and promptly forgot it all afterward; Alice learned her French. We both understood our skills were different, and with that mindset we continued our second year amicably together in Mrs. Olmstead's French class.

Being rivals in French class was bad enough; we also found ourselves in the same biology class. Miss Johnson was our no-nonsense teacher. There were many dedicated longtime teachers at Garfield, and among them were the science instructors teaching core courses. We students had been warned Miss Johnson was a tough teacher, and both Alice and I suspended any socializing during class, earning similar good grades, thus creating harmony between us.

"The final grade for the class shall be the score made on the final examination," Miss Johnson told us. "Write everything you learned about one of the anatomical systems of the human body." On test day, we each blindly picked from a hat the one system we were required to write about. That meant we studied all the systems to prepare for our test. I was lucky; I picked the circulatory system. My subject was readily explainable with many facets to keep me writing steadily to the final bell. Alice was not so lucky; her subject was the nervous system, which was the most complex. It was difficult to comprehend and describe. It was a true "luck of the draw" situation.

Another science teacher at our school was Mr. Schmalle, our charismatic chemistry teacher who worked his magic on his students making them fall in love with the subject––so much so that many later entered colleges as chemistry majors due to his influence. The other classes and teachers were not as noteworthy, and we muddled through our school subjects impatient to begin our outside of classroom social activities.

When I had no pressing homework deadlines, I would walk up the hill a few blocks and south another two blocks to Margaret's house. We were relatively close neighbors, and I came to know her better. She was the youngest child, and her siblings were older with families of their own. She offered me friendship and took me under her wing, though I could be a prickly friend at times. She understood how alone I was; she invited me over to bake cookies, listen to music, or just sit and visit. The wood rocking chair in their living room was the ideal place to sit and rock and read the latest issue of *Time* magazine.

"You're being rude when you park yourself in that rocking chair and bury your nose in a magazine the minute you come in," Margaret said.

"If I satisfy my curiosity and browse through the magazine right away, I don't have to interrupt my visit later."

"You have strange habits."

"Perhaps I just find your house cozy and welcoming. It's easy to settle in and forget I'm a guest. I'll have to remember this for my dream house." Margaret's parents were older, relaxed, and never made a fuss about my visits. The atmosphere in their home was warm and comforting, and I visited often.

It was a great time to be a teenager. I bore no deep scars from wartime racial abuses that older Nisei were often burdened with. Discrimination still existed; we understood those realities. We were accepted as Americans now, and we intended to live lives with freedom to pursue our dreams. For the present, as almost adults, we had choices we could indulge, and we had good friends to share the good times.

Our Sunday after church services ritual began with our two-block walk from the Methodist church to the Buddhist church to meet the Buddhist girls in our group, and take a bus to town to see a movie together.

"There aren't any blockbusters this week. What movie do you want to see?"

"What are the choices?"

"John Garfield in a detective…"

"Forget it."

"Esther Williams…"

"I've seen her swim in a dozen movies already. Can you find something else?"

"There's a movie about old Hawaii and another one that's a tearjerker, it says."

"Can we get an opinion from the rest of you girls?"

"I'm easy. Whatever you decide is fine with me."

"I'll go along with the majority."

"Will you please express a preference?"

"I'm just trying to be agreeable."

"Who's the star in the tearjerker?

"It says Jane Wyman."

We found a group of seats together in the balcony and settled in with our bags of popcorn. The movie was a tearjerker like the advertisement claimed. Alice and a like-minded companion sitting next to her wept continuously with every tragic twist in the plot. The others watched attentively, sniffling at appropriate sad events. Betsy and I were the cynics that afternoon, and we both laughed and snickered at the implausible plot and overwrought drama.

"Just because you didn't like the movie, you didn't have to ruin it for the rest of us by laughing and giggling." Betsy and I were in the dog house. Next time I won't waste my time going to a silly soap opera with these soppy girls.

We organized sleepovers, known as slumber parties in those days. Few of us owned sleeping bags, but most Japanese families owned futons, which served us well on these occasions. We laughed and snacked and talked and talked. We ran through entire scenarios of movies not everyone had seen. Twenty-five years after the retelling of Gunga Din at one of those sleepovers, I caught a showing of the original thirties movie and confirmed the accuracies of their retelling.

A good deal of the time, we were talking about boys. The boys we talked about were Japanese American boys. We made friends and had associations with others without regard to ethnicity and race, especially at Garfield, but we had spent a few formative years segregated from non-Japanese, and our comfort zones were with people of our own kind. Our community was large enough to provide choices, and few defied the miscegenation laws still on the books.

A basketball league for Japanese American teenagers and young adults had been organized, and the teams played at the Buddhist church on Sunday afternoons during the season—our movie going followed the game. The competitions were a big draw, and we girls went to watch the boys. The most consistently winning team was the Chinese American Cathay Post team. All the other teams were Japanese American, and they ended up battling for second place.

Two or three teams that interested us the most were teams made up with guys either our age or a year or two older. The Midgets were mostly fellow classmates we had known from camp or earlier, and we fell into having parties and picnics together more often than with the others.

Various clubs and organizations sponsored dances for the high school and young adult crowd that were usually held at the Buddhist church social hall on a Saturday night, We Reginas decided to sponsor a dance, hoping to make money for our club. We selected a name for our dance, had tickets printed, found someone willing to be the disc jockey, and chose the Methodist church's social hall for its cheaper rent. We sold enough tickets to break even, but it was not a success.

As the hour approached for the dance to begin, the lights in the hall were lowered.

"STOP. I don't sanction this!"

What was Helen Mae saying?

"Girls, turn up the lights this minute."

"But, Helen Mae…"

Our appeals to dim the lights fell on deaf ears. To Helen Mae, lowered lights meant hanky-panky, and she would not allow that during her watch. The lights stayed on, to our dismay.

We were the generation between jitterbugging and rock 'n roll, and we cool cats traversed the dance floor in each other's arms in a very slow dance. Our style of dancing was ingenious and untutored. Lowered lights were appropriate, providing cover for awkward dancers willing to take to the floor doing their "Frankenstein" dance.

Changes

When Helen Mae was reassigned to another mission, the church held one of its potluck lunches after Sunday service as a send-off. We felt it was our duty to attend services that Sunday. As we sat in the pews listening to the sermon, our stomachs growled loudly, competing with the hot water radiators as they belched and gurgled to heat up the chapel. When the service was over, we meandered down to the social hall where the women were taking the wraps off the foodstuffs contributed by the parishioners.

Set on a double-long table in no particular order were trays, bowls, and platters of every description filled with foods of every variety.

A Japanese American potluck buffet offered both American and Japanese foods. The Issei ladies made and brought sushi, teriyaki chicken, and an assortment of bento goodies, while the Nisei women brought casseroles, salads, and baked goods for dessert. Because people brought their most praiseworthy items, there were duplicate selections. The walk around the food-laden table took many turns.

"You have to have a piece of Mrs. Tanaka's Teri-chicken. She makes the best."

"Which one is it?"

"It's at the end of the table next to the potato salad."

"OK, but which is the best sushi?"

"Don't know. Try them all." She was picking up a wiggly strip of *konnyaku* from a *waribako* filled with *onishime*. "I can't resist these. They make me think I'm eating flavored rubber bands."

"There are at least a half dozen different plates of sushi… I'd be a pig to try one of each."

"Then try the spaghetti instead."

"No way, I can eat spaghetti anytime."

"Not as good as my sister's, you won't."

I filled my plate with Japanese food and a generous scoop of potato salad. There's nothing better than a Japanese American potluck. The picnics are great too, but they take second. It doesn't get much better than this. Yum, yum.

By the time Helen May left Seattle, most of us had joined various organizations with more structure, and we Reginas realized we were less a club than a group of friends enjoying each other's company, having fun doing things together. We were confident we were mature enough to proceed without an advisor.

Without warning, Daddey announced we were moving out of the triplex to a different rental two blocks down the hill.

"Huh? Why? What for?" I responded in my usual way. He had anticipated my reaction and was prepared to win me over with answers to questions I had not yet asked.

My commute to school, he assured me, would hardly change, and any other adjustments would be minor. "There are two bedrooms in the duplex, and the rent is lower," he said, hoping to quell any objections before I voiced them.

The two-story house was old, basic, and cheaply built. The original wood siding was covered with the ugly asphalt sheeting imprinted with phony brick patterns, the type once used on cheap remodel jobs. We lived in the upper unit, which was divided into equal quadrants: a parlor, a kitchen and two bedrooms.

The bathroom and a closet shared my bedroom quadrant. The efficient floor plan, with no space wasted on hallways, meant we went through my bedroom to reach the bathroom. My bedroom with its pedestrian lanes was awkward, but the convenience of a bathroom we did not share with other families was a major upgrade. We had taken one-step up and two steps, down. The linoleum on the floor was torn and had lost its corners, and the surface-mounted wire conduits were painted to match the wall color in a vain effort to hide them. Actually, the walls had been painted many times over as many layers of wallpaper, and the multi-layers of paper were peeling and sagging, as they had lost their togetherness in old age. Only Itono would have appreciated its insulation value. The place was a dump, but Daddey made it a home by hanging curtains, purchasing a couple armchairs, and a desk for the parlor.

A trio of newly built houses sat across the street from our abode, and I could not look at them without yearning. They were new and beautiful––no doubt with functional floor plans and modern appliances in multi-cabinet kitchens. How I wished Daddey and I could live in such a house, and live a nice, normal life.

"Midori, to buy house, I have to make payment for many years. If I die, you are too young to make payment. The bank take away house. You lose everything."

There was no point in tempting the gods and risking the longevity Daddey deserved. I had to wait until I grew up; then I would buy a house. Better still, I would design my new house and build it.

SUMMER WORK EXPERIENCE

The summer vacation between our sophomore and junior years came and went without a job, and another attempt to read *Les Miserables* had failed. The following year, I faced the prospect of another jobless summer vacation. To better utilize my time, I enrolled in summer school, and signed up for a couple of elective subjects I could not fit into my regular curriculum. A short time later, I saw a want ad for a mother's helper for a family living in a neighborhood near the university, I kept my fingers crossed, hoping this was the job to change my luck.

Shortly after starting high school, I had taken on a live-in mother's helper job that required a long time-consuming commute to Garfield High School, and my duties consumed most of my personal time. Living away from home while going to school created too many problems and I had quit at the end of two weeks. That experience did not squelch my enthusiasm to try again. Besides, it was a day job. I was hired. I commuted to my job every weekday after morning classes and returned home after the dinner dishes were washed. My weekends were free. The father a psychiatrist, and the three teenaged boys spent the good part of each day out of the house with their own jobs and activities. The mother, whom I was to help, was a perky, unpretentious woman who had me doing odd jobs around the house that I did not think needed doing. All the while, I dodged the huge Airedale terrier that lounged lazily on the kitchen floor wherever I needed to stand.

No doubt, Mrs. Hoedemaker realized within days of my arrival that her new mother's helper was an inept helper. I knew how to wash dishes and iron; other than that, I was an empty slate regarding housecleaning and cooking. Instead of replacing me with a more qualified girl, she changed her expectations and kept me on; assigning projects I was capable of doing. All the while, I observed how life was lived by one family on the other side of town; and she paid me all the while.

My luck had changed—Daddey would have called it karma—to have been exposed to genuine kindness and goodwill; the experience was a positive influence that stayed with me longer than any church sermon.

After a meaningful, well-spent summer, when school started and the inertia of summer was shed, I was ready to charge forward, despite a course load that was heavier than I should have taken on during senior year, when social programs continually crowded our calendar. Lynn, a fellow classmate, also aspired to be an architect, and we two girls intruded the boys' domain by taking physics class. The boys treated us as nonentities as best they could. We went a step further and signed up for architectural drafting and crashed that exclusive boys' club. Now it was Mr. Kelso, the instructor, who chose to ignore our presence when he launched into his tirades lecturing the boys about the real world, while we two girls had to sit and listen. That's when the boys welcomed our presence. "He's cut his talks a lot, and he's really cleaned up his language," Lynn and I were told.

My friends were prudently considering careers in traditional professions, especially teaching. The public schools were only beginning to accept minorities for teaching jobs, and my contemporaries were to become the frontrunners of Japanese American schoolteachers in the region. Joyce, who preferred the physical sciences and took advanced math as an elective, was planning to become a medical technician. Elaine had continued to find interests outside the inane typical teenage girl stuff and had drifted away.

Instead of sitting in study hall, I spent my free period in the school newspaper office, where I edited copy and wrote captions for the Messenger. I followed Margaret as copy manager and found myself composing headlines for the reporters' articles. Senior year was busy and fruitful in accomplishments; however, there was another project I had waited a year to take on.

Funfest

Every spring, Garfield put on its annual Funfest for three nightly performances: a show of skits, revues, and acts, created and performed by various groups of students. Traditionally, junior and senior girls each created their own chorus line revues, while junior and senior boys each put together their raucous skits. The Jewish, Chinese, and Japanese students each put together their own acts, as did various sororities and fraternities. The African American students were not yet as well organized, and often did not have their own act. Planning and practices began in the fall to prepare for tryouts, when the best routines were selected for the show.

As a sophomore, I had been ineligible to participate in the Japanese act, since seniors were in charge, and juniors were invited to take part. I had watched them enviously as an onlooker while they rehearsed a chorus-line routine they had adapted from a recent June Allyson movie. As a junior, I had anxiously waited for the seniors to put together an act. Months passed, and no Funfest meetings were called. We juniors stuck to protocol and made no attempt to usurp the seniors' entitlement, so we waited. The senior organizers did not organize; no Japanese act was prepared for audition, and there was no Japanese act in the Funfest that year. I was crushed.

"I swear I'm going to be the manager of the Japanese act next year when we're seniors, and as God is my witness, we're going to have the best act in next year's Funfest," I had said. "We're making up for this year's failure."

"You're being melodramatic. Having no act is not the end of the world," I was told. The world stayed on course and kept rotating and there was no worse disappointment for the year.

We were seniors at last; I was taking charge and announced... 'I'm the manager for the Japanese act in the next Funfest." My friends were too busy with projects of their own to protest my presumptuous intention; the juniors had no say. Elements for the act had been gestating in my mind since the previous year's disappointment, and I had a basic plot and sequence outlined by the time we held the first meeting. Mae agreed to be assistant manager in charge of the junior class participants. With promises that the after-church meetings and rehearsals at the Buddhist church would start and end promptly, I hoped to maintain the participants' cooperation and enthusiasm.

Funfest Japanese Act participants

As a friendless eighth grader, I had discovered the magic of ballet and had attended performances of dance companies when they toured Seattle. The staging, costumes, music, and the dancing itself created magic; a different make-believe realm than movie musicals. I hoped to capture a bit of the same enchantment. Why not have a doll come to life like Coppelia and give it a Japanese twist?

The toy maker falls asleep, and his toys come to life until he wakes up. The plot was simple, but not so simple squeezing it all into the allotted nine minutes running time. Our longtime students of *Odori*, Marian and Mae, took on the roles of shopkeeper and the Japanese doll. With their combined experience, they choreographed a traditional-style dance that included an over the back fan-toss sequence they practiced until they perfected the maneuver. Good catch. Bravo! Marta, our songstress, was able to find the music of my favorite Japanese song, which she sang while the other two danced their *Odori* duet… A second bravo!

As a concession to popular tastes and to provide a vehicle for more girls to be included, a seven-girl chorus line performed turns and kicks to the *Limehouse Blues*, a tune sounding somewhat Oriental. Joyce was the lead dancer in charge of putting together a dance routine and handling problems with any klutzy dancers. Other girls who did not want a spotlight role but wanted to participate, were tickled to be a part of the idol with moving hands: three junior girls readily agreed to be the "See no evil, hear no evil, speak no evil" monkeys, and a handful of others provided background color by wearing their own beautiful kimonos. I could not find a role for Margaret. After much deliberation, we decided to add a mischievous jester who brings the toys to life with the wave of her wand.

After the dances were set and the sequence of moving toys coordinated, I found a recording studio to cut a record for us for the entire nine-minute act, with music and all the pauses appropriately interspersed. We were able to run through our act fine-tuning the details as many times as necessary and still end the day's rehearsals in short order as promised. We breezed through the tryouts.

We began assembling our costumes. Marian wore an appropriate *Happi* coat and slacks, and the kimono wearers had to dig through their trunks to locate their precious wraps. Everyone else made her own costume. A shortened kimono made of red tulle and garnished with spotlight-catching aluminum-foil flowers was designed for the chorus. Standing posed on steps with hands folded in front, the long kimono sleeves were swung open, exposing the girls' legs as they started their dance routine. "Ah-la! I can see her undies," one mother in the audience exclaimed in Japanese. Our parents were from a different era—annoyingly old-fashioned, but thankfully adept at sewing. The mothers knew how to sew up a kimono without a pattern, even modified kimonos made of unconventional fabric. The idols and monkeys got out their sewing machines and went to work, too. The school agreed to build a doll case but refused to make a papier-mache peach that would collapse to reveal Margaret, who would then jump out to create her mischief. Mae and I took on the task. In the middle of our small living room, we shaped chicken wire, covered it with papier-mache, and painted it peach. It was transported to school prior to final rehearsals.

Stanley, the stage manager, who sat next to me in physics class, asked me to cue him to coordinate spotlight changes, etc., required for our act. We decided I should sit on stage as a doll and cue him with hand signals. Our show was not only a change from previous acts, but the coordinated energy, enthusiasm, and esprit de corps everyone contributed, sparked a magic, and our act was a resounding success. Teamwork is always touted, but it is so essential for success. It had been an exhilarating experience, and for me, the angst from past struggles in school, job failures, and disappointments evaporated. Success builds on lessons learned from past failures as well as past successes; I had a few successes to build on before, now, I felt confident and empowered.

The euphoria evaporated soon enough, and I landed back on earth, but I missed the fun and stimulation of putting together a show. We had a brush with the theater one more time when several of us took on roles from a scene in the play *The Women* for a YTeen program. Future participation in theater would be limited to an audience role. I did remain a movie buff, including oldies, silent, and foreign films. To view a Rudolph Valentino steamer and Jean Cocteau's *Beauty and the Beast*, meant traveling to a faraway theater. About this time, Akira Kurosawa's *Rashomon* was released in American theaters. Times had changed; it was my first exposure to a serious, not overly sentimental Japanese movie and it had a kissing scene. Ah-ya, that was a first. Times had changed...

As the head of the English department, renamed Language Arts, Mr. Wilson could be seen rambling down the hallway in his usual rumpled jacket, oblivious to the commotion around him. He's an eccentric, I thought, and I could not understand how Mrs. Olmstead could speak of him so highly. He was not cut of ordinary cloth like most of us; he was super smart. As a youngster, he had decided to read every book in the local library from A to Z. He admitted he'd only gotten to the books starting with L before abandoning the task. He was listed in Who's Who for writing published verses, when being listed had meaning. During the war, he had been stationed in an intelligence unit in remotest Alaska where he had time to read and think. He decided he could best serve mankind by becoming an educator. Education was the means to dispel ignorance and counter the prevailing evils in the world.

A class offered to seniors––before they left his sphere of influence–– called Cultural Heritage was Mr. Wilson's goal to expose us to examples of man's greater achievements in literature, the arts, music, and to different beliefs, cultures, and traditions likely unknown to us, so that we could achieve a greater understanding of our heritage and subjects not covered in our other studies.

It was a tall order for him to fulfill. We, who religiously listened to the Hit Parade for the latest hit song, were blown away when Beethoven's Fifth Symphony was played. The recording was on a scratchy acetate disc, but the essence was all there. We clamored to hear it to the end, but class was over, and unruly underclassmen were storming the door to be let in. We 'd only touched on a few subjects in the short time we had, but my curiosity was aroused. My view of the world had been expanded by another dedicated teacher.

Extracurricular activities, along with our studies, were coming to an end. We were busy cornering friends and acquaintances to sign our Annuals as the final school day arrived. As a member of the prom decoration committee, I spent a few hours at the private club with the committee before getting home to put the finishing touches on the prom dress I had designed and sewn to wear later that evening. We rushed across town to Meany Hall on the university campus wearing ill-fitting caps and gowns for our commencement program.

A generous friend of ours surprised us with a boxful of double-carnation leis from Hawaii, which he distributed. Wearing the garlands made us feel as beautiful as the flowers and like celebrities to boot. After the graduation ceremony ended and with diplomas in hand, we made another rush home to dress for the prom——the event we had dreamed of since who remembers when. The dance ended in the early morning hours. When I woke up the next day, it was hard to believe my high school years were over.

Changing Jobs

Yoshi applied for a job with the railroad company before his age disqualified him from being hired. The benefits and pay were better than hotel service work, and the job provided a pension on retirement. He was physically fit and looked younger than his age, so he was readily hired. Vanity did not wither and die with age. "I look twenty years younger, *neh?*" he said as he inspected his face in the mirror. Satisfied, he smiled broadly. "I very lucky."

Cleaning the passenger and dining compartments as well as the train's kitchen was a blue-collar job; he was a *rodosha-nin*, a laborer. He had avoided work considered laborer's jobs since the time spent in Kobe while he was waiting for a ship assignment before coming to America. A few such jobs had crept into his resume though he mostly had taken on service jobs. He set aside his pride for the real monetary benefits the new job offered. He worked hard, and his usual nervous energy made him a rushing, slapdash worker with little finesse, but he got the job done plus some. His coworkers welcomed his cooperative attitude and work ethics. The cooks could depend on him for extra help, which they rewarded with small treats to eat. Yoshi's sweet tooth for pastries, pies, and cakes remained undiminished.

On Saturdays, Yoshi continued to work at the hotel doing jobs not covered by the regular janitor. The extra income he earned allowed him to buy a car. It was a luxury he had not had since he sold the old Model A to Kitty when he was interned to Puyallup. The car of choice was a brand-new Ford sedan. The world beyond now lay at his feet and gas pedal.

His concerns for my daily welfare were now minimal, and like a child with a new toy, Yoshi was off to visit acquaintances, attend gatherings, and travel about with friends. They drove up to Mt. Rainier in the fall when the wildflowers were in bloom throughout the meadows, to Hood Canal to visit the beachfront home where he and Aiko had worked shortly after my birth, and further on to the ocean to dig for clams and collect oysters.

After the first autumn rain, he went in search of *matsutake* mushrooms in the foothills of the Cascades and the woodlands of Shelton, joining the hordes of others who went hunting for the special mushrooms so prized by the Japanese. This was a new sport for Yoshi. Before the war, he did not have the time to spend a day driving to forests and trudging in the woods looking for the elusive edible fungi; neither did most Japanese at that time. Sawmill workers had sometimes found them growing in the woods near the mill camps where they were housed. After their harvests, it was farmers in the valley who had the time to go out in search of mushrooms. Hori-*san*, Hayame's husband, had years of experience wandering through the woods in his search. He was a living repository for choice sites where the *matsutake* could be found. Pickers were leery of telling others where they found their specimens to keep others from picking clean their favored sites. The secrecy prevailed until the picker became too old to roam the hills alone and passed on the information to a trusted driver.

Yoshi still spent many of his non-working hours contemplating, composing a new poem, or reworking one he had been formulating through the day, days, or for weeks. So deep-rooted was the habit now, Yoshi fretted and fussed if he missed a day. He diligently submitted his work to various *tanka* poetry competitions held in Japan, including the prestigious Imperial New Year's contest. When the subject for the following year's poem was announced, he wasted little time waiting for inspiration and began writing, then rewriting and refining a poem for eventual submittal; making sure he made the deadline. Yoshi's submissions were rejected every year, but he continued composing a new poem incorporating the new theme, always hoping his luck would work a miracle with a winning poem. And all the while, he continued writing everyday odes as usual.

The high light of each month was the meetings with his Tanka-kai poetry group. There was comfort relaxing in the company of longtime friends. Any quirks in their personalities or habits were known and accepted. Strong-willed Mrs. Itoi could be depended on to offer a contrary opinion when others masked their true opinions, and Mrs. Niguma would not contradict anyone. Once in a while, Mr. Mihara showed up when he was not too involved in community programs. Handsome Mrs. Nakagawa hailed from Mie prefecture too, from an interior mountainous region far north of Yoshi's seaside village. He felt a special affinity toward her as a fellow Mie native.

"Nakagawa-*san*, you're sure you're not descended from *ninjas*?"

"Don't be ridiculous. My family were farmers. They were not assassins."

"Ninjas worked regular jobs, and did their dirty work on assignment in secret. And they came from the mountains where you come from."

"I heard the same stories you did, Nomura-*san*. If there were any ninjas living in my neighborhood, I never knew who they were."

"We lived too far south to be involved in that kind of bloodthirsty business––piracy perhaps. We weren't as steady on our feet as you farmers."

Yoshi's special friendship with Mrs. Esaki endured. They maintained a social relationship as they had in camp, except they saw each other less often. She worked as a sewing machine operator in a clothes-manufacturing workshop, as did many Issei and older Nisei women after the war. It was a behind-the-scenes job requiring a minimal knowledge of English, ideal for immigrant hires. Like other families with both spouses working, they began making headway financially. The telephone became a popular tool for social communication.

"Think how convenient it would have been if we all had telephones in camp," the conversation began.

"I think about the times I walked ten long blocks to visit a friend, only to find they were out."

"Well, I can think of lotta other inconveniences worse than not having a phone."

"Just consider yourself lucky to be living in a postwar era with all our modern luxuries––if you can afford them." And so it was.

Beginning College

Things were the same, and they were different that summer. Mrs. Hoedemaker hired me again for the summer, a job I took on gladly. Since my weekends were free, I joined others on picnics to Lake Wilderness. Practically no one owned his or her own car yet, and the family car was usually off-limits. Our transportation was the black panel truck Kenzo managed to borrow from his dad. He drove with his girlfriend at his side in the front cab while the rest of us, girls and boys, managed to roll with the turns on the floor in back of the van which was windowless except for the portholes in the back door. On weekdays, the truck was used to transport the freshly made satsuma-age, the deep-fried fishcakes that were a side business of their grocery store. When we back-of-the-truck passengers emerged, we reeked of deep-fried fishcake. It was like leaving a poorly vented fish-and-chips joint. After the long ride to our picnic destination, we no longer noticed the deep-fried smell––though others certainly did.

The group was not as clearly defined any longer; our gatherings encompassed a broader range of ages. There were pairings and breakups; we were growing up. I had no boyfriend. We were entering another stage in our lives, and I was anxious to start new adventures and did not need distractions––was what I said.

Gale had begun her new adventures as soon as school ended, electing to start her work career in the Health Sciences department at the university. The rest of us arrived on campus in the fall, taking freshmen classes on the main campus. Whatever thoughts we might have had about going away to college were only fleeting notions, since every one of us knew our parents could not afford such an expense. My own dreams of attending an East Coast college lasted several nanoseconds. The University of Washington was a city bus ride from home, the in-state tuition was affordable, and any student graduating from a high school in the state of Washington qualified to attend the university. There were no SAT tests, enrollment limits, or quotas yet. Grades were generally marked on a curve, and any quarter a student's grade average fell below a C meant probation. Two probations in a row and the student was dropped from college. Period.

The bus stop was a short two blocks down the hill from home. After it routed through downtown, the bus headed north to the university, making it a long ride, but otherwise convenient since no transfers were required. Once on the spacious campus, our varied class schedules had us independently crisscrossing from building to building without seeing a familiar face. The designated meeting place was the main floor reading room in the library. Little serious studying or reading took place there, but by merely sitting there, an acquaintance was likely to pass through looking for someone to talk to, too.

We could be recognized by the uniformity of our apparel. The regulation navy-blue pleated skirts with white middy shirts we had worn at least once a week in high school was too juvenile for college wear, and we had tossed them. We instead wore our long, straight wool skirts just above our socks and white-and-brown saddle shoes. Our skirts were so tight and long, we practically hobbled, and running to classes on opposite sides of campus was well-nigh impossible, but being stylishly current was still more important. Square plaid scarves protected our heads in inclement weather; we neither used nor carried umbrellas since we considered them encumbrances.

Greek-lettered fraternities and sororities at the university continued to be exclusive, but other organizations had begun inviting minorities to join. A prior generation of Japanese students had founded their own club's years before. The men's group owned a large residential building across the street from campus with facilities for a handful of live-ins, and a social meeting space for Japanese American students. We girls joined the Valedas, the Japanese girls' social organization, which was a continuation of our high school groups, and made up of a broader range of girls attending college who were not Garfield grads. Our exposure to a wider circle of acquaintances had yet to be other than basically Japanese. The Reginas were no longer a club, as we had dispersed, spending more time with friends with similar personal and career interests, and with boyfriends.

There was a huge disconnect from what I had learned in high school and what I was expected to know in college. Freshman English 101 was like a foreign language. Our assignment was to write a theme paper of five hundred words relating to an incident in our lives. Applicable references and footnotes were to be included. Footnotes?

The sallow-complexioned teaching assistant sat curled in his seat scanning my paper marked with comments and corrections he had made earlier. The private conference was to review my submittal titled "A True Experience," which lay on the table in front of him, bloodied with his red ink marks.

"The circumstances you bring up in your paper are unfamiliar to me. I have to assume it is based on fact, since you were not given a fiction assignment," he said.

"What? Didn't you ever hear about relocation camps like Minidoka?"

"No, never."

"Really? That's where we spent the war years."

"That such a facility was given an Indian name is incongruous."

"I don't know why they gave it an Indian name. No one ever said."

"There's another word I have marked which has been misused: Caucasian."

"Caucasians are white people."

"Caucasians are people of the Caucasus region near the Black Sea in Soviet Russia. You have used the word incorrectly."

"Caucasian is the polite way we identify white people like you. There are other, not-so-nice names used, too."

"I thought to be 'nice,' I would point out the most obvious areas requiring correction. The entire premise of your paper is preposterous, and your 'camp' is decidedly camp."

Freshman English was the trap to trip up students from inflated grade averages. The second two quarters were not as frustrating as the first. Margaret breezed through all three quarters as usual, and we blinked in wonder. Her ability was never obvious or on display; she just consistently managed to get top grades, whether it was a social science distribution class with hundreds of other freshmen or a small lab class.

Those huge auditorium lecture classes were daunting, and I never got to know a soul in those classes. However, our physics and math for Architecture majors were peppered with familiar faces who were to be my classmates the next few years.

ARCHITECTURE STUDIES

When my second year started, with the mornings mired in fog, I trudged to my math for Architecture students' class. I had failed the third quarter, and I was unhappy to be repeating the course. The math-wizard teaching assistant had been totally unsympathetic when I wrote "Too damn hard" to a problem I had spent hours trying to solve without success. His half-page reply was a lecture: "Young ladies do not use such language, etc." When I entered the makeup class, it was full of more familiar faces; we were all repeating the class, so the stigma of flunking was shared and bonding.

Our basic design studio class for Architecture, Interior Design, and Industrial Design majors met three hours a day, four days a week, in the basement of Architecture Hall, a holdover building from the Alaska

Yukon Exposition of 1906. We were seated alphabetically, much as they would do in grammar school. We sat at long rows of desks facing the blackboards. The class was large; we filled the two large studios to capacity. One-third of the students were giggling interiors majors who came down from the Art Building on upper campus to meet and mix with the male Architecture students. A handful of male industrial design majors disassociated themselves from the mob. They were too pragmatic for the aesthete blathering that floated about. Most of us entered college straight from high school; we were fresh and unquestioning. There was also a large segment of Korean War veterans who were older and who had returned to finish their educations; they were focused, and held a different view of the world.

The mission of the seven instructors/critics was to impart design concepts to a largely unexposed group of students who had not heard of Dadaism, Beaux Arts, and the like. The projects were diverse and stimulating, which I soaked up like a sponge, though my results were uneven. Creativity could not be turned on and off like a spigot. Everyone's favorite critic was George Tsutakawa, an instructor from the art department, whose advice was always positive. He could find an element, often miniscule in any godawful design that could be developed into a viable solution; his advice always encouraged. Then there were the two who critiqued with sarcasm and insults, leaving us crushed like roadkill.

We noticed before long that fellow student Dick was consistently getting the top A for his projects. A few years studying at an art school in New York was an advantage, but his exceptional drawing ability was a gift. He read and was immersed in theory and philosophy too intangible for most of us.

"Dick reminds me of that architect in The Fountainhead. Gary Cooper played him in the movie. Did you see the movie or read the book?" Norton, my desk neighbor had asked. I was familiar with both and I agreed. Dick actually looked more an architect than Cooper, and his aloof independence resembled Olivier's movie *Hamlet*. He was tall and blond with a deeply chiseled profile that resembled a rough-hewn marble bust before the sculptor had smoothed the edges. His desert boots and casual appearance preceded the trend.

My Garfield classmate Lynn changed her mind about becoming an architect. She dropped the basic design class, changed her major, and was gone.

The following school year, the girls from the Interiors department and the Industrial Design clique returned to their respective buildings on upper campus. We Architecture majors were entering the professional phase of our five-year course of study, and we moved upstairs to roomier, high-ceilinged, second-floor studios. We numbered over eighty students, although more than a handful had already dropped out of the program. Desks were still assigned alphabetically, and Norton and I were desk neighbors another year.

Each quarter, two consecutive five-week design problems were assigned. The written program was distributed on the first day of the five-week segment along with a short discussion followed by questions and answers. We had five weeks to develop a solution and prepare drawings to submit for grading. Our Architecture design professors, who we referred to as profs or crits, were available to advise us on our preliminary schemes once or twice a week. If we were diligent, our design concepts were finalized by the end of the fourth week, giving us a week to prepare the final drawings, which were due at 5:00 p.m. on Friday of the fifth week.

Our studio classes were from 2:00 to 5:00 p.m. five days a week, but creative inspiration keeps its own hours, and we students came and went to class according to our creative impulses or whims. My ideas percolated in my head before I put them on paper. The unproductive hours accumulated, and the usual scramble to complete the presentation drawings was on again. The Thursday night prior to the Friday deadline was an all-night cram session few managed to avoid. The Architecture building remained open through the night to accommodate the third, fourth and fifth-year Architecture students, who all had design projects due the next day.

The charrette was a tradition all Architecture students were expected to undergo and endure, working through a sleepless night to finish their projects, much like the rigors medical interns undergo before becoming physicians. It was a test of one's mettle, a rite of passage.

There was always too much to do in too little time. The pressure was intense, but as the Thursday nights wore on, our energy waned along with our concentration. We drank cup after cup of coffee to counter our drowsiness, because we had to stay awake and press on. It wasn't uncommon for a student so overcome with fatigue to find an empty corner to catch a few minutes of sleep, and the really weary returning to their apartments to sleep on a bed. But dawn came far too soon, and they returned to their drawings with another burst of wakefulness. Unfortunately, since they were further from completion, they had to work faster.

Another form of torture was the Wednesday ten-hour sketch problem. The assignment was made available at noon, and the drawn solution was due at 10:00 p.m. Quick problem solving and a swift artistic hand were required. The best submittal was awarded one and a half points. Lesser submittals received either half or one point. All others were marked X—a dreaded "ding." In order to pass to the next level, students were required to earn a minimum of three points. It was not an easy task to reinvent a picnic table or bicycle rack or a small footbridge for a creek when inspiration failed. A last "double-points" three-day watercolor painting sketch problem enabled nearly everyone to earn the required points.

When we had moved to the upstairs design studios, our desks were real drafting tables, and we sat on high wooden stools. It was days after the start of the school year, but I was still fiddling, trying to adjust the tilt of the drafting surface of my table to a comfortable angle.

"Hi, I'm Mae-Lin. I think we're the only girls taking design studio," she said with a broad smile. Her desk was in the other room, and we had not communicated before.

"I'm surprised to see you here. Weren't you one of the girls from the Interior Design department?"

"I was, but I decided to switch to Architecture. It's so much more interesting and challenging than Interiors."

"You'll have to take Architectural Engineering and Physics and…"

"Oh, I don't mind those classes," she said. "It's the social science classes that I find difficult, especially Sociology."

Math and science were not my forte, but there was no mystery about Sociology. "You don't have problems with the hard classes, so why do you find Sociology so difficult?" I asked.

"In class, they discuss subjects which are not mentioned in the textbook. I have no idea what they're talking about. How am I to know about such things? When they include it in the exams, I have no answers."

"What things did they discuss? Can you give me an example?"

"Yes, yes. They talked about panty raids. I was the only person who had never heard of such things. Everyone else knew, and it wasn't in our textbook."

That was her Achilles heel. Recent cultural or social phenomena familiar to those who lived in America were not necessarily common knowledge to immigrants who had only recently arrived in our country. Mae-Lin's father was a professor at the university, and they had recently fled the Communist takeover of China.

At Garfield, the smaller Chinese contingent and we Japanese mixed at school, but though we were both second-generation children of immigrant parents, we moved in our own separate circles, and I never knew one well enough to call a friend.

Mae-Lin was a marvel, and I found her refreshing to be with. She was friendly and open without hidden agendas, and she lacked pretense. She mentioned the Japanese bombings of her homeland in passing and generously withheld any word of subsequent atrocities committed by warrior invaders who may have shared a common ancestor with me. There were endless other things to talk and laugh about, which we did often. Instead of being rivals, we became friends.

That attitude prevailed through much of the class, as the veterans brought a real sense of generosity that we were all in there together with the same goal: everyone to finish with a degree.

I found my way to the library reading room less often as I became involved with my design assignments. All our other classes were for majors, and most were held in the Architecture building, allowing us to walk from one to the other without leaving the building. Our desks became our home on campus.

As third-year students, my friends were involved in the demands of their own majors, a wider range of friends and activities, and their steady boyfriends. Elaine and Alice had already left the fold and married. Sami arrived in town with her family and became an integral part of the community; her father was the new minister of the Methodist church. A new batch of Japanese American habitués migrated to the reading room, including veterans returning from the Korean War, though they were less apt to join in the idle chatter that flowed in our corner of the library. Missing were male students being drafted into service. I was also drifting away from the social circle and my ties to friends, by absenting myself from the reading room. I felt a sense of loss in the beginning, but there were choices to be made. I needed to wean myself from distractions and become independent. My interests revolved around architecture; I said other things mattered less.

The reality was different; I had met someone who mattered as much, if not more. He was the oldest brother of the three from Hawaii who had moved to Seattle when their father became the rector of Seattle's Japanese Episcopal church. We shared similar interests, he was Christian, and there was no mother-in-law in the picture to complicate our lives; all attributes I thought necessary for avoiding major future conflicts in a life together. David was my beloved; we eloped.

Architecture had been reduced to second priority as love and marriage brought on new responsibilities and unanticipated complications. The draft had finally caught up with my new husband as his deferments ran out. I dropped out of college at the end of the school year.

My goals to acquire a degree and become an architect crashed. I was twenty-one, married, and pregnant, with a husband away in the armed services. My new role of wife and then mother had to be nurtured. As I told Daddey each new episode of my new life, he only said, "I see." There were no further comments––after all, it was his daughter's karma.

We lived with Daddey until the downstairs unit of the duplex became available for us to rent and to be independent from my father. Son Michael was born, and a year later, daughter Lorraine joined the family.

Yoshi acquired a new name. "Daddey" no longer sufficed. The moniker served him well through the years while I was growing up and we shared life's uncertainties. It was a hybrid name. Mother, in her campaign to Americanize us, had decided he should be called Daddy. He had softened the sharp "dee" ending to sound more agreeable, just as the Japanese customarily do by switching syllables when a combination word can be made to roll off the tongue more smoothly. Sushi becomes *zushi* when combined with *maki* to become *maki-zushi*. Whether with an s or z, it is a rolled sushi in English. I no longer cringed at our mutual mispronunciation, an embarrassment I felt during my smart-aleck adolescence. As I had grown older, I realized the phonic twist gave him a unique name rather than the generic one shared by all fathers.

Grandpa evolved to Grampa, the same lazy-mouth process, and it became Yoshi's permanent name for the rest of his life. Yoshi loved his grandchildren. It mattered not at all what they called him. The first born, a boy, a grandson who filled that void of the son he never had. That energetic, rambunctious little boy who was a magnet for everything little boys should not touch, investigate, attempt, or disassemble always found refuge in Grampa's quarters when he was scolded by his parents for doing something naughty. The granddaughter who arrived the following year made the two a pair, a double-trouble twosome.

The father/daughter relationship between Daddey and I had had its rocky moments early on––a genteel way of describing those sometime tumultuous situations––but it eased as I grew up. Mostly we lived in harmony when we knew to hold our tongues, refraining from telling the other what to do and avoiding making judgmental remarks. When Daddey became Grampa, he also transferred his affections to his grandchildren, and I was relegated to his Grandchildren's Mother. He relinquished his parental responsibilities that he assumed after Aiko's passing. His status changed from single parent to footloose bachelor, and I asked him if he considered marriage again.

"Grampa, it's OK if I have a stepmother now," I said. "You can find a wife and not be lonely."

"Maybe I single too long. I no want someone tell me do zhis, do zhat, we go visit, we go store, we go…" Apparently he had been considering his options and had reached a decision. "If I marry, no more time to read book and write poem."

"You're getting old…"

"No, not so old. I can have many sweetheart, *neh*."

The children also had a second grandfather who lived in Minneapolis. He baptized each newborn grandchild before they were a month old. Each child had the required quota of godparents, but they had no grandmother. The two grandfathers had been single parents the past dozen years or more; they shared similar experiences, although their dissimilarities were also great.

"I came home from work many times to a house smelling of burnt rice," Grampa's counterpart said. "The boys were responsible to have a pot of rice cooked each day, but inattention resulted in burnt rice, so they had quickly cooked a second batch thinking I would not notice."

"That was never my problem. I had a daughter who never cooked," Grampa said

"Washing the clothes after the boys went to sleep…"

"Yes, leaning over the rim of a bathtub scrubbing clothes was a chore without the luxury of a washing machine."

"When we moved to Kauai, I hired a house-girl to help with the chores for a few hours a day."

"Did you ever consider remarriage? You are handsome man. Many women must have been interested in being your wife."

"Ha, ha, ha, Nomura-*san*, my faith doesn't require celibacy; I wanted the boys to finish school first. But since you asked, there was a persistent woman here in Seattle who proposed we get together. We were completely unsuited: all she thought about was her business and…"

"Money! She was a widow…"

"With no children. She kept sending a go-between for a meeting, so I reluctantly agreed to meet her."

"I think we were both introduced to the same woman!"

CHAPTER 18

The Job, 1957-1966

WHENEVER SEPTEMBER ARRIVED WITH ITS cool, misty, back-to-school weather, a deep regret and sense of failure inevitably returned. I had quit. I had no college degree and no job skills.

My military dependents' check barely covered all our expenses no matter how prudently I budgeted. The Sears Roebuck wringer washing machine was not a luxury when diapers from two babies had to be washed daily. We bought the cheapest model available, but making the monthly payments meant the children went without shoes until they walked. The half-coal, half-gas kitchen stove was a challenge, but I was learning to cook.

As I sat at the kitchen table in the evening, flying insects began buzzing around the lightbulb. The bugs kept increasing by the day. Husband from Hawaii identified the termites and found they had eaten their way through the wood floor under the linoleum. Hundreds of insects were wiggling their way into our bedroom. Shades of cockroaches——these bugs were not shy. They neither ran away nor hid, and they were aggressive. I hated them. The landlord's quick fix eliminated the bug problem; however, the burrowed floorboards were not replaced. We slept in the living room after that.

The washer and the laundry tub were located outside the house by the coal shelter. I was washing diapers. I was tired and cold and the rain dripped through cracks of the corrugated tin roof. I had my Scarlet O'Hara moment: Damn it all. This is only temporary, we're on a detour, and things will get better eventually. It might take a while, but we'll both finish college and get our degrees. That's when the movie ended. In real life, not much changed.

David fulfilled his two years of military service spent mostly in nearby Fort Lewis. Upon his discharge, he went to work at Boeing as a draftsman, and I was a full-time housewife and mother. It was not what we had envisioned for our future. We were as poor as the proverbial church mice, and I had no new ideas how we could climb out of our dark financial pit. Nor were there any paths directing us toward the long-term goals we had once hoped to achieve; any return to finish school was now impossible. No amount of Scarlett O'Hara "God be my witness" vows could alter the reality of our situation. No miracles happened. I never expected any, but I needed guidance to show me a way to get back on track. The messenger came in the guise of a mailman. He was an acquaintance who had married an upperclassman I knew from school. The last time I saw her, we were trying to pass our required swimming test in the women's pool on campus. So much had changed since.

It was the onset of summer, and I was outdoors basking in the June sun during the short interval of quiet while the children took their midday nap. I saw the mailman walking his route across the street, and I waited for him to reach our mailbox. We exchanged greetings, and briefly updated each other on our current circumstances.

"We've been struggling too," he said. But things were beginning to look up since his wife got a job working at The Restaurant. "Say, if you're interested, there's an opening now. A gal is getting married and her fiancé told her: "No wife of mine is going to work," so she quit. They're looking. Give them a call, and fill out an application." He gave me the name of the head waitress to contact and wished me success before continuing on his rounds.

The Restaurant was a first-tier eatery, very expensive, and specialized in grilled foods. The owner came to Seattle from Hawaii with the intent of duplicating the format of his successful restaurant in Honolulu. The restaurant's décor was an extravagant mix of the tropics modified by northwest woodsy. Japanese waitresses wearing kimonos with their long sleeves fluttering in passing, added to the exotic ambience. This was not a Japanese restaurant; therefore, the women were required to speak English. When the initial staffing for his restaurant began, the owner could not find a pool of experienced Japanese American waitresses as was available in Hawaii. In Seattle, there was no tradition for local Nisei and Sansei to have worked as waitresses, except in family-owned ethnic restaurants. In that era, mainstream eateries did not hire Japanese for jobs serving the public. In the local community, many considered working as a waitress was demeaning, which compounded the reluctance Nisei women felt about seeking work there. With wise counsel, the owner contacted and persuaded a well-respected woman in the community who was in difficult circumstances to convince other women that taking a job at The Restaurant would not lower their images or reputations. Instead, their association with the premier dining establishment, which The Restaurant aspired to become, should be seen as prestigious. It was an opportunity to set an example of excellence for those who followed; earning a decent income was an incentive, too. The first group of waitstaff at The Restaurant did indeed, start the traditions for their successors, and set standards of working hard, working well, and working with smarts. Those samurai ancestors everyone claimed to have, could look down from the heavens and witness their female descendants as they carried forth with their *bushido* spirit.

Kai and I applied at the same time, and were both hired. Luckily, I had never heard gossip about The Restaurant and was not forewarned about the job and people working there, or of the now well-established set of standards and tradition; I started as a true innocent. I was so happy and giddy to be hired, finally a real job. I vowed to succeed as a skilled and valued employee. I was capable, and by applying myself, I could achieve my goals. It would take sustained resolve and endurance. *Gambatte.*

Since there was no separate employee entrance, we entered at the front door under The Restaurant's low-ceilinged porte cochere the customers used. The frameless glass door and sidelights bordered by the rough-cut stone walls enhanced the sense of entry into a tropical den. On stepping out from the low-ceilinged entry into the dining room proper with its soaring roof, the two-story stone wall and proportionately oversized fire-place blocked our way and view, requiring us to proceed with a turn to face the reception desk. Alternatively, a guest made his or her way up the stairs to a private dining area or down a half level to the lounge. The blend of exotic Polynesia and Pacific Northwest rustic was carried throughout the space. The featured copper hood above the grill was flanked by long, narrow gas torches. A huge copper chandelier hung from the ceiling, providing artistic décor without providing much light, and a kitschy stuffed Mahi Mahi fish trophy hung on a wall above the liquor case. Two sides of the main dining room opened to the lower level seating area, with slanting glass windows allowing both levels to share the panorama of lake and neighborhoods stretching below and beyond to the University of Washington and further still. Beyond the waterway, the hulking, rusty buildings and smokestacks of the gas plant held stage center. Standing west of that, another landmark; the Grandma's Cookies sign was too prominent to ignore, especially at night when it glowed bold and bright for all to see.

The Restaurant became the success envisioned by the owner. The original structure, designed by architect Roland Terry and partner, which had opened in December 1950, was deemed ready for an addition to accommodate more dining space, offices, and other spaces overlooked in the original design.

The existing building did not include a dressing room for the waitresses. The owner corrected the omission by erecting a wood shed for that purpose. The lean-to was positioned just outside the restaurant's rear door and inside a screen fence, thus hiding it from the busy arterial running along the other side of the fence. It was barely larger than a handicapped parking space at a grocery store. In Hawaii, the waitresses arrived at work wearing their kimonos. Passersby undoubtedly thought it charming and colorful in that touristy area of Waikiki. This was not the case in Seattle, where a kimono was never worn as streetwear; it was reserved for ceremonial occasions. Otherwise, the wearer was marked as a curiosity or as "straight off the boat." We were still trying to blend in and be fully accepted as Americans.

Though a contradiction, the women wore kimonos without protest while working; it was a uniform, a somewhat cumbersome one, but it was not street clothes. The women changed into their uniforms at the work-place. The changing room shack was not only minimal in size, but also had no amenities. The space heater was barely adequate in winter, and the open door provided ventilation in the summer. By the time I arrived, the stray cat that had given birth to kittens among the scattered *zori* and fallen sashes was long gone along with her brood.

The Kimono

We walked past the dishwashing compartment, past peeled potatoes in cylindrical containers, and heads of romaine on the drain boards as we skirted through the kitchen. Masa, who had designated herself in charge of breaking in the two new hires, was leading the way.

"You're lucky. We got a batch of new kimonos not too long ago. You'll be able to wear a new kimono on your first day," Masa said as we reached the shack.

"This is the dressing room?" Kai asked.

"They've promised us a new one, big enough for all of us to dress at the same time."

"When will that be?"

"Construction work begins in a few months, after the busy summer months." We entered the closet crammed with Japanese wear and slippers in disarray on the floor. Masa was oblivious to the mess as she started her search. "You'll have to find your way to the downtown union office. The Restaurant is a union shop, and you have to join the Waitresses' Union within two weeks; actually, sooner the better."

I was crestfallen. This job venture had already cost monies. I had borrowed from our car insurance and baby-shoes fund. At Higo's Store on Jackson, I had purchased *tabi*, *zori's*, and an *obi*, which were part of my uniform, and now I had a union initiation fee and months of dues to pay in advance. I calculated a sum equaling two months of my wages.

Masa continued, "Remember, no nail polish or perfume. And go buy a decent hairnet. The Health Department requires it."

"A hairnet? I've never worn one."

"You'll wear one now. Don't get the type that mashes your hair down, making you look like someone's granny. We all buy ours at Woolworth. They have a brand that makes you look like you're not wearing a net."

She pulled out a kimono from the rack and handed it to Kai. The pattern was not particularly attractive, but no one was bound to notice since everyone inevitably focused on Kai's pretty face. Masa finally came up with a second kimono.

"Lucky I found this. It must be the last one. It's for you." She handed it to me. There was good reason it was the last one, the bottom of the barrel. It was so ugly no one else would have been seen in it alive or dead. How to describe its ugliness? The fancies of paisley print, it was not. It was closer to a junkie's grotesque hallucinations. Only a depraved mind could have concocted the conglomeration of mis-shapen globs, splats, splotches, bleeps, and blobs spattered on white, each curiously suspended not quite equidistant one from another. And the unblended distinct primary and secondary colors screamed for at-tention. All the icky images from Pandora's Box had found their way to the bizarro kimono; it was ugly.

"Do I have to wear that?" I asked. "Can't I wear one of those kimonos hanging there?" I pointed to dozens upon dozens of kimonos crammed onto the sagging clothes pole that ran the length of the shack.

"Those kimonos belong to other girls," Masa said.

"All of them? Isn't there one other kimono I can wear? There must be ten dozen kimonos hanging here."

"Tomorrow you can go buy your own, if you don't like this one."

Masa managed to find an *obi* for me, and she patiently showed me how to dress myself in a kimono. I knew the rudiments only, and I wished the patient mothers who dressed us before the *odori* performances were here to dress me now.

"Remember, left over right, opposite to the American way. You'll know you've worn it the wrong way when you can't tuck your tickets smoothly in the fold by your chest."

"How's that?"

"You'll know soon enough." She was warming up a bit. "Good job. These ties are good and long. Did you use old sheets to make the ties?"

"I was lucky and found one I could rip up." I knew how crucial those strings were to properly fit the "one size fits all" kimonos to the wearer.

"You wouldn't believe the number of girls who come to work here who've never worn a kimono before, except as kids. They bring ties the length of shoestrings the first day."

The *obi's* that were not pre-knotted required a second person to cinch the wide waistband and make the knot, which is tied in the back. I was not a stranger to dressing in a kimono, but I had forgotten how tightly the twice-wound *obi* around my midsection was pulled, crushing breasts and ribs, before the knot was tied. I was sure Masa's sadistic streak was raging when my *obi* was tightened then cinched again ever more tightly, then yanked with a final torso-turning tug, knocking all the air out of my lungs. With great skill, the *obi* strands were woven, twisted, and pinched then knotted to create a bow, which had to stay tight and in place for hours.

"It feels great when you're properly tied together, doesn't it?" commented my tormentor.

I was still gasping for air, so I merely nodded my head. "Oh, by the way, we already have someone named Midori working here," she said nonchalantly. "It's too confusing to have two girls with the same name, so you'll be called Dori. Got that?"

Kai finished dressing first, and she traipsed into the dining room to wait for Masa and me. She looked appropriately Japanese in her kimono, and she looked like she belonged there.

"You the new babe...er...girl? What's your name?" asked; the man stoking the fire in the grill pit.

"Hi, I'm Kai," she said as she smiled.

"Kai? Hubba, hubba."

"Now you have to tell me your name."

"He's Joe, the chef. He runs the kitchen," Masa said, interrupting the tête-à-tête as she came on the scene. She walked over to the broiler to face the chef. "Joe, for your information, Kai's a married woman…with children."

"Masa, now why are you telling me that?"

I strode out into the still-empty dining room like a gladiator gallantly marching into the arena to confront the horde of fierce and bloodthirsty antagonists. Actually, I was shaking in my *zori's* that clacked and flapped as I walked. I didn't shuffle along slightly pigeon-toed as proper Japanese ladies do; therefore, I clacked when the back of my slippers slapped my heel, and the overlapping folded opening at the bottom of my kimono flapped open with each giant stride I took.

Joe watched the spectacle. "Masa, what is that?"

"She's our other new busgirl, Dori." I was beckoned and introduced to the chef.

"Hello, new girl," he said.

A few early shift waitresses were going about their chores in the dining room, and when they saw me and my outfit, they gasped in disbelief then shook bodily as they suppressed their laughter. Not only was my walk ungainly, but my bony elbows and arms also kept poking out from the open sides of my kimono sleeves. Kai managed to look like a Japanese doll; the contrast we presented was all the more painful for me.

Masa was one of the original waitresses; she had started on day one. She was a consummate professional, and she expected everyone else to perform up to her standards. The head waitress job had eluded her, and since diplomacy was not her forte, she felt it was just as well; not having a title allowed her to kibitz from the sidelines, saying whatever she had on her mind. She was adamant that any new hires be trained properly, and she took it upon herself to teach them their duties and responsibilities when she considered the training being undertaken too lax. She was doing just that, giving Kai and me instructions on the chores we were expected to do when we arrived each day. "Before you change into your kimonos, you'll…"

We were interrupted. "TOMI!" hollered the man with a loosened bow tie hanging from his tuxedo shirt collar. He threw his dinner jacket on a chair and resumed his pacing. He once again bellowed out to the rafters, "TOMI! Where the HELL are you?"

A woman came scurrying out of the kitchen with dish towel in hand. "Rudy, what's the emergency?"

His voice, at the same fever pitch, yelled, "DAMN IT, Tomi! Will you tell me what, why…?" Heads popped out of the kitchen, and the bartenders leaned over the counter trying to get a glimpse of what was happening in the dining room. The perpetrator was suddenly aware everyone had stopped what he or she was doing. All eyes and ears were directed toward him, waiting to hear what had brought on his latest tirade. He lowered his voice and hissed, "That godawful what-you-call-it. We're not running a carnie sideshow here. And don't deny you haven't seen it. What makes you think? How did you allow it?"

He spat out the words in rapid-fire succession.

"Oh, you must have noticed the ki-mo-no our new busgirl is wearing. Yes?" Tomi asked, enunciating each word carefully for all eavesdroppers to hear.

"What else would I be talking about? *Por favo*r."

"You don't like it, I gather."

"This is no goddamn joke, Tomi."

"Well, it's just one of the new kimonos The Restaurant finally managed to buy for us girls. Our new girl needed a kimono, so she's wearing one."

"Jesus! Goddamn it all!" Rudy screeched as he seethed with renewed anguish. He collapsed into a chair and sat without uttering a word. With focused concentration and a minute of deliberate breathing, the steam and smoke settled. "OK. I got your point, damn it. I'll make sure future purchases are more selective."

"Thanks, Rudy. We don't ask for much." Tomi started back toward the kitchen.

"Tomi, you could have just told me…"

"A picture is worth a thousand words, they say."

"Since that's the case, why don't you just shut up?"

The late-shift waitresses began arriving at the restaurant, unaware of the incident just past. As they walked through the main dining hall on their way to the dressing shed, they exchanged their customary greetings to coworkers along the way. As they walked through, they noticed the new girl with that godawful kimono who would be working in their midst.

"I didn't know we were that desperate for help," said the first woman. "It's sure different from the old days. They would never allow something like that to be seen on the floor."

"What's important is whether she's a good, willing worker," her companion said.

"If not, we'll make sure she either learns or she leaves. Right?"

"Oh, don't be so hard on them. Not everyone is Miz Perfect like you."

"I say, if they don't perform, they shouldn't be paid."

"Lucky for them, the rest of us don't expect the impossible."

"Disperse your hard-earned cash as you like. I intend to keep mine."

Beginning Duties

I had been watching for her arrival, the one person I knew, she whose husband had led me here. The random parade of staff had passed through without my catching sight of her. Then she appeared, somewhat harried and breathless as she entered the dining room. She stopped and laughed; she had spied me.

Laughing and gasping as she walked toward me, she asked, "What happened? That kimono…" The words choked in her throat.

"It's not the only indignity; you get to keep your name, Midori. Mine's been changed to Dori."

"With Kai and you working here, I have seniority now, and I can keep my name. And I don't have to wear a kimono like that!" My friend Midori had not worked at the restaurant long, and her seniority was still a low-status one. She was not tough as nails and would never harden; she remained considerate and cordial whatever the circumstances. If I did not perform my duties as expected, I certainly did not want her to be blamed for my shortcomings or for bringing me on. I sensed deciphering the social dynamics in play was the crux for getting along with my coworkers in this tony restaurant, and it would be more challenging than performing the demanding physical work. I had to prove to them all that I was up to the challenge.

Our preliminary chores completed, we were given instructions on our duties once diners arrived at The Restaurant. Tomi let Masa continue the teaching chores, saving herself for the inevitable miscues that were bound to occur with two new and inept personnel aimlessly shuffling around the floor and repeatedly asking what they should be doing next.

"As soon as customers are shown to a table, pick up the water pitcher and wait by the table as they are being seated. Then fill each glass and say, 'Good evening.' And don't forget to smile! If no one follows with the butter, you get the butter and put two pats on their butter plates."

"Keep ashtrays on each table empty and clean. It's the busgirl's responsibility. Water, butter, ashtrays––remember that. We must provide service. Our customers pay a lot of money; we provide excellent food and excellent service. Remember that!"

My chores and duties increased exponentially, and I tried to keep up with everyone's demands. I was at the bottom of the hierarchal system. I was at the beck and call of all the other waitresses and staff.

The pressures to provide "the service" permeated the staff, and commands were usually short and curt. There was no room for thin skins; it was a survival course.

"You have to be more useful around here. You're expected to start serving drinks from the bar. Learn the types of liquor, brands we carry, and the names of all popular mixed drinks. The sequence to call drinks to the bartender is: neat, over, water, soda, seven, and ginger; bourbon before scotch. Memorize that."

"Serve to the left, and take from the right."

"Follow the person serving coffee with the cream and sugar tray."

"Crumb the table immediately after the dinner plates are removed and leave the favors."

"Don't just stand around––ever! If nothing else, go around and change ashtrays.

"Tuck the ends of your sleeves in the folds of your obi. You just swept that plate with your sleeves!"

At the end of work each night, my *obi* had inevitably loosened and fallen a few inches, and the toothless rayon fabric of my kimono, hung in sagging folds at the bodice, exposing my neck. Below my *obi*, the once-overlapping layers of my kimono no longer bound my legs, which then allowed me to race about the floor. No amount of hidden ties could hold the uniform in place. I had wondered why our kimono collars were kept tight to our necks, contrary to the low, nape-revealing curvature of the traditional collar placement. Such contrived openness would have accelerated the disassembling of our uniforms. We submitted our kimonos to wholly untraditional stretching, turning, and twisting for hours more than they could endure, and their shapes collapsed before the wearer did. "Perhaps we can find another kimono for you, Dori. They don't all lose their shape like that by the end of the night," a waitress said.

Being released from the stigma of that godawful kimono invigorated my determination to do well, and I learned the lessons taught and watched the others' examples. There could be no distractions; concentration on the tasks at hand was essential to avoid mistakes, anticipate the sequence of tasks coming up, and to work quickly and efficiently. We were never allowed to waver from providing service. Our customers, in turn, were usually considerate and as gracious as anyone could wish. Satisfying the staff was a more difficult task.

The work was demanding and physically exhausting, and we were drained of all energy at the end of a busy shift. Any cobwebs and clutter in my brain were swept away each night from the workout. I was shedding any shyness of strangers, and I was learning to eat humble pie without comment. There was much to learn; I had to succeed.

MONEY IS STILL SCARCE

We were not suddenly living on easy street. On the contrary, the minimum wage was still less than a dollar an hour, and as a new busgirl, I was not entitled to a share of the gratuities until the waitresses deemed my assistance was of value; and the dollar amount contributed depended on the generosity of the individual waitress. Ms. Scrooge wannabes were scarce but not unknown. An IRS investigation descended shortly after my arrival; since my tenure was so short, they did not waste their time with me or Kai. However, the ordeal of individual interviews was unsettling for the staff, and a noticeable tightening of their purse strings followed.

It had taken the estimated two months for me to break even with start-up costs associated with the job. With that behind us, we were at last, a family with two people working. We continued living on a lean budget, much as we had done while trying to make ends meet on a military allotment, except I no longer had to ask for an extension to pay the auto insurance premium when the salesman came to the door to collect. The children could finally have shoes to wear when they learned to walk. We felt it was time to trade in our "rainy day leaks like a sieve" car for a slightly newer, used "no leaks" model. I had considered the Goodwill store that sold secondhand merchandise just blocks down the hill from our home, an extravagance and too expensive except to browse; it might be affordable now. We saved diligently, intent on climbing up and out of a dark-bottomed hole.

Once I was promoted to waitress, our coffers filled more quickly, and we began making plans. The first plan we implemented was a sideways move. By emptying our savings account, we were able to make a down payment on a small two-bedroom house with a daylight basement. In moving to Beacon Hill, we were moving out and away from our Central District roots, much as other Nisei and Sansei had been doing. Located in a quiet residential neighborhood of similar-sized homes old and new, it reminded me of a place where Dick and Jane could have romped. The fenced backyard provided an area where the children could play and vent their surplus energies, and there was space to grow flowers along its borders. The house was not a dream house, but it had features closer to those dreams than anything I had previously called home. Grampa agreed to live in the daylight basement. By living with us, he remained close to his grandchildren, and the rent he paid we used for the mortgage payments. With that in place, David could quit work, go back to school, and get his degree. I would wait my turn until he finished.

Instead of returning to architecture studies, he decided to major in Urban Planning.

"What kind of major is city planning?" I asked.

"It's called Urban Planning," he corrected.

"They're the stray group who sat at desks outside our studios in Architecture Hall," I said with an elitist snub. "A couple of the guys in my class switched over by changing their major. They decided they did not want to be architects anymore."

"Well, I guess I'll be joining them," he said. "Planning encompasses an entire area or region, not only one building. It's an up-and-coming profession."

"You can't convince me it's very interesting."

"I've been giving it a lot of thought, and I'm sure it's better suited for me. I wouldn't make a very good architect. Drawing details of window and door frames eight hours a day would be boring."

I was devastated. I had envisioned our becoming a husband-and-wife team of architects. My initial disappointment and slow acceptance of his decision changed. Dreams be dashed… in the real world, he and I could never work harmoniously together for eight hours every day. Just as our life together was less than harmonious the other sixteen hours of the day, twenty-four hours of togetherness every day would not have worked. It was best we follow our own career paths independently.

We were disappointed when David garnered only two years of credit applicable toward an urban planning degree. His schooling would take another three years. I worked at The Restaurant at night, David went to school during the day, and Grampa was usually available to babysit when there was a gap in our schedules. The plan proceeded smoothly the first year.

During the second year of David's studies, I was expecting our third child, so I worked until summer arrived then took a leave of absence. David worked at Boeing until he returned to school in the fall. Daughter Julia arrived and rounded out our family.

Grampa's new hobby kept him busy snapping pictures of his new granddaughter, and his garden of flowers. They provided new inspiration for his poems too.

Within a month, Grandfather Otani arrived to baptize the newborn grandchild. He had recently remarried, but he came alone, so we waited until a future visit to meet the children's new grandmother. The two grandfathers no longer had conversations about averted wife prospects.

Our savings were just about depleted when I returned to work. It did not take long to get back into the frantic pace required to provide service, even during a late winter snowstorm, when Seattleite's prudently stayed home and off the streets. The underlying ice below the snowpack always makes navigating a car in the city of hills a kamikaze venture after a snowstorm, and longtime city folk do not press their luck so foolishly.

"We'll only have a skeleton crew going in to work today; I'm letting the others stay home, including all the busgirls," Tomi said to me on the phone. "I'll pick you up extra early to make sure we get there in time to do the prep work before opening."

"How many reservations are on the book?" I asked.

"Rudy said two tables. He thinks not more than a dozen customers will show up tonight. Not to worry, there will be five of us to take care of twelve diners."

That evening, a total of seventy-five hungry people came to The Restaurant.

"You call this snow? Not where we come from."

"What's the matter with people in Seattle? Are they all wimps? Can't drive in the snow?"

The out-of-town customers showed no sympathy, and we needed roller skates to provide service.

First Graduation

David had additional babysitting chores along with studies, but the end of school was in sight.

We had little time for outside activities, which meant foregoing get-togethers with my longtime friends and missing their bridal showers when they were scheduled on my workdays. I was a peripheral participant in their social orbit. Gale persevered with her career while the others had gone en masse to the university. Seven diligently kept to their studies and received their degrees; working at their career choices a few years, marrying, and then starting families. Those were the days when married women with school-aged children were stay-at-home housewives. They did not leave their families to go out to work until their children were older. Two contrarian dropouts were to earn degrees the hard way, after marriage and children, and each pursued a career thereafter. It was a matter of priorities.

My friend Margaret died. She had been central in my life during our high school years, when such stable friendships are invaluable, but we had drifted apart in college as our pursuits diverged. The regret was that her life and potential had ended too soon. If we had known, we would have nurtured the friendship with greater care. I was left with only past memories.

When June and graduation finally arrived, David had his degree in hand, and I had survived his three-year ordeal. With the children in bed upstairs and Grampa downstairs, David and I went out for a quiet celebratory dinner. Afterward, we migrated to Chinatown to prolong the celebration.

We turned the corner into the empty Maynard alley. The alley was a dark, nondescript roadway with a single lighted doorway at mid-block. No sign identified its presence, although light filtering through the adjacent glass-block window indicated there was life inside.

David pushed the discreetly positioned doorbell. We could hear noise and voices as a small panel slid open and shut behind the glass wall. The door's lock clicked, and we pulled the door open and entered. The storied "bottle club" was a favorite Asian after-hours haunt that I had heard of but had never been to before.

I saw a dingy bar crowded with imbibers——a loose fraternity of people who knew each other either because they hung out there, were in search of friends to hang out with for the evening, or just not yet ready to call it a night. It was a weekend crowd, and the customers spilled onto the tables and chairs around a small dance floor with a jukebox in the corner. The crowd became boisterous and thicker as the night wore on, and everyone present became a friend.

"What's behind the door over there in the back?" I asked.

"Restrooms."

"Some guys must be sleeping in there, because they never come back."

"What are you, the restroom monitor?"

My single drink was affecting me. I accidently knocked over my near-empty glass, and as I mopped up the spill, a second, full drink appeared on the table.

"For your missus, Dave," said a man at the bar as he raised his own glass in salute. I had never met him before. He soon made his way to our table and sat down. "Hey, we haven't seen you lately. Where you been keeping yourself?"

"I went back to school, so I've been staying sober," David answered. No one ever makes introductions at a bar, and none were forthcoming.

It hardly mattered that formalities had not been made as we exchanged stories as though we were longtime friends.

"I still think it's weird people keep disappearing. Maybe they're getting shanghaied in a back room," I said.

"Where? You mean here?"

"Yeah, my wife's curious. She thinks there's some hanky-panky going on in the back."

"Missus, there's nothing sinister going on in here. Men go up the back stairs to deposit their money in the Bank of China even though they almost never make withdrawals."

"Ha, ha, ha. Ho, ho, ho," the two men roared.

"It's all legit. This is Chinatown." They resumed their laughing.

I was not feeling well. David had stayed sober and managed to get me out of the Wah Mee Club while I could still walk to the car.

Rather than work for the government, David was hired by a small, private company, providing consulting and planning expertise to municipalities and regional agencies that were being inundated with new governmental regulations. Among the most urgent requirements for cities and towns was to have a comprehensive plan in place in order to implement a zoning code. David had been right that urban planning was a new and important field of study and work. The group of coworkers who gathered at the company in those years became lifelong friends.

A World's Fair

Meanwhile, the service trade was gearing up for the opening of the World's Fair in Seattle the following year. The Restaurant was no exception in anticipating a stellar business year. We were told, "Every night will be a Saturday home game football night–– be prepared." Those UW Saturday football nights were the busiest nights of the entire year, when well-heeled alumni and Huskies fans still venting their energies came to celebrate, whether the home team had won or lost. To be that busy each night would be exhausting, but the unique experience of being "crazy busy" was one I could not pass up; it was a time to test my skills as a waitress and the opportunity to replenish our family's depleted coffers.

Although there was the typical amount of staff turnover, a core of dedicated women had worked at The Restaurant many years, a few since the opening or shortly thereafter; they were the experienced backbone of the waitstaff. They had been instrumental in setting the rigorous standards that we were expected to maintain. My own rough start was due in part because I did not take commands graciously and I shied from talking to strangers. Once those basic deficiencies were overcome, the real lessons followed: To always be alert and observe, anticipate and follow through. Be courteous and smile. What I once considered harsh was the steel-edged samurai spirit still alive in the descendent daughters. I came to accept their ways and to admire their values.

The Restaurant was now a premiere dining establishment in the city, and visiting celebrities and notables often came as guests. We did our best to treat them without fanfare and learned firsthand some were truly wonderful human beings, some among them were assholes, and most fell somewhere in between, like the rest of us ordinary folk; therefore, we ought not become too impressed by their publicity.

Unexpectedly, Tomi and Masa announced their resignations. They had been lured away with promises of better opportunities at a new establishment that was scheduled to open before the start of the fair. Several others joined the two in the new venture, and another handful decided they had long delayed going on to other types of work and it was time to move on. The rest of us were shocked and distressed. We wondered how we could carry on without the veteran crew. We did, and it was a lesson to be learned: No one is indispensable.

Meaningful changes were taking place in American society. A wider range of jobs was opening up to minorities, including white-collar jobs, and civil service positions for government work followed suit. With a greater spectrum of job opportunities, fewer Nisei and Sansei were inclined to work as waitresses.

After the war, another generation of Japanese women left their homeland to live in America. They were young brides married to American GIs. Generally bilingual and with greater assimilation into American culture than their predecessors from decades ago, these women identified as "war brides" began to fill the void by taking manual jobs such as waitressing, as seamstresses, and the like.

The Restaurant changed their policy of hiring only Japanese women to include other Asians. The diversified waitstaff now consisting of Japanese, Chinese, and Korean women, American-born and foreign-born, carried on the tradition of service with only minor adjustments.

Rudy, the manager/maître d', left for the East Coast when he was offered a similar job with a restaurant chain. Born in England and of Italian heritage, he trained in Europe for a professional career in the restaurant trade. He was the last such European-trained professional to manage The Restaurant. A young, typically American fellow replaced him. He was less experienced, and had ambitions other than to be a maître d'. The customers hardly noticed the difference, but the rest of us did.

Serving excellent food was a mainstay of the restaurant, and despite the personnel changes disrupting the front of the house, Joe still ruled the kitchen and controlled all food-related matters like a tyrant; he kept the kitchen running like a well-oiled machine. Maintaining the quality of foods served and kepping tight reins on extraneous food expenditures; he also kept a well-scrubbed, spotless kitchen. Joe had come from Honolulu to open the Seattle restaurant and had stayed; here he became an iconic figure contributing to The Restaurant's mystique.

Dick was still the first person to greet customers as they drove up to the entry. He was the parking attendant extraordinaire who magically conjured up a departing guest's car so it was waiting at the door when he or she exited The Restaurant. The many lucrative opportunities offered him did not dissuade him from forfeiting the independence he had working evenings parking cars.

Ruthie was the cocktail waitress par excellence who memorized customers' drink orders as they were ordered, the preferred cocktails of frequent guests, and of former-frequent guests who reappeared even after many years' absence. The lounge was her domain, separate from the dining room. She alone served the drinks and collected payment for drinks served in the lounge. During the Blue Laws era, when customers were not allowed to carry their own cocktail glasses from bar to dining table, Ruthie managed to transfer unfinished drink glasses to the rightful imbibers seated in any of the thirty-two tables in the dining room and collect payment. Without skipping a beat she skillfully attended to her other customers crowded around numerous exotic wood-slab tables and the piano bar as well.

She had been the single experienced hire and non-Japanese female who started at The Restaurant's opening. She continued her tenure as bar hostess, and we were happy she did. We dining room waitresses had learned her feats were impossible to duplicate even on a moderately busy night. We took our turns working as the bar hostess on Ruthie's day off.

"Ruthie called in sick today, so you'll have to work in the bar tonight," the head waitress said upon my arrival.

"No. No, you're wrong. I just worked in the bar a couple of weeks ago. My turn doesn't come around that fast."

"Sorry, but I don't have anyone else to put in there today. They're too new or... You understand." Forever excused from bar duty was the stand-in who had become so overwhelmed, she stood frozen in the middle of the chaos and cried. We all sympathized; we had all felt the same at times. Only our tears forgot to flow.

Serving the first round of guests was manageable. Then the complications set in. Guests at various tables were escorted to tables in the dining room, leaving their drinks behind. I had to deliver the glasses to them.

By the time I returned, a new party was seated at the table in the bar clamoring to order their drinks. Other tables were empty of people, their unfinished drinks waiting to be delivered.

"Hurry up and deliver the drinks on those tables. I need them. People have been waiting too long."

"Where did you take them? Need to know the table number."

"Oh, Miss… Another round of drinks here. Tell the bartender to use Beefeaters in my martini and give me an onion and an olive, will you? I'm hungry."

"Take this drink back. I wanted my Scotch on the rocks."

"Table five going to table twenty-one, and table eighteen is asking for their drinks."

"Sweetheart, what's that drink I had the other night? You know the one I liked with the cherry?" "Just have your usual, dear. The girl is waiting for your order."

"Table two going to table ten."

"Here, pass this on to the piano player and tell him to play some Sinatra songs. That's a good girl."

"We need another round here, and don't forget my twist."

Damn, what drink needs the twist? Damn, all these bar bills that haven't followed their owners. Gotta go find them in the dining room, or the drinks are on me. Damn, when did they fill those window tables with new customers? When is this night going to end?

Most of the real old-timers were gone, and I was now considered one——albeit a new old-timer. I was one of only a few who could remember a time when they called a shack a dressing room. I found myself chastising newcomers when they made complaints about our dressing room. The windowed basement dressing room was long and narrow, with heat in winter and air-conditioning in summer, and a private WC compartment. On one side of the room hung the entire collection of kimonos on the room-length supporting pole. A continuous counter and vanity mirror ran along the opposite wall, reflecting the hodgepodge expanse of kimonos and making the collection impossible to ignore.

Waitstaff at The Restaurant

I sometimes wondered if my godawful kimono might somehow have escaped the occasional "throw out the old" purges that were undertaken when the clothes pole showed signs of collapsing. Could it still be lurking behind a batch of prettier keepers? I wondered. I bought my own *yukata*, the generally blue-and-white patterned cotton kimonos worn in the summer, which had become the preferred uniform. Though less formal, they were machine washable, making them immensely more practical. The cotton fabric did not shift, and I remained tidy and presentable at the end of the night instead of falling apart. I had also become skilled at tying the obi and cinching it as tightly as Masa had on my first day, and my victims cried for mercy.

"Aiiyah!" said Janice as she walked back to the broiler where Joe was presiding over the grill. "Fifty-Cents Mr. More says he didn't get enough French fries. Will you get me a side dish of fries? Please."

"If you ask nicely, I will."

"I'm serious, Joe. Look, he's watching us…"

Mr. More was a regular who usually dined alone. On occasion, he brought a guest. He came early and was often the first diner of the evening.

He sat at the same upper-level table overlooking the dining area below and the expanded view through the windows. It was the best table in the house, he claimed. Rather than a cozy hideaway, his table faced a busy aisle where he watched the parade of customers pass in front of him. He could see the entire upper-level dining room, the goings-on at the broiler, and the traffic going in and out of the kitchen. His strategically located table was where we waitresses could not ignore him. He always ordered the same ground steak, which was the euphemism for hamburger, with accompanying French fries and dinner roll, plus an order of the basic green salad and coffee. His order never varied, and his guests were always persuaded to order the same items, too. And he always left the same tip of fifty cents.

"Aiiyah, we're going to have a crazy night tonight. It all started with Fifty-Cents Mr. More asking for more fries. I can feel trouble in my bones."

"Don't be so superstitious, Janice." She had kept her own name, as did all the new hires. When the waitstaff became diversified, the names did too; the kimono uniform remained unchanged.

"Girls, cut the gossip, and go pick up the dinner plates!"

Sure enough, Joe was ringing his bell for pickup, and we had not noticed. We rushed to the broiler. "You girls aren't paying attention!" he scolded us. Once the grilled meats were placed on the hot dinner plates, it was imperative they be served while the food was piping hot.

The Restaurant did not use tray service. With practiced skill using folded napkins as hot pads, we quickly and carefully placed a third napkin on our wrists, enabling us to carry at least three hot dinner plates at a time. The chances for a mishap generally kept us from adding additional plates to our arms.

"Condiments!" snapped Janice to the busgirl as we passed the busing stand with plates of sizzling steaks and baked potatoes.

We served the diners what they had ordered without our having to ask. As we had picked up the plates, we had both looked at the penciled chart made by the waitress who took the order. Other waitresses rushed past us to pick up the sides, and we returned to our own stations to continue servicing our own tables.

"I told you we're going to have a terrible night. Those downstairs girls were still visiting. I think we'll end up picking up their plates all night long."

"You may be right after all. Look who just came in the door."

Most of our customers were gracious and accommodating. Well-bred and crusty or not, our guests put on their company manners when they came to dine. Of course, there were those who behaved badly; a handful dined frequently enough for us to remember their names, and we prepared ourselves for an ordeal when they appeared. They were demanding, complaining, and insulting; their pleasure was to make others miserable.

The busgirl was out of sight, so Janice picked up the water pitcher to greet her new table.

"*Gomen, gomen* (sorry, sorry)," said the absent busgirl as she rushed by with the butter pats. "I was in the kitchen making coffee. I made a mess, and I was cleaning it up."

The evening progressed with missed cues; everything was out of sync.

"Behind you... BEHIND YOU!" said the alarmed waitress, who adroitly rebalanced the plates she was carrying.

The girl who was leading had stopped suddenly, causing the near collision; she glanced back sheepishly. "Sorry," she said as she rushed off. Joe was at the broiler, where flames were shooting up above the grill, charring a customer's steak to a desired crust. He was clanging his little high-pitched bell and adding to the general commotion. "Penthouse orders, Penthouse orders!"

We interrupted ourselves and rushed to the broiler to pick up an armful of hot dinner plates and headed for the service stairs, scampered up with plates still balanced, continued through an accessory service area and out to the sweeping dining aerie where private parties were held. The territorial view was even more encompassing than in the general dining rooms below. No dumbwaiter was installed, and we had to carry up all supplies and foods.

As we ran back down to pick another armful of hot dinners, we were mentally prioritizing and sequencing the things that had to be done at our own tables: Tables six and three, waiting for their food. Take order on table four, unless they're having another round of drinks. Hopefully, Reiko's finished tossing salads number seven… Darn, I should have put in their dinner order. There's probably a backup of orders due to Penthouse.

I picked up another armful of dinner plates; taking the risk, I held two and lined up two more on my left arm and carried the fifth in my right hand. Since each plate merely held a baked potato, garnish, and steak without sauce, the maneuver was doable. Besides, I had my customers to tend to and could not spare the time to make a third trip up to the Penthouse.

Check to see if table five finished…Must clear plates.

Check for coffee. Add up bill for table two.

I was dropping off the napkin hot pads when plump, baby-faced Meiko came up to the broiler, saying, "Joe… Joe-ooo. Table nineteen man say I tell you, 'You have Rocky Mountain oyster on menu today?'"

Joe smiled broadly and chuckled, "You go tell Mr. Cody, no Rocky Mountain oysters today. Delivery man still on mountain, can't make delivery."

"Huh?"

"You just go back and tell Mr. Cody what I said. Go, go."

A hearty bellow shot up from the lower level. A man was guffawing loudly, broadcasting his merriment distinctly above the din in the dining room. Mr. Cody tested any innocent, new hire, and he was beside himself when he found another victim.

A few minutes later, Meiko was asking us, "Why is oysters so funny?"

"Because, Mr. Cody's oysters are bull testicles." "*Nani?* What's that?"

"Go back to your work. Kay will tell you later."

"Reiko, did you take the saltshaker off table five?" I asked my associate. We were working seven upper-level tables together instead of working individually on three or four tables.

"No, I didn't. I thought you did." She quickly walked over to the table and looked for the missing property. She returned quickly and reported, "The lady on the end has a very nice black beaded evening bag that is bulging at the seams. She can barely close it. Shame on her."

We routinely placed a matched set of wood salt shaker and pepper grinder on the table when taking a dinner order, and we removed them when the dinner plates were removed. Each waitress was responsible for three sets. If any set disappeared, the waitress was responsible for replacing it at her expense unless the loss was reported to the manager at the time of its disappearance. He had the choice of confronting the sticky-fingered customer or allowing the cost of the shakers to be added to the bill, or, to avoid a problem altogether, he replaced them at the restaurant's expense.

No sooner had we cleared a table and had set it up again than a new set of customers was seated. "Take their order right away. They've been waiting in the bar for almost one hour," we were warned.

"Come sing Happy Birthday on table twenty."

I deferred joining the songfest. My new customers needed something to eat; I had to take their dinner order. Their ill humor would usually dissipate with full stomachs, and they would be transformed into civil human beings again.

A loud chorus of the happy birthday song with a Japanese accent rang out. On rare occasions, there were enough American-born singers to make it sound right. Usually it sounded like a congratulatory for who knows? "Hop-py boss-day tsu you-u!"

When new diners were not seated as quickly as a table was cleared and Joe's assistant took over at the broiler, we knew the evening was slowing toward an end. The pace of our walk slowed, and our focus blurred.

"*Hara ga het-ta,*" I said to no one in particular as I unloaded an armful of spent plates onto the dishwasher's trough.

"Ladies never use that kind of language. That's men talk; lower working class talk," Minnie, who overheard my complaint, lectured me.

"I just said I'm hungry."

"Ladies would say '*onaka ga sui-te imasu*' or…" She floated out of the kitchen cradling two wooden salad bowls in her arms, finishing her Japanese lesson as she stepped back into the dining room.

That sounds too genteel to me. "I'm ravenous!"

It was Minnie who minced the English language and got away with it. Absolutely no one was offended when she asked, "Drink before eat?" Any other waitress would have been fired.

At the end of the evening when most of the customers had departed and the late-shift waitresses were still on duty, the off-duty waitstaff ate their snacks and relaxed. We were so pumped with adrenaline, our nervous energy had to be eased down slowly. The Japan-born women automatically reverted to conversing in Japanese among themselves, and my ear became attuned to hearing Japanese spoken again. They used modern idioms and incorporated terms used currently in Japan. We Nisei had learned much of our Japanese language from the Issei, who had emigrated from Japan fifty or more years before, and most used the grammar and terminologies of that era, the Meiji era. The early settlers' speech was laced with archaic words and terms that newer arrivals from Japan considered outrageously funny. It was their turn to think we spoke strangely.

"That vegetable is called *kah-be-ji*. That's American word."

"What?"

"*Katsudo shashin* is like a 'silent movie.' A movie is *eiga*," said Kay. She had started a few months after me and we had witnessed incidents and had common experiences that had forged a shared kinship.

"Remember when Kinu overfilled her water pitcher, got bumped, and those ice cubes rolled down the woman's neck and down her back?"

"Too bad the lady was wearing a backless dress." Unfortunately, the service was not perfect; there were glitches.

"Ha, ha… And that time you had your hair and eyebrows singed!"

"I didn't know what happened. Actually, it wasn't very funny." The bartender had been asked to flame an ice cream sundae, and no matter how much liquor he poured on the cold dessert, it did not flame. As the bar hostess that day, I stood opposite the counter watching the failed attempts. In desperation, the bartender picked up the bottle of 151-proof rum and held it horizontally with the lighter's flame positioned to ignite the alcohol as it left the bottle. The half-empty bottle became a blowtorch shooting flames across at me.

"You're supposed to flame that damn dessert––NOT me!" I bellowed.

"Sorry. You hurt?" The smell of burnt hair lingered. And a new policy was adopted: No more lit desserts, with the exception of sparklers on birthday cakes.

"And the time a customer sitting at table three suddenly keeled over and his face fell onto his dinner plate. The woman with him didn't know what to do; we waitresses didn't know what to do. It was a busy night; a really busy night..."

"So, what happened? Couldn't you give him a napkin?"

"The man died. It was very sudden."

"That reminds me of another death. Our new busgirls' broken English wasn't charming like Minnie's, and none of us understood her 'to-kay' meant turkey."

"I remember her. Her English was funny, but she spoke Japanese with a weird accent, too," said Kay.

"Well, her husband sometimes came to The Restaurant near closing time, looking for her. He would walk around the dining room to find her. He was really creepy, and we were relieved she quit so we didn't have to see him again."

Kay finished the tale, "A couple of months later, the police came here to talk to anyone who knew her. No one knew her well. Someone asked if she was missing;

"She's not missing," they said. "We found her murdered."

She didn't deserve that kind of bad luck.

Once the fair ended and the nightly pandemonium and exuberance concluded, things returned to hectic normal and relative quiet. Work proceeded at a saner pace, and we were no longer tested daily. I had honed my skills of working quickly and efficiently, continually anticipating and prioritizing tasks. And I had met a large cast of people with whom I learned to work cooperatively, to temper expectations by not prejudging people, and to smile even under stress.

For Thanksgiving, we each received a twelve-pound turkey to take home and cook for the holiday. Christmas was the only other holiday when The Restaurant closed and we celebrated with family. New Year's Eve meant a work-shift extending into the early morning hours of the new year. At midnight, the waitstaff joined the full house of revelers and celebrated with a complimentary glass of champagne——to be sipped as we worked, of course. The one night of free drinks went to our heads, and a second glass of bubbly made us usually temperate imbibers giddy and a bit tipsy. Well after the last customers left for home, we were reluctant to do the same. We were exhausted but not yet willing to call it a day.

"Say, have you seen the chalkboard in the men's restroom?"

"What were you girls doing in the men's room?"

"Using the toilet, of course; it's closer than the ladies' room, and we had to go bad."

"We'll have to rethink giving you girls any champagne next New Year."

"Jim, don't be such a fuddy-duddy. We only get free drinks once a year."

"We can't have you girls drinking up the profits."

"Look, you switched brands, and that second bottle was a cheaper champagne. We might only drink once a year, but we can tell the difference."

"Fifteen girls, and two bottles of champagne have this effect on you? Unbelievable," our manager said in disbelief.

"Yeah, we're actually easy dates. You only had to open the third bottle because Taki's been guzzling it down like water."

"She's a pretty lady, probably beautiful once, but she's a lush now."
"Don't compare her to the rest of us ordinary human beings; she had a different upbringing, if her mother was truly a rich man's kept geisha as she claims."

"What's that got to do with the way she drinks?"

"Hey, girls, guess what Sallie and I read on the men's room chalkboard: 'Hooray! Hooray! The first of May. Outdoor screwing starts today!'"

"For real? Someone wrote that in such a high-tone restaurant? I gotta see for myself."

"Girls! Stay out of there. Go home and sober up."

The time had come for me to reset my priorities, to return to my goal to acquire my degree, and to become an architect––so help me God.

CHAPTER 19

The Profession, 1963-1970

"…AND I'VE DECIDED TO GO back to school next fall," I said as a parting remark to David when he called home one day.

"So when did you decide that?" he asked.

"Hmm, I think I decided yesterday. I've been thinking about it for a long time."

"So why now?"

"That was the agreement. You'd go back, and you did. Now it's my turn."

"It's not going to be easy."

"You'll have to get used to it. I haven't worked out all the details yet." I waited but got no further response. "We'll have to buy me a car."

"You don't drive."

"I'll learn," I said as I hung up the phone.

In the eight years after I had dropped out, the School of Architecture within the College of Arts and Sciences had been upgraded to the College of Architecture and Urban Planning. Extensive curriculum and requirement changes had taken place in the eight years that complicated my reentry to the college. All credits I had earned in my freshman and sophomore years were accepted, per se, and applicable third-year credits already earned were accepted; however, any deficiencies had to be fulfilled before I could enroll in fourth-year classes of the five-year program. I had a half-point deficiency in the studio class, which could not be made up because the sketch problem exercises had been dropped from the program. I had to repeat a studio class. My coveted degree required another three years of studies.

My old classmate who had once brought to mind the hero from the pages of The Fountainhead was now teaching full-time at the college. As an academic, he spent his days expounding design theories, leaving the practice of designing and constructing real structures to others. He now wore a three-piece suit with buttoned vest instead of the T-shirts and jeans with desert sandals that had been his uniform as a student. Other former classmates were either working with architectural firms in the area or further away, or had changed their pursuits to other fields of endeavor. Mae-Lin was now a wife and mother and had followed her husband down to Southern California.

Unlike my former classmates who had gone on with their lives, I was reverting back into a college student and feeling middle-aged among youngsters who had been in junior high school when I was previously on campus. I eased into my studies by enrolling as a part-time student and took newly required third-year courses. I was also auditing the first-year structural engineering class since I had retained little from my long-ago classes; although, I still remembered an engineer's washer was the ring to tighten a joint, not the appliance used for washing clothes. Pocket calculators were not yet available, so relearning how to use a slide rule was essential for the second-year engineering classes that were required for credit the following year. I had not used the device in the intervening years. There was little socializing in these core classes, allowing me to sit on the sidelines and focus on learning the subject fundamentals and observe my new classmates while wondering how I would fit in.

After the first hour of our two-hour engineering class, our instructor dismissed the class early due to another commitment he had that day. Rather than parking myself in the library, a place no longer occupied by friends and acquaintances, I walked to the non-descript, smallish lunchroom I had discovered at the start of the school year. Without a desk in the design studio, I had no home on campus, so the room had become a convenient resting place. Positioned across the corridor from the main dining room in the Student Union building, there was little traffic flow to the row of vending machines just inside the door. The foods displayed and dispensed were unappetizing snacks and sweets. Otherwise, the room was filled with tables and chairs ideal for brown baggers to eat their lunches while studying. The sounds emitting from the television hanging in a corner provided white noise except on occasions when enthusiastic soap opera addicts descended to watch an episode of their favorite drama. It was an ideal place for me to work on my homework assignments between scheduled classes. I had an extra-long wait for my next class at one o'clock that afternoon.

Above the buzz in the room, the TV announcer was talking rapidly… people running…Secret Service men…the motorcade… anxiety dripping with every phrase. My concentration on problem solving vanished as I listened to descriptions of actions unfolding, trying to comprehend the scope of what was happening. A few others in the room caught wind of a major news event in progress; alarmed, they too reacted to the TV broadcast in the same way.

"Did you hear that? Listen…" "What? Where?"

"Hey, quiet, guys. I'm trying to hear this. Something serious has happened…"

"Crank up the volume!"

The room became deathly quiet now with people in suspended animation all straining to discern what was taking place through the breathless words of the newscasters. The room began filling up as more people filed in, who when realizing the implications of what was being said, fell silent and in disbelief. Someone had shot our President.

My naïve idealistic belief that we had advanced as a civilization whose people espoused nobler values and whose actions reflected those nobler motives was shot down to earth and to reality that day. It's not an automatic progression that we advance ever upward to higher moral levels. Our noble dreams were peppered with holes. What hand did providence play in releasing us from the classroom early that one day so we might hear firsthand the tragic events as they unfolded, and enable us to contemplate the significance of the tragedy and reflect?

The previous warm-up year proved invaluable when I enrolled as a full-time fourth-year student. By auditing three-quarters of structural engineering, I felt emboldened enough to muddle through a second year and keep up with the others. Despite an urban myth that Asians excel at math, I was that exception lacking numbers genes to master the subject. Term paper assignments forced me to write in complete sentences again. And there was a new "style" of architecture, Brutalism. The cutting-edge Modernism of the fifties I had been immersed in before was now considered passé by the academics. To learn that architecture undergoes design trends was an awakening. I had to rethink and expand my design base to accept and incorporate the new.

The young, especially those who are creative, are eager adherents of whatever is new and innovative, and the band of four English lads sporting long hair were the latest rage; I learned who the Beatles were early on. Exposure to new ideas and experiences was not limited to architecture.

College enrollment at the university had ballooned; as a consequence, auxiliary spaces in nearby off-campus buildings were being used for design studio classes. That first quarter, I was in the group assigned to the vacated retail space one block west of campus. With storefront windows bordering the sidewalk along two sides of our studio, peering eyes of passersby made us feel we were working in a fishbowl. Physically removed from the hub of Architecture Hall, our headquarters building, we had minimal supervision. Removed, too, from classmates located in other makeshift off-campus spaces, our isolated group achieved a semblance of cohesion, aiding my reentry into that rarefied world of architectural design studies. The creative design process itself had not changed during the years I was a dropout; the personnel had changed.

Our studio problem required us to design a campus plan for a new community college sited on an undeveloped woodland area north of the city. Because the assignment was less structural design and more site planning, we were required to prepare a site plan drawing and a site model of our proposed solution, to be completed for submittal in the standard five weeks. The lengthy seven-page typed program was distributed, and a discussion session took place on the first day; we were then on our own.

Once our meeting was over, the studio cleared as students headed out for coffee or for home——anywhere other than their desks. These students followed the same routines as my earlier classmates, and design solutions still needed to gestate. Just as slowly tentative schemes flitted through our heads; we scribbled the ideas on sketch paper before they vanished. We worked and reworked the schematics in a continuous stream, unrolling flimsy sketch tissue as we sketched. Only the worthy ideas were torn off the roll and kept aside, the rest were vigorously crumpled to relieve frustrations. Tossing the paper balls, those having missed the trash basket stayed on the floor as evidence that geniuses were hard at work. Pencils and paper were essential tools for creativity prior to the use of computers.

As time grew short and deadlines loomed, we settled on a concept, refined it, and began the presentation drawings. In this case, we were also required to make a model of our design proposal.

Our models grew and overwhelmed our desks. Each student's model consumed large quantities of Styrofoam boards and space, and remnants of cut-up boards littered the studio floor. Industriously working like Christmas elves, though oblivious to the upcoming holidays, we kept busy cutting undulating curves on sheet after sheet of the foam boards and set one on top of the other to mimic the contours of the site's terrain. We belatedly learned how much more labor-intensive model making was compared to drawing a site plan.

"Methinks they erred when they wrote up this program. Every model is larger than a desktop, leaving us no room to work on our drawings."

"It's not for us to question why…"

"So why is my model twice as high as everyone else's?" Arnie asked no one in particular. His model was obviously nonconforming.

"Methinks your contours are out of scale. We all used board thickness to show five-foot elevations. Methinks your boards represent ten feet on your model."

"For real? How did I screw up?"

Others gathered around to give an assessment. "You bought thicker boards than the rest of us. Yup, you're toast."

"Damn. What was I thinking?"

"Better to start over. You've lost a lot of time. Good luck."

"Forget the luck; what I need is a good stiff drink to ease the pain."

"Whoa on the drink. Alcohol and X-acto knives don't mix when you're cutting contours on a foam board."

"You cut yourself, the injury heals. Try explaining the blood on your nice white model; you won't get much sympathy. You'll really need good luck."

The site design assignment was a different aspect of design my fellow classmates had not previously been exposed to, but I had gained some familiarity since it was David's line of work, allowing me to join the other students on a level playing field. We all worked under pressure and stress. It was not the real world, but it was an intensely stimulating place to be, and it was exhilarating to be involved again.

The next quarter, we moved back to the main building and to the same studio rooms of nine years before. Several old professors were gone, including "The Great White Father" as well as Dean Herman, who had taught Architecture History to a full auditorium each quarter. It had been a favorite two-credit distribution course that non-majors could easily sit through and watch a slideshow. Younger professors had joined the faculty, bringing fresh insights and ideas, but many of the old traditions lingered on. The entire class was finally united, and I found myself one of three females among the throng of male students who were almost ten years younger than me. There were a few military veterans, but the majority of young men were intent on staying in school to keep their deferments and avoid the Draft. The problems in Vietnam were escalating. A different mind-set prevailed among the students. I was not a part of their generation.

We approached design subjectively from different points-of-view, but in our other classes, the old rules of objectivity still reigned. The architectural history for majors was a grueling memory test. Early morning classes on lighting, acoustics, and heating, venting, and air-conditioning, were bracing at that early hour. Many of our lecturers were practitioners with their own consulting businesses available to teach either early or late in the day. Our school hours were long.

I had survived, and my second year of structural engineering classes was coming to an end in two months. The course was no longer an alien mine-field, though I was far from mastering the subject. "Architects can hire pro-fessional structural engineers to do the calculations. Don't worry about it," someone had said to me. Nevertheless, I had to complete the class, and I made it a point to be punctual, hoping some knowledge might be absorbed by osmosis. It was early, and I sat on my high stool at my high desk waiting for class to begin. Other students shuffled in, and Professor Torrence was or-ganizing his papers at the front of the room. My chair began swaying as I sat, and creaks and rattles sounded forth. Tables were moving and, looking up, I saw the ceiling suspension system was undulating. I scooted under my table.

"STAY WHERE YOU ARE! Do not leave the room!" Torrence cried out.

Panicked students heading for the exit stopped in their tracks. A few crawled under their desks as I had. The walls swooned and swayed, and the floor bounced beneath us. A student staggered through the door, gasping, "That hallway's like a roller coaster out there. I think I'm going to be sick."

No response. Everyone was spooked at the incredulous sensations we were feeling. The moving stopped, and everything came to rest, perfectly still as before.

"Let's get back to our desks. I think it appropriate to skip a chapter or two and begin this session with seismic forces on buildings."

The class was unusually attentive; we had all experienced the tremors firsthand, and we were especially sensitive to the importance of earth-quake safety factors in building design.

"Since our class is being held in the general engineering build-ing here on campus, I have full confidence the building's engineers overdesigned their own building with a hefty safety factor. However, I did worry the architects hadn't employed the same precautions regarding their responsibilities," said Professor Torrence. An engineer bashing architects again.

The university offered no classes for architecture majors during the summer, and we were encouraged to broaden our scope of expertise. We were, after all, the modern Renaissance men. My summers meant working at The Restaurant to earn monies for my tuition, books, and supplies. In addition, I saved to pay for Julia's nursery school expenses for the school year. The Japanese Baptist church was still operating a nursery school with bus service. Julia was smaller and quieter than most, and she accepted her routine of attending school without protest. Luckily, she did not follow my example by quitting after a single day's trial. She proved she had more perseverance.

During the school year, Michael and Lorraine were latchkey children who returned home before others in the family. A favorite TV program, Dark Shadows, aired shortly after school, which ensured their prompt walk home, where Morgan and other favorite stuffed toys waited for their homecoming. They were also responsible for cooking rice and setting the table before my return from school. As children of single-parent homes ourselves, David and I understood children were capable of assuming responsibilities and gainfully utilizing their free time. Their adventures during those free times are their stories to tell. I could no longer linger after school; dinner had to be prepared, and my homework started at eight when the children went to bed.

Our cozy two-bedroom home was a model built after the war that managed to contain the five of us on the upper level with the help of a large deck and fenced yard. Grampa's living quarters were the semi-finished daylight basement he shared with the washing machine and furnace. The wood-panel-finished walls were improvements the previous owner had hammered to the studs. It was crudely put together improvements, but we had a place that felt like home.

Yoshi's grandchildren

The children could traipse down the stairs to visit Grampa whenever they needed a treat from one of his containers filled with candies of all sorts, or when they wanted a respite from the nagging and scolding they had to endure upstairs.

"You *Pon-keen-he-do*," Grampa called out as two pairs of feet scampered up the stairs. The two mischief-makers were laughing merrily as they escaped their antagonist.

"Grampa sure sounds angry. What have you two been up to?" I asked.

"Nothing," they both said as one.

"Confess. You both smell like Old Spice aftershave lotion, and you don't shave yet. Sounds like you two were messing with Grampa's things."

"Sorta…but he called us a bad name."

"He never calls innocent kids Pumpkin Head without good reason."

The two innocents roared with more laughter. "He was calling us Pumpkin Head? I thought *Pon-keen-he-do* was a Japanese swear word."

That was Grampa's extent in scolding his grandchildren, although he often told them, "Go upstairs to Mommy and Daddy."

They usually found sanctuary in their *Ojii-chan*'s apartment but not always.

LAST YEAR OF SCHOOL

The same cool, dewy mornings that announced the start of school in September during the years I was a dropout, had also engendered a deep sense of remorse for having quit before reaching my goal. Now, as a fifth-year student, it was my last year of school toward my degree––banishing that mark of failure––and I was experiencing far less anxiety than in the past.

We were introduced to subjects related to our major, including site planning, landscape design, and several reality-driven courses like Professional Practice and Contract Drawings. In real life, we would begin our careers as draftsmen preparing contract drawings, the blueprints for construction. After a quarter of lectures explaining practical features of construction, the following quarter, we had to apply that knowledge and to prepare a set of real working drawings. We were divided into teams of seven with each team member responsible for one page of our group's set of drawings. We learned almost immediately that it was almost impossible to get seven architects-to-be to agree on anything, including the time and place for a meeting. We finally settled on each member's responsibility, and we worked independently as much as possible; thereby solving the dilemma of conflicting schedules and egos. My assigned page was to draw and dimension the building elevations and identify materials used. They had given me an acceptable assignment, unlike one fellow's page full of bathroom plans and details.

We team members were standing around as a group getting pointers pertinent to our assignment.

"The team's page layout, including title blocks, etc., should be consistent. Decide as a group…" the assistant instructor was telling us when he turned toward me and asked, "So why are you taking up space here?"

I was taken by surprise; it came out of the blue. The question was out of context. "What? What space?"

"You're a female, a dilettante female taking up space a boy could have had. You're denying a deserving boy the opportunity to go on and spend his life practicing architecture."

I could not believe what I heard. Is he serious? It's the nineteen-sixties! I thought such discrimination no longer existed. Yes, it's a cliché. Yes, it's trite and hackneyed, but it's not just a platitude; people believe it. Sexism is not dead. The words were said directly to me in all seriousness by a university assistant professor. I earned my space just like the others.

"I'm here to get a degree and to become an architect." I bit my tongue to keep from saying more. I was outraged; I was burning up inside and my face flashed red like a pulsating signal light. Warning…Warning…keep your cool…Keep your cool.

Everyone heard the exchange; no one said a word. I was accustomed to fighting my own battles by now. I would follow protocol and report my grievance to a superior. The next day, the supervising professor got a loud earful from me, all without one word of profanity. I could not let my anger jeopardize my student status and be thrown out of school. I was not aware an accounting of the incident had been reported to our lead instructor before our head-to-head. Stay the course and finish. *Gam-batte*.

The tradition of keeping the architecture building open through the night before a design problem deadline was still in effect, and students endured the twenty-four-hour-plus marathon charrette. My all-night charrette's no longer took place at school; I worked alone at home. After sending the children off to their school in the morning, I drove to Architecture Hall to finish my presentation.

I raced up the stairs to our second-floor design studio and waded through a sea of wadded tracing paper balls, discarded wrappings of all sorts, and layers of paper debris ignominiously brushed off desks and strewn through the aisles. I dropped my Strathmore presentation boards on my desk and swung my plastic toolbox loaded with drawing implements on top.

"Sorry, I thought you were working at home the rest of the day," said my desk neighbor as he retrieved his belongings from under my boards.

"I was, but I'm finishing up here."

A couple of radios placed in opposite corners of the large studio room were tuned to the same radio station, blaring out the latest popular hits at high volume in stereophonic sound. Whenever a Beatles song played, the sleepless ragtag crew became energized choristers who did their best to drown out the song from the radio as they sang in full voice, off-key with wrong lyrics, in an attempt to ward off effects of lost sleep. Strangely, no other popular music group inspired as many spontaneous sing-alongs, though the students were all familiar with the popular tunes of the day. Silly chatter and inane exchanges between various exhausted students floated up above the noise from the radios.

"Oh-o-o… Yester-r-r-day! Tomorrow this'll all be…yesterr-r-day-y."

"You'll never make it as a singer; you had better keep on drawing."

"I need a banjo backup. Where's our banjo player?"

"He's busy trying to finish. We just got a few more hours-s-s."

The students who had reluctantly gone off to get some sleep wandered back to resume work on their projects, now under greater pressure to meet the deadline. They joined the all-nighters who had managed to work through the night without sleep. With unbrushed teeth covered by what felt like fur and grit, dark stubble covering their unshaven cheeks and chins, and blood-shot eyes, they worked on. The assemblage of unbathed bodies added to the scent.

"It's really close in here. We should air out the place. Why don't they open the windows?" I asked my neighbor, Larry.

"We can't have campus cops coming down here confiscating radios. Next thing you know, they'd be taking our coffeemakers. Without the songs and caffeine, there's no way we'd make it to five." "Hang the radios and coffeepots, if they saw this mountain of paper, they'd call it a fire hazard and clear the building. We'd all be in a fine fix," said Bob, my other desk neighbor.

After a while, I noticed neither the aroma nor heard the radio, although everyone hummed along whenever their favorite music played.

"I gotta eat something. Anyone else wanna go to the Coffee Corral?" someone called out.

"Can't spare the time. How about bringing back some donuts?"

We were in a state of exhaustion, frantically racing time. Two classmates entered the room, each with a roll of blue-line prints under their arms. They playfully kicked up the trashed paper on the floor as they made their way to their desks.

"Will you get that smelly ammonia-permeated print from under my nose?" the stressed student hissed. "It smells like wet diapers."

"Just thought it'd bring you out of your stupor, buddy."

"You don't have to rub them on my nose. Yeah, you're letting me know you finished. All you gotta do is tape it on your boards and turn it in."

"Smart boy! It's all a matter of timing."

"Then how about giving me a hand?"

"Tsk, tsk. Old Dean Doyle doesn't approve. Hell, they accused Alex of getting help from other unknown persons last year, and they lowered his grade one point."

"And he was innocent, poor guy. That was a raw deal." "Why didn't he speak up?"

"He didn't have a mouthpiece to back up his denials. He needed a lawyer man to defend him."

"I didn't hear about it till later. It was a bad situation. Not much any of us could have done about it. We're captive slaves here toiling under a dictatorship; it's an autocratic regime."

"Just have to finish this here project, take my last finals, and I'm outta here!"

"Hope…all my troubles melt aaa-way…"

"Any plans for the summer, Jon?"

"Yup, I'm heading for Japan. Decided I had to see them sacred temples for myself after looking at Haag's slides in his landscape class. I might stay over there for a year if my money doesn't run out."

"I'll be in grad school somewhere. I've got no itch to see Southeast Asia or Vietnam. Japan's too close."

I was being addressed. "Sylvia, so will I be disappointed when I get to Japan?"

"Haven't been there, but by most accounts, it's worth a visit. Wish I was going with you."

Our "crits" stayed away the last couple days during our push to finish. It was not healthy or safe to meet the half-crazed students.

As our five o'clock deadline approached, the tension mounted as the majority of students added the finishing touches to their presentations. Add titles, number the boards, erase guidelines, oops, add a few more shadow lines…so many details. Constantly checking the clock, finally the time came when we put down our pencils, gathered up our boards, and headed toward the stairs to race down to the jury room. A clerk standing by the door checked in our submitted work. We were done. It was a relief greater than submitting an income tax to the IRS before the deadline, because we had no late submittal clauses without dire penalties. We climbed back upstairs leisurely as other students galloped past us as they made their way down.

"Hold the doors open, we're coming."

"Jeez, I think I forgot to put my name on my drawings."

The door was slammed shut at the hour; laggards lost half a grade point.

With projects accepted and secured, we returned to our desks, sweeping all discarded sketches and extraneous papers onto the floor without crushing them into tension-relieving balls and adding them to the voluminous piles already covering the floor. The good janitors had everything swept up before daybreak.

I gathered my drawing supplies and put them away to take home later. Now wide awake, I drove home, cooked dinner, and fell asleep when the children went to bed.

Life experiences during my years away from college had made me sensible and pragmatic, and it affected my design solutions. Practical and grounded inhibited creative design; my design solutions did not soar.

Our last quarter of studio was the ten-week thesis project of our own choosing. My proposal for a Japanese American Cultural and Community Center was accepted. I chose to locate the facility on a hillside in the Rainier Valley not too distant from the traditional hub of the community. I had more than a passing knowledge of and interest in the theme, and it was sited in an area I knew well. This last school project was my last chance to go for broke. It was a last opportunity to write a program and design a dream facility with no regard to budgets. I envisioned a modern building touched with distinct but subtle Japanese idioms and a good dash of Katsura Imperial Villa aesthetics for good measure. Ten weeks of concentrated effort had passed quickly.

The schedule for critiques of our projects was posted. Each student had the opportunity to validate his or her design solution with the instructors who judged and graded the completed work. I had once witnessed a student skillfully talk his minimally realized drawings into a decent grade. A good sales job always helped the cause.

Setting aside my reluctance to defend myself, and comfortable with my subject, I set forth selling my thesis project during this critique.

"I deliberately selected this hillside site so it would overlook the accessible commercial activities below yet be removed from them. The trees and natural vegetation existing…"

"Japanese idioms are more prominent in the smaller classrooms, where traditional arts and crafts would be taught, such as *odori* or Japanese dance, the *koto*, which is a long wooden instrument, ikebana…"

"The library would contain both… And poetry groups could gather for meetings and have tea after…"

My thesis subject and site location were one I understood and knew better than my jury. I wanted to believe I had been smart in my choices; I knew my subject matter, and my proposed design solution was on target. It was a good karma day for me. The "crits" were not always as unquestioning or as accepting for those who followed that day, and they were at times merciless––a few would leave bloody from the cutting criticism meted out.

This arena was not full of mercy and grace; you had to be a survivor.

We had endured, and it was time to get on with our lives. Most took a respite before continuing on to graduate school or going on to jobs practicing architecture for pay. Classmate Merle and her husband traveled Europe by rail that summer. David and I joined the exodus, and we flew to Hawaii while Grampa babysat the children. The trip was my reward for finishing school, and for David, it was a homecoming after an eighteen-year absence from the islands.

I had promised to work the summer months at The Restaurant before looking for a career job in the fall. They had been accommodating while I went back to school by scheduling shifts for me to work during school vacations. It was the tenth summer of my working there. Things had changed since my inauspicious beginnings in that godawful kimono. I felt more than a tinge of sadness at leaving the attractive ambiance of The Restaurant and relinquishing a work routine imbued with so many memories. When it was time for me to leave, I said my farewells: "Good-bye, Grandma's Cookies sign and The Gas Works, the stuffed Mahi Mahi in the bar, Joe's bell at the copper-hooded broiler, and stair climb to the Penthouse. Next time I see you, it'll cost me a bundle to eat here."

On occasion, I find myself back at The Restaurant in my dreams and awkwardly wearing a kimono again.

"But I haven't worked here for a long time," I say. "Things have been moved around and changed." What was once familiar appears askew in a surreal setting. "And I'm not up to date on menu items and prices."

"We'll put you on a slow station. You'll be able to handle that."

When were they seated? They're ready to order their dinner now? They have no water or butter yet. We're out of sequence.

"Behind you! Your order's ready to be picked up."

The salad needs to be tossed, desserts to be served, dinner plates to be removed. Why is everything so messed up?

"Clear that table, we have customers waiting."

Work faster, faster. Why can't I move quickly, and why won't my brains mesh smoothly? Why do I keep coming back here to work? Like all dreams, answers are never forthcoming.

Job Hunting

Finding a job was more difficult than anticipated. I had no connections or networks. The economy was healthy, yet no one was willing to hire me.

"No, I don't type. I was looking for a job as a draftsman–– an architectural draftsman."

"We're a small office, and everyone contributes. We're not able to train anyone. Sorry," they said.

It's impossible to have experience when no one is willing to hire you in the first place to get that experience. It's a conundrum.

The Boeing Company was hiring, but they were not interested in a draftsman with no experience, with or without a degree; they had applicants aplenty with experience, they said. The interview took place in a cavernous arena of tables lined row after identical row where the window walls were lined with offices for the titled employees. The prevailing quiet was suddenly broken by a din that became louder and more persistent as desk drawers rumbled open and mingled with shuffling papers. The hour bell rang out, and the hall cleared of people like in a practiced fire drill; absolutely everyone disappeared out to lunch. I would disappear in such a well-ordered cog. I did not regret not getting a job there.

Job interviews were more formal in the larger architectural firms than at smaller offices and their responses more practiced.

"We're looking for permanent workers," my interviewer said.

"I'm applying for a full-time job. It's written on my application."

"Don't try and pass that on me. I won't buy it. You'll work until summer then quit to take care of your kids. And it says here you have three."

I was dumbfounded. I shook my head.

"That has no bearing…"

He interrupted, "We have nothing against you people. We've got a boy here from Manila and another boy from Taiwan." He stood up and gathered his papers. "You'll find your way out?"

In the real world, chauvinists, racists, and narrow-minded "…ists" of all sorts still existed unencumbered by regulations intended to promote equality. Such issues had to be dealt with as they were encountered.

Humbled by the rejections, my ego bruised, I resolved to prove my worth. I'd done it before, and I would do so again; someone had to take a chance and hire me. I did not invoke any Scarlett O'Hara oaths this time, although I felt my determination as deeply as before. Months passed as I languished. Soon, I would be competing with another batch of architecture graduates applying for jobs too. I finally checked in with an unlikely architectural job placement source, the state employment office. Government agencies were rarely a good source for job seekers looking for creative dream jobs, but I was desperate. A few weeks later, they led me to an office in the industrial area south of downtown. Large architectural firms locate themselves in or near the central business district or on the periphery. Smaller offices are apt to locate anywhere the ambiance and amenities lead them. Big or small, they do not locate in industrial areas among factories and warehouses. I was willing to find my way there.

A development company with several in-house architects designing storage and industrial buildings was starting up its own production division to prepare construction drawings and documents speedily. This allowed the owner full control of the design, details, and construction of the buildings he built and owned. His sales staff leased out space in his buildings, the property managers maintained them, and the accounting department logged in the rent.

In the hierarchy of architectural establishments, working for an internationally recognized architect ranked highest in esteem, followed by a nationally famous architect or firm. The esteem quotient decreased in stages to near bottom where a job with a development company dwelled. The purists snubbed their noses at the "sellouts" plying their trade in a company other than purely architectural. On the bottom of the prestige level were those who found work with a developer/contractor who constructed their own buildings; design professionals who worked for them were designated contemptible "conflict of interest" traitors. I was hired by a developer/contractor firm.

Egan, a registered architect, had been hired to head up the new production department. He had one draftsman in place. Dan had hired on hoping to be a designer, and he was open about his disappointment to be working under Egan's thumb. I was the second draftsperson in the department. Others were hired and joined us. Those with experience were older men who were unlikely to be hired by A-1 architectural firms, and the younger ones were summer hires between real jobs or those who finally found their first job to put on their resumes. The economy was booming, and architectural firms were hiring––despite their response to my inquiries––and they were picking and selecting the cream. My coworkers and I had not made that grade.

We were still half a dozen in the drafting room when Egan announced Dan's departure from the company. I gained seniority after three weeks on the job, and I became a job captain. The design staff and newly hired staff with years of drafting experience answered my questions and guided me along as I learned while I worked. The opportunities opened up, I plunged in, and I loved the challenge and the work.

The company was expanding in scope as well as size, and the variety and types of buildings the company began constructing expanded, too. The warehouse remained the mainstay of the business, and by standardizing features of the structure we could comfortably produce a set of contract drawings in three weeks and submit for a building permit. Egan, ever eager to win his brownie points from higher-ups, never varied the time schedule of three weeks regardless of the building's complexity compared to a simple warehouse. We in the drafting room had to complete the project in three weeks. We each took responsibility for completing one sheet of the set and cursed Egan as we ground out the drawings to meet his promised deadlines. The charrette's had prepared us to work under pressure to meet deadlines, though we never worked so late that we went without sleep. The radio in the drafting room was inevitably turned up as soon as workers in other parts of the office went home to their dinners. How else would one hear the first on-air playing of Sgt. Pepper's Lonely Hearts Club Band?

Unlike our school projects, in the real world we had to communicate with each other and coordinate drawings to be accurate, and we conferred with consultants who understood our time constraints since the drawings we labored to produce were made into real buildings. We collaborated with the project engineers and field supervisors to construct a structure "on time and within budget."

Most significantly, the difference between schoolwork and a job: we were paid for the work we did and we no longer had all night charette's.

CAREER WORK

"Sylvia, you didn't provide enough space next to the beam for the equipment box. What do you propose we do?" Ernie, the building's project engineer, said.

I looked at the drawings, and he was right. I studied it, and there was no easy solution. Changes to fix the problem would be costly. The oversight loomed large, and I was crushed. There was no escape; I finally asked him what could be done.

"That's my job, to fix the problem. I thought you should know," he said. "Don't worry about it."

"I'm sooo relieved," I said.

"Sorry, I should have told you earlier, the men in the field will fix it."

Constructing a building could be like giving birth: often painful during the labor but followed by relief and joy afterward.

I went to see Bob, one of the design architects in the next room. Their unit had also expanded and included an artist named Uga, the Estonian, whose specialty was drawing pretty pictures of proposed buildings. As an adjunct for Sales, it was a specialty now accomplished by computer graphics. The paintings always looked better than the real buildings by strategically placing trees and foliage to hide any building blemishes, with the sun always shining brightly on the scene.

"Was that Ernie I saw you talking to?" Bob asked.

"Yes, why do you ask?"

"I'm surprised he's still here."

"Where's he going?"

"Didn't you hear? He burst into Chuck's office demanding a hearing. He told him off with a lot of desk banging. It got loud, so Roger stepped in before they came to blows."

"Nice Ernie told off Little Napoleon, his boss? Of all people, I liked working with him. He must have been really mad. Guess he'll be leaving."

"Ernie wasn't always an inside man. He was a field superintendent. He must have had his fill of office BS."

"I'll miss him. I wonder who's taking over as project engineer on my building."

"Karl's been assigned."

"Is Napoleon trying to sabotage Ernie's project by putting the Storm Trooper in charge of it?"

"That's only a rumor Chuck started. Karl's from the old country, but it's stretching it to say he was a member of the SS."

"Humm…that time Karl closed his office door…" He had whispered: "…the concentration camps operated to house gypsies and lunatics. The number of Jews in the camps has been totally overstated."

"What's that about Karl?"

"Never mind."

We were a potpourri of individuals, mostly new hires stretching and testing our wings in our new jobs. On the first day on the job, I had been taken to each office and introduced as the newly hired "employee number thirty-two." The practice was soon abandoned as hiring escalated, and within months the employee count reached near one hundred. We were strangers trying to work together; in a civilized way, that is, with gnashing teeth and steamy seething on occasion. Meshing the diverse temperaments and egos of a diverse workforce that included tradesmen and professionals into a cohesive smooth-running company was still a goal, but whatever the internal conflicts, we were united with heightened esprit de corps when attacked by outsiders.

The commands emanated from the corner office/conference room from where Mr. B ran his company. The imposing nine-foot-tall door leading into his office was kept closed, although an open-door policy prevailed elsewhere. We in the drafting room were far removed from the inner sanctum, which his advisers, confidants, and department heads entered with a degree of trepidation.

Not that he was inaccessible or unsocial, he was quite the opposite, however, he was a man completely consumed with his work developing and overseeing his real estate holdings. The multifaceted company was created to aid him in that task. His fierce intensity beamed laser sharp through his eyes when he sought to reveal data and facts needed for decision making. Exacting in his expectations, he did not suffer fools. An error might be excused the first time; never a second time. A piercing look could wound those it was directed toward. We did our best to meet his expectations.

The pace and variety of projects made for a job that was never dull.

FAMILY ACTIVITIES

During the school year, the children had less time to get into mischief. In the summer, they were enrolled in every sort of activity that could be crammed into their schedule: swimming lessons, self-defense classes, gymnastics, arts and crafts, YMCA day camps and Camp Orkila sessions on Orcas Island. They were happiest when they had a few weeks of real vacation from enrichment classes before school began again.

Grampa retired from his job cleaning railroad cars. His small pension stretched to cover his expenses, primarily for his car and a few indulgences, including his memberships in various organizations keeping his social life healthy. The Old Peoples Club welcomed all elderly Nikkei regardless of their other affiliations. As the senior citizen Issei's moved beyond mere old age, their numbers decreased, making the organization-sponsored dinners and events opportunities to gather and socialize as they became less mobile. Attending the gatherings to greet longtime acquaintances was worthwhile, for soon enough it would be their names in the obituary column. A New Year's party in late January was always the most popular and best attended event with catered *obento's* featuring the celebratory foods they no longer prepared themselves.

Sightseeing tours to scenic localities and cities in the western United States often included a stop in Reno, Nevada. The tours were kept affordable, and since Yoshi was among the younger, still agile members, he could not pass up visiting a place new to him–– better still was when someone else did the driving. Brimming with energy and enthusiasm, he claimed his ride down and up the Grand Canyon on a mule was exhilarating, forgetting not everyone was immune to heights as he was. In Reno, he played the slot machines and Keno, his favorite game of chance. The gaudy souvenirs he carried home to display in his room were usually "made in Japan."

He relished his new leisure time to do as he wished. Every day, he tended his border garden of flowers, an activity denied him for years. Puttering among his plants kept him moving. Photographing his blooms, first with a still camera then later with a movie camera to capture bird sightings as they came to visit his garden, occupied his good-weather days. Seattle's frequent sunless rainy days gave Yoshi unencumbered time for reading and his poetry. Life was good and he felt he had been lucky.

The local Japanese-language newspaper continued to publish a number of topical tanka poems each week, and Yoshi continued to contribute his poems. Much as a byline journalist selects subjects of interest or concern to write about, Yoshi began writing thirty-one *On* poems about subjects weighing on his mind. The new tanka poems emerging from Japan were bending the rigid rules and shirking old taboos, and they had begun incorporating topical subjects in their compositions. By adopting the new, relaxed format, Yoshi had found he could express his own views about the world. He was a younger Yoshi again. But he signed them by Osei.

When the Walter McCarran Immigration and Naturalization Act was passed by Congress in 1952, hundreds of discriminatory laws including the 1924 Exclusion Act with its "ineligibility for citizenship" clause were voided, Issei became eligible for citizenship. Yoshi became a naturalized citizen of the United States soon after, and finally, he became free of his illegal immigrant status. As an American with rights to free speech and self-expression, Yoshi used the familiar thirty-one *onji* form to speak up on controversial issues along with the mundane. It had been a long, twisted journey, one undertaken while remaining silent.

The Seattle Tanka-kai poetry group meetings continued to be scheduled every month—the get-together Yoshi never missed. He still attended the singing Shigin Group. His best friends were still Mrs. Esaki and her sister and their husbands.

Hayame, his former mother-in-law, returned to Seattle with her husband and now lived a few miles away, close enough to reestablish their ties and routinely play friendly games of Hana, a Japanese card game.

Grampa kept shaking his head.

"What's wrong, Grampa? Are you having girlfriend problems?"

"She is very nice woman. I never hear her say mean thing about other people. I no understand." "Who did what?"

"Hayame-*san*, you grandma, she cheat when we play Hana."

"Ohoo… *Obaa-san* cheats playing cards?"

"We bet only little bit money. Lose maybe one or two dollar sometimes. But people see she cheat and no wanna play cards with her anymore."

"Why don't you quit, too?"

"Like I say, she is kind, good person. She never complain; always *niko niko* happy when she play Hana. Only bad thing, she sneak look at card, not her card." He paused and came up with another thought. "Hmm… maybe second not-so-good thing: her house look like junkyard."

Obaa-san was the same person I remembered; she had not changed nor had her habits, but I had no idea how long she had been a card shark.

We were closer to living the American dream. With college degrees, David and I had jobs in our specialties, which we had worked so long to attain. The angst and stress had diminished along with those dreams of flying barely high enough to miss telephone poles and power lines. Try harder, go faster, and fly higher. Try as I might, I could not soar free. I was glad to be rid of those dreams.

Whenever we had accumulated a little money in our savings in the past, we had depleted it in short order. We were ready to repeat it again. Our once-cute little house was way too small for the six of us; the children had grown. The logical remedy to our problem was to find a building site on which to build a larger house. We found a prospective building parcel a couple miles away and showed Grampa the location for his endorsement.

"No *kes-ki*," he said.

"If you stand here in this corner of the lot, you can see the top of the hill way to the south."

"Only little bit view."

A technicality made it impossible to build a house on the site, so we did not buy the lot, and we continued the search. We found a site with a view, Grampa approved, and I began making mental plans for the house. We would build once we completed making payments on the land. I designed a house beyond our means though still far from the mansion of my dreams.

A Downturn

The once-booming economy was beginning to lose its luster, and development was feeling the effects sooner than other businesses. We in the drafting room were asked to take early vacations. It was an opportune time to take two weeks off from work, and by adding a third unpaid week, the contract drawings for our house were completed and submitted for a building permit. We hired Carl, a contractor who had built friend George's house earlier. He agreed to work on an hourly basis. We broke ground in March with Grampa, our son Michael, plus a high school student we paid to assist Carl to be his go-fer. Friend Dick along with David contributed with their sweat equity on weekends.

At work, a pink slip or two or three began accompanying paychecks. The pattern of layoffs continued every two weeks, and those of us who remained were doomed to sit and wonder which week would be our turn to be laid off. The revised company organization chart showed the diminished ranks of lower-echelon workers without a similar dismissal rate of titled, higher-paid employees who sat in private offices; another case of too many chiefs as the workers bees were laid off. I was promoted to designer and moved to that department as the company made bids to win outside projects. As interest rates climbed, the in-house projects dried up and our overhead costs were too high to be competitive. Our industry was in a downturn, although there was little evidence of it elsewhere. The office morale was dismal, and holding a company picnic was not approved. We employees decided to schedule a potluck picnic of our own to dispel the gloom.

A day before the scheduled picnic, we were told departmental meetings were to be held at nine o'clock sharp.

"Design and production staff to meet in the drafting room. Cancel all other appointments; no one is excused from attending their meeting." Other departments were holding their own meetings at the same hour.

"The company is being reorganized," Bob announced in starting the meeting. "Instead of different departments based on their functions, three teams will be formed: Teams A, B, and C. Each team will consist of project engineers, estimators, designers, and draftsmen. The leasing and accounting areas are undergoing their own reorganization. Not everyone will have a job after today."

The room was abuzz. Everyone knew what was coming. "Who's being cut? How many?"

"We'll have to figure that out," Bob answered. "What I was given are the names of people assigned to each team. These I will read. If your name is not called and you are not assigned to a team, we can assume you no longer have a job here."

"Ass-backward as usual," commented a disgruntled employee. "Just let the man continue."

"Team A's project engineers are…"

Everyone listened intently to the names being read. Team B's names were called. The room was full of people whose names had not been called–including mine. He was reading names for Team C—finally, finally—he called my name. I still have a job; I'm on Team C. I rejoiced in silence; I could continue to pay Carl to work on our house. When the meeting ended, those who still had jobs and the newly jobless opted to take an early martini lunch. As people straggled back to the office after their liquid lunch, good-byes were exchanged with ex-employees who decided to forego the next day's picnic. The consensus was that it was too late to cancel the company employees' (and families') picnic, and it proceeded in the same chaotic, freewheeling way of a typical picnic. Youngsters ran around and drank their fill of soda pop; the adults maintained a veneer of cheer and light ambivalence, keeping darker anxieties at bay. Overtones of an Irish wake permeated the air.

At the end of the year, the company undertook a second reorganization. Select employees formed an independent company and moved to offices elsewhere. I had survived the upheavals and continued working at the company, which was now smaller than it had been when I was first hired two and a half years before. We were a one-core team, and communication from Mr. B was filtered only once, and often it was direct. It was a lean, efficient company to survive the times, a time when a billboard read: "Will the last person leaving Seattle please turn off the lights?" became its iconic slogan.

The House is completed

Early in the year, we had paid little heed to the first faint signs of the recession to come, and we had optimistically decided to proceed with construction of our house. The steep hillside site providing Grampa his view was composed of clay soil, which hindered excavation without heavy machinery. It rained and rained until early spring. Staging the foundation work took months rather than weeks as we dealt with wet clay slurry, and forming and erecting the concrete walls was tediously slow. "There's enough steel rebar and concrete in the foundation to support an apartment," Carl wisecracked in frustration.

The rains stopped, and the structure of the house finally began to take shape. Grampa was still sufficiently agile and sure of foot, and he walked the heavy beams with impunity as he helped set the joists on the beams, as it stood in skeleton form high above the hillside below. Carl, with his thick Swedish accent, and Grampa, with his Japanese pronunciations, managed to communicate without constraint in mangled English. The two immigrants from opposite sides of the world labored cooperatively, each respectful of the other's work and personal ethics. The construction progressed steadily during the dry-weather months, and a roof was installed before the rains returned in autumn.

We moved into the barely finished house in mid-December. Mirrors for the bathrooms had not yet arrived, and five of us, who had to go to work or school, took turns using the one handheld mirror we owned, checking ourselves before heading out the door. The mirror was the only item left from the set of matched grooming tools that had traveled with us to camp and back. Such sets were once popular and Grampa may have received it as a wedding gift. If so, the heirloom turned out to be a utilitarian necessity.

House under construction

The furniture we owned fit comfortably in our family room. We did have the foresight to order new mattresses on rolling metal frames for all bedrooms. Five people doing homework on the dinner table made purchasing desks and chairs for the children's rooms a priority; other furnishings could come later. Wall-to-wall carpeting installed a few days before New Year's meant we could have a party for all who helped us move.

Our house was not the ultimate dream house that kept me mentally occupied through the years. That ever evolving creation with no real-world constraints such as site conditions, utility connections, regulating codes, and a budget, will remain a dream. We had built a real house we could call home, that fit our family's needs and with a few added amenities, including a living room that could accommodate a ten-foot tall Christmas tree.

A portion of the daylight basement designated as Grampa's apartment was promptly hung with pictures; Grampa was mindless of the number of nails pounded into the plasterboard. The exposed horizontal studs used as shelves in previous dwellings were covered and hidden in the new house, so Grampa displayed his collection of memorabilia on tabletops as most people do. From his windows, he looked at the view. There was a glimpse of the bay below where the waters only nibbled the shore. He may have missed hearing the ocean's crashing waves, but he was close enough to a body of water, and he was content to watch others sail the waters in their pleasure boats.

In the evening, he had a different distraction. His snug sitting room's main components were his television set and his lounge chair. The visual activity and the noise from the set kept him company. His favorite programs were the boxing matches when he swung arms and fists with short jabs, and his grunts alternated with commands as he coached the pugilists on the screen, all the while sitting in his oversized recliner chair.

"I go see boxing in Madison Square Garden," he said to anyone who asked. His interest in the sport went a long way back. We never understood why such an easygoing, mild-mannered, kind human being relished watching men pummeling each other senseless. There are less violent sports, we reminded him. He kept football and baseball games on his screen for the noise but rarely watched them with real interest. The one exception was horse racing. He no longer bet on the ponies, but he maintained his interest in the Triple Crown winners.

"You would have won money if you bet on Orange Juice," I said.

"Too bad, I no believe five-year-old daughter pick winner," he answered, remembering the irony of the long-ago incident.

Grampa considered the house incomplete until the surrounding landscaping complemented the structure. He began his campaign to replace the bramble, wild blackberries, and weeds with his favorite plants and flowers. The project was never ending as the weeds continued to compete for space in his garden. His battle to keep the invaders at bay included buying an arsenal of supplies at the nearby Mizuki Nursery & Plant Store and charging it all to "my son-in-law Day-bee." His special affinity for flowers meant patches of blooming florals of every sort. Grampa planted a bed of Peonies here, Asters there, and perennials, annuals, and Buttercups here, there, and everywhere. It was a landscaping nightmare, but nobody noticed the hodgepodge when the flowers blossomed.

"Backyard too cold for tomatoes, sun too short," he lamented as his tomatoes refused to ripen. "Next year I plant flowers. More better."

The phone call from Aunt Kimi was unexpected. "Was Aiko-*san's* mother's name Itono?" she asked. "Mama doesn't remember." It was understandable Hayame did not remember her predecessor's name; she had never met her.

"Why are you calling long distance to ask such a question?"

"I was notified that if Itono Michihira was a relative, her ashes stored at the Seattle Buddhist church had to be claimed."

"Itono never lived in Seattle. How did her remains find their way here?" When the Buddhist church in the valley relocated, the stored ashes of former parishioners were moved to the larger Seattle Temple, where they languished, sadly forgotten until they were rediscovered during a remodeling project. A large stash of ashes in urns, boxes, and paper bags were found; many had no identification. "No wonder Aiko didn't know where her mother was buried. She was resting at the church," Grampa said.

He retrieved the ashes and had them buried alongside her daughter Aiko's urn. He planned to join them later.

Visit to Japan

It's incredible I'm returning to Japan; I had given up hope years ago. It's like a dream. Yoshi was lost in his thoughts. I never crossed the Pacific by ship as these other people did, but we'll be flying in c louds, which will take mere hours and not weeks. Air travel has the benefit of speed; nevertheless, I'll miss the pleasures of travel by sea with sightings of Pacific islands and watching the ocean disappear into the horizon.

Yoshi bounced off his seat and paced the floor while clearing his throat in that telltale nervous habit of his. He cleared his throat again, and recognizing the sound, I knew he had not wandered too far away.

The waiting area at the departure gate was crowded and noisy with travelers, their relatives and friends all in attendance, leaving little room for him to wander. He stared blankly at the ceiling, then out the windows toward the bustling activity on the tarmac. A poem was budding in his mind. I recognized that state of inattentive animation of his when a new poem was in the works. I knew not to interrupt him at such times, so I sat and watched the crowd of mostly Japanese in our waiting area. I found no familiar faces. There was still time before boarding, and I wanted the assurance Grampa was safely on the plane to Japan making his long-delayed return. It was only a visit since America was now his home.

"Nomura-*san*, Nomura-*san*," a woman nearby called out.

Grampa snapped out of his reverie and walked toward the caller. "Hallo, hallo…"

"Nomura-san, you stand there so calm and collected, unlike the rest of us. So, how many previous trips have you made to Japan?"

"This is my first time back since I left fifty years ago."

"This is my third trip back, and I'm as nervous as the first time." She wanted to chat to forestall her growing anxiety. "Everything is so different now. I don't feel like I belong. I'm treated like a guest in my ancestral home. When I return to America, I want to go back and see Japan again."

"Unfortunately, my family home was washed out to sea by a tsunami shortly after the war. I'm sure our village will be unrecognizable."

"Our home was outside of Hiroshima in the country. It wasn't damaged by the bomb during the war. Since then, the city has kept growing and spreading toward our home and covering the greenery and open areas. We are now inside the city. It's a pity."

"I have *shinseki*, relatives, with a similar problem. A photograph of their home in the thirties shows their house surrounded by trees and vegetation. They said their neighbors recently built a market and put the parking lot next to their garden."

"So what part of Hiroshima are you from?"

"My wife's family is from Hiroshima. I come from Mie."

"Hmm. Don't meet many people from Mie. I went to Ise and visited the Shinto shrine and the Pearl Island in Toba City. It's very scenic in that area."

"That's true...that part of Japan is unforgettable. My *mura* is further south..." He saw the ocean inlet between the tree-studded cliffs in his mind's eye, and he ached to be there. A shiver coursed through his body, waking his senses in anticipation of realizing a long-held dream. The seeds of his new poem withered. All he could think about was home and his village by the sea. *Mukashi, mukashi...* a long time ago.

CHAPTER 20

Epilogue

Yoshi traveled to Japan several times more, yet he was always happy when he returned to America and to accustomed comforts and the conveniences he took for granted that were not always available on those travels. As soon as the gifts and trinkets he picked up in Japan were distributed to friends and family and his stories were told and retold, he began planning his next trip with map in hand, searching for places not yet visited but worth exploring next time. His greatest pleasure, however, was the embracing company of kinfolk he had walked away from as a youth.

"An old man like me cannot sit on the floor for hours anymore. I think I inherited my preference to sit on chairs from our Chinese ancestors," he said to his nephew. His legs stretched in front of him, hogging an expanse on the tatami like a foreigner. Etiquette decreed he sit with legs unobtrusively tucked by his side or folded under him, compact and contained. He was reminded of those agonizing nights he sat ramrod straight on aching legs as the *zabuton* beneath him lost its loft and the task of memorizing Buddhist scriptures continued into the night.

"*Oji-san*, Uncle, we don't have Chinese ancestors, just as we have no samurai ancestors."

"You're wrong on both counts, nephew," Yoshi said. "Our grandmother, your great-grandmother, had the family name Hayashi. When the Chinese arrived in Japan, they continued using their Chinese ideogram but adopted the Japanese pronunciation of their name. Centuries ago, an artisan came from China and became our ancestor." When Yoshi was not limited by lack of vocabulary and the unfathomable grammatical rules of his second language, Yoshi could babble endlessly to his heart's content, especially on his favorite subjects.

"Yoshi, we would have been disciplined for speaking heresy. We were taught the Japanese race is pure," older brother Seinojo had said. "You're saying we're hybrids. And in what convoluted way did we acquire those samurai ancestors you speak of?"

"Like every other immigrant who came to America and claimed samurai ancestry. Out of self-defense, I decided to find some samurai forebears for our family tree and honor our name."

"Our name is so commonplace, we're almost as numerous as Suzuki… Sorry, continue…"

"Well, you know as well as me that the villagers who populate the rugged seacoast areas in these parts came from other parts of Japan. We're not an indigenous people. When the Taira fought the Minamoto's in the Genpei Wars, there were members of the defeated forces who fled for their lives rather than stay and be slaughtered."

"*Nani*? Samurai fled rather than fight to their death? They didn't all commit honorable *seppuku*?"

"That's nonsense. How could they take revenge if they all died? A number of warriors on the defeated side who escaped to areas out of reach of their enemies had to be hardy to reach this part of the island. They're our samurai ancestors."

"The Genpei Wars took place almost a thousand years ago. Couldn't you have found a more recent direct line? Secondly, I don't like the idea we may be descendants of cowards who didn't fight to the finish."

"The connection is somewhat vague, but the lineage to the Taira is better than an obscure clan."

Seinojo smiled as he saw his younger brother transformed into the little twerp full of bravado who had to be rescued from time to time. "Yoshi, you always liked reading history books. It's unfortunate we weren't able to send you on to high school. Perhaps that was just as well. If you had stayed here, you wouldn't have had the opportunities you had in America."

The four siblings who had lived to adulthood and were living at war's start managed to survive and were now seniors. Yasue, Yoshi's mother, died during the war. Kakichi, his father, experienced the great tsunami, and he died not long after the event. The trauma and hardships brought on by the war and tidal wave surely shortened his life, the family said.

Earthquake rumblings are common in Japan; this particular undersea quake sucked the waters of the ocean far away from shore. They saw in the distance that wall of water holding back the sea. The villagers, as if by instinct, knew to flee out of harm's way. Most dropped whatever they were doing and ran as fast as they could, scrambling up the hills, as high up as they could go. A few could not leave behind their valuables, so they gathered up a handful of possessions before dashing out and running toward the high ground to join the others who were making their way up the mountain. The ocean came roaring in led by that wall of water, and the sea invaded the land and crushed everything within its wake. Further inland, the waters churned and tossed objects before dumping debris, furnishings, and possessions helter-skelter along its path as the waters swept back to sea with its bounty of goods.

"We had five minutes to make our escape," claimed survivors. Those who delayed their escape as they collected their valuables perished with their collectibles.

The remote, nonstrategic location of their village saved them from direct damage during the war, but nature's forces wreaked its own havoc of destruction on the village. The family's home was demolished; they lost everything except their lives.

Yoshi realized how lucky he had been to be living in America. The wartime dislocations, the tribulations of camp life, and the general upheavals he'd experienced due to the war were mere inconveniences compared to his siblings' trials.

Seinojo and his son started a small *ryokan* in Kamisaki and carried on while many younger villagers began leaving for urban areas, where greater opportunities and abundant distractions abounded. Sister Kimiko was widowed and living with her son and daughter-in-law sufficiently close to the *ryokan* to visit and sip tea with the family often.

In the years following the war, as Japan began its reconstruction and the populace began their recovery, younger brother Hiromu, who had been stationed in Manchuria, had not returned home. The family had received a heavily censored letter from him indicating he was alive and in Siberia. After the war, the Russians had been reluctantly releasing Japanese prisoners of war. The process dragged on for years as the Japanese demanded the return of their soldiers, while the Russians kept denying their existence. As another batch of Japanese POWs were "found," they were returned. Seinojo and the family continued to wait, but the brother was never among the returnees. The Russians claimed all their POWs had been released; there were no more. "Not true," the Japanese said. "There are others." Ten years after the end of World War II, the Russians miraculously found some more Japanese prisoners in Siberia. "These are absolutely the last ones," the Russians again said. Brother Hiromu returned home.

As a military officer, Hiromu was able to have his family live with him in Manchuria. He was stationed in an area near the border when Russia entered the war, just as the war was ending. Hiromu was captured by the Russians and sent off to Siberia as a prisoner of war. His wife and two children had fled the chaos surrounding them and their fate was unknown. Upon his return, Hiromu followed a cold ten-year-old trail looking for his family, making inquiries of anyone who might know what happened and where they might have gone, with no results.

Hiromu remarried, started a new family, and lived in Ise, though he visited Kamisaki often.

More than two decades later, Japanese who had been stranded in China as youths and had become curious to find relatives living in Japan became subjects of the media by broadcasting and promoting their searches in television programs and in newspapers. Hiromu's daughter was one of the searchers, and the reunion between father and daughter made good copy. Her mother and younger brother had died during their escape...

She, the daughter, had been taken in by a Chinese family and adopted. Now married with children of her own, memories of her earlier life made her curious and had given her a desire to close the circle.

Grampa Nomura, Grandpa Otani and David

Grampa's second return to Japan followed a few short years after the first trip when he received word that Seinojo's illness was diagnosed as terminal. Yoshi hastily packed his bags for an extended stay in Japan. His brother was ambulatory and his family nursed him at home. He was often comatose from sedatives to ease his pain.

Yoshi was given a room away from the commotion of the ryokan's public areas and family living quarters, and he tried to stay out of the family's way while they did their chores running their business. He fell into a routine; at times, he sat with his brother and read to him, hoping he recognized the voice through the drug inflicted haze. At other times, he watched television in the sickroom and made random comments, although his companion was unlikely to reply. The volume was set low to mitigate sounds escaping through the sliding shoji screen walls. Yoshi's bad ear had gone completely deaf, and his good ear needed louder and louder stimuli. Hearing loss is such a gradual phenomenon, he had not noticed how much quieter his surroundings were. Audible sounds joined the white background noise, becoming ever softer. Japanese-centric programs and news broadcasts filled the TV screen that communicated in a language he understood, although it reached him as silent entertainment.

Yoshi was being called. He tossed his futon aside, sat up, and looked around. It was still early morning and the household was not yet awake to start the morning chores. The feeling was so strong he gathered his *yukata* around him, tossed on a robe, crept out of his quarters and walked quickly down the shoji-lined hallway toward Seinojo's room. Upon entering, he detected no changes to his brother's condition.

"*Ni-san*, did you call me?" Yoshi asked softly and put his hand over his brother's, which lay over the covers. "I heard you, big brother. I'm here." There was no response. Yoshi kept stroking his brother's hand. How strange to be stroking his hand for the first time in our lives, he thought. Affection was never demonstrated physically in the past in this way. Seinojo had always been the macho presence who had kept the bullies at bay when Yoshi was young, and his brother's special privileges as *chonan* had never blunted his sense of generosity in their relationship.

There was a brief flutter of the eyelids, and the lips parted as Yoshi watched. He gave a momentary squeeze to the limp hand of his brother, and he knew Seinojo was gone. He sat silently on the cushioned tatami, communing with memories as tears flowed.

"*Oji-san*, Uncle, why are you here?" asked the startled niece when she opened the shoji to the sickroom.

"Seinojo called, and he died," Yoshi answered.

The funeral that followed was elaborate. Yoshi had missed all the services held for his kinfolk in the past half-century, and he was heartened he had returned to take part in memorializing his brother. As he sat through the services, sections of the sutra came to mind; not all had been forgotten.

A phenomenan common to immigrants, but true to a greater degree among the Issei populace who could neither send for parents to join them in America nor themselves leave America and return to Japan, was a first generation that did not experience any direct responsibility for their elderly parents, for their end-of-life care, or for ultimately dealing with their deaths. They had been spared that duty. This was true for Yoshi, and he realized this during his brother's dying days.

Since there was no urgency to hurry home, Yoshi went about tying a few loose ends while still in Japan. Uncle Sutekichi, whose stories of travel to foreign lands had set Yoshi on the path to see the world, and who had urged him to seek his fortune abroad, was long gone, but a son still lived. When Sutekichi ended his self-imposed exile, he returned from Australia alone, leaving behind his son. The son made his home in the subcontinent; he married and had children. He survived them all, and as a very old man, he returned to Japan to die among kin. Yoshi went to meet this cousin who had also spent more years abroad than in Japan. He had also learned to speak a great deal more of their adopted language. Their experiences living in two different English-speaking countries were dissimilar, and ultimately the stories of Cousin Kajuro's misadventures interested the old man the most. "To think my little brother turned into such a rascal," he said. "But I can understand his interest in women. Heh, heh."

Yoshi felt compelled to take one other side trip. The route was as circuitous as he remembered. He had only made the trip twice before, on foot and on unpaved trails. Traveling in a coach on paved roads was a different experience. Yoshi's cousin greeted him warmly like a long-lost brother, although the younger man had no memory of him. This cousin from America who had studied the sutras before him was such a distracted student he had smoothed the way for him who followed. "Absolutely no one is as thickheaded as Yoshi," his father had often said as he praised his son for his good efforts.

"I heard so much about you when I was growing up, Yoshi. I'm very appreciative you came to visit me," said the younger cousin as they sat and sipped their tea.

Yoshi laughed. "I hope what was said wasn't all bad. Your father had taken on the difficult task of making me into a devout disciple of Buddha, but it was not my karma. I was already corrupted when I arrived. I was as happy as your parents were when you were born. With a rightful heir to the priesthood, I could return to earthly pleasures."

The structure was austere and familiar, and the temple grounds they walked had changed little in the intervening years. "I liked tending the grounds best and helping your mother with her chores when I lived here," Yoshi said.

"I can understand why Mother said she lost a son when you left."

Back home in America, Yoshi lost his revered status as elderly uncle, *Oji-san*, and reverted back to Grampa who lived downstairs and took care of the garden. His grandchildren were busy with their own lives, but they continued to find him a convenient and willing driver when they needed a ride, especially when they were running late for school——that is, until they got their own driver's licenses.

Just as watching boxing on television released Yoshi's submerged aggression, driving a car had the same curative properties. His lead foot pressed deep on the gas pedal; he bolted from start to speed limit within seconds, accompanied by VA-ROOM-M-M, a roar resembling a Harley Davidson in passing gear. Perhaps his deaf ear and his failing other ear needed really loud sounds for reassurance his motor was running. He knew gas and brake, and hardly anything in between. Like many other Issei who grew up without automobiles, Yoshi had no long-standing familiarity with its mechanics from youth; he was a poor driver.

"Gotta-dama sagana bi-ch!" he shouted at errant drivers.

Sometimes the swearing got worse. "Fa-ga yu!"

"Wow, Grampa swore up a storm while he was driving today," daughter Lorraine said. "He's not a very good influence for young kids like Julia."

"You mean the food curse, Kan-ten Sakana Spinach?" "Nope, it sounded almost like the real thing: Goddamn…" "That's enough, I get the picture."

No one was riding with him the morning he was driving to *Obaa-san's* house. Grampa had received an early morning call from Hayame telling him her husband had died, and they were waiting for the priest to perform services before the body was taken away. Grampa never made it there. Somewhere between home and *Obaa-san's* house, he crashed into another car. He was taken to the hospital with internal bleeding, and his car was totaled.

His injury was not life threatening, and he was expected to recover without complications. He who seldom complained began grumbling. "The doctors, they lie. I die soon."

"*Nani?* What makes you think that?" we said.

"Look-see, big scar, big operation. die soon."

"Nothing of the sort. You'll probably live to be 103 years old if you don't have any more accidents," the doctor said.

Grampa decided he was an invalid waiting to die at age eighty-eight. His wounds healed before his mental attitude. He no longer tended the garden or even wandered outdoors. The poem factory was shuttered; instead, he napped or watched television. His local Japanese-language newspaper subscription continued, and he read the obituaries to note the Issei acquaintances he had outlived. Usually news of a longtime poetry cohort's death came to him by phone, and sadly the number grew. Shocking was the information Mineko Esaki had died.

"But she is not so old. How can this be?" he asked.

"She was a hit-and-run victim. They found her body on the side of the road several days ago. She had no identification; nobody knew who she was. The police finally found someone to identify her," the caller said.

The remorse Yoshi felt did not translate into a new poem. He sat and contemplated the way their karmas had diverged. She had found another interest in her life, and though they remained friends, they had drifted apart. She had so much bad luck during her life. The pity is it never changed, and bad luck followed her to the end.

As if his death sentence had been suspended, Grampa's survival instincts returned. He began to believe the doctors had been right that his death was not imminent, and he should take steps to prolong his life. Most importantly, he would conserve his energy and avoid all exercise "Less use means longer wear and longer life," he reasoned. Then the person who once ate whatever was placed in front of him without comment, became a picky eater, and his appetite for sweets diminished, too. Without sugar fueling his nervous energy, he was less of a presence. Many years passed.

"No. I no wanna ninety-nine-year birthday party!" Grampa was adamant. "It is bad luck. People have party, and they die."

We did not celebrate Grampa's last double-digit birthday. The next year, we celebrated his one hundred years with a party. There were enough longtime friends and newer ones to help him celebrate, but many were gone. The Japanese counsel arranged a visit to the house and presented him with a metal commemorating his centennial year. The president sent a letter of congratulation (which we requested), and Social Security and the railroad union from which he had retired also sent him plaques.

He developed pneumonia and was recovering. "Maybe I live to 113 years old, world's oldest man, *neh*," Grampa said.

His illness had depleted much of his energy reserve, and he was weak and frail. He appeared to be slumbering or comatose a good part of the time, with unexpected periods of lucidity. The winter gloom was giving way to bouts of sunny days, and we hoped his spirits would brighten along with the flowers blooming outside. One morning, I prepared him for his breakfast, and he was wonderfully alert.

"Midori, I was thinking I haven't tasted any *kani* for a long time. Do you think we can have some *kani* to eat?"

"Hmmm, maybe," I said. He hardly eats anything. He even ignores his Jell-O, and he wants to eat crab? It will upset his stomach.

He barely touched his breakfast, so I went to the fish market, bought a crab, shelled it, and set aside choice bits for his lunch.

"Midori a bowl of noodles would taste so good. Noodles are my favorite."

"OK, OK. Do you want the fat *udon* or thin *somen*?"

"Me see, maybe *somen* be OK today."

We still had a package of special *somen* from Japan we had received from a friend. I prepared a large bowl of noodles for his requested lunch. Grampa guzzled up the noodles like a man who hadn't eaten in weeks. Expertly manipulating his chopsticks with his gnarled fingers, as soon as the strands of *somen* entered his mouth, he slurped, accompanied by the appropriate sounds Japanese make when consuming noodles. The noodles slithered down his throat barely chewed, and drinking the broth when the noodles were all consumed.

"There's some *kani* for you on the plate."

"How nice, I haven't eaten any in a long time." He had forgotten he requested it. "Maybe for dessert, watermelon…"

"*Nani?* What did you say?"

"Midori, do we have any watermelon?"

"Grampa, there's no watermelon in the grocery stores."

"*So neh.* Too early for watermelon from Yakima; too cold east of mountain now." "Huh?"

He reverted to his silent reveries after the meal. How I wished he would wake up again and ask to taste his favorite foods, whatever they were. A week passed with barely a word uttered and no further calls for room service.

I opened the bedroom drapes; "Good morning, Grampa."

He was awake, and smiling. "Midori, I have something to tell you. Soon I go away." He whispered.

"Where are you going, Grampa?" I asked as calmly as I could muster.

"They say so. They say I go away."

"Who told you that?" I asked slowly, although the spooky conversation had my heart and mind racing.

"*Kami-sama* tell me."

I hesitated to ask him which of his gods it was. I was glad there was one looking in on him.

Grampa died within the week, on the fourth day of the month. A letter from Yoshi's younger brother arrived two days later informing us their sister Kimiko had died a week before.

Grampa came rushing past me in the *gasa-gasa* way of his when he was in a hurry––that is, before his car accident. "Wait a minute." This isn't happening. Grampa died; he's gone. "Grampa? Stop! Where are you going?"

He stopped and turned around. "Oh. Midori…" He walked back up the slope toward me.

"Why are you in such a hurry?" I asked.

"I go on tour, go sightseeing. My friends, they are waiting for me." A distance down the path, a group of people were milling about eager for their excursion to begin. They were chattering and laughing, and on seeing him, they waved, urging him to join them.

"Nomura-*san, ko-chira oide na sai.* Come this way…"

"I go, *neh*," he said apologetically and ran off toward them, not the old, infirm man. He was Daddey, still young and energetic, the father I best remembered. When he reached the gathering, he turned and waved to me.

"Good-bye Daddy." And a good-bye to Yoshi, George, Osei, Grampa. "Have a nice safe journey."

Yoshi sightseeing in Japan

AUTHOR'S NOTES

⤚ᓚ

WHEN DAUGHTERS JULIA AND LORRAINE asked me to write down Grampa's stories of his early life, they were not particularly interested in his growing up years in Japan. It was his stories of adventures at sea and his bachelor days in New York City that piqued their curiosity. That the old man they knew, who tended the garden, wrote poetry, and who willingly shared his bountiful supply of candy, could have once been a freewheeling young adventurer was difficult for them to fathom: grandfathers are ancient relics who have always been old.

Grampa left behind his sojourner's life style when he traveled west to Seattle and took on responsibilities; he became a settler. The Japanese living on the West Coast had sailed east to America several decades earlier and they had encountered far different challenges than he had confronted while living on the East Coast. However, on joining the immigrant community in Seattle, Grampa's life morphed into a more conventional immigrant experience. My mother had been born into that community and knew it well, but she passed on before I had a chance to ask her about her stories.

War was declared and America was engulfed in a world-wide conflict. We knew we had the wrong connections; we shared the same ancestry as the enemy. My father and I, along with more than 110,000 other persons of Japanese ancestry living on the West Coast, were sent to internment camps far from our homes. I was seven years old when the War began. I was not precocious as some, and I had little comprehension of what the grownups were up to. Mother was not around to furnish explanations and adults rarely bothered to share information with children, instead, they brushed us off with: "Just follow the rules and stay out of trouble."

There are now volumes of scholarly works, government data, and poignant personal narratives written about the evacuation and the camps. For readers desiring in-depth information about those events, I suggest consulting such resources for enlightenment. I was a kid in the dark and the historical implications may have eluded me, but, I did retain a head full of memories about our life in camp. They were the experiences, observations, and concerns of a child still in grammar school, but, they were remembered incidents, not tales handed down from second or third person sources. I decided to join the story line and make "Grampa's story" a two-person memoir and continue documenting our resettlement after the war and beyond from my point of view.

When my father and I returned to Seattle after the war, we began living a "normal" life. Normalcy is not the stuff of books, but as time passed, technology advanced and changes in our ethos occurred while I was distracted and our once normal experiences became curiosities of a bygone era when using paper and pencil was the norm before the arrival of computers. Quaint, may describe those times, but they add context to the story being told

I had wanted to share my father's story from early on. A first attempt was foiled by the incursion of those pesky flying termites that invaded our abode. The bugs were quickly banished; the real problem remained; my writing was overwrought and it was a wasted effort. The project was set aside for other pressing priorities for years. Since Grampa was healthy and active, there was no urgency to gather notes and restart the writing process, I thought. That is, until his auto accident precipitated his physical decline. He remembered the core of his stories and anecdotes, but the timeline and details began shifting from one telling to the next; data were scrambled and had to be reconstructed. Names of family members and relatives never varied, therefore those names remain unchanged in the text although the similarity of several names is bound to create confusion.

New names, however, have been selected for lost names and name changes have been assigned to others to protect their privacy.

In the decades between the first attempt to put our story on paper and this final draft, my writing had evolved, but architectural specifications are not literary works, and input was needed. In acknowledgement: the manuscript was thoughtfully manicured and edited by Brigitte. And Team Four members and those who followed at CreateSpace were helpful throughout. Bruce Rutledge's Chin Music Press came to my rescue and shaped the appearance of the first version. Thank you all and an arigato to Lorraine too..

A last note: we had celebrated Grampa's 100th birthday before the holidays and though Grampa spent most of the day sleeping, he was lucid at times and we would talk. One day not long before his passing, he spoke the name, Odai. I had never heard the name mentioned before. "Who is she?" I asked. He answered with tears. She had stayed hidden all the years I knew my father. There were some things he wanted to keep close to his heart and take with him.

I never thought it would take so long to write this book. The look back revisiting and reviewing the past has had its rewards and it was worth the journey. I am glad you joined me. My goal has been to inform and entertain you, Julia, Lorraine, Michael and David. Now it's time to focus forward in the years still left for me.

Sylvia Otani

NAMES

⎯⤙

Abigail: Cousin's girlfriend

Agnes: Nurse at Firland Sanitarium

Aiko Michihira: Yoshi's wife, Midori's mother

Amie: Worked at Spokane diner, married to Kazuo

Arai-*san*: Yoshi's *sensei*/friend in camp

Architecture instructors and students: Alex, Arnie, Dean Doyle, Dean Herman, Dick, Larry, Mae-Lin, Merle, Norton, George Tsutakawa, Mr. Torrence

Beam, J.T. and Mrs.: Yoshi's employer in Brinnon, Washington

Botan (Peony): Kajuro's friend in New York City

Buckner, Dr. and Mrs.: Seattle surgeon and wife who employed Ujimoto's

Camp Minidoka Block 19 residents: Hidaka's, Mrs. Mori, Shibata-*san*, Shigeno-*san*, Suzuki Tamura-*san*, Wada-*san*, Mrs. Watanabe, and Mrs. Yamagishi

Camp Minidoka classmates/schoolmates: Betty, Dorothy, Frank, Gladys, Hana, Homer, Kathleen, Kazu, Keiji, Kinu, Kewpie, Lily, Richard, Robert, and Tai

Camp Minidoka teachers: Miss Queen, Miss Keck, Mrs. Sampson, and Mrs. Sparks

Carl: Contractor/carpenter who built our house

Chisato: Yoshi's sister (child #7)

Developer's office coworkers: Bob, Chuck, Dan, Egan, Ernie, Karl, Roger, and Uga

Owner/boss: Mr. B

Donovan, Miss: Teacher in Spokane

Emi *Oba-san*: Yoshi's aunt, Shoshun's wife

Faye: Hostess/part-owner of restaurant in New York City

FBI agents: Bob Pringle and Ron McHugh

Frances: Midori's friend in Spokane

Furuya, Masajiro: Early Issei businessman in Seattle

Hagiya, Rev. Paul: Minister at Methodist church

Hamayo: Midori's aunt, Hayame's daughter

Hanako: Maid, mother of Sutekichi

Hashimoto, Mr. and Mrs.: Neighbors in fourplex on Yesler hill

Hayame/Obaa-san: Midori's step-grandmother, Masaichi's 2nd wife

Helen Mae: Missionary worker at Methodist church

Helga: Maid at Hofheimer's

Hiroko: Housemaid

Hiromu: Yoshi's younger brother (child #11)

Hiyama, Mr.: Hayame's friend

Hoedemaker, Mrs.: Midori's employer

Hofheimer, Mr. and Mrs.: Yoshi's employers in New York City

Hofheimer children: Eileen, Alice, Joyce, and Natalie

Hori, Shigeichi: Hayame's second husband

Ijima, Mr.: Hotel owner in Spokane

Ito Nomura: Wife of Yoshi's Uncle Ryokichi

Itono, Sasaki: Midori's grandmother, Masaichi's 1st wife

Izumi: Yoshi's village girlfriend

Jim: Hotel clerk in New York City Joe, Mr.: Manager of College Club

Josef House nurses and personnel: Miss Ahern, Miss Evers, Mrs. Engle, Miss Finke, Miss Palmer, and Mrs. Morris (head nurse)

Josef House patients: Agnes, Cathy, Deanna, Estelle, Ethel, June, Millie, Sue, and Sonny

Kajiro: Yoshi's paternal grandfather

Kajuro: Yoshi's cousin, Sutekichi's son

Kakichi: Yoshi's father, son of Kajiro

Kanjiro Sasaki: Masaichi's wife Itono's brother
Katsujiro: Yoshi's paternal uncle
Katsumi: Midori's uncle, Hayame's son
Kawachi: Yoshi's employee at arcade
Kihei: Yoshi's great-grandfather, Kajiro's father
Kimiko: Yoshi's sister (child #8)
Kimiye: Midori's aunt, Hayame's daughter
Kitty: Pastry chef at hotel where Yoshi worked
Kobayashi: Co-owner/chef at New York City restaurant, Faye's husband
Koga: Seaman on Yoshi's first ship
Koji: Yoshi's friend in New York City
Lewis, Mrs.: Second grade teacher at Bailey Gatzert
Mahan, Miss: Principal of Bailey Gatzert School
Marie Nomura: Next-door neighbor in camp
Market acquaintances: Kazuko, Ken, and Kimi-*chan*
Masae: Midori's aunt, Hayame's daughter
Masaichi Michihira: Aiko's father, Midori's grandfather
Mat-*san*/Git-*san*: Old family friend from valley days
Min: Yoshi's friend in Seattle, husband of Miyo
Min and Bill: Owners of diner in Spokane
Mineko Esaki: Yoshi's friend and tanka poet
Minoura: Quartermaster on Yoshi's first ship
Mototaro: Yoshi's maternal uncle, Yasue's physician brother
Momoko: Yoshi's classmate living in Ise
Nakamura, Mrs.: Family friend in Seattle
Noboru: Yoshi's younger brother (child #9)
Nomura, George Yoichiro: Neighbor in camp
Nomura, George Yoshitsugu: Midori's father
Odai: Nursemaid/household help
Poetry group members: Mrs. Itoi, Mr. Mihara, Mrs. Nakagawa, and Mrs. Niguma
Puyallup friends and neighbors: Bette, Gloria, Mrs. Hidaka, Molly, Mukai's

Reginas: Alice, Betsy, Elaine, Fumiko, Gale, Joyce, Kate, Margaret, Marian, Marta, and Sumi (honorary member)

Rembe, Dr.: Physician advisor

Ryokichi: Yoshi's paternal uncle, husband to Ito Sachiko: Customer at arcade

Sadako: Yoshi's classmate living in Ise

Saito: Third-class officer aboard Yoshi's third ship

Seattle schoolmates and acquaintances: Harold, Mary, Mae

Seattle schoolteachers: Miss Johnson, Mr. Kelso, Mrs. Kendell, Mrs. Olmstead, Mr. Perry, Miss Purdy, Mr. Schmalle, and Mr. Wilson

Seinojo: Yoshi's older brother

Seto-*san*: Kobe boardinghouse owner

Shiro: Yoshi's younger brother (child #10)

Shitoshi: Yoshi's younger brother (child #12)

Shoichi: Yoshi's cousin, Sutekichi's son

Shoshun: Yoshi's uncle, mother Yasue's brother

Shozo: Yoshi's cousin, Sutekichi's son

Spokane classmates: Billy, Joe, Keith, Melody, Raymond, Roderick, Russell, and T.J.

Susumu: Yoshi's physician cousin

Sutekichi: Yoshi's (half) uncle, Kajiro's son

Tadao: Family store employee, Sutekichi's adoptive father

Tainaka-*san*: Village fisherman

Tameko: Yoshi's older sister (child #4)

Terada, Mr. and Mrs.: Family friends on Yesler Hill

The Restaurant employees: Janice, Joe (head chef), Kai, Kay, Masa, Midori, Mieko, Minnie, Reiko, Rudy (manager), Taki, and Tomi (head waitress)

Torao: Yoshi's cousin, Sutekichi's son

Taro: Yoshi's boyhood friend

Uchida Grandfather: Mother Yasue's father

Umae: Yoshi's sister (child #6)

Ujimoto, Mr. and Mrs.: Family friends employed by Dr. Buckner

Waterhouse, Miss: Midori's kindergarten teacher
Yae: Yoshi's paternal grandmother
Yamagishi, Mrs.: Mother of friend in camp
Yamamoto: Yoshi's employee at arcade
Yasue: Yoshi's mother
Yoko, Aunt: Next-door neighbor Marie's aunt
Yoshino: Cousin Kajuro's partner in arcade business
Yosuke: Yoshi's classmate
Yozo: Midori's kindergarten classmate from Japan
Yukimasa: Yoshi's cousin, son of Ito and Ryokichi
Yuriko: Friend of Yoshi's two friends in Ise
Zentaro: Farm worker in the valley

GLOSSARY

Ai-te: (To be) companion
Anata: You, dear (how wife addresses her husband)
Attari mae: That's what/how it should be, it's what is right
Bachi-ga-attaru: Retribution will strike (you)
Bai-shaku-nin: Go-between, marriage broker
Banzai!: Hurrah!
Beppin: Beautiful (woman)
Bon Odori: Buddhist summer festival (for the dead) with (folk) dancing
Busai-ki: Unattractive
Butsudan: Buddhist household shrine
Chan-*bara*: Samurai sword fight movie (slang)
Chonan: First-son heir
Chotto: Small amount, wait a minute
Chusha: Vaccination
Dai-ji: Treasured
Dai-suki-na: Best liked
Da-le?: Who is it/there?
Dango: Dumpling
Dango-jiru: (flour) Dumpling soup
Dojo: Martial arts school/training hall
Do-mo: Thank you (shortened version)
Don-na: Master, husband
Enryo: Reserve

Furoshiki: Cloth wrapper (to carry package/present)

Gai-jin: Foreigner

Gan-batte: Persevere

Ga-sa, ga-sa: This way and that way, fussy

Giri: Sense of obligation/duty

Geta: Wooden footwear

Gohan: Cooked rice

Gomen-nasai: Sorry, apologies

Goza: Woven straw mat

Gozonji-deska: Are you acquainted?

Hai: Yes

Hai-byo: Tuberculosis

Haku-jin: White person, Caucasian

Hara ga het-ta/Onaka ga suite masu: I'm hungry

Hayaku: Quickly, hurry up

Hazukashii: Shy

Hinotama: Fireball

Hon-to: The truth

Iie: No

Irashai: Welcome

I-ro-ha-ni: Beginning kana syllabary

Issei: First generation, migrated from Japan

Itai: Hurts

Jizu: Buddhist prayer beads

Kami-kaze: Divine wind

Kami-sama: God

Kani: Crab

Kanji: Chinese ideogram adopted for Japanese language

Kanoshii: Nostalgic

Karasu to isho-ni, kaeri-mashi: Let's return home with the crows.

Katana: Sword

Katsudo shashin/Eiga/sinema: Movies

Kawaiso: Pitiful

Kendo: "Way of the sword" martial arts

Ken-jin: Person from (same) prefecture

Kenjin-kai: Organization for people from same prefecture

Keski: View

Kibei: Born-in-America Nisei educated in Japan

Kichi-gai: Crazy Kigo; nature or seasonal word in a tanka poem

Kimpira gobo: Slivered burdock root cooked and flavored

Kinako: Sweetened, powdered soybean

Katakana: Japanese syllabary

Ko-hi: Coffee

Koge: Bottom crust of cooked rice; soccrat in Spanish

Komaru: Worrisome

Koto: Japanese musical stringed instrument

Kozo: An acolyte or fledgling

Mada: Not yet

Megane: Eyeglasses

Mise: Shop

Mi-ru-ku: Milk

Miso: Mashed fermented soybean paste

Mizu: Water

Mochi: Sweet rice paste

Mochi tsuki: Action of crushing the rice into paste

Mura: Village

Nakado: Go-between, baishaku-nin

Moshi-moshi: Hello (used mostly on the phone)

Mukashi: Long time ago

Musubi: Rice ball

Nashi: Asian pear

Musume-san: Young girl

Nani: What?

Neh (*Ne* or *na*): Sentence-ending emphasis or to elicit confirmation; Right?

Nigi-yaka: Noisy

Nihon Gakko: Japanese school Nihonmachi: Japantown

Nikkei: People of Japanese ancestry
Ni-san: Older brother
Nisei: Second generation, born in America to Issei parents
Nishime: Japanese simmered stew
Noren: Short curtain often hung in kitchen doorway
Obaa-san/Obaachan: Grandmother
Oba-san: Aunt
Obento: Lunch in a box/container
Ocha: Tea
Ocha-zuke: Tea poured on cooked rice
Odori: Japanese dance
Ogamu: Worship, give respect
Ohagi: Sweet bean/rice treat
Oishi: Delicious
Ojo-san: Young lady
Okaa-san: Mother
Okan: *Sake* decanter
Okashi: Sweet treats
Okyo: Buddhist scripture
Okazu: Meal's main course
On: Accent words in *tanka* poems
Onei-san: Older sister
Onigiri: Cooked rice ball
Otoo-san: Father
Oya-koko: Filial respect
Rodoshe-nin: Laborer
Romaji: Romanized (Latin) spelling
Ryokan: Japanese-style inn
Sake: Rice wine
Samisen: Japanese three-stringed musical instrument
Satsuma-age: Deep-fried fish cake
Sayonara: Good-bye
Sensei: Teacher

Seppuku: Hara-kiri: suicide by disembowelment
Shakuhachi: Japanese bamboo flute
Shikata-ga-nai: Accept the situation/inevitable; be resigned to fate
Shin-nen Omedeto: Happy New Year
Shinpai-nai: Not to worry
Shinseki: A relative
Shoji: Sliding wood panel screen
Shoyu: Soy sauce
Somen: Thin Japanese wheat noodles
Sugoi: Amazingly Taiko: Japanese drum
Takuwan: Pickled daikon
Tanka: Waka poems
Tanomi-masu: Request
Tatami: Woven mat flooring
Teru Bozu: Temple disciple
Uguisu: Japanese nightingale
Umeboshi: Pickled plum
Uta-kai: Poetry club
Wari-bako: Stackable box containers
WRA: War Relocation Authority
Yame-nasai: Please stop it
Yonsei: Third generation, born to Nisei parents
Yukata: Cotton kimono usually for summer wear
Zabuton: Cushion
Zenzai: Sweetened bean "soup" with mochi
Zori: Footwear, flip-flops
Zoo-zoo-ben: A regional Japanese dialect

Words translated as used in text. Dictionary definitions recommended for precise translations and references for nuances of the language.

Made in the USA
San Bernardino, CA
15 May 2018